Foundations of Modern Econometrics

A Unified Approach

Foundations of Modern Econometrics

A Unified Approach

Yongmiao Hong
Cornell University, USA

World Scientific

NEW JERSEY • LONDON • SINGAPORE • BEIJING • SHANGHAI • HONG KONG • TAIPEI • CHENNAI • TOKYO

Published by

World Scientific Publishing Co. Pte. Ltd.
5 Toh Tuck Link, Singapore 596224
USA office: 27 Warren Street, Suite 401-402, Hackensack, NJ 07601
UK office: 57 Shelton Street, Covent Garden, London WC2H 9HE

Library of Congress Control Number: 2020029689

British Library Cataloguing-in-Publication Data
A catalogue record for this book is available from the British Library.

FOUNDATIONS OF MODERN ECONOMETRICS
A Unified Approach

ISBN 978-981-122-018-0 (hardcover)
ISBN 978-981-122-019-7 (ebook for institutions)
ISBN 978-981-122-020-3 (ebook for individuals)

For any available supplementary material, please visit
https://www.worldscientific.com/worldscibooks/10.1142/11824#t=suppl

Preface

Modern economies are full of uncertainties and risk. Economics studies resource allocations in an uncertain market environment. As a generally applicable quantitative analytic tool for uncertain events, probability and statistics have been playing an important role in economic research. Econometrics is statistical analysis of economic and financial data. In the past four decades or so, economics has witnessed a so-called "empirical revolution" in its research paradigm, and as the main methodology in empirical studies in economics, econometrics has been playing an important role. It has become an indispensable part of training in modern economics, business and management. This book develops a coherent set of econometric theory, methods and tools for economic models. It is written as a textbook for graduate students in economics, business, management, statistics, applied mathematics, and related fields. It can also be used as a reference book on econometric theory by scholars who may be interested in both theoretical and applied econometrics.

The book is organized in a coherent manner. Chapter 1 is an introduction to econometrics. It first describes two most important features of modern economics, namely mathematical modeling and empirical validation, and then discusses the role of econometrics as a methodology in empirical studies in economics. A number of motivating economic examples are given to illustrate how econometrics can be used in empirical studies. Finally, it points out the limitations of econometrics due to the fact that an economy is not a repeatedly controlled experiment. Assumptions and careful interpretations are needed when conducting empirical studies in economics.

Chapter 2 provides a general regression analysis. Regression analysis is modeling, estimation, inference, and specification analysis of the conditional mean of economic variables of interest given a set of explanatory variables. It is most widely applied in economics. Among many other things, this chapter interprets the mean squared error and its optimizer—conditional mean, which lays down the probability-theoretic foundation for least squares estimation. In particular, it provides an interpretation for the least squares estimator and its relationship with the true parameter value of a correctly specified regression model. The importance of correct model specification for valid economic interpretation of model parameters is emphasized.

Chapter 3 introduces the classical linear regression analysis. A set of classical assumptions are first given and discussed, and conventional statistical procedures for estimation, inference, and hypothesis testing are then introduced. The roles of conditional homoskedasticity, serial uncorrelatedness, and normality of the disturbance of a linear regression model are analyzed in a finite sample econometric theory. We also discuss the generalized least squares estimation as an efficient estimation method for a linear regression model when the variance-covariance matrix is known up to a constant. In particular, the generalized least squares estimation is interpreted as an ordinary least squares estimation of a suitably transformed regression model via conditional variance scaling and autocorrelation filtering. Chapter 3 is the foundation of modern econometrics and the starting point for us to present modern econometric theory.

The subsequent Chapters 4 to 7 are the generalizations of classical linear regression analysis when various classical assumptions fail. A large sample theoretic approach is taken. For this purpose, Chapter 4 first reviews basic analytic methods and tools in large sample or asymptotic theory, and then relaxes the normality and conditional homoskedasticity assumptions, two key conditions assumed in the classical linear regression modeling. For simplicity, it is assumed that the observed data are generated from an independent and identically distributed random sample. It is shown that while the finite distributional theory is no longer valid, the classical statistical procedures are still approximately applicable when the sample size is large, provided conditional homoskedasticity holds. In contrast, if the data displays conditional heteroskedasticity, classical statistical procedures are not applicable even for large samples, and heteroskedasticity-robust procedures will be called for. Tests for existence of conditional heteroskedasticity in a linear regression framework are introduced.

Chapter 5 extends the linear regression theory to stationary time series data. First, it introduces a variety of basic concepts in time series analysis.

Then it shows that the large sample theory for independent and identically distributed random samples carries over to ergodic stationary time series data if the regression error follows a martingale difference sequence. We introduce tests for serial correlation, and tests for conditional heteroskedasticity and autoregressive conditional heteroskedasticity in a time series regression framework. We also discuss the impact of autoregressive conditional heteroskedasticity on inferences of static time series regressions and dynamic time series regressions respectively.

Chapter 6 extends the large sample theory to a very general case where there exist conditional heteroskedasticity and autocorrelation in a linear regression model. In this case, the classical regression theory cannot be used, and a long-run variance-covariance matrix estimator is called for to validate statistical inferences in a time series regression framework.

Chapter 7 is the instrumental variables estimation for linear regression models, where the regression disturbance is correlated with regressors. This can arise due to measurement errors, simultaneous equations biases, omitted variables, and other various reasons. When the regression error is correlated with the regressors, we usually call that there exists endogeneity. In Chapter 7, a two-stage least squares estimation method and related statistical inference procedures are fully exploited to deal with endogeneity. This is a popular procedure to estimate an economic causal relationship when data are not generated from a randomized or controlled experiment. We also introduce Hausman's (1978) test for endogeneity.

Chapter 8 introduces the generalized method of moments, which is a popular estimation method for possibly nonlinear econometric models characterized as a set of moment conditions. Indeed, most economic theories, such as rational expectations in macroeconomics, can be formulated by a moment condition. The generalized method of moments is particularly suitable to estimate model parameters contained in the moment conditions for which the conditional distribution is usually not available. It also provides a convenient framework to view many econometric estimation methods.

Chapter 9 introduces the maximum likelihood estimation and quasi-maximum likelihood estimation methods for conditional probability models and many other nonlinear econometric models, such as discrete choice models, censored regression models, truncated regression models, duration or survival models, and volatility models. We exploit important implications of correct specification of a conditional distribution model, and discuss the analogy between the martingale difference sequence property of the score function and serial uncorrelatedness of the regression error as well as the analogy between the conditional information equality and conditional homoskedasticity. These links provide a great help in understanding the large sample properties of the maximum likelihood estimator and the quasi-maximum likelihood estimator.

Chapter 10 first summarizes the main contents covered in Chapters 2 to 9. Then starting from a review of the key assumptions of a classical linear regression model, this chapter describes how modern econometrics has been developed by generalizing the classical assumptions. Finally, it discusses some opportunities and challenges which Big data brings to modern econometrics.

This book has several important features. First, it covers, in a progressive manner, various econometrics models and related methods from conditional means to possibly nonlinear conditional moments to the entire conditional distributions, and this is achieved in a unified and coherent framework. There exists a strong logical link among the materials covered in different chapters of the book.

Second, the book provides various intuitions, explanations and potential applications for important econometric concepts, theories and methods from an economic perspective. Economic examples are also provided to motivate important econometric methods and models. Such training is indispensable in teaching and learning econometrics.

Third, the book emphasizes basic training in asymptotic analysis. It first provides a brief review of asymptotic analytic methods and tools, and then show how they are used to develop the econometric theory in each chapter. Asymptotic analysis helps readers gain deep insight into modern econometric theory, particularly the conditions under which the econometric theory, methods and models are valid and applicable. By going through various chapters in this book progressively, readers will learn how to do asymptotic analysis for econometric models. Such skills are useful not only for those students who intend to work on theoretical econometrics, but also for those who intend to work on applied subjects in economics because with such analytic skills, readers will be able to understand more specialized or more advanced econometrics textbooks.

As a prerequisite, students are required to have a solid background in probability and statistics equivalent in both context and level to the textbook entitled as *Probability and Statistics for Economists* by Hong (2017). The present book is based on my lecture notes taught at Cornell University, Renmin University of China, Shandong University, Shanghai Jiaotong University, Tsinghua University, and Xiamen University, where graduate students have provided detailed comments on these notes. I'd like to thank, particularly, Lichun Chen, Yuhan Chi, Liyuan Cui, Tom DiCiccio, Ying Fang, Zhonghao Fu, Nick Kiefer, Xiaoyi Peng, Xia Wang, Jilin Wu, Xiliang Zhao and Zengguang Zhong for their help in my writing of this textbook. Last but not least, I'd also like to thank National Science Foundation of China for its support via the basic scientific center project (NSFC Project No. 71988101) entitled as "economic modeling and economic policy studies".

Yongmiao Hong
Ernest S. Liu Professor of Economics & International Studies
Department of Economics & Department of Statistics and Data Science
Cornell University, Ithaca, U.S.A.

Contents

Preface v

1. Introduction to Econometrics 1

1.1 Introduction 1
1.2 Quantitative Features of Modern Economics 2
1.3 Mathematical Modeling 4
1.4 Empirical Validation 6
1.5 Illustrative Examples 10
1.6 Limitations of Econometric Analysis 20
1.7 Conclusion 24
Exercise 1 26

2. General Regression Analysis 27

2.1 Conditional Probability Distribution 27
2.2 Conditional Mean and Regression Analysis 30
2.3 Linear Regression Modeling 43
2.4 Correct Model Specification for Conditional Mean 49
2.5 Conclusion 57
Exercise 2 60

3. Classical Linear Regression Models 67

3.1 Framework and Assumptions 67
3.2 Ordinary Least Squares (OLS) Estimation 74
3.3 Goodness of Fit and Model Selection Criteria 78
3.4 Consistency and Efficiency of the OLS Estimator 86
3.5 Sampling Distribution of the OLS Estimator 94
3.6 Variance Estimation for the OLS Estimator 96

3.7 Hypothesis Testing . . . 99
3.8 Applications . . . 117
3.9 Generalized Least Squares Estimation . . . 124
3.10 Conclusion . . . 134
Exercise 3 . . . 137

4. Linear Regression Models with Independent Observations 149

4.1 Introduction to Asymptotic Theory . . . 149
4.2 Framework and Assumptions . . . 166
4.3 Consistency of the OLS Estimator . . . 168
4.4 Asymptotic Normality of the OLS Estimator . . . 170
4.5 Asymptotic Variance Estimation . . . 173
4.6 Hypothesis Testing . . . 178
4.7 Testing for Conditional Homoskedasticity . . . 184
4.8 Conclusion . . . 188
Exercise 4 . . . 190

5. Linear Regression Models with Dependent Observations 197

5.1 Introduction to Time Series Analysis . . . 197
5.2 Framework and Assumptions . . . 222
5.3 Consistency of the OLS Estimator . . . 226
5.4 Asymptotic Normality of the OLS Estimator . . . 227
5.5 Asymptotic Variance Estimation for the OLS Estimator . 229
5.6 Hypothesis Testing . . . 233
5.7 Testing for Conditional Heteroskedasticity and Autoregressive Conditional Heteroskedasticity . . . 241
5.8 Testing for Serial Correlation . . . 245
5.9 Conclusion . . . 255
Exercise 5 . . . 256

6. Linear Regression Models Under Conditional Heteroskedasticity and Autocorrelation 265

6.1 Motivation . . . 265
6.2 Framework and Assumptions . . . 268
6.3 Long-Run Variance-Covariance Matrix Estimation . . . 270
6.4 Consistency of the OLS Estimator . . . 277
6.5 Asymptotic Normality of the OLS Estimator . . . 278
6.6 Hypothesis Testing . . . 279

6.7 Testing Whether Long-Run Variance-Covariance Matrix Estimation Is Needed . . . 282
6.8 Ornut-Cochrane Procedure . . . 286
6.9 Conclusion . . . 288
Exercise 6 . . . 290

7. Instrumental Variables Regression 293

7.1 Motivation . . . 293
7.2 Framework and Assumptions . . . 303
7.3 Two-Stage Least Squares (2SLS) Estimation . . . 307
7.4 Consistency of the 2SLS Estimator . . . 309
7.5 Asymptotic Normality of the 2SLS Estimator . . . 311
7.6 Interpretation and Estimation of Asymptotic Variance-Covariance Matrix of the 2SLS Estimator . . . 313
7.7 Hypothesis Testing . . . 322
7.8 Hausman's Test . . . 324
7.9 Conclusion . . . 329
Exercise 7 . . . 334

8. Generalized Method of Moments Estimation 343

8.1 Introduction to Method of Moments Estimation . . . 343
8.2 Generalized Method of Moments (GMM) Estimation . . . 346
8.3 Consistency of the GMM Estimator . . . 353
8.4 Asymptotic Normality of the GMM Estimator . . . 356
8.5 Asymptotic Efficiency of the GMM Estimator . . . 361
8.6 Two-Stage Asymptotically Most Efficient GMM Estimation . . . 363
8.7 Asymptotic Variance-Covariance Matrix Estimation . . . 366
8.8 Hypothesis Testing . . . 367
8.9 Model Specification Testing . . . 369
8.10 Conclusion . . . 374
Exercise 8 . . . 377

9. Maximum Likelihood Estimation and Quasi-Maximum Likelihood Estimation 383

9.1 Motivation . . . 384
9.2 Maximum Likelihood Estimation (MLE) and Quasi-MLE (QMLE) . . . 391

9.3 Statistical Properties of MLE/QMLE 400
9.4 Correct Model Specification and Its Implications 402
9.5 Asymptotic Distribution of MLE 409
9.6 Consistent Estimation of Asymptotic Variance-Covariance Matrix of MLE 413
9.7 Parameter Hypothesis Testing Under Correct Model Specification 414
9.8 Model Misspecification for Conditional Probability Distribution and Its Implications 423
9.9 Asymptotic Distribution of QMLE 436
9.10 Asymptotic Variance Estimation of QMLE 438
9.11 Hypothesis Testing Under Model Misspecification 439
9.12 Specification Testing for Conditional Probability Distribution Model 443
9.13 Conclusion 448
Exercise 9 450

10. Modern Econometrics: Retrospect and Prospect 457

10.1 Summary of Book 457
10.2 Assumptions of Classical Econometrics 461
10.3 From Normality to Nonnormality 463
10.4 From Independent and Identically Distributed Disturbances to Conditional Heteroskedasticity and Autocorrelation 464
10.5 From Linear to Nonlinear Models 466
10.6 From Exogeneity to Endogeneity 469
10.7 From Correct Model Specification to Model Misspecification 471
10.8 From Stationarity to Nonstationarity 474
10.9 From Econometric Models to Economic Theories 477
10.10 From Traditional Data to Big Data 479
10.11 Conclusion 483
Exercise 10 485

Bibliography 487

Index 499

Chapter 1

Introduction to Econometrics

Abstract: Econometrics has become an integral part of training in modern economics and business. Together with microeconomics and macroeconomics, econometrics has been taught as one of the three core courses in most undergraduate and graduate economic programs in the world. This chapter discusses the philosophy and methodology of econometrics in economic research, the roles and limitations of econometrics, and the differences between econometrics and mathematical economics as well as mathematical statistics. A variety of illustrative econometric examples are given, which cover various fields of economics and finance.

Keywords: Data Generating Process (DGP), Econometrics, Probability law, Quantitative analysis, Statistics

1.1 Introduction

Econometrics has become an integrated part of teaching and research in modern economics. The importance of econometrics has been increasingly recognized over the past several decades. In this chapter, we will discuss the philosophy and methodology of econometrics in economic research. First, we will discuss the quantitative feature of modern economics, and the differences between econometrics and mathematical economics as well as mathematical statistics. Then we will focus on the important roles of econometrics as a fundamental methodology in economic research via a variety of illustrative economic examples including the consumption function, marginal propensity to consume and multipliers, rational expectations models and dynamic asset pricing, the constant return to scale and regulations, evaluation of effects of economic reforms in a transitional economy, the efficient market hypothesis, modeling uncertainty and volatility, and duration analysis in labor economics and finance. These examples range from econometric analysis of the conditional mean to the conditional variance and the conditional distribution of economic variables of interest, given a suitable information set. We will also discuss the limitations of econometrics, mainly due to the nonexperimental nature of economic data and the time-varying nature of econometric structures.

1.2 Quantitative Features of Modern Economics

Modern market economies are full of uncertainties and risk. When economic agents make decisions, the outcomes are usually unknown in advance and economic agents will take this uncertainty into account in their decision-making. Modern economics is a study on scarce resource allocations in an uncertain market environment. Generally speaking, modern economics can be roughly classified into four categories: macroeconomics, microeconomics, financial economics, and econometrics. Of them, macroeconomics, microeconomics and econometrics now constitute the core courses for most economic doctoral programs in the world, while financial economics is now mainly being taught in business and management schools.

Most doctoral programs in economics emphasize quantitative analysis. Quantitative analysis consists of mathematical modeling and statistical-based empirical studies. To understand the roles of quantitative analysis, it may be useful to first describe the general process of modern economic research. Like most natural science, the general methodology of modern economic research can be roughly summarized as follows:

- *Step 1*: Data collection and summary of empirical stylized facts. The so-called empirical stylized facts are often summarized from observed economic data. For example, in microeconomics, a well-known stylized fact is the Engel curve, which characterizes that the share of a consumer's expenditure on food out of her or his total income will vary as his/her income changes; in macroeconomics, a well-known stylized fact is the Phillips (1958) curve, which characterizes a negative correlation between the inflation rate and the unemployment rate in an aggregate economy; and in finance, a well-known stylized fact about financial markets is volatility clustering, that is, a high volatility today tends to be followed by another high volatility tomorrow, a low volatility today tends to be followed by another low volatility tomorrow, and both patterns alternate over time. The empirical stylized facts often serve as a starting point for economic research. For example, the development of unit root and cointegration econometrics was mainly motivated by the empirical study of Nelson and Plosser (1982) who documented that most macroeconomic time series are unit root processes.

- *Step 2*: Development of economic theories/models. With the empirical stylized facts in mind, economists then develop an economic theory or model in order to explain them, among other things. This usually calls for specifying a mathematical model of economic theory. In fact, the objective of economic modeling is not merely to explain the stylized facts, but to understand the mechanism governing the economy and to predict the future evolution of the economy.
- *Step 3*: Empirical verification of economic models. Often, economic theory only suggests a qualitative economic relationship. It does not provide any concrete functional form. In the process of transforming a mathematical model into an empirically testable econometric model, one often has to assume some functional form, up to some unknown model parameters. One needs to estimate unknown model parameters based on the observed data, and check whether the econometric model is adequate. An adequate model should be at least consistent with the observed data, particularly with the empirical stylized facts.
- *Step 4*: Applications. After an econometric model passes the empirical evaluation, it can then be used to test economic theories or hypotheses, to forecast future evolution of the economy, and to conduct policy evaluation and make policy recommendations.

For an excellent example highlighting these four steps, see Gujarati (2006, Section 1.3) on labor force participation. We note that not every economist or every research paper has to complete these four steps. In fact, it is not uncommon that each economist may only work on research belonging to a certain stage in his/her entire academic lifetime.

From the general methodology of economic research, we see that modern economics has two important features: one is mathematical modeling for economic theory, and the other is statistical-based empirical analysis for economic phenomena. These two features arise from the effort of several generations of economists to make economics a "science". To be a science, any theory must fulfill two criteria: one is logical consistency and coherency in theory itself, and the other is consistency between theory and stylized facts. Mathematics and econometrics serve to help fulfill these two criteria respectively. Indeed, this has been the main objective of the Econometric Society. The setup of the Nobel Memorial Prize in economics in 1969 may be viewed as the recognition of economics as a science in the academic profession, and the first Nobel prizes in economics were given to two well-known econometricians—Ragnar Frisch and Jan Tinbergen.

1.3 Mathematical Modeling

We first discuss the role of mathematical modeling in economics. Why do we need mathematics and mathematical models in economics? It should be pointed out that there are many ways or tools (e.g., graphical methods, verbal descriptions, and mathematical models) to present economic theory. Mathematics is just one of them. To ensure logical consistency of the theory, it is not necessary to use mathematics. Chinese medicine is an excellent example of science without using mathematical modeling. However, mathematics is well-known as the most rigorous logical language. Any theory, when it can be represented by the mathematical language, will ensure its logical consistency and coherency, thus indicating that it has achieved a rather sophisticated level. Indeed, as Karl Marx pointed out, the use of mathematics is an indication of the mature development of a science.

It has been a long history to use mathematics in economics. In his *Mathematical Principles of the Wealth Theory*, Cournot (1838) was among the earliest to use mathematics in economic analysis. Although the *marginal revolution* in economics, which provides a cornerstone for modern economics, was not proposed with the help of mathematics, it was quickly found in the economic profession that the marginal concepts, such as marginal utility, marginal productivity and marginal cost, correspond to the derivative concepts in calculus. Walras (1874), a mathematical economist, heavily used mathematics to develop his general equilibrium theory. The game theory, which was proposed by Von Neumann and Morgenstern (1944) and now becomes a core in modern microeconomics, originated from a branch in mathematics.

Why does economics need mathematics? Briefly speaking, mathematics plays a number of important roles in economics. First, the mathematical language can summarize the essence of a theory in a rather concise manner. For example, macroeconomics studies relationships between aggregate economic variables (e.g., Gross Domestic Product (GDP), consumption, unemployment, inflation, interest rate, and exchange rate). A very important macroeconomic theory was proposed by Keynes (1936). The classical Keynesian theory can be summarized by two simple mathematical equations:

$$\text{National Income identity: } Y = C + I + G,$$
$$\text{Consumption function: } C = \alpha + \beta Y,$$

where Y is income, C is consumption, I is private investment, G is government spending, α is the "survival level" consumption, and β is the marginal propensity to consume. Substituting the consumption function into the income identity, arranging terms, and taking a partial derivative, we can obtain the multiplier effect of government spending

$$\frac{\partial Y}{\partial G} = \frac{1}{1-\beta}.$$

Thus, the essence of the Keynesian theory can be effectively summarized by two mathematical equations.

Second, complicated logical analysis in economics can be greatly simplified by using mathematics. In introductory economics, economic analysis can be done by verbal descriptions or graphical representations. These methods are very intuitive and easy to grasp. One example is the partial equilibrium analysis where a market equilibrium can be characterized by the intersection of the demand curve and the supply curve. However, in many cases, economic analysis cannot be done easily by verbal languages or graphical representations. One example is the general equilibrium theory first proposed by Walras (1874). This theory addresses a fundamental problem in economics, namely whether the market force can achieve an equilibrium for a competitive market economy where there exist many markets and when there exist mutual interactions between different markets. Suppose there are n goods, with demand $D_i(P)$, supply $S_i(P)$ for good i, where $P = (P_1, P_2, ..., P_n)'$ is a price vector for n goods. Then the general equilibrium analysis addresses whether there exists an equilibrium price vector P^* such that all markets are clear simultaneously:

$$D_i(P^*) = S_i(P^*) \text{ for all } i \in \{1, ..., n\}.$$

Conceptually simple, it is rather challenging to provide a definite answer because both the demand and supply functions could be highly nonlinear. In fact, Walras was unable to establish this theory formally. It was satisfactorily solved by Arrow and Debreu many years later, when they used the fixed point theorem in mathematics to prove the existence of an equilibrium price vector. The power and magic of mathematics was clearly demonstrated in the development of the general equilibrium theory in economics.

Third, mathematical modeling is a necessary path to empirical verification of an economic theory. Most economic and financial phenomena are in form of data (indeed we are in a digital era!). We need to "digitalize" economic theory so as to link the economic theory to the observed data. In particular, one needs to formulate economic theory into an empirically testable mathematical model whose functional form or important structural model parameters will be estimated from the observed data.

1.4 Empirical Validation

We now turn to discuss the second feature of modern economics: statistical-based empirical analysis of an economic theory. Why is statistical-based empirical analysis of an economic theory important? The use of mathematics, although it can ensure logical consistency of a theory itself, cannot ensure that economics is a science. An economic theory would be useless from a practical point of view if the underlying assumptions are incorrect or unrealistic. This is the case even if the mathematical treatment is free of errors and elegant. As pointed out earlier, to be a science, an economic theory must be consistent with reality. That is, it must be able to explain historical stylized facts and predict future economic phenomena.

How to check a theory or model empirically? Or how to validate an economic theory? In practice, it is rather difficult or even impossible to check whether the underlying assumptions of an economic theory or model are correct. Nevertheless, one can confront the implications of an economic theory with the observed data to check if they are consistent. In the early stage of economics, empirical validation was often conducted by case studies or indirect verifications. For example, in his well-known *Wealth of Nations*, Adam Smith (1776) explained the advantage of specialization using a case study example. Such a method is still useful nowadays, but is no longer sufficient for modern economic analysis, because economic phenomena are much more complicated while data may be limited. For rigorous empirical analysis, we need to use econometrics. Econometrics is the field of economics that concerns itself with the application of mathematical statistics and the tools of statistical inference to the empirical measurement of relationships postulated by economic theory. It was founded as a scientific discipline around 1930 as marked by the founding of the Econometric Society and the creation of the most influential economic journal—*Econometrica* in 1933.

Econometrics has witnessed a rather rapid development in the past several decades, for a number of reasons. First, there is a need for empirical verification of economic theory, for forecasts using economic models, and for quantitative evaluation of economic policies and programs. Second, there are more and more high-quality economic data available. Third, advance in computing technology has made the cost of computation cheaper and cheaper over time. In the 1950s and 1960s, economists used electromechanical desk calculators to calculate regressions. Before 1970, it sometimes took up to 24 hours to receive the result from one regression, but now we do it in less than a second. The speed of computing grows faster than the speed of data accumulation.

Although not explicitly stated in most of the econometric literature, modern econometrics is essentially built upon the following fundamental axioms:

- Any economy can be viewed as a stochastic process governed by some probability law.
- Any economic phenomenon, as often summarized in form of data, can be reviewed as a realization of this stochastic Data Generating Process (DGP).

There is no way to verify these axioms. They are the philosophic views of econometricians toward an economy. Not every economist or even econometrician agrees with this view. For example, some economists view an economy as a deterministic chaotic process which can generate seemingly random numbers. However, most economists and econometricians (e.g., Granger and Teräsvirta 1993, Lucas 1977) view that there are a lot of uncertainty in an economy, and they are best described by stochastic factors rather than deterministic systems. For instance, the multiplier-accelerator model of Samuelson (1939) is characterized by a deterministic second-order difference equation for aggregate output. Over a certain range of parameters, this equation produces deterministic cycles with a constant period of business cycles. Without doubt this model sheds deep insight into macroeconomic fluctuations. Nevertheless, a stochastic framework will provide a more realistic basis for analysis of periodicity in economics, because the observed periods of business cycles never occur evenly in any economy.

Frisch (1933) demonstrates that a structural propagation mechanism can convert uncorrelated stochastic impulses into cyclical outputs with uneven, stochastic periodicity. Indeed, although not all uncertainties can be well characterized by probability theory, probability is the best quantitative analytic tool to describe uncertainties. The probability law of this stochastic economic system, which characterizes the evolution of the economy, can be viewed as the "law of economic motions." Accordingly, the tools and methods of mathematical statistics will provide the operating principles.

One important implication of the fundamental axioms is that one should not hope to determine precise, and deterministic economic relationships, as do the models of demand, production, and aggregate consumption in standard micro- and macro-economic textbooks. No model could encompass the myriad essentially random aspects of economic life (i.e., no precise point forecast is possible, using a statistical terminology). Instead, one can only postulate some stochastic economic relationships. The purpose of econometrics is to infer the probability law of the economic system using observed data. Economic theory usually takes a form of imposing certain restrictions on the probability law. Thus, one can test economic theories or hypotheses by checking the validity of these restrictions.

It should be emphasized that the role of mathematics is different from the role of econometrics. The main task of mathematical economics is to express economic theory in the mathematical form of equations (or models) without regard to measurability or empirical verification of economic theory. Mathematics can check whether the reasoning process of an economic theory is correct and sometime can give surprising results and conclusions. However, it cannot check whether an economic theory can explain reality. To check whether a theory is consistent with reality, one needs econometrics. Econometrics is a fundamental methodology in the process of economic analysis. Like the development of a natural science, the development of economic theory is a process of refuting the existing theories which cannot explain newly arising empirical stylized facts and developing new theories which can explain them. Econometrics rather than mathematics plays a crucial role in this process. There is no absolutely correct or universally applicable economic theory. Any economic theory can only explain the reality at certain stage, and therefore, is a "relative truth" in the sense that it is consistent with historical data available at that time. An economic theory may not be rejected due to limited data information. It is possible that more than one economic theory or model coexist simultaneously, because data does not contain sufficient information to distinguish the true one (if any) from false ones. When new data becomes available, a theory that can explain the historical data well may not explain the new data well and thus will be refuted. In many cases, new econometric methods can lead to new discovery and call for new development of economic theory.

Econometrics is not simply an application of a general theory of mathematical statistics to economic data. Although mathematical statistics provides many of the operating tools used in econometrics, econometrics often needs special methods because of the unique nature of economic data, and the unique nature of economic problems at hand. One example is the generalized method of moment estimation (Hansen 1982), which was proposed by econometricians aiming to estimate rational expectations models which only impose certain conditional moment restrictions characterized by the Euler equation and the conditional distribution of economic processes is unknown (thus, the classical maximum likelihood estimation cannot be used). The development of unit root and cointegration (e.g., Engle and Granger 1987, Phillips 1987), which is a core in modern time series econometrics, has been mainly motivated from Nelson and Plosser's (1982) empirical documentation that most macroeconomic time series display unit root behaviors. Thus, it is necessary to provide an econometric theory for unit root and cointegrated systems because the standard statistical inference theory is no longer applicable. The emergence of financial econometrics is also due to the fact that financial time series display some unique features such as persistent volatility clustering, heavy tails, infrequent but large jumps, and serially uncorrelated but not independent asset returns. Financial applications, such as financial risk management, hedging and derivatives pricing, often call for modeling for volatilities and the entire conditional probability distributions of asset returns. The features of financial data and the objectives of financial applications make the use of standard time series analysis quite limited, and therefore, call for the development of financial econometrics. Labor economics is another example which shows how labor economics and econometrics have benefited from each other. Labor economics has advanced quickly over the last few decades because of availability of high-quality labor data and rigorous empirical verification of hypotheses and theories on labor economics. On the other hand, microeconometrics, particularly panel data econometrics, has also advanced quickly due to the increasing availability of microeconomic data and the need to develop econometric theory to accommodate the features of microeconomic data (e.g., censoring and endogeneity).

In the first issue of *Econometrica*, the founder of the Econometric Society, Fisher (1933), nicely summarizes the objective of the Econometric Society and main features of econometrics: "Its main object shall be to promote studies that aim at a unification of the theoretical-quantitative and the empirical-quantitative approach to economic problems and that are penetrated by constructive and rigorous thinking similar to that which has come to dominate the natural sciences.

...

But there are several aspects of the quantitative approach to economics, and no single one of these aspects, taken by itself, should be confounded with econometrics. Thus, econometrics is by no means the same as economic statistics. Nor is it identical with what we call general economic theory, although a considerable portion of this theory has a definitely quantitative character. Nor should econometrics be taken as synonomous [sic] with the application of mathematics to economics. Experience has shown that each of these three view-points, that of statistics, economic theory, and mathematics, is a necessary, but not by itself a sufficient, condition for a real understanding of the quantitative relations in modern economic life. It is the *unification* of all three that is powerful. And it is this unification that constitutes econometrics." Like advanced calculus, probability and statistics are indispensable mathematical tools in econometrics and economics.

1.5 Illustrative Examples

Specifically, econometrics can play the following roles in economics:

- Examine how well an economic theory can explain historical economic data (particularly the important stylized facts);
- Test validity of economic theories and hypotheses;
- Predict the future evolution of the economy;
- Conduct policy evaluation and make policy recommendations.

To appreciate the roles of modern econometrics in economic analysis, we now discuss a number of illustrative econometric examples in various fields of economics and finance.

Example 1.1. [Keynesian Model, Multiplier and Policy Recommendation]: The simplest Keynesian model can be described by the system of equations

$$\begin{cases} Y_t = C_t + I_t + G_t, \\ C_t = \alpha + \beta Y_t + \varepsilon_t, \end{cases}$$

where Y_t is aggregate income, C_t is private consumption, I_t is private investment, G_t is government spending, and ε_t is consumption shock. The parameters α and β can have appealing economic interpretations: α is survival level consumption, and β is the marginal propensity to consume. The multiplier of the income with respect to government spending is

$$\frac{\partial Y_t}{\partial G_t} = \frac{1}{1-\beta},$$

which depends on the Marginal Propensity to Consume (MPC) β.

To assess the effect of fiscal policies on the economy, it is important to know the magnitude of β. For example, suppose the Chinese government wants to maintain a steady growth rate (e.g., an annual 8%) for its economy by active fiscal policy. It has to figure out how many government bonds to be issued each year. Insufficient government spending will jeopardize the goal of achieving the desired growth rate, but excessive government spending will cause budget deficit in the long run. The Chinese government has to balance these conflicting effects and this crucially depends on the knowledge of the value of β. Economic theory can only suggest a positive qualitative relationship between income and consumption. It never tells exactly what β should be for a given economy. It is conceivable that β differs from country to country, because cultural factors may have impact on the consumption behavior of an economy. It is also conceivable that β will depend on the stage of economic development in an economy. Fortunately, econometrics offers a feasible way to estimate β from observed data. In fact, economic theory even does not suggest a specific functional form for the consumption function. The linear functional form for the consumption is assumed for convenience, not implied by economic theory. Econometrics can provide a consistent estimation procedure for the unknown consumption function. This is called the nonparametric method (see, e.g., Härdle 1990, Pagan and Ullah 1999).

Example 1.2. [Rational Expectations and Dynamic Asset Pricing Models]: Suppose a representative agent has a constant relative risk aversion utility

$$U = \sum_{t=0}^{n} \beta^t u(C_t) = \sum_{t=0}^{n} \beta^t \frac{C_t^\gamma - 1}{\gamma},$$

where $\beta > 0$ is the agent's time discount factor, $\gamma \geq 0$ is the risk aversion parameter, $u(\cdot)$ is the agent's utility function in each time period, and C_t is consumption during period t. Let the information available to the agent at time t be represented by the σ-algebra I_t—in the sense that any variable whose value is known at time t is presumed to be I_t-measurable, and let $R_t = P_t/P_{t-1}$ be the gross return to an asset acquired at time $t-1$ at a price of P_{t-1}. The agent's optimization problem is to choose a sequence of consumptions $\{C_t\}$ over time to

$$\max_{\{C_t\}} E(U)$$

subject to the intertemporal budget constraint

$$C_t + P_t q_t \leq W_t + P_t q_{t-1},$$

where q_t is the quantity of the asset purchased at time t and W_t is the agent's period t income. Define the marginal rate of intertemporal substitution

$$\text{MRS}_{t+1}(\theta) = \frac{\frac{\partial u(C_{t+1})}{\partial C_{t+1}}}{\frac{\partial u(C_t)}{\partial C_t}} = \left(\frac{C_{t+1}}{C_t}\right)^{\gamma-1},$$

where model parameter vector $\theta = (\beta, \gamma)'$. Then the First Order Condition (FOC) of the agent's optimization problem can be characterized by

$$E\left[\beta \text{MRS}_{t+1}(\theta) R_{t+1} | I_t\right] = 1.$$

That is, the marginal rate of intertemporal substitution discounts gross returns to unity. This FOC is usually called the Euler equation of the economic system (see Hansen and Singleton 1982 for more discussion).

How to estimate this model? How to test validity of a rational expectations model? Here, the traditional popular maximum likelihood estimation method cannot be used, because one does not know the conditional distribution of economic variables of interest. Nevertheless, econometricians have developed a consistent estimation method based on the conditional moment condition or the Euler equation, which does not require knowledge of the conditional distribution of the data generating process. This method is called the generalized method of moments (see Hansen 1982).

In the empirical literature, it was documented that the empirical estimates of risk aversion parameter γ are often too small to justify the substantial difference between the observed returns on stock markets and bond markets (e.g., Mehra and Prescott 1985). This is the well-known equity premium puzzle. To resolve this puzzle, effort has been devoted to the development of new economic models with time-varying and large risk aversion. An example is Campbell and Cochrance's (1999) consumption-based capital asset pricing model. This story confirms our earlier statement that econometric analysis calls for new economic theory after documenting the inadequacy of the existing model.

Example 1.3. [Production Function and Hypothesis of Constant Return to Scale]: Suppose that for some industry, there are two inputs—labor L_i and capital stock K_i, and one output Y_i, where i is the index for firm i. The production function of firm i is a mapping from inputs (L_i, K_i) to output Y_i:

$$Y_i = \exp(\varepsilon_i)F(L_i, K_i),$$

where ε_i is a stochastic factor (e.g., the uncertain weather condition if Y_i is an agricultural product). An important economic hypothesis is that the production technology displays a Constant Return to Scale (CRS), which is defined as follows:

$$\lambda F(L_i, K_i) = F(\lambda L_i, \lambda K_i) \text{ for all } \lambda > 0.$$

CRS is a necessary condition for the existence of a long-run equilibrium of a competitive market economy. If CRS does not hold for some industry, and the technology displays the Increasing Return to Scale (IRS), the industry will lead to natural monopoly. Government regulation is then necessary to protect consumers' welfare. Therefore, testing CRS versus IRS has important policy implication, namely whether regulation is necessary.

A conventional approach to testing CRS is to assume that the production function is a Cobb-Douglas function:

$$F(L_i, K_i) = A\exp(\varepsilon_i)L_i^{\alpha}K_i^{\beta}.$$

Then CRS becomes a mathematical restriction on parameters (α, β):

$$\mathbf{H}_0 : \alpha + \beta = 1.$$

If $a + \beta > 1$, the production technology displays IRS.

In statistics, a popular procedure to test one-dimensional parameter restriction is the classical Student's t-test. Unfortunately, this procedure is not suitable for many cross-sectional economic data, which usually display conditional heteroskedasticity (e.g., a larger firm has a larger output variation). One needs to use a robust and heteroskedasticity-consistent test procedure, originally proposed in White (1980).

It should be emphasized that CRS is equivalent to the statistical hypothesis $\mathbf{H}_0 : \alpha + \beta = 1$ under the assumption that the production technology is a Cobb-Douglas function. This additional condition is not part of the CRS hypothesis and is called an auxiliary assumption. If the auxiliary assumption is incorrect, the statistical hypothesis $\mathbf{H}_0 : \alpha + \beta = 1$ will not be equivalent to CRS. Correct model specification is essential for a valid conclusion and interpretation for the econometric inference.

Example 1.4. [Effect of Economic Reforms in Transitional Economy]: We now consider an extended Cobb-Douglas production function (after taking a logarithmic operation)

$$\ln Y_{it} = \ln A_{it} + \alpha \ln L_{it} + \beta \ln K_{it} + \gamma \text{Bonus}_{it} + \delta \text{Contract}_{it} + \varepsilon_{it},$$

where i is the index for firm $i \in \{1, ..., N\}$, and t is the index for year $t \in \{1, ..., T\}$, Bonus_{it} is the proportion of bonus out of total wage bill, and Contract_{it} is the proportion of workers who have signed a fixed-term contract. This is an example of the so-called panel data model (see, e.g., Hsiao 2003).

Paying bonuses and signing fixed-term contracts were two innovative incentive reforms in the Chinese state-owned enterprises in the 1980s, compared to the fixed wage and life-time employment systems in the pre-reform era. Economic theory predicts that the introduction of the bonus and contract systems provides stronger incentives for workers to work harder, thus increasing the productivity of a firm (see Groves, Hong, McMillan and Naughton 1994).

To examine the effects of these incentive reforms, we consider the null statistical hypothesis

$$\mathbf{H}_0 : \gamma = \delta = 0.$$

It appears that the classical t-tests or F-tests would serve our purpose here, if we can assume conditional homoskedasticity. Unfortunately, this cannot be used because there may well exist the other way of causation from Y_{it}

to Bonus_{it} : a productive firm may pay its workers higher bonuses regardless of their efforts. This will cause correlation between the bonuses and the error term u_{it}, rendering the Ordinary Least Squares (OLS) estimator inconsistent and invalidating the classical t-tests or F-tests. Fortunately, econometricians have developed an important estimation procedure called Instrumental Variables (IV) estimation, which can effectively filter out the impact of the causation from output to bonus and obtain a consistent estimator for the bonus parameter. Related hypothesis test procedures can be used to check whether bonus and contract reforms can increase firm productivity. IV regression has been a popular methodology to identify economic causal relationships based on nonexperimental observations.

In evaluating the effect of economic reforms, we have turned an economic hypothesis—that introducing bonuses and contract systems has no effect on productivity—into a statistical hypothesis $\mathbf{H}_0 : \delta = \gamma = 0$. When the hypothesis $\mathbf{H}_0 : \delta = \gamma = 0$ is not rejected, we should not conclude that the reforms have no effect. This is because the extended production function model, where the reforms are specified additively, is only one of many ways to check the effect of the reforms. For example, one could also specify the model such that the reforms affect the marginal productivities of labor and capital (i.e., the coefficients of labor and capital). Thus, when the hypothesis $\mathbf{H}_0 : \delta = \gamma = 0$ is not rejected, we can only say that we do not find evidence against the economic hypothesis that the reforms have no effect. We should not conclude that the reforms have no effect.

Example 1.5. [Efficient Market Hypothesis (EMH) and Predictability of Financial Returns]: Let Y_t be the stock return in period t, and let $I_{t-1} = \{Y_{t-1}, Y_{t-2}, ...\}$ be the information set containing the history of past stock returns. The weak form of EMH states that it is impossible to predict future stock returns using the history of past stock returns:

$$E(Y_t|I_{t-1}) = E(Y_t).$$

The left hand side, the so-called conditional mean of Y_t given I_{t-1}, is the expected return that can be obtained when one is fully using the information available at time $t-1$. The right hand side, the unconditional mean of Y_t, is the expected market average return in the long-run; it is the expected return of a buy-and-hold trading strategy. When EMH holds, the past information of stock returns has no predictive power for future stock returns. An important implication of EMH is that mutual fund managers will have no informational advantage over layman investors.

EMH is a model-free hypothesis. One simple way to test EMH is to consider the following AutoRegressive (AR) model

$$Y_t = \alpha_0 + \sum_{j=1}^{p} \alpha_j Y_{t-j} + \varepsilon_t,$$

where p is a pre-selected number of lags, and ε_t is a random disturbance. This linear model is called an AR(p) model. EMH implies

$$\mathbf{H}_0 : \alpha_1 = \alpha_2 = \cdots = \alpha_p = 0.$$

Any nonzero coefficient $\alpha_j, 1 \leq j \leq p$, is evidence against EMH. Thus, to test EMH, one can test whether the α_j are jointly zero. The classical F-test in a linear regression model can be used to test the hypothesis $\mathbf{H}_0$ when $\text{var}(\varepsilon_t|I_{t-1}) = \sigma^2$, i.e., when there exists conditional homoskedasticity. However, EMH may coexist with volatility clustering, which is one of the most important empirical stylized facts of financial markets and which implies that $\text{var}(\varepsilon_t|I_{t-1})$ is time-varying. Therefore, the standard F-test statistic cannot be used here, even asymptotically. Similarly, the popular Box and Pierce's (1970) portmanteau Q test, which is based on the sum of the first p squared sample autocorrelations, also cannot be used, because its asymptotic χ^2 distribution is invalid in presence of autoregressive conditional heteroskedasticity. One has to use procedures that are robust to conditional heteroskedasticity.

Like the discussion in Example 1.4, when one rejects the null hypothesis $\mathbf{H}_0$ that the α_j are jointly zero, we have evidence against EMH. Furthermore, the linear AR(p) model has predictive ability for asset returns. However, when one fails to reject the hypothesis $\mathbf{H}_0$ that the α_j are jointly zero, one can only conclude that we do not find evidence against EMH. One cannot conclude that EMH holds. The reason is, again, that the linear AR(p) model is one of many possibilities to check EMH (see, e.g., Hong and Lee 2005, for more discussion).

Example 1.6. [Volatility Clustering and ARCH Model]: Since the 1970s, oil crisis, the floating foreign exchanges system, and the high interest rate policy in the U.S. have stimulated a lot of uncertainty in the world economy. Economic agents have to incorporate the uncertainty in their decision-making. How to measure uncertainty has become an important issue.

In economics, volatility is a key instrument for measuring uncertainty and risk in finance. This concept is important to investigate information flows and volatility spillover, financial contagions between financial markets, options pricing, and calculation of Value at Risk (VaR).

Volatility can be measured by the conditional variance of asset return Y_t given the information available at time $t-1$:

$$\sigma_t^2 \equiv var(Y_t|I_{t-1}) = E\left[(Y_t - E(Y_t|I_{t-1}))^2|I_{t-1}\right].$$

An example of the conditional variance is the AutoRegressive Conditional Heteroskedasticity (ARCH) model, originally proposed by Engle (1982). An ARCH(q) model assumes that

$$\begin{cases} Y_t = \mu_t + \varepsilon_t, \\ \varepsilon_t = \sigma_t z_t, \\ \mu_t = E(Y_t|I_{t-1}), \\ \sigma_t^2 = \alpha + \sum_{j=1}^{q} \beta_j \varepsilon_{t-j}^2, \qquad \alpha > 0, \beta > 0, \\ \{z_t\} \sim \text{IID}(0,1), \end{cases}$$

where IID stands for Independent and Identically Distributed. This model can explain a well-known stylized fact in financial markets—volatility clustering: a high volatility tends to be followed by another high volatility, and a small volatility tends to be followed by another small volatility. It can also explain the non-Gaussian heavy tail of asset returns. More sophisticated volatility models, such as Bollerslev's (1986) Generalized ARCH or GARCH model, have been developed in time series econometrics.

In practice, an important issue is how to estimate a volatility model. Here, the models for the conditional mean μ_t and the conditional variance σ_t^2 are assumed to be correctly specified, but the conditional distribution of Y_t is unknown, because the distribution of the standardized innovation $\{z_t\}$ is unknown. Thus, the popular Maximum Likelihood Estimation (MLE) method cannot be used. Nevertheless, one can assume that $\{z_t\}$ is IID $N(0,1)$ or follows other plausible distribution. Under this assumption, we can obtain a conditional distribution of Y_t given I_{t-1} and estimate model parameters using the MLE procedure. Although $\{z_t\}$ is not necessarily IID $N(0,1)$ and we know this, the estimator obtained this way is still consistent for the true model parameters. However, because the conditional distribution of z_t given I_{t-1} is likely to be misspecified, the asymptotic variance of this estimator is generally larger than that of MLE (which is based on the true distribution of $\{z_t\}$). This is the cost one has to pay not knowing the true distribution of $\{z_t\}$. This method is called the Quasi-MLE, or QMLE (see, e.g., White 1982 and 1994). Inference procedures based on QMLE are different from those based on MLE. For example, the popular likelihood ratio test cannot be used. The difference comes from the fact that the asymptotic variance of QMLE is different from that of MLE, just like the fact that the asymptotic variance of the OLS estimator under conditional heteroskedasticity is different from that of the OLS estimator under conditional homoskedasticity. Incorrect calculation of the asymptotic variance estimator for QMLE will lead to misleading inference and conclusion (see White 1982, 1994 for more discussion).

Example 1.7. [Modeling Economic Durations]: Suppose we are interested in the time it takes for an unemployed person to find a job, the time that elapses between two trades or two price changes, the time length of a strike, the time length before a cancer patient dies, the time length before a financial crisis (e.g., credit default risk) comes out, the time length before a startup technology firm goes bankrupt, and the time length before a family gets out of poverty. Such analysis is called duration analysis or survival analysis.

In practice, the main interest often lies in the question of how long a duration will continue, given that it has not finished yet. The so-called hazard rate or hazard function measures the chance that the duration will end now, given that it has not ended before. This hazard rate therefore can be interpreted as the chance to find a job, to trade, to end a strike, etc.

Suppose random variable T_i is the duration from a population distribution with Probability Density Function (PDF) $f(t)$ and Cumulative Distribution Function (CDF) $F(t)$. Then the survival function is

$$S(t) = P(T_i > t) = 1 - F(t),$$

and the hazard rate

$$\lambda(t) = \lim_{\delta \to 0^+} \frac{P(t < T_i \leq t + \delta | T_i > t)}{\delta} = \frac{f(t)}{S(t)}.$$

Intuitively, the hazard rate $\lambda(t)$ is the instantaneous probability that an event of interest will end at time t given that it has lasted for period t. Note that the specification of $\lambda(t)$ is equivalent to a specification of the PDF $f(t)$. But $\lambda(t)$ is more interpretable from an economic point of view.

The hazard rate may not be the same for all individuals. To control heterogeneity across individuals, we assume that the individual-specific hazard rate depends on some individual characteristics X_i via the form

$$\lambda_i(t) = \exp(X_i'\beta)\lambda(t).$$

This is called the proportional hazard model, originally proposed by Cox (1972). The parameter

$$\beta = \frac{\partial}{\partial X_i} \ln \lambda_i(t) = \frac{1}{\lambda_i(t)} \frac{\partial}{\partial X_i} \lambda_i(t)$$

can be interpreted as the marginal relative effect of X_i on the hazard rate of individual i. Inference of β will allow one to examine how individual characteristics affect the duration of interest. For example, suppose T_i is the unemployment duration for individual i, then the inference of β will allow us to examine how individual characteristics, such as age, education and gender, can affect the unemployment duration. This will provide important policy implication on labor markets.

Because one can obtain the conditional PDF of Y_i given X_i

$$f_i(t) = \lambda_i(t)S_i(t),$$

where the survival function $S_i(t) = \exp[-\int_0^t \lambda_i(s)ds]$, we can estimate β by the MLE method.

For an excellent survey on duration analysis in labor economics, see Kiefer (1988), and for a complete and detailed account, see Lancaster (1990). Duration analysis has been also widely used in credit risk modeling in the recent financial literature.

The above examples, although not exhaustive, illustrate how econometric models and tools can be used in economic analysis. As noted earlier, an economy can be completely characterized by the probability law governing the economy. In practice, which attributes (e.g., conditional moments) of the probability law should be used depends on the nature of the economic problem at hand. In other words, different economic problems will require modeling different attributes of the probability law and thus require different econometric models and methods. In particular, it is not necessary to specify a model for the entire conditional distribution function for all economic applications. This can be seen clearly from the above examples.

1.6 Limitations of Econometric Analysis

Although the general methodology of economic research is very similar to that of natural science, in general, economics and finance have not reached the mature stage that natural science (e.g., physics) has achieved. In particular, the prediction in economics and finance is not as precise as natural science (see, e.g., Granger 2001, for an assessment of macroeconomic forecasting practice).

Why?

Like any other statistical analysis, econometrics is the analysis of the "average behavior" of a large number of realizations, or the outcomes of a large number of random experiments with the same or similar features. However, economic data are not produced by a large number of repeated random experiments, due to the fact that an economy is not a controlled experiment. Most economic data are nonexperimental in their nature. This imposes some limitations on econometric analysis.

First, as a simplification of reality, economic theory or model can only capture the main or most important factors, but the observed data is the joint outcome of many factors together, and some of them are unknown and unaccounted for. These unknown factors are well presented but their influences are ignored in economic modeling. This is unlike natural science, where one can remove secondary factors via controlled experiments. In the realm of economics, we are only passive observers; most data collected in economics are nonexperimental in that the data collecting agency may not have direct control over the data. As a result, it has been rather difficult, although not impossible, to identify the causal relationships among economic variables. The recently emerging field of experimental economics can help somehow, because it studies the behavior of economic agents under controlled experiments (see, e.g., Samuelson 2005). In other words, experimental economics controls the data generating process so that data is produced by the factors under study. Nevertheless, the scope of experimental economics is limited in many applications. One can hardly imagine how an economy with 1.3 billion of people can be experimented. For example, can we repeat the economic reforms in China and former Eastern European Socialist countries?

Second, an economy is an irreversible or non-repeatable system. A consequence of this is that data observed are a single realization of economic variables. For example, we consider the annual Chinese GDP growth rate $\{Y_t\}$ over the past two decades:

Y_{1997}	Y_{1998}	Y_{1999}	Y_{2000}	Y_{2001}	Y_{2002}	Y_{2003}	Y_{2004}	Y_{2005}	Y_{2006}	Y_{2007}
9.2%	7.8%	7.7%	8.5%	8.3%	9.1%	10.0%	10.1%	11.4%	12.7%	14.2%

Y_{2008}	Y_{2009}	Y_{2010}	Y_{2011}	Y_{2012}	Y_{2013}	Y_{2014}	Y_{2015}	Y_{2016}	Y_{2017}	Y_{2018}
9.7%	9.4%	10.6%	9.6%	7.9%	7.8%	7.3%	6.9%	6.7%	6.8%	6.6%

GDP growths in different years should be viewed as different random variables, and each variable Y_t only has one realization! There is no way to conduct statistical analysis if one random variable only has a single realization. As noted earlier, statistical analysis studies the "average" behavior of a large number of realizations from the same data generating process. To conduct statistical analysis of economic data, economists and econometricians often assume some time-invarying "common features" of an economic system so as to use time series data or cross-sectional data of different economic variables. These common features are usually termed as "stationarity" or "homogeneity" of the economic system. With these assumptions, one can consider that the observed data are generated from the same population or populations with similar characters. Economists and econometricians assume that the conditions needed to employ the tools of statistical inference hold, but this is rather difficult, if not impossible, to check in practice.

Third, economic relationships are often changing over time for an economy. Regime shifts and structural changes are rather a rule than an exception, due to technology shocks and changes in preferences, population structure and institution arrangements. A well-known example is the so-called *Great Moderation* of the U.S. macroeconomy, whose volatilities have been declining since the 1980s (e.g., Bernanke 2004). Figures 1.1 and 1.2 are the time series plots of annual U.S. GDP growth rates and U.S. inflation rates, from which one can see that volatilities of U.S. GDP growth rates and inflation rates have been declining since mid-1980s. Indeed, similar and perhaps more striking phenomena can also been observed for Chinese GDP growth rates and inflation rates. Figures 1.3 and 1.4 show that the volatilities of Chinese GDP growth rates and inflation rates have been declining since the 1990s. An unstable economic relationship makes it difficult for out-of-sample forecasts and policy-making. With a structural break, an economic model that was performing well in the past may not forecast well in the future. Over the past several decades, econometricians have made some progress to copy with the time-varying feature of an economic system. Chow's (1960) test, for example, can be used to check

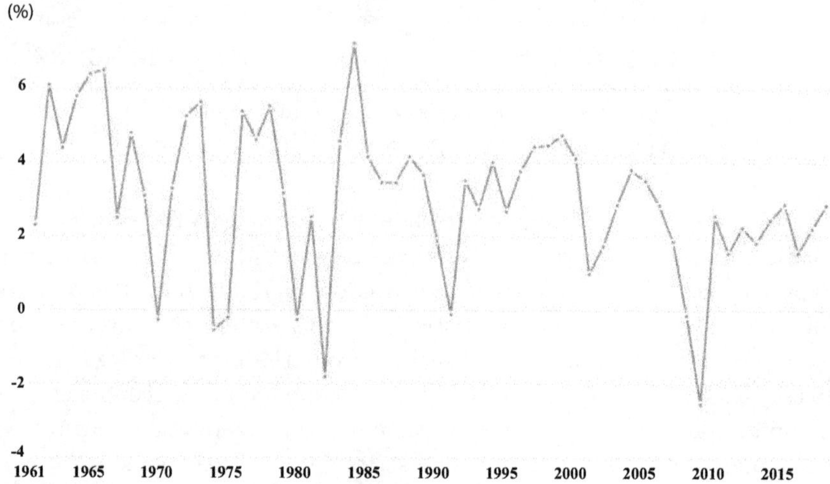

Figure 1.1 Time series plots of annual U.S. GDP growth rates.
Data source: http://data.worldbank.org

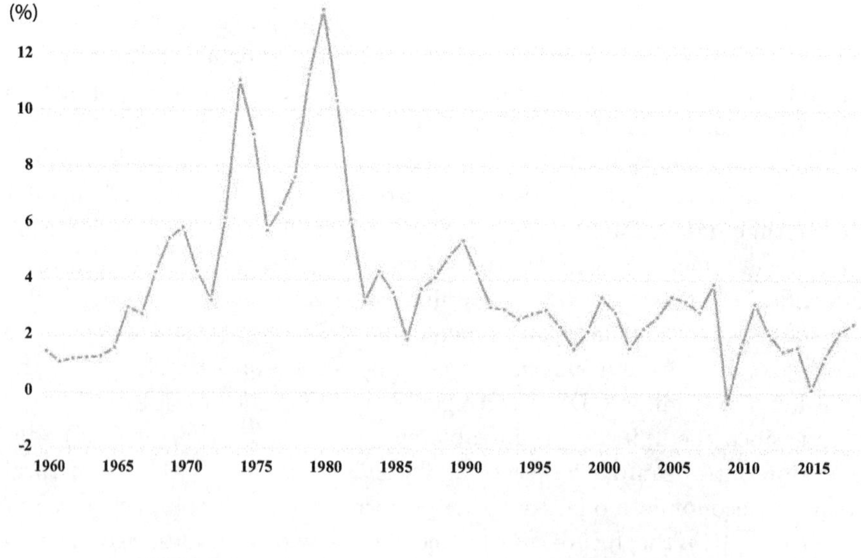

Figure 1.2 Time series plots of annual U.S. inflation rates.
Data source: http://data.worldbank.org

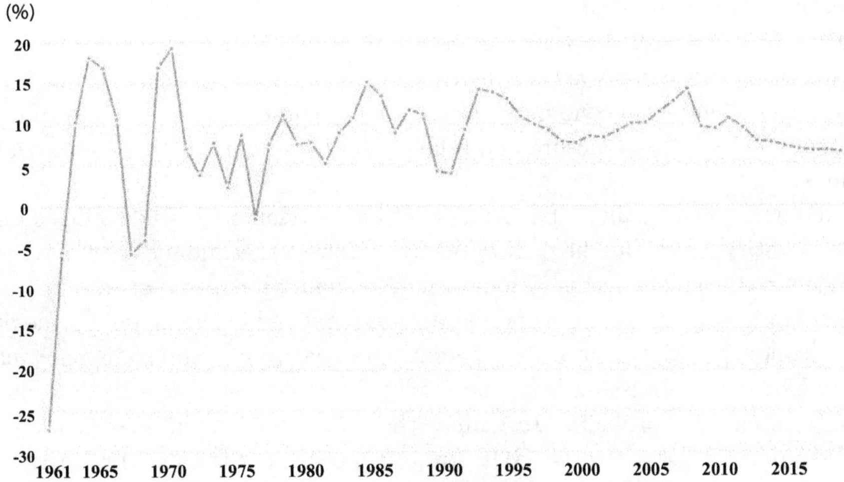

Figure 1.3 Time series plots of Chinese GDP growth rates.
Data source: http://data.worldbank.org

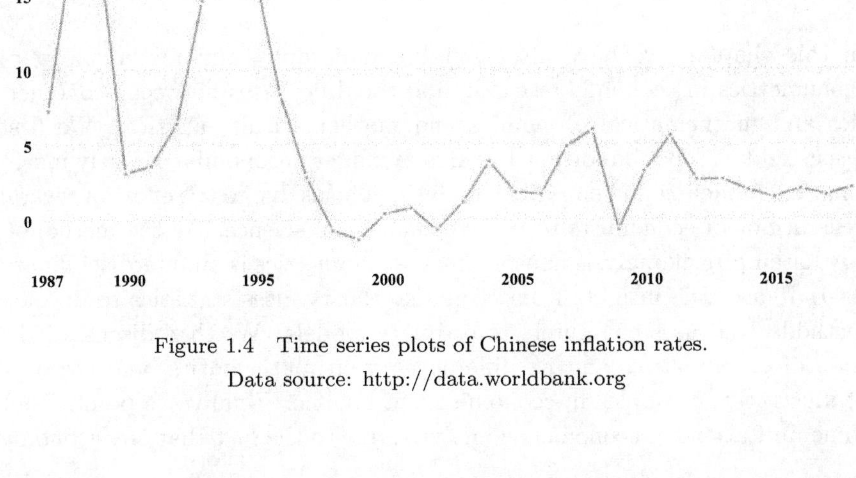

Figure 1.4 Time series plots of Chinese inflation rates.
Data source: http://data.worldbank.org

whether there exist structural breaks. Engle's (1982) volatility model can be used to forecast time-varying volatility using historical asset returns. Nevertheless, the time-varying feature of an economic system always imposes a challenge for economic forecasts. This is quite different from natural sciences, where the structure and relationships are more or less stable over time.

Fourth, data quality. The success of any econometric study hinges on the quantity as well as the quality of data. However, economic data may be subject to various defects. The data may be badly measured or may correspond only vaguely to the economic variables defined in the model. Some of the economic variables may be inherently unmeasurable, and some relevant variables may be missing from the model. Moreover, sample selection bias will also cause a problem. In China, there may have been a tendency to over-report or estimate the GDP growth rates given the existing institutional promotion mechanism for local government officials. All these data problems remain even in the current era of Big data, which consists of both structured and unstructured data. The latter includes data in form of texts, graphs, voices and videos. Of course, the advances in computer technology and artificial intelligence, the development of statistical sampling theory and practice can help improve the quality of economic data. For example, the use of scanning machines makes every transaction data available.

The above features of economic data and economic systems together unavoidably impose some limitations for econometrics to achieve the same mature stage as the natural science.

1.7 Conclusion

In this chapter, we have discussed the philosophy and methodology of econometrics in economic research, and the differences between econometrics and mathematical economics and mathematical statistics. We first discussed two most important features of modern economics, namely mathematical modeling and empirical analysis. This is due to the effort of several generations of economists to make economics a science. As the methodology for empirical analysis in economics, econometrics is an interdisciplinary field. It uses the insights from economic theory, uses statistics to develop methods, and uses computers to estimate models. We then discussed the roles of econometrics and its differences from mathematics, via a variety of illustrative examples in economics and finance. Finally, we pointed out some limitations of econometric analysis, due to the fact that any economy is not a controlled experiment and so most observed economic data are nonexperimental in nature. It should be emphasized that these limitations are not only the limitations of econometrics, but of economics as a whole.

Exercise 1

1.1. Discuss the differences of the roles of mathematics and econometrics in economic research.

1.2. What are the fundamental axioms of econometrics? Discuss their roles and implications.

1.3. What are the limitations of econometric analysis? Discuss possible ways to alleviate the impact of these limits.

1.4. How do you perceive the roles of econometrics in decision-making in economics and business?

Chapter 2

General Regression Analysis

Abstract: This chapter introduces *regression analysis*, the most popular statistical tool to explore the dependence of one variable (say Y) on others (say X). The variable Y is called the dependent variable or response variable, and X is called the independent variable or explanatory variable. The regression relationship between X and Y can be used to study the effect of X on Y or to predict Y using X. We motivate the importance of the regression function from both the economic and statistical perspectives, and characterize the condition for correct specification of a linear model for the regression function, which is shown to be crucial for a valid economic interpretation of model parameters.

Keywords: Conditional distribution, Conditional mean, Consumption function, Correct model specification, Linear regression model, Marginal Propensity to Consume (MPC), Model misspecification, Regression

2.1 Conditional Probability Distribution

Throughout this book, we use the following notational conventions: capital letters (e.g., Y) denote random variables or random vectors, lower case letters (e.g., y) denote realizations of random variables.

We assume that $Z = (Y, X')'$ is a random vector with $E(Y^2) < \infty$, where Y is a scalar, X is a $(k+1) \times 1$ vector of variables with its first component being a constant, and X' denotes the transpose of X. Given this assumption, the conditional mean $E(Y|X)$ exists and is well-defined.

Statistically speaking, the relationship between two random variables or vectors X (e.g., oil price change) and Y (e.g., economic growth) can be characterized by their joint distribution function. Suppose $(X', Y)'$ are continuous random vectors, and the joint Probability Density Function (PDF)

of $(X', Y)'$ is $f(x, y)$. Then the marginal PDF of X is

$$f_X(x) = \int_{-\infty}^{\infty} f(x, y)dy,$$

and the conditional PDF of Y given $X = x$ is

$$f_{Y|X}(y|x) = \frac{f(x, y)}{f_X(x)},$$

provided $f_X(x) > 0$. The conditional PDF $f_{Y|X}(y|x)$ completely describes how Y depends on X. In other words, it characterizes a predictive relationship of Y using X. With this conditional PDF $f_{Y|X}(y|x)$, we can compute the following quantities:

- conditional mean

$$\begin{aligned} E(Y|x) &\equiv E(Y|X = x) \\ &= \int_{-\infty}^{\infty} y f_{Y|X}(y|x)dy; \end{aligned}$$

- conditional variance

$$\begin{aligned} \text{var}(Y|x) &\equiv \text{var}(Y|X = x) \\ &= \int_{-\infty}^{\infty} [y - E(Y|x)]^2 f_{Y|X}(y|x)dy \\ &= E(Y^2|x) - [E(Y|x)]^2; \end{aligned}$$

- conditional skewness

$$S(Y|x) = \frac{E\{[Y - E(Y|x)]^3|x\}}{[\text{var}(Y|x)]^{3/2}};$$

- conditional kurtosis

$$K(Y|x) = \frac{E\{[Y - E(Y|x)]^4|x\}}{[\text{var}(Y|x)]^2};$$

- α-conditional quantile $Q(x, \alpha)$, which is determined by the following equation:

$$P[Y \leq Q(X, \alpha)|X = x] = \alpha \in (0, 1).$$

Note that when $\alpha = \frac{1}{2}$, $Q(x, \frac{1}{2})$ is the conditional median, which is the cutoff point or threshold that divides the population into two equal halves, conditional on $X = x$.

The class of conditional moments is a summary characterization of the conditional distribution $f_{Y|X}(y|x)$. A mathematical model (i.e., an assumed functional form with a finite number of unknown parameters) for a conditional moment is called an econometric model for that conditional moment.

Question: Which moment to model and use in practice?

It depends on economic applications. For some applications, we only need to model the first conditional moment, namely the conditional mean. For example, asset pricing aims at explaining excess asset returns by systematic risk factors. An asset pricing model is essentially a model for the conditional mean of asset returns on risk factors. For others, we may have to model higher order conditional moments and even the entire conditional distribution. In econometric practice, the most popular models are the first two conditional moments, namely the conditional mean and conditional variance. There is no need to model the entire conditional distribution of Y given X when only certain conditional moments are needed. For example, when the conditional mean is of concern, there is no need to model the conditional variance or impose restrictive conditions on it.

The conditional moments, and more generally the conditional probability distribution of Y given X, are not the causal relationship from X to Y. They are a predictive relationship from a statistical perspective. That is, one can use the information on X to predict the distribution of Y or its attributes. These probability concepts cannot tell whether the change in Y is caused by the change in X. Such causal interpretation has to reply on economic theory. Economic theory usually hypothesizes that a change in Y is caused by a change in X, i.e., there exists a causal relationship from X to Y. If such an economic causal relationship exists, we will find a predictive relationship from X to Y. On the other hand, a documented predictive relationship from X to Y may not be caused by an economic causal relationship from X to Y. For example, it is possible that both X and Y are positively correlated due to their dependence on a common factor. As a result, we will find a predictive relationship from X to Y, although they do not have any causal relationship. In fact, it is well-known in econometrics that some economic variables that trend consistently upwards over time are highly correlated even in the absence of any causal relationship between them. Such strong correlations are called spurious relationships. One of the most important goals of econometric analysis is to identify economic causal relationships using nonexperimental observations.

2.2 Conditional Mean and Regression Analysis

We now focus on the first conditional moment, $E(Y|X)$, which is called the regression function of Y on X, where Y is called the regressand, and X is called the regressor vector. We note that the $(k+1) \times 1$ regressor vector X is usually constructed from a set of economic explanatory variables. For example, $X = (1, Z, Z^2, ..., Z^k)'$, where Z is an economic variable such as income or age. The term "regression" is used to signify a predictive relationship between Y and X.

Definition 2.1. [Regression Function]: The conditional mean $E(Y|X)$ is called a regression function of Y on X.

Many economic theories can be characterized by the conditional mean $E(Y|X)$ of Y given X, provided X and Y are suitably defined. Most, though not all, of dynamic economic theories and/or dynamic optimization models, such as rational expectations, efficient market hypothesis (EMH), expectations hypothesis, and optimal dynamic asset pricing, have important implications on (and only on) the conditional mean of underlying economic variables given the information available to economic agents (e.g., Cochrane 2001, Ljungqvist and Sargent 2002). For example, the classical efficient market hypothesis states that the expected asset return given the information available, is zero, or at most, is constant over time; the optimal dynamic asset pricing theory implies that the expectation of the pricing error given the information available is zero for each asset (Cochrane 2001). Although economic theory may suggest a nonlinear relationship, it does not give a completely specified functional form for the conditional mean of economic variables. It is therefore important to model the conditional mean properly.

The term "regression" was coined by Galton (1877, 1885) in the nineteenth century to describe a biological phenomenon. The phenomenon was that the heights of descendants of tall ancestors tend to regress down towards a normal average, a phenomenon also known as regression toward the mean. For Galton, regression had only this biological meaning, but his work was later extended by Yule (1897) and Pearson (1903) to a more general statistical context. In the work of Yule and Pearson, the joint distribution of the response and explanatory variables is assumed to be normal. This assumption was weakened by Fisher (1922, 1925), who assumed that the conditional distribution of the response variable is normal, but the joint distribution need not be. In this respect, Fisher's assumption is closer to Gauss' (1821) formulation.

Most commonly, regression analysis is concerned with the conditional expectation of the dependent variable or response variable given the explanatory variables, that is, the average value of the dependent variable when the explanatory variables are fixed. Less commonly, the focus can also be on a quantile, or other location parameter of the conditional distribution of the dependent variable given the explanatory variables. For the case of a conditional quantile, one usually calls it the quantile regression function. In all cases, a function of the explanatory variables is loosely called the regression function.

Conditional mean analysis or regression analysis is one of the most popular statistical methods in econometrics, and has wide applications in economics. For example, it can be used to estimate economic relationships, test economic hypotheses, predict the future evolution of the economy, and conduct policy evaluation. Below are a few commonly seen examples.

Example 2.1. [Consumption Function]: Let Y be consumption, X be disposable income. Then $E(Y|X) = C(X)$ is called a consumption function, which signifies how consumption depends on income. The first derivative of the consumption function $C(X)$ is called the Marginal Propensity to Consume (MPC):

$$MPC = C'(X) = \frac{dE(Y|X)}{dX}.$$

MPC is a very important concept in Keynes' multiplier effect analysis. Furthermore, if Y denotes food consumption, then according to Engel's law, MPC is a decreasing function of X. Therefore, one can verify Engel's law by empirically testing whether $C'(X)$ is a decreasing function of X.

Example 2.2. [Production Function]: Let Y be output, X be labor, capital and raw materials. Then the regression function $E(Y|X) = F(X)$ is called a production function, which tells too much output can be produced given the amount of inputs X. Most well-known examples of production functions are the Cobb-Douglas and translog functions (see, Christiansen *et al.* 1971 and 1973). A production function can be used to test the Constant Return to Scale (CRS) hypothesis. CRS is defined as follows:

$$\lambda F(X) = F(\lambda X) \text{ for all } \lambda > 0.$$

Example 2.3. [Cost Function]: Let Y be the production cost to produce output X. Then the regression function $E(Y|X) = C(X)$ is called a cost function. For a monopolistic firm or industry, its marginal cost is a decreasing function of output X, namely,

$$\frac{dE(Y|X)}{dX} = C'(X) > 0,$$

$$\frac{d^2E(Y|X)}{dX^2} = C''(X) < 0.$$

This property implies that the cost function for a monopolistic firm is a nonlinear function of output X. Therefore, a linear regression function of X is inappropriate.

Before modeling $E(Y|X)$, we first discuss some probabilistic properties of $E(Y|X)$.

Lemma 2.1. $E[E(Y|X)] = E(Y)$.

Proof: The result follows immediately from applying the law of iterated expectations below.

Lemma 2.2. ***[Law of Iterated Expectations]:*** *For any measurable function $G(X, Y)$,*

$$E[G(X,Y)] = E\{E[G(X,Y)|X]\},$$

provided the expectation $E[G(X, Y)]$ exists.

Proof: We consider the case of the joint continuous distribution of $(Y, X')'$ only. By the multiplication rule that the joint PDF $f(x, y) =$

$f_{Y|X}(y|x)f_X(x)$, we have

$$\begin{aligned} E[G(X,Y)] &= \int_{-\infty}^{\infty}\int_{-\infty}^{\infty} G(x,y)f_{XY}(x,y)dxdy \\ &= \int_{-\infty}^{\infty}\int_{-\infty}^{\infty} G(x,y)f_{Y|X}(y|x)f_X(x)dxdy \\ &= \int_{-\infty}^{\infty}\left[\int_{-\infty}^{\infty} G(x,y)f_{Y|X}(y|x)dy\right] f_X(x)dx \\ &= \int_{-\infty}^{\infty} E[G(X,Y)|X=x]f_X(x)dx \\ &= E\{E[G(X,Y)|X]\}, \end{aligned}$$

where the operator $E(\cdot|X)$ is the expectation with respect to $f_{Y|X}(\cdot|X)$, and the operator $E(\cdot)$ is the expectation with respect to the marginal PDF $f_X(\cdot)$ of X. The law of iterated expectations is also called the law of total expectations in probability theory. This completes the proof.

Question: How to interpret the law of iterated expectations from an economic perspective?

We now provide some examples.

Example 2.4. Suppose Y is wage, and X is a gender dummy variable, taking value 1 if an employee is female and value 0 if an employee is male. Then

$$\begin{aligned} E(Y|X=1) &= \text{ average wage of a female worker}, \\ E(Y|X=0) &= \text{ average wage of a male worker}, \end{aligned}$$

and the overall average wage

$$\begin{aligned} E(Y) &= E[E(Y|X)] \\ &= P(X=1)E(Y|X=1) + P(X=0)E(Y|X=0), \end{aligned}$$

where $P(X=1)$ is the proportion of female employees in the labor force, and $P(X=0)$ is the proportion of the male employees in the labor force. The use of the law of iterated expectations here thus provides some insight into the income distribution between genders.

Example 2.5. Suppose Y is an asset return and we have two information sets: I and J, where $I \subset J$ so that all information in I is contained in J but J contains some extra information. Then we have a conditional version of the law of iterated expectations says that

$$E(Y|I) = E[E(Y|J)|I]$$

or equivalently

$$E\{[Y - E(Y|J)|I]\} = 0,$$

where $Y - E(Y|J)$ is the prediction error using the superior information set J. The conditional law of iterated expectations says that one cannot use a limited information I to predict the prediction error one would make if one had superior information J. In other words, the larger information set J has superior forecasting power than the information set I. See Campbell, Lo and MacKinlay (1997, p.23) for more discussion.

Question: Why is $E(Y|X)$ important from a statistical perspective?

Suppose we are interested in predicting Y using some function $g(X)$ of X, and we use a so-called Mean Squared Error (MSE) criterion to evaluate how well $g(X)$ approximates Y. Then the optimal predictor under the MSE criterion is the conditional mean, as will be shown below.

We first define the MSE criterion. Intuitively, MSE is the average of the squared deviations between the predictor $g(X)$ and the actual outcome Y.

Definition 2.2. **[MSE]:** Suppose function $g(X)$ is used to predict Y. Then the mean squared error of function $g(X)$ is defined as

$$\text{MSE}(g) = E\left[Y - g(X)\right]^2,$$

provided the expectation exists.

The theorem below states that $E(Y|X)$ minimizes MSE.

Theorem 2.1. ***[Optimality of E(Y|X)]:*** *The regression function $E(Y|X)$ is the solution to the optimization problem*

$$\begin{aligned} E(Y|X) &= \arg\min_{g \in \mathbb{F}} \text{MSE(g)} \\ &= \arg\min_{g \in \mathbb{F}} E[Y - g(X)]^2, \end{aligned}$$

where $\mathbb{F}$ *is the space of all measurable and square-integrable functions*

$$\mathbb{F} = \left\{ g(\cdot)\colon \int_{-\infty}^{\infty} g^2(x) f_X(x) dx < \infty \right\}.$$

Proof: We will use the variance and squared-bias decomposition technique. Put

$$g_o(X) \equiv E(Y|X).$$

Then

$$\begin{aligned}
\text{MSE}(g) &= E[Y - g(X)]^2 \\
&= E\left[Y - g_o(X) + g_o(X) - g(X)\right]^2 \\
&= E\left[Y - g_o(X)\right]^2 + E\left[g_o(X) - g(X)\right]^2 \\
&\quad + 2E\{[Y - g_o(X)]\left[g_o(X) - g(X)\right]\} \\
&= E\left[Y - g_o(X)\right]^2 + E\left[g_o(X) - g(X)\right]^2,
\end{aligned}$$

where the cross-product term

$$E\{[Y - g_o(X)]\left[g_o(X) - g(X)\right]\} = 0$$

by the law of iterated expectations and the fact that $E\{[Y - g_o(X)]|X\} = 0$ almost surely.

In the above MSE decomposition, the first term $E[Y - g_o(X)]^2$ is the quadratic variation of the prediction error of the regression function $g_o(X)$. This does not depend on the choice of function $g(X)$. The second term $E[g_o(X) - g(X)]^2$ is the quadratic variation of the approximation error of $g(X)$ for $g_o(X)$. This term achieves its minimum of zero if and only if one chooses $g(X) = g_o(X)$ a.s. Because the first term $E[Y - g_o(X)]^2$ does not depend on $g(X)$, minimizing MSE(g) is equivalent to minimizing the second term $E[g_o(X) - g(X)]^2$. Therefore, the optimal solution for minimizing MSE(g) is given by $g^*(X) = g_o(X)$. This completes the proof.

MSE is a popular statistical criterion for measuring precision of a predictor $g(X)$ for Y. It has at least two advantages: first, it can be analyzed conveniently, and second, it has a nice decomposition of a variance component and a squared-bias component.

However, MSE is one of many possible criteria for measuring goodness of the predictor $g(X)$ for Y. In general, any increasing function of the absolute value $|Y - g(X)|$ can be used to measure the goodness of fit for the predictor $g(X)$. For example, the Mean Absolute Error (MAE)

$$\text{MAE}(g) = E|Y - g(X)|$$

is also a reasonable statistical criterion.

It should be emphasized that different criteria have different optimizers. For example, the optimizer for MAE(g) is the conditional median, rather than the conditional mean. The conditional median, say $m(x)$, is defined as the solution to

$$\int_{-\infty}^{m} f_{Y|X}(y|x)dy = \frac{1}{2}.$$

In other words, $m(x)$ divides the conditional population distribution into two equal halves.

Example 2.6. Let the joint PDF $f_{XY}(x, y) = e^{-y}$ for $0 < x < y < \infty$. Find $E(Y|X)$ and $\text{var}(Y|X)$.

Solution: We first find the conditional PDF $f_{Y|X}(y|x)$. The marginal PDF of X

$$\begin{aligned} f_X(x) &= \int_{-\infty}^{\infty} f_{XY}(x, y)dy \\ &= \int_{x}^{\infty} e^{-y}dy \\ &= e^{-x} \text{ for } 0 < x < \infty. \end{aligned}$$

Therefore,

$$\begin{aligned} f_{Y|X}(y|x) &= \frac{f_{XY}(x, y)}{f_X(x)} \\ &= e^{-(y-x)} \text{ for } 0 < x < y < \infty. \end{aligned}$$

Then

$$\begin{aligned} E(Y|x) &= \int_{-\infty}^{\infty} y f_{Y|X}(y|x)dy \\ &= \int_{x}^{\infty} ye^{-(y-x)}dy \\ &= e^{x}\int_{x}^{\infty} ye^{-y}dy \\ &= -e^{x}\int_{x}^{\infty} yde^{-y} \\ &= 1 + x. \end{aligned}$$

Thus, the regression function $E(Y|X)$ is linear in X.

To compute $\mathrm{var}(Y|X)$, we will use the formula

$$\mathrm{var}(Y|X) = E(Y^2|X) - [E(Y|X)]^2 .$$

Because

$$\begin{aligned}
E(Y^2|x) &= \int_{-\infty}^{\infty} y^2 f_{Y|X}(y|x) dy \\
&= \int_{x}^{\infty} y^2 e^{-(y-x)} dy \\
&= e^x \int_{x}^{\infty} y^2 e^{-y} dy \\
&= -e^x \int_{x}^{\infty} y^2 de^{-y} \text{ where } de^{-y} = -e^{-y}dy \\
&= (-e^x)\left(y^2 e^{-y}|_x^\infty - \int_{x}^{\infty} e^{-y} dy^2 \right) \\
&= (-e^x)\left(0 - x^2 e^{-x} - 2\int_{x}^{\infty} y e^{-y} dy \right) \\
&= x^2 + 2e^x \int_{x}^{\infty} y e^{-y} dy \\
&= x^2 + 2\int_{x}^{\infty} y e^{-(y-x)} dy \\
&= x^2 + 2(1+x),
\end{aligned}$$

we have

$$\begin{aligned}
\mathrm{var}(Y|x) &= E(Y^2|x) - [E(Y|x)]^2 \\
&= x^2 + 2(1+x) - (1+x)^2 \\
&= 1.
\end{aligned}$$

The conditional variance of Y given X does not depend on X. That is, X has no effect on the conditional variance of Y.

The above example shows that while the conditional mean of Y given X is a linear function of X, the conditional variance of Y may not depend on X. This is essentially the assumption made in the classical linear regression model (see Chapter 3). Another example for which we have a linear regression function with constant conditional variance is when X and Y are jointly normally distributed.

Example 2.7. Suppose X and Y follow a bivariate normal distribution, denoted as $BN(\mu_1, \mu_2, \sigma_1^2, \sigma_2^2, \rho)$, such that their joint PDF

$$f_{XY}(x,y) = \frac{1}{2\pi\sigma_1\sigma_2\sqrt{1-\rho^2}} \exp\left\{-\frac{1}{2(1-\rho^2)}\left[\left(\frac{x-\mu_1}{\sigma_1}\right)^2 - 2\rho\left(\frac{x-\mu_1}{\sigma_1}\right)\left(\frac{y-\mu_2}{\sigma_2}\right) + \left(\frac{y-\mu_2}{\sigma_2}\right)^2\right]\right\}.$$

Show: (1) $E(Y|X) = \mu_2 + \frac{\sigma_2}{\sigma_1}\rho(X-\mu_1)$; (2) $\text{var}(Y|X) = \sigma_2^2(1-\rho^2)$.

Solution: Left as an exercise. In fact, it can be shown that conditional on X, Y follows a normal distribution with mean $E(Y|X)$ and variance $\text{var}(Y|X)$ given above.

Theorem 2.2. ***[Regression Identity]:*** *Suppose $E(Y|X)$ exists. Then we can always write*

$$Y = E(Y|X) + \varepsilon,$$

where ε is called the regression disturbance and has the property that

$$E(\varepsilon|X) = 0.$$

Proof: Put $\varepsilon = Y - E(Y|X)$. Then

$$Y = E(Y|X) + \varepsilon,$$

where

$$\begin{aligned} E(\varepsilon|X) &= E\{[Y - E(Y|X)]|X\} \\ &= E(Y|X) - E[g_o(X)|X] \\ &= E(Y|X) - g_o(X) \\ &= 0. \end{aligned}$$

The regression function $E(Y|X)$ can be used to predict the expected value of Y using the information of X. In regression analysis, an important issue is the direction of causation between Y and X. In practice, one often hopes to check whether Y "depends" on or can be "explained" by X, with help of economic theory. For this reason, Y is called the dependent variable, and X is called the explanatory variable or vector. However, it should be emphasized that the regression function $E(Y|X)$ itself does not tell any economic causal relationship between Y and X.

The random variable ε represents the part of Y that is not captured by $E(Y|X)$. It is usually called a *noise* or a *disturbance*, because it "disturbs" an otherwise stable or deterministic relationship between Y and X. On the other hand, the regression function $E(Y|X)$ is called a *signal.*

The property that $E(\varepsilon|X) = 0$ implies that the regression disturbance ε contains no systematic information of X that can be used to predict the expected value of Y. In other words, all information of X that can be used to predict the expectation of Y has been completely summarized by $E(Y|X)$. The condition $E(\varepsilon|X) = 0$ is crucial for the validity of economic interpretation of model parameters, as will be seen shortly.

The property that $E(\varepsilon|X) = 0$ implies that the unconditional mean of ε is zero:

$$E(\varepsilon) = E[E(\varepsilon|X)] = 0$$

and that ε is orthogonal to X:

$$\begin{aligned} E(X\varepsilon) &= E\left[E(X\varepsilon|X)\right] \\ &= E\left[XE(\varepsilon|X)\right] \\ &= E(X \cdot 0) \\ &= 0. \end{aligned}$$

Since $E(\varepsilon) = 0$, we have $E(X\varepsilon) = \mathrm{cov}(X, \varepsilon)$. Thus, the orthogonality condition $E(X\varepsilon) = 0$ means that X and ε are uncorrelated.

In fact, ε is orthogonal to any measurable function of X, i.e., $E[\varepsilon h(X)] = 0$ for any measurable function $h(\cdot)$. This implies that we cannot predict the mean of ε by using any possible model $h(X)$, no matter it is linear or nonlinear.

Question: Is $E(\varepsilon|X) = 0$ equivalent to $E[\varepsilon h(X)] = 0$ for all measurable $h(\cdot)$?

The answer is yes. See Exercise 2.15 at the end of this chapter for more discussion on this challenging problem.

It is possible that $E(\varepsilon|X) = 0$ but $\mathrm{var}(\varepsilon|X)$ is a function of X. If $\mathrm{var}(\varepsilon|X) = \sigma^2 > 0$, the conditional variance of ε does not depend on the value of X, and we say that there exists *conditional homoskedasticity* for ε. This is also known as homogeneity of conditional variance. In this case, X cannot be used to predict the (quadratic) variation of Y. On the other hand, if $\mathrm{var}(\varepsilon|X) \neq \sigma^2$ for any constant $\sigma^2 > 0$, the conditional variance of ε depends on the value of X, and we say that there exists *conditional heteroskedasticity*. Figures 2.1 and 2.2 provide a data illustration of conditional homoskedasticity and conditional heteroskedasticity respectively. Conditional heteroskedasticity is a rule rather than an exception for most economic data. Granger and Machina (2006) provide various interesting examples to illustrate how conditional heteroskedasticity can arise in economics. The existence of conditional heteroskedasticity has huge impact on statistical inferences. In particular, econometric inference procedures of regression analysis are usually different, depending on whether there exists conditional heteroskedasticity. For example, the so-called classical t-test and F-test are invalid under conditional heteroskedasticity (see Chapter 3 for the introduction of the t-test and F-test). This will be emphasized and discussed in detail in subsequent chapters.

Example 2.8. Suppose

$$\varepsilon = \eta\sqrt{\beta_0 + \beta_1 X^2},$$

where random variables X and η are independent, and $E(\eta) = 0$, $\text{var}(\eta) = 1$. Find $E(\varepsilon|X)$ and $\text{var}(\varepsilon|X)$.

Solution:

$$\begin{aligned} E(\varepsilon|X) &= E\left[\eta\sqrt{\beta_0 + \beta_1 X^2}\,|X\right] \\ &= \sqrt{\beta_0 + \beta_1 X^2}E(\eta|X) \\ &= \sqrt{\beta_0 + \beta_1 X^2}E(\eta) \\ &= \sqrt{\beta_0 + \beta_1 X^2}\cdot 0 \\ &= 0. \end{aligned}$$

Next,

$$\begin{aligned} \text{var}(\varepsilon|X) &= E\left\{[\varepsilon - E(\varepsilon|X)]^2|X\right\} \\ &= E(\varepsilon^2|X) \\ &= E[\eta^2(\beta_0 + \beta_1 X^2)|X] \\ &= (\beta_0 + \beta_1 X^2)E(\eta^2|X) \\ &= (\beta_0 + \beta_1 X^2)\cdot 1 \\ &= \beta_0 + \beta_1 X^2. \end{aligned}$$

Although the conditional mean ε given X is identically zero, the conditional variance of ε given X depends on X.

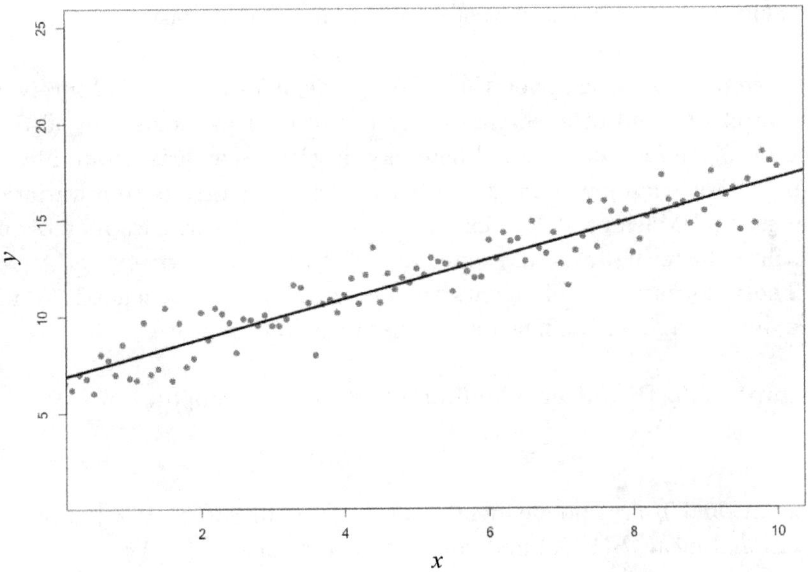

Figure 2.1 Scatter plots of a linear regression with conditional homoskedasticity.

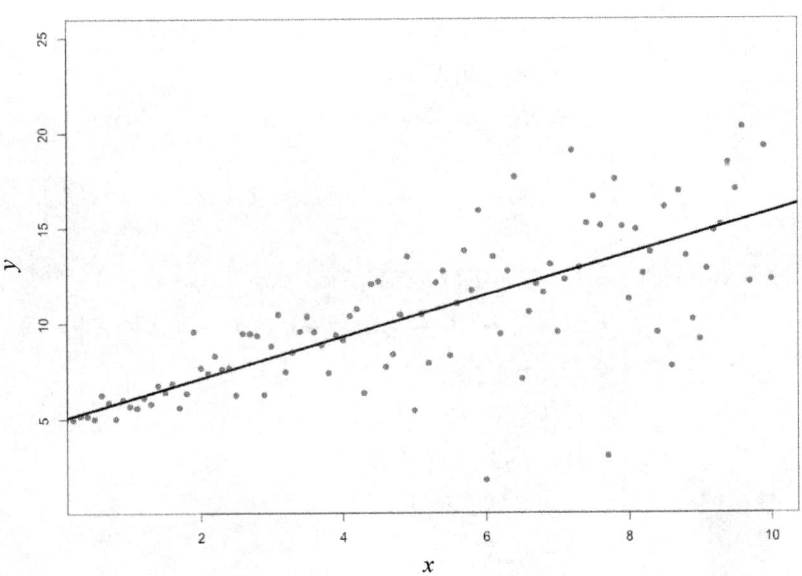

Figure 2.2 Scatter plots of a linear regression with conditional heteroskedasticity.

Question: Why may there exist conditional heteroskedasticity?

Generally speaking, given that $E(Y|X)$ depends on X, it is conceivable that $\text{var}(Y|X)$ and other higher order conditional moments may also depend on X. In fact, conditional heteroskedasticity may arise from different sources. For example, a larger firm may have a larger output variation. Granger and Machina (2006) explain why economic variables may display volatility clustering from an economic structural perspective.

The following example shows that conditional heteroskedasticity may arise due to random coefficients in a data generating process.

Example 2.9. [Random Coefficient Process]: Suppose

$$Y = \beta_0 + (\beta_1 + \beta_2\eta)X + \eta,$$

where X and η are independent, and $E(\eta) = 0$, $\text{var}(\eta) = \sigma_\eta^2$. Find the conditional mean $E(Y|X)$ and conditional variance $\text{var}(Y|X)$.

Solution: (1)

$$\begin{aligned} E(Y|X) &= \beta_0 + E[(\beta_1 + \beta_2\eta)X|X] + E(\eta|X) \\ &= \beta_0 + \beta_1 X + \beta_2 X E(\eta|X) + E(\eta|X) \\ &= \beta_0 + \beta_1 X + \beta_2 X E(\eta) + E(\eta) \\ &= \beta_0 + \beta_1 X + \beta_2 X \cdot 0 + 0 \\ &= \beta_0 + \beta_1 X. \end{aligned}$$

(2)

$$\begin{aligned} \text{var}(Y|X) &= E\left[(Y - E(Y|X))^2|X\right] \\ &= E\left\{[\beta_0 + (\beta_1 + \beta_2\eta)X + \eta - \beta_0 - \beta_1 X]^2|X\right\} \\ &= E\left[(\beta_2 X\eta + \eta)^2|X\right] \\ &= E\left[(\beta_2 X + 1)^2\eta^2|X\right] \\ &= (1 + \beta_2 X)^2 E(\eta^2|X) \\ &= (1 + \beta_2 X)^2 E(\eta^2) \\ &= (1 + \beta_2 X)^2 \sigma_\eta^2. \end{aligned}$$

The random coefficient process has been used to explain why the conditional variance may depend on the regressor X. We can write this process as

$$Y = \beta_0 + \beta_1 X + \varepsilon,$$

where

$$\varepsilon = (1 + \beta_2 X)\eta.$$

Note that $E(\varepsilon|X) = 0$ but $\text{var}(\varepsilon|X) = (1 + \eta_2 X)^2 \sigma_\eta^2$.

2.3 Linear Regression Modeling

As we have known above, the conditional mean $g_o(X) \equiv E(Y|X)$ is the solution to the MSE optimization problem

$$\min_{g \in \mathbb{F}} E[Y - g(X)]^2,$$

where $\mathbb{F}$ is a class of functions that includes all measurable and square-integrable functions, i.e.,

$$\mathbb{F} = \left\{ g : \mathbb{R}^{k+1} \to \mathbb{R} \;\middle|\; \int g^2(x) f_X(x) dx < \infty \right\}.$$

In general, the regression function $E(Y|X)$ is an unknown functional form of X. Economic theory usually suggests a qualitative relationship between X and Y (e.g., the cost of production is an increasing function of output X), but it never suggests a concrete functional form. One needs to use some mathematical model to approximate $g_o(X)$.

Question: How to model the conditional mean $E(Y|X) = g_o(X)$?

In econometrics, a most popular modeling strategy is the parametric approach, which assumes a known functional form for $g_o(X)$, up to some unknown parameters. In particular, one usually uses a class of linear functions to approximate $g_o(x)$, which is simple and easy to interpret. This is the approach we will take in most of this book.

We first introduce a class of affine functions.

Definition 2.3. [Affine Function]: Denote

$$X = \begin{pmatrix} 1 \\ X_1 \\ \vdots \\ X_k \end{pmatrix}, \; \beta = \begin{pmatrix} \beta_0 \\ \beta_1 \\ \vdots \\ \beta_k \end{pmatrix}.$$

Then the class of affine functions is defined as

$$\begin{aligned}\mathbb{A} &= \left\{g : \mathbb{R}^{k+1} \to \mathbb{R} : g(X) = \beta_0 + \sum_{j=1}^{k} \beta_j X_j, \beta_j \in \mathbb{R}\right\} \\ &= \left\{g : \mathbb{R}^{k+1} \to \mathbb{R} \mid g(X) = \beta' X\right\}.\end{aligned}$$

Here, there is no restriction on the values of parameter vector β. For this class of functions, the functional form is known to be linear in both regressor variables X and parameters β; the unknown is the $(k+1) \times 1$ vector β.

From an econometric point of view, the key feature of $\mathbb{A}$ is that $g(X) = X'\beta$ is linear in both regressor vector X and parameter vector β. We emphasize that the regressor vector X are constructed from a set of economic explanatory variables. The regressor vector X can be a vector of different economic explanatory variables; it can also be a vector of economic explanatory variables and their nonlinear transformations. For example, when $k = 1$, we can assume

$$g(X) = \beta_0 + \beta_1 X_1 + \beta_2 X_1^2,$$

or

$$g(X) = \beta_0 + \beta_1 \ln X_1,$$

where X_1 is an economic explanatory variable (e.g., income). The corresponding regressor vectors in these cases are $X = (1, X_1, X_1^2)'$ and $X = (1, \ln X_1)'$ respectively. Obviously, the dependent variable Y is always linear in regressor vector X but it may be nonlinear in economic variable X_1. Such models are called linear regression models. Conversely, a nonlinear regression model for $g_o(X)$ means a known parametric functional form $g(X, \beta)$ which is nonlinear in regression vector X and parameter vector β. An example is the so-called logistic regression model

$$g(X, \beta) = \frac{1}{1 + \exp(-X'\beta)}.$$

Nonlinear regression models can be handled using the analytic tools developed in Chapters 8 and 9. See more discussion there.

We now solve the constrained minimization problem

$$\min_{g \in \mathbb{A}} E[Y - g(X)]^2 = \min_{\beta \in \mathbb{R}^{k+1}} E(Y - X'\beta)^2.$$

The solution

$$g^*(X) = X'\beta^*$$

is called the best linear least squares predictor for Y, and β^* is called the best least squares approximation coefficient vector.

Theorem 2.3. ***[Best Linear Least Squares Prediction]:*** *Suppose $E(Y^2) < \infty$ and the $(k+1) \times (k+1)$ matrix $E(XX')$ is nonsingular. Then the best linear least squares predictor that solves*

$$\min_{g \in \mathbb{A}} E[Y - g(X)]^2 = \min_{\beta \in \mathbb{R}^{k+1}} E(Y - X'\beta)^2$$

is the linear function

$$g^*(X) = X'\beta^*,$$

where the optimizing coefficient vector

$$\beta^* = [E(XX')]^{-1}E(XY).$$

Proof: First, noting that

$$\min_{g \in \mathbb{A}} E[Y - g(X)]^2 = \min_{\beta \in \mathbb{R}^{k+1}} E(Y - X'\beta)^2,$$

we first find the FOC:

$$\frac{d}{d\beta}E(Y - X'\beta)^2|_{\beta=\beta^*} = 0.$$

The left hand side

$$\begin{aligned}
\frac{d}{d\beta}E(Y - X'\beta)^2 &= E\left[\frac{\partial}{\partial\beta}(Y - X'\beta)^2\right] \\
&= E\left[2(Y - X'\beta)\frac{\partial}{\partial\beta}(-X'\beta)\right] \\
&= -2E\left[(Y - X'\beta)\frac{\partial}{\partial\beta}(X'\beta)\right] \\
&= -2E[X(Y - X'\beta)].
\end{aligned}$$

Therefore, FOC implies that

$$E[X(Y - X'\beta^*)] = 0$$

or

$$E(XY) = E(XX')\beta^*.$$

Multiplying the inverse of $E(XX')$, we obtain

$$\beta^* = [E(XX')]^{-1}E(XY).$$

It remains to check the Second Order Condition (SOC): the Hessian matrix

$$\frac{d^2}{d\beta d\beta'}E(Y - X'\beta)^2 = 2E(XX')$$

is positive definite provided $E(XX')$ is nonsingular (why?). Therefore, β^* is a global minimizer. This completes the proof.

The moment condition $E(Y^2) < \infty$ ensures that $E(Y|X)$ exists and is well-defined. When the $(k+1) \times (k+1)$ matrix

$$E(XX') = \begin{bmatrix} 1 & E(X_1) & E(X_2) & \cdots & E(X_k) \\ E(X_1) & E(X_1^2) & E(X_1X_2) & \cdots & E(X_1X_k) \\ E(X_2) & E(X_2X_1) & E(X_2^2) & \cdots & \\ \vdots & \vdots & & & \\ E(X_k) & E(X_kX_1) & & & E(X_k^2) \end{bmatrix}$$

is nonsingular and $E(XY)$ exists, the best linear least squares approximation coefficient β^* is always well-defined, no matter whether $E(Y|X)$ is linear or nonlinear in X.

To gain insight into the nature of β^*, we consider a simple bivariate linear regression model where $\beta = (\beta_0, \beta_1)'$ and $X = (1, X_1)'$. Then the slope and intercept coefficients are, respectively,

$$\beta_1^* = \frac{\text{cov}(Y, X_1)}{\text{var}(X_1)},$$

$$\beta_0^* = E(Y) - \beta_1^* E(X_1).$$

Thus, the best linear least squares approximation coefficient β_1^* is proportional to $\text{cov}(Y, X_1)$. In other words, β_1^* captures the dependence between Y and X_1 that is measurable by $\text{cov}(Y, X_1)$. It will miss the dependence between Y and X_1 that cannot be measured by $\text{cov}(Y, X_1)$. Therefore, linear regression analysis is essentially *correlation analysis*.

On the other hand, White (1980) shows that if a Taylor series expansion (up to certain order) is used to approximate $E(Y|X)$, then the best linear least squares approximation coefficients of the Taylor series expansion model cannot identify the derivatives of $E(Y|X)$, unless $E(Y|X)$ is a linear function of X. In other words, the best linear least squares approximation coefficient β^* are not proportional to the derivatives of $E(Y|X)$ in the Taylor series expansion. For example, if $E(Y|X) = \beta_0^o + \beta_1^o X + \beta_2^o X^2$, then the last two components of the best least squares approximation coefficient vector β^* are not proportional to the first two derivatives of $E(Y|X)$.

In general, the best linear least squares predictor

$$g^*(X) \equiv X'\beta^* \neq E(Y|X).$$

An important question is what happens if $g^*(X) = X'\beta^* \neq E(Y|X)$? In particular, what is the interpretation of β^*?

We now discuss the relationship between the best linear least squares prediction and a linear regression model.

Definition 2.4. [Linear Regression Model]: The specification

$$Y = X'\beta + u, \ \beta \in \mathbb{R}^{k+1},$$

is called a linear regression model, where u is the regression model disturbance or regression model error. If $k = 1$, it is called a bivariate linear regression model or a straight line regression model. If $k > 1$, it is called a multiple linear regression model.

The linear regression model is an artificial specification. Nothing ensures that the regression function is linear, namely $E(Y|X) = X'\beta^o$ for some β^o. In other words, the linear model may not contain the true regression function $g_o(X) \equiv E(Y|X)$. However, even if $g_o(X)$ is not a linear function of X, the linear regression model $Y = X'\beta + u$ may still have some predictive ability although it is a misspecified model for $E(Y|X)$.

We first characterize the relationship between the best linear least squares approximation and the linear regression model.

Theorem 2.4. *Suppose the conditions of Theorem 2.3 hold. Let*

$$Y = X'\beta + u,$$

and let β^* be the best linear least squares approximation coefficient. Then

$$\beta = \beta^*$$

if and only if the following orthogonality condition holds:

$$E(Xu) = 0.$$

Proof: From the linear regression model $Y = X'\beta + u$, we have $u = Y - X'\beta$, and so

$$E(Xu) = E(XY) - E(XX')\beta.$$

(1) Necessity: If $\beta = \beta^*$, then

$$\begin{aligned} E(Xu) &= E(XY) - E(XX')\beta^* \\ &= E(XY) - E(XX')[E(XX')]^{-1}E(XY) \\ &= 0. \end{aligned}$$

(2) Sufficiency: If $E(Xu) = 0$, then

$$\begin{aligned} E(Xu) &= E(XY) - E(XX')\beta \\ &= 0. \end{aligned}$$

From this and the fact that $E(XX')$ is nonsingular, we have

$$\beta = [E(XX')]^{-1}E(XY) \equiv \beta^*.$$

This completes the proof.

Theorem 2.4 implies that no matter whether $E(Y|X)$ is linear or nonlinear in X, we can always write

$$Y = X'\beta + u$$

for some $\beta = \beta^*$ such that the orthogonality condition $E(Xu) = 0$ holds, where $u = Y - X'\beta^*$.

The orthogonality condition $E(Xu) = 0$ is fundamentally linked with the best least squares optimizer. If β is the best linear least squares coefficient β^*, then the disturbance u must be orthogonal to X. On the other hand, if X is orthogonal to u, then β must be the least squares minimizer β^*. Essentially the orthogonality between X and ε is the FOC of the best linear least squares problem! In other words, the orthogonality condition $E(Xu) = 0$ will always hold as long as the MSE criterion is used to obtain the best linear prediction. Note that when X contains an intercept, the orthogonality condition $E(Xu) = 0$ implies that $E(u) = 0$. In this case, we have $E(Xu) = \text{cov}(X, u)$. In other words, the orthogonality condition is equivalent to uncorrelatedness between X and u. This implies that u does not contain any component that can be predicted by a linear function of X.

The condition $E(Xu) = 0$ is fundamentally different from the condition $E(u|X) = 0$. The latter implies the former but not vice versa. In other words, $E(u|X) = 0$ implies $E(Xu) = 0$ but it is possible that $E(Xu) = 0$ and $E(u|X) \neq 0$. This can be illustrated by the following example.

Example 2.10. Suppose $u = (X^2 - 1) + \varepsilon$, where X and ε are independent N(0,1) random variables. Then

$$\begin{aligned} E(u|X) &= X^2 - 1 \neq 0, \text{ but} \\ E(Xu) &= E[X(X^2 - 1)] + E(X\varepsilon) \\ &= E(X^3) - E(X) + E(X)E(\varepsilon) \\ &= 0. \end{aligned}$$

2.4 Correct Model Specification for Conditional Mean

Question: What is the characterization of correct model specification for conditional mean?

Definition 2.5. [Correct Model Specification for Conditional Mean]: The linear regression model

$$Y = X'\beta + u, \ \beta \in \mathbb{R}^{k+1},$$

is said to be correctly specified for $E(Y|X)$ if

$$E(Y|X) = X'\beta^o \text{ for some parameter value } \beta^o \in \mathbb{R}^{k+1}.$$

On the other hand, if

$$E(Y|X) \neq X'\beta \text{ for all } \beta \in \mathbb{R}^{k+1},$$

then the linear regression model is said to be misspecified for $E(Y|X)$.

The class of linear regression models contains an infinite number of linear functions, each corresponding to a particular value of β. When the linear model is correctly specified, a linear function corresponding to some β^o will coincide with $g_o(X)$. The coefficient β^o is called the "true parameter value" or "true model parameter", because now it has a meaningful economic interpretation as the expected marginal effect of X on Y:

$$\beta^o = \frac{\partial E(Y|X)}{\partial X}.$$

For example, when Y is consumption and X is income, β^o is the MPC.

When β^o is a vector, the component

$$\beta_j^o = \frac{\partial E(Y|X)}{\partial X_j}, \qquad 1 \leq j \leq k,$$

is the partial expected marginal effect of regressor X_j on Y when holding all other regressor variables in X fixed. This is also called *ceteris paribus* expected marginal effect of X_j on Y. The term *ceteris paribus* means other things being equal.

We emphasize that the distinction between regressors and explanatory variables is important for the interpretation of parameter value β^o. For example, we consider a linear consumption model

$$Y = \beta_0^o + \beta_1^o X_1 + u,$$

where Y is consumption, X_1 is income, and $E(u|X_1) = 0$. This is a linear regression model where the consumption-income relationship is linear. The expected MPC is given by

$$\frac{\partial E(Y|X_1)}{\partial X_1} = \beta_1^o.$$

Now suppose we have a quadratic consumption function

$$Y = \beta_0^o + \beta_1^o X_1 + \beta_2^o X_1^2 + u.$$

This is still a linear regression model but the consumption-income relationship is nonlinear. As a result, the expected MPC is given by

$$\frac{\partial E(Y|X_1)}{\partial X_1} = \beta_1^o + 2\beta_2^o X_1,$$

which depends on the income level.

Question: What is the interpretation of the intercept coefficient β_0^o when a linear regression model is correctly specified for $g_o(X)$?

The intercept β_0^o corresponds to the intercept $X_0 = 1$, which is always uncorrelated with any other random variables. It captures the "average effect" on Y from all possible factors rather than the explanatory variables in X_t. For example, consider the standard Capital Asset Pricing Model (CAPM)

$$E(Y|X) = \beta_0^o + \beta_1^o X_1,$$

where Y is the excess portfolio return (i.e., the difference between a portfolio return and a risk-free rate) and X_1 is the excess market portfolio return (i.e., the difference between the market portfolio return and a risk-free rate). Here, β_0^o represents the average pricing error. When CAPM holds, $\beta_0^o = 0$. Thus, if the DGP has $\beta_0^o > 0$, CAPM underprices the portfolio. If $\beta_0^o < 0$, CAPM overprices the portfolio.

No economic theory ensures that the functional form of $E(Y|X)$ must be linear in X. Nonlinear functional form in X is a generic possibility. A linear regression model is misspecified for $E(Y|X)$ when, for example, $E(Y|X)$ is a nonlinear function of X. Therefore, we must be very cautious about the economic interpretation of linear coefficients.

By definition, a linear regression model $Y = X'\beta + u$ is correctly specified for $E(Y|X)$ if and only if there exists some parameter value β^o such that

$$E(u|X) = 0,$$

where $u = Y - X'\beta$. In Chapter 7, we shall introduce a popular model specification test called Hausman's (1978) test for $E(u|X) = 0$. Below we examine the relationship between the regression model error u and the true disturbance $\varepsilon = Y - E(Y|X)$.

Theorem 2.5. *If the linear regression model*

$$Y = X'\beta + u$$

is correctly specified for $E(Y|X)$, *then*

(1) $Y = X'\beta^o + \varepsilon$ *for some* β^o *and* ε, *where* $E(\varepsilon|X) = 0$;

(2) $\beta^* = \beta^o$.

Proof: (1) If the linear regression model is correctly specified for $E(Y|X)$, then $E(Y|X) = X'\beta^o$ for some parameter value β^o.

On the other hand, we always have the regression identity $Y = E(Y|X) + \varepsilon$, where $E(\varepsilon|X) = 0$. Combining these two equations gives result (1) immediately.

(2) From Part (1), we have

$$\begin{aligned} E(X\varepsilon) &= E[XE(\varepsilon|X)] \\ &= E(X \cdot 0) \\ &= 0. \end{aligned}$$

It follows that the orthogonality condition holds for $Y = X'\beta^o + \varepsilon$. Therefore, we have $\beta^* = \beta^o$ by a previous theorem (which one?).

Theorem 2.5(1) implies $E(Y|X) = X'\beta^o$ under correct model specification for $E(Y|X)$. This, together with Theorem 2.5(2), implies that when a linear regression model is correctly specified, the conditional mean $E(Y|X)$ will coincide with the best linear least squares predictor $g^*(X) = X'\beta^*$.

Under correct model specification, the best linear least squares approximation coefficient β^* is equal to the true marginal effect parameter β^o. In other words, β^* can be interpreted as the true parameter value β^o when (and only when) the linear regression model is correctly specified.

Question: What happens if the linear regression model

$$Y = X'\beta + u,$$

where $E(Xu) = 0$, is misspecified for $E(Y|X)$? In other words, what happens if $E(Xu) = 0$ but $E(u|X) \neq 0$?

In this case, the regression function

$$\begin{aligned} E(Y|X) &= X'\beta + E(u|X) \\ &\neq X'\beta. \end{aligned}$$

There exists some neglected structure in u that can be exploited to improve the prediction of Y using X. A misspecified model always yields suboptimal predictions. A correctly specified model yields optimal predictions in terms of MSE.

Example 2.11. Consider the following DGP

$$Y = 1 + \frac{1}{2}X_1 + \frac{1}{4}(X_1^2 - 1) + \varepsilon,$$

where X_1 and ε are mutually independent $N(0,1)$.

(1) Find the conditional mean $E(Y|X_1)$ and $\frac{d}{dX_1}E(Y|X_1)$, the marginal effect of X_1 on Y.

Suppose now a linear regression model

$$\begin{aligned} Y &= \beta_0 + \beta_1 X_1 + u \\ &= X'\beta + u, \end{aligned}$$

where $X = (X_0, X_1)' = (1, X_1)'$, is specified to approximate this DGP.

(2) Find the best least squares approximation coefficient β^* and the best linear least squares predictor $g^*_{\mathbb{A}}(X) = X'\beta^*$.

(3) Let $u = Y - X'\beta^*$. Show $E(Xu) = 0$.

(4) Check if the true marginal effect $\frac{d}{dX_1}E(Y|X_1)$ is equal to β_1^*, the model-implied marginal effect.

Solution: (1) Given that X_1 and u are independent, we obtain

$$E(Y|X_1) = 1 + \frac{1}{2}X_1 + \frac{1}{4}(X_1^2 - 1),$$

$$\frac{d}{dX_1}E(Y|X_1) = \frac{1}{2} + \frac{1}{2}X_1.$$

(2) Using the best least squares approximation coefficient formula, we have

$$\begin{aligned} \beta^* &= [E(XX')]^{-1} E(XY) \\ &= \begin{bmatrix} 1 & 0 \\ 0 & 1 \end{bmatrix}^{-1} \begin{bmatrix} 1 \\ \frac{1}{2} \end{bmatrix} \\ &= \begin{bmatrix} 1 \\ \frac{1}{2} \end{bmatrix}. \end{aligned}$$

Hence, we have

$$g^*(X) = X'\beta^* = 1 + \frac{1}{2}X_1.$$

(3) By definition and Part (2), we have

$$\begin{aligned} u &= Y - X'\beta^* \\ &= Y - (\beta_0^* + \beta_1^* X_1) \\ &= \frac{1}{4}(X_1^2 - 1) + \varepsilon. \end{aligned}$$

It follows that

$$\begin{aligned} E(Xu) &= E\left\{ \begin{array}{c} 1 \cdot \left[\frac{1}{4}(X_1^2 - 1) + \varepsilon\right] \\ X_1 \cdot \left[\frac{1}{4}(X_1^2 - 1) + \varepsilon\right] \end{array} \right\} \\ &= \begin{bmatrix} 0 \\ 0 \end{bmatrix}, \end{aligned}$$

although

$$E(u|X_1) = \frac{1}{4}(X_1^2 - 1) \neq 0.$$

(4) No, because

$$\frac{d}{dX_1}E(Y|X_1) = \frac{1}{2} + \frac{1}{2}X_1 \neq \beta_1^* = \frac{1}{2}.$$

The marginal effect depends on the level of X_1, rather than only on a constant. Therefore, the condition $E(Xu) = 0$ is not sufficient for the validity of the economic interpretation for β_1^* as the marginal effect.

Any parametric regression model is subject to potential model misspecification. This can occur due to the use of a misspecified functional form, as well as the existence of omitted variables which are correlated with the existing regressors, among other things. In econometrics, there exists a modeling strategy which is free of model misspecification when a data set is sufficiently large. This modeling strategy is called a nonparametric approach, which does not assume any functional form for $E(Y|X)$ but let data speak for the true relationship. We now introduce the basic idea of a nonparametric approach.

Nonparametric modeling is a statistical method that can model the unknown function arbitrarily well without having to know the functional form of $E(Y|X)$. To illustrate the basic idea of nonparametric modeling, suppose $g_o(x)$ is a smooth function of x. Then we can expand $g_o(x)$ using a set of orthonormal "basis" functions $\{\psi_j(x)\}_{j=0}^{\infty}$:

$$g_o(x) = \sum_{j=0}^{\infty} \beta_j \psi_j(x) \text{ for } x \in \text{support}(X),$$

where the Fourier coefficient

$$\beta_j = \int_{-\infty}^{\infty} g_o(x)\psi_j(x)dx$$

and

$$\int_{-\infty}^{\infty} \psi_i(x)\psi_j(x)dx = \delta_{ij} \equiv \begin{cases} 1 & \text{if } i = j, \\ 0 & \text{if } i \neq j. \end{cases}$$

The function δ_{ij} is called the Kronecker delta.

Example 2.12. Suppose $g_o(x) = x^2$ where $x \in [-\pi, \pi]$. Then

$$\begin{aligned} g_o(x) &= \frac{\pi^2}{3} - 4\left[\cos(x) - \frac{\cos(2x)}{2^2} + \frac{\cos(3x)}{3^2} - \cdots\right] \\ &= \frac{\pi^2}{3} - 4\sum_{j=1}^{\infty}(-1)^{j-1}\frac{\cos(jx)}{j^2}. \end{aligned}$$

Example 2.13. Suppose

$$g_o(x) = \begin{cases} -1 & \text{if } -\pi < x < 0, \\ 0 & \text{if } x = 0, \\ 1 & \text{if } 0 < x < \pi. \end{cases}$$

Then

$$\begin{aligned} g_o(x) &= \frac{4}{\pi}\left[\sin(x) + \frac{\sin(3x)}{3} + \frac{\sin(5x)}{5} + \cdots\right] \\ &= \frac{4}{\pi}\sum_{j=0}^{\infty}\frac{\sin[(2j+1)x]}{(2j+1)}. \end{aligned}$$

Generally, suppose $g_o(x)$ is square-integrable. We have

$$\begin{aligned} \int_{-\pi}^{\pi} g_o^2(x)dx &= \sum_{j=0}^{\infty}\sum_{k=0}^{\infty}\beta_j\beta_k \int_{-\pi}^{\pi}\psi_j(x)\psi_k(x)dx \\ &= \sum_{j=0}^{\infty}\sum_{k=0}^{\infty}\beta_j\beta_k\delta_{jk} \text{ by orthonormality of } \{\psi_j(\cdot)\} \\ &= \sum_{j=0}^{\infty}\beta_j^2 < \infty, \end{aligned}$$

Therefore, $\beta_j \to 0$ as $j \to \infty$. That is, the Fourier coefficient β_j will eventually vanish to zero as the order j goes to infinity. This motivates us to use the following truncated approximation:

$$g_p(x) = \sum_{j=0}^{p}\beta_j\psi_j(x),$$

where p is the order of bases. The bias of $g_p(x)$ from $g_o(x)$ is

$$\begin{aligned} B_p(x) &= g_o(x) - g_p(x) \\ &= \sum_{j=p+1}^{\infty}\beta_j\psi_j(x). \end{aligned}$$

The bias $B_p(x)$ vanishes to zero as the truncation order p increases. Figures 2.3 and 2.4 illustrate the biases with various choices of p for the functions in Examples 2.12 and 2.13 respectively.

The coefficients $\{\beta_j\}$ are unknown in practice, so we have to estimate them using an observed random sample $\{Y_t, X_t\}_{t=1}^n$, where n is the sample size. We consider a linear regression

$$Y_t = \sum_{j=0}^{p} \beta_j \psi_j(X_t) + u_t, \qquad t = 1, ..., n.$$

Obviously, we need to let $p = p(n) \to \infty$ as $n \to \infty$ to ensure that the bias $B_p(x)$ vanishes to zero as $n \to \infty$. However, we should not let p grow to infinity too fast, because otherwise there will be too much sampling variation in parameter estimators due to too many unknown parameters. This requires $p/n \to 0$ as $n \to \infty$.

The nonparametric approach just described is called *nonparametric series regression* (see, e.g., Andrews 1991, Hong and White 1995, Pons 2019). There are many nonparametric methods available in the literature. Another popular nonparametric method is called *kernel smoothing*, which is based on the idea of the Taylor series expansion in a local region. See Härdle (1990)

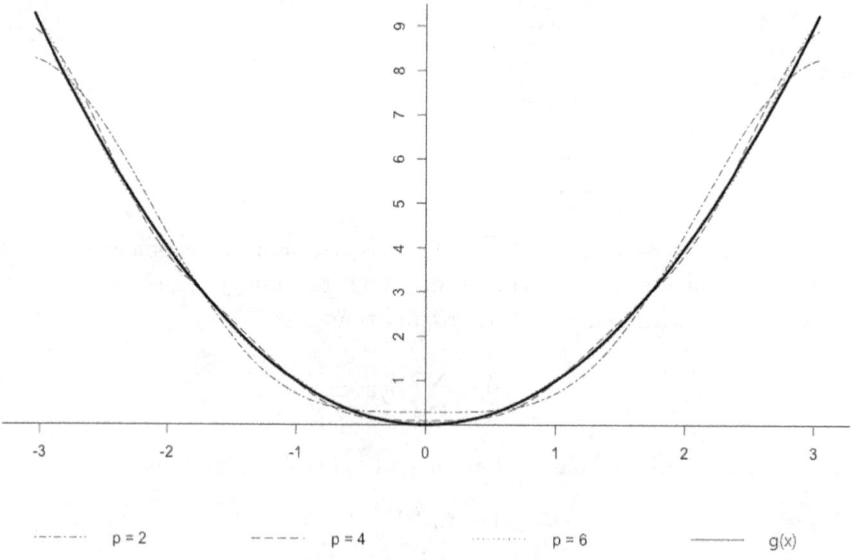

Figure 2.3 Fourier series approximation to the quadratic function in Example 2.12.

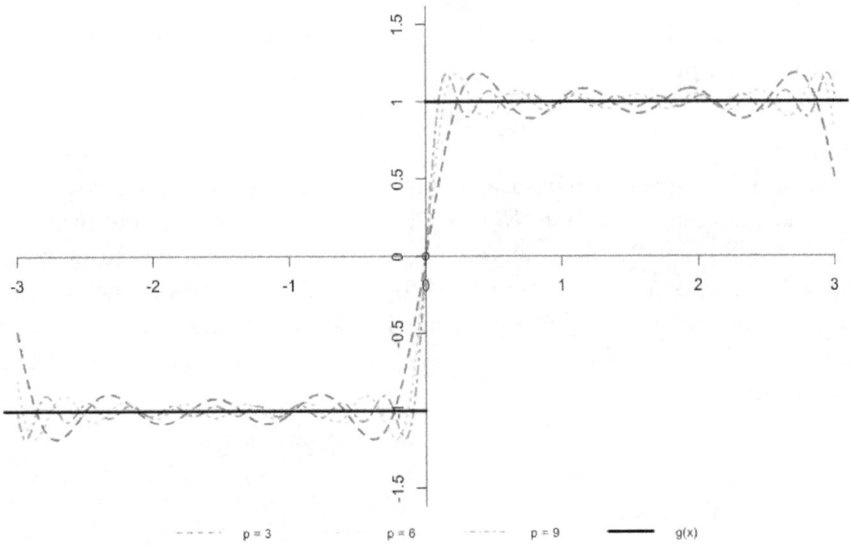

Figure 2.4 Fourier series approximation to the step function Example 2.13.

and Fan and Gijbels (1996) for more discussion on kernel smoothing and local polynomial smoothing. The key feature of nonparametric modeling is that it does not specify a concrete functional form or model but rather estimates the unknown true function from data. As can be seen above, nonparametric series regression is easy to use and understand, because it is a natural extension of linear regression with the number of regressors increasing with the sample size n.

The nonparametric approach is flexible and powerful, but it generally requires a large data set for precise estimation because there are a large number of unknown parameters. Moreover, there is little economic interpretation for it (e.g., it is difficult to give economic interpretation for the coefficients $\{\beta_j\}$). Nonparametric analysis is usually treated in a separate and more advanced econometric course (see more discussion in Chapter 10).

2.5 Conclusion

Most economic theories (e.g., rational expectations theory) have implications on and only on the conditional mean of the underlying economic variable given some suitable information set. The conditional mean $E(Y|X)$ is called the regression function of Y on X. In this chapter, we have shown that the regression function $E(Y|X)$ is the optimal solution to the MSE minimization problem

$$\min_{g\in\mathbb{F}} E[Y - g(X)]^2,$$

where $\mathbb{F}$ is the space of measurable and square-integrable functions.

The regression function $E(Y|X)$ is generally unknown, because economic theory usually does not tell a concrete functional form. In practice, one usually uses a parametric model for $E(Y|X)$ that has a known functional form but with a finite number of unknown parameters. When we restrict $g(X)$ to $\mathbb{A} = \{g : \mathbb{R}^K \to \mathbb{R} \mid g(x) = x'\beta\}$, a class of affine functions, the optimal predictor that solves

$$\min_{g\in\mathbb{A}} E[Y - g(X)]^2 = \min_{\beta\in R^K} E(Y - X'\beta)^2$$

is $g^*(X) = X'\beta^*$, where

$$\beta^* = [E(XX')]^{-1}E(XY)$$

is called the best linear least squares approximation coefficient. The best linear least squares predictor $g^*_A(X) = X'\beta^*$ is always well-defined, no matter whether $E(Y|X)$ is linear in X.

Suppose we write

$$Y = X'\beta + u.$$

Then $\beta = \beta^*$ if and only if

$$E(Xu) = 0.$$

This orthogonality condition is actually the first order condition for the best linear least squares minimization problem. It does not guarantee correct specification of a linear regression model. A linear regression model is correctly specified for $E(Y|X)$ if $E(Y|X) = X'\beta^o$ for some parameter value β^o, which is equivalent to the condition that

$$E(u|X) = 0,$$

where $u = Y - X'\beta^o$. That is, correct model specification for $E(Y|X)$ holds if and only if the conditional mean of the linear regression model error is zero when evaluated at some parameter value β^o. For a correctly specified linear regression model, Y is linear in regressor vector X and parameter vector β. If the regressor vector X is obtained from a set of economic explanatory variables and their nonlinear transformations, then Y will have a nonlinear relationship with economic explanatory variables despite its linear relationship with regressor vector X.

We note that $E(u|X) = 0$ is equivalent to the condition that $E[uh(X)] = 0$ for all measurable functions $h(\cdot)$. When $E(Y|X) = X'\beta^o$ for some parameter value β^o, we have $\beta^* = \beta^o$. That is, the best linear least squares approximation coefficient β^* will coincide with the true model parameter β^o and can be interpreted as the expected marginal effect of X on Y. The condition $E(u|X) = 0$ fundamentally differs from $E(Xu) = 0$. The former is crucial for validity of economic interpretation of the coefficient β^* as the true model parameter β^o. The orthogonality condition $E(Xu) = 0$ does not guarantee this interpretation. Correct model specification is important for economic interpretation of model coefficient and for optimal predictions.

An econometric model aims to provide a concise and reasonably accurate reflection of the data generating process. By disregarding less relevant aspects of the data, the model helps to obtain a better understanding of the main aspects of the DGP. This implies that an econometric model will never provide a completely accurate description of the DGP. Therefore, the concept of a "true model" does not make much practical sense. It reflects an idealized situation that allows us to obtain mathematically exact results. The idea is that similar results hold approximately true if the model is a reasonably accurate approximation of the DGP.

The main purpose of this chapter is to provide a general idea of regression analysis and to shed some light on the nature and limitation of linear regression models, which have been popularly used in econometrics and will be the subject of study in Chapters 3 to 7.

Exercise 2

2.1. Put $\varepsilon = Y - E(Y|X)$. Show $\text{var}(Y|X) = \text{var}(\varepsilon|X)$.

2.2. Show $\text{var}(Y) = \text{var}[E(Y|X)] + \text{var}[Y - E(Y|X)]$, and provide an interpretation for this result.

2.3. Suppose X and Y follow a bivariate normal distribution with joint PDF

$$f_{XY}(x,y) = \frac{1}{2\pi\sigma_1\sigma_2\sqrt{1-\rho^2}} \exp\left\{ -\frac{1}{2(1-\rho^2)} \left[\left(\frac{x-\mu_1}{\sigma_1}\right)^2 \right.\right.$$
$$\left.\left. -2\rho\left(\frac{x-\mu_1}{\sigma_1}\right)\left(\frac{y-\mu_2}{\sigma_2}\right) + \left(\frac{y-\mu_2}{\sigma_2}\right)^2 \right] \right\},$$

where $-1 < \rho < 1, -\infty < \mu_1, \mu_2 < \infty, 0 < \sigma_1, \sigma_2 < \infty$. Find:

(1) $E(Y|X)$.

(2) $\text{var}(Y|X)$. *[Hint: Use the change of variable method for integration and the fact that* $\int_{-\infty}^{\infty} \frac{1}{\sqrt{2\pi}} e^{\frac{1}{2}x^2} dx = 1$.*]*

2.4. Suppose $Z \equiv (Y, X')'$ is a stochastic process such that the conditional mean $g_o(X) \equiv E(Y|X)$ exists, where X is a $(k+1) \times 1$ random vector. Suppose one uses a model (or a function) $g(X)$ to predict Y. A popular evaluation criterion for model $g(X)$ is the mean squared error $\text{MSE}(g) \equiv E[Y - g(X)]^2$.

(1) Show that the optimal predictor $g^*(X)$ for Y that minimizes $\text{MSE}(g)$ is the conditional mean $g_o(X)$; namely, $g^*(X) = g_o(X)$.

(2) Put $\varepsilon \equiv Y - g_o(X)$, which is called the true regression disturbance. Show that $E(\varepsilon|X) = 0$ and interpret this result.

2.5. The choices of model $g(X)$ in Exercise 2.4 are very general. Suppose that we now restrict our choice of $g(X)$ to a linear (or affine) models $\{g_{\mathbb{A}}(X) = X'\beta\}$, where β is a $(k+1) \times 1$ parameter. One can choose a linear function $g_{\mathbb{A}}(X)$ by choosing a value for parameter β. Different values of β give different linear functions $g_{\mathbb{A}}(X)$. The best linear predictor g_L^* that minimizes the mean squared error criterion is defined as $g_{\mathbb{A}}^*(X) \equiv X'\beta^*$, where

$$\beta^* \equiv \arg\min_{\beta \in \mathbb{R}^{k+1}} E(Y - X'\beta)^2$$

is called the optimal linear least squares approximation coefficient.

(1) Show that

$$\beta^* = [E(XX')]^{-1}E(XY).$$

(2) Define $u^* \equiv Y - X'\beta^*$. Show that $E(Xu^*) = 0$, where 0 is a $(k+1)\times 1$ zero vector.

(3) Suppose the conditional mean $g_o(X) = X'\beta^o$ for some parameter value β^o. Then we say that the linear model $g_{\mathbb{A}}(X)$ is correctly specified for conditional mean $g_o(X)$, and β^o is the true model parameter of the DGP. Show that $\beta^* = \beta^o$ and $E(u^*|X) = 0$.

(4) Suppose the conditional mean $g_o(X) \neq X'\beta$ for any value of β. Then we say that the linear model $g_{\mathbb{A}}(X)$ is misspecified for conditional mean $g_o(X)$. Check if $E(u^*|X) = 0$ and discuss its implication.

2.6. Suppose $Y = \beta_0^* + \beta_1^* X_1 + u$, where Y and X_1 are scalars, and $\beta^* = (\beta_0^*, \beta_1^*)'$ is the best linear least squares approximation coefficient.

(1) Show that $\beta_1^* = \text{cov}(Y, X_1)/\sigma_{X_1}^2$ and $\beta_0^* = E(Y) - \beta_1^* E(X)$, and the mean squared error

$$E[Y - (\beta_0^* + \beta_1^* X_1)]^2 = \sigma_Y^2(1 - \rho_{X_1Y}^2),$$

where $\sigma_Y^2 = \text{var}(Y)$ and ρ_{X_1Y} is the correlation coefficient between Y and X_1. This implies that linear regression modeling is essentially a correlation analysis.

(2) Suppose in addition Y and X_1 follow a bivariate normal distribution. Show $E(Y|X_1) = \beta_0^* + \beta_1^* X_1$ and $\text{var}(Y|X_1) = \sigma_Y^2(1 - \rho_{X_1Y}^2)$. That is, the conditional mean of Y given X_1 coincides with the best linear least squares predictor and the conditional variance of Y given X_1 is equal to the mean squared error of the best linear least squares predictor.

2.7. Suppose a function $g(X)$ is used to predict Y, and the evaluation criterion is the Mean Absolute Error (MAE), defined as $\text{MSE}(g) = E|Y - g(X)|$. Show that the optimal solution to minimize $\text{MSE}(g)$ is the conditional median of Y given X.

2.8. Suppose

$$Y = \beta_0 + \beta_1 X_1 + |X_1|\varepsilon,$$

where $E(X_1) = 0$, $\text{var}(X_1) = \sigma_{X_1}^2 > 0$, $E(\varepsilon) = 0$, $\text{var}(\varepsilon) = \sigma_\varepsilon^2 > 0$, and ε and X_1 are independent. Both β_0 and β_1 are scalar constants.

(1) Find $E(Y|X_1)$.

(2) Find $\text{var}(Y|X_1)$.
(3) Show that $\beta_1 = 0$ if and only if $\text{cov}(X_1, Y) = 0$.

2.9. Suppose an aggregate consumption function is given by

$$Y = 1 + 0.5X_1 + \frac{1}{4}(X_1^2 - 1) + \varepsilon,$$

where $X_1 \sim N(0,1), \varepsilon \sim N(0,1)$, and X_1 is independent of ε.
(1) Find the conditional mean $g_o(X) \equiv E(Y|X)$, where $X \equiv (1, X_1)'$.
(2) Find the MPC $\frac{d}{dX_1} g_o(X)$.
(3) Suppose we use a linear model

$$Y = X'\beta + u = \beta_0 + \beta_1 X_1 + u$$

where $\beta \equiv (\beta_0, \beta_1)'$ to predict Y. Find the best linear least squares approximation coefficient β^* and the best linear least squares predictor $g_{\mathbb{A}}^*(X) \equiv X'\beta^*$.

(4) Compute the partial derivative of the linear model $\frac{d}{dX_1} g_{\mathbb{A}}^*(X)$, and compare it with the MPC in Part (2). Discuss the results you obtain.

2.10. Put $g_o(X) = E(Y|X)$, where $X = (1, X_1)'$. Then we have

$$Y = g_o(X) + \varepsilon,$$

where $E(\varepsilon|X) = 0$.

Consider a first order Taylor series expansion of $g_o(X)$ around $\mu_1 = E(X_1)$:

$$\begin{aligned} g_o(X) &\approx g_o(\mu_1) + g_o'(\mu_1)(X_1 - \mu_1) \\ &= [g_o(\mu_1) - \mu g_o'(\mu_1)] + g_o'(\mu_1)X_1. \end{aligned}$$

Suppose $\beta^* = (\beta_0^*, \beta_1^*)'$ is the best linear least squares approximation coefficient. That is, we consider the following linear regression model

$$Y = \beta_0^* + \beta_1^* X + u.$$

Is it true that $\beta_1^* = g_o'(\mu_1)$? Provide your reasoning.

2.11. Suppose a DGP is given by

$$Y = 0.8X_1X_2 + \varepsilon,$$

where $X_1 \sim N(0,1), X_2 \sim N(0,1), \varepsilon \sim N(0,1)$, and X_1, X_2 and ε are mutually independent. Put $X = (1, X_1, X_2)'$.

(1) Is Y predictable in mean using information X?
(2) Suppose we use a linear regression model

$$\begin{aligned} g_{\mathbb{A}}(X) &= X'\beta + u \\ &= \beta_0 + \beta_1 X_1 + \beta_2 X_2 + u \end{aligned}$$

to predict Y. Does this linear regression model have any predicting power? Explain.

2.12. Suppose we have

$$Y = a + bX + u,$$

where u is a random variable with $E(u) = 0$, $\text{var}(u) = \sigma_u^2 > 0$, and it is orthogonal to X in the sense $E(Xu) = 0$. This is called a linear regression model. The random variable u can be viewed as a disturbance to an otherwise perfect linear relationship $Y = a + bX$. Show that the correlation coefficient between X and Y is

$$\rho_{XY} = \frac{b}{\sqrt{b^2 + \sigma_u^2/\sigma_X^2}}.$$

Note that magnitude of ρ_{XY} depends on the ratio $\sigma_\varepsilon^2/\sigma_X^2$, which is usually called the noise-to-signal ratio.

2.13. Suppose X and Y are random variables such that $E(Y|X) = 7 - \frac{1}{4}X$ and $E(X|Y) = 10 - Y$. Determine the correlation between X and Y.

2.14. Show that $E(u|X) = 0$ if and only if $E[h(X)u] = 0$ for any measurable functions $h(\cdot)$.

2.15. Suppose $E(u|X)$ exists, X is a bounded random variable, and $h(X)$ is an arbitrary measurable function. Put $g(X) = E(\varepsilon|X)$ and assume that $E[g^2(X)] < \infty$.

(1) Show that if $g(X) = 0$, then $E[\varepsilon h(X)] = 0$.

(2) Show that if $E[\varepsilon h(X)] = 0$, then $E(\varepsilon|X) = 0$. *[Hint: Consider $h(X) = e^{tX}$ for t in a small neighborhood containing* 0. *Given that X is bounded, we can expand*

$$g(X) = \sum_{j=0}^{\infty} \beta_j X^j$$

where $\beta_j = \int_{-\infty}^{\infty} g(x)x^j f_X(x)dx$ *is the Fourier coefficient, where* $f_X(x)$ *is the PDF of* X*. Then*

$$\begin{aligned} E(\varepsilon e^{tX}) &= E\left[E(\varepsilon|X)e^{tX}\right] \\ &= E\left[g(X)e^{tX}\right] \\ &= \sum_{j=0}^{\infty} \frac{t^j}{j!} E\left[g(X)X^j\right] \\ &= \sum_{j=0}^{\infty} \frac{t^j}{j!} \beta_j \end{aligned}$$

for all t in a small neighborhood containing 0.]

2.16. Consider a general regression model

$$Y_t = g(X_t) + u_t,$$

where $g(X_t)$ is a possibly nonlinear model for $E(Y_t|X_t)$. Show that $E(u_t|X_t) = 0$ if and only if $g(X_t) = E(Y_t|X_t)$.

2.17. Consider the following Nonlinear Least Squares (NLS) problem

$$\min_{\beta \in \mathbf{R}^{k+1}} E\left[Y - g(X, \beta)\right]^2,$$

where $g(X, \beta)$ is possibly a nonlinear function of β. [An example is a logistic regression model where $g(X, \beta) = \frac{1}{1+\exp(-X'\beta)}$.] Suppose $E\left[\frac{\partial}{\partial \beta} g(X, \beta) \frac{\partial}{\partial \beta'} g(X, \beta)\right]$ is a $(k+1) \times (k+1)$ bounded and nonsingular matrix for all $\beta \in \mathbf{R}^{k+1}$, where $\frac{\partial}{\partial \beta'} g(X, \beta)$ is the transpose of the $(k+1) \times 1$ column vector $\frac{\partial}{\partial \beta} g(X, \beta)$.

(1) Derive the FOC for the best NLS approximation coefficient β^* (say).

(2) Put $Y = g(X, \beta) + u$. Show that $\beta = \beta^*$ if and only if $E\left[u \frac{\partial}{\partial \beta} g(X, \beta^*)\right] = 0$. Do we have $E(Xu) = 0$ when $g(X, \beta)$ is nonlinear in β?

(3) The nonlinear regression model $g(X, \beta)$ is said to be correctly specified for $E(Y|X)$ if there exists some unknown parameter value β^o such that $E(Y|X) = g(X, \beta^o)$ with probability one. Here, β^o can be interpreted as a true model parameter. Show that $\beta^* = \beta^o$ if and only if the model $g(X, \beta)$ is correctly specified for $E(Y|X)$.

(4) Do we have $E(u|X) = 0$, where $u = Y - g(X, \beta^o)$ for some parameter value β^o, when the model $g(X, \beta)$ is correctly specified?

(5) If $E(u|X) = 0$, where $u = Y - g(X, \beta^o)$ for some parameter value β^o, is $g(X, \beta)$ correctly specified for $E(Y|X)$?

2.18. Consider the following causal nexus: Variable X_1 is directly affected by variable X_3 and unobserved variables v_1, v_2. Variable X_2 is directly affected by X_1 and an unobserved variable v_3, and it is indirectly affected by X_3 and the other unobserved variables v_1, v_2 via its link with X_1. Variable Y is directly affected by X_1 and X_2, and it is indirectly affected by X_3 and the other unobserved variables v_1, v_2 via its link with X_1. Note that X_1 has both direct and indirect effects on Y. (By a direct effect of a variable on Y it is meant that a change in that variable will cause a change in Y while holding all other variables affecting Y constant. In other words, if a variable has a *ceteris paribus* effect on Y, it is called to have a direct effect on Y.) Also, note that an unobserved disturbance u has a direct effect on Y and it has no linkage at all to any of the other variables. Assume that (Y, X_1, X_2, X_3) are all observable, and their relationships, if any, will be linear.

(1) Consider a linear regression model

$$Y = \beta_0 + \beta_1 X_1 + \beta_2 X_2 + u.$$

Is this model correctly specified for $E(Y|X_1, X_2)$? Explain.

(2) Derive the expression of $E(Y|X_1, X_2, X_3)$. Does X_3 have any additional explanatory power for Y given the presence of X_1 and X_3? Explain.

2.19. Comment on the following statement: "All econometric models are approximations of the economic system of interest and are therefore misspecified. Therefore, there is no need to check correct model specification in practice."

Chapter 3

Classical Linear Regression Models

Abstract: In this chapter, we will introduce the classical linear regression theory, including the classical model assumptions, the statistical properties of the Ordinary Least Squares (OLS) estimator, the t-test and the F-test, as well as the Generalized Least Squares (GLS) estimator and related statistical procedures. This chapter will serve as a starting point from which we will develop modern econometric theory.

Keywords: Autocorrelation, Classical linear regression, Conditional heteroskedasticity, Conditional homoskedasticity, F-test, GLS, Hypothesis testing, Mean Squared Error (MSE), Model selection criterion, Multicollinearity, Normal distribution, OLS, R^2, t-test, Strict exogeneity

3.1 Framework and Assumptions

Suppose we have an observed random sample $\{Z_t\}_{t=1}^n$ of size n, where $Z_t = (Y_t, X_t')'$, Y_t is a scalar, $X_t = (1, X_{1t}, X_{2t}, ..., X_{kt})'$ is a $(k+1) \times 1$ vector, t is an index (either cross-sectional unit or time period) for observations, and n is the sample size. We are interested in making inference of the conditional mean $E(Y_t|X_t)$ using an observed realization (i.e., a data set) of the random sample $\{Y_t, X_t'\}'$, $t = 1, ..., n$.

Throughout this book, we set $K \equiv k + 1$, the number of regressors which contains k economic variables and an intercept. The index t may denote an individual unit (e.g., a firm, a household, and a country) for a cross-sectional data, or denote a time period (e.g., day, week, month and year) in a time series data.

We first provide and discuss the assumptions of the classical linear regression theory.

Assumption 3.1. [Linearity]: $\{Z_t = (Y_t, X_t')'\}_{t=1}^n$ is an observable random sample of size n, with

$$Y_t = X_t'\beta^o + \varepsilon_t, \qquad t = 1, ..., n,$$

where β^o is a $K \times 1$ unknown parameter vector, and ε_t is an unobservable disturbance.

In Assumption 3.1, Y_t is the dependent variable (or regressand), X_t is the vector of regressors (or independent variables), and β^o is the regression coefficient vector. The unobserved disturbance ε_t captures all other factors which influence the dependent variable Y_t other than the regressors in X_t.

When the linear model is correctly specified for the conditional mean $E(Y_t|X_t)$, i.e., when $E(\varepsilon_t|X_t) = 0$, the parameter

$$\beta^o = \frac{d}{dX_t} E(Y_t|X_t)$$

can be interpreted as the expected marginal effect of X_t on Y_t and its magnitude is called the true parameter value. We note that

$$\beta_j^o = \frac{\partial}{\partial X_{jt}} E(Y_t|X_t), \qquad j = 1, ..., k,$$

is the expected marginal effect of X_{jt} on Y_t, holding all other regressors constant. This is the so-called *ceteris paribus* expected marginal effect of X_{jt} on Y_t.

The key notion of *linearity* in the classical linear regression model is that the regression model is linear in both regressor vector X_t and parameter vector β^o. We emphasize that the regressor vector X_t can be a set of different economic explanatory variables, or can be a set of economic explanatory variables and their nonlinear transformations. The regressors themselves in X_t can be nonlinear functions of the same underlying economic variable, each one transformed differently. An example is a polynomial regression, which uses linear regression to fit the response variable as an arbitrary polynomial function of an economic variable. This makes linear regression an extremely powerful inference method. The linearity of a regression model is actually only a restriction on linearity of parameter vector β^o. It allows nonlinear relationships between Y_t and original economic variables.

Question: Does Assumption 3.1 imply a causal relationship from X_t to Y_t?

Not necessarily. As Kendall and Stuart (1961, Vol.2, Ch.26, p.279) point out, "a statistical relationship, however strong and however suggestive, can never establish causal connection. Our ideas of causation must come from outside statistics ultimately, from some theory or other." Assumption 3.1 only implies a predictive relationship: given X_t, can we predict Y_t linearly?

Denote

$$\begin{aligned} Y &= (Y_1, ..., Y_n)', && n \times 1, \\ \varepsilon &= (\varepsilon_1, ..., \varepsilon_n)', && n \times 1, \\ \mathbf{X} &= (X_1, ..., X_n)', && n \times K. \end{aligned}$$

where the t-th row of $\mathbf{X}$ is $X_t' = (1, X_{1t}, ..., X_{kt})$. With these matrix notations, we have a compact expression for Assumption 3.1:

$$\begin{aligned} Y &= \mathbf{X}\beta^o + \varepsilon, \\ n \times 1 &= (n \times K)(K \times 1) + n \times 1. \end{aligned}$$

The second assumption is a strict exogeneity condition.

Assumption 3.2. [Strict Exogeneity]:

$$E(\varepsilon_t|\mathbf{X}) = E(\varepsilon_t|X_1, ..., X_t, ..., X_n) = 0, \qquad t = 1, ..., n.$$

The relationship between the disturbance ε_t and the regressors $\{X_t\}$ is a crucial consideration in formulating a linear regression model. More precisely, Assumption 3.2 may be called strict exogeneity in *mean*. It suggests that the mean values of ε_t does not depend on the value of regressors $\{X_t\}_{t=1}^n$. If t is a time index, then Assumption 3.2 indicates that the mean value of ε_t does not depend on the past, current and future values of the regressors. Among other things, Assumption 3.2 implies correct model specification for $E(Y_t|X_t)$. This is because Assumption 3.2 implies $E(\varepsilon_t|X_t) = 0$ by conditional expectation. Therefore, we have $E(\varepsilon_t) = 0$ by the law of iterated expectations. The strict exogeneity condition implies that for each observation, the value X_t is determined by the factors outside the regression model under study.

Under Assumption 3.2, we have $E(X_s\varepsilon_t) = 0$ for any (t, s), where $t, s \in \{1, ..., n\}$. This follows because

$$\begin{aligned} E(X_s\varepsilon_t) &= E[E(X_s\varepsilon_t|\mathbf{X})] \\ &= E[X_s E(\varepsilon_t|\mathbf{X})] \\ &= E(X_s \cdot 0) \\ &= 0. \end{aligned}$$

Given $E(\varepsilon_t) = 0$, $E(X_s\varepsilon_t) = 0$ implies $\text{cov}(X_s, \varepsilon_t) = 0$ for all $t, s \in \{1, ..., n\}$.

Because $\mathbf{X}$ contains regressors $\{X_s\}$ for both $s \leq t$ and $s > t$, Assumption 3.2 essentially requires that the error ε_t do not depend on both the past and future values of regressors if t is a time index. This rules out dynamic time series models for which ε_t may be correlated with the future values of regressors (because the future values of regressors depend on the current shocks), as is illustrated in the following example.

Example 3.1. [Autoregressive Model]: Consider a first order autoregressive model, denoted as AR(1),

$$\begin{aligned} Y_t &= \beta_0 + \beta_1 Y_{t-1} + \varepsilon_t, \qquad t = 1, ..., n, \\ &= X_t'\beta + \varepsilon_t, \\ \{\varepsilon_t\} &\sim \text{IID}(0, \sigma^2), \end{aligned}$$

where $X_t = (1, Y_{t-1})'$. This is a dynamic regression model because the term $\beta_1 Y_{t-1}$ represents the "memory" or "feedback" of the past into the present value of the process, which induces a correlation between Y_t and the past. The term autoregression refers to the regression of Y_t on its own past values. The parameter β_1 determines the amount of feedback, with a large absolute value of β_1 resulting in more feedback. The disturbance ε_t can be viewed as representing the effect of "new information" that is revealed at time t. Information that is truly new cannot be anticipated so that the effects of today's new information should be unrelated to the effects of yesterday's news in the sense that $E(\varepsilon_t|X_t) = 0$. Here, we make a stronger assumption that we can model the effect of new information as an IID$(0, \sigma^2)$ sequence.

Obviously, $E(X_t\varepsilon_t) = E(X_t)E(\varepsilon_t) = 0$ but $E(X_{t+1}\varepsilon_t) \neq 0$. Thus, we have $E(\varepsilon_t|\mathbf{X}) \neq 0$, and so Assumption 3.2 does not hold. Here, the lagged dependent variable Y_{t-1} in the regressor vector X_t is called a predetermined variable, since it is orthogonal to ε_t but depends on the past history of $\{\varepsilon_t\}$.

In Chapter 5, we will consider linear regression models with dependent observations, which will include Example 3.1 as a special case. In fact, the main reason of imposing Assumption 3.2 is to obtain a finite sample distribution theory. For a large sample theory (i.e., an asymptotic theory as $n \to \infty$), the strict exogeneity condition will not be needed.

In a time series context, strict exogeneity implies that the explanatory variables in X_t do not react to the shocks in the past, current and future periods. Intuitively, the values of X_t are completely determined by factors outside the regression model, and so they are called *strictly exogenous variables*. In econometrics, there are various alternative definitions of exogeneity. For example, one definition assumes that ε_t and $\mathbf{X}$ are independent. Another example is that $\mathbf{X}$ is nonstochastic. This rules out conditional heteroskedasticity (i.e., $\text{var}(\varepsilon_t|\mathbf{X})$ depends on $\mathbf{X}$). In Assumption 3.2, we still allow for conditional heteroskedasticity, because we do not assume that ε_t and $\mathbf{X}$ are independent. We only assume that the conditional mean $E(\varepsilon_t|\mathbf{X})$ does not depend on $\mathbf{X}$. The case that ε and $\mathbf{X}$ are independent or $\mathbf{X}$ is nonstochastic is called *strong exogeneity*.

Below we consider two special cases.

Case I: X Is Nonstochastic

Question: What happens to Assumption 3.2 if $\mathbf{X}$ is nonstochastic?

If $\mathbf{X}$ is nonstochastic, Assumption 3.2 becomes

$$E(\varepsilon_t|\mathbf{X}) = E(\varepsilon_t) = 0.$$

An example of nonstochastic $\mathbf{X}$ is $X_t = (1, t, ..., t^k)'$, where t is a time variable. This corresponds to a time-trend regression model

$$\begin{aligned} Y_t &= X_t'\beta^o + \varepsilon_t \\ &= \sum_{j=0}^{k} \beta_j^o t^j + \varepsilon_t. \end{aligned}$$

Case II: $\{Z_t = (Y_t, X_t')'\}_{t=1}^n$ Is an IID Random Sample

Question: What happens to Assumption 3.2 if $Z_t = (Y_t, X_t')'$ is an independent random sample (i.e., Z_t and Z_s are independent whenever $t \neq s$, although Y_t and X_t may not be independent)?

When $\{Z_t\}$ is IID, Assumption 3.2 becomes

$$\begin{aligned} E(\varepsilon_t|\mathbf{X}) &= E(\varepsilon_t|X_1, X_2, ...X_t, ..., X_n) \\ &= E(\varepsilon_t|X_t) \\ &= 0. \end{aligned}$$

In other words, when $\{Z_t\}$ is IID, $E(\varepsilon_t|\mathbf{X}) = 0$ is equivalent to $E(\varepsilon_t|X_t) = 0$.

Assumption 3.3. **[Nonsingularity]:** (a) The minimum eigenvalue of the $K \times K$ square matrix $\mathbf{X}'\mathbf{X} = \sum_{t=1}^{n} X_t X_t'$ is nonsingular, and (b) with probability one,

$$\lambda_{\min}(\mathbf{X}'\mathbf{X}) \to \infty \text{ as } n \to \infty.$$

Assumption 3.3(a) rules out multicollinearity among the $(k+1)$ regressors in X_t. Multicollinearity refers to a situation in which two or more explanatory variables in a multiple regression model are linearly related. For example, we have exact or perfect multicollinearity if the correlation between two explanatory variables is equal to 1 or -1. More specifically, we say that there exists multicollinearity or perfect multicollinearity among the X_t if for all $t \in \{1, ..., n\}$, the variable X_{jt} for some $j \in \{0, 1, ..., k\}$ is a linear combination of the other $K-1$ column variables $\{X_{it}, i \neq j\}$. In this case, the matrix $\mathbf{X}'\mathbf{X}$ is singular, and as a consequence, the true model parameter β^o in Assumption 3.1 is not identifiable. Of course, perfect multicollinearity is rare in practice.

The nonsingularity of $\mathbf{X}'\mathbf{X}$ implies that $\mathbf{X}$ must be of full rank of $K = k+1$. Thus, we need $K \leq n$. That is, the number of regressors cannot be larger than the sample size. This is a necessary condition for identification of the true parameter value β^o.

The eigenvalue λ of a square matrix A is characterized by the system of linear equations:

$$\det(A - \lambda I) = 0,$$

where $\det(\cdot)$ denotes the determinant of a square matrix, and I is an identity matrix with the same dimension as A.

It is well-known that the eigenvalue λ can be used to summarize information contained in a matrix (recall the popular principal component analysis). Assumption 3.3 implies that new information must be available as the sample size $n \to \infty$ (i.e., X_t should not only have same repeated values as t increases).

Intuitively, if there is no variation in the values of the X_t, it will be difficult to determine the relationship between Y_t and X_t (indeed, the purpose of classical linear regression is to investigate how a change in X_t causes a change in Y_t). Figures 3.1 and 3.2 show that it is easier to estimate the true parameter values when there are large variations in X_t than there are small variations in X_t.

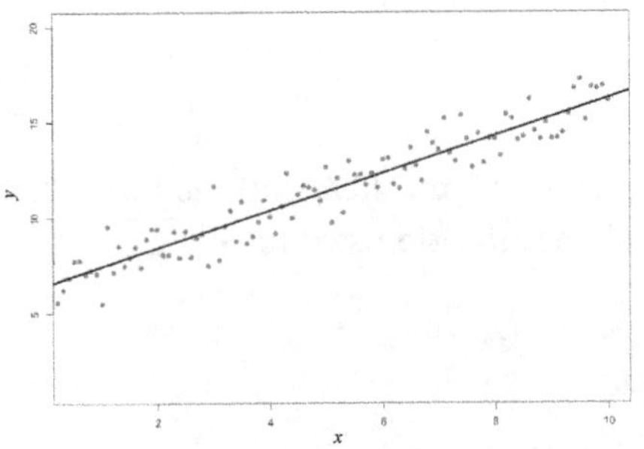

Figure 3.1 Scatter plots of a linear regression with large changes in X_t.

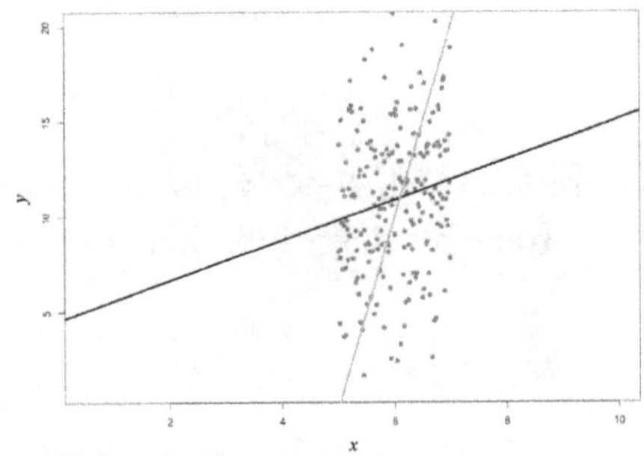

Figure 3.2 Scatter plots of a linear regression with small changes in X_t.

In certain sense, one may call $\mathbf{X}'\mathbf{X}$ the "information matrix" of the random sample $\mathbf{X}$ because it is a measure of the information contained in $\mathbf{X}$. The magnitude of $\mathbf{X}'\mathbf{X}$ will affect the preciseness of parameter estimation for β^o. Indeed, as will be shown below, the condition that $\lambda_{\min}(\mathbf{X}'\mathbf{X}) \to \infty$ as $n \to \infty$ ensures that variance of the OLS estimator will vanish to zero as $n \to \infty$. This rules out a possibility called near-multicollinearity that there is an approximate linear relationship among two or more explanatory variables such that although $\mathbf{X}'\mathbf{X}$ is nonsingular, its minimum eigenvalue $\lambda_{\min}(\mathbf{X}'\mathbf{X})$ does not grow with the sample size n. When $\lambda_{\min}(\mathbf{X}'\mathbf{X})$ does not grow with n, the OLS estimator is well-defined and has a well-behaved finite sample distribution, but its variance never vanishes to zero as $n \to \infty$. In other words, in the near-multicollinearity case where $\lambda_{\min}(\mathbf{X}'\mathbf{X})$ does not grow with n, the OLS estimator will never converge to the true parameter value β^o, although it will still have a well-defined finite sample distribution.

Question: Why can the eigenvalue λ be used as a measure of the information contained in $\mathbf{X}'\mathbf{X}$?

Assumption 3.4. [Spherical Error Variance]:

(a) [Conditional Homoskedasticity]:

$$E(\varepsilon_t^2|\mathbf{X}) = \sigma^2 > 0, \qquad t = 1, ..., n;$$

(b) [Conditional Non-Autocorrelation]:

$$E(\varepsilon_t\varepsilon_s|\mathbf{X}) = 0, \qquad t \neq s, t, s \in \{1, ..., n\}.$$

We can write Assumption 3.4 as

$$E(\varepsilon_t\varepsilon_s|\mathbf{X}) = \sigma^2\delta_{ts},$$

where $\delta_{ts} = 1$ if $t = s$ and $\delta_{ts} = 0$ otherwise. In mathematics, δ_{ts} is called the Kronecker delta function. Under this assumption, we have

$$\begin{aligned} var(\varepsilon_t|\mathbf{X}) &= E(\varepsilon_t^2|\mathbf{X}) - [E(\varepsilon_t|\mathbf{X})]^2 \\ &= E(\varepsilon_t^2|\mathbf{X}) \\ &= \sigma^2 \end{aligned}$$

and

$$\begin{aligned} cov(\varepsilon_t, \varepsilon_s|\mathbf{X}) &= E(\varepsilon_t\varepsilon_s|\mathbf{X}) \\ &= 0 \text{ for all } t \neq s. \end{aligned}$$

By the law of iterated expectations, Assumption 3.4(b) implies that $\text{var}(\varepsilon_t) = \sigma^2$ for all $t = 1, ..., n$, the so-called unconditional homoskedasticity. Similarly, Assumption 3.4(a) implies $\text{cov}(\varepsilon_t, \varepsilon_s) = 0$ for all $t \neq s$. Thus, there exists no serial correlation between ε_t and its lagged values when t is an index for time, or there exists no spatial correlation between the disturbances associated with different cross-sectional units when t is an index for the cross-sectional unit (e.g., consumer, firm and household). In either case, we say that there exists no autocorrelation in $\{\varepsilon_t\}$.

Assumption 3.4 does not imply that ε_t and $\mathbf{X}$ are independent. It allows the possibility that the conditional higher order moments (e.g., skewness and kurtosis) of ε_t depend on $\mathbf{X}$.

We can write Assumptions 3.2 and 3.4 compactly as follows:

$$E(\varepsilon|\mathbf{X}) = 0 \text{ and } E(\varepsilon\varepsilon'|\mathbf{X}) = \sigma^2\mathbf{I},$$

where $\mathbf{I} \equiv I_n$ is an $n \times n$ identity matrix.

3.2 Ordinary Least Squares (OLS) Estimation

Question: How to estimate the true model parameter β^o using an observed data set generated from the random sample $\{Z_t\}_{t=1}^n$, where $Z_t = (Y_t, X_t')'$?

Definition 3.1. [OLS Estimator]: Suppose Assumptions 3.1 and 3.3(a) hold. Define the Sum of Squared Residuals (SSR) of the linear regression model $Y_t = X_t'\beta + u_t$ as

$$\begin{aligned} SSR(\beta) &\equiv (Y - \mathbf{X}\beta)'(Y - \mathbf{X}\beta) \\ &= \sum_{t=1}^{n} (Y_t - X_t'\beta)^2. \end{aligned}$$

Then the OLS estimator $\hat{\beta}$ is the solution to

$$\hat{\beta} = \arg\min_{\beta \in \mathbb{R}^K} SSR(\beta).$$

Note that $SSR(\beta)$ is the sum of squared model errors $\{u_t = Y_t - X_t'\beta\}$, with equal weighting for each t.

Theorem 3.1. ***[Existence of the OLS Estimator]:*** *Under Assumptions 3.1 and 3.3, the OLS estimator $\hat{\beta}$ exists and*

$$\begin{aligned} \hat{\beta} &= (\mathbf{X}'\mathbf{X})^{-1}\mathbf{X}'Y \\ &= \left(\sum_{t=1}^{n} X_t X_t' \right)^{-1} \sum_{t=1}^{n} X_t Y_t \\ &= \left(\frac{1}{n} \sum_{t=1}^{n} X_t X_t' \right)^{-1} \frac{1}{n} \sum_{t=1}^{n} X_t Y_t. \end{aligned}$$

The last expression will be useful for our asymptotic analysis in subsequent chapters.

Proof: Using the formula that for an $K \times 1$ vector A and $K \times 1$ vector β, the derivative

$$\frac{\partial (A'\beta)}{\partial \beta} = A,$$

we have

$$\begin{aligned}
\frac{dSSR(\beta)}{d\beta} &= \frac{d}{d\beta}\sum_{t=1}^{n}(Y_t - X_t'\beta)^2 \\
&= \sum_{t=1}^{n}\frac{\partial}{\partial\beta}(Y_t - X_t'\beta)^2 \\
&= \sum_{t=1}^{n}2(Y_t - X_t'\beta)\frac{\partial}{\partial\beta}(Y_t - X_t'\beta) \\
&= -2\sum_{t=1}^{n}X_t(Y_t - X_t'\beta) \\
&= -2\mathbf{X}'(Y - \mathbf{X}\beta).
\end{aligned}$$

The OLS estimator must satisfy the FOC:

$$\begin{aligned}
-2\mathbf{X}'(Y - \mathbf{X}\hat{\beta}) &= 0, \\
\mathbf{X}'(Y - \mathbf{X}\hat{\beta}) &= 0, \\
\mathbf{X}'Y - (\mathbf{X}'\mathbf{X})\hat{\beta} &= 0.
\end{aligned}$$

It follows that

$$(\mathbf{X}'\mathbf{X})\hat{\beta} = \mathbf{X}'Y.$$

By Assumption 3.3, $\mathbf{X}'\mathbf{X}$ is nonsingular. Thus,

$$\hat{\beta} = (\mathbf{X}'\mathbf{X})^{-1}\mathbf{X}'Y.$$

Checking the SOC, we have the $K \times K$ Hessian matrix

$$\begin{aligned}
\frac{\partial^2 SSR(\beta)}{\partial\beta\partial\beta'} &= -2\sum_{t=1}^{n}\frac{\partial}{\partial\beta'}\left[(Y_t - X_t'\beta)X_t\right] \\
&= 2\mathbf{X}'\mathbf{X}
\end{aligned}$$

is positive definite given $\lambda_{\min}(\mathbf{X}'\mathbf{X}) > 0$. Thus, $\hat{\beta}$ is a global minimizer. Note that for the existence of $\hat{\beta}$, we only need that $\mathbf{X}'\mathbf{X}$ is nonsingular, which is implied by the condition that $\lambda_{\min}(\mathbf{X}'\mathbf{X}) \to \infty$ as $n \to \infty$ but it does not require that $\lambda_{\min}(\mathbf{X}'\mathbf{X}) \to \infty$ as $n \to \infty$. This completes the proof.

Suppose $Z_t = \{Y_t, X_t'\}', t = 1, ..., n$, is an IID random sample of size n. Consider the SSR scaled by n^{-1} :

$$\frac{SSR(\beta)}{n} = \frac{1}{n}\sum_{t=1}^{n}(Y_t - X_t'\beta)^2$$

and its minimizer

$$\hat{\beta} = \left(\frac{1}{n}\sum_{t=1}^{n} X_t X_t'\right)^{-1} \frac{1}{n}\sum_{t=1}^{n} X_t Y_t.$$

These are the sample analogs of the population MSE criterion

$$\text{MSE}(\beta) = E(Y_t - X_t'\beta)^2$$

and its minimizer

$$\beta^* \equiv \left[E(X_t X_t')\right]^{-1} E(X_t Y_t).$$

That is, $SSR(\beta)$, after scaled by n^{-1}, is the sample analogue of MSE(β), and the OLS estimator $\hat{\beta}$ is the sample analogue of the best least squares approximation coefficient β^*.

Put

$$\hat{Y}_t \equiv X_t'\hat{\beta}.$$

This is called the fitted value (or predicted value) for observation Y_t, and

$$e_t \equiv Y_t - \hat{Y}_t$$

is called the estimated residual (or prediction error) for observation Y_t. Note that

$$\begin{aligned} e_t &= Y_t - \hat{Y}_t \\ &= (X_t'\beta^o + \varepsilon_t) - X_t'\hat{\beta} \\ &= \varepsilon_t - X_t'(\hat{\beta} - \beta^o), \end{aligned}$$

where ε_t is the unavoidable true disturbance ε_t, and $X_t'(\hat{\beta} - \beta^o)$ is an estimation error, which is smaller when a larger data set is available (so $\hat{\beta}$ becomes closer to β^o).

The FOC implies that the estimated residual $e = Y - \mathbf{X}\hat{\beta}$ is orthogonal to regressors $\mathbf{X}$ in the sense that

$$\mathbf{X}'e = \sum_{t=1}^{n} X_t e_t = 0.$$

This is the consequence of the very nature of the OLS estimation, as implied by the FOC of $\min_{\beta \in R^K} SSR(\beta)$. It always holds no matter whether $E(\varepsilon_t|\mathbf{X}) = 0$ (note that we do not impose Assumption 3.2 in Theorem 3.1). Note that if X_t contains the intercept, then $\mathbf{X}'e = 0$ implies $\sum_{t=1}^n e_t = 0$.

The earliest form of regression was the OLS method, which was introduced by Legendre (1805) and Gauss (1809), who both applied the method to the problem of determining, from astronomical observations, the orbits of bodies about the Sun (mostly comets, but also later the then newly discovered minor planets).

3.3 Goodness of Fit and Model Selection Criteria

Question: How well does the linear regression model fit the data? That is, how well does a linear regression model explain the variations of the observed data of $\{Y_t\}_{t=1}^n$?

We need some criteria or some measures to characterize goodness of fit.

We first introduce two measures for goodness of fit. The first measure is called the uncentered squared multi-correlation coefficient R^2.

Definition 3.2. [Uncentered R^2]: The uncentered squared multi-correlation coefficient is defined as

$$R_{uc}^2 = \frac{\hat{Y}'\hat{Y}}{Y'Y} = 1 - \frac{e'e}{Y'Y},$$

where the second equality follows from the FOC of the OLS estimation.

The measure R_{uc}^2 has a nice interpretation: the proportion of the uncentered sample quadratic variation in the dependent variables $\{Y_t\}$ that can be attributed to the uncentered sample quadratic variation of the predicted values $\{\hat{Y}_t\}$. Note that we always have $0 \le R_{uc}^2 \le 1$.

Next, we define a closely related measure called centered R^2.

Definition 3.3. [Centered R^2: Coefficient of Determination]: The coefficient of determination

$$R^2 \equiv 1 - \frac{\sum_{t=1}^n e_t^2}{\sum_{t=1}^n (Y_t - \bar{Y})^2},$$

where $\bar{Y} = n^{-1}\sum_{t=1}^n Y_t$ is the sample mean.

When X_t contains the intercept, we have the following orthogonal decomposition:

$$\begin{aligned}\sum_{t=1}^{n}(Y_t-\bar{Y})^2 &= \sum_{t=1}^{n}(\hat{Y}_t-\bar{Y}+Y_t-\hat{Y}_t)^2\\ &= \sum_{t=1}^{n}(\hat{Y}_t-\bar{Y})^2+\sum_{t=1}^{n}e_t^2+2\sum_{t=1}^{n}(\hat{Y}_t-\bar{Y})e_t\\ &= \sum_{t=1}^{n}(\hat{Y}_t-\bar{Y})^2+\sum_{t=1}^{n}e_t^2,\end{aligned}$$

where the cross-product term

$$\begin{aligned}\sum_{t=1}^{n}(\hat{Y}_t-\bar{Y})e_t &= \sum_{t=1}^{n}\hat{Y}_te_t-\bar{Y}\sum_{t=1}^{n}e_t\\ &= \hat{\beta}'\sum_{t=1}^{n}X_te_t-\bar{Y}\sum_{t=1}^{n}e_t\\ &= \hat{\beta}'(\mathbf{X}'e)-\bar{Y}\sum_{t=1}^{n}e_t\\ &= \hat{\beta}'\cdot 0-\bar{Y}\cdot 0\\ &= 0,\end{aligned}$$

where we have made use of the facts that $\mathbf{X}'e = 0$ and $\sum_{t=1}^{n} e_t = 0$ from the FOC of the OLS estimation and the fact that X_t contains the intercept (i.e., $X_{0t} = 1$). It follows that

$$\begin{aligned}R^2 &\equiv 1-\frac{e'e}{\sum_{t=1}^{n}(Y_t-\bar{Y})^2}\\ &= \frac{\sum_{t=1}^{n}(Y_t-\bar{Y})^2-\sum_{t=1}^{n}e_t^2}{\sum_{t=1}^{n}(Y_t-\bar{Y})^2}\\ &= \frac{\sum_{t=1}^{n}(\hat{Y}_t-\bar{Y})^2}{\sum_{t=1}^{n}(Y_t-\bar{Y})^2},\end{aligned}$$

and consequently we have

$$0 \le R^2 \le 1.$$

Question: Can R^2 be negative?

Yes, this is possible. If X_t does not contain the intercept, then the orthogonal decomposition identity

$$\sum_{t=1}^{n}(Y_t - \bar{Y})^2 = \sum_{t=1}^{n}(\hat{Y}_t - \bar{Y})^2 + \sum_{t=1}^{n} e_t^2$$

generally no longer holds. As a consequence, R^2 may be negative when there is no intercept! This is because the cross-product term

$$2\sum_{t=1}^{n}(\hat{Y}_t - \bar{Y})e_t$$

may be negative.

When X_t contains an intercept, the centered R^2 has a similar interpretation to the uncentered R^2_{uc}. That is, R^2 measures the proportion of the sample variance of $\{Y_t\}_{t=1}^n$ that can be explained by the linear predictor of X_t.

Example 3.2. [CAPM and Economic Interpretation of R^2]: The classical CAPM is characterized by the equation

$$r_{it} - r_{ft} = \alpha_i + \beta_i(r_{mt} - r_{ft}) + \varepsilon_{it}, \qquad t = 1, ..., n,$$

where r_{it} is the return on portfolio (or asset) i, r_{ft} is the return on a risk-free asset, and r_{mt} is the return on the market portfolio. Here, $r_{it} - r_{ft}$ is the risk premium of portfolio i, $r_{mt} - r_{ft}$ is the risk premium of the market portfolio, which is the only systematic market risk factor, and ε_{it} is the idiosyncratic risk which can be eliminated by diversification if the ε_{it} are uncorrelated across different assets (see Hong 2017, Example 6.6, Chapter 6). In this model, R^2 has an interesting economic interpretation: it is the proportion of the risk of portfolio i (as measured by the sample variance of its risk premium $r_{it} - r_{ft}$) that is attributed to the market risk factor $(r_{mt} - r_{ft})$. In contrast, $1 - R^2$ is the proportion of the risk of portfolio i that is contributed by idiosyncratic risk factor ε_{it}.

In fact, the centered R^2 is the squared sample correlation between $\{Y_t\}_{t=1}^n$ and $\{\hat{Y}_t\}_{t=1}^n$, as is shown below.

Theorem 3.2. $R^2 = \hat{\rho}^2_{Y\hat{Y}}$, *where* $\hat{\rho}_{Y\hat{Y}}$ *is the sample correlation between* $\{Y_t\}_{t=1}^n$ *and* $\{\hat{Y}_t\}_{t=1}^n$.

Proof: Left as an exercise.

Since the fitted value $\hat{Y}_t = X_t'\hat{\beta} = \hat{\beta}_0 + \sum_{j=1}^k \hat{\beta}_j X_{jt}$ is a linear combination of $\{X_{jt}\}_{j=1}^k$, R may be viewed as a multiple sample correlation between Y_t and $\{X_{jt}\}_{j=1}^k$, and this is why R^2 is called the squared multiple sample correlation coefficient.

For any given random sample $\{Y_t, X_t'\}', t = 1, ..., n$, R^2 is nondecreasing in the number of explanatory variables X_t. In other words, the more explanatory variables are added in the linear regression, the higher R^2 is. This is always true no matter whether X_t has any true explanatory power for Y_t, as is stated below.

Theorem 3.3. *Suppose* $\{Y_t, X_{1t}, ..., X_{(k+q)t}\}', t = 1, ..., n$, *is a random sample, and Assumptions 3.1 and 3.3(a) hold. Let* R_1^2 *be the centered* R^2 *from the linear regression*

$$Y_t = X_t'\beta + u_t,$$

where $X_t = (1, X_{1t}, ..., X_{kt})'$, *and* β *is a* $K \times 1$ *parameter vector; also,* R_2^2 *is the centered* R^2 *from the extended linear regression*

$$Y_t = \tilde{X}_t'\gamma + v_t,$$

where $\tilde{X}_t = (1, X_{1t}, ..., X_{kt}, X_{(k+1)t}, ..., X_{(k+q)t})'$,*and* γ *is a* $(K+q) \times 1$ *parameter vector. Then*

$$R_2^2 \geq R_1^2.$$

Proof: By definition, we have

$$R_1^2 = 1 - \frac{e'e}{\sum_{t=1}^n (Y_t - \bar{Y})^2},$$

$$R_2^2 = 1 - \frac{\tilde{e}'\tilde{e}}{\sum_{t=1}^n (Y_t - \bar{Y})^2},$$

where e is the estimated residual vector from the regression of Y on $\mathbf{X}$, and $\tilde{e}$ is the estimated residual vector from the regression of Y on $\tilde{\mathbf{X}}$. It suffices to show $\tilde{e}'\tilde{e} \leq e'e$. Because the OLS estimator $\hat{\gamma} = (\tilde{\mathbf{X}}'\tilde{\mathbf{X}})^{-1}\tilde{\mathbf{X}}'Y$ minimizes $SSR(\gamma)$ for the extended model, we have

$$\tilde{e}'\tilde{e} = \sum_{t=1}^n (Y_t - \tilde{X}_t'\hat{\gamma})^2 \leq \sum_{t=1}^n (Y_t - \tilde{X}_t'\gamma)^2 \text{ for all } \gamma \in \mathbb{R}^{K+q}.$$

Now we choose

$$\gamma = (\hat{\beta}', 0')',$$

where $\hat{\beta} = (\mathbf{X}'\mathbf{X})^{-1}\mathbf{X}'Y$ is the OLS estimator from the first regression. It follows that

$$\begin{aligned}
\tilde{e}'\tilde{e} &\le \sum_{t=1}^{n}\left(Y_t - \sum_{j=0}^{k}\hat{\beta}_j X_{jt} - \sum_{j=k+1}^{k+q} 0\cdot X_{jt}\right)^2 \\
&= \sum_{t=1}^{n}(Y_t - X_t'\hat{\beta})^2 \\
&= e'e.
\end{aligned}$$

Hence, we have $R_1^2 \le R_2^2$. This completes the proof.

Question: What is the implication of Theorem 3.3?

The measure R^2 can be used to compare models with the same number of predictors, but it is not a useful criterion for comparing models of different sizes because it is biased in favor of large models.

The measure R^2 is not a suitable criterion for correct model specification. It is a measure for sampling variation rather than a measure of population. A high value of R^2 does not necessarily imply correct model specification, and correct model specification also does not necessarily imply a high value of R^2.

Strictly speaking, R^2 is a measure merely of statistical association with nothing to say about causality. High values of R^2 are often very easy to achieve when dealing with economic time series data, even when the causal link between two variables is extremely tenuous or perhaps nonexistent. For example, in the so-called spurious regression where the dependent variable Y_t and the regressors X_t have no causal relationship but they display similar trending behaviors over time, it is often found that R^2 is close to unity (Granger and Newbold 1974, and Phillips 1986).

Finally, R^2 is a measure of the strength of linear association between the dependent variable Y_t and the regressors X_t (see Exercise 3.2). It is not a suitable measure for goodness of fit of a nonlinear regression model where $E(Y_t|X_t)$ is a nonlinear function of X_t.

Question: How to interpret R^2 for the linear regression model

$$\ln Y_t = \beta_0 + \beta_1 \ln L_t + \beta_2 \ln K_t + \varepsilon_t,$$

where Y_t is output, L_t is labor and K_t is capital?

The centered R^2 is the proportion of the total sample variations in $\ln Y_t$ that can be attributed to the sample variations in $\ln L_t$ and $\ln K_t$. It is not the proportion of the sample quadratic variations in Y_t that can be attributed to the sample variations of L_t and K_t. In other words, it is inappropriate to compare the R^2 from the regression of Y_t on L_t and K_t and the R^2 from the regression of $\ln Y_t$ on $\ln L_t$ and $\ln K_t$.

Question: Does a high R^2 value imply a precise estimation for β^o?

The discussion above implies that R^2 is not a suitable criterion for model selection. Often, a large number of potential predictors are available, but we do not necessarily want to include all of them. There are two conflicting factors to consider: on one hand, a larger model has less systematic bias and it would give the best predictions if all parameters could be estimated without error. On the other hand, when unknown parameters are replaced by estimates, the prediction becomes less accurate, and this effect is worse when there are more parameters to estimate. An important idea in statistics is to use a simple model to capture essential information contained in data as much as possible. This is often called the KISS principle, namely "*Keep It Sophisticatedly Simple*"!

Below, we introduce three popular model selection criteria that reflect such an idea.

(1) Akaike Information Criterion (AIC)

A linear regression model can be selected by minimizing the following AIC criterion with a suitable choice of K:

$$AIC = \ln(s^2) + \frac{2K}{n}$$

where

$$s^2 = e'e/(n - K),$$

is called the residual variance estimator for $E(\varepsilon_t^2) = \sigma^2$, and $K = k + 1$ is the number of regressors. The first term $\ln s^2$ is a measure for goodness of fit, and the second term $2K/n$ is a measure for model complexity. AIC is proposed by Akaike (1973).

(2) Bayesian Information Criterion (BIC, Schwarz (1978))

A linear regression model can be selected by minimizing the following criterion with a suitable choice of K:

$$BIC = \ln(s^2) + \frac{K \ln(n)}{n}.$$

This is called the Bayesian Information Criterion (BIC), proposed by Schwarz (1978).

Both AIC and BIC try to trade off the goodness of fit to data measured by $\ln(s^2)$ with the desire to use as few parameters as possible. When $\ln n \geq 2$, which is the case when $n > 7$, BIC gives a heavier penalty for model complexity than AIC, which is measured by the number of estimated parameters (relative to the sample size n). As a consequence, BIC will choose a more parsimonious linear regression model than AIC.

The difference between AIC and BIC is due to the way they are constructed. AIC is designed to select a model that will predict best and is less concerned than BIC with having a few too many parameters. BIC is designed to select the true value of K exactly. Under certain regularity conditions, BIC is strongly consistent in the sense that it determines the true model asymptotically (i.e., as $n \to \infty$), whereas for AIC an overparameterized model will emerge no matter how large the sample is. Of course, such properties are not necessarily guaranteed in finite samples. In practice, the best AIC model is usually close to the best BIC model and often they deliver the same model.

(3) Adjusted R^2

In addition to AIC and BIC, there are other criteria such as $\bar{R}^2$, the so-called adjusted R^2 that can also be used to select a linear regression model. The adjusted R^2, denoted as $\bar{R}^2$, is defined as

$$\bar{R}^2 = 1 - \frac{e'e/(n-K)}{(Y-\bar{Y})'(Y-\bar{Y})/(n-1)}.$$

This differs from

$$R^2 = 1 - \frac{e'e}{(Y-\bar{Y})'(Y-\bar{Y})}.$$

In $\bar{R}^2$, the adjustment is made according to the degrees of freedom, or the number of regressors in X_t. It may be shown that

$$\bar{R}^2 = 1 - \frac{n-1}{n-K}(1 - R^2).$$

We note that $\bar{R}^2$ may take a negative value although there is an intercept in X_t. It does not have as straightforward an interpretation as R^2 does.

To gain insight into $\bar{R}^2$, let us look at the numerator of the ratio in the definition of $\bar{R}^2$, because the denominator does not depend on K. The numerator itself is a ratio. Adding a regressor to the regression will cause both $e'e$ and $n-K$ to decrease. If $e'e$ decreases proportionally more than $n-K$ decreases, the ratio in the numerator will decrease and so $\bar{R}^2$ will increase. By contrast, if $e'e$ decreases proportionally less than $n-K$ decreases, $\bar{R}^2$ will decrease. We note that the decrease in the number of degrees of freedom, $n - K$, is linked to the "statistical cost" of adding another regressor to the regression.

All aforementioned model criteria are structured in terms of the estimated residual variance s^2 plus a penalty adjustment involving the number of estimated parameters, and it is in the extent of this penalty that the criteria differ. For more discussion about these and other selection criteria, see Judge *et al.* (1985, Section 7.5).

Question: Why is it not a good practice to use a complicated model?

A complicated model contains many unknown parameters. Given a fixed amount of data information, parameter estimation will become less precise if more parameters have to be estimated. As a consequence, the out-of-sample forecast for Y_t may become less precise than the forecast of a simpler model. The latter may have a larger bias but more precise parameter estimates. Intuitively, a complicated model is too flexible in the sense that it may capture not only systematic components but also some features in the data which will not show up again. Thus, it cannot forecast futures well.

In many applications especially with a relatively large number of regressors, the matrix $\mathbf{X}'\mathbf{X}$ may be close to a singular matrix when there exists near-multicollinearity in regressors. As a result, the OLS estimator $\hat{\beta}$ will not be stable, inducing a large variance in its MSE. One solution is to restrict the magnitude of β by considering the following estimator

$$\begin{aligned}\hat{\beta} &= (Y - \mathbf{X}\beta)'(Y - \mathbf{X}\beta) + \lambda\beta'\beta \\ &= (\mathbf{X}'\mathbf{X} + \lambda I)^{-1}\mathbf{X}'Y\end{aligned}$$

where λ is a tuning parameter which controls the weight on the magnitude of β measured by the sum of its squared components. This is called a ridge regression estimator. When $\lambda = 0$, the ridge regression estimator becomes the OLS estimator. The introduction of λ makes the ridge regression estimator $\hat{\beta}$ more stable than the OLS estimator. This reduces the variance of $\hat{\beta}$ at a cost of bias. Overall, the MSE of the ridge regression estimator of $\hat{\beta}$ will be smaller than that of the OLS estimator.

When there exists a high-dimensional set of regressors (particularly when the number of regressors K may be larger than the sample size n), many parameters in β may be zero or small enough to be negligible. This is called sparsity of a high-dimensional linear regression. When K is larger than the sample size n, the OLS estimation is simply impossible, because $\mathbf{X}'\mathbf{X}$ is singular. In this case, one can consider the following estimator

$$\hat{\beta} = \min_{\beta}(Y - \mathbf{X}\beta)'(Y - \mathbf{X}\beta) + \lambda|\beta|_1,$$

where $|\beta|_1 = \sum_{j=0}^{k} |\beta_j|$ is the L_1-norm of β. This is called the Least Absolute Shrinkage and Selection Operator (LASSO) estimator, which, unlike the ridge regression estimator, sets those small coefficients directly equal to zero. The LASSO estimator substantially reduces the variance of $\hat{\beta}$ at a cost of bias, which usually leads to a large reduction in the MSE of $\hat{\beta}$ when there exists a high-dimensional vector of regressors. For more discussion, interested readers are referred to Tibshirani (1996).

3.4 Consistency and Efficiency of the OLS Estimator

We now investigate the statistical properties of the OLS estimator $\hat{\beta}$. We are interested in addressing the following basic questions:

- Is $\hat{\beta}$ a good estimator for β^o (consistency)?
- Is $\hat{\beta}$ the best estimator (efficiency)?
- What is the sampling distribution of $\hat{\beta}$ (normality)?

Note that the distribution of $\hat{\beta}$ is called the sampling distribution of $\hat{\beta}$, because $\hat{\beta}$ is a function of the random sample $\{Z_t\}_{t=1}^n$, where $Z_t = (Y_t, X_t')'$.

The sampling distribution of $\hat{\beta}$ is useful for any statistical inference involving $\hat{\beta}$, such as confidence interval estimation and hypothesis testing.

To investigate the statistical properties of $\hat{\beta}$, we first state some useful lemmas.

Lemma 3.1. *Under Assumptions 3.1 and 3.3(a), we have:*

(1)

$$\mathbf{X}'e = 0.$$

(2)

$$\hat{\beta} - \beta^o = (\mathbf{X}'\mathbf{X})^{-1}\mathbf{X}'\varepsilon.$$

(3) Define an $n \times n$ projection matrix

$$\mathbf{P} = \mathbf{X}(\mathbf{X}'\mathbf{X})^{-1}\mathbf{X}'$$

and

$$\mathbf{M} = \mathbf{I} - \mathbf{P}.$$

Then both matrices $\mathbf{P}$ and $\mathbf{M}$ are symmetric (i.e., $\mathbf{P} = \mathbf{P}'$ and $\mathbf{M} = \mathbf{M}'$) and idempotent (i.e., $\mathbf{P}^2 = \mathbf{P}, \mathbf{M}^2 = \mathbf{M}$), with

$$\mathbf{P}\mathbf{X} = \mathbf{X},$$
$$\mathbf{M}\mathbf{X} = 0.$$

(4)

$$SSR(\hat{\beta}) = e'e = Y'\mathbf{M}Y = \varepsilon'\mathbf{M}\varepsilon.$$

Proof: (1) The result follows immediately from the FOC of the OLS estimator.

(2) Because $\hat{\beta} = (\mathbf{X}'\mathbf{X})^{-1}\mathbf{X}'Y$ and $Y = \mathbf{X}\beta^o + \varepsilon$, we have

$$\begin{aligned}\hat{\beta} - \beta^o &= (\mathbf{X}'\mathbf{X})^{-1}\mathbf{X}'(\mathbf{X}\beta^o + \varepsilon) - \beta^o \\ &= (\mathbf{X}'\mathbf{X})^{-1}\mathbf{X}'\varepsilon.\end{aligned}$$

(3) $\mathbf{P}$ is idempotent because

$$\begin{aligned}\mathbf{P}^2 &= \mathbf{PP} \\ &= [\mathbf{X}(\mathbf{X}'\mathbf{X})^{-1}\mathbf{X}'][\mathbf{X}(\mathbf{X}'\mathbf{X})^{-1}\mathbf{X}'] \\ &= \mathbf{X}(\mathbf{X}'\mathbf{X})^{-1}\mathbf{X}' \\ &= \mathbf{P}.\end{aligned}$$

Similarly we can show $\mathbf{M}^2 = \mathbf{M}$.

(4) By the definition of $\mathbf{M}$, we have

$$\begin{aligned}e &= Y - \mathbf{X}\hat{\beta} \\ &= Y - \mathbf{X}(\mathbf{X}'\mathbf{X})^{-1}\mathbf{X}'Y \\ &= [\mathbf{I} - \mathbf{X}(\mathbf{X}'\mathbf{X})^{-1}\mathbf{X}']Y \\ &= \mathbf{M}Y \\ &= \mathbf{M}(\mathbf{X}\beta^o + \varepsilon) \\ &= \mathbf{M}\mathbf{X}\beta^o + \mathbf{M}\varepsilon \\ &= \mathbf{M}\varepsilon\end{aligned}$$

given $\mathbf{MX} = 0$. It follows that

$$\begin{aligned}SSR(\hat{\beta}) &= e'e \\ &= (\mathbf{M}\varepsilon)'(\mathbf{M}\varepsilon) \\ &= \varepsilon'\mathbf{M}^2\varepsilon \\ &= \varepsilon'\mathbf{M}\varepsilon,\end{aligned}$$

where the last equality follows from $\mathbf{M}^2 = \mathbf{M}$.

We now investigate the statistical properties of $\hat{\beta}$.

Theorem 3.4. *Suppose Assumptions 3.1 to 3.3(a) and 3.4 hold. Then*

(1) [Unbiasedness] $E(\hat{\beta}|\mathbf{X}) = \beta^o$ *and* $E(\hat{\beta}) = \beta^o$.

(2) [Vanishing Variance]

$$\begin{aligned}var(\hat{\beta}|\mathbf{X}) &= E\left[(\hat{\beta} - E\hat{\beta})(\hat{\beta} - E\hat{\beta})'|\mathbf{X}\right] \\ &= \sigma^2(\mathbf{X}'\mathbf{X})^{-1}.\end{aligned}$$

If in addition Assumption 3.3(b) holds, then for any $K \times 1$ *vector* τ *such that* $\tau'\tau = 1$, *we have*

$$\tau' var(\hat{\beta}|\mathbf{X})\tau \to 0 \text{ as } n \to \infty.$$

(3) [Orthogonality Between e and $\hat{\beta}$*]*

$$cov(\hat{\beta}, e|\mathbf{X}) = E\{[\hat{\beta} - E(\hat{\beta}|\mathbf{X})]e'|\mathbf{X}\} = 0.$$

(4) [Gauss-Markov Theorem]

$$var(\hat{b}|\mathbf{X}) - var(\hat{\beta}|\mathbf{X}) \text{ is Positive Semi-Definite (PSD)}$$

for any unbiased estimator $\hat{b}$ *that is linear in* Y *with* $E(\hat{b}|\mathbf{X}) = \beta^o$.

(5) [Sample Residual Variance Estimator]

$$s^2 = e'e/(n-K) = \frac{1}{n-K}\sum_{t=1}^{n} e_t^2$$

is unbiased for $\sigma^2 = E(\varepsilon_t^2)$. *That is,* $E(s^2|\mathbf{X}) = \sigma^2$.

Proof: (1) Given $\hat{\beta} - \beta^o = (\mathbf{X}'\mathbf{X})^{-1}\mathbf{X}'\varepsilon$, we have

$$\begin{aligned} E[(\hat{\beta} - \beta^o)|\mathbf{X}] &= E[(\mathbf{X}'\mathbf{X})^{-1}\mathbf{X}'\varepsilon|\mathbf{X}] \\ &= (\mathbf{X}'\mathbf{X})^{-1}\mathbf{X}'E(\varepsilon|\mathbf{X}) \\ &= (\mathbf{X}'\mathbf{X})^{-1}\mathbf{X}'0 \\ &= 0. \end{aligned}$$

(2) Given $\hat{\beta} - \beta^o = (\mathbf{X}'\mathbf{X})^{-1}\mathbf{X}'\varepsilon$ and $E(\varepsilon\varepsilon'|\mathbf{X}) = \sigma^2\mathbf{I}$, we have

$$\begin{aligned} \text{var}(\hat{\beta}|\mathbf{X}) &\equiv E\left\{\left[\hat{\beta} - E(\hat{\beta}|\mathbf{X})\right]\left[\hat{\beta} - E(\hat{\beta}|\mathbf{X})\right]'|\mathbf{X}\right\} \\ &= E\left[(\hat{\beta} - \beta^o)(\hat{\beta} - \beta^o)'|\mathbf{X}\right] \\ &= E[(\mathbf{X}'\mathbf{X})^{-1}\mathbf{X}'\varepsilon\varepsilon'\mathbf{X}(\mathbf{X}'\mathbf{X})^{-1}|\mathbf{X}] \\ &= (\mathbf{X}'\mathbf{X})^{-1}\mathbf{X}'E(\varepsilon\varepsilon'|\mathbf{X})\mathbf{X}(\mathbf{X}'\mathbf{X})^{-1} \\ &= (\mathbf{X}'\mathbf{X})^{-1}\mathbf{X}'\sigma^2\mathbf{I}\mathbf{X}(\mathbf{X}'\mathbf{X})^{-1} \\ &= \sigma^2(\mathbf{X}'\mathbf{X})^{-1}\mathbf{X}'\mathbf{X}(\mathbf{X}'\mathbf{X})^{-1} \\ &= \sigma^2(\mathbf{X}'\mathbf{X})^{-1}. \end{aligned}$$

Note that Assumption 3.4 is crucial here to obtain the expression of $\sigma^2(\mathbf{X}'\mathbf{X})^{-1}$ for $\mathrm{var}(\hat{\beta}|\mathbf{X})$. Moreover, for any $\tau \in \mathbb{R}^K$ such that $\tau'\tau = 1$, we have, with probability one,

$$\begin{aligned}\tau'\mathrm{var}(\hat{\beta}|\mathbf{X})\tau &= \sigma^2\tau'(\mathbf{X}'\mathbf{X})^{-1}\tau \\ &\leq \sigma^2\lambda_{\max}[(\mathbf{X}'\mathbf{X})^{-1}] \\ &= \sigma^2\lambda_{\min}^{-1}(\mathbf{X}'\mathbf{X}) \\ &\to 0\end{aligned}$$

given $\lambda_{\min}(\mathbf{X}'\mathbf{X}) \to \infty$ as $n \to \infty$. Note that the condition that $\lambda_{\min}(\mathbf{X}'\mathbf{X}) \to \infty$ ensures that $\mathrm{var}(\hat{\beta}|\mathbf{X})$ vanishes to zero as $n \to \infty$.

(3) Given $\hat{\beta} - \beta^o = (\mathbf{X}'\mathbf{X})^{-1}\mathbf{X}'\varepsilon$, $e = Y - \mathbf{X}\hat{\beta} = \mathbf{M}Y = \mathbf{M}\varepsilon$ (since $\mathbf{MX} = 0$ by Lemma 3.1(3)), and $E(e) = 0$, we have

$$\begin{aligned}\mathrm{cov}(\hat{\beta}, e|\mathbf{X}) &= E\left\{\left[\hat{\beta} - E(\hat{\beta}|\mathbf{X})\right][e - E(e|\mathbf{X})]'\,|\mathbf{X}\right\} \\ &= E\left[(\hat{\beta} - \beta^o)e'|\mathbf{X}\right] \\ &= E[(\mathbf{X}'\mathbf{X})^{-1}\mathbf{X}'\varepsilon\varepsilon'\mathbf{M}|\mathbf{X}] \\ &= (\mathbf{X}'\mathbf{X})^{-1}\mathbf{X}'E(\varepsilon\varepsilon'|\mathbf{X})\mathbf{M} \\ &= (\mathbf{X}'\mathbf{X})^{-1}\mathbf{X}'\sigma^2\mathbf{I}\mathbf{M} \\ &= \sigma^2(\mathbf{X}'\mathbf{X})^{-1}\mathbf{X}'\mathbf{M} \\ &= 0.\end{aligned}$$

Again, Assumption 3.4 plays a crucial role in ensuring zero correlation between $\hat{\beta}$ and e.

(4) Consider a linear estimator

$$\hat{b} = \mathbf{C}'Y,$$

where $\mathbf{C} = C(\mathbf{X})$ is an $n \times K$ matrix depending on $\mathbf{X}$. It is unbiased for β^o regardless of the value of β^o if and only if

$$\begin{aligned}E(\hat{b}|\mathbf{X}) &= \mathbf{C}'\mathbf{X}\beta^o + \mathbf{C}'E(\varepsilon|\mathbf{X}) \\ &= \mathbf{C}'\mathbf{X}\beta^o \\ &= \beta^o.\end{aligned}$$

This follows if and only if

$$\mathbf{C}'\mathbf{X} = \mathbf{I}.$$

Because

$$\begin{aligned}
\hat{b} &= \mathbf{C}'Y \\
&= \mathbf{C}'(\mathbf{X}\beta^o + \varepsilon) \\
&= \mathbf{C}'\mathbf{X}\beta^o + \mathbf{C}'\varepsilon \\
&= \beta^o + \mathbf{C}'\varepsilon,
\end{aligned}$$

the variance of the linear estimator $\hat{b}$

$$\begin{aligned}
\mathrm{var}(\hat{b}|\mathbf{X}) &= E\left\{[\hat{b} - E(\hat{b}|\mathbf{X})][\hat{b} - E(\hat{b}|\mathbf{X})]'|\mathbf{X}\right\} \\
&= E\left[(\hat{b} - \beta^o)(\hat{b} - \beta^o)'|\mathbf{X}\right] \\
&= E\left[\mathbf{C}'\varepsilon\varepsilon'\mathbf{C}|\mathbf{X}\right] \\
&= \mathbf{C}'E(\varepsilon\varepsilon'|\mathbf{X})\mathbf{C} \\
&- \mathbf{C}'\sigma^2\mathbf{I}\mathbf{C} \\
&= \sigma^2\mathbf{C}'\mathbf{C}.
\end{aligned}$$

Using $\mathbf{C}'\mathbf{X} = \mathbf{I}$, we now have

$$\begin{aligned}
\mathrm{var}(\hat{b}|\mathbf{X}) - \mathrm{var}(\hat{\beta}|\mathbf{X}) &= \sigma^2\mathbf{C}'\mathbf{C} - \sigma^2(\mathbf{X}'\mathbf{X})^{-1} \\
&= \sigma^2[\mathbf{C}'\mathbf{C} - \mathbf{C}'\mathbf{X}(\mathbf{X}'\mathbf{X})^{-1}\mathbf{X}'\mathbf{C}] \\
&= \sigma^2\mathbf{C}'[\mathbf{I} - \mathbf{X}(\mathbf{X}'\mathbf{X})^{-1}\mathbf{X}']\mathbf{C} \\
&= \sigma^2\mathbf{C}'\mathbf{M}\mathbf{C} \\
&= \sigma^2\mathbf{C}'\mathbf{M}\mathbf{M}\mathbf{C} \\
&= \sigma^2\mathbf{C}'\mathbf{M}'\mathbf{M}\mathbf{C} \\
&= \sigma^2(\mathbf{M}\mathbf{C})'(\mathbf{M}\mathbf{C}) \\
&= \sigma^2\mathbf{D}'\mathbf{D},
\end{aligned}$$

which is PSD. Here we have used the fact that for any real-valued matrix $\mathbf{D}$, the squared matrix $\mathbf{D}'\mathbf{D}$ is always PSD. (How to show this?)

(5) Because $e'e = \varepsilon'\mathbf{M}\varepsilon$ and $\mathrm{tr}(AB) = \mathrm{tr}(BA)$, where $\mathrm{tr}(\cdot)$ denotes the trace operator, we have

$$\begin{aligned} E(e'e|\mathbf{X}) &= E(\varepsilon'\mathbf{M}\varepsilon|\mathbf{X}) \\ &= E[\mathrm{tr}(\varepsilon'\mathbf{M}\varepsilon)|\mathbf{X}] \\ &= E[\mathrm{tr}(\varepsilon\varepsilon'\mathbf{M})|\mathbf{X}] \\ &= \mathrm{tr}[E(\varepsilon\varepsilon'|\mathbf{X})\mathbf{M}] \\ &= \mathrm{tr}(\sigma^2\mathbf{I}\mathbf{M}) \\ &= \sigma^2\mathrm{tr}(\mathbf{M}) \\ &= \sigma^2(n-K) \end{aligned}$$

where

$$\begin{aligned} \mathrm{tr}(\mathbf{M}) &= \mathrm{tr}(\mathbf{I}) - \mathrm{tr}[\mathbf{X}(\mathbf{X}'\mathbf{X})^{-1}\mathbf{X}'] \\ &= \mathrm{tr}(\mathbf{I}) - \mathrm{tr}[\mathbf{X}'\mathbf{X}(\mathbf{X}'\mathbf{X})^{-1}] \\ &= n - K, \end{aligned}$$

using $\mathrm{tr}(AB) = \mathrm{tr}(BA)$ again. It follows that

$$\begin{aligned} E(s^2|\mathbf{X}) &= \frac{E(e'e|\mathbf{X})}{n-K} \\ &= \frac{\sigma^2(n-K)}{(n-K)} \\ &= \sigma^2. \end{aligned}$$

We note that the sample residual variance estimator s^2 can be viewed as a generalization of the sample variance $S_n^2 = (n-1)^{-1}\sum_{t=1}^n (Y_t - \bar{Y}_n)^2$ of random sample $\{Y_t\}_{t=1}^n$. This completes the proof.

The unbiasedness property of $\hat{\beta}$ for β^o in Theorem 3.4(1) follows from the strict exogeneity condition in Assumption 3.2. In general, different regressors are correlated with each other. As a result, to obtain an unbiased estimator for any parameter of interest, β_i^o say, that is associated with regressor X_{it}, it is important to include all other possible correlated regressors $\{X_{jt}, j = i\}$. All other regressors which we are not interested in are called control regressors. For example, in labor economics we may be interested in estimating the effect of the return on education (measured by the number of schooling). Because education and experience are correlated, we need to control for experience in regression in order to obtain an unbiased estimation for the effect of education. Intuitively, the observation for the dependent variable is the total effect from all regressors subject to stochastic disturbances, we have to control for (i.e., take into account) the effect of all other regressors in order to correctly estimate the *ceteris paribus* effect of the variable of interest X_{it} on Y_t.

Both Theorems 3.4(1) and (2) imply that the conditional MSE

$$\begin{aligned}\text{MSE}(\hat{\beta}|\mathbf{X}) &= E\left\{[\hat{\beta} - E(\hat{\beta}|\mathbf{X})][\hat{\beta} - E(\hat{\beta}|\mathbf{X})]|\mathbf{X}\right\} \\ &= E[(\hat{\beta} - \beta^o)(\hat{\beta} - \beta^o)'|\mathbf{X}] \\ &= \text{var}(\hat{\beta}|\mathbf{X}) + \text{Bias}(\hat{\beta}|\mathbf{X})\text{Bias}(\hat{\beta}|\mathbf{X})' \\ &= \text{var}(\hat{\beta}|\mathbf{X}) \\ &\to 0 \text{ as } n \to \infty,\end{aligned}$$

where we have used the fact that the bias

$$\text{Bias}(\hat{\beta}|\mathbf{X}) \equiv E(\hat{\beta}|\mathbf{X}) - \beta^o = 0.$$

Recall that MSE measures how close an estimator $\hat{\beta}$ is to the target parameter β^o.

Theorem 3.4(4), which is usually called the Gauss-Markov theorem, implies that $\hat{\beta}$ is the Best Linear Unbiased Estimator (BLUE) for β^o because $\text{var}(\hat{\beta}|\mathbf{X})$ is the smallest among all unbiased linear estimators for β^o. Carl F. Gauss is a well-known German mathematician and astronomer, who published a seminal work on the theory of OLS estimation, including a version of the Gauss–Markov theorem (Gauss 1921).

Formally, we can define a related concept for comparing two unbiased estimators:

Definition 3.4. [Efficiency]: An unbiased estimator $\hat{\beta}$ of parameter β^o is more efficient than another unbiased estimator $\hat{b}$ of parameter β^o if

$$\text{var}(\hat{b}|\mathbf{X}) - \text{var}(\hat{\beta}|\mathbf{X}) \text{ is PSD.}$$

When $\hat{\beta}$ is more efficient than $\hat{b}$, we have that for any $\tau \in \mathbb{R}^K$ such that $\tau'\tau = 1$,

$$\tau' \left[\text{var}(\hat{b}|\mathbf{X}) - \text{var}(\hat{\beta}|\mathbf{X})\right] \tau \geq 0.$$

Choosing $\tau = (1, 0, ..., 0)'$, for example, we have

$$\mathrm{var}(\hat{b}_0) - \mathrm{var}(\hat{\beta}_0) \geq 0.$$

We note that the OLS estimator $\hat{\beta}$ is still BLUE even when there exists near-multicollinearity, where $\lambda_{\min}(\mathbf{X}'\mathbf{X})$ does not grow with the sample size n, and $\mathrm{var}(\hat{\beta}|\mathbf{X})$ does not vanish to zero as $n \to \infty$. Near-multicollinearity is essentially a sample or data problem which we cannot remedy when the objective is to estimate the unknown parameter value β^o.

3.5 Sampling Distribution of the OLS Estimator

To obtain the finite sample sampling distribution of $\hat{\beta}$, we impose the normality assumption on ε.

Assumption 3.5. [Conditional Normality]: $\varepsilon|\mathbf{X} \sim N(0, \sigma^2\mathbf{I})$.

Assumption 3.5 implies both Assumptions 3.2 ($E(\varepsilon|\mathbf{X}) = 0$) and 3.4 ($E(\varepsilon\varepsilon|\mathbf{X}) = \sigma^2\mathbf{I}$). Moreover, under Assumption 3.5, the conditional PDF of ε given $\mathbf{X}$ is

$$f(\varepsilon|\mathbf{X}) = \frac{1}{(\sqrt{2\pi\sigma^2})^n} \exp\left(-\frac{\varepsilon'\varepsilon}{2\sigma^2}\right) = f(\varepsilon),$$

which does not depend on $\mathbf{X}$, so the disturbance ε is independent of $\mathbf{X}$. Thus, every conditional moment of ε given $\mathbf{X}$ does not depend on $\mathbf{X}$.

The normal distribution is also called the Gaussian distribution named after Gauss. It is assumed here so that we can derive the finite sample distributions of $\hat{\beta}$ and related statistics, i.e., the distributions of $\hat{\beta}$ and related statistics when the sample size n is a finite integer. This assumption may be reasonable for observations that are computed as the averages of the outcomes of many repeated experiments, due to the effect of the so-called Central Limit Theorem (CLT). This may occur in physics, for example. In economics, the normality assumption may not always be reasonable. For example, many high-frequency financial time series usually display heavy tails (with kurtosis larger than 3).

Question: What is the sampling distribution of $\hat{\beta}$?

From Lemma 3.1(2), we can write

$$\begin{aligned}\hat{\beta} - \beta^o &= (\mathbf{X}'\mathbf{X})^{-1}\mathbf{X}'\varepsilon \\ &= (\mathbf{X}'\mathbf{X})^{-1}\sum_{t=1}^{n} X_t\varepsilon_t \\ &= \sum_{t=1}^{n} C_t\varepsilon_t,\end{aligned}$$

where the weighting vector

$$C_t = (\mathbf{X}'\mathbf{X})^{-1}X_t$$

is called the leverage of observation X_t. Conditional on $\mathbf{X}$, $\hat{\beta} - \beta^o$ is a linear combination of ε, and so it follows a normal distribution given Assumption 3.5.

Theorem 3.5. ***[Normality of the OLS Estimator]:*** *Under Assumptions 3.1, 3.3(a) and 3.5,*

$$(\hat{\beta} - \beta^o)|\mathbf{X} \sim N[0, \sigma^2(\mathbf{X}'\mathbf{X})^{-1}].$$

Proof: Conditional on $\mathbf{X}$, $\hat{\beta} - \beta^o$ is a weighted sum of independent normal random variables $\{\varepsilon_t\}$, and so it is also normally distributed given Assumption 3.5. This follows from the so-called reproductive property of the normal distribution.

We note that the OLS estimator $\hat{\beta}$ still has the conditional finite sample normal distribution $N[\beta^o, \sigma^2(\mathbf{X}'\mathbf{X})^{-1}]$ even when there exists near-multicollinearity, where $\lambda_{\min}(\mathbf{X}'\mathbf{X})$ does not grow with the sample size n and $\text{var}(\hat{\beta}|\mathbf{X})$ does not vanish to zero as $n \to \infty$.

A corollary follows immediately.

Corollary 3.1. ***[Normality of $R(\hat{\beta} - \beta^o)$]:*** *Suppose Assumptions 3.1, 3.3(a) and 3.5 hold. Then for any nonstochastic $J \times K$ matrix R, we have*

$$R(\hat{\beta} - \beta^o)|\mathbf{X} \sim N[0, \sigma^2 R(\mathbf{X}'\mathbf{X})^{-1}R'].$$

Proof: Conditional on $\mathbf{X}$, $\hat{\beta} - \beta^o$ is normally distributed. Therefore, conditional on $\mathbf{X}$, the linear combination $R(\hat{\beta} - \beta^o)$ is also normally distributed, with

$$E[R(\hat{\beta} - \beta^o)|\mathbf{X}] = RE[(\hat{\beta} - \beta^o)|\mathbf{X}] = R \cdot 0 = 0$$

and

$$\begin{aligned}\operatorname{var}[R(\hat{\beta} - \beta^o)|\mathbf{X}] &= E\Big\{R(\hat{\beta} - \beta^o)\Big[R(\hat{\beta} - \beta^o)\Big]'\Big|\mathbf{X}\Big\} \\ &= E\Big[R(\hat{\beta} - \beta^o)(\hat{\beta} - \beta^o)'R'|\mathbf{X}\Big] \\ &= RE\Big[(\hat{\beta} - \beta^o)(\hat{\beta} - \beta^o)'|\mathbf{X}\Big]R' \\ &= R\operatorname{var}(\hat{\beta}|\mathbf{X})R' \\ &= \sigma^2 R(\mathbf{X}'\mathbf{X})^{-1}R'.\end{aligned}$$

It follows that

$$R(\hat{\beta} - \beta^o)|\mathbf{X} \sim N(0, \sigma^2 R(\mathbf{X}'\mathbf{X})^{-1}R').$$

Question: What is the role of the $J \times K$ nonstochastic matrix R?

The $J \times K$ matrix R is a selection matrix. For example, when $R = (1, 0, ..., 0)$, we then have $R(\hat{\beta} - \beta^o) = \hat{\beta}_0 - \beta_0^o$.

Question: Why would we like to know the sampling distribution of $R(\hat{\beta} - \beta^o)$?

This will be useful for confidence interval estimation and hypothesis testing.

3.6 Variance Estimation for the OLS Estimator

Since $\operatorname{var}(\varepsilon_t) = \sigma^2$ is unknown, $\operatorname{var}[R(\hat{\beta} - \beta^o)|\mathbf{X}] = \sigma^2 R(\mathbf{X}'\mathbf{X})^{-1}R'$ is unknown. We need to estimate σ^2. We can use the sample residual variance estimator

$$s^2 = e'e/(n - K).$$

In order to investigate the statistical properties of s^2, we first provide a lemma.

Lemma 3.2. *[Quadratic Form of Normal Random Variables]: If $v \sim N(0, \mathbf{I})$ and Q is an $n \times n$ nonstochastic symmetric idempotent matrix with rank $q \leq n$, then the quadratic form*

$$v'Qv \sim \chi_q^2,$$

where χ_q^2 denotes a Chi-square distribution with q degrees of freedom.

In our application, we set $v = \varepsilon/\sigma \sim N(0, \mathbf{I})$, and $Q = \mathbf{M}$. Since $\text{rank}(\mathbf{M}) = n - K$, it follows that

$$\left.\frac{e'e}{\sigma^2}\right| \mathbf{X} \sim \chi^2_{n-K}.$$

Theorem 3.6. ***[Residual Variance Estimator]:*** *Suppose Assumptions 3.1, 3.3(a) and 3.5 hold. Then we have for all $n > K$, (1)*

$$\left.\frac{(n-K)s^2}{\sigma^2}\right| \mathbf{X} = \left.\frac{e'e}{\sigma^2}\right| \mathbf{X} \sim \chi^2_{n-K};$$

(2) conditional on $\mathbf{X}$, s^2 and $\hat{\beta}$ are independent.

Proof: (1) Because $e = \mathbf{M}\varepsilon$, we have

$$\frac{e'e}{\sigma^2} = \frac{\varepsilon'\mathbf{M}\varepsilon}{\sigma^2} = \left(\frac{\varepsilon}{\sigma}\right)' \mathbf{M} \left(\frac{\varepsilon}{\sigma}\right).$$

In addition, because $\varepsilon|\mathbf{X} \sim N(0, \sigma^2\mathbf{I})$, and $\mathbf{M}$ is an idempotent matrix with rank equal to $n - K$ (as has been shown earlier), we have the quadratic form

$$\frac{e'e}{\sigma^2} = \left.\frac{\varepsilon'\mathbf{M}\varepsilon}{\sigma^2}\right| \mathbf{X} \sim \chi^2_{n-K}$$

by Lemma 3.2.

(2) Next, we show that s^2 and $\hat{\beta}$ are independent. Because $s^2 = e'e/(n-K)$ is a function of e, it suffices to show that e and $\hat{\beta}$ are independent. This follows immediately because conditional on $\mathbf{X}$, both e and $\hat{\beta}$ are jointly normally distributed and they are uncorrelated. It is well-known that for a joint normal distribution, zero correlation is equivalent to independence.

It remains to show that e and $\hat{\beta}$ are jointly normally distributed. For this purpose, we write

$$\begin{aligned} \begin{bmatrix} e \\ \hat{\beta} - \beta^o \end{bmatrix} &= \begin{bmatrix} \mathbf{M}\varepsilon \\ (\mathbf{X}'\mathbf{X})^{-1}\mathbf{X}'\varepsilon \end{bmatrix} \\ &= \begin{bmatrix} \mathbf{M} \\ (\mathbf{X}'\mathbf{X})^{-1}\mathbf{X}' \end{bmatrix} \varepsilon. \end{aligned}$$

Because $\varepsilon|\mathbf{X} \sim N(0, \sigma^2\mathbf{I})$, the linear combination of

$$\begin{bmatrix} \mathbf{M} \\ (\mathbf{X}'\mathbf{X})^{-1}\mathbf{X}' \end{bmatrix} \varepsilon$$

is also normally distributed conditional on $\mathbf{X}$. It follows that conditional on $\mathbf{X}$, e and $\hat{\beta}$ are independent given $\text{cov}(\hat{\beta}, e|\mathbf{X}) = 0$. This completes the proof.

To discuss the implication of Theorem 3.6, we review the properties of χ^2_q. Suppose q is a positive integer, and $\{Z_i\}_{i=1}^q$ is an IID sequence of $N(0,1)$ random variables. Then the random variable

$$\chi^2 = \sum_{i=1}^q Z_i^2$$

follows a χ^2_q distribution.

The χ^2_q distribution is nonsymmetric and has long right tails. It has $E(\chi^2_q) = q$ and $\text{var}(\chi^2_q) = 2q$ respectively.

Based on these properties of a χ^2 distribution, Theorem 3.6(1) implies

$$E\left[\left.\frac{(n-K)s^2}{\sigma^2}\right|\mathbf{X}\right] = n - K$$

or

$$\frac{(n-K)}{\sigma^2}E(s^2|\mathbf{X}) = n - K.$$

It follows that $E(s^2|\mathbf{X}) = \sigma^2$. Note that we have shown this result in Theorem 3.4(5), with a more tedious approach but under a more general condition.

Theorem 3.6(1) also implies

$$\text{var}\left[\left.\frac{(n-K)s^2}{\sigma^2}\right|\mathbf{X}\right] = 2(n - K).$$

It follows that

$$\begin{aligned}\text{var}(s^2|\mathbf{X}) &= \frac{2\sigma^4}{n-K} \\ &\to 0 \text{ as } n \to \infty.\end{aligned}$$

Both Theorems 3.6(1) and (2) imply that the conditional MSE of s^2

$$\begin{aligned}\text{MSE}(s^2|\mathbf{X}) &= E\left[(s^2 - \sigma^2)^2|\mathbf{X}\right] \\ &= \text{var}(s^2|\mathbf{X}) + [E(s^2|\mathbf{X}) - \sigma^2]^2 \\ &\to 0 \text{ as } n \to \infty.\end{aligned}$$

Thus, s^2 is a good estimator for σ^2.

The sample residual variance $s^2 = e'e/(n-K)$ is a generalization of the sample variance $S_n^2 = (n-1)^{-1}\sum_{t=1}^{n}(Y_t - \bar{Y}_n)^2$ for the random sample $\{Y_t\}_{t=1}^{n}$. The factor $n-K$ is called the number of the degrees of freedom of the estimated residual sample $\{e_t\}_{t=1}^{n}$. To gain intuition why the number of the degrees of freedom is equal to $n-K$, note that the original sample $\{Z_t\}_{t=1}^{n} = \{(Y_t, X_t')'\}_{t=1}^{n}$ has n observations, which can be viewed to have n degrees of freedom. Now when estimating σ^2, we have to use the estimated residual sample $\{e_t\}_{t=1}^{n}$. These n estimated residuals are not linearly independent because they have to satisfy the FOC of the OLS estimation, namely,

$$\mathbf{X}'e = 0,$$
$$(K \times n) \times (n \times 1) = (K \times 1).$$

The FOC imposes K restrictions on $\{e_t\}_{t=1}^{n}$, conditional on $\mathbf{X}$. These K restrictions are needed in order to estimate K unknown parameters β^o. They can be used to obtain the remaining K estimated residuals $\{e_{T-K+1}, ..., e_T\}$ from the first $n-K$ estimated residuals $\{e_1, ..., e_{n-K}\}$ if the latter have been available. Thus, the number of the remaining degrees of freedom of e is $n-K$. Note that the sample variance S_n^2 is the residual variance estimator for $Y_t = \beta_0^o + \varepsilon_t$, a linear regression model with an intercept only.

Question: Why are the sampling distributions of $\hat{\beta}$ and s^2 useful in practice?

They are useful in confidence interval estimation and hypothesis testing on model parameters. We note that conditional independence between $\hat{\beta}$ and s^2 in Theorem 3.6(2) is crucial for deriving the sampling distributions of the popular t-test and F-test statistics, which will be introduced shortly. The Student's t-distribution and F-distribution are very important in confidence interval estimation and hypothesis testing. In this book, we will mainly focus on hypothesis testing. Statistically speaking, confidence interval estimation and hypothesis testing are the two sides of the same coin.

3.7 Hypothesis Testing

We now use the sampling distributions of $\hat{\beta}$ and s^2 to develop test procedures for hypotheses of interest. We consider testing the following linear hypothesis in form of

$$\mathbf{H}_0 : R\beta^o = r,$$
$$(J \times K)(K \times 1) = J \times 1,$$

where R is a $J \times K$ nonstochastic matrix called the selection matrix, and J is the number of restrictions. We assume that R is of full rank and $J \leq K$.

It is important to emphasize that we will test $\mathbf{H}_0$ under correct model specification for $E(Y_t|X_t)$.

We first provide a few motivating examples for hypothesis testing.

Example 3.3. [Reforms Have No Effect]: Consider the extended production function

$$\ln(Y_t) = \beta_0 + \beta_1 \ln(L_t) + \beta_2 \ln(K_t) + \beta_3 AU_t + \beta_4 PS_t + \varepsilon_t,$$

where AU_t is a dummy variable indicating whether a state-owned enterprise t is granted autonomy, and PS_t is the profit share of the state-owned enterprise t with the state.

Suppose we are interested in testing whether autonomy AU_t has an effect on productivity. Then we can write the null hypothesis

$$\mathbf{H}_0^a : \beta_3^o = 0.$$

This is equivalent to the choices of

$$\beta^o = (\beta_0, \beta_1, \beta_2, \beta_3, \beta_4)',$$
$$R = (0, 0, 0, 1, 0),$$
$$r = 0.$$

If we are interested in testing whether profit sharing has an effect on productivity, we can consider the null hypothesis

$$\mathbf{H}_0^b : \beta_4^o = 0.$$

Alternatively, to test whether the production technology exhibits CRS, we can write the null hypothesis as follows:

$$\mathbf{H}_0^c : \beta_1^o + \beta_2^o = 1.$$

This is equivalent to the choice of $R = (0, 1, 1, 0, 0)$ and $r = 1$.

Finally, if we are interested in examining the joint effect of both autonomy and profit sharing, we can test the hypothesis that neither autonomy nor profit sharing has impact:

$$\mathbf{H}_0^d : \beta_3^o = \beta_4^o = 0.$$

This is equivalent to the choice of

$$R = \begin{bmatrix} 0 & 0 & 0 & 1 & 0 \\ 0 & 0 & 0 & 0 & 1 \end{bmatrix},$$

$$r = \begin{bmatrix} 0 \\ 0 \end{bmatrix}.$$

Example 3.4. [Optimal Prediction for Future Spot Exchange Rate]: Consider

$$S_{t+\tau} = \beta_0 + \beta_1 F_t(\tau) + \varepsilon_{t+\tau}, \qquad t = 1, ..., n,$$

where $S_{t+\tau}$ is the spot exchange rate at period $t + \tau$, and $F_t(\tau)$ is the forward exchange rate, namely the period t's price for the foreign currency to be delivered at period $t + \tau$. The null hypothesis of interest is that the forward exchange rate $F_t(\tau)$ is an optimal predictor for the future spot rate $S_{t+\tau}$ in the sense that $E(S_{t+\tau}|I_t) = F_t(\tau)$, where I_t is the information set available at time t. This is actually called the *expectations hypothesis* in economics and finance. Given the above specification, this hypothesis can be written as

$$\mathbf{H}_0^e : \beta_0^o = 0, \beta_1^o = 1,$$

and $E(\varepsilon_{t+\tau}|I_t) = 0$. This is equivalent to the choice of

$$R = \begin{bmatrix} 1 & 0 \\ 0 & 1 \end{bmatrix}, r = \begin{bmatrix} 0 \\ 1 \end{bmatrix}.$$

All examples considered above can be formulated with a suitable specification of R, where R is a $J \times K$ matrix in the null hypothesis

$$\mathbf{H}_0 : R\beta^o = r,$$

where r is a $J \times 1$ vector.

We now introduce the basic idea of hypothesis testing. To test the null hypothesis

$$\mathbf{H}_0 : R\beta^o = r,$$

we can consider the statistic

$$R\hat{\beta} - r$$

and check if this difference is significantly different from zero.

Under $\mathbf{H}_0 : R\beta^o = r$, we have

$$\begin{aligned} R\hat{\beta} - r &= R\hat{\beta} - R\beta^o \\ &= R(\hat{\beta} - \beta^o) \\ &\to 0 \text{ as } n \to \infty \end{aligned}$$

because $\hat{\beta} - \beta^o \to 0$ as $n \to \infty$ in terms of MSE.

Under the alternative to $\mathbf{H}_0$, $R\beta^o \neq r$, but we still have $\hat{\beta} - \beta^o \to 0$ in terms of MSE. It follows that

$$\begin{aligned} R\hat{\beta} - r &= R(\hat{\beta} - \beta^o) + R\beta^o - r \\ &\to R\beta^o - r \neq 0 \end{aligned}$$

as $n \to \infty$, where the convergence is in terms of MSE. In other words, $R\hat{\beta} - r$ will converge to a nonzero limit, $R\beta^o - r$.

The fact that the behavior of $R\hat{\beta} - r$ is different under $\mathbf{H}_0$ and under the alternative hypothesis to $\mathbf{H}_0$ provides a basis to construct hypothesis tests. In particular, we can test $\mathbf{H}_0$ by examining whether $R\hat{\beta} - r$ is significantly different from zero.

Question: How large should the magnitude of the absolute value of the difference $R\hat{\beta} - r$ be in order to claim that $R\hat{\beta} - r$ is significantly different from zero?

For this purpose, we need a decision rule which specifies a threshold value with which we can compare the (absolute) values of $R\hat{\beta} - r$. Because $R\hat{\beta} - r$ is a random variable and so it can take many (possibly an infinite number of) values. Given a data set, we only obtain one realization of $R\hat{\beta} - r$. Whether a realization of $R\hat{\beta} - r$ is close to zero should be judged using the critical value of the sampling distribution of $R\hat{\beta} - r$ under the null hypothesis $\mathbf{H}_0$, which depends on the sample size n and the pre-selected significance level $\alpha \in (0, 1)$.

Question: What is the sampling distribution of $R\hat{\beta} - r$ under $\mathbf{H}_0$?

Because

$$R(\hat{\beta} - \beta^o)|\mathbf{X} \sim N(0, \sigma^2 R(\mathbf{X}'\mathbf{X})^{-1}R'),$$

we have that conditional on $\mathbf{X}$,

$$\begin{aligned} R\hat{\beta} - r &= R(\hat{\beta} - \beta^o) + R\beta^o - r \\ &\sim N(R\beta^o - r, \sigma^2 R(\mathbf{X}'\mathbf{X})^{-1}R'). \end{aligned}$$

Corollary 3.2. *Under Assumptions 3.1, 3.3 and 3.5, and* $\mathbf{H}_0 : R\beta^o = r$, *we have for each* $n > K$,

$$(R\hat{\beta} - r)|\mathbf{X} \sim N(0, \sigma^2 R(\mathbf{X}'\mathbf{X})^{-1}R').$$

The difference $R\hat{\beta} - r$ cannot be used as a test statistic for $\mathbf{H}_0$, because σ^2 is unknown and thus there is no way to calculate the critical values of the sampling distribution of $R\hat{\beta} - r$.

Question: How to construct a feasible (i.e., computable) test statistic?

The form of test statistics will differ depending on whether we have $J = 1$ or $J > 1$. We first consider the case of $J = 1$.

Case I: *t*-Test

Recall that under $\mathbf{H}_0$,

$$(R\hat{\beta} - r)|\mathbf{X} \sim N(0, \sigma^2 R(\mathbf{X}'\mathbf{X})^{-1}R').$$

When $J = 1$, the conditional variance

$$\text{var}[(R\hat{\beta} - r)|\mathbf{X}] = \sigma^2 R(\mathbf{X}'\mathbf{X})^{-1}R'$$

is a scalar. It follows that conditional on $\mathbf{X}$, we have

$$\begin{aligned} \frac{R\hat{\beta} - r}{\sqrt{\text{var}[(R\hat{\beta} - r)|\mathbf{X}]}} &= \frac{R\hat{\beta} - r}{\sqrt{\sigma^2 R(\mathbf{X}'\mathbf{X})^{-1}R'}} \\ &\sim N(0, 1). \end{aligned}$$

Question: What is the unconditional distribution of

$$\frac{R\hat{\beta} - r}{\sqrt{\sigma^2 R(\mathbf{X}'\mathbf{X})^{-1}R'}}?$$

The unconditional distribution is also $N(0, 1)$.

However, σ^2 is unknown, so we cannot use the ratio

$$\frac{R\hat{\beta} - r}{\sqrt{\sigma^2 R(\mathbf{X}'\mathbf{X})^{-1}R'}}$$

as a test statistic. Instead, we have to replace σ^2 by s^2, which is a good estimator for σ^2. This gives a feasible (i.e., computable) test statistic

$$T = \frac{R\hat{\beta} - r}{\sqrt{s^2 R(\mathbf{X}'\mathbf{X})^{-1}R'}}.$$

However, the test statistic T will be no longer normally distributed under $\mathbf{H}_0$. Instead,

$$\begin{aligned} T &= \frac{R\hat{\beta} - r}{\sqrt{s^2 R(\mathbf{X}'\mathbf{X})^{-1}R'}} \\ &= \frac{\frac{R\hat{\beta}-r}{\sqrt{\sigma^2 R(\mathbf{X}'\mathbf{X})^{-1}R'}}}{\sqrt{\frac{(n-K)s^2}{\sigma^2}/(n-K)}} \\ &\sim \frac{N(0,1)}{\sqrt{\chi^2_{n-K}/(n-K)}} \\ &\sim t_{n-K}, \end{aligned}$$

where t_{n-K} denotes a Student's t-distribution with $n-K$ degrees of freedom. Note that the numerator and denominator are mutually independent conditional on $\mathbf{X}$, because $\hat{\beta}$ and s^2 are mutually independent conditional on $\mathbf{X}$. The feasible statistic T is called a t-test statistic because it follows the Student's t_{n-K} distribution.

We now briefly review the properties of the Student's t_q-distribution. Suppose $Z \sim N(0,1)$ and $V \sim \chi^2_q$, and both Z and V are independent. Then the ratio

$$\frac{Z}{\sqrt{V/q}} \sim t_q.$$

The t_q-distribution is symmetric about 0 with heavier tails than the $N(0,1)$ distribution. The smaller number of the degrees of freedom, the heavier tails it has. When $q \to \infty$, $t_q \to N(0,1)$. This implies that we have

$$T = \frac{R\hat{\beta} - r}{\sqrt{s^2 R(\mathbf{X}'\mathbf{X})^{-1}R'}} \xrightarrow{d} N(0,1) \text{ as } n \to \infty,$$

where $\xrightarrow{d}$ denotes convergence in distribution. This result has a very important implication in practice: for a large sample size n, it makes no difference to use either the critical values from t_{n-K} or from $N(0,1)$.

Question: What is convergence in distribution?

Definition 3.5. [Convergence in Distribution]: Suppose $\{Z_n, n = 1, 2, ...\}$ is a sequence of random variables/vectors with Cumulative Distribution Functions (CDFs) $F_n(z) = P(Z_n \leq z)$, and Z is a random variable/vector with CDF $F(z) = P(Z \leq z)$. We say that Z_n converges to Z in distribution if the distribution of Z_n converges to the distribution of Z at all continuity points; namely,

$$\lim_{n\to\infty} F_n(z) = F(z)$$

or

$$F_n(z) \to F(z) \text{ as } n \to \infty$$

for any continuity point z (i.e., for any point at which $F(z)$ is continuous). We use the notation $Z_n \xrightarrow{d} Z$. The distribution of Z is called the asymptotic or limiting distribution of Z_n.

In practice, Z_n is a test statistic or a parameter estimator, and often its sampling distribution $F_n(z)$ is either unknown or very complicated, but $F(z)$ is known or very simple. As long as $Z_n \xrightarrow{d} Z$, then we can use $F(z)$ as an approximation to $F_n(z)$. This gives a convenient procedure for statistical inference. The potential cost is that the approximation of $F_n(z)$ to $F(z)$ may not be good enough in finite samples (i.e., when n is finite). How good the approximation is will depend on the DGP and the sample size n.

With the obtained sampling distribution of the test statistic T, we now provide a decision rule for testing $\mathbf{H}_0$ when $J = 1$.

(1) Decision Rule of the t-Test Based on Critical Values:

- Reject $\mathbf{H}_0 : R\beta^o = r$ at a prespecified significance level $\alpha \in (0, 1)$ if

$$|T| > C_{t_{n-K}, \frac{\alpha}{2}},$$

where $C_{t_{n-K},\frac{\alpha}{2}}$ is the so-called upper-tailed critical value of the t_{n-K} distribution at level $\frac{\alpha}{2}$, which is determined by

$$P\left(t_{n-K} > C_{t_{n-K},\frac{\alpha}{2}}\right) = \frac{\alpha}{2}$$

or equivalently

$$P\left(|t_{n-K}| > C_{t_{n-K},\frac{\alpha}{2}}\right) = \alpha.$$

- Do not reject $\mathbf{H}_0$ at the significance level α if

$$|T| \leq C_{t_{n-K},\frac{\alpha}{2}}.$$

Figure 3.3 illustrates the acceptance and rejection regions of a t-test based on the Student's t_{10}-distribution.

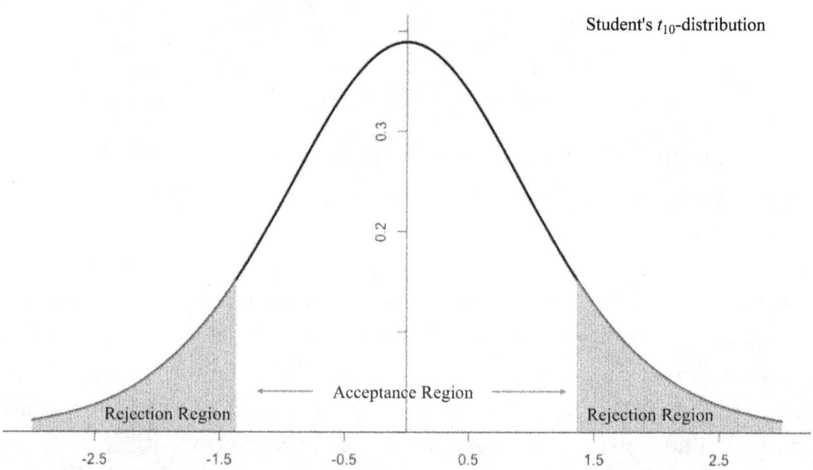

Figure 3.3 Acceptance and rejection regions of a t-test.

In testing $\mathbf{H}_0$, there exist two types of errors, due to the limited information about the population in a given random sample $\{Z_t\}_{t=1}^n$. One possibility is that $\mathbf{H}_0$ is true but we reject it. This is called the "Type I error". The significance level α is the probability of making the Type I error. If

$$P\left(|T| > C_{t_{n-K},\frac{\alpha}{2}} | \mathbf{H}_0\right) = \alpha,$$

we say that the decision rule is a test with size α. The reason that the Type I error exists is that under $\mathbf{H}_0$, the t-test statistic T follows the Student's t_{n-K} distribution and so can take values larger than the critical value with small probability.

On the other hand, the probability $P(|T| > C_{t_{n-K},\frac{\alpha}{2}} \,|\, \mathbf{H}_0$ is false) is called the power function of a size α test. When

$$P\Big(|T| > C_{t_{n-K},\frac{\alpha}{2}} \,|\, \mathbf{H}_0 \text{ is false}\Big) < 1,$$

there exists a possibility that one may fail to reject $\mathbf{H}_0$ when it is false. This is called the "Type II error".

Ideally one would like to minimize both the Type I error and Type II error, but this is impossible for any given finite sample. In practice, one usually presets the level for Type I error, the so-called significance level, and then minimizes the Type II error. Conventional choices for significance level α are 10%, 5% and 1% respectively.

Next, we describe an alternative but equivalent decision rule for testing $\mathbf{H}_0$ when $J = 1$, using the so-called P-value of test statistic T.

Given an observed data set $\mathbf{z}^n = \{z_t = (y_t, x_t')'\}_{t=1}^n$, which is a realization of the random sample $\mathbf{Z}^n = \{Z_t = (Y_t, X_t')'\}_{t=1}^n$, we can compute a realization (i.e., a number) for the t-test statistic T, namely

$$T(\mathbf{z}^n) = \frac{R\hat{\beta} - r}{\sqrt{s^2 R(\mathbf{x}'\mathbf{x})^{-1}R'}}.$$

Then the probability

$$\begin{aligned} p(\mathbf{z}^n) &= P\left[|T| > |T(\mathbf{z}^n)| \,|\, \mathbf{H}_0\right] \\ &= P\left[|t_{n-K}| > |T(\mathbf{z}^n)|\right], \end{aligned}$$

is called the P-value (i.e., probability value) of the test statistic T given that $\mathbf{z}^n = \{z_t = (y_t, x_t')'\}_{t=1}^n$ is observed, where t_{n-K} is a Student's t random variable with $n - K$ degrees of freedom, and $T(\mathbf{z}^n)$ is a realization of the test statistic $T = T(\mathbf{Z}^n)$ given the observed data $\mathbf{z}^n$. Intuitively, the P-value is the smallest value of significance level α for which the null hypothesis is rejected. Here, it is the tail probability that the absolute value of a Student's t_{n-K} random variable is larger than that of the test statistic $T(\mathbf{z}^n)$. If this probability is rather small relative to the significance level, then it is unlikely that the test statistic $T(\mathbf{Z}^n)$ will follow the Student's t_{n-K} distribution. As a result, the null hypothesis is likely to be false.

The above decision rule can be described equivalently as follows.

(2) Decision Rule Based on the P-value:

- Reject $\mathbf{H}_0$ at the significance level α if $p(\mathbf{z}^n) < \alpha$.
- Do not reject $\mathbf{H}_0$ at the significance level α if $p(\mathbf{z}^n) \geq \alpha$.

A small P-value is evidence against the null hypothesis. A large P-value shows that the data are consistent with the null hypothesis.

Question: What are the advantages and disadvantages of using P-values versus using critical values?

P-values are more informative than only rejecting/accepting the null hypothesis at some significance level α. A P-value is the smallest significance level at which a null hypothesis can be rejected. It not only tells us whether the null hypothesis should be accepted or rejected, but it also tells us whether the decision to accept or reject the null hypothesis is a close call.

Most statistical software reports P-values of parameter estimates. This is much more convenient than asking the user to specify significance level α and then reporting whether the null hypothesis is accepted or rejected for that α.

When we reject a null hypothesis, we often say there is a statistically significant effect. This does not mean that there is an effect of practical importance (i.e., an effect of economic importance). This is because when large samples are used, small and practically unimportant effects are likely to be statistically significant.

The t-test and associated procedures just introduced are valid even when there exists near-multicollinearity, where $\lambda_{\min}(\mathbf{X}'\mathbf{X})$ does not grow with the sample size n and $\text{var}(\hat{\beta}|\mathbf{X})$ does not vanish to zero as $n \to \infty$. However, the degree of near-multicollinearity, as measured by sample correlations between explanatory variables, will affect the precision of the OLS estimator $\hat{\beta}$. Other things being equal, the higher degree of near-multicollinearity, the larger the variance of $\hat{\beta}$. As a result, the t-statistic is often insignificant even when the null hypothesis $\mathbf{H}_0$ is false.

We now provide some examples of t-tests.

Example 3.5. [Reforms Have No Effects (Continued)]: We first consider testing the null hypothesis

$$\mathbf{H}_0^a : \beta_3 = 0,$$

where β_3 is the coefficient of the autonomy AU_t in the extended production function regression model. This is equivalent to the selection of $R = (0, 0, 0, 1, 0)$. In this case, we have

$$\begin{aligned} s^2 R(\mathbf{X}'\mathbf{X})^{-1}R' &= \left[s^2(\mathbf{X}'\mathbf{X})^{-1}\right]_{(4,4)} \\ &= S^2_{\hat{\beta}_3} \end{aligned}$$

which is the estimator of $\text{var}(\hat{\beta}_3|\mathbf{X})$. The squared root of $\text{var}(\hat{\beta}_3|X)$ is called the standard error of estimator $\hat{\beta}_3$, and $S_{\hat{\beta}_3}$ is called the estimated standard error of $\hat{\beta}_3$. The t-test statistic

$$\begin{aligned} T &= \frac{R\hat{\beta} - r}{\sqrt{s^2 R(\mathbf{X}'\mathbf{X})^{-1}R'}} \\ &= \frac{\hat{\beta}_3}{\sqrt{S^2_{\hat{\beta}_3}}} \\ &\sim t_{n-K}. \end{aligned}$$

Next, we consider testing the CRS hypothesis

$$\mathbf{H}_0^c : \beta_1 + \beta_2 = 1,$$

which corresponds to $R = (0, 1, 1, 0, 0)$ and $r = 1$. In this case,

$$\begin{aligned} s^2 R(\mathbf{X}'\mathbf{X})^{-1}R' &= S^2_{\hat{\beta}_1} + S^2_{\hat{\beta}_2} + 2\widehat{\text{cov}}(\hat{\beta}_1, \hat{\beta}_2) \\ &= \left[s^2(\mathbf{X}'\mathbf{X})^{-1}\right]_{(2,2)} \\ &\quad + \left[s^2(\mathbf{X}'\mathbf{X})^{-1}\right]_{(3,3)} \\ &\quad + 2\left[s^2(\mathbf{X}'\mathbf{X})^{-1}\right]_{(2,3)} \\ &= S^2_{\hat{\beta}+\hat{\beta}_2}, \end{aligned}$$

which is the estimator of $\text{var}(\hat{\beta}_1 + \hat{\beta}_2|\mathbf{X})$. Here, $\widehat{\text{cov}}(\hat{\beta}_1, \hat{\beta}_2)$ is the estimator for $\text{cov}(\hat{\beta}_1, \hat{\beta}_2|\mathbf{X})$, the covariance between $\hat{\beta}_1$ and $\hat{\beta}_2$ conditional on $\mathbf{X}$.

The t-test statistic is

$$\begin{aligned} T &= \frac{R\hat{\beta} - r}{\sqrt{s^2 R(\mathbf{X}'\mathbf{X})^{-1}R'}} \\ &= \frac{\hat{\beta}_1 + \hat{\beta}_2 - 1}{S_{\hat{\beta}_1+\hat{\beta}_2}} \\ &\sim t_{n-K}. \end{aligned}$$

Case II: *F*-Testing

Question: How to construct a test statistic for $\mathbf{H}_0$ if $J > 1$?

We first state a useful lemma.

Lemma 3.3. *[Quadratic Form of Normal Random Variables]: If a $q \times 1$ random vector $Z \sim N(0, V)$, where $V = var(Z)$ is a nonsingular $q \times q$ variance-covariance matrix, then*

$$Z'V^{-1}Z \sim \chi^2_q.$$

Proof: Because V is symmetric and positive definite, we can find a symmetric and invertible matrix $V^{1/2}$ such that

$$V^{1/2}V^{1/2} = V,$$

and

$$V^{-1/2}V^{-1/2} = V^{-1}.$$

Question: What is this decomposition called?

Now, define

$$Y = V^{-1/2}Z.$$

Then we have $E(Y) = 0$, and

$$\begin{aligned}
\text{var}(Y) &= E\{[Y - E(Y)][Y - E(Y)]'\} \\
&= E(YY') \\
&= E(V^{-1/2}ZZ'V^{-1/2}) \\
&= V^{-1/2}E(ZZ')V^{-1/2} \\
&= V^{-1/2}VV^{-1/2} \\
&= V^{-1/2}V^{1/2}V^{1/2}V^{-1/2} \\
&= I,
\end{aligned}$$

where I is a $q \times q$ identity matrix. It follows that $Y \sim N(0, I)$. Therefore, we have

$$Y'Y \sim \chi^2_q.$$

Applying this lemma, and using the result that

$$(R\hat{\beta} - r)|\mathbf{X} \sim N[0, \sigma^2 R(\mathbf{X}'\mathbf{X})^{-1}R']$$

under $\mathbf{H}_0$, we have the quadratic form

$$(R\hat{\beta} - r)'[\sigma^2 R(\mathbf{X}'\mathbf{X})^{-1}R']^{-1}(R\hat{\beta} - r) \sim \chi^2_J$$

conditional on $\mathbf{X}$, or

$$\frac{(R\hat{\beta} - r)'[R(\mathbf{X}'\mathbf{X})^{-1}R']^{-1}(R\hat{\beta} - r)}{\sigma^2} \sim \chi^2_J$$

conditional on $\mathbf{X}$.

Because χ^2_J does not depend on $\mathbf{X}$, therefore, we also have

$$\frac{(R\hat{\beta} - r)'[R(\mathbf{X}'\mathbf{X})^{-1}R']^{-1}(R\hat{\beta} - r)}{\sigma^2} \sim \chi^2_J$$

unconditionally.

Like in constructing a t-test statistic, we should replace σ^2 by s^2 in the left hand side:

$$\frac{(R\hat{\beta} - r)'[R(\mathbf{X}'\mathbf{X})^{-1}R']^{-1}(R\hat{\beta} - r)}{s^2}.$$

The replacement of σ^2 by s^2 renders the distribution of the quadratic form no longer Chi-squared. Instead, after proper scaling, the quadratic form will follow a so-called F-distribution with degrees of freedom equal to $(J, n-K)$.

To under this result, we first review the properties of the F-distribution. Suppose $U \sim \chi^2_p$ and $V \sim \chi^2_q$, and both U and V are independent. Then the ratio

$$\frac{U/p}{V/q} \sim F_{p,q}$$

is called to follow an $F_{p,q}$ distribution with degrees of freedom (p, q). The reason that this distribution is called an F-distribution is that it is named after R. A. Fisher, a well-known statistician in the 20th century. It is similar to the shape of a χ^2 distribution with a long right tail. An $F_{p,q}$ random variable F has the following properties:

- (a) If $F \sim F_{p,q}$, then $F^{-1} \sim F_{q,p}$.
- (b) $t_q^2 \sim F_{1,q}$.
- (c) Given any fixed integer p, $p \cdot F_{p,q} \to \chi^2_p$ as $q \to \infty$.

Property (b) implies that when $J = 1$, using either the t-test or the F-test will deliver the same conclusion. Property (c) implies that the conclusions based on $F_{p,q}$ and on $p \cdot F_{p,q}$ using the χ_p^2 approximation will be approximately the same when q is sufficiently large.

Now, we can show that the quadratic form scaled by J, namely,

$$\begin{aligned} F &\equiv \frac{(R\hat{\beta} - r)'[R(\mathbf{X}'\mathbf{X})^{-1}R']^{-1}(R\hat{\beta} - r)/J}{s^2} \\ &= \frac{\frac{(R\hat{\beta}-r)'[R(\mathbf{X}'\mathbf{X})^{-1}R']^{-1}(R\hat{\beta}-r)}{\sigma^2}/J}{\frac{(n-K)s^2}{\sigma^2}/(n-K)} \\ &\sim F_{J,n-K}, \end{aligned}$$

where conditional on $\mathbf{X}$, the numerator

$$\frac{(R\hat{\beta} - r)'[R(\mathbf{X}'\mathbf{X})^{-1}R']^{-1}(R\hat{\beta} - r)}{\sigma^2} \sim \chi_J^2,$$

the denominator

$$\frac{(n-K)s^2}{\sigma^2} \sim \chi_{n-K}^2,$$

and they are mutually independent. As a result, we obtain the $F_{J,n-K}$ distribution. The statistic F is called the F-test statistic.

Theorem 3.7. ***[F-Test]:*** *Suppose Assumptions 3.1, 3.3(a) and 3.5 hold. Then under* $\mathbf{H}_0 : R\beta^o = r$, *we have*

$$\begin{aligned} F &= \frac{(R\hat{\beta} - r)'[R(\mathbf{X}'\mathbf{X})^{-1}R']^{-1}(R\hat{\beta} - r)/J}{s^2} \\ &\sim F_{J,n-K} \end{aligned}$$

for all $n > K$.

Figure 3.4 illustrates the acceptance and rejection regions of an F-test based on the $F_{4,22}$ distribution.

A practical issue now is how to compute the F-statistic. One can of course compute the F-test statistic using the above definition of the F-test statistic. However, there is a very convenient alternative way to compute the F-test statistic. We now introduce this method.

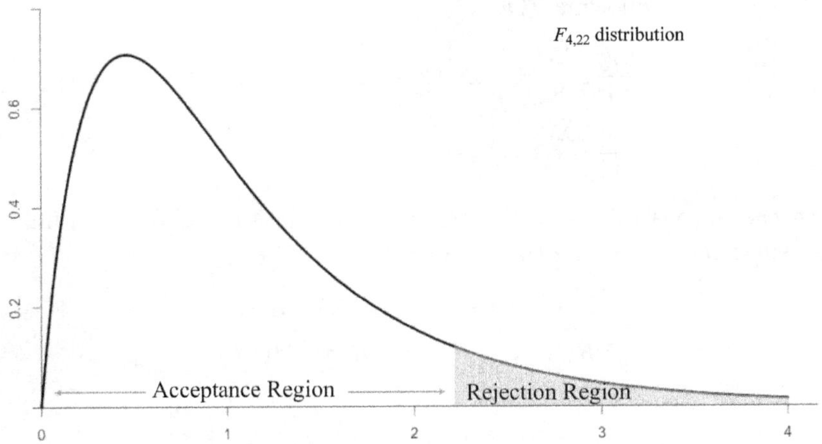

Figure 3.4 Acceptance and rejection regions of an F-test.

Theorem 3.8. *Suppose Assumptions 3.1 and 3.3(a) hold. Let $e'e$ be the SSR from the unrestricted model*

$$Y = \mathbf{X}\beta^o + \varepsilon.$$

Let $\tilde{e}'\tilde{e}$ be the SSR from the restricted model

$$Y = \mathbf{X}\beta^o + \varepsilon$$

subject to

$$R\beta^o = r,$$

where $\tilde{\beta}$ is the restricted OLS estimator. Then under $\mathbf{H}_0$, the F-test statistic can be written as

$$F = \frac{(\tilde{e}'\tilde{e} - e'e)/J}{e'e/(n-K)} \sim F_{J,n-K}.$$

Proof: Let $\tilde{\beta}$ be the OLS estimator under $\mathbf{H}_0$; that is,

$$\tilde{\beta} = \arg \min_{\beta \in R^K} (Y - \mathbf{X}\beta)'(Y - \mathbf{X}\beta)$$

subject to the constraint that $R\beta = r$. We first form the Lagrangian function

$$L(\beta, \lambda) = (Y - \mathbf{X}\beta)'(Y - \mathbf{X}\beta) + 2\lambda'(r - R\beta),$$

where λ is a $J \times 1$ vector called the Lagrange multiplier.

We have the following FOCs:

$$\frac{\partial L(\tilde{\beta},\tilde{\lambda})}{\partial \beta} = -2\mathbf{X}'(Y-\mathbf{X}\tilde{\beta}) - 2R'\tilde{\lambda} = 0,$$
$$\frac{\partial L(\tilde{\beta},\tilde{\lambda})}{\partial \lambda} = 2(r-R\tilde{\beta}) = 0.$$

With the unconstrained OLS estimator $\hat{\beta} = (\mathbf{X}'\mathbf{X})^{-1}\mathbf{X}'Y$, and from the first equation of FOC, we can obtain

$$-(\hat{\beta}-\tilde{\beta}) = (\mathbf{X}'\mathbf{X})^{-1}R'\tilde{\lambda},$$
$$R(\mathbf{X}'\mathbf{X})^{-1}R'\tilde{\lambda} = -R(\hat{\beta}-\tilde{\beta}).$$

Hence, the Lagrange multiplier

$$\begin{aligned}\tilde{\lambda} &= -[R(\mathbf{X}'\mathbf{X})^{-1}R']^{-1}R(\hat{\beta}-\tilde{\beta})\\ &= -[R(\mathbf{X}'\mathbf{X})^{-1}R']^{-1}(R\hat{\beta}-r),\end{aligned}$$

where we have made use of the constraint that $R\tilde{\beta} = r$. It follows that

$$\hat{\beta}-\tilde{\beta} = (\mathbf{X}'\mathbf{X})^{-1}R'[R(\mathbf{X}'\mathbf{X})^{-1}R']^{-1}(R\hat{\beta}-r).$$

Now,

$$\begin{aligned}\tilde{e} &= Y-\mathbf{X}\tilde{\beta}\\ &= Y-\mathbf{X}\hat{\beta}+\mathbf{X}(\hat{\beta}-\tilde{\beta})\\ &= e+\mathbf{X}(\hat{\beta}-\tilde{\beta}).\end{aligned}$$

It follows that

$$\begin{aligned}\tilde{e}'\tilde{e} &= e'e+(\hat{\beta}-\tilde{\beta})'\mathbf{X}'\mathbf{X}(\hat{\beta}-\tilde{\beta})\\ &= e'e+(R\hat{\beta}-r)'[R(\mathbf{X}'\mathbf{X})^{-1}R']^{-1}(R\hat{\beta}-r).\end{aligned}$$

We have

$$(R\hat{\beta}-r)'[R(\mathbf{X}'\mathbf{X})^{-1}R']^{-1}(R\hat{\beta}-r) = \tilde{e}'\tilde{e}-e'e$$

and

$$\begin{aligned}F &= \frac{(R\hat{\beta}-r)'[R(\mathbf{X}'\mathbf{X})^{-1}R']^{-1}(R\hat{\beta}-r)/J}{s^2}\\ &= \frac{(\tilde{e}'\tilde{e}-e'e)/J}{e'e/(n-K)}.\end{aligned}$$

This completes the proof.

Thus, the F-statistic is rather convenient to compute. One only needs to compute SSRs in order to compute it Intuitively, the SSR of the unrestricted regression model is always larger than or at least equal to that of the restricted regression model. When the null hypothesis $\mathbf{H}_0$ is true (i.e., when the parameter restriction is valid), the SSR of the restricted model is more or less similar to that of the unrestricted model, subject to the difference due to sampling variations. If the SSR of the restricted model is sufficiently larger than that of the unrestricted, then there exists evidence against $\mathbf{H}_0$. How large a difference between them is considered as sufficiently large to reject $\mathbf{H}_0$ is determined by the critical value of the associated F-distribution.

Question: What is the interpretation for the Lagrange multiplier $\tilde{\lambda}$?

Recall that we have obtained the relation that

$$\begin{aligned}\tilde{\lambda} &= -[R(\mathbf{X}'\mathbf{X})^{-1}R']^{-1}R(\hat{\beta} - \tilde{\beta})\\ &= -[R(\mathbf{X}'\mathbf{X})^{-1}R']^{-1}(R\hat{\beta} - r).\end{aligned}$$

Thus, $\tilde{\lambda}$ is an indicator of the departure of $R\hat{\beta}$ from r. That is, the value of $\tilde{\lambda}$ will indicate whether $R\hat{\beta} - r$ is significantly different from zero.

Question: What happens to the distribution of F when $n \to \infty$?

Recall the important property of the $F_{p,q}$ distribution that $p \cdot F_{p,q} \xrightarrow{d} \chi_p^2$ when $q \to \infty$. Since our F-statistic for $\mathbf{H}_0$ follows an $F_{J,n-K}$ distribution, it follows that under $\mathbf{H}_0$, the quadratic form

$$\begin{aligned}J \cdot F &= \frac{(R\hat{\beta} - r)' \left[R(\mathbf{X}'\mathbf{X})^{-1}R'\right]^{-1} (R\hat{\beta} - r)}{s^2}\\ &\xrightarrow{d} \chi_J^2 \text{ as } n \to \infty.\end{aligned}$$

This implies that the limiting distribution of $J \cdot F$ is the same as that of the quadratic form

$$\frac{(R\hat{\beta} - r)' \left[R(\mathbf{X}'\mathbf{X})^{-1}R'\right]^{-1} (R\hat{\beta} - r)}{\sigma^2}.$$

That is, replacing σ^2 by s^2 does not change the limiting distribution.

We formally state this result below.

Theorem 3.9. ***[Wald Test]:*** *Suppose Assumptions 3.1, 3.3(a) and 3.5 hold. Then under* $\mathbf{H}_0$*, we have the Wald test statistic*

$$W = J \cdot F = \frac{(R\hat{\beta} - r)'[R(\mathbf{X}'\mathbf{X})^{-1}R']^{-1}(R\hat{\beta} - r)}{s^2} \xrightarrow{d} \chi^2_J$$

as $n \to \infty$.

This result implies that when n is sufficiently large, using the F-statistic and the exact $F_{J,n-K}$ distribution and using the quadratic form W and the simpler χ^2_J approximation will make no essential difference in statistical inference. The Wald test is applicable only when n is large.

Figure 3.5 illustrates the acceptance and rejection regions of a Wald test based on the χ^2_{15} distribution.

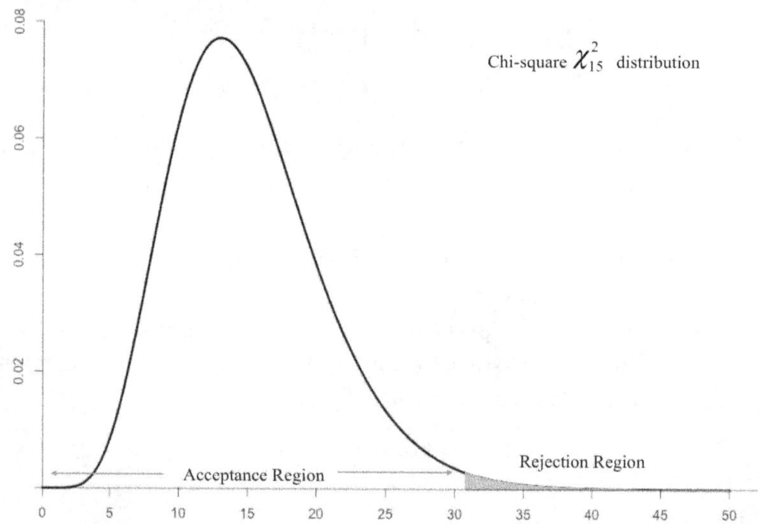

Figure 3.5 Acceptance and rejection regions of a Wald test.

It is important to note that in Theorem 3.9, the Wald test statistic W is proportional to the F-test statistic. This holds under conditional homoskedasticity. Under conditional heteroskedasticity, we can define a robust Wald test statistic, but the relationship of $W = J \cdot F$ will no longer hold.

3.8 Applications

We now consider some special but important cases often encountered in economics and finance.

Case I: Testing for Joint Significance of Explanatory Variables

Consider a linear regression model

$$\begin{aligned} Y_t &= X_t'\beta^o + \varepsilon_t \\ &= \beta_0^o + \sum_{j=1}^{k} \beta_j^o X_{jt} + \varepsilon_t. \end{aligned}$$

We are interested in testing the combined effect of all the regressors except the intercept. The null hypothesis is

$$\mathbf{H}_0 : \beta_j^o = 0 \text{ for } 1 \leq j \leq k,$$

which implies that none of the explanatory variables influences Y_t.
The alternative hypothesis is

$$\mathbf{H}_A : \ \beta_j^o \neq 0 \text{ at least for some } \beta_j^o, \qquad j = 1, ..., k.$$

One can use the F-test and

$$F \sim F_{k,n-(k+1)}.$$

In fact, the restricted model under $\mathbf{H}_0$ is very simple:

$$Y_t = \beta_0^o + \varepsilon_t.$$

The restricted OLS estimator $\tilde{\beta} = (\bar{Y}, 0, ..., 0)'$. It follows that

$$\tilde{e} = Y - \mathbf{X}\tilde{\beta} = Y - \bar{Y}.$$

Hence, we have

$$\tilde{e}'\tilde{e} = (Y - \bar{Y})'(Y - \bar{Y}).$$

Recall the definition of R^2 :

$$\begin{aligned} R^2 &= 1 - \frac{e'e}{(Y - \bar{Y})'(Y - \bar{Y})} \\ &= 1 - \frac{e'e}{\tilde{e}'\tilde{e}}. \end{aligned}$$

It follows that

$$\begin{aligned} F &= \frac{(\tilde{e}'\tilde{e} - e'e)/k}{e'e/(n-k-1)} \\ &= \frac{(1 - \frac{e'e}{\tilde{e}'\tilde{e}})/k}{\frac{e'e}{\tilde{e}'\tilde{e}}/(n-k-1)} \\ &= \frac{R^2/k}{(1-R^2)/(n-k-1)}. \end{aligned}$$

Thus, it suffices to run one regression, namely the unrestricted model in this case. We emphasize that this formula is valid only when one is testing for $\mathbf{H}_0 : \beta_j^o = 0$ for all $1 \leq j \leq k$.

Example 3.6. [Testing EMH]: Suppose Y_t is the exchange rate return in period t, and I_{t-1} is the information available at time $t-1$. Then a classical version of EMH can be stated as follows:

$$E(Y_t|I_{t-1}) = E(Y_t).$$

To check whether exchange rate changes are unpredictable using the past history of exchange rate changes, we specify a linear regression model

$$Y_t = X_t'\beta^o + \varepsilon_t,$$

where

$$X_t = (1, Y_{t-1}, ..., Y_{t-k})'.$$

Under EMH, we have

$$\mathbf{H}_0 : \beta_j^o = 0 \text{ for all } j = 1, ..., k.$$

If the alternative

$$\mathbf{H}_A : \beta_j^o \neq 0 \text{ at least for some } j \in \{1, ..., k\}$$

holds, then exchange rate changes are predictable using the past information.

Question: What is the appropriate interpretation if $\mathbf{H}_0$ is not rejected?

Note that there exists a gap between EMH and $\mathbf{H}_0$, because the linear regression model is just one of many ways to check EMH. It is possible that exchange rate changes are not predictable using a linear autoregressive model, but are predictable using a suitable nonlinear autoregressive model.

Thus, when $\mathbf{H}_0$ is not rejected, at most we can only say that no evidence against the efficiency hypothesis is found. We should not conclude that EMH holds.

Strictly speaking, the current finite sample distribution theory (Assumption 3.2: $E(\varepsilon_t|\mathbf{X}) = 0$) rules out this application, which is a dynamic time series regression model. However, we will justify in Chapter 5 that

$$\begin{aligned} k \cdot F &= \frac{R^2}{(1-R^2)/(n-k-1)} \\ &\xrightarrow{d} \chi^2_k \end{aligned}$$

under conditional homoskedasticity even for a linear dynamic regression model.

In fact, we can use a simpler version when n is large:

$$(n-k-1)R^2 \xrightarrow{d} \chi^2_k.$$

This follows from Slutsky's theorem because $R^2 \xrightarrow{p} 0$ under $\mathbf{H}_0$. Although Assumption 3.5 is not needed for this result, conditional homoskedasticity is still needed, which rules out AutoRegressive Conditional Heteroskedasticity (ARCH) in the time series context. There usually exist significant ARCH effects in high-frequency financial time series data.

Below is a concrete numerical example.

Example 3.7. [Consumption Function and Wealth Effect]: Let Y_t denote consumption, X_{1t} labor income, and X_{2t} liquidity asset wealth. A regression estimation gives

$$\begin{aligned} Y_t = \underset{[1.77]}{33.88} - \underset{[-0.74]}{26.00}X_{1t} + \underset{[0.77]}{6.71}X_{2t} + e_t, \qquad R^2 = 0.742, n = 25. \end{aligned}$$

where the numbers inside $[\cdot]$ are t-statistics.

Suppose we are interested in whether labor income or liquidity asset wealth has impact on consumption. We can use the F-test statistic,

$$\begin{aligned} F &= \frac{R^2/2}{(1-R^2)/(n-3)} \\ &= (0.742/2)/[(1-0.742)/(25-3)] \\ &= 31.636 \\ &\sim F_{2,22}. \end{aligned}$$

Comparing it with the critical value 4.38 of $F_{2,22}$ at the 5% significance level, we reject the null hypothesis that neither income nor liquidity asset has impact on consumption at the 5% significance level.

Case II: Testing for Omitted Variables (or Testing for No Effect)

Suppose $\mathbf{X} = (\mathbf{X}^{(1)}, \mathbf{X}^{(2)})$, where $\mathbf{X}^{(1)}$ is an $n \times (k_1 + 1)$ matrix and $\mathbf{X}^{(2)}$ is an $n \times k_2$ matrix. A random vector $X_t^{(2)}$ has no explanatory power for the conditional expectation of Y_t if

$$E(Y_t|X_t) = E(Y_t|X_t^{(1)}).$$

Alternatively, it has explanatory power for the conditional expectation of Y_t if

$$E(Y_t|X_t) \neq E(Y_t|X_t^{(1)}).$$

When $X_t^{(2)}$ has explaining power for Y_t but is not included in the regression, we say that $X_t^{(2)}$ is an omitted random variable or vector. Note that the omitted variables problem is model-free. In particular, it does not assume that the conditional mean is a linear regression model.

We note that the vector $X_t^{(2)}$ of omitted variables is our primary interest. The set of variables, $X_t^{(1)}$, is not our direct interest, but they have to be included in the regression because $X_t^{(1)}$ is generally correlated with $X_t^{(2)}$. The random variables in $X_t^{(1)}$ are called control variables. In scientific experimentation, a control variable is an experimental factor which is held constant and unchanged throughout the course of the study. Control variables could strongly influence experimental results, so they were not held constant during the experiment in order to test the relationship of the dependent and independent variables. In economics, due to the nonexperimental nature of observed economic data, the variables in $X_t^{(1)}$ are allowed to change during the sample period, but the inclusion of variables in $X_t^{(1)}$ will help purge their impact of the dependent variable Y_t so that one can focus on examining the effect of the omitted variables in $X_t^{(2)}$. The variables in $X_t^{(1)}$ are still called control variables.

Question: How to test whether the variables in $X_t^{(2)}$ are omitted variables in the linear regression context?

Consider the restricted linear regression model

$$Y_t = \beta_0 + \beta_1 X_{1t} + \cdots + \beta_{k_1} X_{k_1 t} + \varepsilon_t.$$

Suppose we have additional k_2 variables $(X_{(k_1+1)t}, ..., X_{(k_1+k_2)t})$, and so we consider the unrestricted linear regression model

$$\begin{aligned} Y_t = \beta_0 + \beta_1 X_{1t} + \cdots + \beta_{k_1} X_{k_1 t} \\ + \beta_{k_1+1} X_{(k_1+1)t} + \cdots + \beta_{(k_1+k_2)} X_{(k_1+k_2)t} + \varepsilon_t. \end{aligned}$$

The null hypothesis is that the additional variables have no effect on Y_t. If this is the case, then

$$\mathbf{H}_0 : \beta_{k_1+1} = \beta_{k_1+2} = \cdots = \beta_{k_1+k_2} = 0.$$

The alternative is that at least one of the additional variables has effect on Y_t.

The F-test statistic is

$$F = \frac{(\tilde{e}'\tilde{e} - e'e)/k_2}{e'e/(n - k_1 - k_2 - 1)} \sim F_{k_2, n-(k_1+k_2+1)}.$$

Question: Suppose we reject the null hypothesis. Then some important explanatory variables are omitted, and they should be included in the regression. On the other hand, if the F-test statistic does not reject the null hypothesis $\mathbf{H}_0$, can we say that there is no omitted variable?

No. There may exist a nonlinear relationship for the additional variables which a linear regression specification cannot capture.

Suppose rejection occurs. Then there exists evidence against $\mathbf{H}_0$. However, if no rejection occurs, then we can only say that we find no evidence against $\mathbf{H}_0$ (which is not the same as the statement that reforms have no effect). It is possible that the effect of $X_t^{(2)}$ is of nonlinear form. In this case, we may obtain a zero coefficient for $X_t^{(2)}$, because the linear specification may not be able to capture it.

Example 3.8. [Testing for Effect of Reforms]: Consider the extended production function

$$\begin{aligned} Y_t = \beta_0 + \beta_1 \ln(L_t) + \beta_2 \ln(K_t) \\ + \beta_3 AU_t + \beta_4 PS_t + \beta_5 CM_t + \varepsilon_t, \end{aligned}$$

where AU_t is the autonomy dummy, PS_t is the profit sharing ratio, and CM_t is the dummy for change of manager. The null hypothesis of interest here is that none of the three reforms has impact:

$$\mathbf{H}_0 : \beta_3 = \beta_4 = \beta_5 = 0.$$

We can use the F-test, and $F \sim F_{3,n-6}$ under $\mathbf{H}_0$.

Example 3.9. [Testing for Granger Causality]: Consider two time series $\{Y_t, Z_t\}$, where t is the time index, $I_{t-1}^Y = \{Y_{t-1}, ..., Y_1\}$ and $I_{t-1}^Z = \{Z_{t-1}, ..., Z_1\}$. For example, Y_t is the GDP growth rate, and Z_t is the money supply growth rate. We say that Z_t does not Granger-cause Y_t in conditional mean with respect to $I_{t-1} = \{I_{t-1}^{(Y)}, I_{t-1}^{(Z)}\}$ if

$$E\left[Y_t | I_{t-1}^{(Y)}, I_{t-1}^{(Z)}\right] = E\left[Y_t | I_{t-1}^{(Y)}\right].$$

In other words, the lagged variables of Z_t have no impact on the current Y_t.

In time series analysis, Granger causality is defined in terms of incremental predictability rather than the real cause-effect relationship. From an econometric point of view, it is a test of omitted variables in a time series context. It is first introduced by Granger (1969).

Question: How to test Granger causality?

Consider now a linear regression model

$$\begin{aligned} Y_t = \beta_0 + \beta_1 Y_{t-1} + \cdots + \beta_p Y_{t-p} \\ + \beta_{p+1} Z_{t-1} + \cdots + \beta_{p+q} Z_{t-q} + \varepsilon_t. \end{aligned}$$

Under non-Granger causality, we have

$$\mathbf{H}_0 : \beta_{p+1} = \cdots = \beta_{p+q} = 0.$$

Granger (1969) proposes an F-test statistic

$$F \sim F_{q,n-(p+q+1)}.$$

The current econometric theory (Assumption 3.2: $E(\varepsilon_t|\mathbf{X}) = 0$) actually rules out this application, because it is a dynamic regression model. However, we will justify in Chapter 5 that under $\mathbf{H}_0$,

$$q \cdot F \xrightarrow{d} \chi_q^2$$

as $n \to \infty$ under conditional homoskedasticity even for a linear dynamic regression model.

Example 3.10. [Testing for Structural Changes]: Consider a bivariate regression model

$$Y_t = \beta_0 + \beta_1 X_{1t} + \varepsilon_t,$$

where t is a time index, and $\{X_t\}$ and $\{\varepsilon_t\}$ are mutually independent. Suppose there exist changes after $t = t_0$, i.e., there exist structural changes. We can consider the extended regression model:

$$\begin{aligned} Y_t &= (\beta_0 + \alpha_0 D_t) + (\beta_1 + \alpha_1 D_t) X_{1t} + \varepsilon_t \\ &= \beta_0 + \beta_1 X_{1t} + \alpha_0 D_t + \alpha_1 (D_t X_{1t}) + \varepsilon_t, \end{aligned}$$

where $D_t = 1$ if $t > t_0$ and $D_t = 0$ otherwise. The variable D_t is called a time dummy variable, indicating whether it is a pre- or post-structural break period.

The null hypothesis of no structural change is

$$\mathbf{H}_0 : \alpha_0 = \alpha_1 = 0.$$

The alternative hypothesis that there exists a structural change is

$$\mathbf{H}_A : \alpha_0 \neq 0 \text{ or } \alpha_1 \neq 0.$$

The F-test statistic

$$F \sim F_{2,n-4}.$$

The idea of such a test is first proposed by Chow (1960).

Case III: Testing for Linear Restrictions

Example 3.11. [Testing for CRS]: Consider the extended production function

$$\ln(Y_t) = \beta_0 + \beta_1 \ln(L_t) + \beta_2 \ln(K_t) + \beta_3 AU_t + \beta_4 PS_t + \beta_5 CM_t + \varepsilon_t.$$

We will test the null hypothesis of CRS:

$$\mathbf{H}_0 : \beta_1 + \beta_2 = 1.$$

The alternative hypothesis is

$$\mathbf{H}_0 : \beta_1 + \beta_2 \neq 1.$$

What is the restricted model under $\mathbf{H}_0$? It is given by

$$\ln(Y_t) = \beta_0 + \beta_1 \ln(L_t) + (1 - \beta_1) \ln(K_t) + \beta_3 AU_t + \beta_4 PS_t + \beta_5 CM_t + \varepsilon_t$$

or equivalently

$$\ln(Y_t/K_t) = \beta_0 + \beta_1 \ln(L_t/K_t) + \beta_3 AU_t + \beta_4 CON_t + \beta_5 CM_t + \varepsilon_t.$$

The F-test statistic

$$F \sim F_{1,n-6}.$$

Because there is only one restriction, both t- and F- tests are applicable to test CRS.

Example 3.12. [Wage Determination]: Consider the wage function

$$W_t = \beta_0 + \beta_1 P_t + \beta_2 P_{t-1} + \beta_3 U_t + \beta_4 V_t + \beta_5 W_{t-1} + \varepsilon_t,$$

where W_t is wage, P_t is price, U_t is unemployment, and V_t is the number of unfilled vacancies.

We will test the null hypothesis

$$\mathbf{H}_0 : \beta_1 + \beta_2 = 0, \beta_3 + \beta_4 = 0, \text{ and } \beta_5 = 1.$$

Question: What is the economic interpretation of the null hypothesis $\mathbf{H}_0$?

Under $\mathbf{H}_0$, we have the restricted wage equation:

$$\Delta W_t = \beta_0 + \beta_1 \Delta P_t + \beta_4 D_t + \varepsilon_t,$$

where $\Delta W_t = W_t - W_{t-1}$ is the wage growth rate, $\Delta P_t = P_t - P_{t-1}$ is the inflation rate, and $D_t = V_t - U_t$ is an index for excess job supply. This implies that the wage increase depends on the inflation rate and the excess labor supply.

The F-test statistic for $\mathbf{H}_0$ is

$$F \sim F_{3,n-6}.$$

3.9 Generalized Least Squares Estimation

Question: The classical linear regression theory crucially depends on the assumption that $\varepsilon|\mathbf{X} \sim N(0, \sigma^2\mathbf{I})$, or equivalently $\{\varepsilon_t\} \sim$ IID $N(0, \sigma^2)$, and $\{X_t\}$ and $\{\varepsilon_t\}$ are mutually independent. What may happen if some classical assumptions do not hold?

Question: Under what conditions, will the existing procedures and results in the previous sections still be approximately true?

Assumption 3.5 is crucial for us to derive the finite sample distributions of the OLS estimator $\hat{\beta}$ and related test statistics, but it is unrealistic for many economic and financial data. In particular, there may exist conditional heteroskedasticity and/or autocorrelation in $\{\varepsilon_t\}$. Suppose Assumption 3.5 is replaced by the following condition:

Assumption 3.6. $\varepsilon|\mathbf{X} \sim N(0, \sigma^2\mathbf{V})$, where $0 < \sigma^2 < \infty$ is unknown and $\mathbf{V} = V(\mathbf{X})$ is a known $n \times n$ symmetric, finite and positive definite matrix.

Assumption 3.6 implies that

$$\begin{aligned} \text{var}(\varepsilon|\mathbf{X}) &= E(\varepsilon\varepsilon'|\mathbf{X}) \\ &= \sigma^2\mathbf{V} = \sigma^2 V(\mathbf{X}) \end{aligned}$$

is known up to constant σ^2. It allows for conditional heteroskedasticity of known form.

It is also possible that $\mathbf{V}$ is not a diagonal matrix. Thus, $\text{cov}(\varepsilon_t, \varepsilon_s|\mathbf{X})$ may not be zero. In other words, Assumption 3.6 allows conditional autocorrelation of known form. If t is a time index, this implies that there exists serial correlation of known form. If t is an index for cross-sectional units, this implies that there exists spatial correlation of known form.

However, the assumption that $\mathbf{V}$ is known is still restrictive from a practical point of view. In practice, $\mathbf{V}$ usually has an unknown form.

Question: What is the statistical property of the OLS estimator $\hat{\beta}$ under Assumption 3.6?

Theorem 3.10. *Suppose Assumptions 3.1, 3.3(a) and 3.6 hold. Then*

(1) [Unbiasedness]:

$$E(\hat{\beta}|\mathbf{X}) = \beta^o \text{ and } E(\hat{\beta}) = \beta^o.$$

(2) [Variance]:

$$\begin{aligned} \text{var}(\hat{\beta}|\mathbf{X}) &= \sigma^2(\mathbf{X}'\mathbf{X})^{-1}\mathbf{X}'\mathbf{V}\mathbf{X}(\mathbf{X}'\mathbf{X})^{-1} \\ &\neq \sigma^2(\mathbf{X}'\mathbf{X})^{-1}. \end{aligned}$$

(3) [Normal Distribution]:

$$(\hat{\beta} - \beta^o)|\mathbf{X} \sim N(0, \sigma^2(\mathbf{X}'\mathbf{X})^{-1}\mathbf{X}'\mathbf{V}\mathbf{X}(\mathbf{X}'\mathbf{X})^{-1}).$$

(4) [Non-Zero Correlation Between $\hat{\beta}$ and e]: Generally,

$$cov(\hat{\beta}, e|\mathbf{X}) \neq 0.$$

Proof: (1) Using $\hat{\beta} - \beta^o = (\mathbf{X}'\mathbf{X})^{-1}\mathbf{X}'\varepsilon$, we have

$$\begin{aligned} E[(\hat{\beta} - \beta^o)|\mathbf{X}] &= (\mathbf{X}'\mathbf{X})^{-1}\mathbf{X}'E(\varepsilon|\mathbf{X}) \\ &= (\mathbf{X}'\mathbf{X})^{-1}\mathbf{X}'0 \\ &= 0. \end{aligned}$$

(2)

$$\begin{aligned} \text{var}(\hat{\beta}|\mathbf{X}) &= E[(\hat{\beta} - \beta^o)(\hat{\beta} - \beta^o)'|\mathbf{X}] \\ &= E[(\mathbf{X}'\mathbf{X})^{-1}\mathbf{X}'\varepsilon\varepsilon'\mathbf{X}(\mathbf{X}'\mathbf{X})^{-1}|\mathbf{X}] \\ &= (\mathbf{X}'\mathbf{X})^{-1}\mathbf{X}'E(\varepsilon\varepsilon'|\mathbf{X})\mathbf{X}(\mathbf{X}'\mathbf{X})^{-1} \\ &= \sigma^2(\mathbf{X}'\mathbf{X})^{-1}\mathbf{X}'\mathbf{V}\mathbf{X}(\mathbf{X}'\mathbf{X})^{-1}. \end{aligned}$$

Note that we cannot further simplify the expression here because $\mathbf{V} \neq \mathbf{I}$.
(3) Because

$$\begin{aligned} \hat{\beta} - \beta^o &= (\mathbf{X}'\mathbf{X})^{-1}\mathbf{X}'\varepsilon \\ &= \sum_{t=1}^{n} C_t\varepsilon_t, \end{aligned}$$

where the weighting vector

$$C_t = (\mathbf{X}'\mathbf{X})^{-1}X_t,$$

$\hat{\beta} - \beta^o$ follows a normal distribution given $\mathbf{X}$, because it is a sum of normal random variables. As a result, conditional on $\mathbf{X}$,

$$\hat{\beta} - \beta^o \sim N(0, \sigma^2(\mathbf{X}'\mathbf{X})^{-1}\mathbf{X}'\mathbf{V}\mathbf{X}(\mathbf{X}'\mathbf{X})^{-1}).$$

(4)

$$\begin{aligned} \text{cov}(\hat{\beta}, e|\mathbf{X}) &= E[(\hat{\beta} - \beta^o)e'|\mathbf{X}] \\ &= E[(\mathbf{X}'\mathbf{X})^{-1}\mathbf{X}'\varepsilon\varepsilon'M|\mathbf{X}] \\ &= (\mathbf{X}'\mathbf{X})^{-1}\mathbf{X}'E(\varepsilon\varepsilon'|\mathbf{X})M \\ &= \sigma^2(\mathbf{X}'\mathbf{X})^{-1}\mathbf{X}'\mathbf{V}M \\ &\neq 0 \end{aligned}$$

because $\mathbf{X}'\mathbf{V}\mathbf{M} \neq 0$. We can see that it is conditional heteroskedasticity and/or autocorrelation in $\{\varepsilon_t\}$ that cause $\hat{\beta}$ to be correlated with e.

The OLS estimator $\hat{\beta}$ is still unbiased and one can show that its variance goes to zero as $n \to \infty$. Thus, it converges to β^o in the sense of MSE.

However, the variance of the OLS estimator $\hat{\beta}$ does no longer have the simple expression of $\sigma^2(\mathbf{X}'\mathbf{X})^{-1}$ under Assumption 3.6. As a consequence, the classical t- and F-test statistics are invalid because they are based on an incorrect variance-covariance matrix of $\hat{\beta}$. That is, they use an incorrect expression of $\sigma^2(\mathbf{X}'\mathbf{X})^{-1}$ rather than the correct variance formula of $\sigma^2(\mathbf{X}'\mathbf{X})^{-1}\mathbf{X}'\mathbf{V}\mathbf{X}(\mathbf{X}'\mathbf{X})^{-1}$.

Theorem 3.10(4) implies that even if we can obtain a consistent estimator for $\sigma^2(\mathbf{X}'\mathbf{X})^{-1}\mathbf{X}'\mathbf{V}\mathbf{X}(\mathbf{X}'\mathbf{X})^{-1}$ and use it to construct tests, we can no longer obtain the Student's t-distribution and F-distribution, because the numerator and the denominator in defining the classical t- and F-test statistics are no longer independent.

To solve the aforementioned problems, we now introduce a new estimation method called the Generalized Least Squares (GLS) estimation. We first state a useful lemma.

Lemma 3.4. ***[Cholesky's Decomposition]:*** *For any $n \times n$ symmetric positive definite matrix $\mathbf{V}$, we can always write*

$$\begin{aligned}\mathbf{V}^{-1} &= \mathbf{C}'\mathbf{C},\\ \mathbf{V} &= \mathbf{C}^{-1}(\mathbf{C}')^{-1}\end{aligned}$$

where $\mathbf{C}$ is an $n \times n$ nonsingular matrix.

This is called Cholesky's factorization. Note that $\mathbf{C}$ may not be symmetric.

Consider the original linear regression model:

$$Y = \mathbf{X}\beta^o + \varepsilon.$$

If we multiply the equation by $\mathbf{C}$, we obtain the transformed regression model

$$\begin{aligned}\mathbf{C}Y &= (\mathbf{C}\mathbf{X})\beta^o + \mathbf{C}\varepsilon, \text{ or}\\ Y^* &= \mathbf{X}^*\beta^o + \varepsilon^*,\end{aligned}$$

where $Y^* = \mathbf{C}Y, \mathbf{X}^* = \mathbf{C}\mathbf{X}$ and $\varepsilon^* = \mathbf{C}\varepsilon$. Then the OLS estimator of this transformed model

$$\begin{aligned}\hat{\beta}^* &= (\mathbf{X}^{*\prime}\mathbf{X}^*)^{-1}\mathbf{X}^{*\prime}Y^* \\ &= (\mathbf{X}'\mathbf{C}'\mathbf{C}\mathbf{X})^{-1}(\mathbf{X}'\mathbf{C}'\mathbf{C}Y) \\ &= (\mathbf{X}'\mathbf{V}^{-1}\mathbf{X})^{-1}\mathbf{X}'\mathbf{V}^{-1}Y\end{aligned}$$

is called the GLS estimator.

Question: What is the nature of the GLS estimator?

Observe that

$$\begin{aligned}E(\varepsilon^*|\mathbf{X}) &= E(\mathbf{C}\varepsilon|\mathbf{X}) \\ &= \mathbf{C}E(\varepsilon|\mathbf{X}) \\ &= \mathbf{C}\cdot 0 \\ &= 0.\end{aligned}$$

Also, note that

$$\begin{aligned}\mathrm{var}(\varepsilon^*|\mathbf{X}) &= E[\varepsilon^*\varepsilon^{*\prime}|\mathbf{X}] \\ &= E[\mathbf{C}\varepsilon\varepsilon'\mathbf{C}'|\mathbf{X}] \\ &= \mathbf{C}E(\varepsilon\varepsilon'|\mathbf{X})\mathbf{C}' \\ &= \sigma^2\mathbf{C}\mathbf{V}\mathbf{C}' \\ &= \sigma^2\mathbf{C}[\mathbf{C}^{-1}(\mathbf{C}')^{-1}]\mathbf{C}' \\ &= \sigma^2\mathbf{I}.\end{aligned}$$

It follows from Assumption 3.6 that

$$\varepsilon^*|\mathbf{X} \sim N(0, \sigma^2\mathbf{I}).$$

The transformation makes the new error ε^* conditionally homoskedastic and serially uncorrelated, while maintaining the normality distribution. Suppose that for t, ε_t has a large variance σ_t^2. The transformation $\varepsilon_t^* = \mathbf{C}\varepsilon_t$ will discount ε_t by dividing it by its conditional standard deviation so that ε_t^* becomes conditionally homoskedastic. In addition, the transformation also removes possible correlation between ε_t and $\varepsilon_s, t \neq s$. As a consequence, the GLS estimator becomes BLUE for β^o in term of the Gauss-Markov theorem.

To appreciate how the transformation by matrix $\mathbf{C}$ removes conditional heteroskedasticity and eliminates serial correlation, we now consider two examples.

Example 3.13. [Removing Heteroskedasticity]: Suppose

$$\mathbf{V} = \begin{bmatrix} \sigma_1^2 & 0 & \cdots & 0 \\ 0 & \sigma_2^2 & \cdots & 0 \\ \cdots & \cdots & \cdots & 0 \\ 0 & \cdots & \cdots & \sigma_n^2 \end{bmatrix}.$$

Then

$$\mathbf{C} = \begin{bmatrix} \sigma_1^{-1} & 0 & \cdots & 0 \\ 0 & \sigma_2^{-1} & \cdots & 0 \\ \cdots & \cdots & \cdots & 0 \\ 0 & \cdots & \cdots & \sigma_n^{-1} \end{bmatrix}$$

where $\sigma_i^2 = \sigma_i^2(\mathbf{X}), i = 1, ..., n$, and

$$\varepsilon^* = \mathbf{C}\varepsilon = \left(\frac{\varepsilon_1}{\sigma_1}, \frac{\varepsilon_2}{\sigma_2}, \cdots, \frac{\varepsilon_n}{\sigma_n}\right)'.$$

The transformed regression model is

$$Y_t^* = X_t^{*\prime}\beta^o + \varepsilon_t^*, \qquad t = 1, ..., n,$$

where

$$\begin{aligned} Y_t^* &= Y_t/\sigma_t, \\ X_t^* &= X_t/\sigma_t, \\ \varepsilon_t^* &= \varepsilon_t/\sigma_t. \end{aligned}$$

Example 3.14. [Eliminating Serial Correlation]: Suppose

$$\mathbf{V} = \begin{bmatrix} 1 & \rho & \rho^2 & \cdots & \rho^{n-2} & \rho^{n-1} \\ \rho & 1 & \rho & \cdots & \rho^{n-3} & \rho^{n-2} \\ \rho^2 & \rho & 1 & \cdots & \rho^{n-4} & \rho^{n-3} \\ \cdots & \cdots & \cdots & \cdots & \cdots & \cdots \\ \rho^{n-2} & \rho^{n-3} & \rho^{n-4} & \cdots & 1 & \rho \\ \rho^{n-1} & \rho^{n-2} & \rho^{n-3} & \cdots & \rho & 1 \end{bmatrix}.$$

This matrix actually arises from the following linear regression model $Y_t = X_t'\beta^o + \varepsilon_t$, where $\varepsilon_t = \rho\varepsilon_{t-1} + v_t$, and $\{v_t\}$ is an IID sequence with $E(v_t) = 0$

and $\text{var}(v_t) = \sigma^2$. Then we have

$$\mathbf{V}^{-1} = \begin{bmatrix} 1 & -\rho & 0 & \cdots & 0 & 0 \\ -\rho & 1+\rho^2 & -\rho & \cdots & \rho^{n-3} & 0 \\ 0 & -\rho & 1+\rho^2 & \cdots & \rho^{n-4} & 0 \\ \cdots & \cdots & \cdots & \cdots & \cdots & \cdots \\ 0 & 0 & 0 & \cdots & 1+\rho^2 & -\rho \\ 0 & 0 & 0 & \cdots & -\rho & 1 \end{bmatrix}$$

and

$$\mathbf{C} = \begin{bmatrix} \sqrt{1-\rho^2} & 0 & 0 & \cdots & 0 & 0 \\ -\rho & 1 & 0 & \cdots & 0 & 0 \\ 0 & -\rho & 1 & \cdots & 0 & 0 \\ \cdots & \cdots & \cdots & \cdots & \cdots & \cdots \\ 0 & 0 & 0 & \cdots & 1 & 0 \\ 0 & 0 & 0 & \cdots & -\rho & 1 \end{bmatrix}.$$

It follows that

$$\begin{aligned} \varepsilon^* &= \mathbf{C}\varepsilon \\ &= \begin{bmatrix} \sqrt{1-\rho^2}\varepsilon_1 \\ \varepsilon_2 - \rho\varepsilon_1 \\ \cdots \\ \varepsilon_n - \rho\varepsilon_{n-1} \end{bmatrix}. \end{aligned}$$

The transformed regression model is

$$Y_t^* = X_t^{*\prime}\beta^o + \varepsilon_t^*, t = 1, ..., n,$$

where

$$\begin{aligned} Y_1^* &= \sqrt{1-\rho^2}Y_1, & Y_t^* &= Y_t - \rho Y_{t-1}, t = 2, ..., n, \\ X_1^* &= \sqrt{1-\rho^2}X_1, & X_t^* &= X_t - \rho X_{t-1}, t = 2, ..., n, \\ \varepsilon_1^* &= \sqrt{1-\rho^2}\varepsilon_1, & \varepsilon_t^* &= \varepsilon_t - \rho\varepsilon_{t-1}, t = 2, ..., n. \end{aligned}$$

The $\sqrt{1-\rho^2}$ transformation for $t = 1$ is called the Prais-Winsten transformation.

Theorem 3.11. ***[GLS Estimation]:*** *Under Assumptions 3.1, 3.3(a) and 3.6, and $n > K$, we have*

(1) [Unbiasedness]: $E(\hat{\beta}^*|\mathbf{X}) = \beta^o$ and $E(\hat{\beta}^*) = \beta^o$.

(2) [Variance]: var$(\hat{\beta}^*|\mathbf{X}) = \sigma^2(\mathbf{X}^{*\prime}\mathbf{X}^*)^{-1} = \sigma^2(\mathbf{X}'\mathbf{V}^{-1}\mathbf{X})^{-1}$.
(3) [Orthogonality]: cov$(\hat{\beta}^*, e^*|\mathbf{X}) = 0$, *where* $e^* = Y^* - \mathbf{X}^*\hat{\beta}^*$.
(4) [Gauss-Markov]: $\hat{\beta}^*$ *is BLUE.*
(5) [Residual Variance Estimator]: $E(s^{*2}|\mathbf{X}) = \sigma^2$, *where* $s^{*2} = e^{*\prime}e^*/(n-K)$.

Proof: Results in Parts (1) to (3) follow because the GLS estimator is the OLS estimator of the transformed model.

(4) The transformed model satisfies Assumptions 3.1, 3.3 and 3.5 of the classical regression assumptions with $\varepsilon^*|\mathbf{X}^* \sim N(0, \sigma^2\mathbf{I})$. It follows that the GLS estimator is BLUE by the Gauss-Markov theorem. Result in Part (5) also follows immediately. This completes the proof.

Because $\hat{\beta}^*$ is the OLS estimator of the transformed regression model with IID $N(0, \sigma^2\mathbf{I})$ errors, the t-test and F-test statistics are applicable, and these test statistics are defined as follows:

$$\begin{aligned} T^* &= \frac{R\hat{\beta}^* - r}{\sqrt{s^{*2}R(\mathbf{X}^{*\prime}\mathbf{X}^*)^{-1}R'}} \\ &\sim t_{n-K}, \\ F^* &= \frac{(R\hat{\beta}^* - r)'[R(\mathbf{X}^{*\prime}\mathbf{X}^*)^{-1}R']^{-1}(R\hat{\beta}^* - r)/J}{s^{*2}} \\ &\sim F_{J,n-K}. \end{aligned}$$

It is very important to note that we still have to estimate the proportionality σ^2 in spite of the fact that $\mathbf{V} = V(X)$ is known.

Because the GLS estimator $\hat{\beta}^*$ is BLUE and the OLS estimator $\hat{\beta}$ differs from $\hat{\beta}^*$, namely,

$$\begin{aligned} \hat{\beta}^* &= (\mathbf{X}^{*\prime}\mathbf{X}^*)^{-1}\mathbf{X}^{*\prime}Y^* \\ &= (\mathbf{X}'\mathbf{V}^{-1}\mathbf{X})^{-1}\mathbf{X}'\mathbf{V}^{-1}Y \\ &\neq (\mathbf{X}'\mathbf{X})^{-1}\mathbf{X}'Y = \hat{\beta}, \end{aligned}$$

it follows that the OLS estimator $\hat{\beta}$ cannot be BLUE.

In fact, the most important message of GLS estimation is the insight it provides into the impact of conditional heteroskedasticity and serial correlation on the estimation and inference of the linear regression model. In practice, the GLS estimator is generally not feasible, because the $n \times n$ matrix $\mathbf{V}$ is of unknown form, where $\text{var}(\varepsilon|\mathbf{X}) = \sigma^2\mathbf{V}$.

Question: What are feasible solutions?

There are at least two approaches to dealing with this problem. We now provide some brief discussions.

(1) Approach I: Adaptive Feasible GLS Estimation

In some cases with additional assumptions, we can use a nonparametric estimator $\hat{\mathbf{V}}$ to replace the unknown $\mathbf{V}$, we obtain an adaptive feasible GLS estimator

$$\hat{\beta}_a^* = (\mathbf{X}'\hat{\mathbf{V}}^{-1}\mathbf{X})^{-1}\mathbf{X}'\hat{\mathbf{V}}^{-1}Y,$$

where $\hat{\mathbf{V}}$ is an estimator for $\mathbf{V}$. Because $\mathbf{V}$ is an $n \times n$ unknown matrix and we only have n data points, it is impossible to estimate $\mathbf{V}$ consistently using a sample of size n if we do not impose any restriction on the form of $\mathbf{V}$. In other words, we have to impose some restrictions on $\mathbf{V}$ in order to estimate it consistently. For example, suppose we assume

$$\begin{aligned}\sigma^2\mathbf{V} &= \text{diag}\{\sigma_1^2(\mathbf{X}), ..., \sigma_n^2(\mathbf{X})\} \\ &= \text{diag}\{\sigma^2(X_1), ..., \sigma^2(X_n)\},\end{aligned}$$

where $\text{diag}\{\cdot\}$ is an $n \times n$ diagonal matrix and $\sigma^2(X_t) = E(\varepsilon_t^2|X_t)$ is unknown. The fact that $\sigma^2\mathbf{V}$ is a diagonal matrix can arise when $\text{cov}(\varepsilon_t\varepsilon_s|\mathbf{X}) = 0$ for all $t \neq s$, i.e., when there is no serial correlation. Then we can use a nonparametric kernel estimator

$$\begin{aligned}\hat{\sigma}^2(x) &= \frac{\frac{1}{n}\sum_{t=1}^n e_t^2 \frac{1}{b} K\left(\frac{x-X_t}{b}\right)}{\frac{1}{n}\sum_{t=1}^n \frac{1}{b} K\left(\frac{x-X_t}{b}\right)} \\ &\xrightarrow{p} \sigma^2(x),\end{aligned}$$

where e_t is the estimated OLS residual, and $K(\cdot)$ is a kernel function which is a specified symmetric density function (e.g., $K(u) = (2\pi)^{-1/2}\exp(-\frac{1}{2}u^2)$ if x is a scalar, and $b = b(n)$ is a bandwidth such that $b \to 0, nb \to \infty$ as $n \to \infty$. The finite sample distribution of $\hat{\beta}_a^*$ will be different from the finite sample distribution of $\hat{\beta}^*$, which assumes that $\mathbf{V}$ was known. This is because the sampling errors of the estimator $\hat{\mathbf{V}}$ have some impact on the estimator $\hat{\beta}_a^*$. However, under some suitable conditions on $\hat{\mathbf{V}}$, $\hat{\beta}_a^*$ will share the same asymptotic property as the infeasible GLS estimator $\hat{\beta}^*$ (i.e., the MSE of $\hat{\beta}_a^*$ is approximately equal to the MSE of $\hat{\beta}^*$). In other words, the first stage estimation of $\sigma^2(\cdot)$ has no impact on the asymptotic distribution of $\hat{\beta}_a^*$. For more discussion, see Robinson (1988) and White and Stinchcombe (1991).

(2) Approach II: Heteroskedasticity and Autocorrelation Consistent (HAC) Variance-Covariance Matrix Estimation

The second approach is to continue to use the OLS estimator $\hat{\beta}$ and obtain a consistent estimator for

$$\text{var}(\hat{\beta}|\mathbf{X}) = \sigma^2(\mathbf{X}'\mathbf{X})^{-1}\mathbf{X}'\mathbf{V}\mathbf{X}(\mathbf{X}'\mathbf{X})^{-1}.$$

The classical definitions of t- and F-test statistics cannot be used, because they are based on an incorrect formula for $\text{var}(\hat{\beta}|\mathbf{X})$. However, some modified tests can be obtained by using a consistent estimator for the correct formula for $\text{var}(\hat{\beta}|\mathbf{X})$. The trick is to estimate $\sigma^2\mathbf{X}'\mathbf{V}\mathbf{X}$, which is a $K \times K$ unknown matrix, rather than to estimate $\mathbf{V}$, which is an $n \times n$ unknown matrix, where K is much smaller than the sample size n. However, only asymptotic distributions can be used in this case.

Suppose now we have

$$\begin{aligned} E(\varepsilon\varepsilon'|\mathbf{X}) &= \sigma^2\mathbf{V} \\ &= \text{diag}\{\sigma_1^2(\mathbf{X}), ..., \sigma_n^2(\mathbf{X})\}. \end{aligned}$$

As pointed out earlier, this essentially assumes $E(\varepsilon_t\varepsilon_s|\mathbf{X}) = 0$ for all $t \neq s$. That is, there is no serial correlation in $\{\varepsilon_t\}$ conditional on $\mathbf{X}$. Instead of attempting to estimate $\sigma_t^2(\mathbf{X})$, one can estimate the $K \times K$ matrix $\sigma^2\mathbf{X}'\mathbf{V}\mathbf{X}$ directly.

Question: How to estimate

$$\sigma^2\mathbf{X}'\mathbf{V}\mathbf{X} = \sum_{t=1}^{n} X_t X_t' \sigma_t^2(\mathbf{X})?$$

We can use the following variance estimator

$$\mathbf{X}'\text{D}(e)\text{D}(e)'\mathbf{X} = \sum_{t=1}^{n} X_t X_t' e_t^2,$$

where $\text{D}(e) = \text{diag}(e_1, ..., e_n)$ is an $n \times n$ diagonal matrix with all off-diagonal elements being zero. This is called White's (1980) heteroskedasticity-consistent variance-covariance matrix estimator. See more discussion in Chapter 4.

Question: For $J = 1$, do we have

$$\frac{R\hat{\beta} - r}{\sqrt{R(\mathbf{X}'\mathbf{X})^{-1}\mathbf{X}'\mathrm{D}(e)\mathrm{D}(e)'\mathbf{X}(\mathbf{X}'\mathbf{X})^{-1}R'}} \sim t_{n-K}?$$

For $J > 1$, do we have

$$(R\hat{\beta} - r)' \left[R(\mathbf{X}'\mathbf{X})^{-1}\mathbf{X}'\mathrm{D}(e)\mathrm{D}(e)'\mathbf{X}(\mathbf{X}'\mathbf{X})^{-1}R'\right]^{-1} (R\hat{\beta} - r)/J \sim F_{J,n-K}?$$

No. Although we have standardized both test statistics by the correct variance estimators, we still have $\mathrm{cov}(\hat{\beta}, e|\mathbf{X}) \neq 0$ under Assumption 3.6. This implies that $\hat{\beta}$ and e are not independent, and therefore, we no longer have a t-distribution or an F-distribution in finite samples.

However, when $n \to \infty$, we have

- Case I: When $J = 1$,

$$\frac{R\hat{\beta} - r}{\sqrt{R(\mathbf{X}'\mathbf{X})^{-1}\mathbf{X}'\mathrm{D}(e)\mathrm{D}(e)'\mathbf{X}(\mathbf{X}'\mathbf{X})^{-1}R'}} \xrightarrow{d} N(0, 1).$$

  This can be called a robust t-test.
- Case II: When $J > 1$,

$$(R\hat{\beta} - r)' \left[R(\mathbf{X}'\mathbf{X})^{-1}\mathbf{X}'\mathrm{D}(e)\mathrm{D}(e)'\mathbf{X}(\mathbf{X}'\mathbf{X})^{-1}R'\right]^{-1} (R\hat{\beta} - r) \xrightarrow{d} \chi^2_J.$$

  This is called a robust Wald test statistic.

The above two feasible solutions are based on the assumption that $E(\varepsilon_t\varepsilon_s|\mathbf{X}) = 0$ for all $t \neq s$.

In fact, we can also consistently estimate the limit of $\mathbf{X}'\mathbf{V}\mathbf{X}$ when there exists conditional heteroskedasticity and autocorrelation simultaneously. This is called Heteroskedasticity and Autocorrelation Consistent (HAC) variance-covariance matrix estimation. When there exists serial correlation of unknown form, an alternative solution should be provided. This is discussed in Chapter 6. See also Andrews (1991) and Newey and West (1987, 1994).

3.10 Conclusion

In this chapter, we have presented the econometric theory for the classical linear regression models. We first provide and discuss a set of assumptions on which the classical linear regression model is built. This set of regularity conditions will serve as the starting points from which we will develop modern econometric theory for linear regression models.

We derive the statistical properties of the OLS estimator. In particular, we point out that R^2 is not a suitable model selection criterion, because it is always nondecreasing with the dimension of regressors. Suitable model selection criteria, such as AIC and BIC, are discussed. We show that conditional on the regressor matrix $\mathbf{X}$, the OLS estimator $\hat{\beta}$ is unbiased, has a vanishing variance, and is BLUE. Under the additional conditional normality assumption, we derive the finite sample normal distribution for $\hat{\beta}$, the Chi-squared distribution for $(n-K)s^2/\sigma^2$, as well as the independence between $\hat{\beta}$ and s^2.

Many hypotheses encountered in economics can be formulated as linear restrictions on model parameters. Depending on the number of parameter restrictions, we construct the t-test and the F-test statistics. In the special case of testing the hypothesis that all slope coefficients are jointly zero, we also construct an asymptotically Chi-squared test statistic based on R^2.

When there exist(s) conditional heteroskedasticity and/or autocorrelation, the OLS estimator is still unbiased and has a vanishing variance, but it is no longer BLUE, and $\hat{\beta}$ and s^2 are no longer mutually independent. Under the assumption of a known variance-covariance matrix up to some scale parameter, one can transform the linear regression model by correcting conditional heteroskedasticity and eliminating autocorrelation, so that the transformed regression model has conditionally homoskedastic and uncorrelated errors. The OLS estimator of this transformed linear regression model is called the GLS estimator, which is BLUE. The t-test and F-test statistics are applicable. When the variance-covariance structure is unknown, the GLS estimator becomes infeasible. However, if the error in the original linear regression model is serially uncorrelated (as is the case with independent observations across t), there are two feasible solutions. The first is to use a nonparametric method to obtain a consistent estimator for the conditional variance $\text{var}(\varepsilon_t|X_t)$, and then obtain a feasible plug-in GLS estimator. The second is to use White's (1980) heteroskedasticity-consistent variance-covariance matrix estimator for the OLS estimator $\hat{\beta}$. Both of these two methods are built on the asymptotic theory. When the error of the original linear regression model is serially correlated, a feasible solution to estimate the variance-covariance matrix is provided in Chapter 6.

This chapter is the foundation of modern econometrics. We will relax the most classical assumptions of this chapter and develop modern econometric theory in subsequent chapters. As we will see, existence of heteroskedasticity and/or autocorrelation, endogeneity and model misspecification will significantly change econometric inference procedures and extend the scope of application of econometric methods and models.

It may be noted that most materials in this chapter overlap with Chapter 10 of *Probability and Statistics for Economists* by Hong (2017).

Exercise 3

3.1. Suppose $\mathbf{Y} = \mathbf{X}\beta^o + \varepsilon$, $\mathbf{X}'\mathbf{X}$ is nonsingular. Let $\hat{\beta} = (\mathbf{X}'\mathbf{X})^{-1}\mathbf{X}'\mathbf{Y}$ be the OLS estimator and $e = \mathbf{Y} - \mathbf{X}\hat{\beta}$ be the $n \times 1$ estimated residual vector. Define an $n \times n$ projection matrix $\mathbf{P} = \mathbf{X}(\mathbf{X}'\mathbf{X})^{-1}\mathbf{X}'$ and $\mathbf{M} = \mathbf{I} - \mathbf{P}$, where $\mathbf{I}$ is an $n \times n$ identity matrix. Show:

(1) $\mathbf{X}'e = 0$.

(2) $\hat{\beta} - \beta^o = (\mathbf{X}'\mathbf{X})^{-1}\mathbf{X}'\varepsilon$.

(3) $\mathbf{P}$ and $\mathbf{M}$ are symmetric and idempotent (i.e., $\mathbf{P}^2 = \mathbf{P}, \mathbf{M}^2 = \mathbf{M}$), $\mathbf{PX} = \mathbf{X}$, and $\mathbf{MX} = 0$.

(4) $SSR(\hat{\beta}) \equiv e'e = \mathbf{Y}'\mathbf{MY} = \varepsilon'\mathbf{M}\varepsilon$.

3.2. Consider a bivariate linear regression model

$$Y_t = X_t'\beta^o + \varepsilon_t, \qquad t = 1, ..., n,$$

where $X_t = (X_{0t}, X_{1t})' = (1, X_{1t})'$, and ε_t is a regression disturbance.

(1) Let $\hat{\beta} = (\hat{\beta}_0, \hat{\beta}_1)'$ be the OLS estimator. Show that $\hat{\beta}_0 = \bar{Y} - \hat{\beta}_1\bar{X}_1$, and

$$\begin{aligned}\hat{\beta}_1 &= \frac{\sum_{t=1}^n (X_{1t} - \bar{X}_1)(Y_t - \bar{Y})}{\sum_{t=1}^n (X_{1t} - \bar{X}_1)^2} \\ &= \frac{\sum_{t=1}^n (X_{1t} - \bar{X}_1)Y_t}{\sum_{t=1}^n (X_{1t} - \bar{X}_1)^2} \\ &= \sum_{t=1}^n C_t Y_t,\end{aligned}$$

where $C_t = (X_{1t} - \bar{X}_1)/\sum_{t=1}^n (X_{1t} - \bar{X}_1)^2$.

(2) Suppose $\mathbf{X} = (X_{11}, ..., X_{1n})'$ and $\varepsilon = (\varepsilon_1, ..., \varepsilon_n)'$ are independent. Show that $\text{var}(\hat{\beta}_1|\mathbf{X}) = \sigma_\varepsilon^2/[(n-1)S_{X_1}^2]$, where $S_{X_1}^2$ is the sample variance of $\{X_{1t}\}_{t=1}^n$ and σ_ε^2 is the variance of ε_t. Thus, the more variations in $\{X_{1t}\}$, the more accurate estimation for β_1^o.

(3) Let $\hat{\rho}$ denote the sample correlation between Y_t and X_{1t}; namely,

$$\hat{\rho} = \frac{\sum_{t=1}^n (X_{1t} - \bar{X}_1)(Y_t - \bar{Y})}{\sqrt{\sum_{t=1}^n (X_{1t} - \bar{X}_1)^2 \sum_{t=1}^n (Y_t - \bar{Y})^2}}.$$

Show that $R^2 = \hat{\rho}^2$. Thus, the squared sample correlation between Y and X_1 is the fraction of the sample variation in Y that can be predicted using the linear predictor of X_1. This result also implies that R^2 is a measure of the strength of sample linear association between Y_t and X_{1t}.

3.3. For the OLS estimation of the linear regression model $Y_t = X_t'\beta^o + \varepsilon$, where X_t is a $K \times 1$ vector, show $R^2 = \hat{\rho}^2_{Y\hat{Y}}$, the squared sample correlation between Y_t and $\hat{Y}_t$.

3.4. Does a high value of R^2 imply a precise OLS estimation for the true parameter value β^o in a linear regression model $Y_t = X_t'\beta^o + \varepsilon_t$? Explain.

3.5. You devise a clever economic theory leading to a simple regression, which you fit: $Y_t = \hat{\alpha} + \hat{\beta}X_t + e_t$. Your fit is good, with a high R^2 (denoted as R_1^2) and a large t-statistic (denoted as t_1). Later that evening you have a flash of inspiration: perhaps economics is all wrong, agents are irrational, equilibria do not exist, etc. Perhaps you also have some doubts about whether you derived your equation correctly. Consequently, you fit $X_t = \hat{\alpha}_2 + \hat{\beta}_2 Y_t + e_{2t}$, again finding satisfactory results (a high R_2^2 and a large t-statistic t_2) and confirming your doubts. The next morning you think this through. What are the relationships between the followings:

(1) R_1^2 and R_2^2? Give your reasoning.

(2) $\hat{\beta}$ and $\hat{\beta}_2$? Give your reasoning.

(3) t_1 and t_2? Give your reasoning.

3.6. Suppose $X_t = Q$ for all $t \geq m$, where m is a fixed integer, and Q is a $K \times 1$ constant vector. Do we have $\lambda_{\min}(\mathbf{X}'\mathbf{X}) \to \infty$ as $n \to \infty$? Explain.

3.7. The adjusted R^2, denoted as $\bar{R}^2$, is defined as follows:

$$\bar{R}^2 = 1 - \frac{e'e/(n-K)}{(Y-\bar{Y})'(Y-\bar{Y})/(n-1)}.$$

Show

$$\bar{R}^2 = 1 - \left[\frac{n-1}{n-K}(1-R^2)\right].$$

3.8. *[Effect of Multicollinearity]:* Consider a regression model

$$Y_t = \beta_0 + \beta_1 X_{1t} + \beta_2 X_{2t} + \varepsilon_t.$$

Suppose Assumptions 3.1 to 3.4 hold. Let $\hat{\beta} = (\hat{\beta}_0, \hat{\beta}_1, \hat{\beta}_2)'$ be the OLS estimator. Show

$$\text{var}(\hat{\beta}_1|\mathbf{X}) = \frac{\sigma^2}{(1-\hat{r}^2)\sum_{t=1}^n (X_{1t}-\bar{X}_1)^2},$$

$$\text{var}(\hat{\beta}_2|\mathbf{X}) = \frac{\sigma^2}{(1-\hat{r}^2)\sum_{t=1}^n (X_{2t}-\bar{X}_2)^2},$$

where $\bar{X}_1 = n^{-1}\sum_{t=1}^n X_{1t}, \bar{X}_2 = n^{-1}\sum_{t=1}^n X_{2t}$, and

$$\hat{r}^2 = \frac{\left[\sum_{t=1}^n (X_{1t}-\bar{X}_1)(X_{2t}-\bar{X}_2)\right]^2}{\sum_{t=1}^n (X_{1t}-\bar{X}_1)^2 \sum_{t=1}^n (X_{2t}-\bar{X}_2)^2}.$$

3.9. Consider the linear regression model

$$Y_t = X_t'\beta^o + \varepsilon_t,$$

where $X_t = (1, X_{1t}, ..., X_{kt})'$. Suppose Assumptions 3.1 to 3.3 hold. Let R_j^2 is the coefficient of determination of regressing variable X_{jt} on all the other explanatory variables $\{X_{it}, 0 \le i \le k, i \ne j\}$. Show

$$\operatorname{var}(\hat{\beta}_j|\mathbf{X}) = \frac{\sigma^2}{(1-R_j^2)\sum_{t=1}^n (X_{jt}-\bar{X}_j)^2},$$

where $\bar{X}_j = n^{-1}\sum_{t=1}^n X_{jt}$. The factor $1/(1-R_j^2)$ is called the Variance Inflation Factor (VIF), which is used to measure the degree of multicollinearity among explanatory variables in X_t.

3.10. Suppose Assumptions 3.1, 3.2, 3.3(a), and 3.5 hold, and there exists near-multicollinearity such that $\lambda_{\min}(\mathbf{X}'\mathbf{X})$ is nonzero but does not go to infinity as $n \to \infty$.

(1) Is the OLS estimator $\hat{\beta}$ unbiased for β^o? Give your reasoning.

(2) Is the OLS estimator $\hat{\beta}$ consistent for β^o as $n \to \infty$? Give your reasoning.

(3) Are the t-test and F-test statistics still valid for testing the null hypothesis that $R\beta'^o = r$? Give your reasoning.

3.11. Consider the following estimation results for three separate regressions based on the same data set with $n = 25$. The first is a regression of consumption on income:

$$Y_t = 36.74 + 0.832X_{1t} + e_{1t}, \qquad R^2 = 0.735,$$
$$[1.98][7.98]$$

the second is a regression of consumption on wealth:

$$Y_t = 36.61 + 0.208X_{2t} + e_{2t}, \qquad R^2 = 0.735,$$
$$[1.97][7.99]$$

and the third is a regression of consumption on both income and wealth:

$$Y = 33.88 - 26.00X_{1t} + 6.71X_{2t} + e_t, \qquad R^2 = 0.742.$$
$$[1.77][-0.74][0.77]$$

(1) In the first two separate regressions, we observe significant t-test statistics for income and wealth respectively, but in the third joint regression, both income and wealth are insignificant. What are possible reasons for the apparently conflicting results? Can we conclude that income and wealth have impact on consumption? Explain.

(2) To test neither income nor wealth has impact on consumption, we can use the F-test. Can you reach a decisive conclusion at the 5% significance level? Explain.

3.12. For the regression model $Y_i = \alpha + \beta X_i + \varepsilon_i$ with $X_i \in \{0, 1\}$ a binary variable, $P(\varepsilon_i = -1) = 2/3$, $P(\varepsilon_i = 2) = 1/3$ and $E(\varepsilon_i \varepsilon_j) = 0$ for $i \neq j$.

(1) Is the OLS estimator unbiased?

(2) Is the OLS estimator BLUE?

(3) Give a better estimator.

For Parts (1) to (3), explain briefly but intelligently.

3.13. Consider the following linear regression model

$$Y_t = X_t'\beta^o + u_t, \qquad t = 1, ..., n, \tag{A.3.1}$$

where $u_t = \sigma(X_t)\varepsilon_t$, where $\{X_t\}$ is a nonstochastic process, and $\sigma(X_t)$ is a positive function of X_t such that

$$\Omega = \begin{bmatrix} \sigma^2(X_1) & 0 & 0 & \ldots & 0 \\ 0 & \sigma^2(X_2) & 0 & \ldots & 0 \\ 0 & 0 & \sigma^2(X_3) & \ldots & 0 \\ \ldots & \ldots & \ldots & \ldots & \ldots \\ 0 & 0 & 0 & \ldots & \sigma^2(X_n) \end{bmatrix} = \Omega^{\frac{1}{2}}\Omega^{\frac{1}{2}},$$

with

$$\Omega^{\frac{1}{2}} = \begin{bmatrix} \sigma(X_1) & 0 & 0 & \ldots & 0 \\ 0 & \sigma(X_2) & 0 & \ldots & 0 \\ 0 & 0 & \sigma(X_3) & \ldots & 0 \\ \ldots & \ldots & \ldots & \ldots & \ldots \\ 0 & 0 & 0 & \ldots & \sigma(X_n) \end{bmatrix}.$$

Assume that $\{\varepsilon_t\}$ is IID $N(0, 1)$. Then $\{u_t\}$ is IID $N(0, \sigma^2(X_t))$. This differs from Assumption 3.5 of the classical linear regression analysis, because now $\{u_t\}$ exhibits conditional heteroskedasticity.

Let $\hat{\beta}$ denote the OLS estimator for β^o.

(1) Is $\hat{\beta}$ unbiased for β^o?

(2) Show that $\text{var}(\hat{\beta}) = (\mathbf{X}'\mathbf{X})^{-1}\mathbf{X}'\Omega\mathbf{X}(\mathbf{X}'\mathbf{X})^{-1}$.

Now consider an alternative estimator

$$\begin{aligned}\tilde{\beta} &= (\mathbf{X}'\Omega^{-1}\mathbf{X})^{-1}\mathbf{X}'\Omega^{-1}Y \\ &= \left[\sum_{t=1}^{n}\sigma^{-2}(X_t)X_tX_t'\right]^{-1}\sum_{t=1}^{n}\sigma^{-2}(X_t)X_tY_t.\end{aligned}$$

(3) Is $\tilde{\beta}$ unbiased for β^o?

(4) Show that $\text{var}(\tilde{\beta}) = (\mathbf{X}'\Omega^{-1}\mathbf{X})^{-1}$.

(5) Is $\text{var}(\hat{\beta})-\text{var}(\tilde{\beta})$ PSD? Which estimator, $\hat{\beta}$ or $\tilde{\beta}$, is more efficient?

(6) Is $\tilde{\beta}$ BLUE for β^o? *[Hint: There are several approaches to this question. A simple one is to consider the transformed model*

$$Y_t^* = X_t^{*\prime}\beta^o + \varepsilon_t, \qquad t = 1, ..., n, \tag{A.3.2}$$

where $Y_t^* = Y_t/\sigma(X_t), X_t^* = X_t/\sigma(X_t)$. *This model is obtained from model (A.3.1) after dividing by* $\sigma(X_t)$. *In matrix notation, model (A.3.2) can be written as*

$$Y^* - \mathbf{X}^*\beta^o + \varepsilon,$$

where the $n \times 1$ *vector* $Y^* = \Omega^{-\frac{1}{2}}Y$ *and the* $n \times k$ *matrix* $\mathbf{X}^* = \Omega^{-\frac{1}{2}}\mathbf{X}$.*]*

(7) Construct two test statistics for the null hypothesis of interest $\mathbf{H}_0 : \beta_2^o = 0$. One test is based on $\hat{\beta}$, and the other test is based on $\tilde{\beta}$. What are the finite sample distributions of your test statistics under $\mathbf{H}_0$? Can you tell which test is better?

(8) Construct two test statistics for the null hypothesis of interest $\mathbf{H}_0 : R\beta^o = r$, where R is a $J \times k$ matrix with $J > 1$. One test is based on $\hat{\beta}$, and the other test is based on $\tilde{\beta}$. What are the finite sample distributions of your test statistics under $\mathbf{H}_0$?

3.14. Consider the classical regression model

$$Y_t = X_t'\beta^o + \varepsilon_t.$$

Suppose that we are interested in testing the null hypothesis

$$\mathbf{H}_0 : R\beta^o = r,$$

where R is a $J \times K$ matrix, and r is a $J \times 1$ vector. The F-test statistic is defined as

$$F = \frac{(R\hat{\beta} - r)'[R(X'X)^{-1}R']^{-1}(R\hat{\beta} - r)/J}{s^2}.$$

Show that

$$F = \frac{(\tilde{e}'\tilde{e} - e'e)/J}{e'e/(n-k-1)},$$

where $e'e$ is the SSR from the unrestricted model, and $\tilde{e}'\tilde{e}$ is the SSR from the restricted regression model subject to the restriction $R\beta = r$.

3.15. The F-test statistic is defined as follows:

$$F = \frac{(R\hat{\beta} - r)'[R(\mathbf{X}'\mathbf{X})^{-1}R']^{-1}(R\hat{\beta} - r)/J}{s^2}.$$

Show that

$$\begin{aligned} F &= \frac{\sum_{t=1}^{n}(\hat{Y}_t - \tilde{Y}_t)^2/J}{s^2} \\ &= \frac{(\hat{\beta} - \tilde{\beta})'X'X(\hat{\beta} - \tilde{\beta})/J}{s^2}, \end{aligned}$$

where $\hat{Y}_t = X_t'\hat{\beta}, \tilde{Y}_t = X_t'\tilde{\beta}$, and $\hat{\beta}$ and $\tilde{\beta}$ are the unrestricted and restricted OLS estimators respectively.

3.16. Show that the F-test statistic is equivalent to a quadratic form in $\tilde{\lambda}$, where $\tilde{\lambda}$ is the Lagrange multiplier in the constrained OLS estimation for the linear regression $\mathbf{Y} = \mathbf{X}\beta^o + \varepsilon$. This result implies that the F-test is equivalent to a Lagrange multiplier test.

3.17. Consider the following classical regression model

$$\begin{aligned} Y_t &= X_t'\beta^o + \varepsilon_t \\ &= \beta_0^o + \sum_{j=1}^{k}\beta_j^o X_{jt} + \varepsilon_t, \qquad t = 1, ..., n. \end{aligned} \tag{A.3.3}$$

Suppose that we are interested in testing the null hypothesis

$$\mathbf{H}_0 : \beta_1^o = \beta_2^o = \cdots = \beta_k^o = 0.$$

Then the F-statistic can be written as

$$F = \frac{(\tilde{e}'\tilde{e} - e'e)/k}{e'e/(n-k-1)}.$$

where $e'e$ is the SSR from the unrestricted model (A.3.3), and $\tilde{e}'\tilde{e}$ is the SSR from the restricted model (A.3.4)

$$Y_t = \beta_0^o + \varepsilon_t. \qquad \text{(A.3.4)}$$

(1) Show that under Assumptions 3.1 and 3.3,

$$F = \frac{R^2/k}{(1-R^2)/(n-k-1)},$$

where R^2 is the coefficient of determination of the unrestricted model (A.3.3).

(2) Suppose in addition Assumption 3.5 holds. Show that under $\mathbf{H}_0$,

$$(n-k-1)R^2 \xrightarrow{d} \chi_k^2.$$

3.18. The F-test statistic is defined as follows:

$$F = \frac{(R\hat{\beta} - r)'[R(\mathbf{X}'\mathbf{X})^{-1}R']^{-1}(R\hat{\beta} - r)/J}{s^2}.$$

Show that

$$F = \frac{(1/J)\sum_{t=1}^{n}(\hat{Y}_t - \tilde{Y}_t)^2}{s^2} = \frac{(\hat{\beta} - \tilde{\beta})'X'X(\hat{\beta} - \tilde{\beta})/J}{s^2},$$

where $\hat{Y}_t = X_t'\hat{\beta}, \tilde{Y}_t = X_t'\tilde{\beta}$, and $\hat{\beta}$ and $\tilde{\beta}$ are the unrestricted and restricted OLS estimators respectively.

3.19. *[Structural Change]:* Suppose Assumptions 3.1 and 3.3 hold. Consider the following model on the whole sample:

$$Y_t = X_t'\beta^o + (D_t X_t)'\alpha^o + \varepsilon_t, t = 1, ..., n,$$

where the time dummy variable $D_t = 0$ if $t \leq n_1$ and $D_t = 1$ if $t > n_1$. This model can be written as two separate models:

$$Y_t = X_t'\beta^o + \varepsilon_t, t = 1, ..., n_1$$

and

$$Y_t = X_t'(\beta^o + \alpha^o) + \varepsilon_t, t = n_1 + 1, ..., n.$$

Let SSR_u, SSR_1, and SSR_2 denote the SSRs of the above three regression models via OLS estimation. Show

$$SSR_u = SSR_1 + SSR_2.$$

This identity implies that estimating the first regression model with time dummy variable D_t via the OLS estimation is equivalent to estimating two separate regression models over two subsample periods respectively.

3.20. A quadratic polynomial regression model

$$Y_t = \beta_0 + \beta_1 X_t + \beta_2 X_t^2 + \varepsilon_t$$

is fit to data. Suppose the P-value for the OLS estimator of β_1 was 0.67 and for β_2 was 0.84. Can we accept the hypothesis that β_1 and β_2 are both 0? Explain.

3.21. Suppose $\mathbf{X}'\mathbf{X}$ is a $K \times K$ matrix, and $\mathbf{V}$ is an $n \times n$ matrix, and both $\mathbf{X}'\mathbf{X}$ and $\mathbf{V}$ are symmetric and nonsingular, with the minimum eigenvalue $\lambda_{\min}(\mathbf{X}'\mathbf{X}) \to \infty$ as $n \to \infty$ and $0 < c \leq \lambda_{\max}(\mathbf{V}) \leq C < \infty$. Show that for any $\tau \in R^K$ such that $\tau'\tau = 1$,

$$\tau' \mathrm{var}(\hat{\beta}|\mathbf{X})\tau = \sigma^2 \tau'(\mathbf{X}'\mathbf{X})^{-1}\mathbf{X}'\mathbf{V}\mathbf{X}(\mathbf{X}'\mathbf{X})^{-1}\tau \to 0$$

as $n \to \infty$. Thus, $\mathrm{var}(\hat{\beta}|\mathbf{X})$ vanishes to zero as $n \to \infty$ under conditional heteroskedasticity.

3.22. Suppose the conditions in Exercise 3.13 hold. It can be shown that the variances of the OLS estimator $\hat{\beta}$ and the GLS estimator $\hat{\beta}^*$ are respectively:

$$\mathrm{var}(\hat{\beta}|\mathbf{X}) = \sigma^2(\mathbf{X}'\mathbf{X})^{-1}\mathbf{X}'\mathbf{V}\mathbf{X}(\mathbf{X}'\mathbf{X})^{-1},$$
$$\mathrm{var}(\hat{\beta}^*|\mathbf{X}) = \sigma^2(\mathbf{X}'\mathbf{V}^{-1}\mathbf{X})^{-1}.$$

Show that $\mathrm{var}(\hat{\beta}|\mathbf{X})-$ $\mathrm{var}(\hat{\beta}^*|\mathbf{X})$ is PSD.

3.23. Suppose a DGP is given by

$$Y_t = \beta_1^o X_{1t} + \beta_2^o X_{2t} + \varepsilon_t = X_t'\beta^o + \varepsilon_t,$$

where $X_t = (X_{1t}, X_{2t})'$, $E(X_t X_t')$ is nonsingular, and $E(\varepsilon_t|X_t) = 0$. For simplicity, we further assume that $E(X_{2t}) = 0$ and $E(X_{1t}X_{2t}) \neq 0$.

Now consider the bivariate linear regression model

$$Y_t = \beta_1^o X_{1t} + u_t.$$

(1) Show that if $\beta_2^o \neq 0$, then $E(Y_1|X_t) = X_t'\beta^o \neq E(Y_{1t}|X_{1t})$. That is, there exists an omitted variable (i.e., X_{2t}) in the bivariate regression model.

(2) Show that $E(Y_t|X_{1t}) \neq \beta_1 X_{1t}$ for all β_1. That is, the bivariate linear regression model is misspecified for $E(Y_t|X_{1t})$.

(3) Is the best linear least squares approximation coefficient β_1^* in the bivariate linear regression model equal to β_1^o?

3.24. Suppose a DGP is given by

$$Y_t = \beta_1^o X_{1t} + \beta_2^o X_{2t} + \varepsilon_t = X_t'\beta^o + \varepsilon_t,$$

where $X_t = (X_{1t}, X_{2t})'$, and Assumptions 3.1 to 3.4 hold. (For simplicity, we have assumed no intercept.) Denote the OLS estimator by $\hat{\beta} = (\hat{\beta}_1, \hat{\beta}_2)'$.

If $\beta_2^o = 0$ and we know it, then we can consider a simpler regression

$$Y_t = \beta_1^o X_{1t} + \varepsilon_t.$$

Denote the OLS estimator of this simpler regression as $\tilde{\beta}_1$.

Compare the relative efficiency between $\hat{\beta}_1$ and $\tilde{\beta}_1$. That is, which estimator is better for β_1^o? Give your reasoning.

3.25. Consider a linear regression model $\mathbf{Y} = \mathbf{X}\beta^o + \varepsilon$, where $\varepsilon|\mathbf{X} \sim N(0, \sigma^2\mathbf{V})$, $\mathbf{V} = V(\mathbf{X})$ is a known $n \times n$ nonsingular matrix, and $0 < \sigma^2 < \infty$ is unknown. The GLS estimator $\hat{\beta}^*$ is defined as the OLS estimator of the transformed model

$$\mathbf{Y}^* = \mathbf{X}^*\beta^o + \varepsilon^*,$$

where $\mathbf{Y}^* = \mathbf{CY}, \mathbf{X}^* = C\mathbf{X}, \varepsilon^* = \mathbf{C}\varepsilon$, and $\mathbf{C}$ is an $n \times n$ nonsingular matrix from the factorization $\mathbf{V}^{-1} = CC'$. Is the coefficient of determination R^2 for the transformed model always positive? Explain.

3.26. Suppose Assumption 3.6 is replaced by the following assumption:

Assumption 3.6′: $\varepsilon|\mathbf{X} \sim N(0, \mathbf{V})$, *where* $\mathbf{V} = V(\mathbf{X})$ *is a known* $n \times n$ *symmetrix, finite and positive definite matrix.*

Compared to Assumption 3.6, Assumption 3.6′ assumes that $\text{var}(\varepsilon|\mathbf{X}) = \mathbf{V}$ is completely known and there is no unknown proportionality σ^2. Define the GLS estimator $\hat{\beta}^* = (\mathbf{X}'\mathbf{V}^{-1}\mathbf{X})^{-1}\mathbf{X}'\mathbf{V}^{-1}Y$.

(1) Is $\hat{\beta}^*$ BLUE?

(2) Put $X^* = \mathbf{C}X$ and $s^{*2} = e^{*\prime}e^*/(n-K)$, where $e^* = Y - X^*\hat{\beta}^*$, $\mathbf{C}'\mathbf{C} = \mathbf{V}^{-1}$. Do the usual t-test and F-test statistics defined as

$$T^* = \frac{R\hat{\beta}^* - r}{\sqrt{s^{*2}R(\mathbf{X}^{*\prime}\mathbf{X}^*)^{-1}R'}}, \quad \text{for } J = 1,$$

$$F^* = \frac{(R\hat{\beta}^* - r)'[R(\mathbf{X}^{*\prime}\mathbf{X}^*)^{-1}R']^{-1}(R\hat{\beta}^* - r)/J}{s^{*2}},$$

follow the t_{n-K} and $F_{J,n-K}$ distributions respectively under the null hypothesis that $R\beta = r$? Explain.

(3) Construct two new test statistics:

$$\tilde{T}^* = \frac{R\hat{\beta}^* - r}{\sqrt{R(\mathbf{X}^{*\prime}\mathbf{X}^*)^{-1}R'}}, \quad \text{for } J = 1,$$

$$\tilde{Q}^* = (R\hat{\beta}^* - r)'[R(\mathbf{X}^{*\prime}\mathbf{X}^*)^{-1}R']^{-1}(R\hat{\beta}^* - r), \quad \text{for } J \geq 1.$$

What sampling distributions will these test statistics follow under the null hypothesis that $R\beta = r$? Explain.

(4) Which set of tests, (T^*, F^*) or $(\tilde{T}^*, \tilde{Q}^*)$, is more powerful at the same significance level? Explain. *[Hint: A Student's t-distribution has a heavier tail than $N(0,1)$ and so has a larger critical value at a given significance level.]*

3.27. Consider a linear regression model $Y_t = X_t'\beta^o + \varepsilon_t$, where X_t contains an intercept (i.e., $X_{0t} = 1$). Assume that all conditions for GLS estimation hold. We are interested in testing whether all coefficients except the intercept in the linear regression model are jointly zero.

(1) Do we still have

$$F^* = \frac{R^{*2}/k}{(1 - R^{*2})/(n-k-1)}?$$

Here R^{*2} and F^* are the centered R^2 and the F-test statistic obtained from the GLS estimation. Give your reasoning.

(2) Do we have $(n-K)R^{*2} \xrightarrow{d} \chi^2_k$ as $n \to \infty$ under the null hypothesis? Give your reasoning.

3.28. Consider a linear regression model

$$Y_t = X_t'\beta^o + \varepsilon_t, \qquad t = 1, 2, ..., n,$$

where $\varepsilon_t = \sigma(X_t)v_t$, X_t is a $K \times 1$ nonstochastic vector, and $\sigma(X_t)$ is a positive function of X_t, and $\{v_t\}$ is IID $N(0,1)$.

Let $\hat{\beta} = (\mathbf{X}'\mathbf{X})^{-1}\mathbf{X}'Y$ denote the OLS estimator for β^o, where $\mathbf{X}$ is an $n \times K$ matrix whose t-th row is X_t, and Y is an $n \times 1$ vector whose t-th component is Y_t.

(1) Is $\hat{\beta}$ unbiased for β^o?

(2) Find $\text{var}(\hat{\beta}) = E[(\hat{\beta} - E\hat{\beta})(\hat{\beta} - E\hat{\beta})']$. You may find the following notation useful: $\Omega = \text{diag}\{\sigma^2(X_1), \sigma^2(X_2), ..., \sigma^2(X_n)\}$, i.e., Ω is an $n \times n$ diagonal matrix with the t-th diagonal component equal to $\sigma^2(X_t)$ and all off-diagonal components equal to zero.

Now consider the transformed regression model

$$\frac{1}{\sigma(X_t)} Y_t = \frac{1}{\sigma(X_t)} X_t'\beta^o + v_t$$

or

$$Y_t^* = X_t^{*\prime}\beta^o + v_t,$$

where $Y_t^* = \sigma^{-1}(X_t)Y_t$ and $X_t^* = \sigma^{-1}(X_t)X_t$.

Denote the OLS estimator of this transformed model as $\tilde{\beta}$.

(3) Show $\tilde{\beta} = (X'\Omega^{-1}X)^{-1}X'\Omega^{-1}Y$.

(4) Is $\tilde{\beta}$ unbiased for β^o?

(5) Find $\text{var}(\tilde{\beta})$.

(6) Which estimator, $\hat{\beta}$ or $\tilde{\beta}$, is more efficient in terms of the MSE criterion? Give your reasoning.

(7) Use the difference $R\tilde{\beta} - r$ to construct a test statistic for the null hypothesis of interest $\mathbf{H}_0 : R\beta^o = r$, where R is a $J \times K$ matrix, r is $K \times 1$, and $J > 1$. What is the finite sample distribution of your test statistic under $\mathbf{H}_0$?

3.29. Consider a linear regression model

$$Y_t = X_t'\beta^o + \varepsilon_t, \qquad t = 1, ..., n,$$

where X_t is a $p \times 1$ regressor vector, β^o is a $p \times 1$ unknown vector, and $\{\varepsilon_t\}$ follows an AR(q) process, namely,

$$\varepsilon_t = \sum_{j=1}^{q} \alpha_j \varepsilon_{t-j} + v_t,$$

$$\{v_t\} \sim \text{IID}(0, \sigma_v^2).$$

We assume that the autoregressive coefficients $\{\alpha_j\}_{j=1}^q$ are known but σ_v^2 is unknown. Further assume that $\{X_t\}$ and $\{v_t\}$ are mutually independent.

(1) Find a BLUE estimator for β^o. Explain.

(2) Construct a test statistic for the null hypothesis $\mathbf{H}_0: R\beta^o = r$ and derive its sampling distribution under $\mathbf{H}_0$, where R is a known $J \times p$ nonstochastic matrix and r is a known $J \times 1$ nonstochastic vector. Discuss the cases of $J = 1$ and $J > 1$ respectively.

Chapter 4

Linear Regression Models with Independent Observations

Abstract: When the conditional normality assumption on the regression disturbance does not hold, the OLS estimator no longer has the finite sample normal distribution, and the t-test and F-test statistics no longer follow the Student's t-distribution and F-distribution in finite samples respectively. In this chapter, we show that under the assumption of IID observations with conditional homoskedasticity, the classical t-test and F-test are approximately applicable in large samples. However, under conditional heteroskedasticity, the t-test and F-test statistics are not applicable even when the sample size goes to infinity. Instead, White's (1980) heteroskedasticity-consistent variance-covariance matrix estimator should be used, which yields asymptotically valid confidence interval estimation and hypothesis test procedures. A direct test for conditional heteroskedasticity due to White (1980) is presented. To facilitate asymptotic analysis in this and subsequent chapters, we introduce some basic tools for asymptotic analysis in this chapter.

Keywords: Almost sure convergence, Asymptotic analysis, Asymptotic normality, Central Limit Theorem (CLT), Conditional heteroskedasticity, Conditional homoskedasticity, Consistency, Convergence in distribution, Convergence in probability, Convergence in quadratic mean, IID, Law of Large Numbers (LLN), Slutsky's theorem, White's heteroskedasticity-consistent variance-covariance matrix estimator

4.1 Introduction to Asymptotic Theory

The assumptions of classical linear regression models are rather strong and one may have a hard time finding practical applications where all these assumptions hold exactly. For example, the conditional normality condition on the disturbance ε is crucial to obtain the finite sample distributions of the OLS estimator, the GLS estimator and related test statistics, but it has been documented that most economic and financial data have heavy tails, and so they are not normally distributed. Figures 4.1 plots the histograms of time series data on the U.S. quarterly GDP growth rates, U.S. monthly inflation rates, and U.S. daily 10-year Treasury Bill rates respectively, which indicate that they do not follow a normal distribution.

An interesting question is whether the parameter estimators and test statistics which are based on the same principles as before still make sense

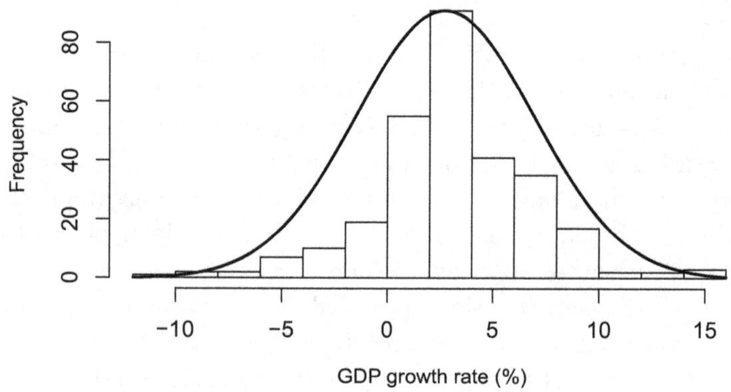

Figure 4.1 (a) Histograms of U.S. quarterly GDP growth rates from 1947-2018. Data source: https://www.macrotrends.net

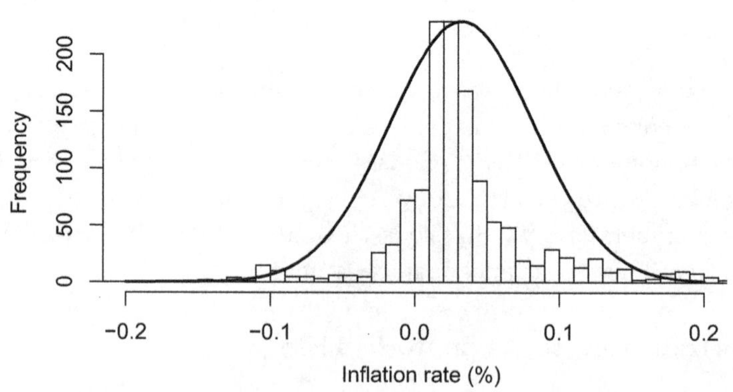

Figure 4.1 (b) Histograms of U.S. monthly inflation rates from 1914-2019. Data source: http://inflationdata.com

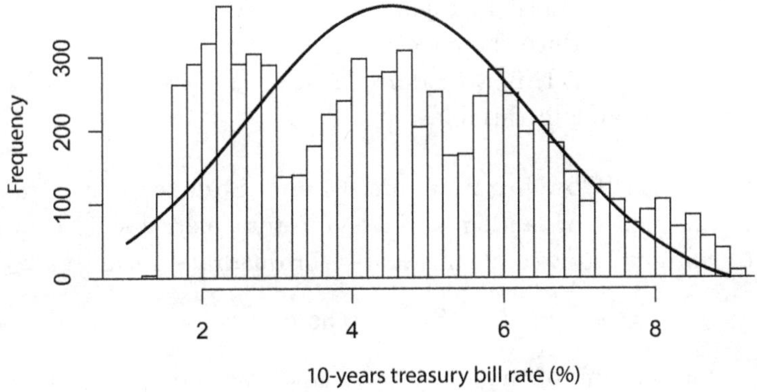

Figure 4.1 (c) Histograms of U.S. daily 10-year Treasury Bill rates from 1990-2019. Data source: https://www.treasury.gov

in this more general setting. In particular, what happens to the OLS estimator, and the t- and F-tests if any of the following assumptions fails:

- strict exogeneity $E(\varepsilon_t|\mathbf{X}) = 0$;
- conditional normality $\varepsilon|\mathbf{X} \sim N(0, \sigma^2 I)$;
- conditional homoskedasticity $\text{var}(\varepsilon_t|\mathbf{X}) = \sigma^2$;
- auto uncorrelatedness $\text{cov}(\varepsilon_t, \varepsilon_s|\mathbf{X}) = 0$ for $t \neq s$.

When classical assumptions are violated, we generally do not know the finite sample statistical properties of the parameter estimators and test statistics anymore. A useful tool to obtain the understanding of the statistical properties of parameter estimators and test statistics in this more general setting is to pretend that we can obtain a limitless number of observations. We can then pose the question how the parameter estimators and test statistics would behave when the number of observations increases without limit. This is called *asymptotic analysis.* In practice, the sample size is always finite. However, the asymptotic properties translate into results that hold true approximately in finite samples, provided that the sample size is large enough. We now need to introduce some basic analytic tools for asymptotic theory. For more systematic introduction of asymptotic theory, see, for example, White (1994, 2001) and Davidson (1994).

To assess how close the OLS estimator $\hat{\beta}$ is to the true parameter value β^o and to derive its asymptotic distribution (after suitable normalization), we briefly review some important convergence concepts and limit theorems.

Most of the materials in this section are borrowed from Hong (2017, Chapter 7). We first introduce the concept of convergence in mean squares (or quadratic mean), which is a distance measure of a sequence of random variables from a random variable.

Definition 4.1. [Convergence in Mean Squares or Quadratic Mean]: A sequence of random variables/vectors/matrices $Z_n, n = 1, 2, ...,$ is said to converge to Z in mean squares (or quadratic mean) as $n \to \infty$ if

$$E||Z_n - Z||^2 \to 0 \text{ as } n \to \infty,$$

where $||\cdot||$ is the sum of the absolute value of each component in $Z_n - Z$.

When Z_n is a vector or a matrix, convergence can be understood as convergence in each element of Z_n. When $Z_n - Z$ is an $l \times m$ matrix, where l and m are fixed positive integers, we can also define the squared norm as

$$||Z_n - Z||^2 = \sum_{t=1}^{l}\sum_{s=1}^{m}[Z_n - Z]^2_{(t,s)}.$$

Note that Z_n converges to Z in mean squares if and only if each component of Z_n converges to the corresponding component of Z in mean squares.

Example 4.1. Suppose $\{Z_t\}$ is IID(μ, σ^2), and $\bar{Z}_n = n^{-1}\sum_{t=1}^{n} Z_t$. Then

$$\bar{Z}_n \overset{q.m.}{\to} \mu.$$

Solution: Because $E(\bar{Z}_n) = \mu$, we have

$$\begin{aligned} E(\bar{Z}_n - \mu)^2 &= \text{var}(\bar{Z}_n) \\ &= \text{var}\left(n^{-1}\sum_{t=1}^{n} Z_t\right) \\ &= \frac{1}{n^2}\text{var}\left(\sum_{t=1}^{n} Z_t\right) \\ &= \frac{1}{n^2}\sum_{t=1}^{n}\text{var}(Z_t) \\ &= \frac{\sigma^2}{n} \\ &\to 0 \text{ as } n \to \infty. \end{aligned}$$

It follows that

$$E(\bar{Z}_n - \mu)^2 = \frac{\sigma^2}{n} \to 0 \text{ as } n \to \infty.$$

Next, we introduce the concept of convergence in probability that is another popular distance measure between a sequence of random variables and a random variable.

Definition 4.2. [Convergence in Probability]: Z_n converges to Z in probability if for any given constant $\epsilon > 0$,

$$\Pr[||Z_n - Z|| > \epsilon] \to 0 \text{ as } n \to \infty$$

or

$$\Pr[||Z_n - Z|| \leq \epsilon] \to 1 \text{ as } n \to \infty.$$

For convergence in probability, we can also write

$$Z_n - Z \xrightarrow{p} 0 \text{ or } Z_n - Z = o_P(1).$$

The notation $o_P(1)$ means that $Z_n - Z$ vanishes to zero in probability. When $Z = b$ is a constant, we can write $Z_n \xrightarrow{p} b$ and $b = p\lim Z_n$ is called the probability limit of Z_n.

Convergence in probability is also called weak convergence or convergence with probability approaching one. When $Z_n \xrightarrow{p} Z$, the probability that the difference $||Z_n - Z||$ exceeds any given small constant ϵ is rather small for all n sufficiently large. In other words, Z_n will be arbitrarily close to Z with very high probability when the sample size n is sufficiently large.

To gain more intuition of the convergence in probability, we define the event

$$A_n(\epsilon) = \{\omega \in \Omega : |Z_n(\omega) - Z(\omega)| > \epsilon\},$$

where ω is a basic outcome in sample space Ω. Then convergence in probability says that the probability of event $A_n(\epsilon)$ may be nonzero for any finite n, but such a probability will eventually vanish to zero as $n \to \infty$. Intuitively, ϵ can be viewed as a pre-specified tolerance level such that one can view that the difference between Z_n and Z_n is small when $|Z_n - Z| \leq \epsilon$, and the difference is large when $|Z_n - Z| > \epsilon$. Thus, when $Z_n \xrightarrow{p} Z$, it becomes less and less likely that the difference $|Z_n - Z|$ is larger than a prespecified constant $\epsilon > 0$. In other words, we have more and more confidence that the difference $|Z_n - Z|$ will be smaller than ϵ as $n \to \infty$.

Lemma 4.1. ***[Weak Law of Large Numbers (WLLN) for an IID Random Sample]:*** *Suppose $\{Z_t\}$ is IID(μ, σ^2), and define $\bar{Z}_n = n^{-1}\sum_{t=1}^n Z_t, n = 1, 2, ...$ Then*

$$\bar{Z}_n \xrightarrow{p} \mu \text{ as } n \to \infty.$$

Proof: For any given constant $\epsilon > 0$, we have by Chebyshev's inequality

$$\begin{aligned}\Pr(|\bar{Z}_n - \mu| > \epsilon) &\le \frac{E(\bar{Z}_n - \mu)^2}{\epsilon^2} \\ &= \frac{\sigma^2}{n\epsilon^2} \to 0 \text{ as } n \to \infty.\end{aligned}$$

Hence,

$$\bar{Z}_n \xrightarrow{p} \mu \text{ as } n \to \infty.$$

This is the so-called Weak Law of Large Numbers (WLLN). In fact, we can weaken the moment condition.

We now provide an economic interpretation of WLLN using an example.

Example 4.2. [Buy and Hold Trading Strategy and Economic Interpretation of WLLN]: In finance, there is a popular trading strategy called buy-and-hold trading strategy. An investor buys a stock at some day and then hold it for a long time period before he sells it out. This is called a buy-and-hold trading strategy. How is the average return of this trading strategy?

Suppose Z_t is the return of the stock in period t, and the returns over different time periods are IID(μ, σ^2). Also assume the investor holds the stock for a total of n periods. Then the average return in each time period is the sample mean

$$\bar{Z} = \frac{1}{n}\sum_{t=1}^n Z_t.$$

When the number n of holding periods is large, we have

$$\bar{Z} \xrightarrow{p} \mu = E(Z_t)$$

as $n \to \infty$. Thus, the average return of the buy-and-hold trading strategy is approximately equal to μ when n is sufficiently large.

In fact, we can relax the moment condition in Lemma 4.1.

Lemma 4.2. ***[WLLN for an IID Random Sample]:*** *Suppose $\{Z_t\}$ is IID with $E(Z_t) = \mu$ and $E|Z_t| < \infty$. Define $\bar{Z}_n = n^{-1}\sum_{t=1}^n Z_t$. Then*

$$\bar{Z}_n \xrightarrow{p} \mu \text{ as } n \to \infty.$$

Question: Why do we need the moment condition $E|Z_t| < \infty$?

We can consider a counter example: suppose $\{Z_t\}$ is a sequence of IID Cauchy(0, 1) random variables whose moments do not exist. Then $\bar{Z}_n \sim$ Cauchy(0, 1) for all $n \geq 1$, and so it does not converge in probability to any constant as $n \to \infty$.

In a similar manner, we can define convergence in probability with order n^α, where α can be a positive or negative constant:

- The sequence of random variables $\{Z_n, n = 1, 2, ...\}$ is said to be of order smaller than n^α in probability if $Z_n/n^\alpha \xrightarrow{p} 0$ as $n \to \infty$. This is denoted as $Z_n = o_P(n^\alpha)$.
- The sequence of random variables $\{Z_n, n = 1, 2, ...\}$ is said to be at most of order n^α in probability if for any given $\delta > 0$, there exist a constant $C = C(\delta) < \infty$ and a finite integer $N = N(\delta)$, such that $P(|Z_n/n^\alpha| > C) < \delta$ for all $n > N$. This is denoted as $Z_n = O_P(n^\alpha)$.

Intuitively, for $Z_n = O_P(n^\alpha)$ with $\alpha > 0$, the order n^α is the fastest growth rate at which Z_n goes to infinity with probability approaching one. When $\alpha < 0$, the order n^α is the slowest convergence rate at which Z_n vanishes to 0 with probability approaching one. In fact, the definition of $Z_n = O_P(n^\alpha)$ delivers as a special case the concept of boundedness in probability.

Definition 4.3. [Boundedness in Probability]: A sequence of random variables/vectors/matrices $\{Z_n\}$ is bounded in probability if for any small constant $\delta > 0$, there exists a constant $C < \infty$ such that

$$P(||Z_n|| > C) \leq \delta$$

as $n \to \infty$. We denote

$$Z_n = O_P(1).$$

Intuitively, when $Z_n = O_P(1)$, the probability that $||Z_n||$ exceeds a very large constant C is arbitrarily small as $n \to \infty$. Or, equivalently, $||Z_n||$ is smaller than C with probability approaching one as $n \to \infty$.

Example 4.3. Suppose $Z_n \sim N(\mu, \sigma^2)$ for all $n \geq 1$. Then

$$Z_n = O_P(1).$$

Solution: For any $\delta > 0$, we always have a sufficiently large constant $C = C(\delta) > 0$ such that

$$\begin{aligned} P(|Z_n| > C) &= 1 - P(-C \leq Z_n \leq C) \\ &= 1 - P\left[\frac{-C-\mu}{\sigma} \leq \frac{Z_n - \mu}{\sigma} \leq \frac{C-\mu}{\sigma}\right] \\ &= 1 - \Phi\left(\frac{C-\mu}{\sigma}\right) + \Phi\left(-\frac{C+\mu}{\sigma}\right) \\ &\leq \delta, \end{aligned}$$

where $\Phi(z) = P(Z \leq z)$ is the CDF of $N(0,1)$. (We can choose C such that $\Phi[(C-\mu)/\sigma] \geq 1 - \frac{1}{2}\delta$ and $\Phi[-(C+\mu)/\sigma] \leq \frac{1}{2}\delta$.)

Question: What is the value of C if $Z_n \sim N(0,1)$?

In this case,

$$\begin{aligned} P(|Z_n| > C) &= 1 - \Phi(C) + \Phi(-C) \\ &= 2[1 - \Phi(C)]. \end{aligned}$$

Suppose we set

$$2[1 - \Phi(C)] = \delta,$$

that is, we set

$$C = \Phi^{-1}\left(1 - \frac{\delta}{2}\right),$$

where $\Phi^{-1}(\cdot)$ is the inverse function of $\Phi(\cdot)$. Then we have

$$P(|Z_n| > C) = \delta.$$

The following lemma provides a convenient way to verify convergence in probability.

Lemma 4.3. *If* $Z_n - Z \xrightarrow{q.m.} 0$, *then* $Z_n - Z \xrightarrow{p} 0$.

Proof: By Chebyshev's inequality, we have

$$P(|Z_n - Z| > \epsilon) \leq \frac{E[Z_n - Z]^2}{\epsilon^2} \to 0$$

for any given $\epsilon > 0$ as $n \to \infty$. This completes the proof.

Example 4.4. Suppose Assumptions 3.1 to 3.4 hold. Does the OLS estimator $\hat{\beta}$ converge in probability to β^o?

Solution: From Theorem 3.5, we have

$$\begin{aligned} \tau' E[(\hat{\beta} - \beta^o)(\hat{\beta} - \beta^o)'|\mathbf{X}]\tau &= \sigma^2 \tau'(\mathbf{X}'\mathbf{X})^{-1}\tau \\ &\leq \sigma^2 \lambda_{\min}^{-1}(\mathbf{X}'\mathbf{X}) \\ &\to 0 \end{aligned}$$

for any $\tau \in R^K, \tau'\tau = 1$ as $n \to \infty$ with probability one. It follows that $E||\hat{\beta} - \beta^o||^2 = E[E(||\hat{\beta} - \beta^o||^2|\mathbf{X})] \to 0$ as $n \to \infty$. Therefore, by Lemma 4.3, we have $\hat{\beta} \xrightarrow{p} \beta^o$.

Example 4.5. Suppose Assumptions 3.1, 3.3 and 3.5 hold. Does the residual variance estimator s^2 converge in probability to σ^2?

Solution: Under the given assumptions and conditional on $\mathbf{X}$,

$$\frac{(n-K)s^2}{\sigma^2} \sim \chi^2_{n-K},$$

and so we have $E(s^2) = \sigma^2$ and $\text{var}(s^2) = \frac{2\sigma^4}{n-K}$. It follows that

$$E(s^2 - \sigma^2)^2 = 2\sigma^4/(n-K) \to 0.$$

Therefore, $s^2 \xrightarrow{q.m.} \sigma^2$ and so $s^2 \xrightarrow{p} \sigma^2$ because convergence in quadratic mean implies convergence in probability.

While convergence in mean squares implies convergence in probability, the converse is not true. We now give an example.

Example 4.6. Suppose

$$Z_n = \begin{cases} 0, \text{ with prob } 1 - \frac{1}{n}, \\ n, \text{ with prob } \frac{1}{n}. \end{cases}$$

Then $Z_n \xrightarrow{p} 0$ as $n \to \infty$ but $E(Z_n - 0)^2 = n \to \infty$. Please verify it.

Solution:

(1) For any given $0 < \varepsilon < 1$, we have

$$P(|Z_n - 0| > \varepsilon) = P(Z_n = n) = \frac{1}{n} \to 0.$$

(2)

$$\begin{aligned} E(Z_n - 0)^2 &= \sum_{z_n \in \{0,n\}} (z_n - 0)^2 f(z_n) \\ &= (0-0)^2 \cdot (1 - n^{-1}) + (n-0)^2 \cdot n^{-1} \\ &= n \to \infty. \end{aligned}$$

Next, we provide another convergence concept called almost sure convergence.

Definition 4.4. [Almost Sure Convergence]: $\{Z_n\}$ converges to Z almost surely as $n \to \infty$ if for any given $\varepsilon > 0$,

$$P\left[\lim_{n\to\infty} ||Z_n - Z|| < \varepsilon\right] = 1.$$

We denote $Z_n - Z \xrightarrow{a.s.} 0$. Almost sure convergence is also called convergence in probability one.

To gain intuition for the concept of almost sure convergence, recall the definition of a random variable: any random variable is a mapping from the sample space Ω to the real line, namely $Z : \Omega \to \mathbb{R}$. Let ω be a basic outcome in the sample space Ω. Define a subset in Ω :

$$A^c = \left\{\omega \in \Omega : \lim_{n\to\infty} Z_n(\omega) = Z(\omega)\right\}.$$

That is, A^c is the set of basic outcomes on which the sequence of $\{Z_n(\cdot)\}$ converges to $Z(\cdot)$ as $n \to \infty$. Then almost sure convergence can be stated as

$$P(A^c) = 1.$$

In other words, the convergent set A^c has probability one to occur.

Similarly, we can define almost sure convergence with order n^α, where α can be a positive or negative constant:

- The sequence of random variables $\{Z_n, n = 1, 2, ...\}$ is said to be of order smaller than n^α with probability one if $Z_n/n^\alpha \xrightarrow{a.s.} 0$ as $n \to \infty$. This is denoted as $Z_n = o_{a.s.}(n^\alpha)$.

- The sequence of random variables $\{Z_n, n = 1, 2, ...\}$ is said to be at most of order n^α with probability one if there exists some large constant $C < \infty$ such that $P(|Z_n/n^\alpha| > C \text{ as } n \to \infty) = 0$. This is denoted as $Z_n = O_{a.s.}(n^\alpha)$.

In particular, when $\alpha = 0$, $Z_n = O_{a.s.}(1)$ implies that with probability one, Z_n is bounded by some large constant for all n sufficiently large.

Example 4.7. Let ω be uniformly distributed on $[0, 1]$, and define

$$Z(\omega) = \omega \text{ for all } \omega \in [0, 1]$$

and

$$Z_n(\omega) = \omega + \omega^n \text{ for } \omega \in [0, 1].$$

Is $Z_n - Z \xrightarrow{a.s.} 0$?

Solution: Consider

$$A^c = \left\{ \omega \in \Omega : \lim_{n\to\infty} |Z_n(\omega) - Z(\omega)| = 0 \right\}.$$

Because for any given $\omega \in [0, 1)$, we always have

$$\begin{aligned} \lim_{n\to\infty} |Z_n(\omega) - Z(\omega)| &= \lim_{n\to\infty} |(\omega + \omega^n) - \omega| \\ &= \lim_{n\to\infty} \omega^n = 0. \end{aligned}$$

In contrast, for $\omega = 1$, we have

$$\lim_{n\to\infty} |Z_n(1) - Z(1)| = 1^n = 1 \neq 0.$$

Thus, $A^c = [0, 1)$ and $P(A^c) = 1$. We also have $P(A) = P(\omega = 1) = 0$.

In probability theory, almost sure convergence is closely related to pointwise convergence (almost everywhere). It is also called strong convergence.

With almost sure convergence, we can now introduce the Strong Law of Large Numbers (SLLN).

Lemma 4.4. ***[SLLN for an IID Random Sample]:*** *Suppose $\{Z_t\}$ is IID with $E(Z_t) = \mu$ and $E|Z_t| < \infty$. Then*

$$\bar{Z}_n \xrightarrow{a.s.} \mu \text{ as } n \to \infty.$$

Almost sure convergence implies convergence in probability, but not vice versa. For simplicity, we will mainly use the concept of convergence in probability in this book.

Lemma 4.5. *If* $Z_n - Z \xrightarrow{a.s.} 0$, *then* $Z_n - Z \xrightarrow{p} 0$.

Question: If $s^2 \xrightarrow{p} \sigma^2$, do we have $s \xrightarrow{p} \sigma$?

Yes, it follows from the following continuity lemma with the choice of $g(s^2) = \sqrt{s^2} = s$.

Lemma 4.6. *[Continuity]: (1) Suppose* $a_n \xrightarrow{p} a$ *and* $b_n \xrightarrow{p} b$, *where* a *and* b *are constants, and* $g(\cdot)$ *and* $h(\cdot)$ *are continuous functions. Then*

$$g(a_n) + h(b_n) \xrightarrow{p} g(a) + h(b),$$

and

$$g(a_n)h(b_n) \xrightarrow{p} g(a)h(b).$$

(2) Similar results hold for almost sure convergence.

Proof: Left as an exercise.

Continuity implies that converge in probability and almost sure convergence carry over to any continuous linear and nonlinear transformation.

In Chapter 3, we have also introduced a concept of convergence in distribution. A sequence of random variables $\{Z_n\}$ converges in distribution to random variable Z if the CDF $F_n(z)$ of random variable Z_n converges to the CDF $F(z)$ of random variable Z at all continuity points (where $F(z)$ is continuous) when $n \to \infty$. Convergence in distribution implies that one can obtain an asymptotic approximation to the exact distribution of Z_n that depends on the positive integer n and the underlying population distribution. In practice, the distribution of Z_n is often rather complicated and even unknown for a finite n. However, if we know the unknown distribution $F_n(\cdot)$ converges to a known distribution $F(\cdot)$ as $n \to \infty$, we can use $F(\cdot)$ to approximate $F_n(\cdot)$ in finite samples, and the resulting approximation errors will be arbitrarily small for n sufficiently large. This provides convenient statistical inferences in practice.

We emphasize that convergence in mean squares, convergence in probability and almost sure convergence all measure the closeness between the random variable Z_n and the random variable Z as $n \to \infty$. This differs from the concept of convergence in distribution, which is defined in terms of the closeness of the CDF $F_n(z)$ of Z_n to the CDF $F(z)$ of Z, not between the closeness of the random variable Z_n to the random variable Z. As a result, for convergence in mean squares, convergence in probability and almost sure convergence, Z_n converges to Z if and only if the convergence of Z_n to Z occurs element by element (that is, each element of Z_n converges to the corresponding element of Z). For the convergence in distribution of Z_n to Z, however, element by element convergence does not imply the convergence in distribution of Z_n to Z, because element-wise convergence in distribution ignores the relationships among the components of Z_n. Nevertheless, $Z_n \xrightarrow{d} Z$ does imply element by element convergence in distribution. That is, convergence in joint distribution implies convergence in marginal distributions.

The main purpose of asymptotic analysis is to derive the large sample distributions of estimators or statistics of interest and use them as approximations in statistical inference. For this purpose, we need to make use of an important limit theorem, namely the Central Limit Theorem (CLT). We now state and prove CLT for an IID random sample, a fundamental limit theorem in probability theory.

Lemma 4.7. *[CLT for an IID Random Sample]:* *Suppose $\{Z_t\}$ is IID(μ, σ^2), and $\bar{Z}_n = n^{-1}\sum_{t=1}^n Z_t$. Then as $n \to \infty$,*

$$\begin{aligned}\frac{\bar{Z}_n - E(\bar{Z}_n)}{\sqrt{var(\bar{Z}_n)}} &= \frac{\bar{Z}_n - \mu}{\sqrt{\sigma^2/n}} \\ &= \frac{\sqrt{n}(\bar{Z}_n - \mu)}{\sigma} \\ &\xrightarrow{d} N(0,1).\end{aligned}$$

Proof: Put

$$Y_t = \frac{Z_t - \mu}{\sigma},$$

and

$$\bar{Y}_n = \frac{1}{n}\sum_{t=1}^n Y_t.$$

Then

$$\frac{\sqrt{n}(\bar{Z}_n - \mu)}{\sigma} = \sqrt{n}\bar{Y}_n.$$

The characteristic function of $\sqrt{n}\,\bar{Y}_n$

$$\begin{aligned}
\phi_n(u) &= E[\exp(\mathbf{i}u\sqrt{n}\bar{Y}_n)], \qquad \mathbf{i} = \sqrt{-1} \\
&= E\left[\exp\left(\frac{\mathbf{i}u}{\sqrt{n}}\sum_{t=1}^{n} Y_t\right)\right] \\
&= \prod_{t=1}^{n} E\left[\exp\left(\frac{\mathbf{i}u}{\sqrt{n}}Y_t\right)\right] \text{ by independence} \\
&= \left[\phi_Y\left(\frac{u}{\sqrt{n}}\right)\right]^n \text{ by identical distribution} \\
&= \left[\phi_Y(0) + \phi'(0)\frac{u}{\sqrt{n}} + \frac{1}{2}\phi''(0)\frac{u^2}{n} + \cdots\right]^n \\
&= \left(1 - \frac{u^2}{2n}\right)^n + o(1) \\
&\to \exp\left(-\frac{u^2}{2}\right) \quad \text{as } n \to \infty,
\end{aligned}$$

where the third equality follows from independence, the fourth equality follows from identical distribution, the fifth equality follows from the Taylor series expansion, and $\phi(0) = 1$, $\phi'(0) = 0$, $\phi''(0) = -1$. Note that $o(1)$ means a reminder term that vanishes to zero as $n \to \infty$, and we have also made use of the fact that $(1 + \frac{a}{n})^n \to e^a$ as $n \to \infty$.

More rigorously, we can show

$$\begin{aligned}
\ln \phi_n(u) &= n \ln \phi_Y\left(\frac{u}{\sqrt{n}}\right) \\
&= \frac{\ln \phi_Y\left(\frac{u}{\sqrt{n}}\right)}{n^{-1}} \\
&\to \frac{u}{2}\lim_{n\to\infty} \frac{\frac{\phi_Y'(u/\sqrt{n})}{\phi_Y(u/\sqrt{n})}}{n^{-1/2}} \\
&= \frac{u^2}{2}\lim_{n\to\infty} \frac{\phi_Y''(u/\sqrt{n})\phi_Y(u/\sqrt{n}) - [\phi_Y'(u/\sqrt{n})]^2}{\phi_Y^2(u/\sqrt{n})} \\
&= -\frac{u^2}{2}.
\end{aligned}$$

It follows that

$$\lim_{n\to\infty} \phi_n(u) = e^{-\frac{1}{2}u^2}.$$

This is the characteristic function of $N(0,1)$. By the uniqueness property of the characteristic function, the asymptotic distribution of

$$\frac{\sqrt{n}(\bar{Z}_n - \mu)}{\sigma}$$

is $N(0,1)$. This completes the proof.

Lemma 4.8. ***[Cramer-Wold Device]:*** *A $p \times 1$ random vector $Z_n \xrightarrow{d} Z$ if and only if for any nonzero $\lambda \in R^p$ such that $\lambda'\lambda = 1$, we have*

$$\lambda' Z_n \xrightarrow{d} \lambda' Z.$$

This lemma is useful for obtaining asymptotic multivariate distributions.

Lemma 4.9. ***[Slutsky's Theorem]:*** *Let $Z_n \xrightarrow{d} Z$, $a_n \xrightarrow{p} a$ and $b_n \xrightarrow{p} b$, where a and b are constants. Then*

$$a_n + b_n Z_n \xrightarrow{d} a + bZ \text{ as } n \to \infty.$$

Example 4.8. Suppose $(X_1, ..., X_n)$ is an IID sequence with mean μ and variance $\sigma^2 < \infty$. Then by CLT for an IID random sample,

$$\frac{\sqrt{n}(\bar{X}_n - \mu)}{\sigma} \xrightarrow{d} N(0,1) \text{ as } n \to \infty.$$

Since $S_n \xrightarrow{p} \sigma$, we have from Slutsky's theorem that

$$\frac{\sqrt{n}(\bar{X}_n - \mu)}{S_n} \xrightarrow{d} N(0,1) \text{ as } n \to \infty.$$

In other words, the replacement of σ by S_n does not change the asymptotic distribution.

Question: If $X_n \xrightarrow{d} X$ and $Y_n \xrightarrow{d} Y$, does $X_n + Y_n \xrightarrow{d} X + Y$?

No. We consider two counter examples.

Example 4.9. X_n and Y_n are independent $N(0,1)$. Then

$$X_n + Y_n \xrightarrow{d} N(0,2).$$

Example 4.10. $X_n = Y_n \sim N(0,1)$ for all $n \geq 1$. Then

$$X_n + Y_n = 2X_n \sim N(0,4).$$

Example 4.11. Suppose Assumptions 3.1, 3.3(a) and 3.5, and the hypothesis $\mathbf{H}_0 : R\beta^o = r$ hold, where R is a $J \times K$ nonstochastic matrix with rank J, r is a $J \times 1$ nonstochastic vector, and $J \leq K$. Then conditional on $\mathbf{X}$, the quadratic form

$$\frac{(R\hat{\beta} - r)'[R(\mathbf{X}'\mathbf{X})^{-1}R']^{-1}(R\hat{\beta} - r)}{\sigma^2} \sim \chi_J^2.$$

Suppose now we replace σ^2 by the residual variance estimator s^2. What is the asymptotic distribution of the quadratic form

$$\frac{(R\hat{\beta} - r)'[R(\mathbf{X}'\mathbf{X})^{-1}R']^{-1}(R\hat{\beta} - r)}{s^2}?$$

Finally, we introduce a lemma which is very useful in deriving the asymptotic distributions of nonlinear statistics (i.e., nonlinear functions of the random sample).

Lemma 4.10. ***[Delta Method]:*** *Suppose* $\sqrt{n}(\bar{Z}_n - \mu)/\sigma \xrightarrow{d} N(0,1)$, *and* $g(\cdot)$ *is continuously differentiable with* $g'(\mu) \neq 0$. *Then as* $n \to \infty$,

$$\sqrt{n}[g(\bar{Z}_n) - g(\mu)] \xrightarrow{d} N(0, [g'(\mu)]^2\sigma^2).$$

Proof: First, because $\sqrt{n}(\bar{Z}_n - \mu)/\sigma \xrightarrow{d} N(0,1)$ implies $\sqrt{n}(\bar{Z}_n - \mu)/\sigma = O_P(1)$, we have $\bar{Z}_n - \mu = O_P(n^{-1/2}) = o_P(1)$.

Next, by the mean value theorem, we have

$$Y_n = g(\bar{Z}_n) = g(\mu) + g'(\bar{\mu}_n)(\bar{Z}_n - \mu),$$

where $\bar{\mu}_n = \lambda\mu + (1-\lambda)\bar{Z}_n$ for $\lambda \in [0,1]$. It follows by Slutsky's theorem that

$$\sqrt{n}\frac{g(\bar{Z}_n) - g(\mu)}{\sigma} = g'(\bar{\mu}_n)\sqrt{n}\frac{\bar{Z}_n - \mu}{\sigma} \\ \xrightarrow{d} N(0, [g'(\mu)]^2),$$

where $g'(\bar{\mu}_n) \xrightarrow{p} g'(\mu)$ given $\bar{\mu}_n \xrightarrow{p} \mu$.

By Slutsky's theorem again, we have

$$\sqrt{n}[Y_n - g(\mu)] \xrightarrow{d} N(0, \sigma^2[g'(\mu)]^2).$$

This completes the proof.

The Delta method is a first order Taylor series approximation in a statistical context. It linearizes a smooth (i.e., differentiable) nonlinear statistic so that CLT can be applied to the linearized statistic. Therefore, it can be viewed as a generalization of CLT from a sample average to a nonlinear statistic. This method is very useful when more than one parameter makes up the function to be estimated and more than one random variable is used in the estimator.

Example 4.12. Suppose $\sqrt{n}(\bar{Z}_n - \mu)/\sigma \xrightarrow{d} N(0,1)$ and $\mu \neq 0$ and $0 < \sigma < \infty$. Find the limiting distribution of $\sqrt{n}(\bar{Z}_n^{-1} - \mu^{-1})$.

Solution: Put $g(\bar{Z}_n) = \bar{Z}_n^{-1}$. Because $\mu \neq 0$, $g(\cdot)$ is continuous at μ. By the mean value theorem, we have

$$g(\bar{Z}_n) = g(\mu) + g'(\bar{\mu}_n)(\bar{Z}_n - \mu),$$

or

$$\bar{Z}_n^{-1} - \mu^{-1} = (-\bar{\mu}_n^{-2})(\bar{Z}_n - \mu),$$

where $\bar{\mu}_n = \lambda\mu + (1-\lambda)\bar{Z}_n \xrightarrow{p} \mu$ given $\bar{Z}_n \xrightarrow{p} \mu$ and $\lambda \in [0,1]$. It follows that

$$\sqrt{n}(\bar{Z}_n^{-1} - \mu^{-1}) = -\frac{\sigma}{\bar{\mu}_n^2}\frac{\sqrt{n}(\bar{Z}_n - \mu)}{\sigma} \\ \xrightarrow{d} N(0, \sigma^2/\mu^4).$$

Taylor series expansions, various convergence concepts, LLN, CLT, and Slutsky's theorem constitute a tool kit of asymptotic analysis. For comprehensive coverage of asymptotic analysis, the readers are referred to White

(1984, 2001) and Davidson (1994). We now use these asymptotic tools to investigate the large sample behavior of the OLS estimator and related statistics in subsequent chapters.

4.2 Framework and Assumptions

We first state the assumptions under which we will establish the asymptotic theory for linear regression models.

Assumption 4.1. [IID Random Sample]: $\{Y_t, X_t'\}_{t=1}^n$ is an observable IID random sample.

Assumption 4.2. [Linearity]:

$$Y_t = X_t'\beta^o + \varepsilon_t, \qquad t = 1, ..., n,$$

for some unknown $K \times 1$ parameter value β^o and some unobservable disturbance ε_t.

Assumption 4.3. [Correct Model Specification]: $E(\varepsilon_t|X_t) = 0$ with $E(\varepsilon_t^2) = \sigma^2 < \infty$.

Assumption 4.4. [Nonsingularity]: The $K \times K$ matrix

$$Q = E(X_t X_t')$$

is nonsingular and finite.

Assumption 4.5. The $K \times K$ matrix $V \equiv \text{var}(X_t\varepsilon_t) = E(X_t X_t' \varepsilon_t^2)$ is symmetric, finite and positive definite.

The IID observations assumption in Assumption 4.1 implies that the asymptotic theory developed in this chapter will be applicable to cross-sectional data, but not to time series data. The observations of the later are usually correlated and will be considered in Chapter 5. Put $Z_t = (Y_t, X_t')'$. Then the IID assumption implies that Z_t and Z_s are independent when $t \neq s$, and the $\{Z_t\}$ have the same distribution for all t. The identical distribution means that the observations are generated from the same DGP, and independence means that different observations contain new information about the DGP.

Assumptions 4.1 and 4.3 imply that the strict exogeneity condition (Assumption 3.2) holds, because we have

$$\begin{aligned} E(\varepsilon_t|\mathbf{X}) &= E(\varepsilon_t|X_1, X_2, ...X_t, ...X_n) \\ &= E(\varepsilon_t|X_t) \\ &= 0. \end{aligned}$$

As one of the most important features of Assumptions 4.1 to 4.5 together, we allow for conditional heteroskedasticity (i.e., $\text{var}(\varepsilon_t|X_t) \neq \sigma^2$), and in particular, we do not assume normality for the conditional distribution of $\varepsilon_t|X_t$. It is possible that $\text{var}(\varepsilon_t|X_t)$ may be correlated with X_t. For example, the variation of the output of a firm may depend on the size of the firm, and the variation of a household may depend on its income level. In economics and finance, conditional heteroskedasticity is more likely to occur in cross-sectional observations than in time series observations, and for time series observations, conditional heteroskedasticity is more likely to occur for high-frequency data than low-frequency data. In this chapter, we will consider the effect of conditional heteroskedasticity in cross-section observations. The effect of conditional heteroskedasticity in time series observations will be considered in Chapter 5.

On the other hand, relaxation of the normality assumption is more realistic for economic and financial data. For example, it has been well documented (Mandelbrot 1963, Fama 1965) that returns on financial assets are not normally distributed. However, the IID assumption on the random sample $\{Y_t, X_t'\}_{t=1}^n$ implies that $\text{cov}(\varepsilon_t, \varepsilon_s) = 0$ for all $t \neq s$. That is, there exists no serial correlation in the regression disturbance, although conditional heteroskedasticity is allowed. We will relax the independence assumptions and consider time series observations in subsequent chapters.

Among other things, Assumption 4.4 implies $E(X_{jt}^2) < \infty$ for $0 \leq j \leq k$. By SLLN for an IID random sample, we have

$$\frac{\mathbf{X}'\mathbf{X}}{n} = \frac{1}{n}\sum_{t=1}^{n} X_t X_t' \overset{a.s.}{\to} E(X_t X_t') = Q$$

as $n \to \infty$. Hence, with probability one, the matrix $\mathbf{X}'\mathbf{X}$ behaves approximately like nQ when n is sufficiently large, whose minimum eigenvalue $\lambda_{\min}(nQ) = n\lambda_{\min}(Q) \to \infty$ at the rate of n. Thus, Assumption 4.4 implies Assumption 3.3.

When X_t contains the intercept, that is, when $X_{0t} = 1$, Assumption 4.5 implies $E(\varepsilon_t^2) < \infty$. If $E(\varepsilon_t^2|X_t) = \sigma^2 < \infty$, i.e., there exists conditional homoskedasticity, then Assumption 4.5 can be ensured by Assumption 4.4. More generally, there exists conditional heteroskedasticity, the moment condition in Assumption 4.5 can be ensured by the moment conditions that $E(\varepsilon_t^4) < \infty$ and $E(X_{jt}^4) < \infty$ for $0 \le j \le k$, because by repeatedly using the Cauchy-Schwarz inequality twice, we have

$$\begin{aligned}|E(\varepsilon_t^2 X_{jt} X_{lt})| &\le [E(\varepsilon_t^4)]^{1/2}[E(X_{jt}^2 X_{lt}^2)]^{1/2} \\ &\le [E(\varepsilon_t^4)]^{1/2}[E(X_{jt}^4)E(X_{lt}^4)]^{1/4},\end{aligned}$$

where $0 \le j,\ l \le k$ and $1 \le t \le n$.

We now address the following questions:

- Consistency of the OLS estimator?
- Asymptotic normality?
- Asymptotic efficiency?
- Confidence interval estimation?
- Hypothesis testing?

In particular, we are interested in knowing whether the statistical properties of the OLS estimator $\hat{\beta}$ and related test statistics derived under the classical linear regression framework are still valid under the current setup, at least when n is large.

4.3 Consistency of the OLS Estimator

Suppose we have an observable random sample $\{Y_t, X_t'\}_{t=1}^n$. Recall that the OLS estimator

$$\begin{aligned}\hat{\beta} &= (\mathbf{X}'\mathbf{X})^{-1}\mathbf{X}'Y \\ &= \left(\frac{\mathbf{X}'\mathbf{X}}{n}\right)^{-1}\frac{\mathbf{X}'Y}{n} \\ &= \hat{Q}^{-1}n^{-1}\sum_{t=1}^n X_t Y_t,\end{aligned}$$

where

$$\hat{Q} = n^{-1}\sum_{t=1}^n X_t X_t'.$$

Substituting $Y_t = X_t'\beta^o + \varepsilon_t$, we obtain

$$\hat{\beta} = \beta^o + \hat{Q}^{-1} n^{-1} \sum_{t=1}^{n} X_t \varepsilon_t.$$

We will consider the consistency of $\hat{\beta}$ directly.

Theorem 4.1. ***[Consistency of the OLS Estimator]:*** *Under Assumptions 4.1 to 4.4, as $n \to \infty$,*

$$\hat{\beta} \xrightarrow{p} \beta^o \text{ or } \hat{\beta} - \beta^o = o_P(1).$$

Proof: Let $C > 0$ be some bounded constant. Also, recall $X_t = (X_{0t}, X_{1t}, ..., X_{kt})'$. First, the moment condition holds: for all $0 \le j \le k$,

$$\begin{aligned} E|X_{jt}\varepsilon_t| &\le (EX_{jt}^2)^{\frac{1}{2}} (E\varepsilon_t^2)^{\frac{1}{2}} \text{ by the Cauchy-Schwarz inequality} \\ &\le C^{\frac{1}{2}} C^{\frac{1}{2}} \\ &\le C, \end{aligned}$$

where $E(X_{jt}^2) \le C$ by Assumption 4.4, and $E(\varepsilon_t^2) \le C$ by Assumption 4.3. It follows from WLLN for an IID random sample (with $Z_t = X_t \varepsilon_t$) that

$$n^{-1} \sum_{t=1}^{n} X_t \varepsilon_t \xrightarrow{p} E(X_t \varepsilon_t) = 0,$$

where

$$\begin{aligned} E(X_t\varepsilon_t) &= E[E(X_t\varepsilon_t|X_t)] \text{ by the law of iterated expectations} \\ &= E[X_t E(\varepsilon_t|X_t)] \\ &= E(X_t \cdot 0) \\ &= 0. \end{aligned}$$

Applying WLLN again (with $Z_t = X_t X_t'$) and noting that

$$E|X_{jt}X_{lt}| \le [E(X_{jt}^2)E(X_{lt}^2)]^{\frac{1}{2}} \le C$$

by the Cauchy-Schwarz inequality for all pairs (j, l), where $0 \le j,\ l \le k$, we have

$$\hat{Q} \xrightarrow{p} E(X_t X_t') = Q.$$

Hence, we have $\hat{Q}^{-1} \xrightarrow{p} Q^{-1}$ by continuity. It follows that

$$\begin{aligned}\hat{\beta} - \beta^o &= (\mathbf{X}'\mathbf{X})^{-1}\mathbf{X}'\varepsilon \\ &= \hat{Q}^{-1} n^{-1} \sum_{t=1}^{n} X_t \varepsilon_t \\ &\xrightarrow{p} Q^{-1} \cdot 0 = 0.\end{aligned}$$

This completes the proof.

From the proof, it can be seen that the correct model specification condition $E(\varepsilon_t|X_t) = 0$ ensures consistency of $\hat{\beta}$.

4.4 Asymptotic Normality of the OLS Estimator

Next, we derive the asymptotic distribution of the OLS estimator $\hat{\beta}$. We first provide a multivariate CLT for an IID random sample.

Lemma 4.11. ***[Multivariate CLT for an IID Random Sample]:*** *Suppose $\{Z_t\}$ is a sequence of IID random vectors with $E(Z_t) = 0$ and var$(Z_t) = E(Z_t Z_t') = V$ is finite and positive definite. Define*

$$\bar{Z}_n = n^{-1} \sum_{t=1}^{n} Z_t.$$

Then as $n \to \infty$,

$$\sqrt{n}\bar{Z}_n \xrightarrow{d} N(0, V)$$

or

$$V^{-\frac{1}{2}} \sqrt{n}\bar{Z}_n \xrightarrow{d} N(0, I).$$

Question: What is the variance-covariance matrix of $\sqrt{n}\bar{Z}_n$?

Lemma 4.11 shows that $V = \text{var}(Z_t)$ is the asymptotic variance of $\sqrt{n}\bar{Z}_n$, that is, the variance of the asymptotic distribution of $\sqrt{n}\bar{Z}_n$. In fact, under the IID condition on $\{Z_t\}_{t=1}^n$, V is also the variance of $\sqrt{n}\bar{Z}_n$:

noting $E(Z_t) = 0$, we have

$$\begin{aligned}
\text{var}(\sqrt{n}\bar{Z}_n) &= \text{var}\left(n^{-\frac{1}{2}}\sum_{t=1}^{n} Z_t\right) \\
&= E\left[\left(n^{-\frac{1}{2}}\sum_{t=1}^{n} Z_t\right)\left(n^{-\frac{1}{2}}\sum_{s=1}^{n} Z_s\right)'\right] \\
&= n^{-1}\sum_{t=1}^{n}\sum_{s=1}^{n} E(Z_t Z_s') \\
&= n^{-1}\sum_{t=1}^{n} E(Z_t Z_t') \\
&= E(Z_t Z_t') \\
&= V.
\end{aligned}$$

In other words, the variance of $\sqrt{n}\bar{Z}_n$ is identical to the variance of each individual random vector Z_t.

Theorem 4.2. ***[Asymptotic Normality of the OLS Estimator]:*** *Under Assumptions 4.1 to 4.5, we have*

$$\sqrt{n}(\hat{\beta} - \beta^o) \xrightarrow{d} N(0, Q^{-1}VQ^{-1})$$

as $n \to \infty$, *where* $V = var(X_t\varepsilon_t) = E(X_t X_t' \varepsilon_t^2)$.

Proof: Recall that

$$\sqrt{n}(\hat{\beta} - \beta^o) = \hat{Q}^{-1} n^{-\frac{1}{2}} \sum_{t=1}^{n} X_t \varepsilon_t.$$

First, we consider the second term

$$n^{-\frac{1}{2}} \sum_{t=1}^{n} X_t \varepsilon_t.$$

Noting that $E(X_t\varepsilon_t) = 0$ by Assumption 4.3, and $\text{var}(X_t\varepsilon_t) = E(X_t X_t' \varepsilon_t^2) = V$, which is finite and positive definite by Assumption 4.5.

Then, by CLT for an IID random sequence $\{Z_t = X_t\varepsilon_t\}$, we have

$$\begin{aligned} n^{-\frac{1}{2}}\sum_{t=1}^{n} X_t\varepsilon_t &= \sqrt{n}\left(n^{-1}\sum_{t=1}^{n} X_t\varepsilon_t\right) \\ &= \sqrt{n}\bar{Z}_n \\ &\xrightarrow{d} Z \sim N(0, V). \end{aligned}$$

On the other hand, as shown earlier, we have

$$\hat{Q} \xrightarrow{p} Q,$$

and so

$$\hat{Q}^{-1} \xrightarrow{p} Q^{-1}$$

given that Q is nonsingular so that the inverse function is continuous and well defined. It follows by Slutsky's theorem that

$$\begin{aligned} \sqrt{n}(\hat{\beta} - \beta^o) &= \hat{Q}^{-1} n^{-\frac{1}{2}}\sum_{t=1}^{n} X_t\varepsilon_t \\ &\xrightarrow{d} Q^{-1}Z \sim N(0, Q^{-1}VQ^{-1}). \end{aligned}$$

This completes the proof.

Theorem 4.2 implies that the asymptotic mean of $\sqrt{n}(\hat{\beta} - \beta^o)$ is equal to 0. That is, the mean of the asymptotic distribution of $\sqrt{n}(\hat{\beta} - \beta^o)$ is 0 when $n \to \infty$. It also implies that the asymptotic variance of $\sqrt{n}(\hat{\beta} - \beta^o)$ is $Q^{-1}VQ^{-1}$. That is, the variance of the asymptotic distribution of $\sqrt{n}(\hat{\beta} - \beta^o)$ is $Q^{-1}VQ^{-1}$ when $n \to \infty$. Because the asymptotic variance is a different concept from the variance of $\sqrt{n}(\hat{\beta} - \beta^o)$, we denote the asymptotic variance of $\sqrt{n}(\hat{\beta} - \beta^o)$ as

$$avar(\sqrt{n}\hat{\beta}) = Q^{-1}VQ^{-1}.$$

We now consider a special case under which we can simplify the expression of avar$(\sqrt{n}\hat{\beta})$.

Assumption 4.6. [Conditional Homoskedasticity]: $E(\varepsilon_t^2|X_t) = \sigma^2$.

Theorem 4.3. *Suppose Assumptions 4.1 to 4.6 hold. Then as $n \to \infty$,*

$$\sqrt{n}(\hat{\beta} - \beta^o) \xrightarrow{d} N(0, \sigma^2 Q^{-1}).$$

Proof: Under Assumption 4.6, we can simplify

$$\begin{aligned} V &= E(X_t X_t' \varepsilon_t^2) \\ &= E[E(X_t X_t' \varepsilon_t^2 | X_t)] \text{ by the law of iterated expectations} \\ &= E[X_t X_t' E(\varepsilon_t^2 | X_t)] \\ &= \sigma^2 E(X_t X_t') \\ &= \sigma^2 Q. \end{aligned}$$

The results follow immediately because

$$Q^{-1} V Q^{-1} = Q^{-1} \sigma^2 Q Q^{-1} = \sigma^2 Q^{-1}.$$

Under conditional homoskedasticity, the asymptotic variance of $\sqrt{n}(\hat{\beta} - \beta^o)$ is

$$\text{avar}(\sqrt{n}\hat{\beta}) = \sigma^2 Q^{-1}.$$

Question: Is the OLS estimator $\hat{\beta}$ BLUE asymptotically (i.e., when $n \to \infty$)?

4.5 Asymptotic Variance Estimation

To construct confidence interval estimators or hypothesis test statistics, we need to estimate the asymptotic variance of $\sqrt{n}(\hat{\beta} - \beta^o)$, $\text{avar}(\sqrt{n}\hat{\beta})$. Because the expression of $\text{avar}(\sqrt{n}\hat{\beta})$ differs under conditional homoskedasticity and conditional heteroskedasticity respectively, we consider consistent estimators for $\text{avar}(\sqrt{n}\hat{\beta})$ under these two cases separately.

Case I: Conditional Homoskedasticity

In this case, the asymptotic variance of $\sqrt{n}(\hat{\beta} - \beta^o)$ is

$$\text{avar}(\sqrt{n}\hat{\beta}) = Q^{-1} V Q^{-1} = \sigma^2 Q^{-1}.$$

Question: How to estimate Q?

Lemma 4.12. *Suppose Assumptions 4.1, 4.2 and 4.4 hold. Then*

$$\hat{Q} = n^{-1} \sum_{t=1}^{n} X_t X_t' \xrightarrow{p} Q.$$

Question: How to estimate σ^2?

Recalling that $\sigma^2 = E(\varepsilon_t^2)$, we use the sample residual variance estimator

$$\begin{aligned} s^2 &= \frac{e'e}{n-K} \\ &= \frac{1}{n-K}\sum_{t=1}^{n} e_t^2 \\ &= \frac{1}{n-K}\sum_{t=1}^{n}(Y_t - X_t'\hat{\beta})^2. \end{aligned}$$

Theorem 4.4. ***[Consistent Estimation of σ^2]:*** *Under Assumptions 4.1 to 4.4, as $n \to \infty$,*

$$s^2 \xrightarrow{p} \sigma^2.$$

Proof: Given that $s^2 = e'e/(n-K)$ and

$$\begin{aligned} e_t &= Y_t - X_t'\hat{\beta} \\ &= \varepsilon_t + X_t'\beta^o - X_t'\hat{\beta} \\ &= \varepsilon_t - X_t'(\hat{\beta} - \beta^o), \end{aligned}$$

we have

$$\begin{aligned} s^2 &= \frac{1}{n-K}\sum_{t=1}^{n}[\varepsilon_t - X_t'(\hat{\beta} - \beta^o)]^2 \\ &= \frac{n}{n-K}\left(n^{-1}\sum_{t=1}^{n}\varepsilon_t^2\right) \\ &\quad + (\hat{\beta} - \beta^o)'\left[(n-K)^{-1}\sum_{t=1}^{n}X_tX_t'\right](\hat{\beta} - \beta^o) \\ &\quad - 2(\hat{\beta} - \beta^o)'(n-K)^{-1}\sum_{t=1}^{n}X_t\varepsilon_t \\ &\xrightarrow{p} 1 \cdot \sigma^2 + 0 \cdot Q \cdot 0 - 2 \cdot 0 \cdot 0 \\ &= \sigma^2 \end{aligned}$$

as $n \to \infty$, given that K is a fixed number (i.e., K does not grow with the sample size n), where we have made use of WLLN in three places respectively.

We can then consistently estimate $\sigma^2 Q^{-1}$ by $s^2\hat{Q}^{-1}$.

Theorem 4.5. *[Asymptotic Variance Estimator of $\sqrt{n}(\hat{\beta}-\beta^o)$]: Under Assumptions 4.1 to 4.4, we have, as $n \to \infty$,*

$$s^2\hat{Q}^{-1} \xrightarrow{p} \sigma^2 Q^{-1}.$$

The asymptotic variance estimator of $\sqrt{n}(\hat{\beta}-\beta^o)$ is

$$s^2\hat{Q}^{-1} = s^2\left(\frac{\mathbf{X}'\mathbf{X}}{n}\right)^{-1}.$$

This is equivalent to saying that the variance estimator of $\hat{\beta}-\beta^o$ is approximately equal to

$$s^2\hat{Q}^{-1}/n = s^2(\mathbf{X}'\mathbf{X})^{-1}$$

when for a large n. Thus, when $n \to \infty$ and there exists conditional homoskedasticity, the asymptotic variance estimator formula of $\hat{\beta}-\beta^o$ coincides with the form of the variance estimator for $\hat{\beta}-\beta^o$ in the classical regression case. Because of this, as will be seen below, the conventional t-test and F-test statistics are still approximately valid for large samples under conditional homoskedasticity.

Case II: Conditional Heteroskedasticity

In this case,

$$\text{avar}(\sqrt{n}\hat{\beta}) = Q^{-1}VQ^{-1},$$

which cannot be simplified.

Question: We can still use $\hat{Q}$ to estimate Q. How to estimate the $K \times K$ matrix $V = E(X_t X_t' \varepsilon_t^2)$?

We can use its sample analog

$$\hat{V} = n^{-1}\sum_{t=1}^{n} X_t X_t' e_t^2 = \frac{\mathbf{X}'\mathrm{D}(e)\mathrm{D}(e)'\mathbf{X}}{n},$$

where

$$\mathrm{D}(e) = diag(e_1, e_2, ..., e_n)$$

is an $n \times n$ diagonal matrix with diagonal elements equal to e_t for $t = 1, ..., n$. To ensure consistency of $\hat{V}$ to V, we impose the following additional moment conditions.

Assumption 4.7. (a) $E(X_{jt}^4) < \infty$ for all $0 \leq j \leq k$; and (b) $E(\varepsilon_t^4) < \infty$.

Lemma 4.13. *Suppose Assumptions 4.1 to 4.5 and 4.7 hold. Then as* $n \to \infty$,

$$\hat{V} \xrightarrow{p} V.$$

Proof: Because $e_t = \varepsilon_t - (\hat{\beta} - \beta^o)' X_t$, we have

$$\begin{aligned}
\hat{V} &= n^{-1} \sum_{t=1}^{n} X_t X_t' \varepsilon_t^2 \\
&\quad + n^{-1} \sum_{t=1}^{n} X_t X_t' [(\hat{\beta} - \beta^o)' X_t X_t' (\hat{\beta} - \beta^o)] \\
&\quad - 2n^{-1} \sum_{t=1}^{n} X_t X_t' [\varepsilon_t X_t' (\hat{\beta} - \beta^o)] \\
&\xrightarrow{p} V + 0 - 2 \cdot 0,
\end{aligned}$$

where for the first term, we have

$$n^{-1} \sum_{t=1}^{n} X_t X_t' \varepsilon_t^2 \xrightarrow{p} E(X_t X_t' \varepsilon_t^2) = V$$

by WLLN and Assumption 4.7, which implies

$$E|X_{it} X_{jt} \varepsilon_t^2| \leq [E(X_{it}^2 X_{jt}^2) E(\varepsilon_t^4)]^{\frac{1}{2}}.$$

For the second term, we have, as $n \to \infty$,

$$\begin{aligned}
& n^{-1} \sum_{t=1}^{n} X_{it} X_{jt} (\hat{\beta} - \beta^o)' X_t X_t' (\hat{\beta} - \beta^o) \\
&= \sum_{l=0}^{k} \sum_{m=0}^{k} (\hat{\beta}_l - \beta_l^o)(\hat{\beta}_m - \beta_m^o) \left(n^{-1} \sum_{t=1}^{n} X_{it} X_{jt} X_{lt} X_{mt} \right) \\
&\xrightarrow{p} 0
\end{aligned}$$

given $\hat{\beta} - \beta^o \xrightarrow{p} 0$, and

$$n^{-1}\sum_{t=1}^{n} X_{it}X_{jt}X_{lt}X_{mt} \xrightarrow{p} E\left(X_{it}X_{jt}X_{lt}X_{mt}\right) = O(1)$$

by WLLN and Assumption 4.7.

Similarly, for the last term, we have

$$\begin{aligned}
&n^{-1}\sum_{t=1}^{n} X_{it}X_{jt}\varepsilon_t X_t'(\hat{\beta} - \beta^o) \\
&= \sum_{l=0}^{k}(\hat{\beta}_l - \beta_l^o)\left(n^{-1}\sum_{t=1}^{n} X_{it}X_{jt}X_{lt}\varepsilon_t\right) \\
&\xrightarrow{p} 0
\end{aligned}$$

given $\hat{\beta} - \beta^o \xrightarrow{p} 0$, and

$$n^{-1}\sum_{t=1}^{n} X_{it}X_{jt}X_{lt}\varepsilon_t \xrightarrow{p} E\left(X_{it}X_{jt}X_{lt}\varepsilon_t\right) = 0$$

by WLLN and Assumption 4.7. This completes the proof.

We now construct a consistent estimator for $\text{avar}(\sqrt{n}\hat{\beta})$ under conditional heteroskedasticity.

Theorem 4.6. ***[Asymptotic Variance Estimator for $\sqrt{n}(\hat{\beta} - \beta^o)$]:*** *Under Assumptions 4.1 to 4.5 and 4.7, we have*

$$\hat{Q}^{-1}\hat{V}\hat{Q}^{-1} \xrightarrow{p} Q^{-1}VQ^{-1}.$$

The form $Q^{-1}VQ^{-1}$ is the so-called White's (1980) heteroskedasticity-consistent variance-covariance matrix of the estimator $\sqrt{n}(\hat{\beta}-\beta^o)$. It follows that when there exists conditional heteroskedasticity, the estimator for the variance of $\hat{\beta}$ is

$$\begin{aligned}
\frac{\hat{Q}^{-1}\hat{V}\hat{Q}^{-1}}{n} &= \frac{(\mathbf{X}'\mathbf{X}/n)^{-1}\hat{V}(\mathbf{X}'\mathbf{X}/n)^{-1}}{n} \\
&= (\mathbf{X}'\mathbf{X})^{-1}\mathbf{X}'\mathrm{D}(e)\mathrm{D}(e)'\mathbf{X}(\mathbf{X}'\mathbf{X})^{-1},
\end{aligned}$$

which differs from the variance estimator $s^2(\mathbf{X}'\mathbf{X})^{-1}$ of $\hat{\beta}$ in the case of conditional homoskedasticity.

Question: What happens if we use $s^2\hat{Q}^{-1}$ as an estimator for avar$[\sqrt{n}(\hat{\beta}-\beta^o)]$ while there exists conditional heteroskedasticity?

Observe that

$$\begin{aligned} V &\equiv E(X_tX_t'\varepsilon_t^2) \\ &= \sigma^2 Q + \text{cov}(X_tX_t', \varepsilon_t^2) \\ &= \sigma^2 Q + \text{cov}[X_tX_t', \sigma^2(X_t)], \end{aligned}$$

where $\sigma^2 = E(\varepsilon_t^2)$, $\sigma^2(X_t) = E(\varepsilon_t^2|X_t)$, and the last equality follows from the law of iterated expectations. Thus, if $\sigma^2(X_t)$ is positively correlated with X_tX_t', $\sigma^2 Q$ will underestimate the true variance-covariance matrix $E(X_tX_t'\varepsilon_t^2)$ in the sense that $V - \sigma^2 Q$ is a positive definite matrix. Consequently, the standard t-test and F-test will overreject the correct null hypothesis at any given significance level, and so are not valid for applications. There will exist substantially larger Type I errors.

Question: What happens if one uses the asymptotic variance estimator $\hat{Q}^{-1}\hat{V}\hat{Q}^{-1}$ but there exists conditional homoskedasticity?

The asymptotic variance estimator $\hat{Q}^{-1}\hat{V}\hat{Q}^{-1}$ is valid in large samples, but it will not perform as well as the estimator $s^2\hat{Q}^{-1}$ in finite samples, because the latter exploits the information of conditional homoskedasticity. It is expected to cause a larger distorted Type I error in finite samples, although it will become asymptotically valid when n is large. For small and finite samples, $s^2\hat{Q}^{-1}$ is a more efficient variance estimator of $\sqrt{n}\hat{\beta}$ under conditional homoskedasticity.

4.6 Hypothesis Testing

Question: How to construct a test statistic for the null hypothesis

$$\mathbf{H}_0 : R\beta^o = r,$$

where R is a $J \times K$ constant matrix, r is a $J \times 1$ constant vector, and $J \leq K$?

We first consider

$$R\hat{\beta} - r = R(\hat{\beta} - \beta^o) + R\beta^o - r.$$

It follows that under $\mathbf{H}_0 : R\beta^o = r$, we have

$$\sqrt{n}(R\hat{\beta} - r) \xrightarrow{d} N(0, RQ^{-1}VQ^{-1}R').$$

The test procedures will differ depending on whether there exists conditional heteroskedasticity. We first consider the case of conditional homoskedasticity.

Case I: Conditional Homoskedasticity

Under conditional homoskedasticity, we have $V = \sigma^2 Q$ and so

$$\sqrt{n}(R\hat{\beta} - r) \xrightarrow{d} N(0, \sigma^2 RQ^{-1}R')$$

when $\mathbf{H}_0$ holds.

When $J = 1$, we can use the conventional t-test statistic for large sample inference.

Theorem 4.7. *[**t-Test**]: Suppose Assumptions 4.1 to 4.4 and 4.6 hold. Then under* $\mathbf{H}_0$ *with* $J = 1$,

$$T = \frac{R\hat{\beta} - r}{\sqrt{s^2 R(\mathbf{X}'\mathbf{X})^{-1}R'}} \xrightarrow{d} N(0, 1)$$

as $n \to \infty$.

Proof: Give $R\sqrt{n}(\hat{\beta} - \beta^o) \xrightarrow{d} N(0, \sigma^2 RQ^{-1}R')$, $R\beta^o = r$ under $\mathbf{H}_0$, and $J = 1$, we have

$$\frac{\sqrt{n}(R\hat{\beta} - r)}{\sqrt{\sigma^2 RQ^{-1}R'}} = \frac{R\sqrt{n}(\hat{\beta} - \beta^o)}{\sqrt{\sigma^2 RQ^{-1}R'}} \xrightarrow{d} N(0, 1).$$

By $\hat{Q} = \mathbf{X}'\mathbf{X}/n \xrightarrow{p} Q$, $s^2 \xrightarrow{p} \sigma^2$ as $n \to \infty$, and Slutsky's theorem, we obtain

$$\frac{\sqrt{n}(R\hat{\beta} - r)}{\sqrt{s^2 R\hat{Q}^{-1}R'}} \xrightarrow{d} N(0, 1).$$

This ratio is the conventional t-test statistic introduced in Chapter 3, namely:

$$\frac{\sqrt{n}(R\hat{\beta} - r)}{\sqrt{s^2 R\hat{Q}^{-1}R'}} = \frac{R\hat{\beta} - r}{\sqrt{s^2 R(\mathbf{X}'\mathbf{X})^{-1}R'}} = T.$$

For $J > 1$, we use a quadratic form test statistic.

Theorem 4.8. ***[Wald Test]:*** *Suppose Assumptions 4.1 to 4.4 and 4.6 hold. Then under* $\mathbf{H}_0$, *as* $n \to \infty$,

$$\begin{aligned} W &\equiv (R\hat{\beta} - r)' \left[s^2 R(\mathbf{X}'\mathbf{X})^{-1} R'\right]^{-1} (R\hat{\beta} - r) \\ &= J \cdot F \\ &\xrightarrow{d} \chi^2_J. \end{aligned}$$

Proof: Under $\mathbf{H}_0 : R\beta^o = r$, $\sqrt{n}(R\hat{\beta} - r) \xrightarrow{d} N(0, \sigma^2 R Q^{-1} R')$ as $n \to \infty$. It follows that the quadratic form

$$\sqrt{n}(R\hat{\beta} - r)' \left(\sigma^2 R Q^{-1} R'\right)^{-1} \sqrt{n}(R\hat{\beta} - r) \xrightarrow{d} \chi^2_J.$$

Also, $s^2 \hat{Q}^{-1} \xrightarrow{p} \sigma^2 Q^{-1}$, so we have by Slutsky's theorem

$$W = \sqrt{n}(R\hat{\beta} - r)' \left(s^2 R \hat{Q}^{-1} R'\right)^{-1} \sqrt{n}(R\hat{\beta} - r) \xrightarrow{d} \chi^2_J,$$

or equivalently

$$\begin{aligned} W &= J \cdot \frac{(R\hat{\beta} - r)'[R(\mathbf{X}'\mathbf{X})^{-1} R']^{-1}(R\hat{\beta} - r)/J}{s^2} \\ &= J \cdot F \\ &\xrightarrow{d} \chi^2_J, \end{aligned}$$

where F is the F-test statistic introduced in Chapter 3.

When $\{\varepsilon_t\}$ is not IID $N(0, \sigma^2)$ conditional on $\mathbf{X}$, we cannot use the F-distribution, but we can still compute the F-statistic and the appropriate test statistic is J times the F-statistic, which is asymptotically χ^2_J under the null hypothesis. That is,

$$J \cdot F = \frac{(\tilde{e}'\tilde{e} - e'e)}{e'e/(n-K)} \xrightarrow{d} \chi^2_J \text{ as } n \to \infty.$$

Because $J \cdot F_{J,n-K}$ converges to χ^2_J as $n \to \infty$, we may interpret Theorem 4.8 in the following way: the classical results for the F-test are still approximately valid under conditional homoskedasticity when n is large.

When the null hypothesis is that all slope coefficients except the intercept are jointly zero, we can use a test statistic based on R^2.

Theorem 4.9. *[$(n-K)R^2$ Test]: Suppose Assumption 4.1 to 4.6 hold, and we are interested in testing the null hypothesis that*

$$\mathbf{H}_0 : \beta_1^o = \beta_2^o = \cdots = \beta_k^o = 0,$$

where $\{\beta_j^o\}$ are the regression coefficients from

$$Y_t = \beta_0^o + \beta_1^o X_{1t} + \cdots + \beta_k^o X_{kt} + \varepsilon_t.$$

Let R^2 be the coefficient of determination from the unrestricted regression model

$$Y_t = X_t'\beta^o + \varepsilon_t.$$

Then under $\mathbf{H}_0$,

$$(n-K)R^2 \xrightarrow{d} \chi_k^2$$

as $n \to \infty$, where $K = k+1$.

Proof: First, recall that in this special case we have

$$\begin{aligned} F &= \frac{R^2/k}{(1-R^2)/(n-k-1)} \\ &= \frac{R^2/k}{(1-R^2)/(n-K)}. \end{aligned}$$

By Theorem 4.8 and noting $J = k$, we have

$$k \cdot F = \frac{(n-K)R^2}{1-R^2} \xrightarrow{d} \chi_k^2$$

as $n \to \infty$ under $\mathbf{H}_0$. This implies that $k \cdot F$ is bounded in probability; that is,

$$\frac{(n-K)R^2}{1-R^2} = O_P(1).$$

Consequently, given that k is a fixed integer,

$$\frac{R^2}{1-R^2} = O_P(n^{-1}) = o_P(1)$$

or

$$R^2 \xrightarrow{p} 0.$$

Therefore, $1 - R^2 \xrightarrow{p} 1$. By Slutsky's theorem, we have

$$\begin{aligned}(n-K)R^2 &= k \cdot \frac{(n-K)R^2/k}{1-R^2}(1-R^2) \\ &= (k \cdot F)(1-R^2) \\ &\xrightarrow{d} \chi^2_k\end{aligned}$$

as $n \to \infty$, or asymptotically equivalently,

$$(n-K)R^2 \xrightarrow{d} \chi^2_k$$

as $n \to \infty$. This completes the proof.

Question: Do we have $nR^2 \xrightarrow{d} \chi^2_k$?

Yes, it follows from Slutsky's theorem and the facts that

$$nR^2 = \frac{n}{n-K}(n-K)R^2 \text{ and } \frac{n}{n-K} \to 1.$$

Question: Which test statistic, $(n-K)R^2$ or nR^2, should be used?

Case II: Conditional Heteroskedasticity

Recall that under $\mathbf{H}_0 : R\beta^o = r$,

$$\begin{aligned}\sqrt{n}(R\hat{\beta} - r) &= R\sqrt{n}(\hat{\beta} - \beta^o) + \sqrt{n}(R\beta^o - r) \\ &= R\sqrt{n}(\hat{\beta} - \beta^o) \\ &\xrightarrow{d} N(0, RQ^{-1}VQ^{-1}R'),\end{aligned}$$

where

$$V = E(X_t X_t' \varepsilon_t^2).$$

Therefore, when $J = 1$, we have

$$\frac{\sqrt{n}(R\hat{\beta} - r)}{\sqrt{RQ^{-1}VQ^{-1}R'}} \xrightarrow{d} N(0,1) \text{ as } n \to \infty.$$

Given $\hat{Q} \xrightarrow{p} Q$ and $\hat{V} \xrightarrow{p} V$, where $\hat{V} = \mathbf{X}'\mathrm{D}(e)\mathrm{D}(e)'\mathbf{X}/n$, and Slutsky's theorem, we can define a robust t-test statistic

$$T_r = \frac{\sqrt{n}(R\hat{\beta} - r)}{\sqrt{R\hat{Q}^{-1}\hat{V}\hat{Q}^{-1}R'}} \xrightarrow{d} N(0,1) \text{ as } n \to \infty$$

when $\mathbf{H}_0$ holds, where the subscript r in T_r indicates robustness. By robustness, we mean that T_r is asymptotically valid no matter whether there exists conditional heteroskedasticity.

Theorem 4.10. ***[Robust t-Test Under Conditional Heteroskedasticity]:*** *Suppose Assumptions 4.1 to 4.5 and 4.7 hold. Then under $\mathbf{H}_0$ with $J = 1$, as $n \to \infty$, the robust t-test statistic*

$$T_r = \frac{\sqrt{n}(R\hat{\beta} - r)}{\sqrt{R\hat{Q}^{-1}\hat{V}\hat{Q}^{-1}R'}} \xrightarrow{d} N(0, 1).$$

When $J > 1$, we have the quadratic form

$$\begin{aligned} W &= \sqrt{n}(R\hat{\beta} - r)' \left(RQ^{-1}VQ^{-1}R'\right)^{-1} \sqrt{n}(R\hat{\beta} - r) \\ &\xrightarrow{d} \chi^2_J \end{aligned}$$

under $\mathbf{H}_0$. Given $\hat{Q} \xrightarrow{p} Q$ and $\hat{V} \xrightarrow{p} V$, the robust Wald test statistic

$$\begin{aligned} W_r &= \sqrt{n}(R\hat{\beta} - r)' \left(R\hat{Q}^{-1}\hat{V}\hat{Q}^{-1}R'\right)^{-1} \sqrt{n}(R\hat{\beta} - r) \\ &\xrightarrow{d} \chi^2_J \end{aligned}$$

by Slutsky's theorem.

We can write W_r equivalently as follows:

$$W_r = (R\hat{\beta} - r)'[R(\mathbf{X}'\mathbf{X})^{-1}\mathbf{X}'\mathrm{D}(e)\mathrm{D}(e)'\mathbf{X}(\mathbf{X}'\mathbf{X})^{-1}R']^{-1}(R\hat{\beta} - r),$$

where we have used the fact that

$$\begin{aligned} \hat{V} &= \frac{1}{n}\sum_{t=1}^{n} X_t e_t e_t X_t' \\ &= \frac{\mathbf{X}'\mathrm{D}(e)\mathrm{D}(e)'\mathbf{X}}{n}, \end{aligned}$$

where $\mathrm{D}(e) = diag(e_1, e_2, ..., e_n)$.

Theorem 4.11. ***[Robust Wald Test Under Conditional Heteroskedasticity]:*** *Suppose Assumptions 4.1 to 4.5 and 4.7 hold. Then under $\mathbf{H}_0$, as $n \to \infty$,*

$$W_r = n(R\hat{\beta} - r)' \left(R\hat{Q}^{-1}\hat{V}\hat{Q}^{-1}R'\right)^{-1} (R\hat{\beta} - r) \xrightarrow{d} \chi^2_J.$$

It is important to emphasize that under conditional heteroskedasticity, the test statistics $J \cdot F$ and $(n-K)R^2$ cannot be used.

Question: What happens if there exists conditional heteroskedasticity but $J \cdot F$ or $(n-K)R^2$ is used in practice?

There will exist substantial distorted Type I errors because $J \cdot F$ or $(n-K)R^2$ will be no longer asymptotically χ^2-distributed under $\mathbf{H}_0$. Therefore, it would deliver misleading conclusions if $J \cdot F$ is used in this case.

Although the general form W_r of the Wald test statistic developed here is asymptotically valid no matter whether there exists conditional homoskedasticity or conditional heteroskedasticity, this general form W_r of test statistic may perform poorly in small samples in the sense that the asymptotic distribution will provide a poor approximation to its finite sample distribution, causing a distorted Type I error in small and finite samples. Thus, if one has information that the disturbance ε_t is conditionally homoskedastic, one should use the test statistics (e.g., $J \cdot F$ and $(n-K)R^2$) derived under conditional homoskedasticity, which will perform better in small sample sizes in the sense that its finite sample distribution will be closer to the asymptotic distribution. Because of this reason, it is important to test whether conditional homoskedasticity holds.

4.7 Testing for Conditional Homoskedasticity

Question: How to test conditional homoskedasticity for $\{\varepsilon_t\}$ in a linear regression model?

There have been many tests for conditional homoskedasticity. Here, we introduce a popular test proposed by White (1980).

Consider the null hypothesis

$$\mathbf{H}_0 : E(\varepsilon_t^2|X_t) = \sigma^2,$$

where ε_t is the regression disturbance in the linear regression model

$$Y_t = X_t'\beta^o + \varepsilon_t.$$

If the null hypothesis $\mathbf{H}_0$ is false, then $E(\varepsilon_t^2|X_t)$ will be a nonnegative function of X_t.

First, suppose ε_t were observed, and we consider the auxiliary regression

$$\begin{aligned}\varepsilon_t^2 &= \gamma_0 + \sum_{j=1}^{k} \gamma_j X_{jt} + \sum_{1 \le j \le l \le k} \gamma_{jl} X_{jt} X_{lt} + v_t \\ &= \gamma' \text{vech}(X_t X_t') + v_t \\ &= \gamma' U_t + v_t,\end{aligned}$$

where $\text{vech}(X_t X_t')$ is the so-called vech (vector half) operator stacks all lower triangular elements of the symmetric matrix $X_t X_t'$ into a $\frac{K(K+1)}{2} \times 1$ column vector. For example, when $X_t = (1, X_{1t}, X_{2t})'$, we have

$$\text{vech}(X_t X_t') = (1, X_{1t}, X_{2t}, X_{1t}^2, X_{1t} X_{2t}, X_{2t}^2)'.$$

For the auxiliary regression, there is a total of $\frac{K(K+1)}{2}$ regressors in U_t. This is essentially regressing ε_t^2 on the intercept, X_t, and the quadratic terms and cross-product terms of X_t. Under $\mathbf{H}_0$, all coefficients except the intercept are jointly zero. Any nonzero coefficients except the intercept will indicate the existence of conditional heteroskedasticity. Thus, we can test $\mathbf{H}_0$ by checking whether all coefficients except the intercept are jointly zero. Assuming that $E(\varepsilon_t^4|X_t) = \mu_4$ (which implies $E(v_t^2|X_t) = \sigma_v^2$ under $\mathbf{H}_0$), we can run an OLS regression and construct a R^2-based test statistic. Under $\mathbf{H}_0$, we can obtain

$$(n - J - 1)\tilde{R}^2 \xrightarrow{d} \chi_J^2,$$

where $J = \frac{K(K+1)}{2} - 1$ is the number of the regressors except the intercept. Unfortunately, ε_t is not observable in practice. However, we can replace ε_t with $e_t = Y_t - X_t'\hat{\beta}$, which is a consistent estimator for ε_t. Thus, we run the following feasible auxiliary regression

$$\begin{aligned}e_t^2 &= \gamma_0 + \sum_{j=1}^{k} \gamma_j X_{jt} + \sum_{1 \le j \le l \le k} \gamma_{jl} X_{jt} X_{lt} + \tilde{v}_t \\ &= \gamma' \text{vech}(X_t X_t') + \tilde{v}_t.\end{aligned}$$

Under $\mathbf{H}_0 : E(\varepsilon_t^2|X_t) = \sigma^2$, the resulting test statistic

$$(n - J - 1)R^2 \xrightarrow{d} \chi_J^2$$

as $n \to \infty$. It can be shown that the replacement of ε_t^2 by e_t^2 has no impact on the asymptotic χ_J^2 distribution of $(n - J - 1)R^2$. The proof, however, is rather tedious. For the details of the proof, see White (1980). Below, we provide some heuristics.

Question: Why does the use of e_t^2 in place of ε_t^2 not affect the asymptotic distribution of $(n-J-1)R^2$?

To explain this, we put $U_t = \text{vech}(X_t X_t')$ and consider the infeasible auxiliary regression

$$\varepsilon_t^2 = U_t'\gamma^o + v_t.$$

We have $\sqrt{n}(\tilde{\gamma}-\gamma^o) \xrightarrow{d} N(0, \sigma_v^2 Q_{\text{UU}}^{-1})$, where $Q_{\text{UU}} = E(U_t U_t')$, and $\tilde{\gamma}$ is the OLS estimator for γ^o. Under $\mathbf{H}_0 : R\gamma^o = 0$, where R is a $J \times J$ diagonal matrix with the first diagonal element being 0 and other diagonal elements being 1, we have

$$\sqrt{n}R\tilde{\gamma} \xrightarrow{d} N(0, \sigma_v^2 R Q_{\text{UU}}^{-1} R'),$$

where $\sigma_v^2 = E(v_t^2)$. This implies $R\tilde{\gamma} = O_P(n^{-1/2})$, which vanishes to zero in probability at rate $n^{-1/2}$. It is this term that yields the asymptotic χ_J^2 distribution for $(n-J-1)\tilde{R}^2$, which is asymptotically equivalent to the test statistic

$$\sqrt{n}(R\tilde{\gamma})'[s_v^2 R\hat{Q}_{\text{UU}}^{-1} R']^{-1}\sqrt{n}R\tilde{\gamma},$$

where s_v^2 is the residual variance estimator for σ_v^2.

Now suppose we replace ε_t^2 with e_t^2, and consider the feasible auxiliary regression

$$e_t^2 = U_t'\gamma^o + \tilde{v}_t.$$

Denote the OLS estimator by $\hat{\gamma}$ in this feasible auxiliary regression. To examine the impact of replacing ε_t^2 by e_t^2, we decompose

$$\begin{aligned} e_t^2 &= \left[\varepsilon_t - X_t'(\hat{\beta}-\beta^o)\right]^2 \\ &= \varepsilon_t^2 + (\hat{\beta}-\beta^o)' X_t X_t'(\hat{\beta}-\beta^o) - 2(\hat{\beta}-\beta^o)' X_t \varepsilon_t \\ &= \gamma' U_t + \tilde{v}_t. \end{aligned}$$

Thus, the OLS estimator $\hat{\gamma}$ can be written as follows:

$$\hat{\gamma} = \tilde{\gamma} + \hat{\delta} + \hat{\eta},$$

where $\tilde{\gamma}$ is the OLS estimator of γ^o in the infeasible auxiliary regression, $\hat{\delta}$ is the effect of the second term, and $\hat{\eta}$ is the effect of the third term. For the third term, $X_t\varepsilon_t$ is uncorrelated with U_t given $E(\varepsilon_t|X_t) = 0$. Therefore, this term, after further scaled by the factor $\hat{\beta}-\beta^o$ that itself vanishes to zero in probability at the rate $n^{-1/2}$, will vanish to zero in probability at a rate n^{-1}, that is, $\hat{\eta} = O_P(n^{-1})$. This is expected to have negligible impact on the asymptotic distribution of the test statistic $(n - J - 1)R^2$. For the second term, X_tX_t' is perfectly correlated with U_t. However, it is scaled by a factor of $||\hat{\beta} - \beta^o||^2$ rather than by $||\hat{\beta} - \beta^o||$. As a consequence, the regression coefficient of $(\hat{\beta} - \beta^o)'X_tX_t'(\hat{\beta} - \beta^o)$ on U_t will also vanish to zero at rate n^{-1}, that is, $\hat{\delta} = O_P(n^{-1})$. Therefore, it also has negligible impact on the asymptotic distribution of $(n - J - 1)R^2$.

Question: How to test conditional homoskedasticity if $E(\varepsilon_t^4|X_t)$ is not a constant (i.e., $E(\varepsilon_t^4|X_t) \neq \mu_4$ for any constant μ_4 under $\mathbf{H}_0$)? This corresponds to the case when v_t displays conditional heteroskedasticity.

Question: Suppose White's (1980) test rejects the null hypothesis of conditional homoskedasticity. Then one can conclude that there exists evidence of conditional heteroskedasticity. What conclusion can one reach if White's test fails to reject $\mathbf{H}_0 : E(\varepsilon_t^2|X_t) = \sigma^2$?

Because White (1980) considers a quadratic alternative to $\mathbf{H}_0$, White's (1980) test may have no power against some conditional heteroskedastic alternatives for which $E(\varepsilon_t^2|X_t)$ does not depend on the quadratic form of X_t but depends on cubic or higher order polynomials of X_t. Thus, when White's test fails to reject $\mathbf{H}_0$, one can only say that we find no evidence against $\mathbf{H}_0$.

However, when White's test fails to reject $\mathbf{H}_0$, we have

$$E(\varepsilon_t^2 X_t X_t') = \sigma^2 E(X_t X_t') = \sigma^2 Q$$

even if $\mathbf{H}_0$ is false. Therefore, one can use the conventional variance-covariance matrix estimator $s^2(\mathbf{X}'\mathbf{X})^{-1}$ for $\sqrt{n}\hat{\beta}$. Indeed, the main motivation for White's (1980) test for conditional heteroskedasticity is whether the heteroskedasticity-consistent variance-covariance matrix of $\sqrt{n}\hat{\beta}$ has to be used, not really whether conditional heteroskedasticity exists. For this purpose, it suffices to regress ε_t^2 or e_t^2 on the quadratic form of X_t. This can be seen from the decomposition

$$V = E(X_t X_t' \varepsilon_t^2) = \sigma^2 Q + \text{cov}(X_t X_t', \varepsilon_t^2),$$

which indicates that $V = \sigma^2 Q$ if and only if ε_t^2 is uncorrelated with $X_t X_t'$.

The validity of White's test and associated interpretation is built upon the assumption that the linear regression model is correctly specified for the conditional mean $E(Y_t|X_t)$. Suppose the linear regression model is not correctly specified, i.e., $E(Y_t|X_t) \neq X_t'\beta$ for all β. Then the OLS estimator $\hat{\beta}$ will converge to

$$\beta^* = [E(X_tX_t')]^{-1}E(X_tY_t),$$

the best linear least squares approximation coefficient, and $E(Y_t|X_t) \neq X_t'\beta^*$. In this case, the estimated residual

$$\begin{aligned} e_t &= Y_t - X_t'\hat{\beta} \\ &= \varepsilon_t + [E(Y_t|X_t) - X_t'\beta^*] + X_t'(\beta^* - \hat{\beta}), \end{aligned}$$

where $\varepsilon_t = Y_t - E(Y_t|X_t)$ is the true disturbance with $E(\varepsilon_t|X_t) = 0$, the estimation error $X_t'(\beta^* - \hat{\beta})$ vanishes to 0 as $n \to \infty$, but the approximation error $E(Y_t|X_t) - X_t'\beta^*$ never disappears. In other words, when the linear regression model is misspecified for $E(Y_t|X_t)$, the estimated residual e_t will contain not only the true disturbance but also the approximation error which is a function of X_t. This will result in a spurious conditional heteroskedasticity when White's test is used. Therefore, before using White's test or any other tests for conditional heteroskedasticity, it is important to first check whether the linear regression model is correctly specified. For tests of correct specification of a linear regression model, see Hausman's test in Chapter 7 and other specification tests mentioned there.

4.8 Conclusion

In this chapter, within the context of IID observations, we have relaxed some key assumptions of the classical linear regression model. In particular, we do not assume conditional normality for the regression disturbance ε_t and allow for conditional heteroskedasticity. Because the exact finite sample distribution of the OLS estimator is generally unknown, we have relied on asymptotic analysis. It is found that for large samples, the results of the OLS estimator $\hat{\beta}$ and related test statistics (e.g., the t-test and F-test statistics) are still applicable under conditional homoskedasticity. Under conditional heteroskedasticity, however, the statistical properties of $\hat{\beta}$ are different from those of $\hat{\beta}$ under conditional homoskedasticity, and as a consequence, the conventional t-test and F-test statistics are invalid even when the sample size $n \to \infty$. One has to use White's (1980) heteroskedasticity-consistent variance-covariance matrix estimator for the OLS estimator $\hat{\beta}$ and use it to construct robust test statistics. A direct test for conditional heteroskedasticity, due to White (1980), is described.

The asymptotic theory provides convenient inference procedures in practice. However, the finite sample distribution of $\hat{\beta}$ may be different from its asymptotic distribution. How well the approximation of the asymptotic distribution for the unknown finite sample distribution depends on the DGP and the sample size of the data. In econometrics, simulation studies have been used to examine how well asymptotic theory can approximate the finite sample distributions of econometric estimators or related statistics. They are the nearest approach that econometricians can make to the laboratory experiments of the physical sciences and are a very useful way of reinforcing or checking the theoretical results. Alternatively, resampling methods called bootstrap have been proposed in econometrics to approximate the finite sample distributions of econometric estimators or related statistics by simulating data on a computer (see, e.g., Hall 1992). In this book, we focus on the use of asymptotic theory.

Exercise 4

4.1. Suppose Assumptions 3.1, 3.3 and 3.5 hold. Show (1) the sample residual variance estimator s^2 converges in probability to σ^2, and (2) s converges in probability to σ.

4.2. Let $Z_1, ..., Z_n$ be a random sample from a population with mean μ and variance σ^2. Show that

$$E\left[\frac{\sqrt{n}(\bar{Z}_n - \mu)}{\sigma}\right] = 0 \text{ and } \mathrm{var}\left[\frac{\sqrt{n}(\bar{Z}_n - \mu)}{\sigma}\right] = 1.$$

4.3. Suppose a sequence of random variables $\{Z_n, n = 1, 2, ...\}$ is defined as

$$\begin{array}{lll} Z_n & \frac{1}{n} & n \\ P_{Z_n} & 1 - \frac{1}{n} & \frac{1}{n}. \end{array}$$

(1) Does Z_n converge in mean squares to 0? Give your reasoning clearly.
(2) Does Z_n converge in probability to 0? Give your reasoning clearly.

4.4. Let the sample space Ω be the closed interval [0,1] with the uniform probability distribution. Define $Z(\omega) = \omega$ for all $\omega \in [0, 1]$. Also, for $n = 1, 2, ...$, define a sequence of random variables

$$Z_n(s) = \begin{cases} \omega + \omega^n & \text{if } \omega \in [0, 1 - n^{-1}], \\ \omega + 1 & \text{if } \omega \in (1 - n^{-1}, 1]. \end{cases}$$

(1) Does Z_n converge in quadratic mean to Z?
(2) Does Z_n converge in probability to Z?
(3) Does Z_n converge almost surely to Z?

4.5. Suppose $g(\cdot)$ is a real-valued continuous function, and $\{Z_n, n = 1, 2, ...\}$ is a sequence of real-valued random variables which converges in probability to random variable Z. Show $g(Z_n) \xrightarrow{p} g(Z)$ as $n \to \infty$.

4.6. Suppose $g(\cdot)$ is a real-valued continuous function, and $\{Z_n, n = 1, 2, ...\}$ is a sequence of real-valued random variables which converges almost surely to random variable Z as $n \to \infty$. Show $g(Z_n) \xrightarrow{a.s.} g(Z)$.

4.7. Suppose $\mathbf{X}^n = (X_1, X_2, ..., X_n)$ is an IID random sample from an $N(0, 1)$ population. Define the sample mean $\bar{X}_n = n^{-1} \sum_{t=1}^{n} X_t$.

(1) What is the sampling distribution of the sample mean $\bar{X}_n$?

(2) Suppose $F_n(\cdot)$ is the cumulative distribution function of $\bar{X}_n$. What is the limit of $F_n(z)$?

(3) Find the asymptotic distribution of $\bar{X}_n$.

(4) Is the asymptotic distribution of $\bar{X}_n$ the same as $\lim_{n\to\infty} F_n(z)$? Explain.

4.8. Define $Z_n = X_n + Y_n$, where $\{X_n\}$ is an IID sequence from an $N(0,1)$ population, $\{Y_n\}$ is a sequence of binary random variables with $P(Y_n = \frac{1}{n}) = 1 - \frac{1}{n}$ and $P(Y_n = n) = \frac{1}{n}$, and X_n and Y_n are mutually independent.

(1) Find the limiting distribution (also called asymptotic distribution) of Z_n.

(2) The mean and variance of the asymptotic distribution are called the asymptotic mean and asymptotic variance respectively. Find $\lim_{n\to\infty} E(Z_n)$ and $\lim_{n\to\infty} \text{var}(Z_n)$. Are they the same as the asymptotic mean and asymptotic variance of Z_n respectively? Show your reasoning.

4.9. Suppose $\sqrt{n}(\bar{X}_n - \mu)/\sigma \xrightarrow{d} N(0,1)$ as $n \to \infty$, and function $g(\cdot)$ is twice continuously differentiable such that $g'(\mu) = 0$ and $g''(\mu) \neq 0$. Then show that as $n \to \infty$,

$$\frac{n\left[g(\bar{X}_n) - g(\mu)\right]}{\sigma^2} \xrightarrow{d} \frac{g''(\mu)}{2}\chi_1^2.$$

4.10. Suppose $\sqrt{n}(\bar{X}_n - \mu)/\sigma \xrightarrow{d} N(0,1)$ as $n \to \infty$, where $-\infty < \mu < \infty$ and $0 < \sigma < \infty$. Find a nondegenerate asymptotic distribution of a suitably normalized version of the following statistics:

(1) $Y_n = \exp(-\bar{X}_n)$.

(2) $Y_n = \bar{X}_n^2$, where $\mu = 0$ in this case.

Give your reasoning.

4.11. Suppose a stochastic process $\{Y_t, X_t'\}_{t=1}^n$ satisfies the following assumptions:

Assumption 1 [Linearity]: $\{Y_t, X_t'\}_{t=1}^n$ is an IID random sample with

$$Y_t = X_t'\beta^o + \varepsilon_t, \qquad t = 1, ..., n,$$

for some unknown parameter β^o and some unobservable disturbance ε_t.

Assumption 2 [IID]: The $K \times K$ matrix $E(X_tX_t') = Q$ is nonsingular and finite.

Assumption 3 [Conditional heteroskedasticity]:

(a) $E(X_t\varepsilon_t) = 0$.

(b) $E(\varepsilon_t^2|X_t) \neq \sigma^2$.

(c) $E(X_{jt}^4) \leq C$ for all $0 \leq j \leq k$, and $E(\varepsilon_t^4) \leq C$ for some $C < \infty$.

(1) Show $\hat{\beta} \xrightarrow{p} \beta^o$ as $n \to \infty$.

(2) Show $\sqrt{n}(\hat{\beta} - \beta^o) \xrightarrow{d} N(0, \Omega)$ as $n \to \infty$, where $\Omega = Q^{-1}VQ^{-1}$, and $V = E(X_tX_t'\varepsilon_t^2)$.

(3) Show that the asymptotic variance estimator

$$\hat{\Omega} = \hat{Q}^{-1}\hat{V}\hat{Q}^{-1} \xrightarrow{p} \Omega \text{ as } n \to \infty,$$

where $\hat{Q} = n^{-1}\sum_{t=1}^n X_tX_t'$ and $\hat{V} = n^{-1}\sum_{t=1}^n X_tX_t'e_t^2$. This is called White's (1980) heteroskedasticity-consistent variance-covariance matrix estimator.

(4) Consider a test for hypothesis $\mathbf{H}_0 : R\beta^o = r$. Does $J \cdot F \xrightarrow{d} \chi_J^2$, where

$$F = \frac{(R\hat{\beta} - r)'[R(\mathbf{X}'\mathbf{X})^{-1}R']^{-1}(R\hat{\beta} - r)/J}{s^2}$$

is the usual F-test statistic? If it does, give the reasoning. If it does not, could you provide an alternative test statistic that converges in distribution to χ_J^2 as $n \to \infty$?

4.12. Put $Q = E(X_tX_t'), V = E(\varepsilon_t^2X_tX_t')$ and $\sigma^2 = E(\varepsilon_t^2)$. Suppose there exists conditional heteroskedasticity, and $\text{cov}(\varepsilon_t^2, X_tX_t') = V - \sigma^2Q$ is PSD, i.e., $\sigma^2(X_t)$ is positively correlated with X_tX_t'. Show that $Q^{-1}VQ^{-1} - \sigma^2Q^{-1}$ is PSD.

4.13. Suppose the following assumptions hold:

Assumption 1: $\{Y_t, X_t'\}_{t=1}^n$ is an IID random sample with

$$Y_t = X_t'\beta^o + \varepsilon_t,$$

for some unknown parameter β^o and unobservable random disturbance ε_t.

Assumption 2: $E(\varepsilon_t|X_t) = 0$.

Assumption 3:

(a) $W_t = W(X_t)$ is a positive function of X_t.

(b) The $K \times K$ matrix $E(X_t W_t X_t') = Q_W$ is finite and nonsingular.

(c) $E(W_t^8) \leq C < \infty$, $E(X_{jt}^8) \leq C < \infty$ for all $0 \leq j \leq k$, and $E(\varepsilon_t^4) \leq C$.

Assumption 4: $V_W = E(W_t^2 X_t X_t' \varepsilon_t^2)$ is finite and nonsingular.

We consider the so-called Weighted Least Squares (WLS) estimator for β^o :

$$\hat{\beta}_W = \left(n^{-1} \sum_{t=1}^{n} X_t W_t X_t' \right)^{-1} n^{-1} \sum_{t=1}^{n} X_t W_t Y_t.$$

(1) Show that $\hat{\beta}_W$ is the solution to the following problem

$$\min_{\beta} \sum_{t=1}^{n} W_t (Y_t - X_t'\beta)^2.$$

(2) Show that $\hat{\beta}_W$ is consistent for β^o.

(3) Show that $\sqrt{n}(\hat{\beta}_W - \beta^o) \xrightarrow{d} N(0, \Omega_W)$ for some $K \times K$ finite and positive definite matrix Ω_W. Obtain the expressions of Ω_W under (i) conditional homoskedasticity $E(\varepsilon_t^2|X_t) = \sigma^2$ and (ii) conditional heteroskedasticity $E(\varepsilon_t^2|X_t) \neq \sigma^2$ respectively.

(4) Propose an estimator $\hat{\Omega}_W$ for Ω_W, and show that $\hat{\Omega}_w$ is consistent for Ω_w under conditional homoskedasticity and conditional heteroskedasticity respectively.

(5) Construct a test statistic for $\mathbf{H}_0 : R\beta^o = r$, where R is a $J \times K$ matrix and r is a $J \times 1$ vector under conditional homoskedasticity and under conditional heteroskedasticity respectively. Derive the asymptotic distribution of the test statistic under $\mathbf{H}_0$ in each case.

(6) Suppose $E(\varepsilon_t^2|X_t) = \sigma^2(X_t)$ is known, and we set $W_t = \sigma^{-1}(X_t)$. Construct a test statistic for $\mathbf{H}_0 : R\beta^o = r$, where R is a $J \times K$ matrix and r is a $J \times 1$ vector. Derive the asymptotic distribution of the test statistic under $\mathbf{H}_0$.

4.14. Consider the problem of testing conditional homoskedasticity ($\mathbf{H}_0 : E(\varepsilon_t^2|X_t) = \sigma^2$) for a linear regression model

$$Y_t = X_t'\beta^o + \varepsilon_t,$$

where X_t is a $K \times 1$ vector consisting of an intercept and explanatory variables. To test conditional homoskedasticity, we consider the auxiliary regression

$$\begin{aligned}\varepsilon_t^2 &= \text{vech}(X_t X_t')'\gamma + v_t \\ &= U_t'\gamma + v_t.\end{aligned}$$

Show that under $\mathbf{H}_0 : E(\varepsilon_t^2|X_t) = \sigma^2$, we have (1) $E(v_t|X_t) = 0$; and (2) $E(v_t^2|X_t) = \sigma_v^2$ if and only if $E(\varepsilon_t^4|X_t) = \mu_4$ for some constant μ_4.

4.15. Consider testing conditional homoskedasticity ($\mathbf{H}_0 : E(\varepsilon_t^2|X_t) = \sigma^2$) for a linear regression model

$$Y_t = X_t'\beta^o + \varepsilon_t,$$

where X_t is a $K \times 1$ vector consisting of an intercept and explanatory variables. To test conditional homoskedasticity, we consider the auxiliary regression

$$\begin{aligned}\varepsilon_t^2 &= \text{vech}(X_t X_t')'\gamma + v_t \\ &= U_t'\gamma + v_t,\end{aligned}$$

where $U_t = \text{vech}(X_t X_t')$ is a $J \times 1$ vector, with $J = K(K+1)/2$. Suppose Assumptions 4.1, 4.2, 4.3, 4.4 and 4.7 in Chapter 4 hold, and $E(\varepsilon_t^4|X_t) = \mu_4$. Assume that $\{\varepsilon_t\}$ is an observable sequence, and denote R^2 be the coefficient of determination of the auxiliary regression. Show that the test statistic $(n - J - 1)R^2 \xrightarrow{d} \chi_J^2$ under the null hypothesis of conditional homoskedasticity for $\{\varepsilon_t\}$. Give your reasoning.

4.16. In Exercise 4.15, the assumption that $\{\varepsilon_t\}$ is observable is not realistic. In practice, we need to replace ε_t by $e_t = Y_t - X_t'\hat{\beta}$, the estimated OLS residual. Provide a heuristic explanation why the replacement of ε_t by e_t has no impact on the asymptotic distribution of the proposed test statistic for conditional homoskedasticity in Exercise 4.15.

4.17. Consider the problem of testing conditional homoskedasticity ($\mathbf{H}_0$: $E(\varepsilon_t^2|X_t) = \sigma^2$) for a linear regression model

$$Y_t = X_t'\beta^o + \varepsilon_t,$$

where X_t is a $K \times 1$ vector consisting of an intercept and explanatory variables. To test conditional homoskedasticity, we consider the auxiliary regression

$$\begin{aligned}\varepsilon_t^2 &= \text{vech}(X_t X_t')'\gamma + v_t \\ &= U_t'\gamma + v_t.\end{aligned}$$

Suppose Assumptions 4.1, 4.2, 4.3, 4.4 and 4.7 of Chapter 4 hold, and $E(\varepsilon_t^4|X_t) \neq \mu_4$. That is, $E(\varepsilon_t^4|X_t)$ is a function of X_t.

(1) Show $\text{var}(v_t|X_t) \neq \sigma_v^2$ under $\mathbf{H}_0$. That is, the disturbance v_t in the auxiliary regression model displays conditional heteroskedasticity.

(2) Suppose ε_t is directly observable. Construct an asymptotically valid test for the null hypothesis $\mathbf{H}_0$ of conditional homoskedasticity of ε_t. Derive the asymptotic distribution of the proposed test statistic and provide your reasoning.

4.18. In Exercise 4.17, the assumption that $\{\varepsilon_t\}$ is observable is not realistic. In practice, we need to replace ε_t by $e_t = Y_t - X_t'\hat{\beta}$, the estimated OLS residual. Provide a heuristic explanation why the replacement of ε_t by e_t has no impact on the asymptotic distribution of the proposed robust test statistic for conditional homoskedasticity in Exercise 4.17.

4.19. Suppose $\{Y_t, X_i'\}_{t=1}^n$ is an IID random sample. Consider a nonlinear regression model

$$Y_t = g(X_t, \beta^o) + \varepsilon_t,$$

where β^o is an unknown $K \times 1$ parameter vector, $E(\varepsilon_t|X_t) = 0$, $E(\varepsilon_t^2|X_t) = \sigma^2$, and σ^2 is an unknown constant. Assume that $g(X_t, \cdot)$ is twice continuously differentiable with respect to β with the $K \times K$ matrices $A(\beta) = E[\frac{\partial g(X_t,\beta)}{\partial \beta}\frac{\partial g(X_t,\beta)}{\partial \beta'}]$ and $B(\beta) = E[\frac{\partial^2 g(X_t,\beta)}{\partial \beta \partial \beta'}]$ finite, nonsingular and continuous for all $\beta \in \Theta$, where Θ is a compact set. We further assume that as $n \to \infty$,

$$\sup_{\beta \in \Theta} \left| \frac{1}{n} \sum_{t=1}^n \frac{\partial g(X_t, \beta)}{\partial \beta} \frac{\partial g(X_t, \beta)}{\partial \beta'} - A(\beta) \right| \xrightarrow{p} 0,$$

$$\sup_{\beta \in \Theta} \left| \frac{1}{n} \sum_{t=1}^n \frac{\partial^2 g(X_t, \beta)}{\partial \beta \partial \beta'} - B(\beta) \right| \xrightarrow{p} 0.$$

The Nonlinear Least Squares (NLS) estimator $\hat{\beta}$ is defined to solve the minimization of the SSR problem, i.e.,

$$\hat{\beta} = \arg\min_{\beta} \sum_{t=1}^n \left[Y_t - g(X_t, \beta)\right]^2.$$

The FOC is

$$\sum_{t=1}^{n} \frac{\partial g(X_t, \hat{\beta})}{\partial \beta}[Y_t - g(X_t, \hat{\beta})] = 0,$$

where $\frac{\partial}{\partial \beta} g(X_t, \beta)$ is a $K \times 1$ vector.

Generally, there exists no closed form expression for $\hat{\beta}$, but it can be shown that $\hat{\beta} \xrightarrow{p} \beta^o$ as $n \to \infty$ and this can be used in answering the questions below. We assume that all necessary regularity conditions hold.

(1) Derive the asymptotic distribution of $\sqrt{n}(\hat{\beta} - \beta^o)$. Give your reasoning.

(2) Construct a Wald-type test for the hypothesis of interest $\mathbf{H}_0 : R(\beta^o) = r$, where $R(\cdot)$ is a $J \times 1$ continuously differentiable vector-valued function, r is a $J \times 1$ known constant vector, and $J > 1$. Derive the asymptotic distribution of the test statistic under $\mathbf{H}_0$. Give your reasoning. [*Hint: The derivative* $R'(\beta) = \frac{d}{d\beta} R(\beta)$ *is a* $J \times K$ *matrix.*]

4.20. Suppose we do not impose the conditional homoskedasticity condition, i.e., we do not assume $E(\varepsilon_t^2|X_t) = \sigma^2$. Resolve the questions in Exercise 4.19.

Chapter 5

Linear Regression Models with Dependent Observations

Abstract: In this chapter, we will show that the asymptotic theory for linear regression models with IID observations carries over to ergodic stationary linear time series regression models with Martingale Difference Sequence (MDS) disturbances. Some basic concepts in time series analysis are introduced, and some tests for serial correlation are described.

Keywords: AutoRegressive Conditional Heteroskedasticity (ARCH), Conditional heteroskedasticity, Difference-stationary process, Dynamic regression model, Ergodicity, Martingale, MDS, Random walk, Serial correlation, Static regression model, Stationarity, Time series, Trend-stationary process, Unit root, White Noise (WN)

5.1 Introduction to Time Series Analysis

The asymptotic theory developed in Chapter 4 is applicable to cross-sectional data (due to the IID random sample assumption). What happens if we have time series data? Could the asymptotic theory for linear regression models with IID observations be applicable to linear regression models with time series observations?

Consider a simple regression model

$$\begin{aligned} Y_t &= X_t'\beta^o + \varepsilon_t \\ &= \beta_0 + \beta_1 Y_{t-1} + \varepsilon_t, \\ \{\varepsilon_t\} &\sim \text{IID}N(0, \sigma^2), \end{aligned}$$

where $X_t = (1, Y_{t-1})'$. This is called a first order AutoRegressive model, denoted as AR(1), which violates the IID assumption for $\{Y_t, X_t'\}_{t=1}^n$ in

Chapter 4. Here, we have

$$E(\varepsilon_t|X_t) = 0$$

but no longer have

$$\begin{aligned} E(\varepsilon_t|\mathbf{X}) &= E(\varepsilon_t|X_1, X_2, ..., X_n) \\ &= 0 \end{aligned}$$

because X_{t+j} contains ε_t when $j > 0$. Hence, Assumption 3.2 (strict exogeneity) fails.

In general, the IID assumption for $\{Y_t, X_t'\}_{t=1}^n$ in Chapter 4 rules out time series data. Most economic and financial data are time series observations.

Question: Under what conditions will the asymptotic theory developed in Chapter 4 carry over to linear regression models with dependent observations?

To establish asymptotic theory for linear regression models with time series observations, we need to introduce some basic concepts in time series.

Question: What is a time series process?

A time series process can be stochastic or deterministic. For example, in chaos theory, a logistic map

$$Z_t = 4Z_{t-1}(1 - Z_{t-1})$$

is a deterministic time series process, which can generate a seemingly uncorrelated sequence. In this book, we only consider stochastic time series processes, which are consistent with the fundamental axiom of modern econometrics discussed in Chapter 1.

Definition 5.1. [Stochastic Time Series Process]: A stochastic time series $\{Z_t\}$ is a sequence of random variables or random vectors indexed by time $t \in \{..., 0, 1, 2, ...\}$ and governed by some probability law (Ω, F, P), where Ω is the sample space, F is a σ-field, and P is a probability measure, with $P : F \to [0, 1]$.

More precisely, we can write $Z_t = Z(t, \cdot)$, and its realization $z_t = Z(t, \omega)$, where $\omega \in \Omega$ is a basic outcome in sample space Ω.

For each ω, we can obtain a sample path $z_t = Z(t, \omega)$ of the process $\{Z_t\}$ as a deterministic function of time t. Different ω's will give different sample paths.

The dynamics of $\{Z_t\}$ is completely determined by the *transition probability* of Z_t, i.e., the *conditional probability* of Z_t given its past history $I_{t-1} = \{Z_{t-1}, Z_{t-2}, ...\}$.

Based on a time series process, we can define a time series random sample. Consider a segment of a time series process $\{Z_t\}$ for $t = 1, ..., n$. This is called a time series random sample of size n, denoted as

$$\mathbf{Z}^n = \{Z_1, ..., Z_n\}'.$$

Any realization of this random sample is called a time series data set, denoted as

$$\mathbf{z}^n = \{z_1, ..., z_n\}'.$$

This corresponds to the occurrence of some specific outcome $\omega \in \Omega$. In theory, a random sample $\mathbf{Z}^n$ can generate many data sets, each corresponding to a specific $\omega \in \Omega$. In reality, however, one only observes a data set for any random sample of an economic time series process, due to the nonexperimental nature of the economic system.

Question: How to characterize the dynamics of the time series process $\{Z_t\}$, namely, how it evolves over time?

Consider the random sample $\mathbf{Z}^n$ where Z_t follows a continuous probability distribution. It is well-known from basic statistics courses that the joint Probability Density Function (PDF) of the random sample $\mathbf{Z}^n$,

$$f_{\mathbf{Z}^n}(\mathbf{z}^n) = f_{Z_1, Z_2, ..., Z_n}(z_1, z_2, ..., z_n), \qquad \mathbf{z}^n \in \mathbb{R}^n,$$

completely captures all the sample information contained in $\mathbf{Z}^n$. With $f_{\mathbf{Z}^n}(\mathbf{z}^n)$, we can, in theory, obtain the sampling distribution of any statistic (e.g., the sample mean estimator, the sample variance estimator, and the $(1 - \alpha)100\%$ confidence interval estimator) that is a function of $\mathbf{Z}^n$.

Now, by sequential partition (repeating the multiplication rule $P(A \cap B) = P(A|B)P(B)$ for any events A and B), we can write

$$f_{\mathbf{Z}^n}(\mathbf{z}^n) = \prod_{t=1}^{n} f_{Z_t|I_{t-1}}(z_t|I_{t-1}),$$

where by convention, for $t = 1$, $f(z_1|I_0) = f(z_1)$, the marginal PDF of Z_1. Thus, the conditional PDF $f_{Z_t|I_{t-1}}(z|I_{t-1})$ completely describes the joint probability distribution of the random sample $\mathbf{Z}^n$. Note that I_{t-1}=$\mathbf{Z}^{t-1}$.

Example 5.1. Let Z_t be the U.S. GDP in quarter t. Then the quarterly records of the U.S. GDP from the second quarter of 1947 to the last quarter of 2017 constitute a time series data set, denoted as $\mathbf{z}^n = (z_1, ..., z_n)'$, with $n = 284$.

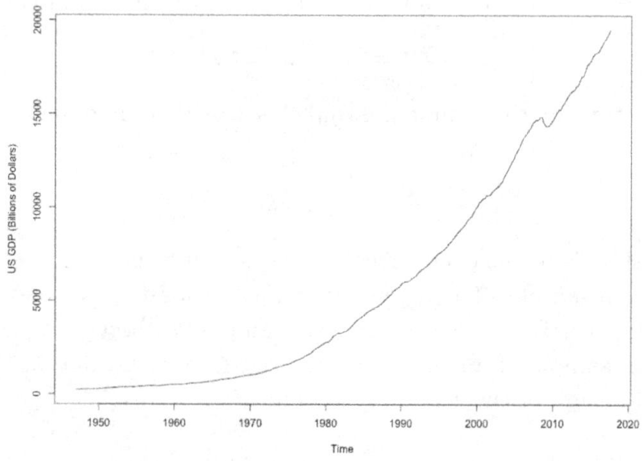

Figure 5.1 Quarterly data of U.S. GDP.
Data source: https://www.macrotrends.net

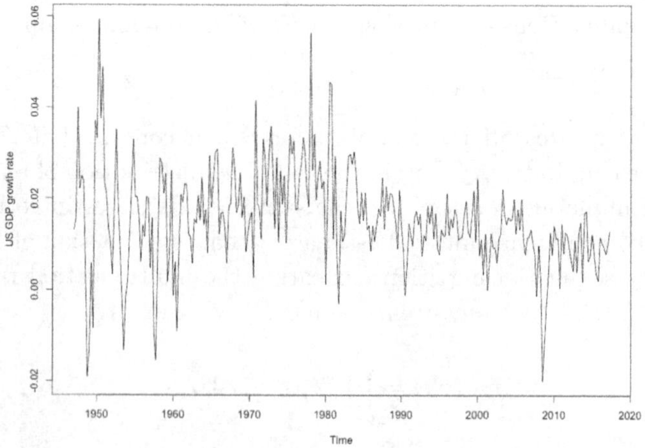

Figure 5.2 Quarterly data of U.S. GDP growth rates.
Data source: https://www.macrotrends.net

Example 5.2. Let Z_t be the Standard and Poor 500 (S&P 500) closing price index at day t. Then the daily records of the S&P 500 index from January 2, 1970 to December 29, 2017 constitute a time series data set, denoted as $\mathbf{z}^n = (z_1, ..., z_n)'$, with $n = 12110$.

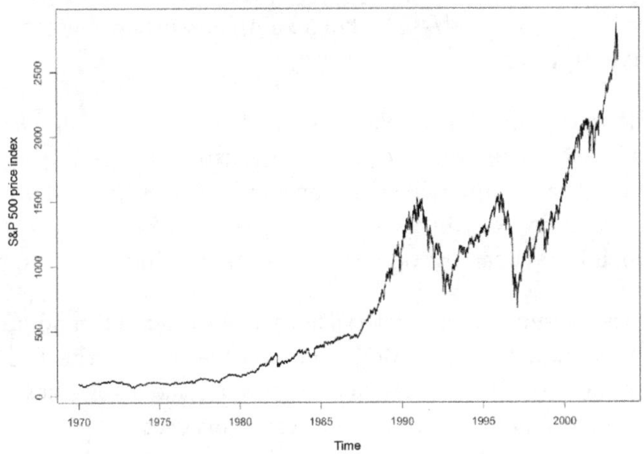

Figure 5.3 Daily data of S&P 500 price index.

Data source: Datastream

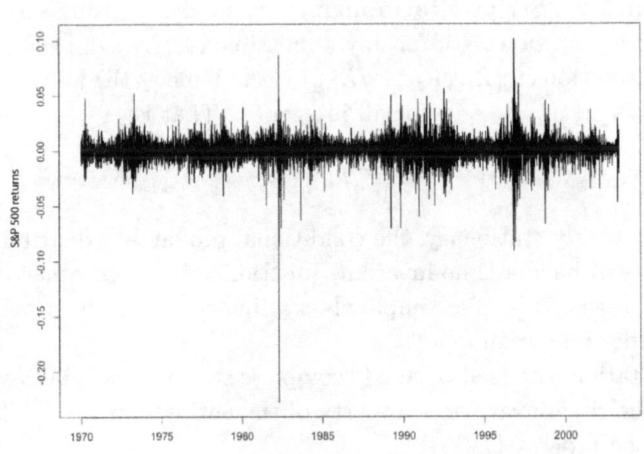

Figure 5.4 Daily data on S&P 500 returns.

Data source: Datastream

Here is a fundamental feature of an economic time series: each random variable Z_t only has one observed realization z_t in practice. It is impossible to obtain more realizations for each economic variable Z_t, due to the nonexperimental nature of the economic system. In order to "aggregate" realizations from different random variables $\{Z_t\}_{t=1}^n$, we need to impose a stationarity assumption, a concept of stability for certain aspects of the probability law $f_{Z_t|I_{t-1}}(z_t|I_{t-1})$. For example, we may need to make the following assumptions:

- The marginal PDF of each Z_t shares some common features (e.g., the same mean, and the same variance).
- The relationship (joint distribution) between Z_t and I_{t-1} is time-invariant in certain aspects (e.g., $\text{cov}(Z_t, Z_{t-j}) = \gamma(j)$ does not depend on time t; it only depends on the time distance j).

With these assumptions, observations from different random variables $\{Z_t\}$ can be viewed to share some common features of the DGP, so that one can conduct statistical inference by pooling them together. These observations over time constitute a time series data set.

We now introduce the concept of stationarity. A stochastic time series $\{Z_t\}$ can be stationary or nonstationary. There are various notions for stationarity. The first is strict stationarity.

Definition 5.2. [Strict Stationarity]: A stochastic time series process $\{Z_t\}$ is strictly stationary if for any admissible $t_1, t_2, ..., t_m$, the joint probability distribution of $\{Z_{t_1}, Z_{t_2}, ..., Z_{t_m}\}$ is the same as the joint distribution of $\{Z_{t_1+k}, Z_{t_2+k}, ..., Z_{t_m+k}\}$ for all integers k. That is,

$$f_{Z_{t_1} Z_{t_2} \cdots Z_{t_m}}(z_1, ..., z_m) = f_{Z_{t_1+k} Z_{t_2+k} \cdots Z_{t_m+k}}(z_1, ..., z_m).$$

If Z_t is strictly stationary, the conditional probability distribution of Z_t given I_{t-1} will have a time-invariant functional form. In other words, the probabilistic structure of a completely stationary process is invariant under a shift of the time origin.

Strict stationarity is also called "complete stationarity", because it characterizes the time-invariance property of the entire joint probability distribution of the process $\{Z_t\}$.

No moment condition on $\{Z_t\}$ is needed when defining strict stationarity. Thus, a strictly stationary process may not have finite moments (e.g., $\text{var}(Z_t) = \infty$). However, if moments (e.g., $E(Z_t)$) and joint product moments (e.g., $E(Z_t Z_{t-j})$) of $\{Z_t\}$ exist, then they are time-invariant when $\{Z_t\}$ is strictly stationary. Moreover, any measurable transformation of a strictly stationary process is strictly stationary.

Strict stationarity implies identical distribution for each Z_t. Thus, although strictly stationary time series data are realizations from different random variables, they can be viewed as realizations from the same (marginal) population distribution.

Example 5.3. [IID Cauchy Sequence]: Suppose $\{Z_t\}$ is an IID Cauchy $(0, 1)$ sequence with marginal PDF

$$f(z) = \frac{1}{\pi(1+z^2)}, \qquad -\infty < z < \infty.$$

Note that Z_t has no moment. Consider $\{Z_{t_1}, ..., Z_{t_m}\}$. Because their joint PDF

$$f_{Z_{t_1} Z_{t_2} ... Z_{t_m}}(z_1, ..., z_m) = \prod_{j=1}^{m} f(z_j)$$

is time-invariant, $\{Z_t\}$ is strictly stationary.

We now introduce another concept of stationarity based on the time-invariance property of the joint product moments of $\{Z_{t_1}, Z_{t_2}, ..., Z_{t_m}\}$.

Definition 5.3. [N-th Order Stationarity]: Let N be a positive integer. The time series process$\{Z_t\}$ is said to be stationary up to order N if, for any admissible $t_1, t_2, ..., t_m$, and any k, all the joint product moments up to order N of $\{Z_{t_1}, Z_{t_2}, ..., Z_{t_m}\}$ exist and are equal to the corresponding joint product moments up to order N *of* $\{Z_{t_1+k}, ..., Z_{t_m+k}\}$. That is,

$$E\left[(Z_{t_1})^{n_1} \cdots (Z_{t_m})^{n_m}\right] = E\left[(Z_{t_1+k})^{n_1} \cdots (Z_{t_m+k})^{n_m}\right],$$

for any k and all nonnegative integers $n_1, ..., n_m$ satisfying $\sum_{j=1}^{m} n_j \leq N$.

Setting $n_2 = n_3 = ... = n_m = 0$, we have

$$E\left[(Z_t)^{n_1}\right] = E\left[(Z_0)^{n_1}\right] \text{ for all } t.$$

On the other hand, for $n_1 + n_2 \leq N$, we have the pairwise joint product moment

$$E[(Z_t)^{n_1}(Z_{t-j})^{n_2}] = E[(Z_0)^{n_1}(Z_{-j})^{n_2}]$$
$$= \text{function of } j,$$

where j is called a lag order.

We now consider a special case: $N = 2$. This yields a concept called weak stationarity.

Definition 5.4. [Weak Stationarity]: A stochastic time series process $\{Z_t\}$ is weakly stationary if

(1) $E(Z_t) = \mu$ for all t;
(2) $\text{var}(Z_t) = \sigma^2 < \infty$ for all t;
(3) $\text{cov}(Z_t, Z_{t-j}) = \gamma(j)$ is only a function of lag order j for all t.

Strict stationarity is defined in terms of the "time invariance" property of the entire probability distribution of the time series process $\{Z_t\}$, while weak-stationarity is defined in terms of the "time-invariance" property in the first two moments (means, variances and covariances) of the process $\{Z_t\}$. Suppose all moments of $\{Z_t\}$ exist. Then it is possible that the first two moments are time-invariant but the higher order moments are time-varying. In other words, a process $\{Z_t\}$ can be weakly stationary but not strictly stationary. However, Example 5.3 shows that a process can be strictly stationary but not weakly stationary, because the first two moments simply do not exist.

Weak stationarity is also called "covariance-stationarity", or "second order stationarity" because it is based on the time-invariance property of the first two moments. It does not require identical distribution for each Z_t. The higher order moments of Z_t can be different for different t's. The definitions from strict stationarity to N-th order stationarity to weak stationarity provide various concepts of stationarity. Hong, Wang and Wang (2017) propose a test for strict stationary and a class of derivative tests for N-th order stationarity including weak stationarity.

Question: Which, strict or weak stationarity, is more restrictive?

We consider two cases:

- Case I: If $E(Z_t^2) < \infty$, then strict stationarity implies weak stationarity.

- Case II: If $E(Z_t^2) = \infty$, then strict stationarity does not imply weak stationarity. In other words, a time series process can be strictly stationary but not weakly stationary.

Example 5.4. An IID Cauchy(0, 1) process is strictly stationary but not weakly stationary.

A special but important weakly stationary time series is a process with zero autocorrelations.

Definition 5.5. [White Noise (WN)]: A weakly stationary time series process $\{Z_t\}$ is a WN (or serially uncorrelated) process if

(1) $E(Z_t) = 0$,
(2) $\text{var}(Z_t) = \sigma^2$,
(3) $\text{cov}(Z_t, Z_{t-j}) = \gamma(j) = 0$ for all $j > 0$.

Later we will explain why such a process is called a WN. The WN assumption is a basic building block for linear time series modeling. Any zero-mean weakly stationary time series process can be decomposed as a linear combination of a WN sequence, and this is called *Wold's decomposition*.

When a WN sequence $\{Z_t\}$ is a Gaussian process (i.e., any finite set $(Z_{t_1}, Z_{t_2}, ..., Z_{t_m})$ of $\{Z_t\}$ has a joint normal distribution), we call $\{Z_t\}$ is a Gaussian WN. For a Gaussian WN process, $\{Z_t\}$ is an IID sequence.

Example 5.5. [AR(1)]: A first order AutoRegressive (AR) process, denoted as AR(1),

$$Z_t = \alpha Z_{t-1} + \varepsilon_t,$$
$$\{\varepsilon_t\} \sim \text{WN}(0, \sigma^2),$$

is weakly stationary if $|\alpha| < 1$ because $Z_t = \sum_{j=0}^{\infty} \alpha^j \varepsilon_{t-j}$, and

$$\begin{aligned} E(Z_t) &= 0, \\ \text{var}(Z_t) &= \frac{\sigma^2}{1-\alpha^2}, \\ \gamma(j) &= \frac{\sigma^2}{1-\alpha^2}\alpha^{|j|}, \qquad j = 0, \pm 1, \pm 2, ... \end{aligned}$$

Here, ε_t may be interpreted as a random shock or an innovation that drives the movement of the process $\{Z_t\}$ over time.

More generally, $\{Z_t\}$ is a p-th order AR process, denoted as AR(p), if

$$Z_t = \alpha_0 + \sum_{j=1}^{p} \alpha_j Z_{t-j} + \varepsilon_t,$$
$$\{\varepsilon_t\} \sim \text{WN}(0, \sigma^2).$$

Example 5.6. [MA(q)]: $\{Z_t\}$ is a q-th order Moving-Average (MA) process, denoted as MA(q), if

$$Z_t = \alpha_0 + \sum_{j=1}^{q} \alpha_j \varepsilon_{t-j} + \varepsilon_t,$$
$$\{\varepsilon_t\} \sim \text{WN}(0, \sigma^2).$$

This is a weakly stationary process. For an MA(q) process, we have $\gamma(j) = 0$ for all $|j| > q$.

Example 5.7. [ARMA(p, q)]: $\{Z_t\}$ is an AutoRegressive-Moving Average (ARMA) process of orders (p, q), denoted as ARMA(p, q), if

$$Z_t = \alpha_0 + \sum_{j=1}^{p} \alpha_j Z_{t-j} + \sum_{j=1}^{q} \beta_j \varepsilon_{t-j} + \varepsilon_t,$$
$$\{\varepsilon_t\} \sim \text{WN}(0, \sigma^2).$$

ARMA models include AR and MA models as special cases. An estimation method for ARMA models can be found in Chapter 9. In practice, the orders of (p, q) can be selected according to the AIC or BIC criterion.

Under rather mild regularity conditions, a zero-mean weakly stationary process can be represented by an MA(∞) process

$$Z_t = \sum_{j=0}^{\infty} \alpha_j \varepsilon_{t-j},$$
$$\{\varepsilon_t\} \sim \text{WN}(0, \sigma^2),$$

where $\sum_{j=1}^{\infty} \alpha_j^2 < \infty$. This is called *Wold's decomposition.* The partial derivative

$$\frac{\partial Z_{t+j}}{\partial \varepsilon_t} = \alpha_j, j = 0, 1, ...$$

is called the impulse response function of the time series process $\{Z_t\}$ with respect to a random shock ε_t. This function characterizes the impact of a random shock ε_t on the immediate and subsequent observations $\{Z_{t+j}, j \geq 0\}$. For a weakly stationary process, the impact of any shock on a future Z_{t+j} will always diminish to zero as the lag order $j \to \infty$, because $\alpha_j \to 0$. The ultimate cumulative impact of ε_t on the process $\{Z_t\}$ is the sum $\sum_{j=0}^{\infty} \alpha_j$. For the example of a weakly stationary AR(1) process,

$$Z_t = \sum_{j=1}^{\infty} \alpha^j \varepsilon_{t-j} + \varepsilon_t.$$

On the other hand, under a suitable condition, a zero-mean weakly stationary time series can also be represented as an AR(∞) process. Such a condition is called the invertibility condition, which allows one to represent the unobservable innovation ε_t as a linear combination of observable observations $\{Z_{t-j}\}_{j=0}^{\infty}$. Invertibility is a crucial condition for time series forecasts.

The function $\gamma(j) = \text{cov}(Z_t, Z_{t-j})$ is called the autocovariance function of the weakly stationary process $\{Z_t\}$, where j is a lag order. It characterizes the (linear) serial dependence of Z_t on its own lagged variable Z_{t-j}. Note that $\gamma(j) = \gamma(-j)$ for all integers j.

The normalized function $\rho(j) = \gamma(j)/\gamma(0)$ is called the autocorrelation function of $\{Z_t\}$. It has the property that $|\rho(j)| \leq 1$. The plot of $\rho(j)$ as a function of j is called the autocorrelogram of the time series process $\{Z_t\}$. It can be used to judge which linear time series model (e.g., AR, MA, or ARMA) should be used to fit a particular time series data set.

We now consider the Fourier transform of the autocovariance function $\gamma(j)$.

Definition 5.6. [Spectral Density Function]: The Fourier transform of $\gamma(j)$

$$h(\omega) = \frac{1}{2\pi} \sum_{j=-\infty}^{\infty} \gamma(j) e^{-\mathbf{i}j\omega}, \qquad \omega \in [-\pi, \pi],$$

where $\mathbf{i} = \sqrt{-1}$, is called the power spectral density function or spectral density function of a weakly stationary time series process $\{Z_t\}$.

The normalized version

$$f(\omega) = \frac{h(\omega)}{\gamma(0)} = \frac{1}{2\pi}\sum_{j=-\infty}^{\infty} \rho(j)e^{-\mathbf{i}j\omega}, \qquad \omega \in [-\pi, \pi],$$

is called the standardized spectral density function of $\{Z_t\}$.

Question: What are the properties of $f(\omega)$?

It can be shown that (1) $f(\omega)$ is real-valued, and $f(\omega) \geq 0$; (2) $\int_{-\pi}^{\pi} f(\omega)d\omega = 1$; and (3) $f(-\omega) = f(\omega)$ for $\omega \in [-\pi, \pi]$.

To gain insight into the special density function $h(\omega)$, we now introduce a frequency domain representation of a weakly stationary time series. Suppose $\{Z_t\}$ is a zero-mean weakly stationary time series. Then there exists a stochastic process $W(\omega)$ such that

$$Z_t = \int_{-\pi}^{\pi} e^{\mathbf{i}t\omega} dW(\omega), \qquad \omega \in [-\pi, \pi],$$

where ω is frequency, $W(\omega)$ is an uncorrelated increment process with $E[dW(\omega)] = 0$ for all $\omega \in [-\pi, \pi]$, and $\text{cov}[dW(\omega), dW(\lambda)] = E|dW(\omega)|^2$ if $\omega = \lambda$ and 0 otherwise. Intuitively, any weakly stationary time series can be decomposed as the "sum" of periodic components of different frequencies which are orthogonal to each other. The magnitude of the periodic components corresponding to frequencies from ω to $\omega + d\omega$ is the incremental component $dW(\omega)$. This is called *Cramer's representation* in time series analysis. Under regularity conditions, it can be shown that $E[dW(\omega)]^2 = h(\omega)d\omega$. Therefore, the spectral density function $h(\omega)$ characterizes the distribution of the strength of various periodic components over frequencies, the so-called spectral distribution of a weakly stationary process $\{Z_t\}$.

The spectral density function $h(\omega)$ is widely used in economic analysis. For example, it can be used to search for business cycles. Specifically, a frequency ω_0 corresponding to a special peak is closely associated with a business cycle with periodicity $T_0 = 2\pi/\omega_0$. Intuitively, time series can be decomposed as the sum of many cyclical components with different frequencies ω, and $h(\omega)$ is the strength or magnitude of the component with frequency ω. When $h(\omega)$ has a peak at ω_0, it means that the cyclical component with frequency ω_0 or periodicity $T_0 = 2\pi/\omega_0$ dominates all other frequencies. Consequently, the whole time series behaves as mainly having a cycle with periodicity T_0.

The functions $h(\omega)$ and $\gamma(j)$ are the Fourier transforms of each other. Thus, they contain the same information on serial dependence in $\{Z_t\}$. In time series analysis, the use of $\gamma(j)$ is called the time domain analysis, and the use of $h(\omega)$ is called the frequency domain analysis. Which tool to use depends on the convenience of the user. In some applications, the use of $\gamma(j)$ is simpler and more intuitive, while in other applications, the use of $h(\omega)$ is more enlightening. This is exactly the same as the case that it is more convenient to speak Chinese in China, while it is more convenient to speak English in the United States. Because of the importance of spectral analysis in macroeconomics, Sargent (1987) devotes one chapter on introduction to spectral analysis in his *Macroeconomic Theory*, 2nd Edition.

Example 5.8. [Hamilton (1994, Section 6.4)]: Business cycles and seasonalities of the U.S. industrial production can be identified respectively by the estimated spectral density function based on monthly data of U.S. industrial production index in the post World War II period.

Example 5.9. [Bizer and Durlauf (1990)]: Based on the historical annual data on the U.S. income tax rates, it is documented that there exists an 8-year cycle in the U.S. income tax rate changes, which is significantly linked to the party (the Republican or the Democrat) status of the U.S. presidents.

For a serially uncorrelated or WN sequence, the spectral density function $h(\omega)$ is flat as a function of frequency ω :

$$\begin{aligned} h(\omega) &= \frac{1}{2\pi}\gamma(0) \\ &= \frac{1}{2\pi}\sigma^2 \text{ for all } \omega \in [-\pi, \pi]. \end{aligned}$$

This is analogous to the power (or energy) spectral density function of a physical white color light. It is for this reason that we call a serially uncorrelated time series a WN process.

Intuitively, a white color light can be decomposed via a lens as the sum of equal magnitude components of different frequencies. That is, a white color light has a flat physical spectral density function.

It is important to point out that a WN may not be IID, as is illustrated by the following example.

Example 5.10. [Engle's (1982) ARCH Model]: Consider a first order AutoRegressive Conditional Heteroskedastic (ARCH) process, denoted as ARCH(1):

$$Z_t = \varepsilon_t h_t^{1/2},$$

$$h_t = \alpha_0 + \alpha_1 Z_{t-1}^2,$$

$$\{\varepsilon_t\} \sim \text{IID}(0,1).$$

This is first proposed by Engle (1982) and it has been widely used to model volatility in economics and finance. We have $E(Z_t|I_{t-1}) = 0$ and $\text{var}(Z_t|I_{t-1}) = h_t$, where $I_{t-1} = \{Z_{t-1}, Z_{t-2}, ...\}$ is the information set containing all past history of Z_t. It can be shown that

$$E(Z_t) = 0,$$

$$\text{cov}(Z_t, Z_{t-j}) = 0 \text{ for } j > 0,$$

$$\text{var}(Z_t) = \frac{\alpha_0}{1-\alpha_1}.$$

When $\alpha_1 < 1$, $\{Z_t\}$ is a stationary WN. But it is not weakly stationary if $\alpha_1 = 1$, because $\text{var}(Z_t) = \infty$. In both cases, $\{Z_t\}$ is strictly stationary (e.g., Nelson 1990).

Although $\{Z_t\}$ is a WN, it is not an IID sequence because the correlation in $\{Z_t^2\}$ is $\text{corr}(Z_t^2, Z_{t-j}^2) = \alpha_1^{|j|}$ for $j = 0, 1, 2, ...$ In other words, an ARCH process is uncorrelated in level but is autocorrelated in squares.

Question: What is the spectral density function $h(\omega)$ of a weakly stationary ARCH(1) process?

Having introduced various concepts of stationarity, we can now discuss nonstationary time series processes. Usually, we call $\{Z_t\}$ a nonstationary time series when it is not covariance-stationary. In time series econometrics, there have been two types of nonstationary processes that display similar sample paths when the sample size is not large but have quite different implications. We first discuss a nonstationary process called trend-stationary process.

Example 5.11. [Trend-Stationary Process]: A time series $\{Z_t\}$ is called a trend-stationary process if

$$Z_t = \alpha_0 + \alpha_1 t + \varepsilon_t,$$

where ε_t is a weakly stationary process with mean 0 and variance σ^2. To see why $\{Z_t\}$ is not weakly stationary, we consider a simplest case where $\{\varepsilon_t\}$ is IID$(0, \sigma^2)$. Then

$$\begin{aligned} E(Z_t) &= \alpha_0 + \alpha_1 t, \\ \text{var}(Z_t) &= \sigma^2, \\ \text{cov}(Z_t, Z_{t-j}) &= 0. \end{aligned}$$

More generally, a trend-stationary time series process can be defined as follows:

$$Z_t = \alpha_0 + \sum_{j=1}^{p} \alpha_j t^j + \varepsilon_t,$$

where $\{\varepsilon_t\}$ is a weakly stationary process. The reason that $\{Z_t\}$ is called trend-stationary is that it will become weakly stationary after the deterministic trend is removed.

Figures 5.5 to 5.7 plots simulated time series data for a linear trend-stationary process with IID, ARCH(1) and AR(1) innovations respectively.

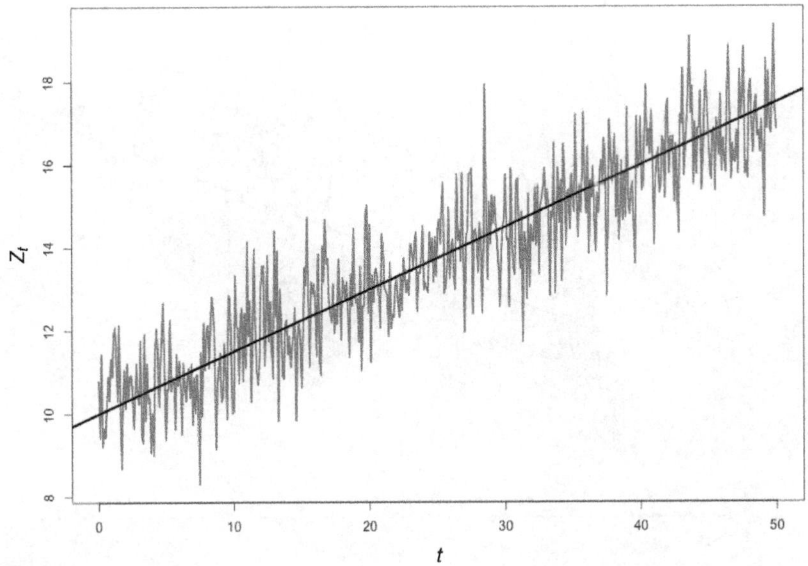

Figure 5.5 A linear trend-stationary process with IID $N(0,1)$ innovations.

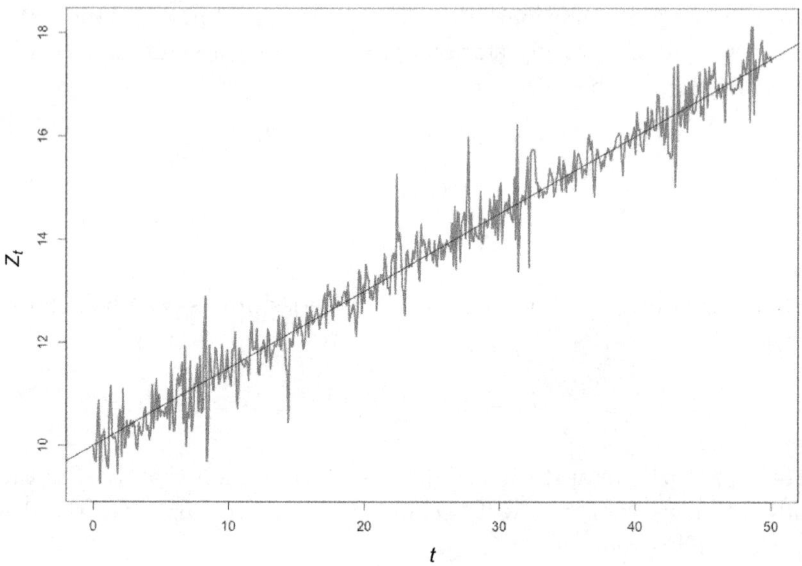

Figure 5.6 A linear trend-stationary process with ARCH(1) innovations.

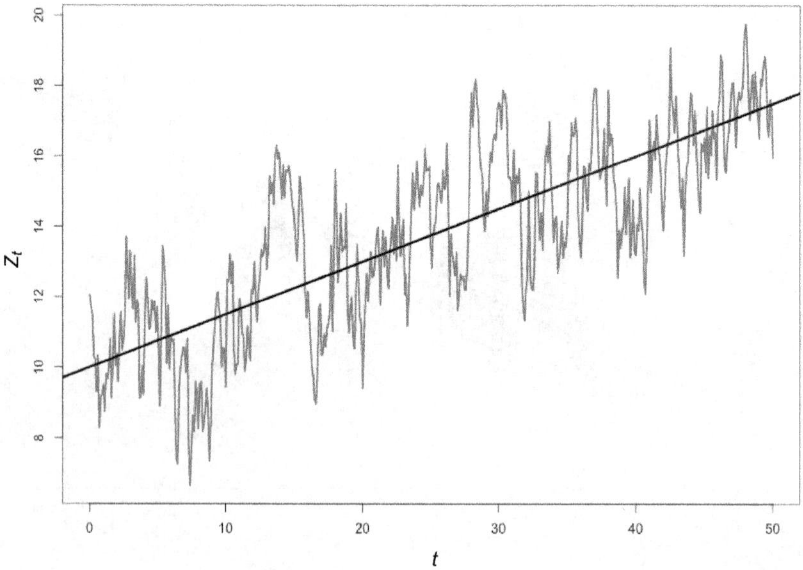

Figure 5.7 A linear trend-stationary process with AR(1) innovations.

Next, we discuss the second type of nonstationary process called difference-stationary process. Again, we start with a special case:

Example 5.12. [Random Walk]: $\{Z_t\}$ is a random walk with a drift if

$$Z_t = \alpha_0 + Z_{t-1} + \varepsilon_t,$$

where $\{\varepsilon_t\}$ is IID$(0, \sigma^2)$. For simplicity, we assume $Z_0 = 0$. Then

$$E(Z_t) = \alpha_0 t,$$

$$\text{var}(Z_t) = \sigma^2 t,$$

$$\text{cov}(Z_t, Z_{t-j}) = \sigma^2 (t - j).$$

Note that for any given j,

$$\text{corr}(Z_t, Z_{t-j}) = \sqrt{\frac{t-j}{t}} \to 1 \text{ as } t \to \infty,$$

which implies that the impact of an infinite past shock on today's behavior never dies out. Indeed, this can be seen more clearly if we write

$$Z_t = Z_0 + \alpha_0 t + \sum_{j=0}^{t-1} \varepsilon_{t-j}.$$

Note that $\{Z_t\}$ has a deterministic linear time trend but with an increasing variance over time. The impulse response function $\partial Z_{t+j}/\partial \varepsilon_t = 1$ for all $j \geq 0$, which never dies off to zero as $j \to \infty$.

There is another nonstationary process called martingale process which is closely related to a random walk.

Definition 5.7. [Martingale]: A time series process $\{Z_t\}$ is a martingale with drift if

$$Z_t = \alpha + Z_{t-1} + \varepsilon_t,$$

and $\{\varepsilon_t\}$ satisfies

$$E(\varepsilon_t | I_{t-1}) = 0 ,$$

where I_{t-1} is the σ-field generated by $\{\varepsilon_{t-1}, \varepsilon_{t-2}, ...\}$. We call that $\{\varepsilon_t\}$ is a Martingale Difference Sequence (MDS).

Question: Why is ε_t called an MDS?

This is so because ε_t is the difference of a martingale process. That is, $\varepsilon_t = Z_t - Z_{t-1}$.

Example 5.13. [Martingale and EMH]: Suppose an asset log-price $\ln P_t$ follows a martingale process, i.e.,

$$\ln P_t = \ln P_{t-1} + \varepsilon_t,$$

where $E(\varepsilon_t | I_{t-1}) = 0$. Then

$$\varepsilon_t = \ln P_t - \ln P_{t-1} \approx \frac{P_t - P_{t-1}}{P_{t-1}}$$

is the asset relative price change or asset return (if there is no dividend) from time $t-1$ to time t, which can be viewed as the proxy for the new information arrival from time $t-1$ to time t that derives the asset price change in the same period. For this reason, ε_t is also called an innovation sequence. The MDS property of ε_t implies that the price change ε_t is unpredictable using the past information available at time $t-1$, and the market is called informationally efficient. Thus, the best predictor for the asset price at time t using the information available at time $t-1$ is P_{t-1}, i.e., $E(P_t | I_{t-1}) = P_{t-1}$.

Question: What is the relationship between a random walk and a martingale?

A random walk is a martingale because IID with zero mean implies $E(\varepsilon_t | I_{t-1}) = E(\varepsilon_t) = 0$. However, the converse is not true.

Example 5.14. Reconsider an ARCH(1) process

$$\varepsilon_t = h_t^{1/2} z_t,$$

$$h_t = \alpha_0 + \alpha_1 \varepsilon_{t-1}^2,$$

$$\{z_t\} \sim \text{IID}(0,1),$$

where $\alpha_0, \alpha_1 > 0$. It follows that

$$E(\varepsilon_t | I_{t-1}) = 0,$$

$$\text{var}(\varepsilon_t | I_{t-1}) = h_t = \alpha_0 + \alpha_1 \varepsilon_{t-1}^2,$$

where I_{t-1} denotes the information available at time $t-1$. Clearly $\{\varepsilon_t\}$ is an MDS but not IID, because its conditional variance h_t is time-varying (depending on the past information set I_{t-1}).

Since the only condition for MDS is $E(\varepsilon_t|I_{t-1}) = 0$, an MDS need not be strictly stationary or weakly stationary. However, if it is assumed that $\text{var}(\varepsilon_t) = \sigma^2$ exists, then an MDS is weakly stationary.

When the variance $E(\varepsilon_t^2)$ exists, we have the following directional relationships:

$$\text{IID} \Longrightarrow \text{MDS} \Longrightarrow \text{WN}.$$

Lemma 5.1. *If $\{\varepsilon_t\}$ is an MDS with $E(\varepsilon_t^2) = \sigma^2 < \infty$, then $\{\varepsilon_t\}$ is a WN.*

Proof: By the law of iterated expectations, we have

$$E(\varepsilon_t) = E[E(\varepsilon_t|I_{t-1})] = 0,$$

and for any $j > 0$,

$$\begin{aligned}
\text{cov}(\varepsilon_t, \varepsilon_{t-j}) &= E(\varepsilon_t\varepsilon_{t-j}) - E(\varepsilon_t)E(\varepsilon_{t-j}) \\
&= E[E(\varepsilon_t\varepsilon_{t-j}|I_{t-1})] \\
&= E[E(\varepsilon_t|I_{t-1})\varepsilon_{t-j}] \\
&= E(0 \cdot \varepsilon_{t-j}) \\
&= 0.
\end{aligned}$$

This implies that an MDS, together with $\text{var}(\varepsilon_t) = \sigma^2$, is a WN.

However, a WN does not imply an MDS, as can be seen from the example below.

Example 5.15. [Nonlinear MA]: Suppose a nonlinear MA process is give as

$$\begin{aligned}
\varepsilon_t &= \alpha z_{t-1}z_{t-2} + z_t, \\
\{z_t\} &\sim \text{IID}(0, 1).
\end{aligned}$$

Then it can be shown that $\{\varepsilon_t\}$ is a WN but not an MDS, because $\text{cov}(\varepsilon_t, \varepsilon_{t-j}) = 0$ for all $j > 0$ but

$$E(\varepsilon_t|I_{t-1}) = \alpha z_{t-1}z_{t-2} \neq 0.$$

Thus, a non-MDS sequence can be a WN.

Figures 5.8 to 5.10 plot simulated data for an IID sequence, a conditionally heteroskedastic MDS, and a non-MDS WN process, respectively.

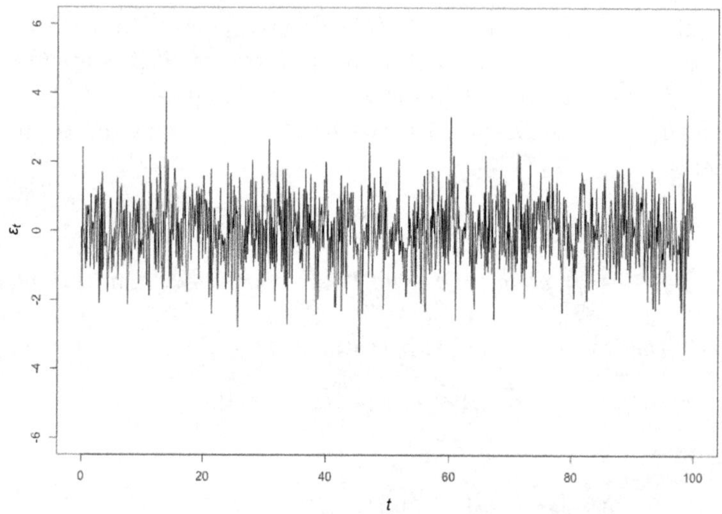

Figure 5.8 Plot of a simulated IID $N(0,1)$ sequence.

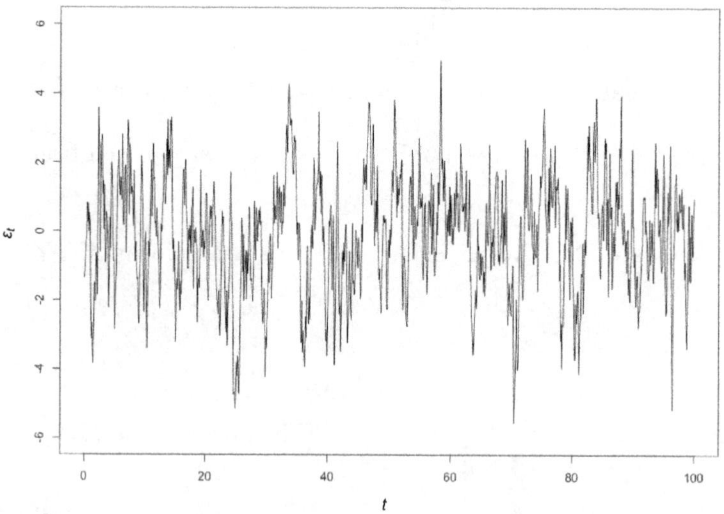

Figure 5.9 Plot of a simulated time series for a conditionally homoskedastic MDS.

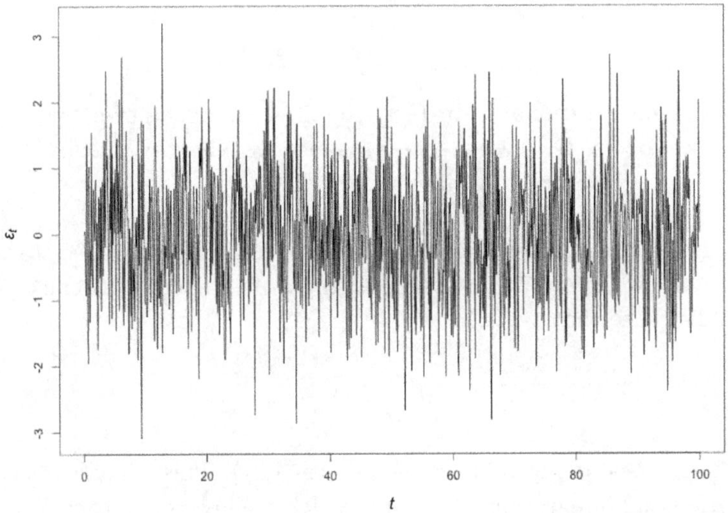

Figure 5.10 Plot of a simulated time series for a non-MDS WN process.

Question: When will the concepts of IID, MDS and WN coincide?

When a stationary process $\{\varepsilon_t\}$ is a stationary Gaussian process if $\{\varepsilon_{t_1}, \varepsilon_{t_2}, ..., \varepsilon_{t_m}\}$ is multivariate normally distributed for any admissible set of integers $\{t_1, t_2, ..., t_m\}$. Unfortunately, an important stylized fact for most economic and financial time series is that they are typically non-Gaussian. Therefore, it is important to emphasize the difference among the concepts of IID, MDS and WN in time series econometrics. They have different probabilistic properties and different implications in economics.

When $\text{var}(\varepsilon_t)$ exists, both random walk and martingale processes are special cases of the so-called unit root process, which is defined below.

Definition 5.8. [Unit Root or Difference-Stationary Process]: $\{Z_t\}$ is a unit root process with drift if

$$Z_t = \alpha_0 + Z_{t-1} + \varepsilon_t,$$

where $\{\varepsilon_t\}$ is covariance-stationary $(0, \sigma^2)$.

The process $\{Z_t\}$ is called a unit root process because its autoregressive coefficient is unity. It is also called a difference-stationary process because its first difference,

$$\Delta Z_t = Z_t - Z_{t-1} = \alpha_0 + \varepsilon_t,$$

becomes weakly stationary. In fact, the first difference of a linear trend-stationary process $Z_t = \alpha_0 + \alpha_1 t + \varepsilon_t$ is also weakly stationary:

$$\Delta Z_t = \alpha_1 + \varepsilon_t - \varepsilon_{t-1}.$$

The inverse of differencing is "integrating". For a difference-stationary process $\{Z_t\}$, we can write it as the integral of the weakly stationary process $\{\varepsilon_t\}$ in the sense that

$$Z_t = \alpha_0 t + Z_0 + \sum_{j=0}^{t-1} \varepsilon_{t-j},$$

where Z_0 is the starting value of the process $\{Z_t\}$. This is analogous to differentiation and integration in calculus which are inverses of each other. For this reason, $\{Z_t\}$ is also called an *Integrated process* of order 1, denoted as $I(1)$. Obviously, a random walk and a martingale process are $I(1)$ processes if the variance of the innovation ε_t is finite. There are various popular tests for unit roots, including those of Dicky and Fuller (1979), Phillips (1987) and Phillips and Perron (1988).

Figures 5.11 to 5.13 plots simulated time series data for a unit root process with IID, ARCH(1) and AR(1) innovations respectively.

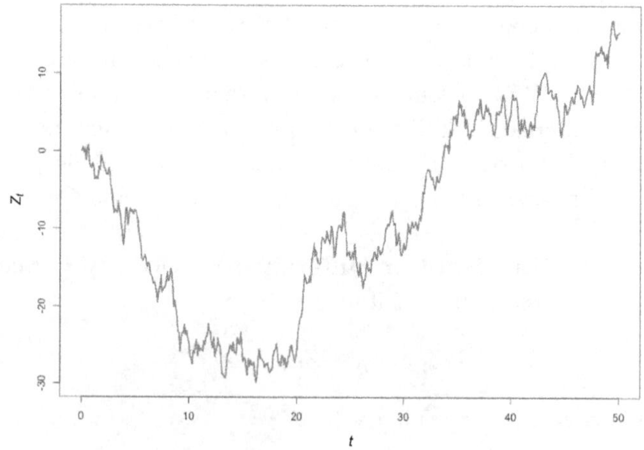

Figure 5.11 Plot of a simulated time series data for a unit root process with IID $N(0,1)$ innovations.

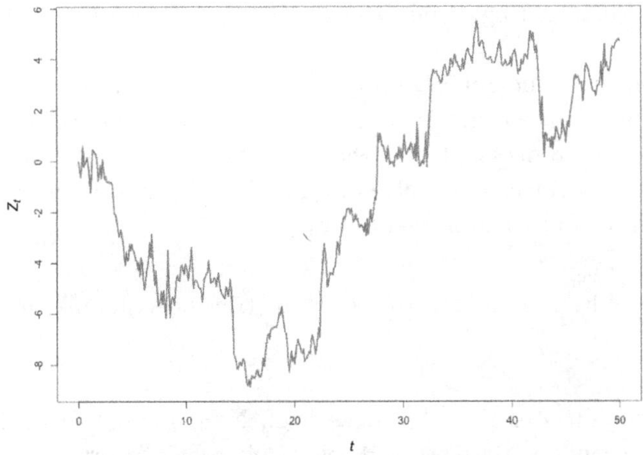

Figure 5.12 Plot of a simulated time series data for a unit root process with ARCH(1) innovations.

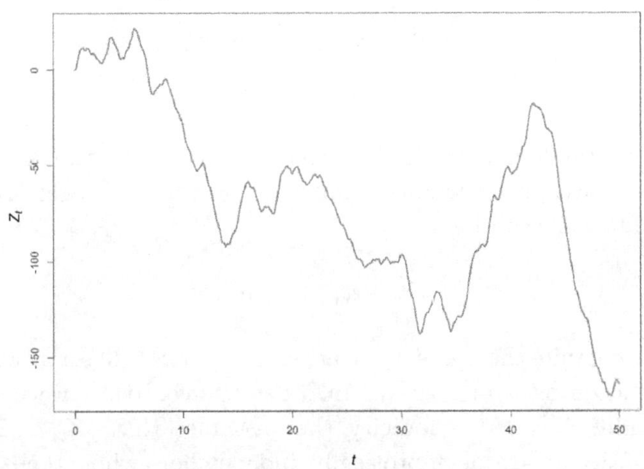

Figure 5.13 Plot of a simulated time series data for a unit root process with AR(1) innovations.

We will assume strict stationarity in most cases in the present and subsequent chapters. This implies that some economic variables have to be transformed before used in the linear regression model $Y_t = X_t'\beta^o + \varepsilon_t$. Otherwise, the asymptotic theory developed here cannot be applied. Indeed, a different asymptotic theory should be developed for unit root processes (see, e.g., Engle and Granger 1987, Phillips 1987, and Hamilton 1994).

In macroeconomics, it is important to check whether a nonstationary macroeconomic time series is trend-stationary or difference-stationary. If it is a unit root process, then a shock to the economy will never die out to zero as time evolves. In contrast, a random shock to a trend-stationary process will die out to zero eventually.

Question: Why has the unit root econometrics been popular in econometrics?

It was found in empirical studies (e.g., Nelson and Plosser 1982) that most macroeconomic time series display unit root properties.

Next, we introduce a concept of asymptotic independence, which imposes certain restrictions on temporal dependence of a time series process.

Consider as an example the following time series

$$\begin{aligned}\mathbf{Z}^n &= (Z_1, Z_2, ..., Z_n)' \\ &= (W, W, ..., W)',\end{aligned}$$

where W is a random variable that does not depend on time index t. Obviously, the stationarity condition holds. However, any realization of this random sample $\mathbf{Z}^n$ will be

$$\mathbf{z}^n = (w, w, ..., w)',$$

i.e., it will contain the same realization w for all n observations (so no new information as n increases). In order to avoid this, we need to impose a condition called ergodicity that assumes that $(Z_t, ..., Z_{t+k})$ and $(Z_{m+t}, ..., Z_{m+t+l})$ are asymptotically independent when their time distance $m \to \infty$.

Statistically speaking, independence or little correlation generates new or more information as the sample size n increases. Recall that X and Y are independent if and only if

$$E[f(X)g(Y)] = E[f(X)]E[g(Y)]$$

for any measurable bounded functions $f(\cdot)$ and $g(\cdot)$. We now extend this definition to define ergodicity.

Definition 5.9. [Ergodicity]: A strictly stationary process $\{Z_t\}$ is said to be ergodic if for any two bounded functions $f : R^{k+1} \to R$ and $g : \mathbb{R}^{l+1} \to \mathbb{R}$,

$$\lim_{m\to\infty} |E[f(Z_t, ..., Z_{t+k})g(Z_{m+t}, ..., Z_{m+t+l})]|$$
$$= |E[f(Z_t, ..., Z_{t+k})]| \cdot |E[g(Z_{m+t}, ..., Z_{m+t+l})]|.$$

Clearly, ergodicity is a notion of asymptotic independence. A strictly stationary process that is ergodic is called ergodic stationary. If $\{Z_t\}$ is ergodic stationary, then $\{f(Z_t)\}$ is also ergodic stationary for any measurable function $f(\cdot)$.

An important implication of ergodicity is that the statistical properties (such as the population mean and variance) of the ergodic time series process can be deduced from a single, sufficiently long sample (realizations) of the process. We now introduce WLLN and CLT for an ergodic time series process.

Theorem 5.1. *[**WLLN for an Ergodic Stationary Random Sample**]: Let $\{Z_t\}$ be an ergodic stationary process with $E(Z_t) = \mu$ and $E|Z_t| < \infty$. Then the sample mean*

$$\bar{Z}_n = n^{-1}\sum_{t=1}^{n} Z_t \xrightarrow{p} \mu \text{ as } n \to \infty.$$

Question: Why do we need to assume ergodicity?

Consider a counter example which does not satisfy the ergodicity condition: $Z_t = W$ for all t. Then the sample mean $\bar{Z}_n = W$, a random variable which will never converge to μ as $n \to \infty$.

Next, we state a CLT for an ergodic stationary MDS random sample.

Theorem 5.2. *[**CLT for an Ergodic Stationary MDS Random Sample**]: Suppose $\{Z_t\}$ is an stationary MDS process, with $var(Z_t) \equiv E(Z_t Z_t') = V$ finite, symmetric and positive definite. Then as $n \to \infty$,*

$$\sqrt{n}\bar{Z}_n = n^{-1/2}\sum_{t=1}^{n} Z_t \xrightarrow{d} N(0, V)$$

or equivalently,

$$V^{-1/2}\sqrt{n}\bar{Z}_n \xrightarrow{d} N(0, I).$$

Question: Is $\text{avar}(\sqrt{n}\bar{Z}_n) = V = \text{var}(Z_t)$? That is, does the asymptotic variance of $\sqrt{n}\bar{Z}_n$ coincide with the individual variance $\text{var}(Z_t)$?
To check this, we have

$$\begin{aligned}
\text{var}(\sqrt{n}\bar{Z}_n) &= E[\sqrt{n}\bar{Z}_n\sqrt{n}\bar{Z}_n'] \\
&= E\left[\left(n^{-1/2}\sum_{t=1}^{n} Z_t\right)\left(n^{-1/2}\sum_{s=1}^{n} Z_s\right)'\right] \\
&= n^{-1}\sum_{t=1}^{n}\sum_{s=1}^{n} E(Z_t Z_s') \\
&= n^{-1}\sum_{t=1}^{n} E(Z_t Z_t') \\
&= E(Z_t Z_t') \\
&= V.
\end{aligned}$$

Here, the MDS property plays a crucial rule in simplifying the asymptotic variance of $\sqrt{n}\bar{Z}_n$ because it implies $\text{cov}(Z_t, Z_s) = 0$ for all $t \neq s$. MDS is one of the most important concepts in modern economics, particularly in macroeconomics, finance, and econometrics. For example, rational expectations theory can be characterized by an expectational error being an MDS.

The basic time series concepts introduced in this section are selective, serving for the purpose of analysis of time series models introduced in this book. For more comprehensive coverage of time series analysis, readers are referred to, e.g., Brockwell and Davies (1991), Hamilton (1994), and Priestley (1981).

5.2 Framework and Assumptions

With the basic time series concepts and analytic tools introduced above, we can now develop an asymptotic theory for linear regression models with time series observations. We first state the assumptions that allow for time series observations.

Assumption 5.1. [Ergodic Stationarity]: The observable stochastic process $\{Y_t, X_t'\}_{t=1}^n$ is ergodic stationary, where Y_t is a random variable and X_t is a $K \times 1$ random vector.

Assumption 5.2. [Linearity]:

$$Y_t = X_t'\beta^o + \varepsilon_t,$$

where β^o is a $K \times 1$ unknown parameter vector, and ε_t is the unobservable disturbance.

Assumption 5.3. [Correct Model Specification]: $E(\varepsilon_t|X_t) = 0$ with $E(\varepsilon_t^2) = \sigma^2 < \infty$.

Assumption 5.4. [Nonsingularity]: The $K \times K$ matrix

$$Q = E(X_t X_t')$$

is symmetric, finite and nonsingular.

Assumption 5.5. [MDS]: $\{X_t\varepsilon_t\}$ is an MDS process with respect to the σ-field generated by $\{X_s\varepsilon_s, s < t\}$ and the $K \times K$ matrix $V \equiv \text{var}(X_t\varepsilon_t) = E(X_t X_t' \varepsilon_t^2)$ is finite and positive definite.

In Assumption 5.1, an ergodic stationary process is a stochastic process which exhibits both stationarity and ergodicity. In essence this implies that the random process will not change its statistical properties over time and that its statistical properties of the process can be inferred from a single, sufficiently long time series sample of the process. The ergodic stationary process $Z_t = \{Y_t, X_t'\}_{t=1}^n$ in Assumption 5.1 can be independent or serially dependent across different time periods. We thus allow for time series observations from a stationary stochastic process.

Under Assumptions 5.1 and 5.2, the linear regression model allows that the regressor vector X_t includes lagged dependent variables and/or lagged explanatory variables. When X_t includes lagged dependent variables, we call the linear regression model a dynamic regression model. When X_t includes lagged explanatory variables, we call the linear regression model a distributional lag model. If X_t does not include any lagged dependent variables, we call the linear regression model a static regression model.

It is important to emphasize that the asymptotic theory to be developed below and in subsequent chapters is not applicable to nonstationary time series. A problem associated with nonstationary time series is the so-called spurious regression or spurious correlation problem. If the dependent variable Y_t and the regressors X_t display similar trending behaviors over time, one is likely to obtain seemly highly "significant" regression coefficients and high values for R^2, even if they do not have any causal relationship. Such results are completely spurious. In fact, the OLS estimator for a nonstationary time series regression model does not follow the asymptotic theory to be developed below. A different asymptotic theory for nonstationary time series regression models has to be used (see, e.g., Engle and Granger 1986, Hamilton 1994, Phillips 1986, 1987). Using the correct asymptotic theory, the seemingly highly "significant" regression coefficient estimators would become insignificant in the spurious regression models.

Unlike the IID case, where $E(\varepsilon_t|X_t) = 0$ is equivalent to the strict exogeneity condition that

$$E(\varepsilon_t|X) = E(\varepsilon_t|X_1, ..., X_t, ..., X_n) = 0,$$

the correct model specification condition $E(\varepsilon_t|X_t) = 0$ is weaker than $E(\varepsilon_t|\mathbf{X}) = 0$ in a time series context. In other words, it is possible that $E(\varepsilon_t|X_t) = 0$ but $E(\varepsilon_t|\mathbf{X}) \neq 0$. Assumption 5.3 allows for the inclusion of predetermined variables in X_t, the lagged dependent variables Y_{t-1}, Y_{t-2}, etc.

For example, suppose $X_t = (1, Y_{t-1})'$. Then we obtain an AR(1) model

$$\begin{aligned} Y_t &= X_t'\beta^o + \varepsilon_t \\ &= \beta_0 + \beta_1 Y_{t-1} + \varepsilon_t, \qquad t = 2, ..., n, \\ \{\varepsilon_t\} &\sim \text{MDS}(0, \sigma^2). \end{aligned}$$

Then $E(\varepsilon_t|X_t) = 0$ holds if $E(\varepsilon_t|I_{t-1}) = 0$, namely if $\{\varepsilon_t\}$ is an MDS, where I_{t-1} is the sigma-field generated by $\{\varepsilon_{t-1}, \varepsilon_{t-2}, ...\}$. However, we generally have $E(\varepsilon_t|X) \neq 0$ because $E(\varepsilon_t X_{t+1}) \neq 0$.

The MDS assumption for $X_t\varepsilon_t$ is a key condition in this chapter. When X_t contains an intercept, the MDS condition for $X_t\varepsilon_t$ in Assumption 5.5 implies that $E(\varepsilon_t|I_{t-1}) = 0$; that is, ε_t is an MDS, where $I_{t-1} = \varepsilon_{t-1}, \varepsilon_{t-2}, ...$

Question: When can an MDS disturbance ε_t arise in economics and finance?

Example 5.16. [Rational Expectations and MDS]: Recall the dynamic asset pricing model under a rational expectations framework in Chapter 1. The behavior of the economic agent is characterized by the Euler equation:

$$E\left[\beta \frac{u'(C_t)}{u'(C_{t-1})} R_t \middle| I_{t-1}\right] = 1$$

or

$$E(M_t R_t | I_{t-1}) = 1,$$

where β is the time discount factor of the representative economic agent, C_t is the consumption, R_t is the asset gross return, and M_t is the stochastic discount factor defined as follows:

$$\begin{aligned} M_t &= \beta \frac{u'(C_t)}{u'(C_{t-1})} \\ &= \beta + \frac{u''(C_{t-1})}{u'(C_{t-1})} \Delta C_t + \text{higher order} \\ &\sim \text{risk discount factor.} \end{aligned}$$

Using the formula that $\text{cov}(X_t, Y_t | I_{t-1}) = E(X_t Y_t | I_{t-1}) - E(X_t | I_{t-1}) E(Y_t | I_{t-1})$ and rearranging, we can write the Euler equation as

$$E(M_t | I_{t-1}) E(R_t | I_{t-1}) + \text{cov}(M_t, R_t | I_{t-1}) = 1.$$

It follows that

$$\begin{aligned} E(R_t | I_{t-1}) &= \frac{1}{E(M_t | I_{t-1})} + \frac{\text{cov}(M_t, R_t | I_{t-1})}{\text{var}(M_t | I_{t-1})} \cdot \frac{-\text{var}(M_t | I_{t-1})}{E(M_t | I_{t-1})} \\ &= \alpha_t + \beta_t \lambda_t, \end{aligned}$$

where $\alpha_t = \alpha(I_{t-1})$ is the risk-free interest rate, $\lambda_t = \lambda(I_{t-1})$ is the market risk, and $\beta_t = \beta(I_{t-1})$ is the price of market risk, or the so-called beta factor.

Equivalently, we can write a regression equation for the asset return

$$R_t = \alpha_t + \beta_t \lambda_t + \varepsilon_t,$$

where ε_t is a stochastic pricing error satisfying

$$E(\varepsilon_t | I_{t-1}) = 0.$$

Note that the parameters α_t and β_t are generally time-varying. The standard CAPM usually assumes $\alpha_{t-1} = \alpha$, $\beta_t = \beta$ and uses some proxies for λ_t.

As in Chapter 4, no normality assumption on $\{\varepsilon_t\}$ is imposed. Furthermore, no conditional homoskedasticity condition is imposed. We now allow that $\text{var}(\varepsilon_t | X_t)$ is a function of X_t. In particular, because X_t may contain lagged dependent variables $Y_{t-1}, Y_{t-2}, \ldots$, $\text{var}(\varepsilon_t | X_t)$ can change over time (e.g., volatility clustering). Volatility clustering is a well-known financial phenomenon where a large volatility today tends to be followed by another large volatility tomorrow, and a small volatility today tends to be followed by another small volatility tomorrow.

Although Assumptions 5.1 to 5.5 allow for temporal dependences between observations, we will still obtain the same asymptotic properties for the OLS estimator and related test procedures as in the IID case. Put it differently, all the large sample properties for the OLS estimator and related tests established under the IID assumption in Chapter 4 remain applicable to time series observations with the stationary MDS assumption for $\{X_t\varepsilon_t\}$, and the MDS condition plays a crucial role here. We now show that this is indeed the case in subsequent sections.

5.3 Consistency of the OLS Estimator

We first investigate the consistency of the OLS estimator $\hat{\beta}$. Recall the OLS estimator

$$\begin{aligned}\hat{\beta} &= (\mathbf{X}'\mathbf{X})^{-1}\mathbf{X}'Y \\ &= \hat{Q}^{-1}n^{-1}\sum_{t=1}^{n} X_tY_t,\end{aligned}$$

where, as before,

$$\hat{Q} = n^{-1}\sum_{t=1}^{n} X_tX_t'.$$

Substituting $Y_t = X_t'\beta^o + \varepsilon_t$ from Assumption 5.2, we have

$$\hat{\beta} - \beta^o = \hat{Q}^{-1}n^{-1}\sum_{t=1}^{n} X_t\varepsilon_t.$$

Theorem 5.3. *[Consistency of the OLS Estimator]: Suppose Assumptions 5.1 to 5.5 hold. Then*

$$\hat{\beta} - \beta^o \xrightarrow{p} 0 \text{ as } n \to \infty.$$

Proof: Because $\{X_t\}$ is ergodic stationary, $\{X_tX_t'\}$ is also ergodic stationary. Thus, given Assumption 5.4, which implies $E|X_{it}X_{jt}| \leq C < \infty$ for $0 \leq i, j \leq k$ and for some constant C, we have

$$\hat{Q} \xrightarrow{p} E(X_tX_t') = Q$$

by WLLN for an ergodic stationary process. Because Q^{-1} exists, by continuity we have

$$\hat{Q}^{-1} \xrightarrow{p} Q^{-1} \text{ as } n \to \infty.$$

Next, we consider $n^{-1}\sum_{t=1}^{n} X_t \varepsilon_t$. Because $\{Y_t, X_t'\}_{t=1}^{n}$ is ergodic stationary, $\varepsilon_t = Y_t - X_t'\beta^o$ is ergodic stationary, and so is $X_t\varepsilon_t$. In addition,

$$E|X_{jt}\varepsilon_t| \leq \left[E(X_{jt}^2)E(\varepsilon_t^2)\right]^{1/2} \leq C < \infty \text{ for } 0 \leq j \leq k$$

by the Cauchy-Schwarz inequality and Assumptions 5.3 and 5.4. It follows that

$$n^{-1}\sum_{t=1}^{n} X_t\varepsilon_t \xrightarrow{p} E(X_t\varepsilon_t) = 0$$

by WLLN for an ergodic stationary process, where

$$\begin{aligned} E(X_t\varepsilon_t) &= E[E(X_t\varepsilon_t|X_t)] \\ &= E[X_t E(\varepsilon_t|X_t)] \\ &= E(X_t \cdot 0) \\ &= 0 \end{aligned}$$

by the law of iterated expectations and Assumption 5.3. Therefore, we have

$$\hat{\beta} - \beta^o = \hat{Q}^{-1}n^{-1}\sum_{t=1}^{n} X_t\varepsilon_t \xrightarrow{p} Q^{-1} \cdot 0 = 0.$$

This completes the proof.

5.4 Asymptotic Normality of the OLS Estimator

Next, we derive the asymptotic distribution of the OLS estimator $\hat{\beta}$.

Theorem 5.4. ***[Asymptotic Normality of the OLS Estimator]:*** *Suppose Assumptions 5.1 to 5.5 hold. Then*

$$\sqrt{n}(\hat{\beta} - \beta^o) \xrightarrow{d} N(0, Q^{-1}VQ^{-1}) \text{ as } n \to \infty.$$

Proof: Recall

$$\sqrt{n}(\hat{\beta} - \beta^o) = \hat{Q}^{-1}n^{-\frac{1}{2}}\sum_{t=1}^{n} X_t\varepsilon_t.$$

First, we consider the second term

$$n^{-\frac{1}{2}}\sum_{t=1}^{n} X_t\varepsilon_t.$$

Because $\{Y_t, X_t'\}_{t=1}^n$ is ergodic stationary, $X_t\varepsilon_t$ is also ergodic stationary. Also, $\{X_t\varepsilon_t\}$ is an MDS with $\text{var}(X_t\varepsilon_t) = E(X_tX_t'\varepsilon_t^2) = V$ being finite and positive definite (Assumption 5.5). By CLT for an ergodic stationary MDS process, we have

$$n^{-\frac{1}{2}}\sum_{t=1}^{n} X_t\varepsilon_t \xrightarrow{d} N(0, V).$$

Moreover, $\hat{Q}^{-1} \xrightarrow{p} Q^{-1}$, as shown earlier. It follows from Slutsky's theorem that

$$\begin{aligned}\sqrt{n}(\hat{\beta} - \beta^o) &= \hat{Q}^{-1}n^{-\frac{1}{2}}\sum_{t=1}^{n} X_t\varepsilon_t \\ &\xrightarrow{d} Q^{-1}N(0, V) \sim N(0, Q^{-1}VQ^{-1}).\end{aligned}$$

This completes the proof.

The asymptotic distribution of $\hat{\beta}$ under Assumptions 5.1 to 5.5 is exactly the same as that of $\hat{\beta}$ in Chapter 4. In particular, the asymptotic mean of $\sqrt{n}(\hat{\beta} - \beta^o)$ is 0, and the asymptotic variance of $\sqrt{n}(\hat{\beta} - \beta^o)$ is $Q^{-1}VQ^{-1}$; we denote

$$\text{avar}(\sqrt{n}\hat{\beta}) = Q^{-1}VQ^{-1}.$$

The asymptotic variance of $\sqrt{n}\hat{\beta}$ can be simplified if there exists conditional homoskedasticity.

Assumption 5.6. $E(\varepsilon_t^2|X_t) = \sigma^2$.

This assumption rules out the possibility that the conditional variance of ε_t changes with X_t. For low-frequency macroeconomic time series, this might be a reasonable assumption. For high-frequency financial time series, however, this assumption will be rather restrictive.

Theorem 5.5. ***[Asymptotic Normality Under Conditional Homoskedasticity]:*** *Suppose Assumptions 5.1 to 5.6 hold. Then*

$$\sqrt{n}(\hat{\beta} - \beta^o) \xrightarrow{d} N(0, \sigma^2 Q^{-1}).$$

Proof: Under Assumption 5.6, we can simplify

$$\begin{aligned} V &= E(X_t X_t' \varepsilon_t^2) \\ &= E[E(X_t X_t' \varepsilon_t^2 | X_t)] \\ &= E[X_t X_t' E(\varepsilon_t^2 | X_t)] \\ &= \sigma^2 E(X_t X_t') \\ &= \sigma^2 Q. \end{aligned}$$

The desired results follow immediately from the previous theorem. This completes the proof.

Under conditional homoskedasticity, the asymptotic variance of $\sqrt{n}(\hat{\beta} - \beta^o)$ is

$$\begin{aligned} \text{avar}(\sqrt{n}\hat{\beta}) &= Q^{-1} V Q^{-1} \\ &= \sigma^2 Q^{-1}. \end{aligned}$$

This is rather convenient to estimate.

5.5 Asymptotic Variance Estimation for the OLS Estimator

To construct confidence interval estimators or hypothesis test statistics, we need to estimate the asymptotic variance of $\sqrt{n}(\hat{\beta} - \beta^o)$, namely $\text{avar}(\sqrt{n}\hat{\beta})$. We consider consistent estimation for $\text{avar}(\sqrt{n}\hat{\beta})$ under conditional homoskedasticity and conditional heteroskedasticity respectively.

Case I: Conditional Homoskedasticity

Under this case, the asymptotic variance of $\sqrt{n}(\hat{\beta} - \beta^o)$ is

$$\text{avar}(\sqrt{n}\hat{\beta}) = Q^{-1} V Q^{-1} = \sigma^2 Q^{-1}.$$

It suffices to have consistent estimators for σ^2 and Q respectively.

Question: How to estimate Q?

Lemma 5.2. *Suppose Assumptions 5.1 and 5.3 hold. Then*

$$\hat{Q} \xrightarrow{p} Q \text{ as } n \to \infty.$$

Question: How to estimate σ^2?

To estimate σ^2, we use the sample residual variance estimator

$$s^2 = \frac{e'e}{n-K}.$$

Theorem 5.6. ***[Consistent Estimation for σ^2]:*** *Under Assumptions 5.1 to 5.5, as $n \to \infty$,*

$$s^2 \xrightarrow{p} \sigma^2.$$

Proof: The proof is analogous to the proof of Theorem 4.4 in Chapter 4. We have

$$\begin{aligned} s^2 &= \frac{1}{n-K}\sum_{t=1}^n e_t^2 \\ &= (n-K)^{-1}\sum_{t=1}^n \varepsilon_t^2 \\ &\quad + (\hat{\beta}-\beta^o)'\left(\frac{1}{n-K}\sum_{t=1}^n X_t X_t'\right)(\hat{\beta}-\beta^o) \\ &\quad - 2(\hat{\beta}-\beta^o)'\frac{1}{n-K}\sum_{t=1}^n X_t\varepsilon_t \\ &\xrightarrow{p} \sigma^2 + 0\cdot Q\cdot 0 - 2\cdot 0\cdot 0 = \sigma^2 \end{aligned}$$

given that K is a fixed number, where we have made use of WLLN for an ergodic stationary process in several places. This completes the proof.

We can then estimate $\text{avar}(\sqrt{n}\hat{\beta}) = \sigma^2 Q^{-1}$ by $s^2\hat{Q}^{-1}$.

Theorem 5.7. ***[Asymptotic Variance Estimator of $\sqrt{n}\hat{\beta}$ Under Conditional Homoskedasticity]:*** *Under Assumptions 5.1 to 5.4, we can consistently estimate the asymptotic variance avar($\sqrt{n}\hat{\beta}$) by*

$$s^2\hat{Q}^{-1} \xrightarrow{p} \sigma^2 Q^{-1}.$$

This implies that the variance estimator of $\hat{\beta}$ is calculated as

$$\frac{s^2\hat{Q}^{-1}}{n} = s^2(\mathbf{X}'\mathbf{X})^{-1},$$

which is the same as in the classical linear regression case.

Case II: Conditional Heteroskedasticity

In this case,

$$\text{avar}(\sqrt{n}\hat{\beta}) = Q^{-1}VQ^{-1}$$

cannot be further simplified.

Question: How to estimate $Q^{-1}VQ^{-1}$?

Question: It is straightforward to estimate Q by $\hat{Q}$. How to estimate $V = E(X_tX_t'\varepsilon_t^2)$?

We can use its sample analog

$$\hat{V} = n^{-1}\sum_{t=1}^{n} X_tX_t'e_t^2.$$

To ensure consistency of $\hat{V}$ for V, we impose the following moment condition:

Assumption 5.7. $E(X_{jt}^4) < \infty$ for $0 \le j \le k$ and $E(\varepsilon_t^4) < \infty$.

Lemma 5.3. *Suppose Assumptions 5.1 to 5.5 and 5.7 hold. Then*

$$\hat{V} \xrightarrow{p} V \text{ as } n \to \infty.$$

Proof: The proof is analogous to the proof of Lemma 4.13 in Chapter 4. Because $e_t = \varepsilon_t - (\hat{\beta} - \beta^o)'X_t$, we have

$$\begin{aligned}\hat{V} &= n^{-1}\sum_{t=1}^{n} X_tX_t'\varepsilon_t^2 \\ &\quad + n^{-1}\sum_{t=1}^{n} X_tX_t'[(\hat{\beta} - \beta^o)'X_tX_t'(\hat{\beta} - \beta^o)] \\ &\quad - 2n^{-1}\sum_{t=1}^{n} X_tX_t'[\varepsilon_tX_t'(\hat{\beta} - \beta^o)] \\ &\xrightarrow{p} V + 0 - 2 \cdot 0,\end{aligned}$$

where for the first term, we have

$$n^{-1}\sum_{t=1}^{n} X_tX_t'\varepsilon_t^2 \xrightarrow{p} E(X_tX_t'\varepsilon_t^2) = V$$

by WLLN for an ergodic stationary process and Assumption 5.5. For the second term, it suffices to show that for any combination (i, j, l, m), where $0 \leq i, j, l, m \leq k$,

$$\begin{aligned}
&n^{-1}\sum_{t=1}^{n} X_{it}X_{jt}[(\hat{\beta}-\beta^o)'X_tX_t'(\hat{\beta}-\beta^o)] \\
&= \sum_{l=0}^{k}\sum_{m=0}^{k}(\hat{\beta}_l-\beta_l^o)(\hat{\beta}_m-\beta_m^o)\left(n^{-1}\sum_{t=1}^{n}X_{it}X_{jt}X_{lt}X_{mt}\right) \\
&\xrightarrow{p} 0,
\end{aligned}$$

which follows from $\hat{\beta}-\beta^o \xrightarrow{p} 0$ and $n^{-1}\sum_{t=1}^{n} X_{it}X_{jt}X_{lt}X_{mt} \xrightarrow{p} E(X_{it}X_{jt}X_{lt}X_{mt}) = O(1)$ by WLLN and Assumption 5.7.

For the last term, it suffices to show

$$\begin{aligned}
&n^{-1}\sum_{t=1}^{n} X_{it}X_{jt}[\varepsilon_t X_t'(\hat{\beta}-\beta^o)] \\
&= \sum_{l=0}^{k}(\hat{\beta}_l-\beta_l^o)\left(n^{-1}\sum_{t=1}^{n}X_{it}X_{jt}X_{lt}\varepsilon_t\right) \\
&\xrightarrow{p} 0,
\end{aligned}$$

which follows from $\hat{\beta}-\beta^o \xrightarrow{p} 0$, $n^{-1}\sum_{t=1}^{n} X_{it}X_{jt}X_{lt}\varepsilon_t \xrightarrow{p} E(X_{it}X_{jt}X_{lt}\varepsilon_t) = 0$ by WLLN for an ergodic stationary process, the law of iterated expectations, and $E(\varepsilon_t|X_t) = 0$.

We have proved the following result.

Theorem 5.8. ***[Asymptotic Variance Estimator for $\sqrt{n}\hat{\beta}$ Under Conditional Heteroskedasticity]:*** *Under Assumptions 5.1 to 5.5 and 5.7, we can consistently estimate avar($\sqrt{n}\hat{\beta}$) by*

$$\hat{Q}^{-1}\hat{V}\hat{Q}^{-1} \xrightarrow{p} Q^{-1}VQ^{-1}.$$

The variance estimator $\hat{Q}^{-1}\hat{V}\hat{Q}^{-1}$ is the so-called White's heteroskedasticity-consistent variance-covariance matrix estimator of the OLS estimator $\sqrt{n}\hat{\beta}$ in a linear time series regression model with MDS disturbances.

5.6 Hypothesis Testing

Question: How to construct a test for the null hypothesis

$$\mathbf{H}_0 : R\beta^o = r,$$

where R is a $J \times K$ constant matrix, and r is a $J \times 1$ constant vector?

Because

$$\sqrt{n}(\hat{\beta} - \beta^o) \xrightarrow{d} N(0, Q^{-1}VQ^{-1}),$$

we have under $\mathbf{H}_0$,

$$\sqrt{n}R(\hat{\beta} - \beta^o) \xrightarrow{d} N(0, RQ^{-1}VQ^{-1}R').$$

When $E(\varepsilon_t^2|X_t) = \sigma^2$, we have $V = \sigma^2 Q$, and so

$$R\sqrt{n}(\hat{\beta} - \beta^o) \xrightarrow{d} N(0, \sigma^2 RQ^{-1}R').$$

The test statistics differ in two cases. We first construct a test under conditional homoskedasticity.

Case I: Conditional Homoskedasticity

When $J = 1$, we can use the conventional t-test statistic for large sample inference.

Theorem 5.9. ***[t-Test Under Conditional Homoskedasticity]:*** *Suppose Assumptions 5.1 to 5.6 hold. Then under* $\mathbf{H}_0$ *with* $J = 1$,

$$T = \frac{R\hat{\beta} - r}{\sqrt{s^2 R(\mathbf{X}'\mathbf{X})^{-1}R'}} \xrightarrow{d} N(0, 1)$$

as $n \to \infty$.

Proof: Given $R\sqrt{n}(\hat{\beta} - \beta^o) \xrightarrow{d} N(0, \sigma^2 RQ^{-1}R')$, $R\beta^o = r$ under $\mathbf{H}_0$, and $J = 1$, we have

$$\frac{\sqrt{n}(R\hat{\beta} - r)}{\sqrt{\sigma^2 RQ^{-1}R'}} \xrightarrow{d} N(0, 1).$$

By Slutsky's theorem and $\hat{Q} = \mathbf{X}'\mathbf{X}/n$, we obtain

$$\frac{\sqrt{n}(R\hat{\beta} - r)}{\sqrt{s^2 R\hat{Q}^{-1}R'}} \xrightarrow{d} N(0, 1).$$

This ratio is the conventional t-test statistic we examined in Chapter 3, namely:

$$\frac{\sqrt{n}(R\hat{\beta}-r)}{\sqrt{s^2 R\hat{Q}^{-1}R'}} = \frac{R\hat{\beta}-r}{\sqrt{s^2 R(\mathbf{X}'\mathbf{X})^{-1}R'}} = T.$$

For $J > 1$, we can consider an asymptotic χ^2 test that is based on the conventional F-statistic.

Theorem 5.10. ***[Wald Test Under Conditional Homoskedasticity]:*** *Suppose Assumptions 5.1 to 5.6 hold. Then under* $\mathbf{H}_0$,

$$W = J \cdot F \xrightarrow{d} \chi^2_J$$

as $n \to \infty$.

Proof: We write

$$R\hat{\beta} - r = R(\hat{\beta} - \beta^o) + R\beta^o - r.$$

Under $\mathbf{H}_0 : R\beta^o = r$, we have

$$\begin{aligned}\sqrt{n}(R\hat{\beta}-r) &= R\sqrt{n}(\hat{\beta}-\beta^o)\\ &\xrightarrow{d} N(0, \sigma^2 RQ^{-1}R').\end{aligned}$$

It follows that the quadratic form

$$\sqrt{n}(R\hat{\beta}-r)'[\sigma^2 RQ^{-1}R']^{-1}\sqrt{n}(R\hat{\beta}-r) \xrightarrow{d} \chi^2_J.$$

Also, because $s^2\hat{Q}^{-1} \xrightarrow{p} \sigma^2 Q^{-1}$, we have the Wald test statistic

$$\begin{aligned}W &= \sqrt{n}(R\hat{\beta}-r)'[s^2 R\hat{Q}^{-1}R']^{-1}\sqrt{n}(R\hat{\beta}-r)\\ &\xrightarrow{d} \chi^2_J\end{aligned}$$

by Slutsky's theorem. This can be written equivalently as follows:

$$W = \frac{(R\hat{\beta}-r)'[R(\mathbf{X}'\mathbf{X})^{-1}R']^{-1}(R\hat{\beta}-r)}{s^2} \xrightarrow{d} \chi^2_J,$$

namely

$$W = J \cdot F \xrightarrow{d} \chi^2_J,$$

where F is the conventional F-test statistic considered in Chapter 3.

We cannot use the F-distribution for a finite sample size n, but we can still compute the F-statistic and the appropriate test statistic is J times the F-statistic, which is asymptotically χ_J^2 as $n \to \infty$. That is,

$$J \cdot F = \frac{(\tilde{e}'\tilde{e} - e'e)}{e'e/(n-K)} \xrightarrow{d} \chi_J^2.$$

Put it differently, the classical F-test statistic is still approximately applicable under Assumptions 5.1 to 5.6 for a large n.

We now give two examples that are not covered under the assumptions of a classical linear regression model.

Example 5.17. [Testing for Granger Causality]: Consider a bivariate time series $\{Y_t, X_t\}$, where t is the time index, $I_{t-1}^{(Y)} = \{Y_{t-1}, ..., Y_1\}$ and $I_{t-1}^{(X)} = \{X_{t-1}, ..., X_1\}$. For example, Y_t is the GDP growth rate, and X_t is the money supply growth rate. We say that X_t does not Granger-cause Y_t in conditional mean with respect to $I_{t-1} = \{I_{t-1}^{(Y)}, I_{t-1}^{(X)}\}$ if

$$E\left[Y_t \middle| I_{t-1}^{(Y)}, I_{t-1}^{(X)}\right] = E\left[Y_t \middle| I_{t-1}^{(Y)}\right].$$

In other words, the lagged variables of X_t have no impact on the current Y_t.

Granger causality is defined in terms of incremental predictability rather than the real cause-effect relationship. From an econometric point of view, it is a test of omitted variables in a time series context. It is first introduced by Granger (1969).

Question: How to test Granger causality?

We consider two approaches to testing Granger causality. The first test is proposed by Granger (1969). Consider a linear regression model

$$\begin{aligned} Y_t = {} & \beta_0 + \beta_1 Y_{t-1} + \cdots + \beta_p Y_{t-p} \\ & + \beta_{p+1} X_{t-1} + \cdots + \beta_{p+q} X_{t-q} + \varepsilon_t. \end{aligned}$$

Under non-Granger causality, we have

$$\mathbf{H}_0 : \beta_{p+1} = \cdots = \beta_{p+q} = 0.$$

The F-test statistic

$$F \sim F_{q, n-(p+q+1)}.$$

The classical regression theory of Chapter 3 (Assumption 3.2: $E(\varepsilon_t|\mathbf{X}) = 0$) rules out this application, because it is a dynamic regression model. However, we have justified in this chapter that under $\mathbf{H}_0$,

$$q \cdot F \xrightarrow{d} \chi^2_q$$

as $n \to \infty$ under conditional homoskedasticity for a linear dynamic regression model.

There is another well-known test for Granger causality proposed by Sims (1980), which is based on the fact that the future cannot cause the present in any notion of causality. To test whether $\{X_t\}$ Granger-causes $\{Y_t\}$, we consider the following linear regression model

$$X_t = \alpha_0 + \sum_{j=1}^{p} \alpha_j X_{t-j} + \sum_{j=1}^{J} \beta_j Y_{t+j} + \sum_{j=1}^{q} \gamma_j Y_{t-j} + u_t.$$

Here, the dependent variable is X_t rather than Y_t. If $\{X_t\}$ Granger-causes $\{Y_t\}$, we expect some relationship between the current X_t and the future values of Y_t. Note that nonzero values for any of $\{\beta_j\}_{j=1}^{J}$ cannot be interpreted as causality from the future values of Y_t to the current X_t, simply because the future cannot cause the present. Nonzero values of any β_j must imply that there exists causality from the current X_t to the future values of Y_t. Therefore, we test the null hypothesis

$$\mathbf{H}_0 : \beta_j = 0 \text{ for } 1 \leq j \leq J.$$

Let F be the associated F-test statistic. Then under $\mathbf{H}_0$,

$$J \cdot F \xrightarrow{d} \chi^2_J$$

as $n \to \infty$ under conditional homoskedasticity. However, it is generally the case that the stochastic disturbance sequence $\{u_t\}$ is serially correlated so that the test statistic $J \cdot F$ cannot be used. Instead, a robustified test statistic for $\mathbf{H}_0$ should be considered, using, e.g., a consistent long-run variance-covariance matrix estimator to be introduced in Chapter 6.

The concept of Granger causality, introduced by Granger (1969), is defined in terms of incremental periodicity of one time series for another in conditional mean. Granger (1980) introduces a concept of general Granger causality in terms of incremental predictability of one time series for another in conditional distribution, and a concept of Granger causality in conditional variance. Hong (2001) develops a test for Granger causality in variance (or volatility spillover), and Wang and Hong (2018) propose a test for general Granger causality in distribution. Furthermore, Hong, Liu and Wang (2009) introduce a concept of Granger causality in risk, and develop a test.

Example 5.18. [Wage Determination]: Consider the wage function

$$\begin{aligned}W_t &= \beta_0 + \beta_1 P_t + \beta_2 P_{t-1} + \beta_3 U_t \\ &\quad + \beta_4 V_t + \beta_5 W_{t-1} + \varepsilon_t,\end{aligned}$$

where W_t is wage, P_t is price, U_t is unemployment, and V_t is the number of unfilled vacancies. We will test the null hypothesis

$$\mathbf{H}_0 : \beta_1 + \beta_2 = 0, \beta_3 + \beta_4 = 0, \text{ and } \beta_5 = 1.$$

Question: What is the economic interpretation of the null hypothesis $\mathbf{H}_0$?

Under $\mathbf{H}_0$, we have the restricted wage model:

$$\Delta W_t = \beta_0 + \beta_1 \Delta P_t + \beta_4 D_t + \varepsilon_t,$$

where $\Delta W_t = W_t - W_{t-1}$ is wage growth rate, $\Delta P_t = P_t - P_{t-1}$ is inflation rate, and $D_t = V_t - U_t$ is an index for excess job supply. This implies that wage increase depends on inflation rate and excess labor supply.

Under $\mathbf{H}_0$, we have

$$3F \xrightarrow{d} \chi^2_3.$$

We now consider a special case of testing for joint significance of all economic variables. More specifically, we are interested in testing the null hypothesis that all slope coefficients are jointly zero in a stationary time series linear regression model

$$\begin{aligned}Y_t &= X_t'\beta^o + \varepsilon_t \\ &= \beta_0^o + \sum_{j=1}^{k} \beta_j^o X_{jt} + \varepsilon_t.\end{aligned}$$

Theorem 5.11. ***[$(n-K)R^2$ Test]:*** *Suppose Assumptions 5.1 to 5.6 hold, and we are interested in testing the null hypothesis that*

$$\mathbf{H}_0 : \beta_1^o = \beta_2^o = \cdots = \beta_k^o = 0,$$

where the β_j^o, $1 \leq j \leq k$, *are the slope coefficients in the linear regression model* $Y_t = X_t'\beta^o + \varepsilon_t$.

Let R^2 *be the coefficient of determination from the unrestricted regression model*

$$Y_t = X_t'\beta^o + \varepsilon_t.$$

Then under $\mathbf{H}_0$,

$$(n-K)R^2 \xrightarrow{d} \chi_k^2.$$

Proof: First, note that as shown earlier, we have in this case,

$$F = \frac{R^2/k}{(1-R^2)/(n-K)}.$$

Here, we have $J = k$, and under $\mathbf{H}_0$,

$$k \cdot F = \frac{(n-K)R^2}{1-R^2} \xrightarrow{d} \chi_k^2.$$

This implies that $k \cdot F$ is bounded in probability; that is,

$$\frac{(n-K)R^2}{1-R^2} = O_P(1).$$

Consequently, given that k is fixed (i.e., k does not grow with the sample size n), we have

$$R^2/(1-R^2) \xrightarrow{p} 0$$

or equivalently,

$$R^2 \xrightarrow{p} 0.$$

Therefore, $1 - R^2 \xrightarrow{p} 1$. By Slutsky's theorem, we have

$$\begin{aligned}(n-K)R^2 &= \frac{(n-K)R^2}{1-R^2} \cdot (1-R^2) \\ &\xrightarrow{d} \chi_k^2.\end{aligned}$$

This completes the proof.

Example 5.19. [Testing EMH]: Suppose Y_t is the exchange rate return in period t, and I_{t-1} is the information available at time $t-1$. Then a classical version of EMH can be stated as follows:

$$E(Y_t|I_{t-1}) = E(Y_t).$$

To check whether exchange rate changes are unpredictable using the past history of exchange rate changes, we specify a linear regression model

$$Y_t = X_t'\beta^o + \varepsilon_t,$$

where

$$X_t = (1, Y_{t-1}, ..., Y_{t-k})'.$$

Under EMH, we have

$$\mathbf{H}_0 : \beta_j^o = 0 \text{ for all } j = 1, ..., k.$$

If the alternative

$$\mathbf{H}_A : \beta_j^o \neq 0 \text{ at least for some } j \in \{1, ..., k\}$$

holds, then exchange rate changes are predictable using the past information.

What is the appropriate interpretation if $\mathbf{H}_0$ is not rejected? Note that there exists a gap between EMH and $\mathbf{H}_0$, because the linear regression model is just one of many ways to check EMH. Thus, if $\mathbf{H}_0$ is not rejected, at most we can only say that no evidence against EMH is found. We should not conclude that EMH holds.

In using $k \cdot F$ or $(n - K)R^2$ statistic to test EMH, although the normality assumption is not needed for this result, we still require conditional homoskedasticity, which rules out ARCH in the dynamic time series regression framework. ARCH arises in high-frequency financial time series processes. In such cases, $(n - K)R^2$ will not follow a Chi-square distribution asymptotically under the null hypothesis.

It may be further noted that the $(n - K)R^2$ test, or any other autocorrelation-based tests, may fail to detect the alternatives which are WN but not MDS. One example is the nonlinear MA process in Example 5.10. In an empirical study, Hong and Lee (2003) document that the changes of several major exchanges are serially uncorrelated but are not MDS.

Case II: Conditional Heteroskedasticity

Next, we construct hypothesis tests for $\mathbf{H}_0$ under conditional heteroskedasticity. Recall that under $\mathbf{H}_0$,

$$\begin{aligned}\sqrt{n}(R\hat{\beta} - r) &= R\sqrt{n}(\hat{\beta} - \beta^o) + \sqrt{n}(R\beta^o - r) \\ &= \sqrt{n}R(\hat{\beta} - \beta^o) \\ &\xrightarrow{d} N(0, RQ^{-1}VQ^{-1}R'),\end{aligned}$$

where $V = E(X_t X_t' \varepsilon_t^2)$.

For $J = 1$, we have

$$\frac{\sqrt{n}(R\hat{\beta} - r)}{\sqrt{RQ^{-1}VQ^{-1}R'}} \xrightarrow{d} N(0,1) \text{ as } n \to \infty.$$

Because $\hat{Q} \xrightarrow{p} Q$ and $\hat{V} \xrightarrow{p} V$, where $\hat{V} = \mathbf{X}'\mathrm{D}(e)\mathrm{D}(e)'\mathbf{X}/n$, we have by Slutsky's theorem that the robust t-test statistic

$$T_r = \frac{\sqrt{n}(R\hat{\beta} - r)}{\sqrt{R\hat{Q}^{-1}\hat{V}\hat{Q}^{-1}R'}} \xrightarrow{d} N(0,1) \text{ as } n \to \infty.$$

Theorem 5.12. ***[Robust t-Test Under Conditional Heteroskedasticity]:*** *Suppose Assumptions 5.1 to 5.5 and 5.7 hold. Then under* $\mathbf{H}_0$ *with* $J = 1$, *as* $n \to \infty$, *the robust t-test statistic*

$$T_r = \frac{\sqrt{n}(R\hat{\beta} - r)}{\sqrt{R\hat{Q}^{-1}\hat{V}\hat{Q}^{-1}R'}} \xrightarrow{d} N(0,1).$$

For $J > 1$, the quadratic form

$$\sqrt{n}(R\hat{\beta} - r)'[RQ^{-1}VQ^{-1}R']^{-1}\sqrt{n}(R\hat{\beta} - r) \xrightarrow{d} \chi^2_J$$

under $\mathbf{H}_0$. Given $\hat{Q} \xrightarrow{p} Q$ and $\hat{V} \xrightarrow{p} V$, where $\hat{V} = \mathbf{X}'\mathrm{D}(e)\mathrm{D}(e)'\mathbf{X}/n$, we have a robust Wald test statistic

$$\begin{aligned}W_r &= n(R\hat{\beta} - r)'[R\hat{Q}^{-1}\hat{V}\hat{Q}^{-1}R']^{-1}(R\hat{\beta} - r) \\ &\xrightarrow{d} \chi^2_J\end{aligned}$$

by Slutsky's theorem. We can equivalently write

$$\begin{aligned}W_r &= (R\hat{\beta} - r)'[R(\mathbf{X}'\mathbf{X})^{-1}\mathbf{X}'\mathrm{D}(e)\mathrm{D}(e)'\mathbf{X}(\mathbf{X}'\mathbf{X})^{-1}R']^{-1}(R\hat{\beta} - r) \\ &\xrightarrow{d} \chi^2_J.\end{aligned}$$

Theorem 5.13. ***[Robust Wald Test Under Conditional Heteroskedasticity]:*** *Suppose Assumptions 5.1 to 5.5 and 5.7 hold. Then under* $\mathbf{H}_0$, *as* $n \to \infty$,

$$W = n(R\hat{\beta} - r)'(R\hat{Q}^{-1}\hat{V}\hat{Q}^{-1}R')^{-1}(R\hat{\beta} - r) \xrightarrow{d} \chi^2_J.$$

Under conditional heteroskedasticity, $J \cdot F$ and $(n-K)R^2$ can no longer be used even when $n \to \infty$, because they do not converge to χ^2_J as $n \to \infty$.

On the other hand, although the general form of the test statistic W_r developed here can be used no matter whether there exists conditional homoskedasticity, W_r may perform poorly in small samples (i.e., the asymptotic χ^2_J approximation may be poor in small samples, or Type I errors are large). Thus, if one has information that the disturbance term is conditionally homoskedastic, one should use the test statistics derived under conditional homoskedasticity, which will perform better in small sample sizes. Because of this reason, it is important to test whether conditional homoskedasticity holds in a time series context.

5.7 Testing for Conditional Heteroskedasticity and Autoregressive Conditional Heteroskedasticity

In this section, we first consider testing conditional heteroskedasticity in a time series regression context.

Question: Can we still use White's (1980) test for conditional heteroskedasticity in a stationary time series linear regression context?

The answer is yes. Although White's (1980) test is developed under the independence assumption, it is also applicable to a time series linear regression model when $\{X_t\varepsilon_t\}$ is an MDS process. Thus, the procedure to implement White's (1980) test as is discussed in Chapter 4 can be used here. Specifically, to test the null hypothesis

$$\mathbf{H}_0 : E(\varepsilon_t^2|X_t) = \sigma^2,$$

where ε_t is the regression disturbance in a stationary time series linear regression model

$$Y_t = X_t'\beta^o + \varepsilon_t,$$

we consider the following feasible auxiliary regression

$$\begin{aligned} e_t^2 &= \gamma_0 + \sum_{j=1}^{k} \gamma_j X_{jt} + \sum_{1 \le j \le l \le k} \gamma_{jl} X_{jt} X_{lt} + \tilde{v}_t \\ &= \gamma' \text{vech}(X_t X_t') + \tilde{v}_t, \end{aligned}$$

where $e_t = Y_t - X_t'\hat{\beta}$ is the estimated OLS residual, and $\text{vech}(X_t X_t')$ is a $\frac{1}{2}K(K+1) \times 1$ vector. Under $\mathbf{H}_0 : E(\varepsilon_t^2|X_t) = \sigma^2$ and $E(\varepsilon_t^4) = \mu_4 < \infty$, the test statistic

$$(n - J - 1)R^2 \xrightarrow{d} \chi_J^2 \text{ as } n \to \infty,$$

where $J = \frac{1}{2}K(K+1)$.

In the time series econometrics, there is an alternative approach to testing conditional heteroskedasticity in an autoregressive time series context. This is Engle's (1982) Lagrange Multiplier (LM) test for ARCH effects in $\{\varepsilon_t\}$.

Consider the regression model

$$\begin{aligned} Y_t &= X_t'\beta^o + \varepsilon_t, \\ \varepsilon_t &= \sigma_t z_t, \\ \{z_t\} &\sim \text{IID}(0, 1), \end{aligned}$$

where $\sigma_t = \sigma(I_{t-1})$ is a nonnegative function of information set $I_{t-1} = \{\varepsilon_{t-1}, \varepsilon_{t-2}, ...\}$. Here, to allow for a possibly time-varying conditional variance of the regression disturbance ε_t given I_{t-1}, ε_t is formulated as the product between a random shock z_t and $\sigma_t = \sigma(I_{t-1})$. When the random shock series $\{z_t\}$ is IID(0, 1), we have

$$\begin{aligned} \text{var}(\varepsilon_t|I_{t-1}) &= E(z_t^2\sigma_t^2|I_{t-1}) \\ &= \sigma_t^2 E(z_t^2|I_{t-1}) \\ &= \sigma_t^2. \end{aligned}$$

That is, σ_t^2 is the conditional variance of ε_t given I_{t-1}. When σ_t^2 is a function of I_{t-1}, the conditional variance of ε_t will change over time, and this is called ARCH.

Suppose there exists a constant σ^2 such that

$$\mathbf{H}_0 : E(\varepsilon_t^2|I_{t-1}) = \sigma^2$$

holds, then $\sigma_t^2 = \sigma^2$ will not change over time. This is called autoregressive conditional homoskedasticity.

To test the null hypothesis $\mathbf{H}_0$ of autoregressive conditional homoskedasticity, we consider the following auxiliary regression for ε_t^2 :

$$\varepsilon_t^2 = \alpha_0 + \sum_{j=1}^{q} \alpha_j \varepsilon_{t-j}^2 + v_t,$$

where $E(v_t|I_{t-1}) = 0$. This is called an ARCH(q) model in Engle (1982). ARCH models can capture a well-known empirical stylized fact called volatility clustering in financial markets, i.e., a high volatility today tends to be followed by another large volatility tomorrow, and a small volatility today tends to be followed by another small volatility tomorrow, and such patterns alternate over time. To see this more clearly, we consider an ARCH(1) model where

$$\sigma_t^2 = \alpha_0 + \alpha_1 \varepsilon_{t-1}^2,$$

where, to ensure nonnegativity of σ_t^2, both α_0 and α_1 are required to be nonnegative parameters. Suppose $0 < \alpha_1 < 1$. Then if ε_{t-1} is an unusually large deviation from its expectation of 0 so that ε_{t-1}^2 is large, then the conditional variance of ε_t is larger than usual. Therefore, ε_t is expected to have an unusually large deviation from its mean of 0, with either direction. Similarly, if ε_{t-1}^2 is usually small, then σ_t^2 is small, and ε_t^2 is expected to be small as well. Because of this behavior, volatility clustering arises.

In addition to volatility clustering, ARCH(1) can also generate heavy tails for ε_t even when the random shock z_t is IID $N(0,1)$. This can be seen from its kurtosis

$$\begin{aligned} K &= \frac{E(\varepsilon_t^4)}{[E(\varepsilon_t^2)]^2} \\ &= \frac{E(z_t^4)(1-\alpha_1^2)}{(1-3\alpha_1^2)} \\ &> 3 \end{aligned}$$

given $\alpha_1 > 0$, where we have made use of the fact that $E(z_t^4) = 3$ for $z_t \sim N(0,1)$.

In an ARCH(q) framework, all autoregressive coefficients $\alpha_j, 1 \le j \le q$, are identically zero when $\mathbf{H}_0$ holds. Thus, we can test $\mathbf{H}_0$ by checking whether all $\alpha_j, 1 \le j \le q$, are jointly zero. If $\alpha_j \neq 0$ for some $1 \le j \le q$, then there exists autocorrelation in $\{\varepsilon_t^2\}$ and $\mathbf{H}_0$ is false.

Observe that with $\varepsilon_t = \sigma_t z_t$ and $\{z_t\}$ is IID(0,1), the disturbance v_t in the auxiliary autoregression model is an IID sequence under $\mathbf{H}_0$, which implies that $E(v_t^2|I_{t-1}) = \sigma_v^2$, i.e., $\{v_t\}$ is conditionally homoskedastic. Thus, when $\mathbf{H}_0$ holds, we have

$$(n-q-1)\tilde{R}^2 \xrightarrow{d} \chi_q^2,$$

where $\tilde{R}^2$ is the centered R^2 from the auxiliary regression for $\{\varepsilon_t^2\}$.

The auxiliary regression for ε_t^2, unfortunately, is infeasible because ε_t is not observable. However, we can replace ε_t by the estimated OLS residual e_t and consider the regression

$$e_t^2 = \alpha_0 + \sum_{j=1}^{q} \alpha_j e_{t-j}^2 + \tilde{v}_t.$$

Then we obtain Engle's (1982) test for ARCH effects:

$$(n-q-1)R^2 \xrightarrow{d} \chi_q^2.$$

Note that the replacement of ε_t by e_t has no impact on the asymptotic distribution of the test statistic, for the same reason as in White's (1980) test for conditional heteroskedasticity. See Chapter 4 for more discussion.

The existence of ARCH effects for $\{\varepsilon_t\}$ does not automatically imply that we have to use White's heteroskedasticity-consistent variance-covariance matrix $Q^{-1}VQ^{-1}$ for the OLS estimator $\hat{\beta}$. Suppose $Y_t = X_t'\beta^o + \varepsilon_t$ is a static time series model such that the two time series $\{X_t\}$ and $\{\varepsilon_t\}$ are independent of each other, and $\{\varepsilon_t\}$ displays ARCH effects, i.e.,

$$\text{var}(\varepsilon_t|I_{t-1}) = \alpha_0 + \sum_{j=1}^{q} \alpha_j \varepsilon_{t-j}^2$$

with at least some $\alpha_j \neq 0, j \in \{1, ..., q\}$. Then Assumption 5.6 still holds because $\text{var}(\varepsilon_t|X_t) = \text{var}(\varepsilon_t) = \sigma^2$ given the assumption that $\{X_t\}$ and $\{\varepsilon_t\}$ are independent. In this case, we have

$$\text{avar}(\sqrt{n}\hat{\beta}) = \sigma^2 Q^{-1}.$$

Next, suppose $Y_t = X_t'\beta^o + \varepsilon_t$ is a dynamic time series regression model such that X_t contains some lagged dependent variables (say Y_{t-1}). Then if $\{\varepsilon_t\}$ displays ARCH effects, Assumption 5.6 may fail because we may have $E(\varepsilon_t^2|X_t) \neq \sigma^2$, which generally occurs when X_t and $\{\varepsilon_{t-j}^2, j = 1, ..., p\}$ are not independent. In this case, we have to use

$$\text{avar}(\sqrt{n}\hat{\beta}) = Q^{-1}VQ^{-1}.$$

5.8 Testing for Serial Correlation

Question: Why is it important to test serial correlation for $\{\varepsilon_t\}$?

We now provide some motivation for doing so. First, we examine the impact of serial correlation in $\{\varepsilon_t\}$ on the asymptotic variance of the OLS estimator $\sqrt{n}\hat{\beta}$. Recall that under Assumptions 5.1 to 5.5,

$$\begin{aligned}\sqrt{n}(\hat{\beta}-\beta^o) &= \hat{Q}^{-1}\frac{1}{\sqrt{n}}\sum_{t=1}^{n} X_t\varepsilon_t \\ &\xrightarrow{d} N(0, Q^{-1}VQ^{-1}),\end{aligned}$$

where $V = \mathrm{var}(X_t\varepsilon_t)$. Among other things, this implies that the asymptotic variance of $n^{-1/2}\sum_{t=1}^{n} X_t\varepsilon_t$ is the same as the variance of $X_t\varepsilon_t$. This follows from the MDS assumption for $\{X_t\varepsilon_t\}$:

$$\begin{aligned}\mathrm{var}\left(n^{-1/2}\sum_{t=1}^{n} X_t\varepsilon_t\right) &= n^{-1}\sum_{t=1}^{n}\sum_{s=1}^{n} E(X_t\varepsilon_t X_s'\varepsilon_s) \\ &= n^{-1}\sum_{t=1}^{n} E(X_tX_t'\varepsilon_t^2) \\ &= E(X_tX_t'\varepsilon_t^2) \\ &= V.\end{aligned}$$

This result will not generally hold if the MDS property for $\{X_t\varepsilon_t\}$ is violated.

Question: How to check $E(X_t\varepsilon_t|I_{t-1}) = 0$, where I_{t-1} is the σ-field generated by $\{X_s\varepsilon_s, s < t\}$?

When X_t contains the intercept, we have that $\{\varepsilon_t\}$ is an MDS with respect to the σ-field generated by $\{\varepsilon_s, s < t\}$, which implies that $\{\varepsilon_t\}$ is serially uncorrelated.

If $\{\varepsilon_t\}$ is serially correlated, then $\{X_t\varepsilon_t\}$ will not be an MDS, and consequently we will generally have $\mathrm{var}(n^{-1/2}\sum_{t=1}^{n} X_t\varepsilon_t) \neq V$. Therefore, serial uncorrelatedness is a necessary condition for the validity of $\mathrm{avar}(\sqrt{n}\hat{\beta}) = Q^{-1}VQ^{-1}$ with $V = E(X_tX_t'\varepsilon_t^2)$.

On the other hand, let us revisit the correct model specification condition that

$$E(\varepsilon_t|X_t) = 0,$$

in a time series context. Note that this condition does not necessarily imply that $\{\varepsilon_t\}$ or $\{X_t\varepsilon_t\}$ is an MDS in a time series context.

To see this, consider the case when

$$Y_t = X_t'\beta^o + \varepsilon_t$$

is a static regression model where $\{X_t\}$ and $\{\varepsilon_t\}$ are mutually independent, or at least when $\text{cov}(X_t, \varepsilon_s) = 0$ for all t, s. Then it is possible that $E(\varepsilon_t|X_t) = 0$ but $\{\varepsilon_t\}$ is serially correlated. An example is that $\{\varepsilon_t\}$ is an AR(1) process but $\{\varepsilon_t\}$ and $\{X_t\}$ are mutually independent. In this case, serial dependence in $\{\varepsilon_t\}$ does not cause inconsistency of the OLS estimator $\hat{\beta}$ to β^o, but we no longer have

$$\text{var}\left(n^{-1/2}\sum_{t=1}^{n} X_t\varepsilon_t\right) = V \equiv \text{var}\,(X_t\varepsilon_t) = E(X_tX_t'\varepsilon_t^2).$$

In other words, the MDS property for $\{\varepsilon_t\}$ is crucial for $\text{var}(n^{-1/2}\sum_{t=1}^{n} X_t\varepsilon_t) = V$ in a static regression model, although it is not needed to ensure $E(\varepsilon_t|X_t) = 0$. For a static regression model, the regressors in X_t are usually called exogenous variables. In particular, if $\{X_t\}$ and $\{\varepsilon_t\}$ are mutually independent, then X_t is called strongly exogenous. If Assumption 3.2 ($E(\varepsilon_t|\mathbf{X}) = 0$) holds, then X_t is called strictly exogenous.

On the other hand, when $Y_t = X_t'\beta^o + \varepsilon_t$ is a dynamic regression model where X_t includes lagged dependent variables such as $\{Y_{t-1}, ..., Y_{t-k}\}$, then X_t and ε_{t-j} are generally not independent for $j > 0$. In this case, the correct model specification condition

$$E(\varepsilon_t|X_t) = 0$$

holds when $\{\varepsilon_t\}$ is an MDS, i.e., $E(\varepsilon_t|I_{t-1}) = 0$, where $I_{t-1} = \{\varepsilon_{t-1}, \varepsilon_{t-2}, ...\}$. If $\{\varepsilon_t\}$ is not an MDS, the condition that $E(\varepsilon_t|X_t) = 0$ generally does not hold. To see this, we consider, for example, an AR(1) model

$$\begin{aligned} Y_t &= \beta_0^o + \beta_1^o Y_{t-1} + \varepsilon_t \\ &= X_t'\beta^o + \varepsilon_t. \end{aligned}$$

Suppose $\{\varepsilon_t\}$ is an MA(1) process, i.e., $\varepsilon_t = \alpha v_{t-1} + v_t$, $\{v_t\} \sim \text{IID}(0, \sigma_v^2)$. Then $E(X_t\varepsilon_t) \neq 0$, and so $E(\varepsilon_t|X_t) \neq 0$. This is in fact an ARMA(1,1) process. When the DGP is an ARMA(1,1) process, the AR(1) model suffers from dynamic misspecification. Thus, to ensure correct specification ($E(Y_t|X_t) = X_t'\beta^o$) of a dynamic regression model in a time series context, it is important to check the MDS property for $\{\varepsilon_t\}$. In this case, tests for MDS can be viewed as specification tests for dynamic regression models.

In time series econometrics such as rational expectations econometrics, correct model specification usually requires that ε_t be an MDS:

$$E(\varepsilon_t|I_{t-1}) = 0,$$

where I_{t-1} is the information set available to the economic agent at time $t-1$. In this content, X_t is usually a subset of I_{t-1}, namely $X_t \in I_{t-1}$. Thus both Assumptions 5.3 and 5.5 hold simultaneously:

$$E(\varepsilon_t|X_t) = E[E(\varepsilon_t|I_{t-1})|X_t] = 0$$

and

$$E(X_t\varepsilon_t|I_{t-1}) = X_t E(\varepsilon_t|I_{t-1}) = 0$$

given that X_t belongs to I_{t-1}.

Question: How to check serial dependence in $\{\varepsilon_t\}$?

To check the MDS property of $\{\varepsilon_t\}$, one may check whether there exists serial correlation in $\{\varepsilon_t\}$. Evidence of serial correlation in $\{\varepsilon_t\}$ will indicate that $\{\varepsilon_t\}$ is not an MDS. The existence of serial correlation may be due to various sources of model misspecification. For example, it may be that in the linear regression model, important explanatory variables are missing (omitted variables), or that the functional relationship is nonlinear (functional form misspecification), or that lagged dependent variables or lagged explanatory variables should have been included as regressors (neglected dynamics or dynamic misspecification). Therefore, tests for serial correlation can also be viewed as a model specification check in a dynamic time series regression context.

We now introduce a number of tests for serial correlation of the disturbance $\{\varepsilon_t\}$ in a linear regression model.

(1) Breusch-Godfrey Test

Consider the null hypothesis

$$\mathbf{H}_0 : E(\varepsilon_t|I_{t-1}) = 0,$$

where $I_{t-1} = \{\varepsilon_{t-1}, \varepsilon_{t-2}, ...\}$, ε_t is the regression disturbance in the stationary time series linear regression model

$$Y_t = X_t'\beta^o + \varepsilon_t,$$

with $E(\varepsilon_t|X_t) = 0$.

We now introduce the Lagrange Multiplier (LM) test for serial correlation originally proposed by Breusch (1978) and Godfrey (1978). Following the vast literature, we will first assume autoregressive conditional homoskedasticity (i.e., $E(\varepsilon_t^2|I_{t-1}) = \sigma^2$) in testing serial correlation for $\{\varepsilon_t\}$. Thus, this method is not suitable for high-frequency financial time series, where volatility clustering has been well-documented. Extensions to conditional heteroskedasticity and ARCH will be discussed later.

First, suppose ε_t is observed, and we consider the auxiliary regression model (an AR(p))

$$\varepsilon_t = \sum_{j=1}^{p} \alpha_j \varepsilon_{t-j} + u_t, \quad t = p+1, ..., n,$$

where $\{u_t\}$ is an MDS. Under $\mathbf{H}_0$, we have $\alpha_j = 0$ for $1 \le j \le p$. Thus, we can test $\mathbf{H}_0$ by checking whether $\{\alpha_j\}_{j=1}^p$ are jointly equal to 0. Given the assumption that $E(\varepsilon_t^2|I_{t-1}) = \sigma^2$, which implies $E(u_t^2|\varepsilon_{t-1}, ..., \varepsilon_{t-p}) = \sigma^2$ under $\mathbf{H}_0$, we can run an OLS auxiliary regression and obtain

$$n\tilde{R}_{uc}^2 \xrightarrow{d} \chi_p^2,$$

where $\tilde{R}_{uc}^2$ is the uncentered R^2 in the auxiliary AR(p) regression (noting that there is no intercept), and p is the number of the regressors.
Unfortunately, ε_t is not observable. However, we can replace ε_t with the estimated OLS residual $e_t = Y_t - X_t'\hat{\beta}$. When $Y_t = X_t'\beta^o + \varepsilon_t$ is a stationary dynamic linear regression model, unlike White's (1980) test for heteroskedasticity of unknown form, this replacement will generally change the asymptotic χ_p^2 distribution of nR_{uc}^2. This follows because the estimation error $X_t'(\hat{\beta} - \beta^o)$ contained in the estimated residual e_t is correlated with the regressors of the auxiliary AR(p) regression and so has nontrivial impact on the asymptotic distribution of the test statistic. To remove the impact of the estimation error $X_t'(\hat{\beta} - \beta^o)$, we can modify the auxiliary regression as follows:

$$\begin{aligned} e_t &= \sum_{j=1}^{K} \gamma_j X_{jt} + \sum_{j=1}^{p} \alpha_j e_{t-j} + u_t \\ &= \gamma' X_t + \sum_{j=1}^{p} \alpha_j e_{t-j} + u_t, \quad t = p+1, ..., n, \end{aligned}$$

where X_t contains the intercept. The inclusion of the regressors X_t in the auxiliary regression will purge the impact of the estimation error $X_t'(\hat{\beta} - \beta^o)$

of the test statistic, because X_t and $X_t'(\hat{\beta} - \beta^o)$ are perfectly correlated. Therefore, the resulting statistic

$$nR^2 \xrightarrow{d} \chi_p^2 \text{ as } n \to \infty$$

under $\mathbf{H}_0 : E(\varepsilon_t|I_{t-1}) = 0$, where R^2 is the centered squared multi-correlation coefficient in the feasible auxiliary regression model.

To further explain why X_t has to be included in the auxiliary AR(p) regression when $Y_t = X_t'\beta^o + \varepsilon_t$ is a dynamic regression model, we assume that X_t contains some lagged dependent variables (say Y_{t-j} for $1 \leq j \leq p$). When we replace ε_t by $e_t = \varepsilon_t - X_t'(\hat{\beta} - \beta^o)$, the estimation error $X_t'(\hat{\beta} - \beta^o)$ will have nontrivial impact on the asymptotic distribution of a test statistic for $\mathbf{H}_0$, because X_t may be correlated with ε_{t-j} (and so with e_{t-j} in the augmented auxiliary AR(p) regression) at least for some lag order $j > 0$. To remove the impact of $X_t'(\hat{\beta} - \beta^o)$, we can add the regressor vector X_t in the auxiliary regression, which is perfectly correlated with the estimation error $X_t'(\hat{\beta} - \beta^o)$, and so can purge its impact. This can be proven rigorously but we do not attempt to do so here, because it would be tedious and offer no more new insight than the above intuition. Below, we provide a heuristic explanation.

First, we consider the infeasible auxiliary AR(p) autoregression $\varepsilon_t = \sum_{j=1}^p \alpha_j^o \varepsilon_{t-j} + u_t$. Under the null hypothesis of no serial correlation, the OLS estimator

$$\sqrt{n}(\tilde{\alpha} - \alpha^o) = \sqrt{n}\tilde{\alpha}$$

converges to an asymptotic normal distribution, which implies $\tilde{\alpha} = O_P(n^{-1/2})$ vanishes in probability at a rate of $n^{-1/2}$. The test statistic $n\tilde{R}_{uc}^2$ is asymptotically equivalent to a quadratic form in $\sqrt{n}\tilde{\alpha}$ which follows an asymptotic χ_p^2 distribution. In other words, the asymptotic distribution of $n\tilde{R}_{uc}^2$ is determined by the asymptotic distribution of $\sqrt{n}\tilde{\alpha}$.

Now, suppose we replace ε_t by $e_t = \varepsilon_t - (\hat{\beta} - \beta^o)'X_t$, and consider the feasible auxiliary AR(p) autoregression

$$e_t = \sum_{j=1}^p \alpha_j^o e_{t-j} + v_t.$$

Suppose the OLS estimator of this feasible auxiliary AR(p) regression is $\hat{\alpha}$. We can then decompose

$$\hat{\alpha} = \tilde{\alpha} - \hat{\delta} + \text{ reminder term},$$

where $\tilde{\alpha}$, as discussed above, is the OLS estimator of regressing ε_t on $\varepsilon_{t-1}, ..., \varepsilon_{t-p}$, and $\hat{\delta}$ is the OLS estimator of regressing $(\hat{\beta} - \beta^o)'X_t$ on $\varepsilon_{t-1}, ..., \varepsilon_{t-p}$. When the regressor vector X_t contains lagged dependent variables so that $E(X_t\varepsilon_{t-j})$ is likely not zero for some $j \in \{1, ..., p\}$, $\hat{\delta}$ will converge to zero at the same rate as $\tilde{\alpha}$, which is $n^{-1/2}$. Because $\hat{\delta} \xrightarrow{p} 0$ at the same rate as $\tilde{\alpha}$, $\hat{\delta}$ will have nontrivial impact on the asymptotic distribution of nR^2_{uc}, where R^2_{uc} is the uncentered R^2 in the feasible auxiliary AR(p) autoregression. To remove the impact of $\hat{\delta}$, we need to include X_t as additional regressors in the feasible auxiliary AR(p) regression.

Question: When do we not need to include X_t in the auxiliary regression?

When we have a static regression model $Y_t = X_t'\beta^o + \varepsilon_t$, where $\text{cov}(X_t, \varepsilon_s) = 0$ for all t, s (so $E(X_t\varepsilon_{t-j}) = 0$ for all $j \in \{1, ..., p\}$), the estimation error $X_t'(\hat{\beta} - \beta^o)$ in e_t has no impact on the asymptotic distribution of nR^2_{uc}. It follows that we do not need to include X_t in the feasible auxiliary AR(p) autoregression. In other words, we can test serial correlation for $\{\varepsilon_t\}$ by running the following auxiliary AR(p) model

$$e_t = \sum_{j=1}^{p} \alpha_j e_{t-j} + u_t.$$

The resulting nR^2_{uc} is asymptotically χ^2_p under the null hypothesis of no serial correlation.

Question: Suppose we have a static regression model, and we include X_t in the auxiliary regression in testing serial correlation of $\{\varepsilon_t\}$. What will happen?

For a static regression model, whether the regressor vector X_t is included in the auxiliary regression has no impact on the asymptotic χ^2_p distribution of nR^2_{uc} or nR^2 under the null hypothesis of no serial correlation in $\{\varepsilon_t\}$. Thus, we will still obtain an asymptotic valid test statistic nR^2 under $\mathbf{H}_0$. In fact, the size performance of the test may be better in finite samples. However, the test may be less powerful in finite samples than the test without including X_t, because X_t may take away some serial correlation in $\{\varepsilon_t\}$ under the alternative to $\mathbf{H}_0$.

Question: What happens if we include an intercept in the auxiliary regression

$$e_t = \alpha_0 + \sum_{j=1}^{p} \alpha_j e_{t-j} + u_t,$$

where e_t is the OLS residual from a static regression model?

With the inclusion of the intercept here, we can then use nR^2 to test serial correlation in $\{\varepsilon_t\}$, which is more convenient to compute than nR^2_{uc}. Most statistical software report R^2 but not R^2_{uc}. Under $\mathbf{H}_0$, $nR^2 \xrightarrow{d} \chi^2_p$. However, the inclusion of the intercept α_0 may have some adverse impact on the power of the test in small samples, because there is an additional parameter to estimate.

As discussed at the beginning of this section, a test for serial correlation can be viewed as a specification test for a dynamic time series regression model, because existence of serial correlation in the estimated model residual $\{e_t\}$ will generally indicate misspecification of a dynamic regression model.

On the other hand, for a static time series regression model, it is possible that the static regression model $Y_t = X_t'\beta^o + \varepsilon_t$ is correctly specified in the sense that $E(\varepsilon_t|X_t) = 0$ but $\{\varepsilon_t\}$ displays serial correlation. In this case, existence of serial correlation in $\{\varepsilon_t\}$ does not affect the consistency of the OLS estimator $\hat{\beta}$ but affects the asymptotic variance and therefore the efficiency of the OLS estimator $\hat{\beta}$.

Question: What happens to a test for serial correlation in $\{\varepsilon_t\}$ if a static time series regression model $Y_t = X_t'\beta^o + \varepsilon_t$ is misspecified?

Since ε_t is unobservable, one always has to use the estimated residual e_t in testing for serial correlation. Because the estimated residual

$$\begin{aligned} e_t &= Y_t - X_t'\hat{\beta} \\ &= \varepsilon_t + [E(Y_t|X_t) - X_t'\beta^*] + X_t'(\beta^* - \hat{\beta}), \end{aligned}$$

it contains the true disturbance $\varepsilon_t = Y_t - E(Y_t|X_t)$ and model approximation error $E(Y_t|X_t) - X_t'\beta^*$, where

$$\beta^* = [E(X_t X_t')]^{-1} E(X_t Y_t)$$

is the best linear least squares approximation coefficient which the OLS estimator $\hat{\beta}$ always converges to as $n \to \infty$. If the static linear regression model is misspecified for $E(Y_t|X_t)$, then the approximation error $E(Y_t|X_t) - X_t'\beta^*$ will never vanish to zero as $n \to \infty$ and this term can cause serial correlation in e_t if X_t is a time series process. Thus, when one finds that there exists serial correlation in the estimated residuals $\{e_t\}$ of a static linear regression model, there exist two possibilities: (a) $\{\varepsilon_t\}$ is serially correlated while the static linear regression model is correctly specified (i.e., $E(\varepsilon_t|X_t) = 0$), and (b) the static linear regression model is misspecified. In the latter case, the OLS estimator $\hat{\beta}$ is generally not consistent for β^o. Therefore, one has to first check correct specification of a static regression model in order to give correct interpretation of any documented serial correlation in the estimated residuals.

(2) Durbin-Watson Test

In the development of tests for serial correlation in regression disturbances, there have been two popular tests that have historical importance. One is the Durbin-Watson test and the other is Durbin's h-test. The Durbin-Watson test is the first formal procedure developed for testing first order serial correlation

$$\varepsilon_t = \rho\varepsilon_{t-1} + u_t, \qquad \{u_t\} \sim \text{IID}\left(0, \sigma^2\right),$$

using the OLS residuals $\{e_t\}_{t=1}^n$ in a static linear regression model $Y_t = X_t'\beta^o + \varepsilon_t$. Durbin and Watson (1950, 1951) propose a test statistic

$$d = \frac{\sum_{t=2}^n (e_t - e_{t-1})^2}{\sum_{t=1}^n e_t^2}.$$

They present tables of bounds at the 0.05, 0.025 and 0.01 significance levels of the d statistic for static regressions with an intercept. Against the one-sided alternative that $\rho > 0$, if d is less than the lower bound d_L, the null hypothesis that $\rho = 0$ is rejected; if d is greater than the upper bound d_U, the null hypothesis is accepted. Otherwise, the test is equivocal. Against the one-sided alternative that $\rho < 0$, $4 - d$ can be used to replace d in the above procedure.

The Durbin-Watson test has been extended to test for lag 4 autocorrelation by Wallis (1972) and for autocorrelation at any lag by Vinod (1973).

The Durbin-Watson d-test is not applicable to dynamic linear regression models, because parameter estimation uncertainty in the OLS estimator $\hat{\beta}$ will have nontrivial impact on the asymptotic distribution of d. Durbin (1970) developed the so-called h-test for first-order autocorrelation in $\{\varepsilon_t\}$

that takes into account parameter estimation uncertainty in $\hat{\beta}$. Consider a simple dynamic linear regression model

$$Y_t = \beta_0^o + \beta_1^o Y_{t-1} + \beta_2^o X_t + \varepsilon_t,$$

where X_t is strictly exogenous. Durbin's h statistic is defined as:

$$h = \hat{\rho}\sqrt{\frac{n}{1 - n \cdot \widehat{\text{var}}}(\hat{\beta}_1)},$$

where $\widehat{\text{var}}(\hat{\beta}_1)$ is an estimator for the variance of $\hat{\beta}_1$, $\hat{\rho}$ is the OLS estimator from regressing e_t on e_{t-1} (in fact, $\hat{\rho} \approx 1 - d/2$). Durbin (1970) shows that $h \xrightarrow{d} N(0,1)$ as $n \to \infty$ under null hypothesis that $\rho = 0$. In fact, Durbin's h-test is asymptotically equivalent to the LM test (with $\rho = 1$) introduced above.

(3) Box-Pierce Test

Define the sample autocovariance function

$$\hat{\gamma}(j) = n^{-1} \sum_{t=j+1}^{n} (e_t - \bar{e})(e_{t-j} - \bar{e}),$$

where $\bar{e} = n^{-1} \sum_{t=1}^{n} e_t$ (this is zero when X_t contains an intercept). The Box and Pierce (1970) portmanteau test statistic is defined as

$$Q(p) = n \sum_{j=1}^{p} \hat{\rho}^2(j),$$

where the sample autocorrelation function

$$\hat{\rho}(j) = \hat{\gamma}(j)/\hat{\gamma}(0).$$

When $\{e_t\}$ is a directly observed data or is the estimated residual from a static regression model, we can show

$$Q(p) \xrightarrow{d} \chi_p^2$$

under the null hypothesis of no serial correlation.

On the other hand, when e_t is an estimated residual from an ARMA(r, s) model

$$Y_t = \alpha_0 + \sum_{j=1}^{r} \alpha_j Y_{t-j} + \sum_{j=1}^{s} \beta_j \varepsilon_{t-j} + \varepsilon_t,$$

then

$$Q(p) \xrightarrow{d} \chi^2_{p-(r+s)} \text{ as } n \to \infty,$$

where $p > r+s$, where the model parameters are estimated by the Maximum Likelihood Estimation (MLE) method. See Box and Pierce (1970) for more details.

To improve small sample performance of the $Q(p)$ test, Ljung and Box (1978) propose a modified $Q(p)$ test statistic:

$$Q^*(p) \equiv n(n+2)\sum_{j=1}^{p}(n-j)^{-1}\hat{\rho}^2(j) \xrightarrow{d} \chi^2_{p-(r+q)}.$$

The modification matches the first two moments of $Q^*(p)$ with those of the χ^2 distribution. This improves the size of the test in small samples, although not the power of the test.

When $\{e_t\}$ is an estimated residual from a dynamic regression model with regressors including both lagged dependent variables and exogenous variables, then the asymptotic distribution of $Q(p)$ becomes generally unknown (Breusch and Pagan 1980). One solution is to modify the $Q(p)$ test statistic as follows:

$$\hat{Q}(p) \equiv n\hat{\rho}'(I-\hat{\Phi})^{-1}\hat{\rho} \xrightarrow{d} \chi^2_p \text{ as } n \to \infty,$$

where $\hat{\rho} = [\hat{\rho}(1), ..., \hat{\rho}(p)]'$, and $\hat{\Phi}$ captures the impact caused by nonzero correlation between $\{X_t\}$ and $\{\varepsilon_{t-j}, 1 \le j \le p\}$. See Hayashi (2000, Section 2.10) for more discussion and the expression of $\hat{\Phi}$.

Like the nR^2 test, the $Q(p)$ test also assumes conditional homoskedasticity and autoregressive conditional homoskedasticity. In fact, it can be shown to be asymptotically equivalent to the nR^2 test statistic when e_t is the estimated residual of a static regression model.

Hong (1996) proposes a class of consistent tests for serial correlation of unknown form for the disturbance in a stationary linear regression model. Of them, one test can be viewed as a generalized Box-Pierce portmanteau test when p grows with sample size n (i.e., $p = p(n) \to \infty$ as $n \to \infty$), where a downward weighting function is introduced to discount higher order lags, and there exists an optimal weighting function to maximize certain power criterion. Interestingly, replacing $\{\varepsilon_t\}$ by the estimated residual $\{e_t\}$ does not affect the asymptotic normal distribution under the null hypothesis of MDS, even in a linear dynamic regression model. Intuitively, parameter estimation uncertainty contained in the estimated residual $\{e_t\}$ produces a correction term of a finite order, which becomes asymptotically negligible as $p \to \infty$.

5.9 Conclusion

In this chapter, we first introduce some basic concepts in time series analysis, and then show that the asymptotic theory established under the IID assumption in Chapter 4 carries over to ergodic stationary linear time series regression models with MDS disturbances. The MDS assumption for the regression disturbances plays a key role. For a static linear regression model, the MDS assumption is crucial for the validity of White's (1980) heteroskedasticity-consistent variance-covariance matrix estimator. For a dynamic linear regression model, the MDS assumption is crucial for correct model specification for the conditional mean $E(Y_t|I_{t-1})$.

To check the validity of the MDS assumption, one can test serial correlation in the regression disturbance. We introduce a number of popular tests for serial correlation and discuss the difference in testing serial correlation between a static regression model and a dynamic regression model.

As in Chapter 4, the form of the asymptotic variance of the OLS estimator depends on whether there exists conditional heteroskedasticity with respect to the regressors of the linear time series regression model. We further discuss how to test conditional heteroskedasticity with respect to explanatory variables and ARCH respectively, and exploit different implications of these two forms of conditional heteroskedasticity for static and dynamic linear regression models respectively.

Exercise 5

5.1. (1) Why is the concept of stationarity important for time series econometrics?

(2) Why is the concept of ergodicity important for time series econometrics? For each part, illustrate your points using concrete examples.

5.2. Suppose a time series $\{Z_t\}$ follows an AR(1) process

$$Z_t = \alpha Z_{t-1} + \varepsilon_t, \{\varepsilon_t\} \sim \text{WN}(0, \sigma^2),$$

where $|\alpha| < 1$.

(1) Find $E(Z_t)$, $\text{var}(Z_t)$, $\text{cov}(Z_t, Z_{t-j})$ and $\text{corr}(Z_t, Z_{t-j})$ for $j = 0, \pm 1, \ldots$.

(2) Is this process weakly stationary? Explain.

(3) If $|\alpha| \geq 1$, is $\{Z_t\}$ weakly stationary? Explain.

5.3. Suppose a time series process $\{Z_t\}$ follows an MA(1) process

$$Z_t = \alpha \varepsilon_{t-1} + \varepsilon_t, \{\varepsilon_t\} \sim \text{WN}(0, \sigma^2).$$

(1) Find $E(Z_t)$, $\text{var}(Z_t)$, $\text{cov}(Z_t, Z_{t-j})$ and $\text{corr}(Z_t, Z_{t-j})$ for $j = 0, \pm 1, \ldots$.

(2) Suppose α is a finite constant. Is $\{Z_t\}$ weakly stationary? Explain.

(3) Given an autocorrelation coefficient $\text{corr}(Z_t, Z_{t-1}) = \rho$ (say), is it possible that there exist two different values for α? Explain.

5.4. Suppose a time series $\{Z_t\}$ follows an ARMA$(1, 1)$ process

$$Z_t = \alpha Z_{t-1} + \beta \varepsilon_{t-1} + \varepsilon_t, \{\varepsilon_t\} \sim \text{WN}(0, \sigma^2),$$

where $|\alpha| < 1$.

(1) Find $E(Z_t)$, $\text{var}(Z_t)$, $\text{cov}(Z_t, Z_{t-j})$ and $\text{corr}(Z_t, Z_{t-j})$ for $j = 0, \pm 1, \ldots$.

(2) Is it weakly stationary? Explain.

(3) Express $\{Z_t\}$ as an AR(∞) process.

(4) Suppose $|\beta| < 1$. Represent $\{Z_t\}$ as an MA(∞) process.

5.5. A weakly stationary ARMA(1,1) process

$$Z_t = \alpha Z_{t-1} - \alpha^{-1} Z_{t-1} + \varepsilon_t, \text{ where } \{\varepsilon_t\} \sim \text{IID}(0, \sigma^2), \text{ and } |\alpha| < 1,$$

is called an *all-pass filter* model. Find the autocorrelation function $\rho(j)$ of $\{Z_t\}$.

5.6. Discuss whether the following relations are true or false. Give your reasoning.

(1) A zero-mean IID sequence is an MDS.
(2) A zero-mean IID sequence is a WN process.
(3) An MDS is a WN process.
(4) A WN process may not be an IID sequence.
(5) A WN process may not be an MDS.

5.7. Suppose a time series $\{X_t\}$ is a Gaussian process, namely, for all integer k, $Z_t \equiv (X_t, X_{t-1}, ..., X_{t-k})'$ follows a joint normal distribution. Show that for a zero-mean stationary Gaussian process $\{X_t\}$, IID, MDS and WN are equivalent to each other in the sense that given one, we can always derive the other two. *[Hint: Examine the PDF of a joint normal distribution.]*

5.8. (1) Suppose that using some statistical test, one finds evidence that there exists serial correlation in $\{\varepsilon_t\}$. Can we conclude that $\{\varepsilon_t\}$ is not an MDS? Give your reasoning.

(2) Suppose one finds that there exists no serial correlation in $\{\varepsilon_t\}$. Can we conclude that $\{\varepsilon_t\}$ is an MDS? Give your reasoning. *[Hint: Consider a nonlinear MA process* $\varepsilon_t = z_{t-1}z_{t-2} + z_t$, *where* $z_t \sim \text{IID}(0, \sigma^2)$.*]*

5.9. Suppose $\{Z_t\}$ is a zero-mean weakly stationary time series process. Then there exists a stochastic process $W(\omega)$ such that

$$Z_t = \int_{-\pi}^{\pi} e^{\mathbf{i}t\omega} dW(\omega), \qquad \omega \in [-\pi, \pi],$$

where $\mathbf{i} = \sqrt{-1}$, ω is frequency, $W(\omega)$ is an uncorrelated increment process with $E[dW(\omega)] = 0$ for all $\omega \in [-\pi, \pi]$, and $\text{cov}[dW(\omega), dW(\lambda)] = E|dW(\omega)|^2$ if $\omega = \lambda$ and 0 otherwise.

(1) Show that the autocovariance function $\gamma(j) = \text{cov}(Z_t, Z_{t-j}) = \int_{-\pi}^{\pi} e^{\mathbf{i}j\omega}|dW(\omega)|^2$. Note that for a zero-mean complex-valued process, $\text{cov}(Z_t, Z_{t-j}) = E(Z_t Z_{t-j}^*)$. $j = 0, \pm 1, \pm 2....$

(2) Show that $\gamma(j) = \int_{-\pi}^{\pi} e^{\mathbf{i}j\omega} h(\omega) d\omega$ if in addition $E|dW(\omega)|^2 = h(\omega)d\omega$. This implies that $\gamma(j)$ is the inverse Fourier transform of the spectral density function $h(\omega)$.

5.10. Suppose $\{Z_t\}_{t=1}^n$ is a random sample of size n from a weakly stationary zero-mean time series process $\{Z_t\}$. Define the discrete Fourier transform

$$D_n(\omega) = n^{-1/2} \sum_{t=1}^{n} Z_t e^{\mathbf{i}t\omega},\ \omega \in [-\pi, \pi],$$

where $\mathbf{i} = \sqrt{-1}$, ω is called a frequency. Intuitively, the discrete Fourier transform $D_n(\omega)$ extracts the periodic component with frequency ω from the time series $\{Z_t\}$. Define

$$\hat{h}_n(\omega) = \frac{1}{2\pi} |D_n(\omega)|^2 .$$

Show that $E\hat{h}_n(\omega) \to h(\omega) = \frac{1}{2\pi} \sum_{j=-\infty}^{\infty} \gamma(j) e^{-\mathbf{i}j\omega}$ as $n \to \infty$, where $\gamma(j) = \text{cov}(Z_t, Z_{t-j})$.

5.11. Suppose $\{Z_t\}$ is a zero-mean weakly stationary process with spectral density function $h(\omega)$ and standardized spectral density function $f(\omega) = h(\omega)/\gamma(0)$. Show that:

(1) $f(\omega)$ is real-valued for all $\omega \in [-\pi, \pi]$.

(2) $f(\omega)$ is a symmetric function, i.e., $f(-\omega) = f(\omega)$.

(3) $\int_{-\pi}^{\pi} f(\omega) d\omega = 1$.

(4) $f(\omega) \geq 0$ for all $\omega \in [-\pi, \pi]$. *[Hint: Consider the limit of* $E|n^{-1/2} \sum_{t=1}^{n} Z_t e^{\mathbf{i}t\omega}|^2$, *the variance of the complex-valued random variable* $n^{-1/2} \sum_{t=1}^{n} Z_t e^{\mathbf{i}t\omega}$*.]*

5.12. Consider an ARCH(1) process in Section 5.1.

(1) Drive the condition(s) under which an ARCH(1) process is weakly stationary.

(2) Drive the spectral density function of a weakly stationary ARCH(1) process.

(3) Can the spectral density function $h(\omega)$ distinguish an IID sequence with a finite variance from a weakly stationary ARCH(1) process? Explain.

5.13. Consider testing the null hypothesis of conditional homoskedasticity ($\mathbf{H}_0 : E(\varepsilon_t^2 | X_t) = \sigma^2$) for a stationary time series regression model

$$Y_t = X_t' \beta^o + \varepsilon_t,$$

where X_t is a $K \times 1$ vector consisting of an intercept and explanatory variables.

To test conditional homoskedasticity, we consider the auxiliary regression

$$\begin{aligned}\varepsilon_t^2 &= \text{vech}(X_tX_t')'\gamma + v_t \\ &= U_t'\gamma + v_t,\end{aligned}$$

where $U_t = \text{vech}(X_tX_t')$ is a $J \times 1$ vector, with $J = K(K+1)/2$. Suppose Assumptions 5.1 to 5.5 and 5.7 hold, and $E(\varepsilon_t^4|X_t) = \mu_4$.

(1) Assume that $\{\varepsilon_t\}$ is observable, and denote R^2 be the coefficient of determination of the auxiliary regression. Show that the test statistic $(n-J-1)R^2 \xrightarrow{d} \chi_J^2$ under $\mathbf{H}_0$. Give your reasoning.

(2) The assumption that $\{\varepsilon_t\}$ is observable in Part (1) is not realistic. Now we replace ε_t by $e_t = Y_t - X_t'\hat{\beta}$, the estimated OLS residual. Provide a heuristic explanation why the replacement of ε_t by e_t does not affect the asymptotic distribution of the proposed test statistic in Part (1).

5.14. Suppose a dynamic linear regression model

$$\begin{aligned}Y_t &= \beta_0^o + \beta_1^o Y_{t-1} + \varepsilon_t \\ &= X_t'\beta^o + \varepsilon_t,\end{aligned}$$

where $X_t = (1, Y_{t-1})'$, satisfies Assumptions 5.1, 5.2 and 5.4. Suppose further that $\{\varepsilon_t\}$ follows an MA(1) process

$$\varepsilon_t = \rho v_{t-1} + v_t, \qquad \{v_t\} \sim \text{IID}(0, \sigma_v^2).$$

Thus, there exists first order serial correlation in $\{\varepsilon_t\}$.

Is the OLS estimator $\hat{\beta}$ consistent for β^o? Explain.

5.15. Suppose a time series linear regression model

$$Y_t = X_t'\beta^o + \varepsilon_t$$

satisfies Assumptions 5.1 to 5.3. This includes both static regression models and dynamic regression models.

(1) Does the condition $E(\varepsilon_t|X_t) = 0$ imply that $\{\varepsilon_t\}$ is a WN? Explain.

(2) If $\{\varepsilon_t\}$ is an MDS, does it imply $E(\varepsilon_t|X_t) = 0$? Explain.

(3) If $\{\varepsilon_t\}$ is serially correlated, does it necessarily imply $E(\varepsilon_t|X_t) \neq 0$, i.e., the linear regression model is misspecified for $E(Y_t|X_t)$? Explain.

5.16. Suppose a static time series linear regression model

$$Y_t = X_t'\beta^o + \varepsilon_t$$

satisfies Assumptions 5.1 to 5.3, and $\{X_t\}$ and $\{\varepsilon_t\}$ are mutually independent.

(1) Derive the asymptotic variance of the OLS estimator $\sqrt{n}\hat{\beta}$ when $\{\varepsilon_t\}$ is an MDS. Give your reasoning.

(2) Is the OLS estimator $\hat{\beta}$ consistent for β^o when there exists serial correlation in $\{\varepsilon_t\}$? Give your reasoning.

(3) Derive the asymptotic variance of the OLS estimator $\sqrt{n}\hat{\beta}$ when there exists serial correlation in $\{\varepsilon_t\}$. Give your reasoning.

5.17. Suppose a linear regression model

$$Y_t = X_t'\beta^o + \varepsilon_t$$

satisfies Assumptions 5.1 to 5.6. We are interested in testing the null hypothesis $\mathbf{H}_0$ that $\{\varepsilon_t\}$ is an MDS. Assume that ε_t is observable.

(1) Consider the auxiliary autoregression

$$\varepsilon_t = \sum_{j=1}^{p} \alpha_j \varepsilon_{t-j} + v_t,\ t = p+1, ..., n.$$

Let $\tilde{R}_{uc}^2$ be the uncentered R^2 from the OLS estimation of this auxiliary autoregression. Show $n\tilde{R}_{uc} \xrightarrow{d} \chi_p^2$ as $n \to \infty$ under $\mathbf{H}_0$.

(2) Now consider an alternative auxiliary autoregression

$$\varepsilon_t = \alpha_0 + \sum_{j=1}^{p} \alpha_j \varepsilon_{t-j} + u_t, \quad t = p+1, ..., n.$$

Let $\tilde{R}^2$ be the centered R^2 from this auxiliary autoregression. Show $n\tilde{R}^2 \xrightarrow{d} \chi_p^2$ as $n \to \infty$ under $\mathbf{H}_0$.

(3) Which test statistic, $n\tilde{R}_{uc}^2$ or $n\tilde{R}^2$, performs better in small and finite samples? Give your heuristic reasoning.

5.18. The assumption that $\{\varepsilon_t\}$ is observable in $\{\varepsilon_t\}$ in Exercise 5.17 is not realistic. In practice, one has to use the estimated OLS residual e_t to replace ε_t. Provide a heuristic explanation for whether or not the replacement of ε_t by e_t affects the asymptotic distribution of the test statistics under the null hypothesis of MDS for $\{\varepsilon_t\}$ in both Parts (1) and (2) of Exercise 5.17. *[Hint: You may need to consider static and dynamic regression models respectively.]*

5.19. Suppose a linear regression model

$$Y_t = X_t'\beta^o + \varepsilon_t$$

satisfies Assumptions 5.1 to 5.5, and $E(\varepsilon_t^2|X_t) \neq \sigma^2$. We are interested in testing the null hypothesis $\mathbf{H}_0$ that $\{\varepsilon_t\}$ is an MDS. Assume that $\{\varepsilon_t\}$ is observable.

Consider the auxiliary autoregression

$$\varepsilon_t = \sum_{j=1}^{p} \alpha_j \varepsilon_{t-j} + v_t, \quad t = p+1, ..., n.$$

(1) Construct an asymptotically valid test statistic for the null hypothesis that $\{\varepsilon_t\}$ is an MDS. Give your reasoning.

(2) Can one use $n\tilde{R}^2_{uc}$ as a test statistic? Explain.

5.20. The assumption that $\{\varepsilon_t\}$ is observable in $\{\varepsilon_t\}$ in Exercise 5.19 is not realistic. In practice, one has to use the estimated OLS residual e_t to replace ε_t. Provide a heuristic explanation for whether or not the replacement of ε_t by e_t affects the asymptotic distribution of the test statistic under the null hypothesis of MDS in Part (1) of Exercise 5.19. *[Hint: You may consider static and dynamic regression models respectively.]*

5.21. Suppose ε_t follows an ARCH(1) process

$$\varepsilon_t = \sigma_t z_t,$$
$$\sigma_t^2 = \alpha_0 + \alpha_1 \varepsilon_{t-1}^2,$$
$$z_t \sim \text{IID } N(0,1).$$

(1) Show $E(\varepsilon_t|I_{t-1}) = 0$ and $\text{cov}(\varepsilon_t, \varepsilon_{t-j}) = 0$ for all $j > 0$, where $I_{t-1} = \{\varepsilon_{t-1}, \varepsilon_{t-2}, ...\}$.

(2) Show $\text{cov}(\varepsilon_t^2, \varepsilon_{t-1}^2) = \alpha_1$.

(3) Show the kurtosis of ε_t is given by

$$K = \frac{E(\varepsilon_t^4)}{[E(\varepsilon_t^2)]^2} = \frac{3(1-\alpha_1^2)}{1-3\alpha_1^2}.$$

Thus, $K > 3$ if $\alpha_1 > 0$.

5.22. An ergodic stationary time series linear regression model is given by

$$\begin{aligned} Y_t &= X_t'\beta^o + \varepsilon_t, \\ \varepsilon_t &= \sigma_t z_t, \\ \sigma_t^2 &= \alpha_0 + \alpha_1 \varepsilon_{t-1}^2, \qquad \alpha_0 > 0, 0 < \alpha_1 < 1, \\ \{z_t\} &\sim \text{IID } N(0,1), \end{aligned}$$

where $\{X_t\}$ and $\{z_t\}$ are mutually independent.

(1) Is the OLS estimator $\hat{\beta}$ consistent for β^o? Explain.

(2) Is $s^2\hat{Q}^{-1}$ a consistent estimator for the asymptotic variance $\text{avar}(\sqrt{n}\hat{\beta})$? Does the existence of ARCH affect the structure of $\text{avar}(\sqrt{n}\hat{\beta})$? Explain.

5.23. Suppose a time series linear regression model

$$Y_t = X_t'\beta^o + \varepsilon_t$$

satisfies Assumptions 5.1 to 5.5. Both static and dynamic regression models are covered.

Suppose there exists ARCH for $\{\varepsilon_t\}$, namely,

$$E(\varepsilon_t^2 | I_{t-1}) = \alpha_0 + \sum_{j=1}^{q} \alpha_j \varepsilon_{t-j}^2,$$

where I_{t-1} is the sigma-field generated by $\{\varepsilon_{t-1}, \varepsilon_{t-2}, ...\}$. Does this imply that one has to use the asymptotic variance formula $Q^{-1}VQ^{-1}$ for $\text{avar}(\sqrt{n}\hat{\beta})$? Explain. *[Hint: Consider static and dynamic regression models respectively.]*

5.24. Suppose a time series linear regression model

$$Y_t = X_t'\beta^o + \varepsilon_t$$

satisfies Assumptions 5.1 to 5.5, and the two time series $\{X_t\}$ and $\{\varepsilon_t\}$ are mutually independent.

Assume that there exists ARCH for $\{\varepsilon_t\}$, namely,

$$E(\varepsilon_t^2 | I_{t-1}) = \alpha_0 + \sum_{j=1}^{q} \alpha_j \varepsilon_{t-j}^2,$$

where I_{t-1} is the sigma-field generated by $\{\varepsilon_{t-1}, \varepsilon_{t-2}, ...\}$. What is the form of $\text{avar}(\sqrt{n}\hat{\beta})$, where $\hat{\beta}$ is the OLS estimator? Give your reasoning.

5.25. Suppose a dynamic linear regression model

$$\begin{aligned} Y_t &= X_t'\beta^o + \varepsilon_t \\ &= \beta_0^o + \beta_1^o Y_{t-1} + \varepsilon_t \end{aligned}$$

satisfies Assumptions 5.1 to 5.5, where $X_t = (1, Y_{t-1})'$. Assume that there exists ARCH for $\{\varepsilon_t\}$:

$$E(\varepsilon_t^2 | I_{t-1}) = \alpha_0 + \alpha_1 Y_{t-1}^2.$$

What is the form of avar$(\sqrt{n}\hat{\beta})$? Here $\hat{\beta}$ is the OLS estimator.

5.26. Suppose a time series linear regression model

$$Y_t = X_t'\beta^o + \varepsilon_t$$

satisfies Assumptions 5.1 to 5.5 and 5.7.

We are interested in testing the null hypothesis of autoregressive conditional homoskedasticity $\mathbf{H}_0 : E(\varepsilon_t^2 | I_{t-1}) = \sigma^2$, where $I_{t-1} = \{\varepsilon_{t-1}, \varepsilon_{t-2}, ...\}$. For this purpose, we assume

$$\varepsilon_t = \sigma_t z_t, \{z_t\} \sim \text{IID}(0, \sigma_z^2),$$

with $E(z_t^4) < \infty$. Consider an auxiliary ARCH(q) model

$$\varepsilon_t^2 = \alpha_0 + \sum_{j=1}^{q} \alpha_j \varepsilon_{t-j}^2 + v_t, \qquad t = q+1, ..., n,$$

where $E(v_t) = 0$. Under $\mathbf{H}_0$, all slope coefficients in the auxiliary ARCH(q) model should be jointly equal to zero.

(1) Show that $E(v_t | I_{t-1}) = 0$ and $E(v_t^2 | I_{t-1}) = \mu_4$ under $\mathbf{H}_0$.

(2) Assume that ε_t is observable. Let $\tilde{R}^2$ be the coefficient of determination in the auxiliary ARCH(q) regression. Show $n\tilde{R}^2 \xrightarrow{d} \chi_q^2$ as $n \to \infty$ under $\mathbf{H}_0$. Give your reasoning.

(3) The assumption that ε_t is observable is not realistic. In practice, one has to use e_t to replace ε_t in the auxiliary ARCH(q) regression. Let R^2 be the coefficient of determination in the feasible auxiliary ARCH(q) regression. Show $nR^2 \xrightarrow{d} \chi_q^2$ as $n \to \infty$ under $\mathbf{H}_0$. This implies that the replacement of ε_t by e_t does not affect the asymptotic distribution of the test statistic.

Chapter 6

Linear Regression Models Under Conditional Heteroskedasticity and Autocorrelation

Abstract: When the regression disturbance $\{\varepsilon_t\}$ displays serial correlation, the asymptotic results in Chapter 5 are no longer applicable, because the asymptotic variance of the OLS estimator will depend on serial correlation in $\{X_t\varepsilon_t\}$. In this chapter, we introduce a method to estimate the asymptotic variance of the OLS estimator in the presence of conditional heteroskedasticity and autocorrelation, and then develop robust test procedures based on it.

Keywords: Cochrane-Orcutt procedure, Heteroskedasticity and Autocorrelation Consistent (HAC) variance-covariance matrix, Kernel function, Long-run variance-covariance matrix, Newey-West estimator, Nonparametric estimation, Spectral density matrix, Variance ratio test

6.1 Motivation

In Chapter 5, we assume that $\{X_t\varepsilon_t\}$ is an MDS. In many economic applications, there may exist serial correlation in the regression disturbance $\{\varepsilon_t\}$. As a consequence, $\{X_t\varepsilon_t\}$ is generally no longer an MDS. We now provide a few examples where $\{\varepsilon_t\}$ is serially correlated.

Example 6.1. [Testing a Zero Population Mean]: Suppose the daily stock return $\{Y_t\}$ is an ergodic stationary process with $E(Y_t) = \mu$. We are interested in testing the null hypothesis

$$\mathbf{H}_0 : \mu = 0$$

versus the alternative hypothesis

$$\mathbf{H}_A : \mu \neq 0.$$

A test for $\mathbf{H}_0$ can be based on the sample mean

$$\bar{Y}_n = n^{-1}\sum_{t=1}^{n} Y_t.$$

By a suitable CLT (see, e.g., White (1984, Theorem 5.15) or Lemma 6.1 below), the sampling distribution of the sample mean $\bar{Y}_n$ scaled by $\sqrt{n}$

$$\sqrt{n}\bar{Y}_n \xrightarrow{d} N(0, V)$$

under $\mathbf{H}_0$, where V is the asymptotic variance of the scaled sample mean:

$$V \equiv \text{avar}\left(\sqrt{n}\bar{Y}_n\right).$$

Because

$$\begin{aligned}\text{var}(\sqrt{n}\bar{Y}_n) = n^{-1}&\sum_{t=1}^{n}\text{var}\,(Y_t)\\ &+ 2n^{-1}\sum_{t=2}^{n-1}\sum_{j=1}^{t-1}\text{cov}(Y_t, Y_{t-j}),\end{aligned}$$

serial correlation in $\{Y_t\}$ is expected to affect the asymptotic variance of $\sqrt{n}\bar{Y}_n$. Thus, unlike in Chapter 5, $\text{avar}(\sqrt{n}\bar{Y}_n)$ is no longer equal to $\text{var}(Y_t)$. Suppose there exists a variance estimator $\hat{V}$ such that $\hat{V} \xrightarrow{p} V$. Then, by Slutsky's theorem, we can construct a robust t-test statistic which is asymptotically $N(0,1)$ under $\mathbf{H}_0$:

$$\frac{\sqrt{n}\bar{Y}_n}{\sqrt{\hat{V}}} \xrightarrow{d} N(0,1).$$

This robust t-test statistic for $\mathbf{H}_0$ is asymptotically valid when there exists serial correlation of unknown form in $\{Y_t\}$.

Example 6.2. [Unbiasedness Hypothesis]: Consider the following linear regression model

$$S_{t+\tau} = \alpha + \beta F_t(\tau) + \varepsilon_{t+\tau},$$

where $S_{t+\tau}$ is the spot foreign exchange rate at time $t+\tau$, $F_t(\tau)$ is the forward exchange rate (with maturity $\tau > 0$) at time t, and the disturbance $\varepsilon_{t+\tau}$ is not observable. Forward currency contracts are agreements to exchange, in the future, fixed amounts of two currencies at prices set today. No money changes hand over until the contract expires or is offset.

It has been a long-standing controversy on whether the current forward rate $F_t(\tau)$, as opposed to the current spot rate S_t, is a better predictor for the future spot rate $S_{t+\tau}$. The unbiasedness hypothesis states that the forward exchange rate (with maturity τ) at time t is the optimal predictor for the spot exchange rate at time $t+\tau$, namely,

$$E(S_{t+\tau}|I_t) = F_t(\tau) \ ,$$

where I_t is the information set available at time t. This implies

$$\mathbf{H}_0 : \alpha = 0, \beta = 1,$$

and

$$E(\varepsilon_{t+\tau}|I_t) = 0 \ , \ t = 1, 2, ...$$

However, with $\tau > 1$, we generally do not have $E(\varepsilon_{t+j}|I_t) = 0$ for $1 \leq j \leq \tau - 1$. Consequently, there exists serial correlation in $\{\varepsilon_t\}$ up to $\tau - 1$ lags under $\mathbf{H}_0$. This will affect the asymptotic variance of the OLS estimator $\sqrt{n}\hat{\beta}$.

Example 6.3. [Long Horizon Return Predictability]: There has been much interest in regressions of asset returns, measured over various horizons, on various forecasting variables. The latter include ratios of price to dividends or earnings, various interest rate measures such as the yield spread between long and short term rates, the quality yield spread between low and high-grade corporate bonds, and the short term interest rate.

Consider a predictive regression

$$Y_{t+h,h} = \beta_0 + \beta_1 r_t + \beta_2(d_t - p_t) + \varepsilon_{t+h,h},$$

where $Y_{t+h,h}$ is the cumulative return over the holding period from time t to time $t+h$, namely,

$$Y_{t+h,h} = \sum_{j=1}^{h} R_{t+j},$$

where R_{t+j} is an asset return in period $t+j$, r_t is the short term interest rate in time t, and $d_t - p_t$ is the log dividend-price ratio, which is expected to be a good proxy for market expectations of future stock returns, because $d_t - p_t$ is equal to the expectation of the sum of all discounted future returns and dividend growth rates. In the empirical finance, there has been an interest in investigating how the predictability of asset returns by various forecasting variables depends on time horizon h. For example, it is expected that $d_t - p_t$ is a better proxy for expectations of long horizon returns than for expectations of short horizon returns. When monthly data is used and $h > 1$, there exists an overlapping for observations on $Y_{t+h,h}$. As a result, the forecast error $\varepsilon_{t+h,h}$ is expected to display serial correlation up to lag order $h - 1$.

Example 6.4. [Relationship Between GDP and Money Supply]: Consider a linear macroeconomic regression model

$$Y_t = \alpha + \beta M_t + \varepsilon_t,$$

where Y_t is GDP growth rate in time t, M_t is money supply growth rate in time t, and ε_t is an unobservable disturbance such that $E(\varepsilon_t|M_t) = 0$ but there may exist persistent serial correlation of unknown form in $\{\varepsilon_t\}$.

Question: What happens to the OLS estimator $\hat{\beta}$ if the disturbance $\{\varepsilon_t\}$ displays conditional heteroskedasticity (i.e., $E(\varepsilon_t^2|X_t) \neq \sigma^2$) and/or autocorrelation (i.e., $\text{cov}(\varepsilon_t, \varepsilon_{t-j}) \neq 0$ at least for some $j > 0$)? In particular, we would like to address the following important issues:

- Is the OLS estimator $\hat{\beta}$ consistent for β^o?
- Is $\hat{\beta}$ asymptotically most efficient?
- Is $\hat{\beta}$, after properly scaled, asymptotically normal?
- Are the test statistics introduced in Chapter 5 applicable for large sample inference?

6.2 Framework and Assumptions

We now state the set of assumptions which allow for conditional heteroskedasticity and serial correlation of unknown form.

Assumption 6.1. [Ergodic Stationarity]: $\{Y_t, X_t'\}_{t=1}^n$ is an observable ergodic stationary process.

Assumption 6.2. [Linearity]:

$$Y_t = X_t'\beta^o + \varepsilon_t,$$

where β^o is a $K \times 1$ unknown parameter vector and ε_t is the unobservable disturbance.

Assumption 6.3. [Correct Model Specification]: $E(\varepsilon_t|X_t) = 0$ almost surely.

Assumption 6.4. [Nonsingularity]: The $K \times K$ matrix

$$Q = E(X_t X_t')$$

is symmetric, finite and nonsingular.

Assumption 6.5. [Long-Run Variance-Covariance Matrix]: (a) For $j = 0, \pm 1, ...,$ define the $K \times K$ autocovariance function of $\{X_t\varepsilon_t\}$

$$\begin{aligned}\Gamma(j) &= \text{cov}(X_t\varepsilon_t, X_{t-j}\varepsilon_{t-j}) \\ &= E(X_t\varepsilon_t\varepsilon_{t-j}X_{t-j}').\end{aligned}$$

Then $\sum_{j=-\infty}^{\infty}||\Gamma(j)|| < \infty$, where $||A|| = \sum_{i=1}^{K}\sum_{j=1}^{K}|A_{(i,j)}|$ for any $K \times K$ matrix, and the long-run variance-covariance matrix

$$V = \sum_{j=-\infty}^{\infty}\Gamma(j)$$

is positive definite.

(b) The conditional expectation

$$E(X_t\varepsilon_t|X_{t-j}\varepsilon_{t-j}, X_{t-j-1}\varepsilon_{t-j-1}, ...) \overset{q.m.}{\to} 0 \text{ as } j \to \infty.$$

(c) $\sum_{j=0}^{\infty}[E(r_j'r_j)]^{1/2} < \infty$, where

$$\begin{aligned}r_j &= E(X_t\varepsilon_t|X_{t-j}\varepsilon_{t-j}, X_{t-j-1}\varepsilon_{t-j-1}, ...) \\ &\quad - E(X_t\varepsilon_t|X_{t-j-1}\varepsilon_{t-j-1}, X_{t-j-2}\varepsilon_{t-j-2}, ...).\end{aligned}$$

Assumptions 6.1 to 6.4 have been assumed in Chapter 5 but Assumption 6.5 is new. Assumption 6.5(a) allows for both conditional heteroskedasticity and autocorrelation of unknown form in $\{\varepsilon_t\}$, and no normality assumption is imposed on $\{\varepsilon_t\}$.

We do not assume that $\{X_t\varepsilon_t\}$ is an MDS, although $E(X_t\varepsilon_t) = 0$ as implied by $E(\varepsilon_t|X_t) = 0$. Note that $E(\varepsilon_t|X_t) = 0$ does not necessarily imply that $\{X_t\varepsilon_t\}$ is an MDS in a time series context. See the aforementioned examples for which $\{X_t\varepsilon_t\}$ is not an MDS.

Assumptions 6.5(b, c) imply that the serial dependence of $X_t\varepsilon_t$ on its past history in term of mean and variance respectively vanishes to zero as the lag order $j \to \infty$. Intuitively, Assumption 6.5(c) may be viewed as the net effect of $X_{t-j}\varepsilon_{t-j}$ on the conditional mean of $X_t\varepsilon_t$. It implies $E(r_j'r_j) \to 0$ as $j \to \infty$.

6.3 Long-Run Variance-Covariance Matrix Estimation

Question: Why are we interested in the long-run variance-covariance matrix V as defined in Assumption 6.5?

Recall that for the OLS estimator $\hat{\beta}$, we have

$$\sqrt{n}(\hat{\beta} - \beta^o) = \hat{Q}^{-1} n^{-1/2} \sum_{t=1}^{n} X_t\varepsilon_t.$$

Suppose a suitable CLT holds for $\{X_t\varepsilon_t\}$ in the present context. That is, suppose

$$n^{-1/2} \sum_{t=1}^{n} X_t\varepsilon_t \xrightarrow{d} N(0, V)$$

as $n \to \infty$, where V is an asymptotic variance-covariance matrix, namely

$$V \equiv \text{avar}\left(n^{-1/2} \sum_{t=1}^{n} X_t\varepsilon_t\right).$$

Then, by Slutsky's theorem, we have

$$\sqrt{n}(\hat{\beta} - \beta^o) \xrightarrow{d} N(0, Q^{-1}VQ^{-1})$$

under suitable regularity conditions.

Now we consider the expression of V. Put

$$g_t = X_t\varepsilon_t.$$

Note that $E(g_t) = 0$ given $E(\varepsilon_t|X_t) = 0$ and the law of iterated expectations. Because $\{g_t\}$ is not an MDS, it may be serially correlated. Thus, the $K \times K$ autocovariance function $\Gamma(j) = \text{cov}(g_t, g_{t-j})$ may not be zero at least for some lag order $j > 0$.

Now we consider the variance-covariance matrix

$$
\begin{aligned}
\operatorname{var}\left(n^{-1/2}\sum_{t=1}^{n} X_t\varepsilon_t\right) &= \operatorname{var}\left(n^{-1/2}\sum_{t=1}^{n} g_t\right) \\
&= E\left[\left(n^{-1/2}\sum_{t=1}^{n} g_t\right)\left(n^{-1/2}\sum_{s=1}^{n} g_s\right)'\right] \\
&= n^{-1}\sum_{t=1}^{n}\sum_{s=1}^{n} E(g_t g_s') \\
&= n^{-1}\sum_{t=1}^{n} E(g_t g_t') \\
&\quad + n^{-1}\sum_{t=2}^{n}\sum_{s=1}^{t-1} E(g_t g_s') \\
&\quad + n^{-1}\sum_{t=1}^{n-1}\sum_{s=t+1}^{n} E(g_t g_s') \\
&= n^{-1}\sum_{t=1}^{n} E(g_t g_t') \\
&\quad + \sum_{j=1}^{n-1} n^{-1}\sum_{t=j+1}^{n} E(g_t g_{t-j}') \\
&\quad + \sum_{j=-(n-1)}^{-1} n^{-1}\sum_{t=1}^{n+j} E(g_t g_{t-j}') \\
&= \sum_{j=-(n-1)}^{n-1} (1-|j|/n)\Gamma(j) \\
&\to \sum_{j=-\infty}^{\infty} \Gamma(j) \text{ as } n\to\infty
\end{aligned}
$$

by dominated convergence. Therefore, we have $V = \sum_{j=-\infty}^{\infty}\Gamma(j)$.

As a special case, when $\{g_t\}$ is an MDS, we have

$$
\begin{aligned}
V \equiv \operatorname{avar}\left(n^{-1/2}\sum_{t=1}^{n} X_t\varepsilon_t\right) &= E(g_t g_t') \\
&= E(X_t X_t'\varepsilon_t^2) \\
&= \Gamma(0).
\end{aligned}
$$

When $\text{cov}(g_t, g_{t-j})$ is PSD for all $j > 0$, the difference $\sum_{j=-\infty}^{\infty}\Gamma(j) - \Gamma(0)$ is a PSD matrix. Intuitively, when $\Gamma(j)$ is PSD, a large deviation of g_t from its mean will tend to be followed by another large deviation. As a result, $V - \Gamma(0)$ is PSD.

Question: How to estimate the long-run variance-covariance matrix V?

It has been a long-standing problem for estimating a long run variance-covariance matrix. An important approach to estimating V is based on the spectral density matrix of time series process $\{X_t\varepsilon_t\}$. To explore the link between the long-run variance-covariance matrix V and the spectral density matrix of $\{X_t\varepsilon_t\}$, we now extend the concept of the spectral density function of a univariate time series to a multivariate time series context.

Definition 6.1. [Spectral Density Matrix]: Suppose $\{g_t = X_t\varepsilon_t\}$ is a $K\times 1$ weakly stationary process with $E(g_t) = 0$ and autocovariance function $\Gamma(j) \equiv \text{cov}(g_t, g_{t-j}) = E(g_t g_{t-j}')$, which is a $K \times K$ matrix. Suppose

$$\sum_{j=-\infty}^{\infty} ||\Gamma(j)|| < \infty.$$

Then the Fourier transform of the autocovariance function $\Gamma(j)$ exists and is given by

$$H(\omega) = \frac{1}{2\pi}\sum_{j=-\infty}^{\infty}\Gamma(j)e^{-\mathbf{i}j\omega}, \qquad \omega \in [-\pi, \pi],$$

where $\mathbf{i} = \sqrt{-1}$. The $K \times K$ matrix-valued function $H(\omega)$ is called the spectral density matrix of the weakly stationary time series vector-valued process $\{g_t\}$.

The inverse Fourier transform of the spectral density matrix is

$$\Gamma(j) = \int_{-\pi}^{\pi} e^{\mathbf{i}j\omega}H(\omega)d\omega.$$

Both $H(\omega)$ and $\Gamma(j)$ are the Fourier transforms of each other. They contain the same information on serial dependence of the process $\{g_t = X_t\varepsilon_t\}$. The spectral density matrix $H(\omega)$ is useful to identify business cycles (see Sargent 1987, *Dynamic Macroeconomics*, 2nd Edition). For example, if g_t is the GDP growth rate at time t, then $H(\omega)$ can be used to identify business cycles of the economy.

Given the definition of the spectral density matrix $H(\omega)$, we have the long-run variance-covariance matrix

$$V = 2\pi H(0) = \sum_{j=-\infty}^{\infty} \Gamma(j).$$

That is, the long-run variance-covariance matrix V is 2π times the spectral density matrix of the time series process $\{g_t\}$ at frequency zero. As will be seen below, this link provides a basis for consistent nonparametric estimation of V.

Question: What are the elements of the $K \times K$ autovariance function $\Gamma(j)$?

Recall that $g_t = (g_{0t}, g_{1t}, ..., g_{kt})'$, where $g_{lt} = X_{lt}\varepsilon_t$ for $0 \leq l \leq k$. Then the $(l+1, m+1)$-th element of $\Gamma(j)$ is

$$\begin{aligned}[\Gamma(j)]_{(l+1,m+1)} &= \Gamma_{lm}(j) \\ &= \text{cov}[g_{lt}, g_{m(t-j)}] \\ &= \text{cov}[X_{lt}\varepsilon_t, X_{m(t-j)}\varepsilon_{(t-j)}],\end{aligned}$$

which is the cross-covariance between $X_{lt}\varepsilon_t$ and $X_{m(t-j)}\varepsilon_{(t-j)}$. We note that

$$\Gamma_{lm}(j) \neq \Gamma_{lm}(-j),$$

because g_t is a vector, not a scalar. Instead, we have

$$\Gamma(j) = \Gamma(-j)',$$

which implies $\Gamma_{lm}(j) = \Gamma_{ml}(-j)$.

Question: What is the $(l+1, m+1)$-th element of $H(\omega)$ when $l \neq m$?

The function

$$H_{lm}(\omega) = \frac{1}{2\pi} \sum_{j=-\infty}^{\infty} \Gamma_{lm}(j)e^{-\mathbf{i}j\omega}$$

is called the cross-spectral density function between $\{g_{lt}\}$ and $\{g_{mt}\}$. The cross-spectrum is very useful in investigating comovements between different economic time series. The popular concept of Granger causality was first defined using the cross-spectrum (see Granger 1969). In general, the cross-spectral density function $H_{lm}(\omega)$ is complex-valued.

We first consider a naive estimation method for V. Given a random sample $\{Y_t, X_t'\}_{t=1}^n$, we can obtain the estimated OLS residual $e_t = Y_t - X_t'\hat{\beta}$ from the linear regression model $Y_t = X_t'\beta^o + \varepsilon_t$. Because

$$V = 2\pi H(0) = \sum_{j=-\infty}^{\infty} \Gamma(j),$$

we first consider a naive estimator

$$\hat{V} = \sum_{j=-(n-1)}^{n-1} \hat{\Gamma}(j),$$

where the sample autocovariance function

$$\hat{\Gamma}(j) = \begin{cases} n^{-1}\sum_{t=j+1}^{n} X_t e_t X_{t-j}' e_{t-j}, \ j = 0, 1, ..., n-1, \\ n^{-1}\sum_{t=1-j}^{n} X_t e_t X_{t-j}' e_{t-j}, \ j = -1, -2, ..., -(n-1). \end{cases}$$

There is no need to subtract the same mean from $X_t e_t$ and $X_{t-j}e_{t-j}$ because $\mathbf{X}'e = \sum_{t=1}^n X_t e_t = 0$. Also, note that the summation over lag orders in $\hat{V}$ extends to the maximum lag order $n-1$ for the sample autocovariance function $\hat{\Gamma}(j)$. Unfortunately, although it can be proven that $\hat{\Gamma}(j)$ is consistent for $\Gamma(j)$ as $n \to \infty$ for each given j, the long-run variance estimator $\hat{V}$ is not consistent for V.

Question: Why?

There are too many estimated terms in the summation over lag orders in $\hat{V}$. In fact, there are n estimated parameters $\{\hat{\Gamma}(j)\}_{j=0}^{n-1}$ in $\hat{V}$. It can be shown that the asymptotic variance estimator $\hat{V}$ defined above is proportional to the ratio of the number of the estimated autocovariance matrices $\{\hat{\Gamma}(j)\}$ to the sample size n, which will not vanish to zero if the number of the estimated autocovariances is the same as or is close to the sample size n.

The above explanation motivates us to consider the following truncated sum

$$\hat{V} = \sum_{j=-p}^{p} \hat{\Gamma}(j),$$

where p is a positive integer. If p is fixed (i.e., p does not grow when the sample size n increases), however, we expect

$$\hat{V} \xrightarrow{p} \sum_{j=-p}^{p} \Gamma(j) \neq 2\pi H(0) = V,$$

because the resulting bias

$$\sum_{j=-p}^{p} \Gamma(j) - V = - \sum_{|j|>p} \Gamma(j)$$

will never vanish to zero as $n \to \infty$ when p is fixed. Hence, we should let p grow to infinity as $n \to \infty$; that is, let $p = p(n) \to \infty$ as $n \to \infty$. The bias will then vanish to zero as $n \to \infty$. Note that the bias is negative when $\Gamma(j)$ is PSD, i.e., when there exists positive autocorrelation in $\{X_t \varepsilon_t\}$.

However, we cannot let p grow as fast as the sample size n. Otherwise, the variance of $\hat{V}$ will never vanish to zero. Therefore, to ensure consistency of $\hat{V}$ to V, we should balance the bias and the variance of $\hat{V}$ properly. This suggests using a truncated variance estimator

$$\hat{V} = \sum_{j=-p_n}^{p_n} \hat{\Gamma}(j),$$

where $p_n \to \infty, p_n/n \to 0$. An example $p_n = n^{1/3}$. Here, p_n is a smoothing parameter and can be viewed as the maximum truncation lag order.

Although this variance estimator is consistent for V, it may not be PSD for all n. To ensure that it is always PSD, we can use a weighted average estimator

$$\hat{V} = \sum_{j=-p_n}^{p_n} k(j/p_n)\hat{\Gamma}(j)$$

where the weighting function $k(\cdot)$ is called a kernel function. An example is the Bartlett kernel

$$k(z) = (1 - |z|)\mathbf{1}(|z| \leq 1),$$

where $\mathbf{1}(\cdot)$ is the indicator function, which takes value 1 if the condition inside holds, and takes value 0 if the condition inside does not hold. Newey and West (1987, 1994) first used this kernel function to estimate V in econometrics. The truncated variance estimator $\hat{V}$ can be viewed as a kernel-based estimator with the use of the truncated kernel $k(z) = \mathbf{1}(|z| \leq 1)$, which assigns equal weighting to each of the first p_n lags. However, unlike the Bartlett kernel, the truncated kernel cannot ensure that $\hat{V}$ is PSD.

In fact, we can consider a more general variance estimator for V:

$$\hat{V} = \sum_{j=1-n}^{n-1} k(j/p_n)\hat{\Gamma}(j),$$

where $k(\cdot)$ may have unbounded support. In fact, any kernel $k : \mathbb{R} \to [-1, 1]$ can be used as long as it is symmetric about 0, and is continuous at all points except a finite number of points on $\mathbb{R}$, with $k(0) = 1$ and $\int_{-\infty}^{\infty} k^2(z)dz < \infty$. At the origin, $k(\cdot)$ attains the maximal value, and the fact that $k(\cdot)$ is square-integrable implies $k(z) \to 0$ as $|z| \to \infty$. This covers kernels with bounded and unbounded supports. When a kernel with unbounded support is used, p_n is no longer a maximum truncation lag order, but it is still a smoothing parameter p_n.

Most kernels are downward-weighting in the sense that $k(z) \to 0$ as $|z| \to \infty$. The use of a downward weighting kernel may enhance estimation efficiency of V because we have $\Gamma(j) \to 0$ as $j \to \infty$ when $\sum_{j=-\infty}^{\infty} ||\Gamma(j)|| < \infty$, and so it is more efficient to assign a larger weight to a lower order j and a smaller weight to a higher order j. Intuitively, although the summation over lag orders in $\hat{V}$ extends to the maximum lag order $n-1$, the lag orders that are much larger than p_n are expected to have negligible contributions to $\hat{V}$, given that $k(\cdot)$ discounts higher order lags. As a result, we have $\hat{V} \xrightarrow{p} V$ as $n \to \infty$.

An example of $k(\cdot)$ that has unbounded support is the Quadratic-Spectral kernel:

$$k(z) = \frac{3}{(\pi z)^2}\left[\frac{\sin(\pi z)}{\pi z} - \cos(\pi z)\right], \quad -\infty < z < \infty.$$

Andrews (1991) uses it to estimate V. This kernel also delivers a PSD matrix. Andrews (1991) shows that the Quadratic-Spectral kernel minimizes the asymptotic MSE of the long-run variance estimator $\hat{V}$ over a class of kernel functions. Figure 6.1 plots the shapes of the truncated, Bartlett, Daniell and Quadratic-Spectral kernels respectively.

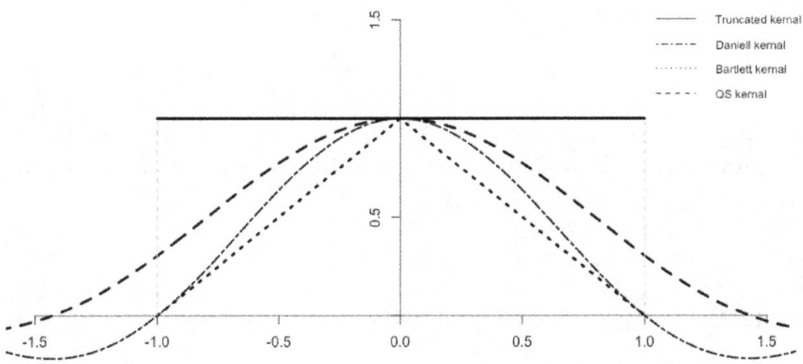

Figure 6.1 Shapes of the truncated, Bartlett, Daniell and Quadratic-Spectral kernels.

Under a set of regularity conditions on the random sample $\{Y_t, X_t'\}_{t=1}^n$, the kernel function $k(\cdot)$, and the lag order p_n (Newey and West 1987, Andrews 1991), we have

$$\hat{V} \xrightarrow{p} V$$

provided $p_n \to \infty, p_n/n \to 0$. There are many rules to satisfy $p_n \to \infty, p_n/n \to 0$. In practice, it is most important to determine an appropriate smoothing parameter p_n. Andrews (1991) and Newey and West (1994) discuss data-driven methods to choose p_n.

For derivations of the asymptotic variance and asymptotic bias of the long-run variance estimator $\hat{V}$, see, e.g., Newey and West (1987, 1994) and Andrews (1991).

6.4 Consistency of the OLS Estimator

When there exist conditional heteroskedasticity and autocorrelation of unknown form in $\{\varepsilon_t\}$, it is very difficult, if not impossible, to use GLS estimation. Instead, the OLS estimator $\hat{\beta}$ is convenient to use in practice. We now investigate the asymptotic properties of the OLS estimator $\hat{\beta}$ when there exist conditional heteroskedasticity and autocorrelation of unknown form.

Theorem 6.1. *Suppose Assumptions 6.1 to 6.5(a) hold. Then*

$$\hat{\beta} \xrightarrow{p} \beta^o \text{ as } n \to \infty.$$

Proof: Recall that we have

$$\hat{\beta} - \beta^o = \hat{Q}^{-1} n^{-1} \sum_{t=1}^{n} X_t \varepsilon_t.$$

By Assumptions 6.1, 6.2 and 6.4 and WLLN for an ergodic stationary process, we have

$$\hat{Q} \xrightarrow{p} Q \text{ and } \hat{Q}^{-1} \xrightarrow{p} Q^{-1}.$$

Similarly, by Assumptions 6.1 to 6.3 and 6.5(a), we have

$$n^{-1} \sum_{t=1}^{n} X_t \varepsilon_t \xrightarrow{p} E(X_t \varepsilon_t) = 0$$

using WLLN for an ergodic stationary process, where $E(X_t\varepsilon_t) = 0$ given Assumption 6.2 ($E(\varepsilon_t|X_t) = 0$) and the law of iterated expectations.

6.5 Asymptotic Normality of the OLS Estimator

To derive the asymptotic distribution of $\sqrt{n}(\hat{\beta} - \beta^o)$, we first provide a CLT for an ergodic stationary time series process.

Lemma 6.1. ***[CLT for a Zero Mean Ergodic Stationary Process (White 1984, Theorem 5.15)]:*** *Suppose $\{Z_t\}$ is an ergodic stationary process with*

(1) $E(Z_t) = 0$;

(2) $V = \sum_{j=-\infty}^{\infty} \Gamma(j)$ is finite and nonsingular, where $\Gamma(j) = E(Z_t Z_{t-j}')$;

(3) $E(Z_t|Z_{t-j}, Z_{t-j-1}, ...) \xrightarrow{q.m.} 0$, as $j \to \infty$;

(4) $\sum_{j=0}^{\infty} [E(r_j' r_j)]^{1/2} < \infty$, where

$$r_j = E(Z_t|Z_{t-j}, Z_{t-j-1}, ...) - E(Z_t|Z_{t-j-1}, Z_{t-j-2}, ...).$$

Then as $n \to \infty$,

$$n^{1/2} \bar{Z}_n = n^{-1/2} \sum_{t=1}^{n} Z_t \xrightarrow{d} N(0, V).$$

Proof: See White (1984, Theorem 5.15).

Theorem 6.2. ***[Asymptotic Normality]:*** *Suppose Assumptions 6.1 to 6.5 hold. Then as $n \to \infty$,*

$$\sqrt{n}(\hat{\beta} - \beta^o) \xrightarrow{d} N(0, Q^{-1}VQ^{-1}),$$

where $V = \sum_{j=-\infty}^{\infty} \Gamma(j)$ is as in Assumption 6.5.

Proof: We now use Lemma 6.1 to derive the asymptotic distribution of $\sqrt{n}(\hat{\beta} - \beta^o)$. Recall that

$$\sqrt{n}(\hat{\beta} - \beta^o) = \hat{Q}^{-1}n^{-1/2}\sum_{t=1}^{n} X_t\varepsilon_t.$$

By Assumptions 6.1 to 6.3 and 6.5 and CLT for an ergodic stationary process, we have

$$n^{-1/2}\sum_{t=1}^{n} X_t\varepsilon_t \xrightarrow{d} N(0, V),$$

where $V = \sum_{j=-\infty}^{\infty} \Gamma(j)$ is as in Assumption 6.5. Also, $\hat{Q} \xrightarrow{p} Q$ and $\hat{Q}^{-1} \xrightarrow{p} Q^{-1}$ by Assumption 6.4 and WLLN for an ergodic stationary process. We then have by Slutsky's theorem

$$\sqrt{n}(\hat{\beta} - \beta^o) \xrightarrow{d} N(0, Q^{-1}VQ^{-1}).$$

6.6 Hypothesis Testing

We now consider testing the null hypothesis

$$\mathbf{H}_0 : R\beta^o = r,$$

where R is a nonstochastic $J \times K$ matrix with full rank, r is a $J \times 1$ nonstochastic vector, and $J \leq K$.

When there exists autocorrelation in $\{X_t\varepsilon_t\}$, there is no need (and in fact there is no way) to consider the cases of conditional homoskedasticity and conditional heteroskedasticity separately. (Why?)

Corollary 6.1. *Suppose Assumptions 6.1 to 6.5 hold. Then under $\mathbf{H}_0$, as $n \to \infty$,*

$$\sqrt{n}(R\hat{\beta} - r) \xrightarrow{d} N(0, RQ^{-1}VQ^{-1}R').$$

We directly assume a consistent estimator $\hat{V}$ for V.

Assumption 6.6. $\hat{V} \xrightarrow{p} V$.

When there exists serial correlation of unknown form, we can estimate V using a nonparametric kernel estimator $\hat{V}$, as described in Section 6.3. In some special scenarios (e.g., Examples 6.2 and 6.3), we may have $\Gamma(j) = 0$ for all $j > p_0$, where p_0 is a fixed lag order. In these cases, we can use the following variance estimator

$$\hat{V} = \sum_{j=-p_0}^{p_0} \hat{\Gamma}(j).$$

It can be shown that $\hat{V} \xrightarrow{p} V$ in this case.

When $J = 1$, we define a robust t-test statistic

$$T_r = \frac{\sqrt{n}(R\hat{\beta} - r)}{\sqrt{R\hat{Q}^{-1}\hat{V}\hat{Q}^{-1}R'}}.$$

When $J > 1$, we define a robust Wald test statistic

$$\begin{aligned} W_r &= n(R\hat{\beta} - r)'[R(\mathbf{X}'\mathbf{X}/n)^{-1}\hat{V}(\mathbf{X}'\mathbf{X}/n)^{-1}R']^{-1}(R\hat{\beta} - r) \\ &\xrightarrow{d} \chi^2_J. \end{aligned}$$

Both test statistics T_r and W_r have employed an asymptotic variance estimator $\hat{V}$ that is robust to conditional heteroskedasticity and autocorrelation of unknown form.

Theorem 6.3. ***[Robust t-Test and Wald Test]:*** *Under Assumptions 6.1 to 6.6 and* $\mathbf{H}_0 : R\beta^o = r$, *we have as* $n \to \infty$,
(1) when $J = 1$,

$$T_r \xrightarrow{d} N(0, 1);$$

(2) when $J \geq 1$,

$$W_r \xrightarrow{d} \chi^2_J.$$

Proof: We shall only show Part (2). By Corollary 6.1, we have as $n \to \infty$,

$$\sqrt{n}(R\hat{\beta} - r) \xrightarrow{d} N(0, RQ^{-1}VQ^{-1}R')$$

under $\mathbf{H}_0$. It follows that the quadratic form

$$\sqrt{n}(R\hat{\beta}-r)'\left(RQ^{-1}VQ^{-1}R'\right)^{-1}\sqrt{n}(R\hat{\beta}-r)\xrightarrow{d}\chi^2_J.$$

By Slutsky's theorem, Assumption 6.6, and $\hat{Q}\xrightarrow{p}Q$ as $n\to\infty$, we have the robust Wald test statistic

$$W_r=n(R\hat{\beta}-r)'\left(R\hat{Q}^{-1}\hat{V}\hat{Q}^{-1}R'\right)^{-1}(R\hat{\beta}-r)\xrightarrow{d}\chi^2_J.$$

Using the expression of $\hat{Q}=\mathbf{X}'\mathbf{X}/n$, we have an equivalent expression for W_r :

$$W_r=n(R\hat{\beta}-r)'[R(\mathbf{X}'\mathbf{X}/n)^{-1}\hat{V}(\mathbf{X}'\mathbf{X}/n)^{-1}R']^{-1}(R\hat{\beta}-r)\xrightarrow{d}\chi^2_J.$$

This completes the proof.

The standard t-test and F-test statistics introduced in Chapter 3 cannot be used when there exist conditional heteroskedasticity and autocorrelation in $\{X_t\varepsilon_t\}$. Moreover, all test statistics introduced in Chapter 5 cannot be used here, because in Chapter 5, it is assumed that $\{X_t\varepsilon_t\}$ is an MDS, which implies that there is no serial correlation in $\{X_t\varepsilon_t\}$.

Question: Can we use the robust t-test statistic T_r and robust Wald test statistic W_r when $\Gamma(j)=0$ for all nonzero j?

Yes. However, they are not ideal test statistics because they may perform poorly in finite samples in the sense that their finite sample distributions may be quite different from the asymptotic distributions. In particular, they usually overreject the correct null hypothesis $\mathbf{H}_0$ in finite samples even if $\Gamma(j)=0$ for all $j\neq 0$. This is due to the fact that such long-run variance estimators $\hat{V}$ as those of Andrews (1991) and Newey and West (1987, 1994) tend to underestimate the true variance in finite samples, as have been documented by various simulation and empirical studies. Therefore, when $\Gamma(j)=0$ for all $j\neq 0$, a better variance estimator is

$$\begin{aligned}\hat{V}&=\hat{\Gamma}(0)\\&=n^{-1}\sum_{t=1}^{n}X_te_te_tX_t'\\&=\mathbf{X}'\mathrm{D}(e)\mathrm{D}(e)'\mathbf{X}/n.\end{aligned}$$

This estimator has made use of the information that there is no serial correlation in $\{X_t\varepsilon_t\}$. It is essentially White's heteroskedasticity consistent variance-covariance matrix estimator (also see Chapter 5).

Question: Why do the robust t-test statistic T_r and robust Wald test statistic W_r tend to overreject a correct null hypothesis $\mathbf{H}_0$ in presence of conditional heteroskedasticity and autocorrelation of unknown form?

We consider the robust t-test as an example. Recall $\hat{V}$ is an estimator for the spectral density $H(0)$ at frequency zero, up to a factor of 2π. When there exists strong positive serial correlation in $\{\varepsilon_t\}$, as is the case for many economic time series, $H(\omega)$ will display a peak or mode at frequency zero. The kernel estimator, which is a local averaging estimator, always tends to underestimate $H(0)$, because it has an asymptotic negative bias. Consequently, the robust t-statistic tends to be a larger statistic value, because it is the ratio of $R\hat{\beta} - r$ to the square root of a variance estimator which tends to be smaller than the true variance. See Andrews (1991) and Newey and West (1994) for more discussions and simulation studies.

6.7 Testing Whether Long-Run Variance-Covariance Matrix Estimation Is Needed

Because of the notorious poor performance of the robust t-test and robust W test even when $\Gamma(j) = 0$ for all $j \neq 0$, it is very important to test whether we really have to use a long-run variance estimator. This is similar to the need for testing conditional heteroskedasticity in Chapters 4 and 5.

Question: How to test whether we need to use a long-run variance-covariance matrix estimator? That is, how to test whether the null hypothesis that

$$\mathbf{H}_0 : 2\pi H(0) \equiv \sum_{j=-\infty}^{\infty} \Gamma(j) = \Gamma(0)?$$

The null hypothesis $\mathbf{H}_0$ can be equivalently written as follows:

$$\mathbf{H}_0 : \sum_{j=1}^{\infty} \Gamma(j) = 0.$$

It can arise from two cases:

- Case I: $\Gamma(j) = 0$ for all $j \neq 0$.
- Case II: $\Gamma(j) \neq 0$ for some $j \neq 0$, but $\sum_{j=1}^{\infty} \Gamma(j) = 0$.

For simplicity, we will consider Case I only. Case II is pathological, although it could occur in practice.

We now provide a test for $\mathbf{H}_0$ under Case I. Here, we assume that $\{X_t\varepsilon_t\}$ is an MDS under $\mathbf{H}_0$. The MDS assumption implies $\mathbf{H}_0$ but not vice versa. This stronger condition greatly simplifies our analysis and the form of a proposed test statistic. See Hong (1997) in a closely related univariate context.

To test the null hypothesis that $\sum_{j=1}^{\infty} \Gamma(j) = 0$, we can use a consistent estimator $\hat{A}$ (say) for $\sum_{j=1}^{\infty} \Gamma(j)$ and then check whether $\hat{A}$ is close to a zero matrix. Any significant difference of $\hat{A}$ from zero will indicate the violation of the null hypothesis, and thus a long-run variance estimator is needed.

To estimate $\sum_{j=1}^{\infty} \Gamma(j)$ consistently, we can use a nonparametric kernel estimator

$$\hat{A} = \sum_{j=1}^{n-1} k(j/p_n)\text{vech}[\hat{\Gamma}(j)],$$

where $k(\cdot)$ is a kernel, and $p_n = p(n) \to \infty$ at a suitable rate as $n \to \infty$. We shall derive the asymptotic distribution of $\hat{A}$ (with suitable scaling) under the assumption that $\{g_t = X_t\varepsilon_t\}$ is an MDS, which implies the null hypothesis $\mathbf{H}_0$ that $\sum_{j=1}^{\infty} \Gamma(j) = 0$. First, we consider the case when $\{g_t = X_t\varepsilon_t\}$ is autoregressively conditionally homoskedastic, namely, $\text{var}(g_t|I_{t-1}) = \text{var}(g_t)$, where $I_{t-1} = \{g_{t-1}, g_{t-2}, ...\}$. In this case, by applying the martingale CLT, we can show that as $n \to \infty$,

$$\left[p\int_0^{\infty} k^2(z)dz\right]^{-1/2} \{\text{vech}[\Gamma(0)]\text{vech}[\Gamma(0)]'\}^{-1/2}\sqrt{n}\hat{A} \xrightarrow{d} N(0, I_{K(K+1)/2}).$$

We then construct a test statistic

$$\begin{aligned} M &= \left[p\int_0^{\infty} k^2(z)dz\right]^{-1} \sqrt{n}\hat{A}' \left\{\text{vech}[\hat{\Gamma}(0)]\text{vech}[\hat{\Gamma}(0)]'\right\}^{-1} \sqrt{n}\hat{A} \\ &\xrightarrow{d} \chi^2_{K(K+1)/2} \text{ as } n \to \infty, \end{aligned}$$

where the convergence in distribution holds under $\mathbf{H}_0$.

Next, we consider the case when $\{g_t = X_t\varepsilon_t\}$ displays ARCH, namely $\text{var}(g_t|I_{t-1}) \neq \text{var}(g_t)$. In this case, the test statistic for $\mathbf{H}_0$ is

$$\hat{M} = \sqrt{n}\hat{A}'\hat{B}^{-1}\sqrt{n}\hat{A},$$

where

$$\hat{B} = \sum_{j=1}^{n-1}\sum_{l=1}^{n-1} k(j/p)k(l/p)\hat{C}(j,l),$$

$$\hat{C}(j,l) = \frac{1}{n}\sum_{t=1+\max(j,l)}^{n-1} \text{vech}(\hat{g}_t\hat{g}_{t-j}')\text{vech}'(\hat{g}_t\hat{g}_{t-l}'),$$

with $\hat{g}_t = X_t e_t$. Under the assumption that $\{g_t = X_t\varepsilon_t\}$ is an MDS, we have

$$\hat{M} \xrightarrow{d} \chi^2_{K(K+1)/2} \text{ as } n \to \infty.$$

This test is robust to ARCH of unknown form for $\{g_t = X_t\varepsilon_t\}$.

In fact, the test statistic just introduced is closely related to a variance ratio test that is popular in financial econometrics. Cochrane (1988) and Poterba and Summers (1988) use the variance ratio test to check the martingale hypothesis or measure persistence of macroeconomic time series. Extending an idea of Cochrane (1988), Lo and MacKinlay (1988) first rigorously present an asymptotic theory for a variance ratio test, and apply it to test the MDS hypothesis of asset returns $\{Y_t\}$. Recall that $\sum_{j=1}^p Y_{t-j}$ is the cumulative asset return over a total of p periods. Then under the MDS hypothesis, which implies $\gamma(j) \equiv \text{cov}(Y_t, Y_{t-j}) = 0$ for all $j > 0$, one has

$$\frac{\text{var}\left(\sum_{j=1}^p Y_{t-j}\right)}{p \cdot \text{var}(Y_t)} = \frac{p\gamma(0) + 2p\sum_{j=1}^p (1-j/p)\gamma(j)}{p\gamma(0)}$$
$$= 1.$$

This unity property of the variance ratio can be used to test the MDS hypothesis because any departure from unity is evidence against the MDS hypothesis.

Under autoregressive conditional homoskedasticity, the variance ratio test is based on the statistic

$$\text{VR}_o \equiv \sqrt{n/p}\sum_{j=1}^p (1-j/p)\hat{\rho}(j)$$
$$= \frac{\pi}{2}\sqrt{n/p}\left[\hat{f}(0) - \frac{1}{2\pi}\right],$$

where

$$\hat{f}(0) = \frac{1}{2\pi}\sum_{j=-p}^{p}\left(1 - \frac{|j|}{p}\right)\hat{\rho}(j)$$

is a kernel-based standardized spectral density estimator at frequency 0, using the Bartlett kernel $K(z) = (1 - |z|)\mathbf{1}(|z| \leq 1)$ and a lag order equal to p. Thus, the variance ratio test essentially checks whether the long-run variance is equal to the individual variance $\gamma(0)$. Because VR_o is based on a spectral density estimator of frequency 0, and because of this, it is particularly powerful against long memory processes, whose autocovariance function decays to zero slowly as the lag order increases and so its spectral density at frequency 0 is infinity (see Robinson 1994).

Under the MDS hypothesis with conditional homoskedasticity for $\{Y_t\}$, Lo and MacKinlay (1988) show that for any fixed p,

$$\text{VR}_o \xrightarrow{d} N[0, 2(2p-1)(p-1)/3p] \text{ as } n \to \infty.$$

In a closely related context, Hong (1997) shows that when $p = p_n \to \infty$, $p_n/n \to 0$ as $n \to \infty$, we have

$$\left[p_n \int_0^\infty k^2(z)dz\right]^{-1/2} \sqrt{n}\sum_{j=1}^{n-1} k(j/p_n)\hat{\rho}(j) \xrightarrow{d} N(0,1).$$

This is the scalar version of the proposed test statistic M in a univariate time series context. When the Bartlett kernel $k(z) = (1 - |z|)\mathbf{1}(|z| \leq 1)$ is used, Hong's (1997) test statistic becomes the variance ratio test statistic VR_o when a large p_n is used, with $\int_0^\infty k^2(z)dz = \int_0^1 (1-z)^2 dz = \frac{1}{3}$. Compared to the variance ratio test, Hong's (1997) test or the proposed M test is applicable when p_n is large, and it employs a general kernel function which usually discounts higher order lags, As a result, Hong's (1997) test or the proposed M test is expected to have good power against the alternatives for which autocorrelation carries over a relatively long distributional lag and the strength of autocorrelation decays to zero slowly as lag order j increases.

When $\{Y_t\}$ displays conditional heteroskedasticity, Lo and MacKinlay (1988) also consider a heteroskedasticity-consistent variance ratio test:

$$\text{VR} \equiv \sqrt{n/p}\sum_{j=1}^{p}(1 - j/p)\hat{\gamma}(j)/\sqrt{\hat{\gamma}_2(j)},$$

where $\hat{\gamma}_2(j)$ is a consistent estimator for the asymptotic variance of $\hat{\gamma}(j)$ under conditional heteroskedasticity. Lo and MacKinlay (1988) assume a fourth order cumulant condition that

$$E\left[(Y_t-\mu)^2(Y_{t-j}-\mu)(Y_{t-l}-\mu)\right]=0, \qquad j,l>0, j\neq l.$$

Intuitively, this condition ensures that the sample autocovariances at different lags are asymptotically uncorrelated; that is, $\text{cov}[\sqrt{n}\hat{\gamma}(j),\sqrt{n}\hat{\gamma}(l)]\to 0$ for all $j\neq l$. As a result, the heteroskedasticity-consistent variance ratio test statistic VR has the same asymptotic distribution as VR_o. However, the condition in the above equation rules out many important volatility processes, such as Nelson's (1991) Exponential GARCH (EGARCH) and Glosten *et al.*'s (1993) Threshold GARCH (TGARCH) models. Moreover, the variance ratio test only exploits the implication of the MDS hypothesis on the spectral density at frequency 0; it does not check the spectral density at nonzero frequencies. As a result, it is not consistent (i.e., it has no asymptotic unit power) against serial correlation of unknown form. See Durlauf (1991) for more discussion.

6.8 Ornut-Cochrane Procedure

Long-run variance estimators are necessary for statistical inference of the OLS estimation in a linear regression model when there exists serial correlation of *unknown form.* If serial correlation in the regression disturbance has of a known form up to some unknown parameters, then simpler statistical inference procedures are possible. One example is the classical Ornut-Cochrane procedure. Consider a linear regression model with serially correlated disturbances:

$$Y_t=X_t'\beta^o+\varepsilon_t,$$

where $E(\varepsilon_t|X_t)=0$ but $\{\varepsilon_t\}$ follows an AR(p) process

$$\varepsilon_t=\sum_{j=1}^{p}\alpha_j\varepsilon_{t-j}+v_t, \{v_t\}\sim \text{IID}(0,\sigma^2),$$

where p is a known fixed order but the autoregressive coefficients $\{\alpha_j\}_{j=1}^p$ are unknown.

The OLS estimator $\hat{\beta}$ is consistent for β^o given $E(X_t\varepsilon_t)=0$ but its asymptotic variance depends on serial correlation in $\{\varepsilon_t\}$. We can consider the following transformed linear regression model

$$\begin{aligned} Y_t - \sum_{j=1}^{p} \alpha_j Y_{t-j} &= \left(X_t - \sum_{j=1}^{p} \alpha_j X_{t-j} \right)' \beta^o + \left(\varepsilon_t - \sum_{j=1}^{p} \alpha_j \varepsilon_{t-j} \right) \\ &= \left(X_t - \sum_{j=1}^{p} \alpha_j X_{t-j} \right)' \beta^o + v_t. \end{aligned}$$

We can write it as follows:

$$Y_t^* = X_t^{*\prime} \beta^o + v_t,$$

where

$$\begin{aligned} Y_t^* &= Y_t - \sum_{j=1}^{p} \alpha_j Y_{t-j}, \\ X_t^* &= X_t - \sum_{j=1}^{p} \alpha_j X_{t-j}. \end{aligned}$$

The OLS estimator $\tilde{\beta}$ of this transformed regression will be consistent for β^o and $\sqrt{n}(\tilde{\beta} - \beta^o)$ will be asymptotically normal:

$$\sqrt{n}(\tilde{\beta} - \beta^o) \xrightarrow{d} N(0, \sigma_v^2 Q_{X^*X^*}^{-1}),$$

where $Q_{X^*X^*} = E(X_t^* X_t^{*\prime})$. The OLS estimator $\tilde{\beta}$ is a GLS estimator discussed in Chapter 3. It is asymptotically BLUE. However, the GLS estimator $\tilde{\beta}$ is infeasible, because $(Y_t^*, X_t^{*'})$ is not available due to the unknown parameters $\{\alpha_j\}_{j=1}^p$. As a solution, one can use an adaptive feasible two-step GLS procedure:

- Step 1: Regress

$$Y_t = X_t' \beta^o + \varepsilon_t, t = 1, ..., n,$$

namely, regress Y_t on X_t and obtain the estimated OLS residual $e_t = Y_t - X_t'\hat{\beta}$. Then run an AR($p$) model

$$e_t = \sum_{j=1}^{p} \alpha_j e_{t-j} + \tilde{v}_t, t = p + 1, ..., n,$$

and obtain the OLS estimators $\{\hat{\alpha}_j\}_{j=1}^p$.

- Step 2: Regress the transformed model

$$\hat{Y}_t^* = \hat{X}_t^{*\prime}\beta^o + v_t^*, t = p+1, ..., n,$$

where $\hat{Y}_t^*$ and $\hat{X}_t^*$ are defined in the same way as Y_t^* and X_t^* respectively, with $\{\hat{\alpha}_j\}_{j=1}^p$ replacing $\{\alpha_j\}_{j=1}^p$. The resulting OLS estimator is denoted as $\tilde{\beta}_a$.

It can be shown that the adaptive feasible GLS estimator $\tilde{\beta}_a$ has the same asymptotic properties as the infeasible GLS estimator $\tilde{\beta}$. In other words, the sampling error resulting from the first step estimation has no impact on the asymptotic properties of the OLS estimator in the second step. The asymptotic variance estimator of $\tilde{\beta}_a$ is given by

$$\hat{s}_v^2 \hat{Q}_{X^*X^*}^{-1},$$

where

$$\hat{s}_v^2 = \frac{1}{n-K}\sum_{t=1}^n \hat{v}_t^{*2},$$

$$\hat{Q}_{X^*X^*} = \frac{1}{n}\sum_{t=1}^n \hat{X}_t^* \hat{X}_t^{*\prime},$$

with $\hat{v}_t = \hat{Y}_t^* - \hat{X}_t^{*\prime}\tilde{\beta}_a$. The t-test statistic which is asymptotically $N(0,1)$ and the $J \cdot F$-test statistic which is asymptotically χ_J^2 from the last stage regression are applicable when the sample size n is large.

The adaptive feasible GLS estimator $\tilde{\beta}_a$ is asymptotically BLUE. This approach is therefore asymptotically more efficient than the OLS-based robust test procedures developed in Section 6.6 of the present chapter, but it is based on the assumption that the AR(p) process for the disturbance $\{\varepsilon_t\}$ is known. The robust test procedures in Section 6.6 are applicable when $\{\varepsilon_t\}$ has conditional heteroskedasticity and serial correlation of unknown form.

6.9 Conclusion

In this chapter, we have first discussed some motivating economic examples where a long-run variance-covariance matrix estimator is needed. Then we discussed consistent estimation of a long-run variance-covariance matrix by a nonparametric kernel method. The asymptotic properties of the OLS estimator are investigated, which calls for the use of a new CLT because

$\{X_t\varepsilon_t\}$ is no longer an MDS. Robust t-test statistic and robust Wald test statistic that are asymptotically valid under conditional heteroskedasticity and autocorrelation of unknown form are then constructed. When there exists serial correlation of unknown form, there is no need (and no way) to separate the cases of conditional homoskedasticity and conditional heteroskedasticity. Because the robust t- and Wald tests may have very poor finite sample performances even if $\{X_t\varepsilon_t\}$ is an MDS, it is desirable to first check whether we really need a long-run variance estimator. We provide such a test. We also introduce a classical estimation method called Ornut-Ochrance procedure when it is known that the regression disturbance follows an AR process with a known order.

Long-run variances have been also widely used in nonstationary time series econometrics such as in the unit root and cointegration literature (e.g., Engle and Granger 1986, Phillips 1987). Unfortunately, it is documented in both simulation studies and empirical applications that regression disturbances display relatively persistent serial dependence, various kernel-based long-run variance estimators tend to underestimate the true long-run variance even if the sample size is large. Intuitively, the spectral density function of a time series process displays a sharp model at frequency zero when there exists persistent serial dependence. Kernel estimators for the spectral density are smoothed local averaging and so tend to suffer from a substantial negative bias. Different approaches have been proposed in the time series literature. For example, a so-called self-normalization technique has been proposed, which, instead of attempting to consistently estimate the long-run variance, replaces the kernel long-run variance estimators by a recursive statistic which converges to a stochastic multiple of the long-run variance. The resulting test statistic will be thus asymptotically free of the long-run variance but a nonstandard distribution arises due to the stochastic proportionality in the denominator. Such a test has substantially better sizes in finite samples, although its power may suffer to certain extent due to the relatively heavy tail of the nonstandard asymptotic distribution. For self-normalization methods, see Shao (2010) for detailed discussion.

Exercise 6

6.1. Suppose Assumptions 6.1 to 6.3 and 6.5(a) hold. Show

$$\begin{aligned}\text{avar}\left(n^{-1/2}\sum_{t=1}^{n} X_t\varepsilon_t\right) &= \lim_{n\to\infty} \text{var}\left(n^{-1/2}\sum_{t=1}^{n} X_t\varepsilon_t\right)\\ &= \sum_{j=-\infty}^{\infty} \Gamma(j).\end{aligned}$$

6.2. Suppose $\Gamma(j) = 0$ for all $j > p_0$, where p_0 is a fixed lag order. An example of this case is Example 6.2 in Section 6.1. In this case, the long-run variance-covariance matrix $V = \sum_{j=-p_0}^{p_0} \Gamma(j)$ and we can estimate it by using the following estimator

$$\hat{V} = \sum_{j=-p_0}^{p_0} \hat{\Gamma}(j)$$

where the sample autocovariance function $\hat{\Gamma}(j)$ is defined as in Section 6.1. Show that for each given lag order j, $\hat{\Gamma}(j) \xrightarrow{p} \Gamma(j)$ as $n \to \infty$.

Given that p_0 is a fixed integer, an important implication that $\hat{\Gamma}(j) \xrightarrow{p} \Gamma(j)$ for each given j as $n \to \infty$ will ensure $\hat{V} \xrightarrow{p} V$ as $n \to \infty$.

6.3. Suppose $\{Y_t\}$ is a stationary time series process with the following spectral density function

$$h(\omega) = \frac{1}{2\pi} \sum_{j=-\infty}^{\infty} \gamma(j) e^{-\mathbf{i}j\omega}.$$

Show that

$$\text{var}\left(\sum_{j=1}^{p} Y_{t-j}\right) \to 2\pi h(0) \text{ as } p \to \infty.$$

6.4. Suppose $\{Y_t\}$ is a weakly stationary process with $\gamma(j) = \text{cov}(Y_t, Y_{t-j})$.

(1) Find an example of $\{Y_t\}$ such that $\sum_{j=1}^{\infty} \gamma(j) = 0$ but there exists at least one $j > 0$, such that $\gamma(j) \neq 0$.

(2) Can the variance ratio test detect the autocorrelation structure of the time series process in Part (1) when the sample size n is sufficiently large?

(3) The variance ratio test is often used to test the MDS hypothesis. If the variance ratio test fails to reject the null hypothesis of MDS, can one conclude that the MDS hypothesis holds? Explain.

6.5. Suppose $\{Y_t\}$ is a zero-mean ergodic stationary time series process with a finite fourth moment, and let $\{Y_t\}_{t=1}^n$ be a random sample with size n. Define the sample autocovariance function

$$\hat{\gamma}(j) = \frac{1}{n} \sum_{t=j+1}^{n} Y_t Y_{t-j}, \qquad j = 0, 1, ...$$

Show $\text{cov}[\hat{\gamma}(j), \hat{\gamma}(l)] = 0$ for $j, l > 0, j \neq l$ if

$$E(Y_t^2 Y_{t-j} Y_{t-l}) = 0 \text{ for } j, l > 0, j \neq l.$$

6.6. Suppose Assumptions 6.1 to 6.5 hold for Example 6.3 in Section 6.1, where $X_t = (1, r_t, d_t - p_t)'$, and $h \geq 1$ is a fixed positive integer.

(1) What is the asymptotic variance of the OLS estimator $\sqrt{n}\hat{\beta}$? Give your reasoning.

(2) Construct an estimator for the asymptotic variance of $\sqrt{n}\hat{\beta}$ and show that it is consistent for the asymptotic variance of $\sqrt{n}\hat{\beta}$. Give your reasoning.

(3) Can we use a kernel-based long-run variance estimator for $\sqrt{n}\hat{\beta}$? Which variance estimator, a kernel-based long-run variance estimator or the variance estimator in Part (2), performs better in finite samples? Explain.

6.7. Suppose Assumptions 6.1 to 6.4 hold, and the disturbance $\{\varepsilon_t\}$ follows an AR(1) process

$$\varepsilon_t = \alpha\varepsilon_{t-1} + v_t, \qquad \{v_t\} \sim \text{IID}(0, \sigma_v^2),$$

where $|\alpha| < 1$ and α is unknown. One can first estimate the linear regression model $Y_t = X_t'\beta^o + \varepsilon_t, t = 1, ..., n$, and obtain the OLS estimator $\hat{\beta}$.

(1) Put $e_t = Y_t - X_t'\hat{\beta}$. Then regress e_t on e_{t-1} and obtain the OLS estimator $\hat{\alpha}$ for the autoregressive coefficient α. Show $\hat{\alpha} \xrightarrow{p} \alpha$ as $n \to \infty$.

(2) Construct a transformed linear regression model

$$\hat{Y}_t^* = \hat{X}_t^{*\prime}\beta^o + v_t^*, \qquad t = 2, ..., n,$$

where $\hat{Y}_t^* = Y_t - \hat{\alpha}Y_{t-1}$ and $\hat{X}_t^* = X_t - \alpha X_{t-1}$, and obtain the OLS estimator $\tilde{\beta}_a$ for this regression. Show that $\tilde{\beta}_a \xrightarrow{p} \beta^o$ as $n \to \infty$.

(3) Show that the asymptotic variance of $\sqrt{n}(\tilde{\beta}_a - \beta^o)$ is $\sigma_v^2 Q_{X^*X^*}^{-1}$, where $Q_{X^*X^*} = E(X_t^* X_t^{*\prime})$, with $X_t^* = X_t - \alpha X_{t-1}$.

(4) Construct an asymptotic variance estimator for $\tilde{\beta}_a$ and show that it is consistent for the avar$(\sqrt{n}\tilde{\beta}_a)$.

(5) Construct a t-test statistic for the null hypothesis $\mathbf{H}_0 : R\beta^o = r$, where R is a $1 \times K$ nonstochastic vector, and r is a constant scalar. Derive the asymptotic distribution of the proposed t-test statistic under $\mathbf{H}_0$.

(6) Construct a Wald test statistic for the null hypothesis $\mathbf{H}_0 : R\beta^o = r$, where R is a $J \times K$ nonstochastic vector, and r is a $J \times 1$ nonstochastic vector. Derive the asymptotic distribution of the proposed Wald test statistic under $\mathbf{H}_0$.

6.8. Consider the Cochrane-Orcutt procedure in Section 6.8. Suppose Assumptions 6.1 to 6.4 hold, $\{\varepsilon_t\}$ follows a stationary AR(p) process $\varepsilon_t = \sum_{j=1}^p \alpha_j \varepsilon_{t-j} + v_t$, where $\{v_t\} \sim \text{IID}(0, \sigma_v^2)$, $0 < \sigma_v^2 < \infty$, and the autoregressive coefficients $\{\alpha_j^o\}_{j=1}^p$ are known. Show:

(1) The Cochrane-Orcutt estimator $\tilde{\beta}$ is consistent for β^o as $n \to \infty$. Give your reasoning.

(2) $\sqrt{n}(\tilde{\beta} - \beta^o)$ follows an asymptotic normal distribution. Give your reasoning.

6.9. Consider the Cochrane-Orcutt procedure in Section 6.8. Suppose Assumptions 6.1 to 6.4 hold, $\{\varepsilon_t\}$ follows a stationary AR(p) process $\varepsilon_t = \sum_{j=1}^p \alpha_j \varepsilon_{t-j} + v_t$, where $\{v_t\} \sim \text{IID}(0, \sigma_v^2)$, $0 < \sigma_v^2 < \infty$, but the autoregressive coefficients $\{\alpha_j^o\}_{j=1}^p$ are unknown. We consider the adaptive feasible Cochrane-Orcutt estimator $\tilde{\beta}_a$ described in Section 6.8.

(1) Show that $\tilde{\beta}_a$ is consistent for β^o as $n \to \infty$. Give your reasoning.

(2) Derive the asymptotic distribution of $\sqrt{n}(\tilde{\beta} - \beta^o)$. Give your reasoning.

(3) Does the first stage estimation of the autoregressive coefficients $\{\alpha_j^o\}_{j=1}^p$ have any impact on the asymptotic distribution of $\sqrt{n}(\tilde{\beta} - \beta^o)$? Explain.

Chapter 7

Instrumental Variables Regression

Abstract: In this chapter we first discuss possibilities that the orthogonality condition $E(\varepsilon_t|X_t) = 0$ may fail, which will generally render inconsistent the OLS estimator for the true model parameter. We then introduce a consistent Two-Stage Least Squares (2SLS) estimator, investigating its statistical properties and providing intuitions for the nature of the 2SLS estimator. Hypothesis tests are constructed. We consider various test procedures corresponding to the cases for which the regression disturbance is an MDS with conditional homoskedasticity, an MDS with conditional heteroskedasticity, and a non-MDS process, respectively. The latter case will require consistent estimation of a long-run variance-covariance matrix. It is important to emphasize that the t-test and F-test statistics obtained from the second stage regression estimation cannot be used even for large samples. Finally, we conclude this chapter by presenting a summary of econometric theory for linear regression models developed in Chapters 2 to 7.

Keywords: Endogeneity, Errors in variables, Hausman's test, Instrumental Variables (IV), Measurement errors, Omitted variables, Orthogonality condition, Simultaneous equations bias, 2SLS

7.1 Motivation

In all previous chapters, we always assumed that $E(\varepsilon_t|X_t) = 0$ holds even when there exist conditional heteroskedasticity and autocorrelation. This ensures consistency of the OLS estimator for the true parameter value β^o.

Questions: When may the condition $E(\varepsilon_t|X_t) = 0$ fail? And, what will happen to the OLS estimator $\hat{\beta}$ if $E(\varepsilon_t|X_t) = 0$ fails?

There are at least three possibilities where $E(\varepsilon_t|X_t) = 0$ may fail. The first is model misspecification (e.g., functional form misspecification or existence of omitted variables). The second is the existence of measurement errors in regressors (also called errors in variables). The third is the estimation of a subset of a simultaneous equations system. We will consider the last two possibilities in this chapter. For the first case (i.e., model misspecification), it may not be meaningful to discuss consistent estimation of the parameters in a misspecified linear regression model except for some special cases such as existence of omitted variables.

We first provide some examples in which $E(\varepsilon_t|X_t) \neq 0$.

Example 7.1. [Errors of Measurements or Errors in Variables]: Often, economic data measure concepts that differ somewhat from those of economic theory. It is therefore important to take into account errors of measurements. This is usually called errors in variables in econometrics. Consider a DGP

$$Y_t^* = \beta_0^o + \beta_1^o X_t^* + u_t, \tag{7.1}$$

where X_t^* is income, Y_t^* is consumption, and $\{u_t\}$ is $\text{IID}(0, \sigma_u^2)$ and is independent of $\{X_t^*\}$.

Suppose both X_t^* and Y_t^* are not observable. The observed variables X_t and Y_t contain measurement errors in the sense that

$$X_t = X_t^* + v_t, \tag{7.2}$$

$$Y_t = Y_t^* + w_t, \tag{7.3}$$

where $\{v_t\}$ and $\{w_t\}$ are measurement errors independent of $\{X_t^*\}$ and $\{Y_t^*\}$, such that $\{v_t\} \sim \text{IID}(0, \sigma_v^2)$ and $\{w_t\} \sim \text{IID}(0, \sigma_w^2)$. We assume that the series $\{v_t\}, \{w_t\}$ and $\{u_t\}$ are all mutually independent of each other.

Because we only observe (X_t, Y_t), we are forced to estimate the following regression model

$$Y_t = \beta_0^o + \beta_1^o X_t + \varepsilon_t, \tag{7.4}$$

where ε_t is some unobservable disturbance.

Clearly, the disturbance ε_t is different from the original (true) disturbance u_t. Although the linear regression model is correctly specified, we no longer have $E(\varepsilon_t|X_t) = 0$ due to the existence of the measurement errors. This is explained below.

Question: If we use the OLS estimator $\hat{\beta}$ to estimate this model, is $\hat{\beta}$ consistent for β^o?

From the general regression analysis in Chapter 2, we have known that the key for the consistency of the OLS estimator $\hat{\beta}$ for β^o is to check if $E(X_t\varepsilon_t) = 0$. From Eqs. (7.1) to (7.3), we have

$$\begin{aligned} Y_t &= Y_t^* + w_t \\ &= (\beta_0^o + \beta_1^o X_t^* + u_t) + w_t, \\ X_t &= X_t^* + v_t. \end{aligned}$$

Therefore, from Eq. (7.4), we obtain

$$\begin{aligned} \varepsilon_t &= Y_t - \beta_0^o - \beta_1^o X_t \\ &= [\beta_0^o + \beta_1^o X_t^* + u_t + w_t] - \beta_0^o - \beta_1^o (X_t^* + v_t) \\ &= u_t + w_t - \beta_1^o v_t. \end{aligned}$$

The regression error ε_t contains the true disturbance u_t and a linear combination of measurement errors.

Now, the expectation

$$\begin{aligned} E(X_t\varepsilon_t) &= E[(X_t^* + v_t)\varepsilon_t] \\ &= E(X_t^*\varepsilon_t) + E(v_t\varepsilon_t) \\ &= 0 - \beta_1^o E(v_t^2) \\ &= -\beta_1^o \sigma_v^2 \\ &\neq 0. \end{aligned}$$

The regressor vector X_t is correlated with the error ε_t. Consequently, by WLLN, the OLS estimator

$$\begin{aligned} \hat{\beta} - \beta^o &= \hat{Q}_{XX}^{-1} n^{-1} \sum_{t=1}^{n} X_t \varepsilon_t \\ &\xrightarrow{p} Q_{XX}^{-1} E(X_t\varepsilon_t) \\ &= -\beta_1^o \sigma_v^2 Q_{XX}^{-1} \neq 0. \end{aligned}$$

In other words, $\hat{\beta}$ is not consistent for β^o due to the existence of the measurement errors in regressors $\{X_t\}$.

Question: What is the effect of the measurement errors $\{w_t\}$ in the dependent variable Y_t?

Example 7.2. [Errors of Measurements in Dependent Variable]: Now we consider a DGP given by

$$Y_t^* = \beta_0^o + \beta_1^o X_t^* + u_t,$$

where X_t^* is income, Y_t^* is consumption, and $\{u_t\}$ is IID$(0, \sigma_u^2)$ and is independent of $\{X_t^*\}$.

Suppose X_t^* is now observed, and Y_t^* is still not observable, such that

$$X_t = X_t^*,$$
$$Y_t = Y_t^* + w_t,$$

where $\{w_t\}$ is IID$(0, \sigma_w^2)$ measurement errors independent of $\{X_t^*\}$ and $\{Y_t^*\}$. We assume that the two series $\{w_t\}$ and $\{u_t\}$ are mutually independent.

Because we only observe (X_t, Y_t), we are forced to estimate the following model

$$Y_t = \beta_0^o + \beta_1^o X_t + \varepsilon_t.$$

Question: If we use the OLS estimator $\hat{\beta}$ to estimate this model, is $\hat{\beta}$ consistent for β^o?

The answer is yes! The measurement errors in Y_t do not cause any trouble for consistent estimation of β^o.

The measurement error in Y_t can be regarded as part of the true regression disturbance. It increases the asymptotic variance of $\sqrt{n}(\hat{\beta} - \beta^o)$, that is, the existence of measurement errors in Y_t renders the estimation of β^o less precise.

Example 7.3. [Errors in Expectations]: Consider a linear regression model

$$Y_t = \beta_0 + \beta_1 X_t^* + u_t,$$

where X_t^* is the economic agent's conditional expectation of X_t at time $t-1$, and $\{u_t\}$ is an IID$(0, \sigma^2)$ sequence with $E(u_t|X_t^*) = 0$. The conditional expectation X_t^* is a latent variable. Examples include the Phillips (1958) curve's based expected inflation rate models in macroeconomics and Friedman's (1957) permanent income hypothesis.

When the economic agent follows rational expectations, then $X_t^* = E(X_t|I_{t-1})$ and we have

$$X_t = X_t^* + v_t,$$

where

$$E(v_t|I_{t-1}) = 0,$$

where I_{t-1} is the information available to the economic agent at time $t-1$. Assume that two error series $\{u_t\}$ and $\{v_t\}$ are mutually independent.

We can consider the following regression model

$$Y_t = \beta_0^o + \beta_1^o X_t + \varepsilon_t,$$

where the error term

$$\varepsilon_t = u_t - \beta_1^o v_t.$$

Since

$$\begin{aligned} E(X_t\varepsilon_t) &= E[(X_t^* + v_t)(u_t - \beta_1^o v_t)] \\ &= -\beta_1^o \sigma_v^2 \\ &\neq 0 \end{aligned}$$

provided $\beta_1^o \neq 0$, the OLS estimator is not consistent for β_1^o.

It may be noted that some forecast variables obtained from survey data have been used for X_t^* in empirical studies in economics.

Example 7.4. [Market Microstructure Noises and Realized Volatility]: Microstructure noise is a deviation from the fundamental value that is induced by the characteristics of the market under consideration, such as bid-ask bounce, discreteness of price change, latency, and asymmetric information of traders. Originally, it comes from the bid-ask bounce, i.e., the fact that even if volatility is zero, there are buyers and sellers at different prices and consequently we observe prices at bid or ask prices, and not at mid-prices. As a result, if we use the classical quadratic variation estimator for the squared volatility: even with an underlying volatility of zero, we will measure a lot of times $(P_{ask} - P_{bid})^2$, where P_{ask} and P_{bid} are the ask and bid prices.

Assume that the unobserved mid-price between time 0 and time T (where T is fixed) follows a discretized arithmetic Brownian motion

$$P_{(i+1)\delta}^* = P_{i\delta}^* + \sigma(i\delta)\sqrt{\delta}v_{i+1},$$

where δ is the sampling interval over time, the square of $\sigma(i\delta)$ is an instantaneous volatility at time $i\delta$, and $\{v_i\}$ is a sequence of IID $N(0,1)$ innovations that derives the movements of the mid-price.

On the other hand, the actual price observed at time $i\delta$ is

$$P_{i\delta} = P^*_{i\delta} + \varepsilon_{i\delta},$$

where $\varepsilon_{i\delta}$ is the market microstructure noise around half a bid-ask spread at time point $i\delta$, explaining why the traded price is not exactly the mid-price. It is assumed that $\varepsilon_{i\delta}$ is independent of the mid-price $P^*_{i\delta}$. For simplicity, we further assume that the market microstructure noises $\{\varepsilon_{i\delta}\}$ are an IID $(0, \sigma^2_\varepsilon)$ sequence. (It is possible that $\{\varepsilon_{i\delta}\}$ may become a serially correlated sequence when the sampling interval δ becomes small.)

Now suppose we are interested in estimating the integrated volatility

$$V = \int_0^T \sigma^2(t)dt,$$

when we have a discretized sample $\{P_{i\delta}\}_{i=1}^n$ of size n over the time period [0,T], with a sampling interval $\delta = T/n$. A popular estimator is called the realized volatility, defined as

$$\hat{V} = \sum_{i=1}^n \left(P_{i\delta} - P_{(i-1)\delta}\right)^2.$$

It can be shown that the estimation bias

$$\begin{aligned} E(\hat{V}) - V &= \sum_{i=1}^n E\left[(P^*_{i\delta} - P^*_{(i-1)\delta}) + (\varepsilon_{i\delta} - \varepsilon_{(i-1)\delta})\right]^2 - V \\ &= \left[\sum_{i=1}^n E(P^*_{i\delta} - P^*_{(i-1)\delta})^2 - V\right] + \sum_{i=1}^n E(\varepsilon_{i\delta} - \varepsilon_{(i-1)\delta})^2 \\ &= 2n\sigma^2_\varepsilon[1 + o(1)] \text{ as } n \to \infty. \end{aligned}$$

This implies that the estimator of the squared volatility increases linearly with the sampling frequency, and this comes only from the microstructure noise. Thus, the microstructure noise is a disturbance that may make high frequency estimates of some parameters (e.g., the realized volatility) inconsistent.

For an excellent account of market microstructure, readers are referred to O'Hara (1995).

Example 7.5. [Omitted Variables]: Consider an earning equation

$$Y_t = X_t'\beta^o + \gamma A_t + u_t,$$

where Y_t is earning, X_t is a vector consisting of working experience and schooling, and A_t is ability which is unobservable, and the disturbance u_t satisfies the condition that $E(u_t|X_t, A_t) = 0$. Because one does not observe ability A_t, one is forced to consider the regression model

$$Y_t = X_t'\beta^o + \varepsilon_t$$

and is interested in knowing the value of parameter vector β^o, the marginal effects of schooling and working experience. However, we have $E(X_t\varepsilon_t) \neq 0$ because A_t is usually correlated with X_t. Obviously, this is a misspecified model but one may be still interested in estimating the parameter value β^o, particularly the rate of return to education.

Example 7.6. [Production-Bonus Causality]: Consider an extended production function DGP

$$\ln(Y_t) = \beta_0^o + \beta_1^o \ln(L_t) + \beta_2^o \ln(K_t) + \beta_3^o B_t + \varepsilon_t,$$

where Y_t, L_t and K_t are output, labor and capital stock respectively, B_t is the proportion of bonus out of total pay, and t is a time index. Without loss of generality, we assume that

$$\begin{aligned} E(\varepsilon_t) &= 0, \\ E[\ln(L_t)\varepsilon_t] &= 0, \\ E[\ln(K_t)\varepsilon_t] &= 0. \end{aligned}$$

Economic theory suggests that the use of bonus in addition to basic wage in state-owned enterprises will provide a stronger incentive for workers to work harder in a transitional economy. This theory can be tested by checking whether $\beta_3^o = 0$. However, the test procedure is complicated because there exists a possibility that when a state-owned enterprise is more productive, it will pay more bonus to workers regardless of their effort. In this case, the OLS estimator $\hat{\beta}_3$ is not consistent for β_3^o and so cannot be used to test the null hypothesis.

Why?

To reflect the fact that a more productive state-owned enterprise pays more bonus to its workers, we can assume a structural equation for bonus:

$$B_t = \alpha_0^o + \alpha_1^o \ln(Y_t) + w_t, \tag{7.5}$$

where $\alpha_1^o > 0$, and $\{w_t\}$ is an IID$(0, \sigma_w^2)$ sequence that is independent of $\{Y_t\}$. For simplicity, we assume that $\{w_t\}$ is independent of $\{\varepsilon_t\}$.

Put $X_t = [1, \ln(L_t), \ln(K_t), B_t]'$. Now, from Eq. (7.5) and then Eq. (7.4), we have

$$\begin{aligned} E(B_t\varepsilon_t) &= E[(\alpha_0^o + \alpha_1^o \ln(Y_t) + w_t)\varepsilon_t] \\ &= \alpha_1^o E[\ln(Y_t)\varepsilon_t] \\ &= \alpha_1^o \beta_3^o E(B_t\varepsilon_t) + \alpha_1^o E(\varepsilon_t^2). \end{aligned}$$

It follows that

$$E(B_t\varepsilon_t) = \frac{\alpha_1^o}{1 - \alpha_1^o \beta_3^o}\sigma^2 \neq 0,$$

where $\sigma^2 = \text{var}(\varepsilon_t)$. Consequently, the OLS estimator $\hat{\beta}_3$ is inconsistent for β_3^o due to the existence of the reserved causality from productivity $\ln(Y_t)$ to bonus B_t. It is now clear why we say that there exists endogeneity if $E(\varepsilon_t|X_t) \neq 0$. When there exists a reserved causality from productivity to bonus, bonus is an endogenous variable because it is determined by productivity. As a result, ε_t is correlated with bonus so that $E(\varepsilon_t|B_t) \neq 0$. In contrast, if there is no reserved causality from productivity to bonus, bonus will be an exogenous variable and $E(\varepsilon_t|B_t) = 0$.

The bias of the OLS estimator for β_3^o in the above model is usually called the simultaneous equation bias because it arises from the fact that the productivity function is but one of the two equations that hold simultaneously. This is a common phenomenon in economics. It is the rule rather than the exception for economic relationships to be embedded in a simultaneous system of equations. Below we consider two more examples with simultaneous equations bias.

Example 7.7. [Simultaneous Equations Bias]: We consider the following simple model of national income determination:

$$C_t = \beta_0^o + \beta_1^o I_t + \varepsilon_t, \tag{7.6}$$

$$I_t = C_t + D_t, \tag{7.7}$$

where I_t is income, C_t is consumption expenditure, and D_t is non-consumption expenditure. The variables I_t and C_t are called endogenous variables, as they are determined by the two-equation model under study. The variable D_t is called an exogenous variable, because it is determined outside the model. We assume that $\{D_t\}$ and $\{\varepsilon_t\}$ are mutually independent, and $\{\varepsilon_t\}$ is IID$(0, \sigma^2)$.

Question: If the OLS estimator $\hat{\beta}$ is applied to the first equation, is it consistent for β^o?

To answer this question, we have from Eq. (7.7)

$$\begin{aligned} E(I_t\varepsilon_t) &= E[(C_t + D_t)\varepsilon_t] \\ &= E(C_t\varepsilon_t) + E(D_t\varepsilon_t) \\ &= \beta_1^o E(I_t\varepsilon_t) + E(\varepsilon_t^2) + 0. \end{aligned}$$

It follows that

$$E(I_t\varepsilon_t) = \frac{1}{1-\beta_1^o}\sigma^2 \neq 0.$$

Thus, $\hat{\beta}$ is not consistent for β^o.

In fact, this bias problem can also be seen from the so-called reduced form model.

Question: What is the reduced form?

Solving for Eqs. (7.6) and (7.7) simultaneously, we can obtain the "reduced forms" that express endogenous variables in terms of exogenous variables and disturbances:

$$C_t = \frac{\beta_0^o}{1-\beta_1^o} + \frac{\beta_1^o}{1-\beta_1^o}D_t + \frac{1}{1-\beta_1^o}\varepsilon_t,$$

$$I_t = \frac{\beta_0^o}{1-\beta_1^o} + \frac{1}{1-\beta_1^o}D_t + \frac{1}{1-\beta_1^o}\varepsilon_t.$$

Obviously, I_t is positively correlated with ε_t (i.e., $E(I_t\varepsilon_t) \neq 0$). Thus, the OLS estimator for the regression of C_t on I_t in Eq. (7.6) will not be consistent for β_1^o, the parameter for MPC. Generally speaking, the OLS estimator for the reduced form is consistent for new parameters, which are functions of original parameters.

Example 7.8. [Wage-Price Spiral Model]: Consider the system of equations

$$W_t = \beta_0^o + \beta_1^o P_t + \beta_2^o D_t + \varepsilon_t, \tag{7.8}$$

$$P_t = \alpha_0^o + \alpha_1^o W_t + v_t, \tag{7.9}$$

where W_t, P_t, D_t are wage, price, and excess demand in the labor market respectively. Eq. (7.8) describes the mechanism of how wage is determined.

In particular, wage depends on price and excess demand for labor. Eq. (7.9) describes how price depends on wage (or income).

Suppose D_t is an exogenous variable, with $E(\varepsilon_t|D_t) = 0$. There are two endogenous variables, W_t and P_t, in the system of equations in (7.8) and (7.9).

Question: Will W_t be correlated with v_t? And, will P_t be correlated with ε_t?

To answer these questions, we first obtain the reduced form equations:

$$W_t = \frac{\beta_0^o + \beta_1^o \alpha_0}{1 - \beta_1^o \alpha_1^o} + \frac{\beta_1^o}{1 - \beta_1^o \alpha_1^o} D_t + \frac{\varepsilon_t + \beta_1^o v_t}{1 - \beta_1^o \alpha_1^o},$$

$$P_t = \frac{\alpha_0^o}{1 - \beta_1^o \alpha_1^o} + \frac{\alpha_1^o \beta_2^o}{1 - \beta_1^o \alpha_1^o} D_t + \frac{\alpha_1^o \varepsilon_t + v_t}{1 - \beta_1^o \alpha_1^o}.$$

Conditional on the exogenous variable D_t, both W_t and P_t are correlated with ε_t and v_t. As a consequence, both the OLS estimator for β_1^o in Eq. (7.8) and the OLS estimator for α_1^o in Eq. (7.9) will be inconsistent.

In this chapter, we will consider a method called Two-Stage Least Squares (2SLS) estimation to obtain consistent estimators for the unknown parameters in all above examples except for the parameter β_2^o in Eq. (7.8) of Example 7.8. No method can deliver a consistent estimator for β_2^o in Eq. (7.8) because it is not identifiable. This is the so-called identification problem of simultaneous equations.

To see why there is no way to obtain a consistent estimator for β_2^o in Eq. (7.8), from Eq. (7.9), we can write

$$W_t = -\frac{\alpha_1^o}{\alpha_2^o} + \frac{1}{\alpha_2^o} P_t - \frac{v_t}{\alpha_2^o}. \tag{7.10}$$

Let a and b be two arbitrary constants. We multiply Eq. (7.8) with a, multiply Eq. (7.10) with b, and then add them together:

$$(a+b)W_t = a\beta_1^o - \frac{b\alpha_1}{\alpha_2} + \left(a\beta_2^o + \frac{b}{\alpha_2}\right) P_t + a\beta_3^o D_t + \left(a\varepsilon_t - \frac{b}{\alpha_2} v_t\right),$$

or

$$\begin{aligned} W_t = &\left[\frac{a\beta_1^o}{a+b} - \frac{b\alpha_1^o}{(a+b)\alpha_2^o}\right] + \frac{1}{a+b}\left(a\beta_2^o + \frac{b}{\alpha_2^o}\right) P_t \\ &+ \frac{a\beta_3^o}{a+b} D_t + \frac{1}{a+b}\left(a\varepsilon_t - \frac{b}{\alpha_2^o} v_t\right). \end{aligned} \tag{7.11}$$

This new equation, (7.11), is a combination of the original wage equation (7.8) and price equation (7.9). It is of the same statistical form as Eq. (7.8). Since a and b are arbitrary, there is an infinite number of parameters that can satisfy Eq. (7.11) and they are all indistinguishable from Eq. (7.8). Consequently, if we use OLS to run regression of W_t on P_t and D_t, or more generally, use any other method to estimate Eq. (7.8) or Eq. (7.11), there is no way to know which model, either Eq. (7.8) or Eq. (7.11), is being estimated. Therefore, there is no way to estimate β_2^o. This is the so-called identification problem for simultaneous equations models. To avoid such identification problems in simultaneous equations, certain conditions are required to make the system of simultaneous equations identifiable. For example, if an extra variable, say money supply growth, is added in the price equation in (7.9), we then obtain

$$P_t = \alpha_0^o + \alpha_1^o W_t + \alpha_2^o M_t + v_t, \tag{7.12}$$

then the system of Eqs. (7.8) and (7.12) becomes identifiable provided $\alpha_2^o \neq 0$, and as a result, the parameters in Eqs. (7.8) and (7.12) can be consistently estimated.

Question: Check why the system of Eqs. (7.8) and (7.12) is identifiable.

We note that for the system of Eqs. (7.8) and (7.9), although Eq. (7.8) cannot be consistently estimated by any method, Eq. (7.9) can be consistently estimated using the method proposed below. For an identifiable system of simultaneous equations with simultaneous equations bias, we can use various methods to estimate them consistently, including 2SLS, the Generalized Method of Moments (GMM) and the Quasi-Maximum Likelihood Estimation (QMLE). These methods will be introduced below and in subsequent chapters.

7.2 Framework and Assumptions

We now provide a set of regularity conditions for our formal analysis in this chapter.

Assumption 7.1. [Ergodic Stationarity]: $\{Y_t, X_t', Z_t'\}_{t=1}^n$ is an observable ergodic stationary stochastic process, where X_t is a $K \times 1$ vector, Z_t is an $l \times 1$ vector, and $l \geq K$.

Assumption 7.2. [Linearity]:

$$Y_t = X_t'\beta^o + \varepsilon_t, \qquad t = 1, ..., n,$$

for some unknown $K \times 1$ parameter vector β^o and some unobservable disturbance ε_t.

Assumption 7.3. [Nonsingularity]: The $K \times K$ matrix

$$Q_{XX} = E(X_t X_t')$$

is symmetric, finite and nonsingular.

Assumption 7.4. [Instrumental Variables (IV) Conditions]:
(a) $E(\varepsilon_t|X) \neq 0$;
(b) $E(\varepsilon_t|Z_t) = 0$;
(c) The $l \times l$ matrix

$$Q_{ZZ} = E(Z_t Z_t')$$

is finite and nonsingular, and the $l \times K$ matrix

$$Q_{ZX} = E(Z_t X_t')$$

is finite and of full rank.

Assumption 7.5. [CLT]: As $n \to \infty$, $n^{-1/2}\sum_{t=1}^n Z_t\varepsilon_t \xrightarrow{d} N(0, V)$ for some $K \times K$ symmetric, finite and nonsingular matrix $V \equiv \text{avar}(n^{-1/2}\sum_{t=1}^n Z_t\varepsilon_t)$.

Assumption 7.1 allows for IID observations and stationary time series observations.

Assumption 7.5 directly assumes that CLT holds. This is called a "high level assumption." It covers three cases: IID, MDS and non-MDS for $\{X_t\varepsilon_t\}$, respectively. For an IID or MDS sequence $\{Z_t\varepsilon_t\}$, we have $V = \text{var}(Z_t\varepsilon_t) = E(Z_t Z_t'\varepsilon_t^2)$. For a non-MDS process $\{Z_t\varepsilon_t\}$, $V = \sum_{j=-\infty}^{\infty}\text{cov}(Z_t\varepsilon_t, Z_{t-j}\varepsilon_{t-j})$ is a long-run variance-covariance matrix.

The random vector Z_t that satisfies Assumption 7.4 is called the instrumental variables (IV) or simply instruments. The concept of IV was first derived by Philip Wright, possibly in coauthorship with his son Sewall Wright, in the context of simultaneous equations in his book *The Tariff on Animal and Vegetable Oils* in 1928. In 1945, Olav Reiersϕl applied the same approach in the context of errors-in-variables models in his dissertation, giving the method its name. For the history of IV regression, readers are referred to Stock and Trebbi (2003).

When $E(\varepsilon_t|X_t) \neq 0$, we usually (but not always) have $E(X_t\varepsilon_t) \neq 0$. As a result, the OLS estimator is not consistent for β^o. Now suppose we have an instrument vector Z_t with $E(\varepsilon_t|Z_t) = 0$, which implies $E(Z_t\varepsilon_t) = 0$. Then we can first project X_t onto Z_t and then run a regression of Y_t on the projection. This will deliver consistent estimation of β^o.

The IV method is often used to estimate causal relationships when controlled experiments are not feasible or when a treatment cannot be successfully delivered to every unit in a randomized or controlled experiment. Intuitively, IV is used when an explanatory variable of interest is correlated with the regression disturbance. A valid instrument induces changes in the explanatory variable but has no effect on the dependent variable, allowing a researcher to uncover the causal effect of the explanatory variable on the dependent variable.

As we shall show, IV methods allow for consistent estimation when explanatory variables are correlated with disturbances in a regression model. Such correlation may occur when changes in the dependent variable change the values of at least one of the explanatory variables ("reversed" causation), when there are omitted variables that affect both the dependent and explanatory variables, or when explanatory variables are subject to measurement errors. Explanatory variables which suffer from one or more of these issues in the context of a regression are sometimes referred to as endogenous variables. In this situation, the OLS method produces biased and inconsistent estimates. However, if an instrument is available, consistent estimates may still be obtained. An instrument is a variable that does not itself belong to the set of explanatory variables but is correlated with endogenous variables. For linear models, Assumptions 7.4(b) and 7.4(c) are two main requirements for IVs. When Assumption 7.4(b) holds, the instrument vector Z_t is called to satisfy the exclusion restriction.

The condition that $l \geq K$ in Assumption 7.1 implies that the number of instruments in Z_t is larger than or at least equal to the number of regressors in X_t.

Question: Why is the condition of $l \geq K$ required?

Question: How to choose instruments Z_t in practice?

First of all, one should analyze which explanatory variables in X_t are endogenous or exogenous. If an explanatory variable is exogenous, then this variable should be included in Z_t, the set of instruments. For example, the constant term should always be included, because a constant is uncorrelated with any random variables. All other exogenous variables in X_t should also be included in Z_t. If k_0 of the K regressors are endogenous, one should find at least k_0 additional instruments.

Most importantly, we should choose an instrument vector Z_t which is closely related to X_t as much as possible. As we will see below, the strength of the correlation between Z_t and X_t affects the magnitude of the asymptotic variance of the 2SLS estimator for β^o which we will propose, although it does not affect the consistency provided the correlation between Z_t and X_t is a non-zero constant.

In time series regression models, it is often reasonable to assume that lagged variables of X_t are not correlated with ε_t. Therefore, we can use lagged values of X_t, for example, X_{t-1}, as an IV. This IV is expected to be highly correlated with X_t if $\{X_t\}$ is a time series process. In light of this, we can choose the set of instruments $Z_t = (1, \ln L_t, \ln K_t, B_{t-1})'$ in estimating Eq. (7.4) in Example 7.1, choose $Z_t = (1, D_t, I_{t-1})'$ in estimating Eq. (7.6) in Example 7.7, choose $Z_t = (1, D_t, P_{t-1})'$ in estimating Eq. (7.8) in Example 7.8. For examples with measurement errors or expectational errors, where $E(X_t\varepsilon_t) \neq 0$ due to the presence of measurement errors or expectational errors, we can choose $Z_t = X_{t-1}$ if the measurement errors or expectational errors in X_t are serially uncorrelated. The expectational errors in X_t are MDS and so are serially uncorrelated in Example 7.3 when the economic agent has rational expectations.

In empirical studies involving IV regressions, it is not rare to find that the correlation between Z_t and X_t is low, that is, the instrument vector Z_t can only explain a small proportion of variations in the endogenous vector X_t. In this case, Z_t is called a weak instrument. In econometrics, this scenario is often modelled that the partial correlation between Z_t and X_t, as measured by $E(Z_tX_t')$, vanishes to zero as the sample size $n \to \infty$, namely, $E(Z_tX_t') = n^{-1/2}C$, where C is an $l \times K$ constant matrix. In this case, IV regressions such as the 2SLS method to be introduced below will not yield consistent estimation of β^o. See Staiger and Stock (1997) for more discussion.

7.3 Two-Stage Least Squares (2SLS) Estimation

Question: Because $E(\varepsilon_t|X_t) \neq 0$, the OLS estimator $\hat{\beta}$ is not consistent for the true parameter value β^o. How to obtain a consistent estimator for β^o in situations similar to the examples described in Section 7.1?

It should be pointed out that when $E(\varepsilon_t|X_t) \neq 0$, endogeneity arises due to various reasons including model misspecification. However, it may still make sense to find out the expected marginal effect of explanatory variables X_t on the dependent variable Y_t, even if the linear regression model is misspecified. For example, although Example 7.5 suffers from an omitted variable problem, one may be still interested in knowing the rate of return to education. This requires consistent estimation of β^o.

We now introduce the 2SLS procedure, which can consistently estimate β^o when $E(\varepsilon_t|X_t) \neq 0$. The 2SLS procedure can be described as follows:

Stage 1: Regress X_t on Z_t via OLS and save the predicted value $\hat{X}_t$. This is the projection of X_t on Z_t.

Here, we consider an auxiliary linear regression model is

$$X_t = \gamma' Z_t + v_t, \qquad t = 1, ..., n,$$

where γ is an $l \times K$ parameter matrix, and v_t is a $K \times 1$ regression error. From Theorem 2.4 in Chapter 2, we have $E(Z_t v_t) = 0$ if and only if γ is the best least squares approximation coefficient, i.e., if and only if

$$\gamma = [E(Z_t Z_t')]^{-1} E(Z_t X_t')$$

In matrix form, we can write

$$\mathbf{X} = \mathbf{Z}\gamma + v,$$

where $\mathbf{X}$ is an $n \times K$ matrix, $\mathbf{Z}$ is an $n \times l$ matrix, γ is an $l \times K$ matrix, and v is an $n \times K$ matrix.

The OLS estimator for γ is

$$\begin{aligned}\hat{\gamma} &= (\mathbf{Z}'\mathbf{Z})^{-1}\mathbf{Z}'\mathbf{X} \\ &= \left(n^{-1}\sum_{t=1}^{n} Z_t Z_t'\right)^{-1} n^{-1}\sum_{t=1}^{n} Z_t X_t'.\end{aligned}$$

The predicted value or the sample projection of X_t on Z_t is

$$\hat{X}_t = \hat{\gamma}' Z_t$$

or in matrix form

$$\hat{\mathbf{X}} = \mathbf{Z}\hat{\gamma} = \mathbf{Z}(\mathbf{Z}'\mathbf{Z})^{-1}\mathbf{Z}'\mathbf{X}.$$

Stage 2: Use the predicted value $\hat{X}_t$ as regressors for Y_t. Regress Y_t on $\hat{X}_t$, and the resulting OLS estimator is called the 2SLS estimator, denoted as $\hat{\beta}_{2SLS}$. This is the regression of Y_t on the projection in the first stage.

Question: Why use the fitted value $\hat{X}_t = \hat{\gamma}' Z_t$ as regressors in the second stage?

We first consider the auxiliary regression

$$X_t = \gamma' Z_t + v_t,$$

where γ is the best linear least squares approximation coefficient, and so v_t is orthogonal to Z_t in the sense $E(Z_t v_t') = 0$. Because $E(Z_t \varepsilon_t) = 0$, the population projection $\gamma' Z_t$ is orthogonal to ε. In general, $v_t = X_t - \gamma' Z_t$, which is orthogonal to Z_t, is correlated with ε_t. In other words, the auxiliary regression in the first stage decomposes X_t into two components: $\gamma' Z_t$ and v_t, where $\gamma' Z_t$ is orthogonal to ε_t, and v_t is correlated with ε_t.

Since the best linear least squares approximation coefficient γ is unknown, we have to replace it with the estimator $\hat{\gamma}$. The fitted value $\hat{X}_t = \hat{\gamma}' Z_t$ is the (sample) projection X_t onto Z_t. The regression of X_t on Z_t purges the component of X_t that is correlated with ε_t so that the projection $\hat{X}_t$ is approximately orthogonal to ε_t given that Z_t is orthogonal to ε_t. The word "approximately" is used here because $\hat{\gamma}$ is an estimator of γ and thus contains some estimation error.

The regression model in the second stage can be written as

$$Y_t = \hat{X}_t' \beta^o + \hat{u}_t$$

or in matrix form

$$Y = \hat{\mathbf{X}}\beta^o + \hat{u}.$$

Note that the disturbance $\hat{u}_t$ is not ε_t because $\hat{X}_t$ is not X_t.

Using $\hat{\mathbf{X}} = \mathbf{Z}\hat{\gamma} = \mathbf{Z}(\mathbf{Z}'\mathbf{Z})^{-1}\mathbf{Z}'\mathbf{X}$, we can write the second stage OLS estimator, namely the 2SLS estimator as follows:

$$
\begin{aligned}
\hat{\beta}_{2SLS} &= (\hat{\mathbf{X}}'\hat{\mathbf{X}})^{-1}\hat{\mathbf{X}}'Y \\
&= [(\mathbf{Z}\hat{\gamma})'(\mathbf{Z}\hat{\gamma})]^{-1}(\mathbf{Z}\hat{\gamma})'Y \\
&= \left\{[\mathbf{Z}(\mathbf{Z}'\mathbf{Z})^{-1}\mathbf{Z}'\mathbf{X}]'[\mathbf{Z}(\mathbf{Z}'\mathbf{Z})^{-1}\mathbf{Z}'\mathbf{X}]\right\}^{-1}[\mathbf{Z}(\mathbf{Z}'\mathbf{Z})^{-1}\mathbf{Z}'\mathbf{X}]'Y \\
&= [\mathbf{X}'\mathbf{Z}(\mathbf{Z}'\mathbf{Z})^{-1}\mathbf{Z}'\mathbf{Z}(\mathbf{Z}'\mathbf{Z})^{-1}\mathbf{Z}'\mathbf{X}]^{-1}\mathbf{X}'\mathbf{Z}(\mathbf{Z}'\mathbf{Z})^{-1}\mathbf{Z}'Y \\
&= [\mathbf{X}'\mathbf{Z}(\mathbf{Z}'\mathbf{Z})^{-1}\mathbf{Z}'\mathbf{X}]^{-1}\mathbf{X}'\mathbf{Z}(\mathbf{Z}'\mathbf{Z})^{-1}\mathbf{Z}'Y \\
&= \left[\frac{\mathbf{X}'\mathbf{Z}}{n}\left(\frac{\mathbf{Z}'\mathbf{Z}}{n}\right)^{-1}\frac{\mathbf{Z}'\mathbf{X}}{n}\right]^{-1}\frac{\mathbf{X}'\mathbf{Z}}{n}\left(\frac{\mathbf{Z}'\mathbf{Z}}{n}\right)^{-1}\frac{\mathbf{Z}'Y}{n}.
\end{aligned}
$$

Using the expression $Y = \mathbf{X}\beta^o + \varepsilon$ from Assumption 7.2, we have

$$
\begin{aligned}
\hat{\beta}_{2SLS} - \beta^o &= \left[\frac{\mathbf{X}'\mathbf{Z}}{n}\left(\frac{\mathbf{Z}'\mathbf{Z}}{n}\right)^{-1}\frac{\mathbf{Z}'\mathbf{X}}{n}\right]^{-1}\frac{\mathbf{X}'\mathbf{Z}}{n}\left(\frac{\mathbf{Z}'\mathbf{Z}}{n}\right)^{-1}\frac{\mathbf{Z}'\varepsilon}{n} \\
&= \left(\hat{Q}_{XZ}\hat{Q}_{ZZ}^{-1}\hat{Q}_{ZX}\right)^{-1}\hat{Q}_{XZ}\hat{Q}_{ZZ}^{-1}\frac{Z'\varepsilon}{n},
\end{aligned}
$$

where

$$
\begin{aligned}
\hat{Q}_{ZZ} &= \frac{\mathbf{Z}'\mathbf{Z}}{n} = n^{-1}\sum_{t=1}^{n} Z_t Z_t', \\
\hat{Q}_{XZ} &= \frac{\mathbf{X}'\mathbf{Z}}{n} = n^{-1}\sum_{t=1}^{n} X_t Z_t', \\
\hat{Q}_{ZX} &= \frac{\mathbf{Z}'\mathbf{X}}{n} = n^{-1}\sum_{t=1}^{n} Z_t X_t' = \hat{Q}_{XZ}'.
\end{aligned}
$$

Question: What are the statistical properties of $\hat{\beta}_{2SLS}$?

7.4 Consistency of the 2SLS Estimator

By WLLN for an ergodic stationary process, we have as $n \to \infty$,

$$
\begin{aligned}
&\hat{Q}_{ZZ} \xrightarrow{p} Q_{ZZ}, \quad l \times l, \\
&\hat{Q}_{XZ} \xrightarrow{p} Q_{XZ}, \quad K \times l, \\
&\frac{Z'\varepsilon}{n} \xrightarrow{p} E(Z_t\varepsilon_t) = 0, \quad l \times 1.
\end{aligned}
$$

Also, $Q_{XZ}Q_{ZZ}^{-1}Q_{ZX}$ is a $K \times K$ symmetric and nonsingular matrix because Q_{XZ} is of full rank, Q_{ZZ} is nonsingular, and $l \geq K$. It follows from continuity that

$$\left(\hat{Q}_{XZ}\hat{Q}_{ZZ}^{-1}\hat{Q}_{ZX}\right)^{-1} \xrightarrow{p} \left(Q_{XZ}Q_{ZZ}^{-1}Q_{ZX}\right)^{-1}.$$

Consequently, we have

$$\hat{\beta}_{2SLS} - \beta^o \xrightarrow{p} \left(Q_{XZ}Q_{ZZ}^{-1}Q_{ZX}\right)^{-1} Q_{XZ}Q_{ZZ}^{-1} \cdot 0 = 0.$$

We now state this consistency result in the following theorem.

Theorem 7.1. ***[Consistency of 2SLS]:*** *Under Assumptions 7.1 to 7.4, as $n \to \infty$,*

$$\hat{\beta}_{2SLS} \xrightarrow{p} \beta^o.$$

To provide intuition why the 2SLS estimator $\hat{\beta}_{2SLS}$ is consistent for β^o, we consider the linear regression model

$$Y_t = X_t'\beta^o + \varepsilon_t.$$

The OLS estimator $\hat{\beta}$ is not consistent for β^o because $E(X_t\varepsilon_t) \neq 0$. Suppose now we decompose the regressor X_t into two components:

$$X_t = \tilde{X}_t + v_t,$$

where $\tilde{X}_t = \gamma' Z_t$ is a projection of X_t on Z_t and so it is orthogonal to ε_t. The other component, $v_t = X_t - \tilde{X}_t$, is generally correlated with ε_t but is uncorrelated with $\tilde{X}_t$. Thus, consistent estimation for β^o is possible if we observe $\tilde{X}_t$ and run the following regression

$$\begin{aligned} Y_t &= X_t'\beta^o + \varepsilon_t \\ &= \tilde{X}_t'\beta^o + (v_t'\beta^o + \varepsilon_t) \\ &= \tilde{X}_t'\beta^o + u_t, \end{aligned}$$

where $u_t = v_t'\beta^o + \varepsilon_t$ is the disturbance when regressing Y_t on $\tilde{X}_t$. Because

$$\begin{aligned} E(\tilde{X}_t u_t) &= \gamma' E(Z_t u_t) \\ &= \gamma' E(Z_t v_t')\beta^o + \gamma' E(Z_t\varepsilon_t) \\ &= 0, \end{aligned}$$

the OLS estimator of regressing Y_t on $\tilde{X}_t$ would be consistent for β^o.

However, $\tilde{X}_t = \gamma' Z_t$ is not observable, so we need to use a proxy, i.e., $\hat{X}_t = \hat{\gamma}' Z_t$, where $\hat{\gamma}$ is the OLS estimator of regressing X_t on Z_t. The corresponding regression model becomes

$$Y_t = \hat{X}_t \beta^o + \hat{u}_t.$$

This results in the 2SLS estimator $\hat{\beta}_{2SLS}$. We note that where $\hat{u}_t \neq u_t$ since $\hat{X}_t \neq \tilde{X}_t$. However, because $\hat{\gamma} \to \gamma$ as $n \to \infty$, we have

$$\hat{u}_t = u_t - (\hat{X}_t - X_t)'\beta^o = u_t - Z_t'(\hat{\gamma} - \gamma)\beta^o$$

will coverage to u_t. Therefore, the estimation error of $\hat{\gamma}$ in the first stage does not affect the consistency of the 2SLS estimator $\hat{\beta}$.

Question: Is 2SLS $\hat{\beta}_{2SLS}$ still consistent for β^o if $E(\varepsilon_t|Z_t) \neq 0$ but $E(Z_t \varepsilon_t) = 0$?

7.5 Asymptotic Normality of the 2SLS Estimator

We now derive the asymptotic distribution of $\hat{\beta}_{2SLS}$. Write

$$\begin{aligned}\sqrt{n}(\hat{\beta}_{2SLS} - \beta^o) &= \left(\hat{Q}_{XZ}\hat{Q}_{ZZ}^{-1}\hat{Q}_{ZX}\right)^{-1}\hat{Q}_{XZ}\hat{Q}_{ZZ}^{-1}\frac{\mathbf{Z}'\varepsilon}{\sqrt{n}} \\ &= \hat{A}\cdot\frac{\mathbf{Z}'\varepsilon}{\sqrt{n}},\end{aligned}$$

where the $K \times l$ matrix

$$\hat{A} = \left(\hat{Q}_{XZ}\hat{Q}_{ZZ}^{-1}\hat{Q}_{ZX}\right)^{-1}\hat{Q}_{XZ}\hat{Q}_{ZZ}^{-1}.$$

By the CLT assumption (Assumption 7.5), we have

$$\frac{\mathbf{Z}'\varepsilon}{\sqrt{n}} = n^{-\frac{1}{2}}\sum_{t=1}^{n} Z_t\varepsilon_t \xrightarrow{d} N(0, V),$$

where V is an $l \times l$ symmetric, finite and nonsingular matrix. By Slutsky's theorem, we have

$$\begin{aligned}\sqrt{n}(\hat{\beta}_{2SLS} - \beta^o) &\xrightarrow{d} \left(Q_{XZ}Q_{ZZ}^{-1}Q_{ZX}\right)^{-1}Q_{XZ}Q_{ZZ}^{-1}\cdot N(0, V) \\ &\sim N(0, AVA') \\ &\sim N(0, \Omega),\end{aligned}$$

where $A = (Q_{XZ}Q_{ZZ}^{-1}Q_{ZX})^{-1}Q_{XZ}Q_{ZZ}^{-1}$ is the probability limit of $\hat{A}$. The asymptotic variance of $\sqrt{n}\hat{\beta}_{2SLS}$

$$\begin{aligned}
\text{avar}(\sqrt{n}\hat{\beta}_{2SLS}) &= \Omega \\
&= AVA' \\
&= \left[\left(Q_{XZ}Q_{ZZ}^{-1}Q_{ZX}\right)^{-1} Q_{XZ}Q_{ZZ}^{-1}\right] V \left[\left(Q_{XZ}Q_{ZZ}^{-1}Q_{ZX}\right)^{-1} Q_{XZ}Q_{ZZ}^{-1}\right]' \\
&= \left(Q_{XZ}Q_{ZZ}^{-1}Q_{ZX}\right)^{-1} Q_{XZ}Q_{ZZ}^{-1}VQ_{ZZ}^{-1}Q_{ZX}\left(Q_{XZ}Q_{ZZ}^{-1}Q_{ZX}\right)^{-1}.
\end{aligned}$$

Theorem 7.2. ***[Asymptotic Normality of 2SLS]:*** *Under Assumptions 7.1 to 7.5, as $n \to \infty$,*

$$\sqrt{n}(\hat{\beta}_{2SLS} - \beta^o) \xrightarrow{d} N(0, \Omega).$$

The estimation of V depends on whether $\{Z_t\varepsilon_t\}$ is an MDS. We first consider the case where $\{Z_t\varepsilon_t\}$ is an MDS. In this case, $V = E(Z_tZ_t'\varepsilon_t^2)$ and so we need not estimate a long-run variance-covariance matrix.

Case I: $\{Z_t\varepsilon_t\}$ Is an Ergodic Stationary MDS

Assumption 7.6. **[MDS]:** (a) $\{Z_t\varepsilon_t\}$ is an MDS; (b) $\text{var}(Z_t\varepsilon_t) = E(Z_tZ_t'\varepsilon_t^2)$ is an $l \times l$ symmetric, finite and nonsingular matrix.

Corollary 7.1. *Under Assumptions 7.1 to 7.4 and 7.6, we have as $n \to \infty$,*

$$\sqrt{n}(\hat{\beta}_{2SLS} - \beta^o) \xrightarrow{d} N(0, \Omega),$$

where Ω is defined as above with $V = E(Z_tZ_t'\varepsilon_t^2)$.

There is no need to estimate a long-run variance-covariance matrix but Ω involves the heteroskedasticity-consistent variance-covariance matrix V.

When $\{Z_t\varepsilon_t\}$ is an MDS with a conditionally homoskedastic disturbance ε_t, the asymptotic variance Ω can be greatly simplified.

Assumption 7.7. **[Conditional Homoskedasticity]:** $E(\varepsilon_t^2|Z_t) = \sigma^2$.

Note that the conditional expectation in Assumption 7.7 is conditional on Z_t, not on X_t. Under this assumption, by the law of iterated expectations, we obtain

$$\begin{aligned} V &= E(Z_t Z_t' \varepsilon_t^2) \\ &= E[Z_t Z_t' E(\varepsilon_t^2 | Z_t)] \\ &= \sigma^2 E(Z_t Z_t') \\ &= \sigma^2 Q_{ZZ}. \end{aligned}$$

It follows that

$$\begin{aligned} \Omega &= (Q_{XZ} Q_{ZZ}^{-1} Q_{ZX})^{-1} Q_{XZ} Q_{ZZ}^{-1} \sigma^2 Q_{ZZ} Q_{ZZ}^{-1} Q_{ZX} (Q_{XZ} Q_{ZZ}^{-1} Q_{ZX})^{-1} \\ &= \sigma^2 (Q_{XZ} Q_{ZZ}^{-1} Q_{ZX})^{-1}. \end{aligned}$$

Corollary 7.2. ***[Asymptotic Normality of 2SLS Under MDS with Conditional Homoskedasticity]:*** *Under Assumptions 7.1 to 7.4, 7.6 and 7.7, we have as $n \to \infty$,*

$$\sqrt{n}(\hat{\beta}_{2SLS} - \beta^o) \xrightarrow{d} N(0, \Omega),$$

where

$$\Omega - \sigma^2 (Q_{XZ} Q_{ZZ}^{-1} Q_{ZX})^{-1}.$$

Case II: $\{Z_t \varepsilon_t\}$ Is an Ergodic Stationary Non-MDS

In this general case, we have

$$V \equiv \text{avar}\left(n^{-1/2} \sum_{t=1}^{n} Z_t \varepsilon_t\right) = \sum_{j=-\infty}^{\infty} \Gamma(j)$$

where $\Gamma(j) = \text{cov}(Z_t \varepsilon_t, Z_{t-j} \varepsilon_{t-j})$. We need to use a consistent long-run variance-covariance matrix estimator for V. When $\{Z_t \varepsilon_t\}$ is not an MDS, there is no need (and in fact there is no way) to consider conditional homoskedasticity and conditional heteroskedasticity separately.

7.6 Interpretation and Estimation of Asymptotic Variance-Covariance Matrix of the 2SLS Estimator

The asymptotic variance-covariance matrix Ω of $\hat{\beta}_{2SLS}$ is so complicated that it will be highly desirable if we can find an interpretation to help understand its structure. What is the nature of $\hat{\beta}_{2SLS}$? How to understand the structure of Ω?

Let us revisit the second stage regression model

$$Y_t = \hat{X}_t'\beta^o + \hat{u}_t,$$

where the regressor

$$\hat{X}_t = \hat{\gamma}' Z_t$$

is the sample projection of X_t on Z_t, and the disturbance $\hat{u}_t = Y_t - \hat{X}_t'\beta^o$. Note that $\hat{u}_t \neq \varepsilon_t$ since $\hat{X}_t \neq X_t$. Given $Y_t = X_t'\beta^o + \varepsilon_t$ from Assumption 7.2, we have

$$\begin{aligned}\hat{u}_t &= Y_t - \hat{X}_t'\beta^o \\ &= \varepsilon_t + (X_t - \hat{X}_t)'\beta^o \\ &= \varepsilon_t + \hat{v}_t'\beta^o,\end{aligned}$$

where ε_t is the true disturbance and $\hat{v}_t \equiv X_t - \hat{X}_t = X_t - \hat{\gamma}' Z_t$. Since $\hat{v}_t$ is the estimated residual from the first stage auxiliary OLS regression

$$\mathbf{X} = \mathbf{Z}\gamma + v,$$

we have the following FOC:

$$\mathbf{Z}'(\mathbf{X} - \hat{\mathbf{X}}) = \mathbf{Z}'\hat{v} = 0.$$

It follows that the 2SLS estimator

$$\begin{aligned}\hat{\beta}_{2SLS} &= (\hat{\mathbf{X}}'\hat{\mathbf{X}})^{-1}\hat{\mathbf{X}}'Y \\ &= (\hat{\mathbf{X}}'\hat{\mathbf{X}})^{-1}\hat{\mathbf{X}}'(\hat{\mathbf{X}}\beta^o + \tilde{\varepsilon}) \\ &= \beta^o + (\hat{\mathbf{X}}'\hat{\mathbf{X}})^{-1}\hat{\mathbf{X}}'(\varepsilon + \hat{v}\beta^o) \\ &= \beta^o + (\hat{\mathbf{X}}'\hat{\mathbf{X}})^{-1}\hat{\mathbf{X}}'\varepsilon\end{aligned}$$

because $\hat{\mathbf{X}}'\hat{v} = \hat{\gamma}'\mathbf{Z}'\hat{v} = 0$ (why?). Therefore, the asymptotic properties of $\hat{\beta}_{2SLS}$ are determined by

$$\begin{aligned}\hat{\beta}_{2SLS} - \beta^o &= (\hat{\mathbf{X}}'\hat{\mathbf{X}})^{-1}\hat{\mathbf{X}}'\varepsilon \\ &= \left(\frac{\hat{\mathbf{X}}'\hat{\mathbf{X}}}{n}\right)^{-1} \frac{\hat{\mathbf{X}}'\varepsilon}{n}.\end{aligned}$$

In other words, the estimated residual $\hat{v} = \mathbf{X} - \hat{\mathbf{X}}$ from the first stage regression has no impact on the statistical properties of $\hat{\beta}_{2SLS}$, although it is a component of $\hat{u}_t$. Thus, when analyzing the asymptotic properties of $\hat{\beta}_{2SLS}$, we can proceed as if we were estimating $Y = \hat{\mathbf{X}}\beta^o + \varepsilon$ by OLS.

Next, recall that we have

$$\begin{aligned}\hat{\mathbf{X}} &= \mathbf{Z}\hat{\gamma},\\ \hat{\gamma} &= (\mathbf{Z}'\mathbf{Z})^{-1}\mathbf{Z}'\mathbf{X}\\ &\xrightarrow{p} Q_{ZZ}^{-1}Q_{ZX} = \gamma.\end{aligned}$$

By WLLN, the sample projection $\hat{X}_t$ converges in probability to the population projection $\tilde{X}_t \equiv \gamma' Z_t$ as $n \to \infty$. That is, $\hat{X}_t$ will become arbitrarily close to $\tilde{X}_t$ as $n \to \infty$. In fact, the estimation error of $\hat{\gamma}$ in the first stage has no impact on the asymptotic properties of $\hat{\beta}_{2SLS}$.

Thus, for interpretational purpose, we can consider the following artificial regression model

$$Y_t = \tilde{X}_t'\beta^o + \varepsilon_t, \tag{7.13}$$

whose infeasible OLS estimator

$$\tilde{\beta} = (\tilde{X}'\tilde{X})^{-1}\tilde{X}'Y.$$

As we will show below, the asymptotic properties of $\hat{\beta}_{2SLS}$ are the same as those of the infeasible OLS estimator $\tilde{\beta}$. This helps a lot in understanding the asymptotic variance-covariance structure of $\sqrt{n}\hat{\beta}_{2SLS}$. It is important to emphasize that the equation in (7.13) is not derived from other equations. It is just a convenient way to understand the nature of $\hat{\beta}_{2SLS}$.

We now show that the asymptotic properties of $\hat{\beta}_{2SLS}$ are the same as those of $\tilde{\beta}$. For the asymptotic normality, observe that

$$\begin{aligned}\sqrt{n}(\tilde{\beta} - \beta^o) &= \hat{Q}_{\tilde{X}\tilde{X}}^{-1}\frac{\tilde{X}'\varepsilon}{\sqrt{n}}\\ &\xrightarrow{d} Q_{\tilde{X}\tilde{X}}^{-1} \cdot N(0, \tilde{V}) \sim N(0, Q_{\tilde{X}\tilde{X}}^{-1}\tilde{V}Q_{\tilde{X}\tilde{X}}^{-1})\end{aligned}$$

using the asymptotic theory in Chapters 5 and 6, where

$$\begin{aligned}Q_{\tilde{X}\tilde{X}} &\equiv E(\tilde{X}_t\tilde{X}_t'),\\ \tilde{V} &\equiv \text{avar}\left(n^{-1/2}\sum_{t=1}^{n}\tilde{X}_t\varepsilon_t\right).\end{aligned}$$

We first consider the case where $\{Z_t\varepsilon_t\}$ is an MDS with conditional homoskedasticity.

Case I: MDS with Conditional Homoskedasticity

Suppose $\{\tilde{X}_t\varepsilon_t\}$ is an MDS, and $E(\varepsilon_t^2|\tilde{X}_t) = \sigma^2$. Then we have

$$\begin{aligned}\tilde{V} &= E(\tilde{X}_t\tilde{X}_t'\varepsilon_t^2) \\ &= \sigma^2 Q_{\tilde{X}\tilde{X}}\end{aligned}$$

by the law of iterated expectations. It follows that

$$\sqrt{n}(\tilde{\beta} - \beta^o) \xrightarrow{d} N(0, \sigma^2 Q_{\tilde{X}\tilde{X}}^{-1}).$$

Because $\tilde{X}_t = \gamma' Z_t$, $\gamma = Q_{ZZ}^{-1}Q_{ZX}$, we have

$$\begin{aligned}Q_{\tilde{X}\tilde{X}} &= E(\tilde{X}_t\tilde{X}_t') \\ &= \gamma' E(Z_t Z_t')\gamma \\ &= \gamma' Q_{ZZ}\gamma \\ &= Q_{XZ}Q_{ZZ}^{-1}Q_{ZZ}Q_{ZZ}^{-1}Q_{ZX} \\ &= Q_{XZ}Q_{ZZ}^{-1}Q_{ZX}.\end{aligned}$$

Therefore,

$$\begin{aligned}\sigma^2 Q_{\tilde{X}\tilde{X}}^{-1} &= \sigma^2\left(Q_{XZ}Q_{ZZ}^{-1}Q_{ZX}\right)^{-1} \\ &= \Omega \equiv \text{avar}(\sqrt{n}\hat{\beta}_{2SLS}).\end{aligned}$$

This implies that the asymptotic distribution of $\tilde{\beta}$ is indeed the same as that of $\hat{\beta}_{2SLS}$ under the MDS disturbances with conditional homoskedasticity.

The asymptotic variance formula

$$\begin{aligned}\text{avar}(\sqrt{n}\hat{\beta}_{2SLS}) &= \sigma^2 Q_{\tilde{X}\tilde{X}}^{-1} \\ &= \sigma^2(\gamma' Q_{ZZ}\gamma)^{-1}\end{aligned}$$

indicates that the asymptotic variance of $\sqrt{n}\hat{\beta}_{2SLS}$ will be large if the correlation between Z_t and X_t, as measured by γ, is weak. Thus, more precise estimation of β^o will be obtained if one chooses the instrument vector Z_t such that Z_t is highly correlated with X_t.

Question: How to estimate Ω under the MDS disturbances with conditional homoskedasticity?

Consider the asymptotic variance estimator

$$\begin{aligned}\hat{\Omega} &= \hat{s}^2 \hat{Q}_{\hat{X}\hat{X}}^{-1} \\ &= \hat{s}^2 \left(\hat{Q}_{XZ}\hat{Q}_{ZZ}^{-1}\hat{Q}_{ZX}\right)^{-1}\end{aligned}$$

where $\hat{s}^2 = \hat{e}'\hat{e}/(n-K)$, $\hat{e} = Y - \mathbf{X}\hat{\beta}_{2SLS}$,

$$\hat{Q}_{\hat{X}\hat{X}} = n^{-1}\sum_{t=1}^{n} \hat{X}_t \hat{X}_t',$$

and $\hat{X}_t = \hat{\gamma}' Z_t$ is the sample projection of X_t on Z_t. Note that we have to use $\hat{X}_t$ rather than $\tilde{X}_t$ because $\tilde{X}_t = \gamma' Z_t$ is unknown.

It should be emphasized that $\hat{e}$ is not the estimated residual from the second stage regression (i.e., not from the regression of Y on $\hat{X}$). This implies that even under conditional homoskedasticity, the conventional t-statistic in the second stage regression does not converge to $N(0,1)$ in distribution, and $J \cdot \hat{F}$ does not converge to χ^2_J where $\hat{F}$ is the F-statistic in the second stage regression.

To show $\hat{\Omega} \xrightarrow{p} \Omega$, we shall show: (a) $\hat{Q}_{\hat{X}\hat{X}}^{-1} \xrightarrow{p} Q_{\tilde{X}\tilde{X}}^{-1}$, and (b) $\hat{s}^2 \xrightarrow{p} \sigma^2$ as $n \to \infty$.

We first show (a). There are two methods for proving this.

Method 1: We shall show $\hat{Q}_{\hat{X}\hat{X}}^{-1} \xrightarrow{p} Q_{\tilde{X}\tilde{X}}^{-1}$ as $n \to \infty$. Because $\hat{X}_t = \hat{\gamma}' Z_t$ and $\hat{\gamma} \xrightarrow{p} \gamma$, we have

$$\begin{aligned}\hat{Q}_{\hat{X}\hat{X}} &= n^{-1}\sum_{t=1}^{n} \hat{X}_t \hat{X}_t' \\ &= \hat{\gamma}'\left(n^{-1}\sum_{t=1}^{n} Z_t Z_t'\right)\hat{\gamma} \\ &= \hat{\gamma}'\hat{Q}_{ZZ}\hat{\gamma} \\ &\xrightarrow{p} \gamma' Q_{ZZ}\gamma \\ &= E[(\gamma' Z_t)(Z_t'\gamma)] \\ &= E(\tilde{X}_t \tilde{X}_t') \\ &= Q_{\tilde{X}\tilde{X}}.\end{aligned}$$

Method 2: We shall show $(\hat{Q}_{XZ}\hat{Q}_{ZZ}^{-1}\hat{Q}_{ZX})^{-1} \xrightarrow{p} (Q_{XZ}Q_{ZZ}^{-1}Q_{ZX})^{-1}$ as $n \to \infty$, which follows immediately from $\hat{Q}_{XZ} \xrightarrow{p} Q_{XZ}$ and $\hat{Q}_{ZZ} \xrightarrow{p} Q_{ZZ}$

by WLLN. This method is more straightforward but less intuitive than the first method.

Next, we shall show (b) $\hat{s}^2 \xrightarrow{p} \sigma^2$ as $n \to \infty$. We decompose

$$\begin{aligned}
\hat{s}^2 &= \frac{\hat{e}'\hat{e}}{n-K} \\
&= \frac{1}{n-K}\sum_{t=1}^{n}(Y_t - X_t'\hat{\beta}_{2SLS})^2 \\
&= \frac{1}{n-K}\sum_{t=1}^{n}[\varepsilon_t - X_t'(\hat{\beta}_{2SLS} - \beta^o)]^2 \\
&= \frac{1}{n-K}\sum_{t=1}^{n}\varepsilon_t^2 \\
&\quad + (\hat{\beta}_{2SLS} - \beta^o)'\frac{1}{n-K}\sum_{t=1}^{n}X_tX_t'(\hat{\beta}_{2SLS} - \beta^o) \\
&\quad - 2(\hat{\beta}_{2SLS} - \beta^o)'\frac{1}{n-K}\sum_{t=1}^{n}X_t\varepsilon_t \\
&\xrightarrow{p} \sigma^2 + 0 \cdot Q_{xx} \cdot 0 - 2 \cdot 0 \cdot E(X_t\varepsilon_t) \\
&= \sigma^2.
\end{aligned}$$

Note that although $E(X_t\varepsilon_t) \neq 0$, the last term still vanishes to zero in probability, because $\hat{\beta}_{2SLS} - \beta^o \xrightarrow{p} 0$.

We have proved the following theorem.

Theorem 7.3. ***[Consistency of $\hat{\Omega}$ Under MDS with Conditional Homoskedasticity]:*** *Under Assumptions 7.1 to 7.4, 7.6 and 7.7, we have as $n \to \infty$,*

$$\hat{\Omega} = \hat{s}^2\hat{Q}_{\hat{X}\hat{X}}^{-1} \xrightarrow{p} \Omega = \sigma^2 Q_{\tilde{X}\tilde{X}}^{-1} = \sigma^2\left(Q_{XZ}Q_{ZZ}^{-1}Q_{ZX}\right)^{-1}.$$

Question: What happens if we replace $\hat{s}^2$ by the sample residual variance estimator $s^2 = e'e/(n-K)$, where $e = Y - \hat{\mathbf{X}}\hat{\beta}_{2SLS}$ is the estimated residual from the second stage regression? Do we still have $s^2 \xrightarrow{p} \sigma^2$?

Case II: $\{Z_t\varepsilon_t\}$ Is an MDS with Conditional Heteroskedasticity

When there exists conditional heteroskedasticity but $\{Z_t\varepsilon_t\}$ is still an MDS, the infeasible OLS estimator $\tilde{\beta}$ in the artificial regression

$$Y = \tilde{X}\beta^o + \varepsilon$$

has the following asymptotic distribution:

$$\sqrt{n}(\tilde{\beta} - \beta^o) \xrightarrow{d} N(0, Q_{\tilde{X}\tilde{X}}^{-1} \tilde{V} Q_{\tilde{X}\tilde{X}}^{-1}),$$

where

$$\tilde{V} = E(\tilde{X}_t \tilde{X}_t' \varepsilon_t^2).$$

Given $\tilde{X}_t = \gamma' Z_t$, $\gamma = Q_{ZZ}^{-1} Q_{ZX}$, $Q_{\tilde{X}\tilde{X}} = \gamma' Q_{ZZ} \gamma$, and $\tilde{V} = \gamma' E(Z_t Z_t' \varepsilon_t^2)\gamma = \gamma' V \gamma$, where $V = E(Z_t Z_t' \varepsilon_t^2)$ under the MDS assumption with conditional heteroskedasticity, we have

$$\begin{aligned}
\text{avar}(\sqrt{n}\tilde{\beta}) &= Q_{\tilde{X}\tilde{X}}^{-1} \tilde{V} Q_{\tilde{X}\tilde{X}}^{-1} \\
&= [E(\tilde{X}_t \tilde{X}_t')]^{-1} E\left(\tilde{X}_t \tilde{X}_t' \varepsilon_t^2\right) [E(\tilde{X}_t \tilde{X}_t')]^{-1} \\
&= [\gamma' E(Z_t Z_t')\gamma]^{-1} \gamma' E(Z_t Z_t' \varepsilon_t^2)\gamma [\gamma' E(Z_t Z_t')\gamma]^{-1} \\
&= \left(Q_{XZ} Q_{ZZ}^{-1} Q_{ZX}\right)^{-1} Q_{XZ} Q_{ZZ}^{-1} V Q_{ZZ}^{-1} Q_{ZX} (Q_{XZ} Q_{ZZ}^{-1} Q_{ZX})^{-1} \\
&= \Omega \equiv \text{ avar}(\sqrt{n}\hat{\beta}_{2SLS}).
\end{aligned}$$

This implies that the asymptotic distribution of the infeasible OLS estimator $\tilde{\beta}$ is the same as that of $\hat{\beta}_{2SLS}$ under MDS with conditional heteroskedasticity. Therefore, the estimator for Ω is

$$\hat{\Omega} = \hat{Q}_{\hat{X}\hat{X}}^{-1} \hat{V}_{\hat{X}\hat{X}} \hat{Q}_{\hat{X}\hat{X}}^{-1},$$

where

$$\begin{aligned}
\hat{V}_{\hat{X}\hat{X}} &= n^{-1} \sum_{t=1}^{n} \hat{X}_t \hat{X}_t' \hat{e}_t^2 \\
&= \hat{\gamma}' \left(n^{-1} \sum_{t=1}^{n} Z_t Z_t' \hat{e}_t^2 \right) \hat{\gamma},
\end{aligned}$$

where $\hat{\gamma} = (\mathbf{Z}'\mathbf{Z})^{-1}\mathbf{Z}'\mathbf{X} = \hat{Q}_{ZZ}^{-1} \hat{Q}_{ZX}$ and $\hat{e}_t = Y_t - X_t' \hat{\beta}_{2SLS}$. This is a White's (1980) heteroskedasticity-consistent variance-covariance matrix estimator for $\hat{\beta}_{2SLS}$.

Now, put

$$\hat{V} \equiv n^{-1} \sum_{t=1}^{n} Z_t Z_t' \hat{e}_t^2.$$

Then

$$\hat{\Omega} = \left(\hat{Q}_{XZ} \hat{Q}_{ZZ}^{-1} \hat{Q}_{ZX}\right)^{-1} \hat{Q}_{XZ} \hat{Q}_{ZZ}^{-1} \hat{V} \hat{Q}_{ZZ}^{-1} \hat{Q}_{ZX} \left(\hat{Q}_{XZ} \hat{Q}_{ZZ}^{-1} \hat{Q}_{ZX}\right)^{-1},$$

where (please check it!)

$$\begin{aligned}\hat{V} &= n^{-1}\sum_{t=1}^{n} Z_t Z_t' \hat{e}_t^2 \\ &\xrightarrow{p} V = E(Z_t Z_t' \varepsilon_t^2)\end{aligned}$$

under suitable regularity conditions.

Question: How to show $\hat{\Omega} \xrightarrow{p} \Omega$ as $n \to \infty$ under MDS with conditional heteroskedasticity?

We first impose a moment condition:

Assumption 7.8. (a) $E(Z_{jt}^4) \leq C$ for some constant $C < \infty$ and for all $0 \leq j \leq l$; and (b) $E(\varepsilon_t^4) < \infty$.

Again, there are two methods to show $\hat{\Omega} \xrightarrow{p} \Omega$ here.

Method 1: We shall show $\hat{Q}_{\hat{X}\hat{X}} \xrightarrow{p} Q_{\tilde{X}\tilde{X}}$ and $\hat{V}_{\hat{X}\hat{X}} \xrightarrow{p} \tilde{V}$. The fact that $\hat{Q}_{\hat{X}\hat{X}} \xrightarrow{p} Q_{\tilde{X}\tilde{X}}$ has been shown earlier in the case of conditional homoskedasticity. To show $\hat{V}_{\hat{X}\hat{X}} \xrightarrow{p} \tilde{V}$, we write

$$\begin{aligned}\hat{V}_{\hat{X}\hat{X}} &= n^{-1}\sum_{t=1}^{n} \hat{X}_t \hat{X}_t \hat{e}_t^2 \\ &= \hat{\gamma}' \left(n^{-1}\sum_{t=1}^{n} Z_t Z_t' \hat{e}_t^2 \right) \hat{\gamma} \\ &= \hat{\gamma}' \hat{V} \hat{\gamma}.\end{aligned}$$

Because $\hat{\gamma} \xrightarrow{p} \gamma$, and following the consistency proof for $n^{-1}\sum_{t=1}^{n} X_t X_t' e_t^2$ in Chapter 4, we can show that

$$\hat{V} = n^{-1}\sum_{t=1}^{n} Z_t Z_t' \hat{e}_t^2 \xrightarrow{p} E(Z_t Z_t' \varepsilon_t^2) = V,$$

under Assumption 7.8. (Please verify it!)

It follows that

$$\begin{aligned}\hat{V}_{\hat{X}\hat{X}} &\xrightarrow{p} \gamma' E(Z_t Z_t' \varepsilon_t^2) \gamma \\ &= E(\tilde{X}_t \tilde{X}_t' \varepsilon_t^2) \\ &= \tilde{V}.\end{aligned}$$

This and $\hat{Q}_{\hat{X}\hat{X}} \xrightarrow{p} Q_{\tilde{X}\tilde{X}}$ imply $\hat{\Omega} \xrightarrow{p} \Omega$.

Method 2: Given that

$$\hat{\Omega} = \left(\hat{Q}_{XZ}\hat{Q}_{ZZ}^{-1}\hat{Q}_{ZX}\right)^{-1}\hat{Q}_{XZ}\hat{Q}_{ZZ}^{-1}\hat{V}\hat{Q}_{ZX}^{-1}\hat{Q}_{ZX}\left(\hat{Q}_{XZ}\hat{Q}_{ZZ}^{-1}\hat{Q}_{ZX}\right)^{-1},$$

it suffices to show $\hat{Q}_{XZ} \xrightarrow{p} Q_{XZ}, \hat{Q}_{ZZ} \xrightarrow{p} Q_{ZZ}$ and $\hat{V} \xrightarrow{p} V$. The first two results immediately follow by WLLN. The last result follows by using a similar reasoning of the consistency proof for $n^{-1}\sum_{t=1}^{n} X_t X_t' e_t^2$ in Chapter 4 or 5.

We now summarize the result derived above.

Theorem 7.4. ***[Consistency of $\hat{\Omega}$ Under MDS with Conditional Heteroskedasticity]:*** *Under Assumptions 7.1 to 7.4, 7.6 and 7.8, we have as $n \to \infty$,*

$$\begin{aligned}\hat{\Omega} &= \hat{Q}_{\hat{X}\hat{X}}^{-1}\hat{V}_{\hat{X}\hat{X}}\hat{Q}_{\hat{X}\hat{X}}^{-1}\\ &\xrightarrow{p} \Omega = Q_{\tilde{X}\tilde{X}}^{-1}\tilde{V}Q_{\tilde{X}\tilde{X}}^{-1}\\ &= (Q_{XZ}Q_{ZZ}^{-1}Q_{ZX})^{-1}Q_{XZ}Q_{ZZ}^{-1}VQ_{ZZ}^{-1}Q_{ZX}(Q_{XZ}Q_{ZZ}^{-1}Q_{ZX})^{-1},\end{aligned}$$

where $\tilde{V} = E(\tilde{X}_t\tilde{X}_t'\varepsilon_t^2)$ and $V = E(Z_t Z_t'\varepsilon_t^2)$.

Case III: $\{Z_t\varepsilon_t\}$ Is an Ergodic Stationary Non-MDS

Finally, we consider a general case where $\{Z_t\varepsilon_t\}$ is not an MDS, which may arise as in the examples discussed in Chapter 6.

In this case, we have $\sqrt{n}(\hat{\beta}_{2SLS} - \beta^o) \xrightarrow{d} N(0, \Omega)$ as $n \to \infty$, where

$$\begin{aligned}\Omega &= Q_{\tilde{X}\tilde{X}}^{-1}\tilde{V}Q_{\tilde{X}\tilde{X}}^{-1}\\ &= (Q_{XZ}Q_{ZZ}^{-1}Q_{ZX})^{-1}Q_{XZ}Q_{ZZ}^{-1}VQ_{ZZ}^{-1}Q_{ZX}(Q_{XZ}Q_{ZZ}^{-1}Q_{ZX})^{-1},\end{aligned}$$

with

$$\tilde{V} = \sum_{j=-\infty}^{\infty}\tilde{\Gamma}(j), \qquad \tilde{\Gamma}(j) = \text{cov}(\tilde{X}_t\varepsilon_t, \tilde{X}_{t-j}\varepsilon_{t-j}),$$

$$V = \sum_{j=-\infty}^{\infty}\Gamma(j), \qquad \Gamma(j) = \text{cov}(Z_t\varepsilon_t, Z_{t-j}\varepsilon_{t-j}).$$

On the other hand, we have

$$\begin{aligned}\text{avar}(\sqrt{n}\tilde{\beta}) &= Q_{\tilde{X}\tilde{X}}^{-1}V_{\tilde{X}\tilde{X}}Q_{\tilde{X}\tilde{X}}^{-1}\\ &= (\gamma' Q_{XX}\gamma)^{-1}\gamma' V\gamma(\gamma' Q_{XX}\gamma)^{-1}\\ &= \Omega \equiv \text{avar}(\sqrt{n}\hat{\beta}_{2SLS}).\end{aligned}$$

Thus, the asymptotic variance of $\sqrt{n}\hat{\beta}_{2sls}$ is the same as that of $\sqrt{n}\tilde{\beta}$ under this general case.

To estimate Ω, we need to use a long-run variance-covariance matrix estimator for V or $\tilde{V}$. We directly assume that we have a consistent estimator $\hat{V}$ for V.

Assumption 7.9. $\hat{V} \xrightarrow{p} V \equiv \sum_{j=-\infty}^{\infty} \Gamma(j)$, where $\Gamma(j) = \text{cov}(Z_t\varepsilon_t, Z_{t-j}\varepsilon_{t-j})$ for $j \geq 0$, and $\Gamma(j) = \Gamma(-j)'$ for $j < 0$.

Since $\tilde{\Gamma}(j) = \gamma'\Gamma(j)\gamma$, a consistent estimator for $\tilde{V} = \sum_{j=-\infty}^{\infty} \tilde{\Gamma}(j)$ can be given by

$$\hat{\gamma}'\hat{V}\hat{\gamma} \xrightarrow{p} \tilde{V} \text{ as } n \to \infty.$$

Theorem 7.5. ***[Consistency of $\hat{\Omega}$ Under Non-MDS]:*** *Under Assumptions 7.1 to 7.4, and 7.9, we have as $n \to \infty$,*

$$\begin{aligned}\hat{\Omega} &= \hat{Q}_{\hat{X}\hat{X}}^{-1}\hat{V}_{\hat{X}\hat{X}}\hat{Q}_{\hat{X}\hat{X}}^{-1} \\ &= (\hat{Q}_{XZ}\hat{Q}_{ZZ}^{-1}\hat{Q}_{ZX})^{-1}\hat{Q}_{XZ}\hat{Q}_{ZZ}^{-1}\hat{V}\hat{Q}_{ZZ}^{-1}\hat{Q}_{ZX}(\hat{Q}_{XZ}\hat{Q}_{ZZ}^{-1}\hat{Q}_{ZX})^{-1} \\ &\xrightarrow{p} \Omega = Q_{\tilde{X}\tilde{X}}^{-1}\tilde{V}Q_{\tilde{X}\tilde{X}}^{-1},\end{aligned}$$

where $\hat{V}_{\hat{X}\hat{X}} = \hat{\gamma}\hat{V}\hat{\gamma}'$ and

$$\Omega = (Q_{XZ}Q_{ZZ}^{-1}Q_{ZX})^{-1}Q_{XZ}Q_{ZZ}^{-1}VQ_{ZZ}^{-1}Q_{ZX}(Q_{XZ}Q_{ZZ}^{-1}Q_{ZX})^{-1}.$$

With a consistent estimator of Ω, we can develop various confidence interval estimators and various tests for the null hypothesis $\mathbf{H}_0 : R\beta^o = r$.

We will consider the latter now.

7.7 Hypothesis Testing

Now, consider the null hypothesis of interest

$$\mathbf{H}_0 : R\beta^o = r,$$

where R is a $J \times K$ nonstochastic matrix with full rank, r is a $J \times 1$ nonstochastic vector, and $J \leq K$. The test statistics will differ depending on whether $\{Z_t\varepsilon_t\}$ is an MDS, and whether $\{\varepsilon_t\}$ is conditionally homoskedastic when $\{Z_t\varepsilon_t\}$ is an MDS. For sake of space, we do not present the results on t-type test statistics here when $J = 1$.

Case I: $\{Z_t\varepsilon_t\}$ Is an MDS with Conditional Homoskedasticity

Theorem 7.6. ***[Wald Test Under Conditional Homoskedasticity]:*** *Put $\hat{e} \equiv Y - \mathbf{X}\hat{\beta}_{2SLS}$. Then under Assumptions 7.1 to 7.4, 7.6 and 7.7, the Wald test statistic*

$$W = \frac{n(R\hat{\beta}_{2SLS} - r)'[R(\hat{\mathbf{X}}'\hat{\mathbf{X}})^{-1}R']^{-1}(R\hat{\beta}_{2SLS} - r)}{\hat{e}'\hat{e}/(n-K)} \xrightarrow{d} \chi^2_J$$

as $n \to \infty$, under $\mathbf{H}_0$.

Proof: The result follows immediately from the asymptotic normality theorem (Corollary 7.2) for $\sqrt{n}(\hat{\beta}_{2SLS} - \beta^o)$, $\mathbf{H}_0$ (which implies $\sqrt{n}(R\hat{\beta}_{2SLS} - r) = R\sqrt{n}(\hat{\beta}_{2SLS} - \beta^o)$), the consistent asymptotic variance estimation theorem (Theorem 7.5), and Slutsky's theorem.

It is important to note that W/J is not the F-statistic from the second stage regression, because $\hat{e}$ is not the estimated residual from the second stage regression.

Therefore, $W \neq J \cdot F$, where

$$F = \frac{(e_r'e_r - e_u'e_u)/J}{e_u'e_u/(n-K)},$$

where e_r and e_u are estimated residuals from the restricted and unrestricted regression models in the second stage regression respectively.

Case II: $\{Z_t\varepsilon_t\}$ Is an Ergodic Stationary MDS with Conditional Heteroskedasticity

Theorem 7.7. ***[Robust Wald Test Under Conditional Heteroskedasticity]:*** *Under Assumptions 7.1 to 7.4, 7.6 and 7.8, the Wald test statistic*

$$\begin{aligned} W_r &\equiv n(R\hat{\beta}_{2SLS} - r)' \left(R\hat{Q}^{-1}_{\hat{X}\hat{X}}\hat{V}_{\hat{X}\hat{X}}\hat{Q}^{-1}_{\hat{X}\hat{X}}R'\right)^{-1} (R\hat{\beta}_{2SLS} - r) \\ &\xrightarrow{d} \chi^2_J \end{aligned}$$

as $n \to \infty$ under $\mathbf{H}_0$, where $\hat{V}_{\hat{X}\hat{X}} = n^{-1}\sum_{t=1}^n \hat{X}_t\hat{X}_t'\hat{e}_t^2$ and $\hat{e}_t = Y_t - X_t'\hat{\beta}_{2SLS}$.

Question: Suppose there exists conditional homoskedasticity but we use W_r. Is W_r an asymptotically valid procedure in this case?

The answer is yes. The robust Wald test statistic W_r is asymptotically valid and so applicable under conditional homoskedasticity. However, the finite sample performance of W_r will be generally less satisfactory than the Wald test statistic W in Theorem 7.6, because the latter makes use of the information of conditional homoskedasticity. In particular, W_r is expected to have a larger discounted Type I error in small and finite samples.

Case III: $\{Z_t\varepsilon_t\}$ Is an Ergodic Stationary Non-MDS

When $\{Z_t\varepsilon_t\}$ is a non-MDS, we can still construct a Wald test which is robust to conditional heteroskedasticity and autocorrelation of unknown form, as is stated below.

Theorem 7.8. ***[Robust Wald Test Under Conditional Heteroskedasticity and Autocorrelation]:*** *Under Assumptions 7.1 to 7.5 and 7.9, the robust Wald test statistic*

$$W_r = n(R\hat{\beta}_{2SLS} - r)' \left(R\hat{Q}_{\hat{X}\hat{X}}^{-1}\hat{V}_{\hat{X}\hat{X}}\hat{Q}_{\hat{X}\hat{X}}^{-1}R'\right)^{-1}(R\hat{\beta}_{2SLS} - r)$$
$$\xrightarrow{d} \chi_J^2$$

under $\mathbf{H}_0$, *where* $\hat{V}_{\hat{X}\hat{X}} = \hat{\gamma}'\hat{V}\hat{\gamma}, \hat{\gamma} = (\mathbf{Z}'\mathbf{Z})^{-1}\mathbf{Z}'\mathbf{X}$ *and* $\hat{V}$ *is a consistent long-run variance-covariance matrix estimator for* $V = \sum_{j=-\infty}^{\infty}\Gamma(j)$ *with* $\Gamma(j) = cov(Z_t\varepsilon_t, Z_{t-j}\varepsilon_{t-j})$ *for* $j \geq 0$ *and* $\Gamma(j) = \Gamma(-j)'$ *for* $j < 0$.

7.8 Hausman's Test

When there exists endogeneity so that $E(X_t\varepsilon_t) \neq 0$, the OLS estimator $\hat{\beta}$ is inconsistent for β^o. Instead, the 2SLS estimator $\hat{\beta}_{2SLS}$ should be used, which involves the choice of the instrument vector Z_t that in turn affects the efficiency of $\hat{\beta}_{2SLS}$. In practice, it is not uncommon that practitioners are not sure whether there exists endogeneity. In this section, we introduce Hausman's (1978) test for endogeneity. The null hypothesis of interest is:

$$\mathbf{H}_0 : E(\varepsilon_t|X_t) = 0.$$

If this null hypothesis is rejected, one has to use the 2SLS estimator $\hat{\beta}_{2SLS}$ provided that one can find a set of instruments for Z_t that satisfies Assumption 7.4.

For simplicity, we impose the following conditions.

Assumption 7.10. (a) $\{(X_t', Z_t')'\varepsilon_t\}$ is an MDS; and (b) $E(\varepsilon_t^2|X_t, Z_t) = \sigma^2$.

Assumptions 7.10 is made for simplicity. They could be relaxed to be a non-MDS process with conditional heteroskedasticity but Hausman's (1978) test statistic to be introduced below should be generalized.

Question: How to test the conditional homoskedasticity assumption that $E(\varepsilon_t^2|X_t, Z_t) = \sigma^2$?

Put $\hat{e}_t = Y_t - X_t'\hat{\beta}_{2SLS}$. Like White's (1980) test for conditional heteroskedasticity in Section 4.7 of Chapter 4, we can run an auxiliary regression of $\hat{e}_t^2$ on vech(U_t'), where $U_t = (X_t', Z_t')'$, a $(K+l) \times 1$ vector. Under the condition that $E(\varepsilon_t^4|X_t, Z_t) = \mu_4$ is a constant, we have $nR^2 \xrightarrow{d} \chi_J^2$ under the null hypothesis of conditional homoskedasticity, where $J = \frac{1}{2}(K+l)(K+l+1) - 1$. Note that X_t and Z_t may contain some common variables. In this case, some redundant variables in vech$(U_t U_t')$ should be eliminated so as to avoid multicollinearity. As a result, the number J of degrees of freedom of the asymptotic Chi-square distribution has to be adjusted.

The basic idea of Hausman's test is under $\mathbf{H}_0 : E(\varepsilon_t|X_t) = 0$, both the OLS estimator $\hat{\beta} = (X'X)^{-1}X'Y$ and the 2SLS estimator $\hat{\beta}_{2SLS}$ are consistent for β^o. They converge to the same limit β^o in probability but it can be shown that $\hat{\beta}$ is an asymptotically efficient estimator while $\hat{\beta}_{2SLS}$ is not. Under the alternatives to $\mathbf{H}_0$, $\hat{\beta}_{2SLS}$ remains to be consistent for β^o but $\hat{\beta}$ is generally not consistent for β^o. Hausman (1978) considers a test for $\mathbf{H}_0$ based on the difference between the two estimators

$$\hat{\beta}_{2SLS} - \hat{\beta},$$

which converges in probability to zero under $\mathbf{H}_0$ but generally to a nonzero constant under the alternatives to $\mathbf{H}_0$, giving the test its power against $\mathbf{H}_0$ when the sample size n is sufficiently large. How large the difference $\hat{\beta}_{2SLS} - \hat{\beta}$ should be in order to be considered as significantly large will be determined by the sampling distribution of $\sqrt{n}(\hat{\beta}_{2SLS} - \hat{\beta})$.

To construct Hausman's (1978) test statistic, we need to derive the asymptotic distribution of $\sqrt{n}(\hat{\beta}_{2SLS} - \hat{\beta})$. For this purpose, we first state a lemma.

Lemma 7.1. *Suppose* $\hat{A} \xrightarrow{p} A$ *and* $\hat{B} = O_P(1)$. *Then* $(\hat{A} - A)\hat{B} \xrightarrow{p} 0$.

We first consider the OLS estimator $\hat{\beta}$. Note that

$$\sqrt{n}(\hat{\beta} - \beta^o) = \hat{Q}_{XX}^{-1} n^{-1/2} \sum_{t=1}^{n} X_t \varepsilon_t$$

where $\hat{Q}_{XX}^{-1} \xrightarrow{p} Q_{XX}^{-1}$ and

$$n^{-1/2} \sum_{t=1}^{n} X_t \varepsilon_t \xrightarrow{d} N(0, \sigma^2 Q_{XX})$$

as $n \to \infty$ by CLT for an ergodic stationary MDS (Theorem 5.2). It follows that $n^{-1/2} \sum_{t=1}^{n} X_t \varepsilon_t = O_P(1)$, and by Lemma 7.1, we have

$$\sqrt{n}(\hat{\beta} - \beta^o) = Q_{XX}^{-1} n^{-1/2} \sum_{t=1}^{n} X_t \varepsilon_t + o_P(1).$$

Similarly, we can obtain

$$\begin{aligned} \sqrt{n}(\hat{\beta}_{2SLS} - \beta^o) &= \hat{A} n^{-1/2} \sum_{t=1}^{n} Z_t \varepsilon_t \\ &= A n^{-1/2} \sum_{t=1}^{n} Z_t \varepsilon_t + o_P(1), \end{aligned}$$

where

$$\begin{aligned} \hat{A} &= (\hat{Q}_{XZ} \hat{Q}_{ZZ}^{-1} \hat{Q}_{ZX})^{-1} \hat{Q}_{XZ} \hat{Q}_{ZZ}^{-1} \\ &\xrightarrow{p} A \equiv (Q_{XZ} Q_{ZZ}^{-1} Q_{ZX})^{-1} Q_{XZ} Q_{ZZ}^{-1} \end{aligned}$$

and $n^{-1/2} \sum_{t=1}^{n} Z_t \varepsilon_t \xrightarrow{d} N(0, \sigma^2 Q_{ZZ})$ as $n \to \infty$ (see Corollary 7.2). It follows by CLT for an ergodic stationary MDS and Assumption 7.10 that as $n \to \infty$,

$$\begin{aligned} \sqrt{n}(\hat{\beta}_{2SLS} - \hat{\beta}) &= n^{-1/2} \sum_{t=1}^{n} \left[(Q_{XZ} Q_{ZZ}^{-1} Q_{ZX})^{-1} Q_{XZ} Q_{ZZ}^{-1} Z_t - Q_{XX}^{-1} X_t \right] \varepsilon_t \\ &\quad + o_P(1) \\ &\xrightarrow{d} N(0, \sigma^2 (Q_{XZ} Q_{ZZ}^{-1} Q_{ZX})^{-1} - \sigma^2 Q_{XX}^{-1}). \end{aligned}$$

Interestingly, the asymptotic variance of $\sqrt{n}(\hat{\beta}_{2SLS} - \hat{\beta})$ is equal to the difference between $\text{avar}(\sqrt{n}\hat{\beta}_{2SLS}) = \sigma^2 (Q_{XZ} Q_{ZZ}^{-1} Q_{ZX})^{-1}$ and $\text{avar}(\sqrt{n}\hat{\beta}) = \sigma^2 Q_{XX}^{-1}$. This follows because the asymptotic covariance between $\sqrt{n}\hat{\beta}_{2SLS}$

and $\sqrt{n}\hat{\beta}$ is equal to $\text{avar}(\sqrt{n}\hat{\beta})$ when $\hat{\beta}$ is an asymptotically efficient estimator under $\mathbf{H}_0$. Hausman (1978) provides an intuition. We note that such a result no longer holds when $\{Z_t\varepsilon_t\}$ is not an MDS and/or $E(\varepsilon_t^2|Z_t) \neq \sigma^2$.

We can now construct a quadratic form

$$\begin{aligned} H &= \frac{n(\hat{\beta}_{2SLS} - \hat{\beta})' \left[(\hat{Q}_{XZ}\hat{Q}_{ZZ}^{-1}\hat{Q}_{ZX})^{-1} - \hat{Q}_{XX}^{-1}\right]^{-1} (\hat{\beta}_{2SLS} - \hat{\beta})}{s^2} \\ &\xrightarrow{d} \chi^2_K \end{aligned}$$

where the convergence in distribution occurs as $n \to \infty$ under the null hypothesis $\mathbf{H}_0$, and $s^2 = e'e/n$ is the sample residual variance estimator based on the estimated OLS residual $e = Y - X\hat{\beta}$. This is called Hausman's (1978) test statistic.

Question: Can we replace the sample residual variance estimator s^2 by $\hat{s}^2 = \hat{e}'\hat{e}/n$, where $\hat{e} = Y - X\hat{\beta}_{2SLS}$? And if so, which estimator, s^2 or $\hat{s}^2$, will give a better power in finite samples?

Theorem 7.9. ***[Hausman's Test for Endogeneity]:*** *Suppose Assumptions 7.1 to 7.4, 7.10 and* $\mathbf{H}_0$ *hold, and* $Q_{XX} - Q_{XZ}Q_{ZZ}^{-1}Q_{ZX}$ *is strictly positive definite. Then as* $n \to \infty$,

$$H \xrightarrow{d} \chi^2_K.$$

We note that in Theorem 7.9,

$$\begin{aligned} \text{avar}[\sqrt{n}(\hat{\beta}_{2SLS} - \hat{\beta})] &= \sigma^2(Q_{XZ}Q_{ZZ}^{-1}Q_{ZX})^{-1} - \sigma^2 Q_{XX}^{-1} \\ &= \text{avar}(\sqrt{n}\hat{\beta}_{2SLS}) - \text{avar}(\sqrt{n}\hat{\beta}). \end{aligned}$$

This simple asymptotic variance-covariance matrix structure is made possible under Assumption 7.10. Suppose there exists conditional heteroskedasticity (i.e., $E(\varepsilon_t^2|X_t, Z_t) \neq \sigma^2$). Then we no longer have the above simple variance-covariance matrix structure for $\text{avar}[\sqrt{n}(\hat{\beta} - \hat{\beta}_{2SLS})]$. However, we can construct a robust Hausman test statistic which will follow an asymptotic χ^2_K distribution under $\mathbf{H}_0$.

Question: How to modify Hausman's test statistic so that it remains asymptotically χ^2_K when there exists conditional heteroskedasticity (i.e., $E(\varepsilon_t^2|X_t, Z_t) \neq \sigma^2$) but $\{(X_t', Z_t')'\varepsilon_t\}$ is still an MDS?

The variance-covariance matrix $(Q_{XZ}Q_{ZZ}^{-1}Q_{ZX})^{-1} - Q_{XX}^{-1}$ may become singular when its rank $J < K$. In this case, we have to modify Hausman's test statistic by using the generalized inverse of the variance-covariance matrix estimator:

$$H = \frac{n(\hat{\beta}_{2SLS} - \hat{\beta})' \left[(\hat{Q}_{XZ}\hat{Q}_{ZZ}^{-1}\hat{Q}_{ZX})^{-1} - \hat{Q}_{XX}^{-1}\right]^{-} (\hat{\beta}_{2SLS} - \hat{\beta})}{s^2}.$$

Note that now $H \xrightarrow{d} \chi_J^2$ under $\mathbf{H}_0$ where $J < K$.

Question: What is the generalized inverse A^- of matrix A?

In fact, Hausman's (1978) test is a general approach to testing model specification, not merely whether endogeneity exists. For example, it can be used to test whether a fixed effect panel data regression model or a random effect panel data regression model should be used. In Hausman (1978), two estimators are compared, one of which is asymptotically efficient under the null hypothesis but inconsistent under the alternative, and the other of which is asymptotically inefficient but consistent under the alternative hypothesis. This approach was extended by White (1981) to compare any two different estimators either of which need not be asymptotically most efficient. The methods of Hausman and White were further generalized by Newey (1985), Tauchen (1985) and White (1990) to construct moment-based tests or m-tests for model specification.

By construction, Hausman's (1978) test is designed to test the null hypothesis $\mathbf{H}_0 : E(\varepsilon_t|X_t) = 0$. When $E(\varepsilon_t|X_t) \neq 0$ but $E(X_t\varepsilon_t) = 0$, both $\hat{\beta}_{2SLS}$ and $\hat{\beta}$ still converge to the same probability limit, rendering Hausman's test to have no asymptotic unit power to reject $\mathbf{H}_0 : E(\varepsilon_t|X_t) = 0$. When a test cannot reject all alternatives to a null hypothesis, we say that the test is not a consistent test. Using a nonparametric series regression, Hong and White (1995) propose a consistent generalized F-test for the null hypothesis $\mathbf{H}_0 : E(\varepsilon_t|X_t) = 0$ for a parametric regression model. See also Fan and Li (2006) and Hong and Lee (2013) for consistent model specification tests.

Hausman's test is used to check whether $E(\varepsilon_t|X_t) = 0$. Suppose this condition fails. Then one has to choose an instrument vector Z_t that satisfies Assumption 7.4. When we choose a set of variables for Z_t, how can we check the validity of Z_t as instruments? In particular, how to check whether $E(\varepsilon_t|Z_t) = 0$? For this purpose, we will consider Sargan's (1958) test or the so-called overidentification test to be introduced in Chapter 8.

7.9 Conclusion

In this chapter, we discuss the possibilities that the orthogonality condition of $E(\varepsilon_t|X_t) = 0$ may fail in practice, which will render inconsistent the OLS estimator for the true model parameter. With the use of IV, we introduce a consistent 2SLS estimator, which is one of the most popular methods to identify economic causal relationships using non-experimental observations. We investigate the statistical properties of the 2SLS estimator and provide interpretations that can enhance deeper understanding of the nature of the 2SLS estimator. We discuss how to construct consistent estimators for the asymptotic variance-covariance matrix of the 2SLS estimator under various scenarios, including MDS with conditional homoskedasticity, MDS with conditional heteroskedasticity, and non-MDS possibly with conditional heteroskedasticity. For the latter, consistent estimation for a long-run variance-covariance matrix is needed. With these consistent asymptotic variance estimators, various hypothesis test procedures are proposed. It is important to emphasize that the conventional t-test and F-test statistics cannot be used even for large samples. We also introduce Hausman's (1978) test to check whether $E(\varepsilon_t|X_t) = 0$ holds.

In fact, the 2SLS procedure is one of several approaches to consistent estimation of model parameters when the condition of $E(\varepsilon_t|X_t) = 0$ fails. There are alternative estimation procedures that also yield consistent estimators. For example, suppose the correlation between X_t and ε_t is caused by the omitted variables problem, namely

$$\varepsilon_t = g(W_t) + u_t,$$

when $E(u_t|X_t, W_t) = 0$ and W_t is a set of omitted variables which are correlated with X_t. This delivers a partially linear regression model

$$Y_t = X_t'\beta^o + g(W_t) + u_t.$$

Because $E(Y_t|W_t) = E(X_t|W_t)'\beta^o + g(W_t)$, we obtain

$$Y_t - E(Y_t|W_t) = [X_t - E(X_t|W_t)]'\beta^o + u_t$$

or

$$Y_t^* = X_t^{*\prime}\beta^o + u_t,$$

where $Y_t^* = Y_t - E(Y_t|W_t)$ and $X_t^* = X_t - E(X_t|W_t)$. Because $E(X_t^* u_t) = 0$, the OLS estimator $\tilde{\beta}^*$ of regressing Y_t^* on X_t^* would be consistent for β^o. However, (Y_t^*, X_t^*) are not observable, so $\tilde{\beta}^*$ is infeasible. Nevertheless, one can first estimate $E(Y_t|W_t)$ and $E(X_t|W_t)$ nonparametrically, and then obtain a feasible OLS estimator which will be consistent for the true model parameter (e.g., Robinson 1988). Specifically, let $\hat{m}_Y(W_t)$ and $\hat{m}_X(W_t)$ be consistent nonparametric estimators for $E(Y_t|W_t)$ and $E(X_t|W_t)$ respectively. Then we can obtain an adaptive feasible OLS estimator

$$\tilde{\beta}_a^* = \left(\sum_{t=1}^n \hat{X}_t^* \hat{X}_t^{*\prime}\right)^{-1} \sum_{t=1}^n \hat{X}_t^* \hat{Y}_t^*,$$

where $\hat{X}_t^* = X_t - \hat{m}_X(W_t)$ and $\hat{Y}_t^* = Y_t - \hat{m}_Y(W_t)$. It can be shown that as $n \to \infty$, $\tilde{\beta}_a^* \xrightarrow{p} \beta^o$ and

$$\sqrt{n}(\tilde{\beta}_a^* - \beta^o) \xrightarrow{d} N(0, Q^{*-1}V^*Q^{*-1}),$$

where $Q^* = E(X_t^* X_t^{*\prime})$ and $V^* = \text{avar}(n^{-1/2}\sum_{t=1}^n X_t^* u_t)$. The first stage nonparametric estimation has no impact on the asymptotic properties of the adaptive feasible OLS estimator $\tilde{\beta}_a$.

Another method to consistently estimate the true model parameter value is to make use of panel data. A panel data is a collection of observations for a total of n cross-sectional units and each of these units has T time series observations over the same time period. This is called a balanced panel data. In contrast, an unbalanced panel data is a collection of observations for a total of n cross-sectional units and each unit may have different lengths of time series observations but with some common overlapping time periods.

With a balanced panel data, we have

$$\begin{aligned} Y_{it} &= X_{it}'\beta^o + \varepsilon_{it} \\ &= X_{it}'\beta^o + \alpha_i + u_{it}, \end{aligned}$$

where α_i is called an individual-specific effect and u_{it} is called an idiosyncratic disturbance such that $E(u_{it}|X_{it}, \alpha_i) = 0$. When α_i is correlated with X_{it}, which may be caused by omitted variables which do not change over time, the panel data model is called a fixed effect panel data model. When α_i is uncorrelated with X_{it}, the panel data model is called a random effect panel data model. Here, we consider a fixed effect panel data model with strictly exogenous variables X_{it}. Because ε_{it} is correlated with X_{it}, the OLS estimator of regressing Y_{it} on X_{it} is not consistent for β^o. However, one can consider the demeaned model

$$Y_{it} - \dot{Y}_{i.} = (X_{it} - \dot{X}_{i.})'\beta^o + (\varepsilon_{it} - \dot{\varepsilon}_{i.}),$$

where $\dot{Y}_{i.} = T^{-1}\sum_{t=1}^{T} Y_{it}$ and similarly for $\dot{X}_{i.}$ and $\dot{\varepsilon}_{i.}$. The demeaning procedure removes the unobservable individual-specific effect and as a result, the OLS estimator for the demeaned model, which is called the within estimator in the panel data literature, will be consistent for the true model parameter β^o. (It should be noted that for a dynamic panel data model where X_{it} is not strictly exogenous, the within estimator is not consistent for β^o when the number of the time periods T is fixed. Different estimation methods have to be used.) See Hsiao (2002) for detailed discussion of panel data econometric models.

Chapters 2 to 7 present a relatively comprehensive econometric theory for linear regression models often encountered in economics and finance. We start with a general regression analysis, discussing the interpretation of a linear regression model, which depends on whether the linear regression model is correctly specified for conditional mean. After discussing the classical linear regression model in Chapter 3, Chapters 4 to 7 discuss various extensions and generalizations when some assumptions in the classical linear regression model are violated. In particular, we consider the scenarios under which the results for classical linear regression models are approximately applicable for large samples. The key conditions are conditional homoskedasticity and serial uncorrelatedness in the disturbance of a correctly specified linear regression model. When there exists conditional heteroskedasticity or serial correlation in the regression disturbance, the results for classical linear regression models are no longer applicable even for large samples; we provide robust asymptotically valid procedures under these scenarios. On the other hand, when linear regression model suffers from endogeneity (i.e., $E(\varepsilon_t|X_t) \neq 0$), Chapter 7 shows that the 2SLS method can be used for consistent estimation of and hypothesis testing on parameters of interest.

The asymptotic theory developed for linear regression models in Chapters 4 to 7 can be easily extended to more complicated, nonlinear models. For example, consider a nonlinear regression model

$$Y_t = g(X_t, \beta^o) + \varepsilon_t,$$

where $E(\varepsilon_t|X_t) = 0$. The Nonlinear Least Squares (NLS) estimator solves the minimization of the SSR problem

$$\hat{\beta} = \arg\min_{\beta} \sum_{t=1}^{n} [Y_t - g(X_t, \beta)]^2 .$$

The FOC is

$$D(\hat{\beta})'e = \sum_{t=1}^{n} \frac{\partial g(X_t, \hat{\beta})}{\partial \beta} \left[Y_t - g(X_t, \hat{\beta}) \right] = 0,$$

where $D(\beta)$ is an $n \times K$ matrix, with the t-th row being $\partial g(X_t, \beta)/\partial \beta$. Although one generally does not have a closed form expression for $\hat{\beta}$, all asymptotic theory and procedures in Chapters 4 to 7 are applicable to the NLS estimator if one replaces X_t by $(\partial/\partial\beta) g(X_t, \beta)$ evaluated at the true parameter value β^o or its consistent estimator $\hat{\beta}$. See also the discussion in Chapters 8 and 9.

The asymptotic theory in Chapters 4 to 7 however, cannot be directly applied to some popular nonlinear models. Examples of such nonlinear models include:

- Nonlinear regression model with endogeneity:

$$Y_t = g(X_t, \beta^o) + \varepsilon_t,$$

  where $E(\varepsilon_t|X_t) \neq 0$;
- Rational expectations model:

$$E\left[m(Z_t, \beta^o)\right] = 0;$$

- Conditional variance model:

$$Y_t = g(X_t, \beta^o) + \sigma(X_t, \beta^o) u_t,$$

  where $g(X_t, \beta)$ is a parametric model for $E(Y_t|X_t), \sigma^2(X_t, \beta)$ is a parametric model for $\text{var}(Y_t|X_t)$, and $\{u_t\}$ is IID$(0, 1)$;
- Conditional probability distribution model of Y_t given X_t:

$$f(y|X_t, \beta).$$

These nonlinear models are not models for conditional mean; they model other characteristics of the conditional distribution of Y_t given X_t. For these models, we need to develop new estimation methods and new asymptotic theory, which we will turn to in subsequent chapters.

One important subject that we do not discuss in detail in Chapters 2 to 7 is model specification testing. Chapter 2 emphasizes the importance of correct model specification for the validity of economic interpretation of model parameters. How to check whether a linear regression model is correctly specified for conditional mean $E(Y_t|X_t)$? This is called model specification testing. Some popular specification tests in econometrics are

Hausman's (1978) test and White's (1981) test which compare two parameter estimators for the same model parameter. Also, see Hong and White's (1995) generalized F-test for model specification using a nonparametric series regression.

Exercise 7

7.1. Suppose $Y_t = X_t'\beta^o + \varepsilon_t$, where Y_t and X_t' are observable and ε_t is not observable. If $E(\varepsilon_t|X_t) \neq 0$, does this always imply that the linear regression model is misspecified for $E(Y_t|X_t)$? In other word, in addition to model misspecification for $E(Y_t|X_t)$, are there any other possibilities which may cause $E(\varepsilon_t|X_t) \neq 0$? Provide some examples to explain.

7.2. Consider Example 7.7 in Section 7.1, where $\{\varepsilon_t\}$ is IID$(0, \sigma_\varepsilon^2)$, $\{v_t\}$ is IID$(0, \sigma_v^2)$, and $\{\varepsilon_t\}$ and $\{v_t\}$ are mutually independent.

(1) Suppose Eqs. (7.8) and (7.9) constitute a system of equations. Explain why the parameter β_2^o is not identifiable.

(2) Suppose now Eqs. (7.8) and (7.12) constitute a system of equations. Explain why the parameter β_2^o becomes identifiable.

(3) Suppose now we have a system of equations: $W_t = \beta_1^o + \beta_2^o P_t + \beta_3^o D_t + \varepsilon_t$ and $P_t = \alpha_1^o + \alpha_2^o W_t + \alpha_3^o D_t + v_t$. Is the parameter β_2^o identifiable? Explain.

7.3. Consider a simple Keynesian national income model

$$C_t = \beta_1^o + \beta_2^o(Y_t - T_t) + \varepsilon_t, \quad (A.7.1)$$

$$T_t = \gamma_1^o + \gamma_2^o Y_t + v_t, \quad (A.7.2)$$

$$Y_t = C_t + G_t, \quad (A.7.3)$$

where C_t, Y_t, T_t, and G_t are consumption, income, tax, and government spending respectively, and $\{\varepsilon_t\}$ and $\{v_t\}$ are IID$(0, \sigma_\varepsilon^2)$ and $(0, \sigma_v^2)$ respectively. Eq. (A.7.1) is a consumption function, Eq. (A.7.2) is a tax function, and Eq. (A.7.3) is an income identity.

(1) Can the OLS estimator $\hat{\beta}$ of Eq. (A.7.1) give consistent estimation for the MPC? Explain.

(2) Suppose G_t is an exogenous variable (i.e., G_t does not depend on both C_t and Y_t). Can G_t be used as a valid IV? If yes, describe a 2SLS procedure. If not, explain.

(3) Suppose the government has to maintain a budget balance such that

$$G_t = T_t + w_t, \quad (A.7.4)$$

where $\{w_t\}$ is IID$(0, \sigma_w^2)$. Could G_t be used as a valid IV? If yes, describe a 2SLS procedure. If not, explain.

7.4. Consider the DGP

$$Y_t = X_t'\beta^o + \varepsilon_t, \tag{A.7.5}$$

where $X_t = (1, X_{1t})'$,

$$X_{1t} = v_t + u_t, \tag{A.7.6}$$

$$\varepsilon_t = w_t + u_t, \tag{A.7.7}$$

where $\{v_t\}, \{u_t\}$ and $\{w_t\}$ are all IID $N(0,1)$, and they are mutually independent.

(1) Is the OLS estimator $\hat{\beta}$ consistent for β^o? Explain.

(2) Suppose $Z_{1t} = w_t - \varepsilon_t$. Is $Z_t = (1, Z_{1t})'$ a valid set of IVs? Explain.

(3) Find an instrument vector and the asymptotic distribution of $\hat{\beta}_{2SLS}$ using this instrument vector. *[Hint: You need to find* $\sqrt{n}(\hat{\beta}_{2SLS} - \beta^o) \xrightarrow{d} N(0, V)$ *for some* V*, where the expression of* V *should be given.]*

(4) To test the hypothesis

$$\mathbf{H}_0 : R\beta^o = r,$$

where R is a $J \times 2$ matrix, and r is a $J \times 1$ vector. Suppose that $\tilde{F}$ is the F-statistic in the second stage regression of 2SLS. Could we use $J \cdot \tilde{F}$ as an asymptotic χ^2_J test? Explain.

7.5. Consider the following demand-supply system:

$$Y_t = \alpha_0^o + \alpha_1^o P_t + \alpha_2^o S_t + \varepsilon_t,$$

$$Y_t = \beta_0^o + \beta_1^o P_t + \beta_2^o C_t + v_t,$$

where the first equation is a model for the demand of certain good, where Y_t is the quantity demanded for the good, P_t is the price of the good, S_t is the price of a substitute, and ε_t is a shock to the demand. The second equation is a model for the supply of the good, where Y_t is the quantity supplied, C_t is the cost of production, and v_t is a shock to the supply. Suppose S_t and C_t are exogenous variables, $\{\varepsilon_t\}$ is IID$(0, \sigma_\varepsilon^2)$ and $\{v_t\}$ is IID$(0, \sigma_v^2)$, and two series $\{\varepsilon_t\}$ and $\{v_t\}$ are independent of each other. We have also assumed that the market is always clear so the quantity demanded is equal to the quantity supplied.

(1) Suppose a 2SLS estimator is used to estimate the demand model with the instrument vector $Z_t = (1, S_t, C_t)'$. Describe the 2SLS procedure. Is the resulting 2SLS $\hat{\alpha}_{2sls}$ consistent for $\alpha^o = (\alpha_0^o, \alpha_1^o, \alpha_2^o)'$? Explain.

(2) Suppose a 2SLS estimator is used to estimate the supply equation with instruments $Z_t = (1, S_t, C_t)'$. Describe the 2SLS procedure. Is the resulting 2SLS $\hat{\beta}_{2SLS}$ consistent for $\beta^o = (\beta_0^o, \beta_1^o, \beta_2^o)'$? Explain.

(3) Suppose $\{\varepsilon_t\}$ and $\{v_t\}$ are contemporaneously correlated, namely, $E(\varepsilon_t v_t) \neq 0$. This can occur when there is a common shock to both the demand and supply of the good. Does this affect the conclusions in Parts (1) and (2)? Explain.

7.6. Show that under Assumptions 7.1 to 7.4, $\hat{\beta}_{2SLS} \xrightarrow{p} \beta^o$ as $n \to \infty$.

7.7. Suppose Assumptions 7.1 to 7.5 hold.

(1) Show that $\sqrt{n}(\hat{\beta}_{2SLS} - \beta^o) \xrightarrow{d} N(0, \Omega)$ as $n \to \infty$, where

$$\Omega = \left(Q_{XZ} Q_{ZZ}^{-1} Q_{ZX}\right)^{-1} Q_{XZ} Q_{ZZ}^{-1} V Q_{ZZ}^{-1} Q_{ZX} (Q_{XZ} Q_{ZZ}^{-1} Q_{ZX})^{-1},$$

and V is given as in Assumption 7.5.

(2) If in addition $\{Z_t \varepsilon_t\}$ is an ergodic stationary MDS with $E(\varepsilon_t^2 | Z_t) = \sigma^2$, show that

$$\Omega = \sigma^2 (Q_{XZ} Q_{ZZ}^{-1} Q_{ZX})^{-1}.$$

7.8. The use of IV ensures consistency of the 2SLS estimator. Explain why and how the choice of IV affects the efficiency of the 2SLS estimator. Suppose Assumptions 7.1 to 7.5 hold.

7.9. Suppose Assumptions 7.1 to 7.4, 7.6 and 7.7 hold, and we are interested in testing the null hypothesis $\mathbf{H}_0 : R\beta^o = r$, where R is a $1 \times K$ constant vector and r is a constant. Construct a t-type test statistic and derive its asymptotic distribution under $\mathbf{H}_0$ in each of the following cases:

(1) $\{Z_t \varepsilon_t\}$ is an MDS, and $E(\varepsilon_t^2 | Z_t) = \sigma^2$. And does a standard t-test statistic from the second stage regression of Y_t on $\hat{X}_t$ follow an asymptotic $N(0, 1)$ distribution under $\mathbf{H}_0$? Explain.

(2) $\{Z_t \varepsilon_t\}$ is an MDS, and $E(\varepsilon_t^2 | Z_t) \neq 0$.

(3) $\{Z_t \varepsilon_t\}$ is a non-MDS.

7.10. Suppose Assumptions 7.1 to 7.4, 7.6 and 7.7 hold.

(1) Define

$$\hat{s}^2 = \frac{\hat{e}'\hat{e}}{n},$$

where $\hat{e} = Y - X\hat{\beta}_{2SLS}$. Show $\hat{s}^2 \xrightarrow{p} \sigma^2 = \text{var}(\varepsilon_t)$ as $n \to \infty$.

(2) Define

$$s^2 = \frac{e'e}{n},$$

where $e = Y - \hat{X}\hat{\beta}_{2SLS}$ is the estimated residual from the second stage regression of Y_t on $\hat{X}_t = \hat{\gamma}'Z_t$. Show that s^2 is not a consistent estimator for σ^2.

7.11. *[2SLS Hypothesis Testing]:* Suppose Assumptions 7.1 to 7.5 hold. Define a F-statistic

$$F = \frac{n(R\hat{\beta}_{2SLS} - r)'(R\hat{Q}_{\hat{X}\hat{X}}^{-1}R')^{-1}(R\hat{\beta}_{2SLS} - r)/J}{e'e/(n-K)},$$

where $e_t = Y_t - \hat{X}_t'\hat{\beta}_{2SLS}$ is the estimated residual from the second stage regression of Y_t on $\hat{X}_t$. Does $J \cdot F \xrightarrow{d} \chi^2_J$ under the null hypothesis $\mathbf{H}_0$: $R\beta^o = r$? If yes, give your reasoning. If not, provide a modification so that the modified test statistic converges to χ^2_J under $\mathbf{H}_0$.

7.12. Let

$$\hat{V} = \frac{1}{n}\sum_{t=1}^{n} Z_t Z_t' \hat{e}_t^2,$$

where $\hat{e}_t = Y_t - X_t'\hat{\beta}_{2SLS}$. Show $\hat{V} \xrightarrow{p} V$ under Assumptions 7.1 to 7.8.

7.13. Suppose the following assumptions hold:

Assumption 1 [Linearity]: $\{Y_t, X_t'\}_{t=1}^n$ is an ergodic stationary process with

$$Y_t = X_t'\beta^o + \varepsilon_t, \qquad t = 1, ..., n,$$

for some unknown $K \times 1$ parameter vector β^o and some unobservable disturbance ε_t.

Assumption 2 [Nonsingularity]: The $K \times K$ matrix

$$Q_{XX} = E(X_t X_t')$$

is nonsingular and finite.

Assumption 3 [Orthogonality]:
(a) $E(\varepsilon_t | X_t) = 0$.

(b) $E(\varepsilon_t|Z_t) = 0$, where Z_t is an $l \times 1$ random vector, with $l \geq K$.
(c) The $l \times l$ matrix

$$Q_{ZZ} = E(Z_t Z_t')$$

is finite and nonsingular, and the $l \times K$ matrix

$$Q_{XZ} = E(Z_t X_t')$$

is finite and of full rank.

Assumption 4: $\{(X_t', Z_t')'\varepsilon_t\}$ is an MDS.

Assumption 5: $E(\varepsilon_t^2|X_t, Z_t) = \sigma^2$.

Under these assumptions, both the OLS estimator

$$\hat{\beta} = (\mathbf{X}'\mathbf{X})^{-1}\mathbf{X}'Y$$

and the 2SLS estimator

$$\hat{\beta}_{2SLS} = [(\mathbf{X}'\mathbf{Z})(\mathbf{Z}'\mathbf{Z})^{-1}\mathbf{Z}'\mathbf{X}]^{-1}\mathbf{X}'\mathbf{Z}(\mathbf{Z}'\mathbf{Z})^{-1}\mathbf{Z}'Y$$

are consistent for β^o.

(1) Show that $\hat{\beta}$ is a special 2SLS estimator $\hat{\beta}_{2SLS}$ with some proper choice of IV.

(2) Which estimator, $\hat{\beta}$ or $\hat{\beta}_{2SLS}$, is more asymptotically efficient? *[Hint: If $\sqrt{n}(\hat{\beta}_1 - \beta^o) \xrightarrow{d} N(0, \Omega_1)$ and $\sqrt{n}(\hat{\beta}_2 - \beta^o) \xrightarrow{d} N(0, \Omega_2)$, then $\hat{\beta}_1$ is asymptotically more efficient than $\hat{\beta}_2$ if and only if $\Omega_2 - \Omega_1$ or $\Omega_1^{-1} - \Omega_2^{-1}$ is PSD.]*

7.14. Consider the linear regression model

$$Y_t = X_t'\beta^o + \varepsilon_t,$$

where $E(X_t\varepsilon_t) \neq 0$. Our purpose is to find a consistent estimation procedure for β^o.

First, consider the artificial regression

$$X_t = \gamma' Z_t + v_t,$$

where X_t is the regressor vector, Z_t is the instrument vector, $\gamma = [E(Z_t Z_t')]^{-1} E(Z_t X_t')$ is the best linear least squares approximation coefficient, and v_t is the $K \times 1$ regression error.

Now, suppose instead of decomposing X_t, we decompose the regression error ε_t as follows:

$$\varepsilon_t = v_t'\rho^o + u_t,$$

where $\rho^o = [E(v_t v_t')]^{-1}E(v_t\varepsilon_t)$ is the best linear least squares approximation coefficient.

Assuming that v_t is observable, we consider the augmented linear regression model

$$Y_t = X_t'\beta^o + v_t'\rho^o + u_t.$$

Show $E[(X_t', v_t)'u_t] = 0$. One important implication of this orthogonality condition is that if v_t is observable then the OLS estimator of regressing Y_t on X_t and v_t will be consistent for $(\beta^{o\prime}, \rho^{o\prime})'$.

7.15. In practice, v_t is unobservable in the first stage regression. However, it can be estimated by the estimated OLS residual

$$\hat{v}_t = X_t - \hat{\gamma}'Z_t = X_t - \hat{X}_t.$$

We now consider the following feasible augmented linear regression model

$$Y_t = X_t'\beta^o + \hat{v}_t'\rho^o + \tilde{u}_t,$$

and we denote the resulting OLS estimator as $\hat{\alpha} = (\hat{\beta}', \hat{\rho}')'$, where $\hat{\beta}$ is the OLS estimator for β^o and $\hat{\rho}$ is the OLS estimator for ρ^o.

Show $\hat{\beta} = \hat{\beta}_{2SLS}$. *[Hint: The following decomposition may be useful: Suppose*

$$A = \begin{bmatrix} B & C' \\ C & D \end{bmatrix}$$

is a nonsingular square matrix, where B is $k_1 \times k_1, C$ is $k_2 \times k_1$ and D is $k_2 \times k_2$. Then

$$A^{-1} = \begin{bmatrix} B^{-1}(I + C'E^{-1}CB^{-1}) & -B'^{-1}C'E^{-1} \\ -E^{-1}CB^{-1} & E^{-1} \end{bmatrix},$$

where $E = D - CB^{-1}C'$.]

7.16. Suppose $\hat{Y}$ is an $n \times 1$ vector of the fitted values of regressing Y_t on Z_t, and $\hat{X}$ is an $n \times K$ matrix of fitted values of regressing X_t on Z_t. Show that $\hat{\beta}_{2SLS}$ is equal to the OLS estimator of regressing $\hat{Y}$ on $\hat{X}$.

7.17. *[Hausman's Test]:* Suppose Assumptions 1, 2, 3(b, c), 4 and 5 in Exercise 7.13 hold. A test for the null hypothesis $\mathbf{H}_0 : E(\varepsilon_t|X_t) = 0$ can be constructed by comparing $\hat{\beta}$ and $\hat{\beta}_{2SLS}$, because they will converge in probability to the same limit β^o under $\mathbf{H}_0$ and generally to different limits under the alternatives to $\mathbf{H}_0$. Assume that $\mathbf{H}_0$ holds.

(1) Show that

$$\sqrt{n}(\hat{\beta} - \beta^o) - Q_{XX}^{-1} \frac{1}{\sqrt{n}} \sum_{t=1}^{n} X_t \varepsilon_t \xrightarrow{p} 0$$

or equivalently

$$\sqrt{n}(\hat{\beta} - \beta^o) = Q_{XX}^{-1} \frac{1}{\sqrt{n}} \sum_{t=1}^{n} X_t \varepsilon_t + o_P(1),$$

where $Q_{XX} = E(X_t X_t')$.

(2) Show that

$$\sqrt{n}(\hat{\beta}_{2SLS} - \beta^o) = Q_{\tilde{X}\tilde{X}}^{-1} \frac{1}{\sqrt{n}} \sum_{t=1}^{n} \tilde{X}_t \varepsilon_t + o_P(1),$$

where $Q_{\tilde{X}\tilde{X}} = E(X_t X_t'), \tilde{X}_t = \gamma' Z_t$ and $\gamma = [E(Z_t Z_t')]^{-1} E(Z_t X_t)$.

(3) Show that

$$\sqrt{n}(\hat{\beta}_{2SLS} - \hat{\beta}) = \frac{1}{\sqrt{n}} \sum_{t=1}^{n} \left\{ Q_{XX}^{-1} X_t - Q_{\tilde{X}\tilde{X}}^{-1} \tilde{X}_t \right\} \varepsilon_t + o_P(1).$$

(4) The asymptotic distribution of $\sqrt{n}(\hat{\beta}_{2SLS} - \hat{\beta})$ is determined by the leading term only in Part (3). Find its asymptotic distribution.

(5) Construct an asymptotically χ^2 test statistic. What is the number of degrees of freedom of the asymptotic χ^2 distribution? Assume that $Q_{XX} - Q_{\tilde{X}\tilde{X}}$ is strictly positive definite.

7.18. Suppose Assumptions 1, 2, 3(b, c) and 4 in Exercise 7.13 hold, $E(X_{jt}^4) < \infty$ for $1 \leq j \leq K$, $E(Z_{jt}^4) < \infty$ for $1 \leq j \leq l$, and $E(\varepsilon_t^4) < \infty$. There may exist conditional heteroskedasticity. Construct a Hausman's type test statistic for $\mathbf{H}_0 : E(\varepsilon_t|X_t) = 0$ and derive its asymptotic distribution under $\mathbf{H}_0$.

7.19. In Theorem 7.9, Hausman's test statistic for the null hypothesis $\mathbf{H}_0 : E(\varepsilon_t|X_t) = 0$ is defined as

$$H = \frac{n(\hat{\beta}_{2SLS} - \hat{\beta})'[(\hat{Q}_{XZ} \hat{Q}_{ZZ}^{-1} \hat{Q}_{ZX})^{-1} - \hat{Q}_{XX}^{-1}]^{-1} (\hat{\beta}_{2SLS} - \hat{\beta})}{s^2},$$

where $s^2 = e'e/(n-K)$, and $e = Y - X\hat{\beta}$ is the estimated OLS residual. Now we define an alternative Hausman's test statistic, denoted as $\hat{H}$, which is the same as H, except that the sample residual variance estimator s^2 is replaced by $\hat{s}^2 = \hat{e}'\hat{e}/(n-K)$, where $\hat{e} = Y - X\hat{\beta}_{2SLS}$.

(1) Show that $\hat{H} \xrightarrow{d} \chi^2_K$ as $n \to \infty$ under $\mathbf{H}_0 : E(\varepsilon_t|X_t) = 0$. Give your reasoning.

(2) Which test, H or $\hat{H}$, will have a smaller Type II error in finite samples when the null hypothesis $\mathbf{H}_0$ is false? Give your reasoning.

7.20. Hausman's test checks the null hypothesis $\mathbf{H}_0$ that $E(\varepsilon_t|X_t) = 0$. It is based on the comparison between two estimators, the OLS estimator $\hat{\beta}$ and the 2SLS estimator $\hat{\beta}_{2SLS}$. These two estimators converge in probability to the same limit under $\mathbf{H}_0$, and generally to different limits under the alternative to $\mathbf{H}_0$.

(1) Is it possible that $\mathbf{H}_0$ is false but $\hat{\beta}$ and β_{2SLS} still converge to the same limit? If yes, give a proof; if not, give an example.

(2) Suppose $\mathbf{H}_0$ is false but $\hat{\beta}$ and β_{2SLS} converge to the same limit. Does Hausman's test have asymptotic unit power to reject $\mathbf{H}_0$ as the sample size $n \to \infty$?

7.21. *[Hausman-White Test]:* Suppose Assumptions 1, 3(b, c), 4 and 5 in Exercise 7.13 hold. A test for the null hypothesis $\mathbf{H}_0 : E(\varepsilon_t|X_t) = 0$ can be constructed by comparing $\hat{\beta}$ and $\hat{\beta}_W$, where $\hat{\beta}_W$ is a Weighted Least Squares (WLS) estimator defined as

$$\hat{\beta}_W = \left(\sum_{t=1}^{n} X_t W_t^2 X_t'\right)^{-1} \sum_{t=1}^{n} W_t X_t Y_t,$$

where $W_t = W(X_t)$ is a weighting function of X_t, and $Q_{WXWX} \equiv E(W_t^2 X_t X_t')$ is finite, symmetric and positive definite. The estimators $\hat{\beta}$ and $\hat{\beta}_W$ will converge in probability to the same limit β^o under $\mathbf{H}_0$ and generally to different limits under the alternatives to $\mathbf{H}_0$. Assume that $\mathbf{H}_0$ holds.

(1) Show $\hat{\beta}_W \to \beta^o$ as $n \to \infty$ under $\mathbf{H}_0$.

(2) Show

$$\sqrt{n}(\hat{\beta}_W - \beta^o) = Q_{WXWX}^{-1} \frac{1}{\sqrt{n}} \sum_{t=1}^{n} W_t X_t \varepsilon_t + o_P(1).$$

(3) Show

$$\sqrt{n}(\hat{\beta}_W - \hat{\beta}) = \frac{1}{\sqrt{n}} \sum_{t=1}^{n} \left(Q_{WXWX}^{-1} W_t - Q_{XX}^{-1} \right) X_t \varepsilon_t + o_P(1).$$

(4) Derive the asymptotic distribution of $\sqrt{n}(\hat{\beta}_W - \hat{\beta})$.

(5) Construct a test statistic of $\mathbf{H}_0$ based on a quadratic form of $\sqrt{n}(\hat{\beta}_W - \hat{\beta})$, and derive its asymptotic distribution under $\mathbf{H}_0$. You can impose any necessary additional moment conditions.

(6) Explain why such a test generally has power when the null hypothesis $\mathbf{H}_0$ is false.

Chapter 8

Generalized Method of Moments Estimation

Abstract: Many economic theories and hypotheses have implications on and only on a moment condition or a set of moment conditions. A popular method to estimate model parameters contained in the moment condition is the Generalized Method of Moments (GMM). In this chapter, we first provide some economic examples for the moment condition, and define the GMM estimator. We then establish the consistency and asymptotic normality of the GMM estimator. Since the asymptotic variance-covariance matrix of a GMM estimator depends on the choice of a weighting matrix, we introduce an asymptotically optimal two-stage GMM estimator with a suitable choice of a weighting matrix. With the construction of a consistent asymptotic variance estimator, we then propose an asymptotically χ^2 Wald test statistic for the hypothesis of interest, and a model specification test for the moment condition.

Keywords: CAPM, Dynamic CAPM, Exact identification, GMM, Instrument, IV estimation, Linear IV estimator, Method of Moments Estimation (MME), Model specification test, Moment condition, Moment matching, Optimal estimation, Overidentification, Rational expectations, Sample moment, Sargan's test, Two-stage GMM estimation, Weighting matrix

8.1 Introduction to Method of Moments Estimation

To motivate the GMM estimation, we first consider a traditional method in statistics which is called the Method of Moments Estimation (MME).

Question: Suppose $f(y, \beta^o)$ is the Probability Density Function (PDF) or the Probability Mass Function (PMF) of a univariate random variable Y_t, where β^o is an unknown true parameter value. How to estimate the unknown parameter value β^o using a realization of the random sample $\{Y_t\}_{t=1}^n$?

The basic idea of MME is to match the sample moments with the population moments obtained under the probability distribution model $f(y, \beta)$. For simplicity, below we consider the case of a continuous distribution for Y_t, so $f(y, \beta)$ is a PDF model. Specifically, MME can be implemented as follows:

Step 1: Compute population moments $\mu_k(\beta^o) \equiv E(Y_t^k)$ under the PDF model $f(y, \beta^o)$.

For example, for $k = 1, 2$, we have

$$\begin{aligned} E(Y_t) &= \int_{-\infty}^{\infty} y f(y, \beta^o) dy = \mu_1(\beta^o) \\ E(Y_t^2) &= \int_{-\infty}^{\infty} y^2 f(y, \beta^o) dy \\ &= \sigma^2(\beta^o) + \mu_1^2(\beta^o), \end{aligned}$$

where $\sigma^2(\beta^o)$ is the variance of Y_t.

Step 2: Compute the sample moments from the random sample $\mathbf{Y}^n = (Y_1, ..., Y_n)'$ of size n:

For example, for $k = 1, 2$, we have

$$\begin{aligned} \hat{m}_1 &= \bar{Y}_n \xrightarrow{p} \mu_1(\beta^o) \\ \hat{m}_2 &= n^{-1} \sum_{t=1}^n Y_t^2 \\ &\xrightarrow{p} E(Y_t^2) = \sigma^2(\beta^o) + \mu_1^2(\beta^o), \end{aligned}$$

where $\sigma^2(\beta^o) = \mu_2(\beta^o) - \mu_1^2(\beta^o)$, and the weak convergence follows by WLLN.

Step 3: Match the sample moments with the corresponding population moments evaluated at some parameter value $\hat{\beta}$:

For example, for $k = 1, 2$, we set

$$\begin{aligned} \hat{m}_1 &= \mu_1(\hat{\beta}), \\ \hat{m}_2 &= \mu_2(\hat{\beta}) = \sigma^2(\hat{\beta}) + \mu_2^2(\hat{\beta}). \end{aligned}$$

Step 4: Solve for the system of equations. The solution $\hat{\beta}$ is called the MME for β^o.

In general, if β is a $K \times 1$ parameter vector, we need K equations of matching moments. We have $\hat{m}_k = \mu_k(\hat{\beta})$ for each n. Since $\hat{m}_k \xrightarrow{p} \mu_k(\beta^o)$ as $n \to \infty$ by WLLN, we expect $\hat{\beta} \equiv \hat{\beta}_n(\mathbf{Y}^n) \xrightarrow{p} \beta^o$ as $n \to \infty$.

We now illustrate MME by two simple examples.

Example 8.1. Suppose the random sample $\{Y_t\}_{t=1}^n \sim$ IID EXP(λ). Find an estimator for λ using MME.

Solution: In our application, $\beta = \lambda$. Because the exponential PDF

$$f(y, \lambda) = \frac{1}{\lambda} e^{-y/\lambda} \text{ for } y > 0,$$

it can be shown that

$$\begin{aligned}\mu(\lambda) = E(Y_t) &= \int_0^\infty y f(y, \lambda) dy \\ &= \int_0^\infty y \frac{1}{\lambda} e^{-y/\lambda} dy \\ &= \lambda.\end{aligned}$$

On the other hand, the first sample moment is the sample mean:

$$\hat{m}_1 = \bar{Y}_n.$$

Matching the sample mean with the population mean evaluated at λ :

$$\hat{m}_1 = \mu(\hat{\lambda}) = \hat{\lambda},$$

we obtain the MME

$$\hat{\lambda} = \hat{m}_1 = \bar{Y}_n.$$

Example 8.2. Suppose the random sample $\{Y_t\}_{t=1}^n \sim \text{IID}N(\mu, \sigma^2)$. Find MME for $\beta^o = (\mu, \sigma^2)'$.

Solution: The first two population moments are

$$\begin{aligned}E(Y_t) &= \mu, \\ E(Y_t^2) &= \sigma^2 + \mu^2.\end{aligned}$$

The first two sample moments are

$$\hat{m}_1 = \bar{Y}_n,$$
$$\hat{m}_2 = \frac{1}{n}\sum_{t=1}^{n} Y_t^2.$$

Matching the first two moments, we have

$$\bar{Y}_n = \hat{\mu},$$
$$\frac{1}{n}\sum_{t=1}^{n} Y_t^2 = \hat{\sigma}^2 + \hat{\mu}^2.$$

It follows that the MME

$$\hat{\mu} = \bar{Y}_n,$$
$$\hat{\sigma}^2 = \frac{1}{n}\sum_{t=1}^{n} Y_t^2 - \bar{Y}_n^2 = \frac{1}{n}\sum_{t=1}^{n}(Y_t - \bar{Y}_n)^2.$$

It is well-known that $\hat{\mu} \xrightarrow{p} \mu$ and $\hat{\sigma}^2 \xrightarrow{p} \sigma^2$ as $n \to \infty$.

8.2 Generalized Method of Moments (GMM) Estimation

Suppose β is a $K \times 1$ parameter vector, and there exists an $l \times 1$ moment function $m_t(\beta)$ such that

$$E[m_t(\beta^o)] = 0 \text{ for some unknown parameter value } \beta^o,$$

where the sub-index t denotes that $m_t(\beta)$ is a function of both β and some random variables indexed by t, and β^o is the true parameter value. For example, in the context of linear regression modelling, we may have

$$m_t(\beta) = X_t(Y_t - X_t'\beta)$$

in the OLS estimation, or

$$m_t(\beta) = Z_t(Y_t - X_t'\beta)$$

in the 2SLS estimation, or more generally in the IV estimation, where Z_t is an $l \times 1$ instrument vector.

If $l = K$, that is, if the number of moment conditions is the same as that of unknown parameters, the model $E[m_t(\beta^o)] = 0$ is called exactly identified. If $l > K$, that is, if the number of moment conditions is more than that of unknown parameters, the model is called overidentified.

The moment condition $E[m_t(\beta^o)] = 0$ may follow from economic and financial theory (e.g., rational expectations and correct asset pricing). We now illustrate this by the following example.

Example 8.3. [CAPM]: Define Y_t as an $L \times 1$ vector of excess returns for L assets (or portfolios of assets) in period t. For these L assets, the excess returns can be explained using the excess market portfolio return:

$$\begin{aligned} Y_t &= \beta_0^o + \beta_1^o R_{mt} + \varepsilon_t \\ &= \beta^{o\prime} X_t + \varepsilon_t, \end{aligned}$$

where $X_t = (1, R_{mt})'$ is a bivariate vector, R_{mt} is the excess market portfolio return, β^o is a $2 \times L$ true parameter matrix, and ε_t is an $L \times 1$ disturbance representing idiosyncratic risk, with $E(\varepsilon_t|X_t) = 0$. This orthogonality condition implies that there exists no systematic pricing bias in any time period. This is the standard CAPM.

Define the $l \times 1$ moment function

$$m_t(\beta) = X_t \otimes (Y_t - \beta' X_t),$$

where $l = 2L$ and $\otimes$ denotes the Kronecker product. When CAPM holds, we have

$$E[m_t(\beta^o)] = 0.$$

These $l \times 1$ moment conditions form a basis to estimate and test CAPM.

In fact, for any measurable function $h : R^2 \to R^l$, CAPM implies

$$E[h(X_t)(Y_t - \beta' X_t)] = 0.$$

This can also be used to estimate CAPM.

Question: How to choose the instruments $h(X_t)$?

Example 8.4. [Dynamic CAPM (Hansen and Singleton 1982)]: Suppose a representative economic agent has a constant relative risk aversion utility over his lifetime

$$U = \sum_{t=0}^{n} \delta^t u(C_t) = \sum_{t=0}^{n} \delta^t \frac{C_t^\gamma - 1}{\gamma},$$

where $u(\cdot)$ is the time-invariant utility function of the economic agent in each time period (we assume $u(c) = (c^\gamma - 1)/\gamma$), δ is the agent's time discount factor, γ is the economic agent's risk aversion parameter, and C_t is the consumption during period t. Let the information available to the agent at time $t-1$ be represented by the sigma-algebra I_{t-1} in the sense that any variable whose value is known at time $t-1$ is presumed to be I_{t-1}-measurable, and let

$$R_t = \frac{P_t}{P_{t-1}} = 1 + \frac{P_t - P_{t-1}}{P_{t-1}}$$

be the gross return to an asset acquired at time $t-1$ at the price of P_{t-1} (we assume no dividend on the asset). The agent's optimization problem is

$$\max_{\{C_t\}} E(U)$$

subject to the intertemporal budget constraint

$$C_t + P_t q_t = Y_t + P_t q_{t-1},$$

where q_t is the quantity of the asset purchased at time t and Y_t is the agent's labor income during period t. Define the marginal rate of intertemporal substitution

$$MRS_t(\gamma) = \frac{\frac{\partial u(C_t)}{\partial C_t}}{\frac{\partial u(C_{t-1})}{\partial C_{t-1}}} = \left(\frac{C_t}{C_{t-1}}\right)^{\gamma-1}.$$

The FOC of the agent optimization problem is characterized by the Euler equation:

$$E\left[\delta^o \mathrm{MRS}_t(\gamma^o) R_t | I_{t-1}\right] = 1 \text{ for some } \beta^o = (\delta^o, \gamma^o)'.$$

That is, the marginal rate of intertemporal substitution discounts gross returns to unity in expectation. Any dynamic CAPM is equivalent to a specification of $\mathrm{MRS}_t(\gamma)$. For more discussion, see Hansen and Singleton (1982) or Cochrane (2001).

We may write the Euler equation as follows:

$$E\left[\{\delta^o \mathrm{MRS}_t(\gamma^o) R_t - 1\} | I_{t-1}\right] = 0.$$

Thus, one may view that $\{\delta \mathrm{MRS}_t(\gamma) R_t - 1\}$ is a generalized model residual which has the MDS property when evaluated at the true structural parameter value $\beta^o = (\delta^o, \gamma^o)'$.

Question: How to estimate the unknown parameter value β^o in a dynamic CAPM?

More generally, how to estimate β^o from any linear or nonlinear econometric model which can be formulated as a set of moment conditions? Note that the joint distribution of the random sample is not given or implied by economic theory; only a set of conditional moments is given.

From the Euler equation, we can induce the following unconditional moment restrictions:

$$E\left[\delta^o \text{MRS}_t(\gamma^o)R_t - 1\right] = 0,$$
$$E\left\{\frac{C_{t-1}}{C_{t-2}}\left[\delta^o \text{MRS}_t(\gamma^o)R_t - 1\right]\right\} = 0,$$
$$E\left\{R_{t-1}\left[\delta^o \text{MRS}_t(\gamma^o)R_t - 1\right]\right\} = 0.$$

Therefore, we can consider the 3×1 sample moments

$$\hat{m}(\beta) = \frac{1}{n}\sum_{t=1}^{n} m_t(\beta),$$

where

$$m_t(\beta) = \left[\delta \text{MRS}_t(\gamma)R_t - 1\right]\left(1, \frac{C_{t-1}}{C_{t-2}}, R_{t-1}\right)'$$

can serve as the basis for estimation. The elements of the vector

$$Z_t \equiv \left(1, \frac{C_{t-1}}{C_{t-2}}, R_{t-1}\right)'$$

are called IVs which are a subset of information set I_{t-1}.

We now define the GMM estimator.

Definition 8.1. [GMM Estimator]: The GMM estimator is

$$\hat{\beta} = \arg\min_{\beta\in\Theta} \hat{m}(\beta)'\hat{W}^{-1}\hat{m}(\beta),$$

where

$$\hat{m}(\beta) = n^{-1}\sum_{t=1}^{n} m_t(\beta)$$

is an $l \times 1$ sample moment vector, β is a $K \times 1$ unknown parameter vector, Θ is a $K \times 1$ dimensional parameter space, and $\hat{W}$ is an $l \times l$ symmetric nonsingular matrix which is possibly data-dependent. Here, we assume $l \geq K$, i.e., the number of moments may be larger than or at least equal to the number of unknown parameters.

Question: Why do we require $l \geq K$ in GMM estimation?

Question: Why is the GMM estimator $\hat{\beta}$ not defined by setting the $l \times 1$ sample moments to zero jointly, namely

$$\hat{m}(\hat{\beta}) = 0?$$

When $l > K$, i.e., when the number of equations is larger than that of unknown parameters, we generally cannot find a solution $\hat{\beta}$ such that $\hat{m}(\hat{\beta}) = 0$. However, we can find a solution $\hat{\beta}$ which makes $\hat{m}(\hat{\beta})$ as close to an $l \times 1$ zero vector as possible by minimizing the quadratic form

$$\hat{m}(\beta)'\hat{m}(\beta) = \sum_{i=1}^{l} \hat{m}_i^2(\beta),$$

where $\hat{m}_i(\beta) = n^{-1}\sum_{t=1}^{n} m_{it}(\beta)$, $i = 1, ..., l$. Since each sample moment component $\hat{m}_i(\beta)$ has a different variance, and $\hat{m}_i(\beta)$ and $\hat{m}_j(\beta)$ may be correlated, we can introduce a weighting matrix $\hat{W}$ and choose $\hat{\beta}$ to minimize a weighted quadratic form in $\hat{m}(\hat{\beta})$, namely

$$\hat{m}(\beta)'\hat{W}^{-1}\hat{m}(\beta).$$

Question: What is the role of $\hat{W}$?

When $\hat{W} = I$, an identity matrix, each of the l component sample moments is weighted equally. If $\hat{W} \neq I$, then the l sample moment components are weighted differently. A suitable choice of weighting matrix $\hat{W}$ can improve the efficiency of the resulting estimator. Here, a natural question is: what is the optimal weighting function for the choice of $\hat{W}$?

Intuitively, the sample moment components which have large sampling variations should be discounted. This is an idea similar to the GLS estimator, which discounts noisy observations by dividing by the conditional standard deviation of the disturbance term and differencing out serial correlations. As we will see soon, an asymptotically optimal weighting matrix $\hat{W}$ should converge to the asymptotic variance-covariance matrix of the sample moment $\hat{m}(\beta^o)$ up to some constant proportionality.

Question: Does the GMM estimator have a closed form expression?

In general, when the moment function $m_t(\beta)$ is nonlinear in parameter β, there is no closed form solution for $\hat{\beta}$. However, there is an important special case where the GMM estimator $\hat{\beta}$ has a closed form. This is the case of so-called linear IV estimation. Specifically, to estimate a linear regression model

$$Y_t = X_t'\beta^o + \varepsilon_t,$$

where $E(\varepsilon_t|X_t) \neq 0$. Suppose there exists an instrument vector Z_t such that $E(\varepsilon_t|Z_t) = 0$. We construct a moment function

$$m_t(\beta) = Z_t(Y_t - X_t'\beta),$$

where Y_t is a scalar, X_t is a $K \times 1$ vector, and Z_t is an $l \times 1$ vector, with $l \geq K$. Then we have

$$E[Z_t(Y_t - X_t'\beta^o)] = 0 \text{ for some } \beta^o.$$

In this case, the GMM estimator, or more precisely, the linear IV estimator, $\hat{\beta}$, solves the following minimization problem:

$$\min_{\beta \in R^K} \hat{m}(\beta)'\hat{W}^{-1}\hat{m}(\beta) = n^{-2} \min_{\beta \in R^K} (Y - \mathbf{X}\beta)'\mathbf{Z}\hat{W}^{-1}\mathbf{Z}'(Y - \mathbf{X}\beta),$$

where

$$\begin{aligned}
\hat{m}(\beta) &= \frac{\mathbf{Z}'(Y - \mathbf{X}\beta)}{n} \\
&= \frac{1}{n}\sum_{t=1}^{n} Z_t(Y_t - X_t'\beta).
\end{aligned}$$

The FOC is given by

$$\begin{aligned}
&\frac{\partial}{\partial\beta}\left[(Y - \mathbf{X}\beta)'\mathbf{Z}\hat{W}^{-1}\mathbf{Z}'(Y - \mathbf{X}\beta)\right]_{\beta=\hat{\beta}} \\
&= -2\mathbf{X}'\mathbf{Z}\hat{W}^{-1}\mathbf{Z}'(Y - \mathbf{X}\hat{\beta}) \\
&= 0.
\end{aligned}$$

It follows that

$$\mathbf{X}'\mathbf{Z}\hat{W}^{-1}\mathbf{Z}'\mathbf{X}\hat{\beta} = \mathbf{X}'\mathbf{Z}\hat{W}^{-1}\mathbf{Z}'Y.$$

When the $K \times l$ matrix $Q_{XZ} = E(X_tZ_t')$ is of full rank of K, the $K \times K$ matrix $Q_{XZ}W^{-1}Q_{ZX}$ is nonsingular. Therefore, $\mathbf{X}'\mathbf{Z}\hat{W}^{-1}\mathbf{Z}'\mathbf{X}$ is not singular at least for large samples, and consequently the GMM estimator $\hat{\beta}$ has the closed form expression:

$$\hat{\beta} = (\mathbf{X}'\mathbf{Z}\hat{W}^{-1}\mathbf{Z}'\mathbf{X})^{-1}\mathbf{X}'\mathbf{Z}\hat{W}^{-1}\mathbf{Z}'Y.$$

This is called a linear IV estimator because it estimates the parameter value β^o in a linear model $Y_t = X_t'\beta^o + \varepsilon_t$.

Theorem 8.1. ***[Linear IV Estimator]:*** *Suppose $m_t(\beta) = Z_t(Y_t - X_t'\beta)$, where Y_t is a scalar variable, Z_t is an $l \times 1$ instrument vector, X_t is a $K \times 1$ explanatory vector, β is a $K \times 1$ parameter vector, with $l \geq K$. Also, with probability one, the $K \times l$ matrix $\mathbf{X}'\mathbf{Z}$ is of full rank K and the $l \times l$ weighting matrix $\hat{W}$ is nonsingular. Then the resulting GMM estimator $\hat{\beta}$ is called a linear IV estimator and has the closed form expression*

$$\hat{\beta} = (\mathbf{X}'\mathbf{Z}\hat{W}^{-1}\mathbf{Z}'\mathbf{X})^{-1}\mathbf{X}'\mathbf{Z}\hat{W}^{-1}\mathbf{Z}'Y.$$

When $l = K$, and Q_{XZ} is nonsingular,

$$\hat{\beta} = (\mathbf{Z}'\mathbf{X})^{-1}\mathbf{Z}'Y.$$

The linear IV estimator $\hat{\beta}$ is used to estimate the unknown true parameter value β^o in a linear regression model $Y_t = X_t'\beta^o + \varepsilon_t$. Note that the IV estimator $\hat{\beta}$ generally depends on the choice of instrument vector Z_t and weighting matrix $\hat{W}$.

Interestingly, the 2SLS estimator $\hat{\beta}_{2SLS}$ considered in Chapter 7 is a special case of the linear IV estimator by choosing

$$\hat{W} = \mathbf{Z}'\mathbf{Z},$$

or more generally, by choosing $\hat{W} = c(\mathbf{Z}'\mathbf{Z})$ for any constant $c \neq 0$.

Question: Is the choice of $\hat{W} = \mathbf{Z}'\mathbf{Z}$ optimal? In other words, is the 2SLS estimator $\hat{\beta}_{2SLS}$ asymptotically efficient in estimating β^o?

However, when $l = K$, the exact identification case, the IV estimator $\hat{\beta}$ does not depend on the choice of $\hat{W}$. This is because in this case the FOC that $\mathbf{X}'\mathbf{Z}\hat{W}^{-1}\mathbf{Z}'(Y - \mathbf{X}\hat{\beta}) = 0$ becomes

$$\mathbf{Z}'(Y - \mathbf{X}\hat{\beta}) = 0,$$
$$(K \times n)(n \times 1) = K \times 1,$$

given $\mathbf{X}'\mathbf{Z}$ and $\hat{W}$ are nonsingular at least for large samples. This yields the linear IV estimator $\hat{\beta} = (\mathbf{Z}'\mathbf{X})^{-1}\mathbf{Z}'Y$ regardless of the choice of weighting matrix $\hat{W}$.

Obviously, the OLS estimator $\hat{\beta} = (\mathbf{X}'\mathbf{X})^{-1}\mathbf{X}'Y$ is a special case of the linear IV estimator by choosing $Z_t = X_t$.

8.3 Consistency of the GMM Estimator

Question: What are the statistical properties of the GMM estimator $\hat{\beta}$?

To investigate the asymptotic properties of the GMM estimator $\hat{\beta}$, we first provide a set of regularity conditions.

Assumption 8.1. [Compactness]: The parameter space Θ is compact (closed and bounded).

Assumption 8.2. [Uniform Convergence]: (a) The moment function $m_t(\beta)$ is an $l \times 1$ measurable function of a random vector indexed by t for each $\beta \in \Theta$, and given each t, $m_t(\beta)$ is continuous in $\beta \in \Theta$ with probability one; (b) $\{m_t(\beta)\}$ is an ergodic stationary process; (c) $\hat{m}(\beta)$ converges uniformly over Θ to $m(\beta) \equiv E[m_t(\beta)]$ in probability in the sense that

$$\sup_{\beta \in \Theta} ||\hat{m}(\beta) - m(\beta)|| \xrightarrow{p} 0,$$

where $||\cdot||$ is an Euclidean norm; (d) $m(\beta)$ is continuous in $\beta \in \Theta$.

Assumption 8.3. [Identification]: There exists a unique parameter value β^o in Θ such that $m(\beta^o) = 0$.

Assumption 8.4. [Weighting Matrix]: $\hat{W} \xrightarrow{p} W$, where W is a nonstochastic $l \times l$ symmetric, finite and nonsingular matrix.

Assumption 8.3 is an identification condition. If the moment condition $m(\beta^o) = 0$ is implied by economic theory, β^o can be viewed as the true model parameter value. Assumptions 8.1 and 8.3 imply that the true model parameter value β^o lies inside the compact parameter space Θ. Compactness is sometimes restrictive, but it greatly simplifies asymptotic analysis and is sometime necessary (as in the case of estimating GARCH models) where some parameters must be restricted to ensure a positive conditional variance estimator.

In many applications such as Examples 8.3 and 8.4, the moment function $m_t(\beta)$ usually has the form

$$m_t(\beta) = h_t \varepsilon_t(\beta)$$

for some weighting function h_t and some error or generalized error term $\varepsilon_t(\beta)$. Assumption 8.2 allows but does not require such a multiplicative form for $m_t(\beta)$. Also, in Assumption 8.2, we impose a UWLLN for $\hat{m}(\beta)$ over Θ. Intuitively, uniform convergence implies that the largest (or worse) deviation between $\hat{m}(\beta)$ and $m(\beta)$ over Θ vanishes to 0 in probability as $n \to \infty$.

Question: How to ensure uniform convergence in probability?

This can be achieved by a suitable UWLLN. For example, when $\{(Y_t, X_t')'\}_{t=1}^n$ is IID, we have the following result:

Lemma 8.1. ***[USLLN for an IID Process]:*** *Let $\{Z_t, t = 1, 2, ...\}$ be an IID sequence of random $d \times 1$ vectors, with common CDF F.*

Let Θ be a compact subset of R^K, and let $q : R^d \times \Theta \to R$ be a function such that $q(\cdot, \beta)$ is measurable for each $\beta \in \Theta$ and $q(z, \cdot)$ is continuous on Θ for each $z \in R^d$.

Suppose there exists a measurable function $D : R^d \to R^+$ such that $|q(z, \beta)| \leq D(z)$ for all $\beta \in \Theta$ and $z \in S$, where S is the support of Z_t and $E[D(Z_t)] < \infty$.

Then

(1) $Q(\beta) = E[q(Z_t, \beta)]$ is continuous on Θ;

(2) $\sup_{\beta \in \Theta} |\hat{Q}(\beta) - Q(\beta)| \to 0$ almost surely as $n \to \infty$, where $\hat{Q}(\beta) = n^{-1} \sum_{t=1}^n q(Z_t, \beta)$.

Proof: See Jennrich (1969, Theorem 2).

For an ergodic time series process, we can use the following USLLN.

Lemma 8.2. ***[USLLN for an Ergodic Stationary Process (Ranga Rao 1962)]:*** *Let (Ω, F, P) be a probability space, and let $T : \Omega \to \Omega$ be a one-to-one measure preserving transformation.*

Let Θ be a compact subset of R^K, and let $q : \Omega \times \Theta \to R$ be a function such that $q(\cdot, \beta)$ is measurable for each $\theta \in \Theta$ and $q(\omega, \cdot)$ is continuous on Θ for each $\omega \in \Omega$.

Suppose there exists a measurable function $D : \Omega \to R^+$ *such that* $|q(\omega, \beta)| \leq D(\omega)$ *for all* $\beta \in \Theta$ *and* $\omega \in \Omega$, *and* $E(D) = \int DdP < \infty$. *If for each* $\beta \in \Theta$, $q_t(\theta) = q(T^t\omega, \beta)$ *is ergodic, then*

(1) $Q(\beta) = E[q_t(\beta)]$ *is continuous on* Θ;

(2) $\sup_{\beta\in\Theta} |\hat{Q}(\beta) - Q(\beta)| \to 0$ *almost surely as* $n \to \infty$, *where* $\hat{Q}(\beta) = n^{-1}\sum_{t=1}^{n} q_t(\beta)$.

Proof: See Ranga Rao (1962).

We note that uniform almost sure convergence implies uniform convergence in probability.

To show consistency of the GMM estimator $\hat{\beta}$ for β^o, we need the following extremum estimator lemma.

Lemma 8.3. ***[Consistency of Extremum Estimator (White 1994)]:*** *Let* $\hat{Q}(\beta)$ *be a stochastic real-valued function of* $\beta \in \Theta$, *and* $Q(\beta)$ *be a nonstochastic real-valued continuous function of* β, *where* Θ *is a compact parameter space. Suppose that for each* β, $\hat{Q}(\beta)$ *is a measurable function of the random sample with sample n, and for each n,* $\hat{Q}(\cdot)$ *is continuous in* $\beta \in \Theta$ *with probability one. Also suppose* $\hat{Q}(\beta) - Q(\beta) \xrightarrow{p} 0$ *uniformly in* $\beta \in \Theta$.

Let $\hat{\beta} = \arg\max_{\beta\in\Theta} \hat{Q}(\beta)$, *and* $\beta^o = \arg\max_{\beta\in\Theta} Q(\beta)$ *is the unique maximizer. Then* $\hat{\beta} - \beta^o \xrightarrow{p} 0$ *as* $n \to \infty$.

Proof: See White (1994, Theorem 3.4).

This lemma continues to hold if we change all convergences in probability to almost sure convergences. We now apply Lemma 8.3 to show the consistency of the GMM estimator $\hat{\beta}$.

Theorem 8.2. ***[Consistency of GMM]:*** *Suppose Assumptions 8.1 to 8.4 hold. Then as* $n \to \infty$,

$$\hat{\beta} \xrightarrow{p} \beta^o.$$

Proof: Put

$$\hat{Q}(\beta) = -\hat{m}(\beta)'\hat{W}^{-1}\hat{m}(\beta)$$

and

$$Q(\beta) = -m(\beta)'W^{-1}m(\beta).$$

Then

$$\begin{aligned}
&\left|\hat{Q}(\beta) - Q(\beta)\right| \\
&= \left|\hat{m}(\beta)'\hat{W}^{-1}\hat{m}(\beta) - m(\beta)'W^{-1}m(\beta)\right| \\
&= \left|[\hat{m}(\beta) - m(\beta) + m(\beta)]'\hat{W}^{-1}[\hat{m}(\beta) - m(\beta) + m(\beta)] - m(\beta)'W^{-1}m(\beta)\right| \\
&\leq \left|[\hat{m}(\beta) - m(\beta)]'\,\hat{W}^{-1}\,[\hat{m}(\beta) - m(\beta)]\right| \\
&\quad + 2\left|m(\beta)'\hat{W}^{-1}\,[\hat{m}(\beta) - m(\beta)]\right| \\
&\quad + \left|m(\beta)'(\hat{W}^{-1} - W^{-1})m(\beta)\right|.
\end{aligned}$$

It follows from Assumptions 8.1, 8.2 and 8.4 that

$$\hat{Q}(\beta) \xrightarrow{p} Q(\beta)$$

uniformly over Θ, and $Q(\cdot) = m(\cdot)'W^{-1}m(\cdot)$ is continuous in β over Θ. Moreover, Assumption 8.3 implies that β^o is the unique minimizer of $Q(\beta)$ over Θ. It follows that $\hat{\beta} \xrightarrow{p} \beta^o$ by the extremum estimator lemma. Note that the proof of the consistency theorem does not require the existence of FOC. This is made possible by using the extremum estimator lemma. This completes the proof of consistency.

8.4 Asymptotic Normality of the GMM Estimator

To derive the asymptotic distribution of the GMM estimator, we impose two additional regularity conditions.

Assumption 8.5. [Interiorness]: β^o is an interior point of Θ.

Assumption 8.6. [CLT]:

(a) For each t, $m_t(\beta)$ is continuously differentiable with respect to $\beta \in \Theta$ with probability one.

(b) As $n \to \infty$,

$$\sqrt{n}\hat{m}(\beta^o) \equiv n^{-1/2}\sum_{t=1}^{n} m_t(\beta^o) \xrightarrow{d} N(0, V_o),$$

where $V_o \equiv \text{avar}[\sqrt{n}\hat{m}(\beta^o)]$ is finite and positive definite.

(c) $\{\frac{\partial m_t(\beta)}{\partial \beta}\}$ obeys UWLLN, i.e.,

$$\sup_{\beta\in\Theta}\left\| n^{-1}\sum_{t=1}^{n}\frac{\partial m_t(\beta)}{\partial \beta} - D(\beta)\right\| \xrightarrow{p} 0,$$

where the $l \times K$ matrix

$$\begin{aligned} D(\beta) &\equiv E\left[\frac{\partial m_t(\beta)}{\partial \beta}\right] \\ &= \frac{dm(\beta)}{d\beta} \end{aligned}$$

is continuous in $\beta \in \Theta$ and is of full rank K.

Question: Why do we need to assume that β^o is an interior point in Θ?

This is because we will have to use a Taylor series expansion. We need to make use of FOC for GMM in order to derive the asymptotic distribution of $\hat{\beta}$.

In Assumption 8.6, we assume both CLT and UWLLN directly. These are called "high-level assumptions." They can be ensured by imposing more primitive conditions on the DGP (e.g., an IID or MDS random sample), and the moment and smoothness conditions on $m_t(\beta)$. For more discussion, see White (1994).

We now establish the asymptotic normality of the GMM estimator $\hat{\beta}$.

Theorem 8.3. ***[Asymptotic Normality of GMM]:*** *Suppose Assumptions 8.1 to 8.6 hold. Then as $n \to \infty$,*

$$\sqrt{n}\left(\hat{\beta} - \beta^o\right) \xrightarrow{d} N(0, \Omega),$$

where

$$\Omega = (D_o' W^{-1} D_o)^{-1} D_o' W^{-1} V_o W^{-1} D_o (D_o' W^{-1} D_o)^{-1},$$

and $D_o \equiv D(\beta^o) = \frac{\partial m(\beta^o)}{\partial \beta}$.

Proof: Because β^o is an interior element in Θ, and $\hat{\beta} \xrightarrow{p} \beta^o$ as $n \to \infty$, we have that $\hat{\beta}$ is an interior element of Θ with probability approaching one as $n \to \infty$.

For n sufficiently large, the FOC for the maximization of $\hat{Q}(\beta) = -\hat{m}(\beta)'\hat{W}^{-1}\hat{m}(\beta)$ is

$$\begin{aligned} 0 &= \left.\frac{d\hat{Q}(\beta)}{d\beta}\right|_{\beta=\hat{\beta}} \\ &= -2\frac{d\hat{m}(\hat{\beta})}{d\beta'}\hat{W}^{-1}\hat{m}(\hat{\beta}), \end{aligned}$$

or

$$\begin{aligned} 0 &= \frac{d\hat{m}(\hat{\beta})}{d\beta'}\hat{W}^{-1}\sqrt{n}\hat{m}(\hat{\beta}), \\ K \times 1 &= (K \times l) \times (l \times l) \times (l \times 1). \end{aligned}$$

Note that $\hat{W}$ is not a function of β. Also, this FOC does not necessarily imply $\hat{m}(\hat{\beta}) = 0$. Instead, it only says that a set (with dimension $K \leq l$) of linear combinations of the l components in $\hat{m}(\hat{\beta})$ are jointly equal to zero. Here, the $l \times K$ matrix $\frac{d\hat{m}(\beta)}{d\beta}$ is the gradient of the $l \times 1$ vector $\hat{m}(\hat{\beta})$ with respect to the $K \times 1$ vector β.

Using a Taylor series expansion around the true parameter value β^o, we have

$$\sqrt{n}\hat{m}(\hat{\beta}) = \sqrt{n}\hat{m}(\beta^o) + \frac{d\hat{m}(\bar{\beta})}{d\beta}\sqrt{n}(\hat{\beta} - \beta^o),$$

where $\bar{\beta} = \lambda\hat{\beta} + (1-\lambda)\beta^o$ lies between $\hat{\beta}$ and β^o, with $\lambda \in [0,1]$. Here, for notational simplicity, we have abused the notation in the expression of $\frac{d\hat{m}(\bar{\beta})}{d\beta}$. Precisely speaking, a different $\bar{\beta}$ is needed for each partial derivative of $\hat{m}(\cdot)$ with respect to each parameter β_j, where $j \in \{1, ..., K\}$.

The first term in the Taylor series expansion is contributed by the sampling randomness of the sample average of the moment functions evaluated at the true parameter value β^o, and the second term is contributed by the randomness of the parameter estimator $\hat{\beta} - \beta^o$. These two terms will jointly determine the asymptotic distribution of the scaled sample moment $\sqrt{n}\hat{m}(\hat{\beta})$.

It follows from FOC that

$$
\begin{aligned}
0 &= \frac{d\hat{m}(\hat{\beta})}{d\beta'}\hat{W}^{-1}\sqrt{n}\hat{m}(\hat{\beta}) \\
&= \frac{d\hat{m}(\hat{\beta})}{d\beta'}\hat{W}^{-1}\sqrt{n}\hat{m}(\beta^o) \\
&\quad + \frac{d\hat{m}(\hat{\beta})}{d\beta'}\hat{W}^{-1}\frac{d\hat{m}(\bar{\beta})}{d\beta}\sqrt{n}(\hat{\beta}-\beta^o).
\end{aligned}
$$

Now let us show that $\frac{d\hat{m}(\hat{\beta})}{d\beta} \xrightarrow{p} D_o \equiv D(\beta^o)$. To show this, consider

$$
\begin{aligned}
&\left\|\frac{d\hat{m}(\hat{\beta})}{d\beta} - D_0\right\| \\
&= \left\|\frac{d\hat{m}(\hat{\beta})}{d\beta} - D(\hat{\beta}) + D(\hat{\beta}) - D(\beta^o)\right\| \\
&\leq \left\|\frac{d\hat{m}(\hat{\beta})}{d\beta} - D(\hat{\beta})\right\| + \left\|D(\hat{\beta}) - D(\beta^o)\right\| \\
&\leq \sup_{\beta\in\Theta}\left\|\frac{d\hat{m}(\beta)}{d\beta} - D(\beta)\right\| + \left\|D(\hat{\beta}) - D(\beta^o)\right\| \\
&\xrightarrow{p} 0
\end{aligned}
$$

by the triangle inequality, Assumption 8.6 (UWLLN, and continuity of $D(\beta)$), and $\hat{\beta}-\beta^o \xrightarrow{p} 0$.

Similarly, because $\bar{\beta} = \lambda\hat{\beta} + (1-\lambda)\beta^o$ for $\lambda \in [0,1]$, we have

$$
||\bar{\beta}-\beta^o|| = ||\lambda(\hat{\beta}-\beta^o)|| \leq ||\hat{\beta}-\beta^o|| \xrightarrow{p} 0.
$$

It follows that

$$
\frac{d\hat{m}(\bar{\beta})}{d\beta} \xrightarrow{p} D_o.
$$

Then the $K \times K$ matrix

$$
D_o' W^{-1} D_o
$$

is nonsingular by Assumptions 8.4 and 8.6. Therefore, for n sufficiently large, the inverse

$$
\left[\frac{d\hat{m}(\hat{\beta})}{d\beta'}\hat{W}^{-1}\frac{d\hat{m}(\bar{\beta})}{d\beta}\right]^{-1}
$$

exists and converges in probability to $(D_o'W^{-1}D_o)^{-1}$. Thus, when n is sufficiently large, we have

$$\begin{aligned}\sqrt{n}(\hat{\beta}-\beta^o) &= -\left[\frac{d\hat{m}(\hat{\beta})}{d\beta'}\hat{W}^{-1}\frac{d\hat{m}(\bar{\beta})}{d\beta}\right]^{-1}\frac{d\hat{m}(\hat{\beta})}{d\beta'}\hat{W}^{-1}\sqrt{n}\hat{m}(\beta^o)\\ &= \hat{A}\sqrt{n}\hat{m}(\beta^o),\end{aligned}$$

where

$$\hat{A} = -\left[\frac{d\hat{m}(\hat{\beta})}{d\beta'}\hat{W}^{-1}\frac{d\hat{m}(\bar{\beta})}{d\beta}\right]^{-1}\frac{d\hat{m}(\hat{\beta})}{d\beta'}\hat{W}^{-1}.$$

By Assumption 8.6(b), and CLT for $\{m_t(\beta^o)\}$, we have

$$\sqrt{n}\hat{m}(\beta^o) \xrightarrow{d} N(0, V_o),$$

where $V_o \equiv \text{avar}[n^{-1/2}\sum_{t=1}^n m_t(\beta^o)]$. Moreover,

$$\begin{aligned}\hat{A} &= -\left[\frac{d\hat{m}(\hat{\beta})}{d\beta'}\hat{W}^{-1}\frac{d\hat{m}(\bar{\beta})}{d\beta}\right]^{-1}\frac{d\hat{m}(\hat{\beta})}{d\beta'}\hat{W}^{-1}\\ &\xrightarrow{p} -\left(D_o'W^{-1}D_o\right)^{-1}D_o'W^{-1} \equiv A.\end{aligned}$$

It follows from Slutsky's theorem that

$$\sqrt{n}(\hat{\beta}-\beta^o) \xrightarrow{d} A\cdot N(0, V_o) \sim N(0, \Omega),$$

where

$$\begin{aligned}\Omega &= AV_oA'\\ &= (D_o'W^{-1}D_o)^{-1}D_o'W^{-1}V_oW^{-1}D_o(D_o'W^{-1}D_o)^{-1}.\end{aligned}$$

This completes the proof.

We observe that the structure of $\text{avar}(\sqrt{n}\hat{\beta})$ is very similar to that of $\text{avar}(\sqrt{n}\hat{\beta}_{2SLS})$. In fact, as pointed out earlier, 2SLS is a special case of the GMM estimator with the choice of

$$\begin{aligned}m_t(\beta) &= Z_t(Y_t - X_t'\beta),\\ W &= E(Z_tZ_t') = Q_{ZZ}.\end{aligned}$$

Similarly, the OLS estimator is a special case of the GMM estimator with the choice of

$$\begin{aligned} m_t(\beta) &= X_t(Y_t - X_t'\beta), \\ W &= E(X_t X_t') = Q_{XX}. \end{aligned}$$

Most econometric estimators can be viewed as a special case of GMM, at least asymptotically. In other words, GMM provides a convenient unified framework to view most econometric estimators. See White (1994) for more discussion.

8.5 Asymptotic Efficiency of the GMM Estimator

Question: There are many possible choices of $\hat{W}$. Is there any optimal choice for $\hat{W}$? If so, what is the optimal choice of $\hat{W}$?

The following theorem shows that the optimal choice of W is given by

$$W = V_o \equiv \text{var}[\sqrt{n}\hat{m}(\beta^o)],$$

namely the optimal limit weighting matrix W is the asymptotic variance-covariance matrix of $\sqrt{n}\hat{m}(\beta^o)$, the $\sqrt{n}$-scaled sample moment function evaluated at the true parameter value β^o.

Theorem 8.4. ***[Asymptotic Efficiency of GMM]:*** *Suppose Assumptions 8.4 and 8.6 hold. Define $\Omega_o = (D_o'V_o^{-1}D_o)^{-1}$, which is obtained by choosing the weighting matrix $W = V_o \equiv avar[\sqrt{n}\hat{m}(\beta^o)]$. Then*

$$\Omega - \Omega_o \textit{ is PSD}$$

where Ω is the asymptotic variance of GMM that corresponds to any finite, symmetric and nonsingular matrix W.

Proof: Observe that $\Omega - \Omega_o$ is PSD if and only if $\Omega_o^{-1} - \Omega^{-1}$ is PSD. We therefore consider

$$\begin{aligned} &\Omega_o^{-1} - \Omega^{-1} \\ &= D_o'V_o^{-1}D_o - D_o'W^{-1}D_o(D_o'W^{-1}V_oW^{-1}D_o)^{-1}D_o'W^{-1}D_o \\ &= D_o'V_o^{-1/2}[I - V_o^{1/2}W^{-1}D_o(D_o'W^{-1}V_oW^{-1}D_o)^{-1}D_o'W^{-1}V_o^{1/2}]V_o^{-1/2}D_o \\ &= D_o'V_o^{-1/2}GV_o^{-1/2}D_o, \end{aligned}$$

where $V_o = V_o^{1/2} V_o^{1/2}$ for some symmetric and nonsingular matrix $V_o^{1/2}$, and

$$G \equiv I - V_o^{1/2} W^{-1} D_o (D_o' W^{-1} V_o W^{-1} D_o)^{-1} D_o' W^{-1} V_o^{1/2}$$

is a symmetric idempotent matrix (i.e., $G = G'$ and $G^2 = G$). It follows that we have

$$\begin{aligned}
\Omega_o^{-1} - \Omega^{-1} &= (D_o' V_o^{-1/2} G)(G V_o^{-1/2} D_o) \\
&= (G V_o^{-1/2} D_o)'(G V_o^{-1/2} D_o) \\
&= B'B \\
&\sim \text{PSD (why?)},
\end{aligned}$$

where $B = G V_o^{-1/2} D_o$ is an $l \times K$ matrix. This completes the proof.

The optimal choice of $W = V_o$ is not unique. The choice of $W = cV_o$ for any nonzero constant c is also optimal.

In practice, the asymptotic variance-covariance matrix V_o is not available. However, we can use a feasible asymptotically optimal choice $\hat{W} = \tilde{V}$, a consistent estimator for $V_o \equiv \text{avar}[\sqrt{n}\hat{m}(\beta^o)]$.

Question: What is the intuition that $\hat{W} = \tilde{V}$ is an optimal weighting matrix?

By UWLLN, we have $\hat{W} \xrightarrow{p} V_o$ as $n \to \infty$, where V_o is the asymptotic variance-covariance matrix of the scaled sample moment vector $\sqrt{n}\hat{m}(\beta^o)$. The use of $\hat{W}^{-1} \xrightarrow{p} V_o^{-1}$, therefore, downweighs the sample moments which have large sampling variations and differences out correlations between different components $\sqrt{n}\hat{m}_i(\beta^o)$ and $\sqrt{n}\hat{m}_j(\beta^o)$ for $i \neq j$, where $i, j = 1, ..., K$. This is similar in spirit to the adaptive feasible GLS estimator in the linear regression model.

As pointed out earlier, the 2SLS estimator $\hat{\beta}_{2SLS}$ is a special case of the GMM estimator with

$$m_t(\beta) = Z_t(Y_t - X_t'\beta)$$

and the choice of weighting matrix

$$W = E(Z_t Z_t') = Q_{ZZ}.$$

Suppose $\{m_t(\beta^o)\}$ is an MDS and $E(\varepsilon_t^2|Z_t) = \sigma^2$, where $\varepsilon_t = Y_t - X_t'\beta^o$. Then

$$\begin{aligned} V_o &= \text{avar}[\sqrt{n}\hat{m}(\beta^o)] \\ &= E\left[m_t(\beta^o)m_t(\beta^o)'\right] \\ &= \sigma^2 Q_{ZZ} \end{aligned}$$

where the last equality follows from the law of iterated expectations and conditional homoskedasticity. Because $W = Q_{ZZ}$ is proportional to V_o, the 2SLS estimator $\hat{\beta}$ is asymptotically optimal in this case. In contrast, when $\{m_t(\beta^o)\}$ is an MDS with conditional heteroskedasticity (i.e., $E(\varepsilon_t^2|Z_t) \neq \sigma^2$) or $\{m_t(\beta^o)\}$ is not an MDS, then the choice of $W = Q_{ZZ}$ does not deliver an asymptotically optimal 2SLS estimator. Instead, the GMM estimator with the choice of $W = V_o = E(Z_t Z_t' \varepsilon_t^2)$ is asymptotically optimal when $\{m_t(\beta^o)\}$ is an MDS with conditional heteroskedasticity. Similarly, the choice of $W = V_o \equiv \sum_{j=-\infty}^{\infty} \Gamma(j)$, where $\Gamma(j) = E(Z_t\varepsilon_t\varepsilon_{t-j}Z_{t-j}')$ for $j \geq 0$ and $\Gamma(j) = \Gamma(-j)'$ for $j < 0$, when $\{m_t(\beta^o)\}$ is not an MDS.

8.6 Two-Stage Asymptotically Most Efficient GMM Estimation

Theorem 8.4 suggests that the following two-stage GMM estimator will be asymptotically optimal.

Step 1: Find a consistent preliminary GMM estimator $\tilde{\beta}$:

$$\tilde{\beta} = \arg\min_{\beta\in\Theta} \hat{m}(\beta)'\tilde{W}^{-1}\hat{m}(\beta),$$

for some preliminary weighting matrix $\tilde{W}$ which converges in probability to some finite and positive definite matrix. For convenience, one can set $\tilde{W} = I$, an $l \times l$ identity matrix. This is not an optimal estimator, but it is a consistent estimator for β^o.

With the preliminary GMM estimator $\tilde{\beta}$, we can construct a preliminary consistent variance estimator $\tilde{V}$ for $V_o \equiv \text{avar}[\sqrt{n}\hat{m}(\beta^o)]$, and choose $\hat{W} = \tilde{V}$.

The construction of $\tilde{V}$ differs in the following two cases, depending on whether $\{m_t(\beta^o)\}$ is an MDS:

Case I: $\{m_t(\beta^o)\}$ Is an Ergodic Stationary MDS

In this case,

$$V_o \equiv \text{avar}[\sqrt{n}\hat{m}(\beta^o)] = E[m_t(\beta^o)m_t(\beta^o)'].$$

The asymptotic variance estimator

$$\tilde{V} = n^{-1}\sum_{t=1}^{n} m_t(\tilde{\beta})m_t(\tilde{\beta})'$$

will be consistent for

$$V_o = E[m_t(\beta^o)m_t(\beta^o)'].$$

Question: How to show that $\tilde{V}$ is consistent for V_o?

We need to assume that $\{n^{-1}\sum_{t=1}^{n} m_t(\beta)m_t(\beta)' - E[m_t(\beta)m_t(\beta)']\}$ satisfies the uniform convergence:

$$\sup_{\beta\in\Theta}\left\| n^{-1}\sum_{t=1}^{n} m_t(\beta)m_t(\beta)' - E[m_t(\beta)m_t(\beta)']\right\| \xrightarrow{p} 0.$$

Also, we need to assume that the $l \times l$ matrix $V(\beta) \equiv E[m_t(\beta)m_t(\beta)']$ is continuous in $\beta \in \Theta$.

Case II: $\{m_t(\beta^o)\}$ Is an Ergodic Stationary Non-MDS

In this case, $V_o \equiv \text{avar}[\sqrt{n}\hat{m}(\beta^o)] = \sum_{j=-\infty}^{\infty}\Gamma(j)$, where $\Gamma(j) = \text{cov}[m_t(\beta^o), m_{t-j}(\beta^o)]$ for $j \geq 0$ and $\Gamma(j) = \Gamma(-j)$ for $j < 0$. Therefore, a consistent long-run variance-covariance matrix estimator is needed:

$$\tilde{V} = \sum_{j=1-n}^{n-1} k(j/p)\tilde{\Gamma}(j),$$

where $k(\cdot)$ is a kernel function, $p = p(n)$ is a smoothing parameter,

$$\tilde{\Gamma}(j) = n^{-1}\sum_{t=j+1}^{n} m_t(\tilde{\beta})m_{t-j}(\tilde{\beta})' \quad \text{for } j \geq 0,$$

and $\tilde{\Gamma}(j) = \tilde{\Gamma}(-j)'$ if $j < 0$. Under regularity conditions, it can be shown that $\tilde{V}$ is consistent for the long-run variance-covariance matrix

$$V_o = \sum_{j=-\infty}^{\infty}\Gamma(j),$$

where $\Gamma(j)$ =cov$[m_t(\beta^o), m_{t-j}(\beta^o)] = E[m_t(\beta^o)m_{t-j}(\beta^o)']$. See more discussion in Chapter 6.

Question: Why do we not need demean when defining $\tilde{\Gamma}(j)$?

Step 2: Choose $\hat{W} = \tilde{V}$, and find an asymptotically optimal GMM estimator $\hat{\beta}$:

$$\hat{\beta} = \arg\min_{\beta\in\Theta} \hat{m}(\beta)'\tilde{V}^{-1}\hat{m}(\beta),$$

where the weighting matrix $\tilde{V}$ does not involve the unknown parameter β. It is a given (stochastic) weighting matrix. This two-stage GMM estimator $\hat{\beta}$ is asymptotically optimal because $\tilde{V} \xrightarrow{p} V_o = \text{avar}[\sqrt{n}\hat{m}(\beta^o)]$ as $n \to \infty$.

Theorem 8.5. ***[Two-Stage Asymptotically Most Efficient GMM Estimator]:*** *Suppose Assumptions 8.1 to 8.3, 8.5 and 8.6 hold, and the first stage weighting matrix $\tilde{W} \xrightarrow{p} W$ for some symmetric finite and positive definite matrix W. Also, suppose $\tilde{V}$ is an asymptotic variance estimator based on the first stage GMM estimation such that $\tilde{V} \xrightarrow{p} V_o \equiv avar[\sqrt{n}\hat{m}(\beta^o)]$ as $n \to \infty$, and $\tilde{V}$ is used as the weighting matrix for the second stage GMM estimation. Let $\hat{\beta}$ be the resulting two-stage GMM estimator. Then*

$$\sqrt{n}(\hat{\beta} - \beta^o) \xrightarrow{d} N(0, \Omega_o) \text{ as } n \to \infty,$$

where $\Omega_o = (D_o' V_o^{-1} D_o)^{-1}$.

Question: Why do we need the two-stage asymptotically optimal GMM estimator?

First, most macroeconomic time series data sets are usually short, and second, the use of instruments Z_t is usually inefficient. These factors lead to a large estimation error so it is desirable to have an asymptotically efficient estimator.

Although the two-stage GMM procedure is asymptotically efficient, one may like to iterate the procedure further until the GMM parameter estimates and the values of the minimized objective function converge. This will alleviate any dependence of the GMM estimator on the choice of the initial weighting matrix $\tilde{W}$, and it may improve the finite sample performance of the GMM estimator when the number of parameters is large (e.g., Ferson and Foerster 1994).

8.7 Asymptotic Variance-Covariance Matrix Estimation

To construct confidence interval estimators and conduct hypothesis test statistics, we need to estimate the asymptotic variance-covariance matrix Ω_o of the $\sqrt{n}$-scaled optimal GMM estimator.

Question: How to estimate $\Omega_o \equiv (D_o' V_o^{-1} D_o)^{-1}$?

We need to estimate both D_o and V_o respectively. To estimate $D_o = E[\frac{\partial m_t(\beta^o)}{\partial \beta}]$, we can use

$$\hat{D} = \frac{d\hat{m}(\hat{\beta})}{d\beta}.$$

We have shown earlier that

$$\hat{D} \xrightarrow{p} D_o \text{ as } n \to \infty.$$

To estimate V_o, we need to consider two cases, MDS and non-MDS, separately.

Case I: $\{m_t(\beta^o)\}$ Is an Ergodic Stationary MDS

In this case,

$$V_o = E[m_t(\beta^o)m_t(\beta^o)'].$$

A consistent variance estimator is

$$\hat{V} = n^{-1}\sum_{t=1}^{n} m_t(\hat{\beta})m_t(\hat{\beta})'.$$

Assuming UWLLN for $\{m_t(\beta)m_t(\beta)'\}$, we can show that $\hat{V}$ is consistent for

$$V_o = E[m_t(\beta^o)m_t(\beta^o)'].$$

Case II: $\{m_t(\beta^o)\}$ Is an Ergodic Stationary Non-MDS

In this case,

$$V_o = \sum_{j=-\infty}^{\infty} \Gamma(j),$$

where $\Gamma(j) = E[m_t(\beta^o)m_{t-j}(\beta^o)']$. A consistent variance estimator is

$$\hat{V} = \sum_{j=1-n}^{n-1} k(j/p)\hat{\Gamma}(j),$$

where $k(\cdot)$ is a kernel function, and

$$\hat{\Gamma}(j) = n^{-1} \sum_{t=j+1}^{n} m_t(\hat{\beta})m_{t-j}(\hat{\beta})' \text{ for } j \geq 0.$$

Under suitable conditions (e.g., Newey and West 1994, Andrews 1991), we can show

$$\hat{V} \xrightarrow{p} V_o$$

but the proof of this is beyond the scope of this course.

To cover both cases, we directly impose the following "high-level assumption":

Assumption 8.7. $\hat{V} - V_o \xrightarrow{p} 0$ as $n \to \infty$, where $V_o \equiv \text{avar}[\sqrt{n}\hat{m}(\beta^o)]$.

Theorem 8.6. ***[Asymptotic Variance Estimator for Two-Stage Asymptotically Optimal GMM Estimator]:*** *Suppose Assumptions 8.1 to 8.7 hold. Then*

$$\hat{\Omega}_o \equiv (\hat{D}'\hat{V}^{-1}\hat{D})^{-1} \xrightarrow{p} \Omega_o \text{ as } n \to \infty.$$

8.8 Hypothesis Testing

We now consider testing the hypothesis of interest

$$\mathbf{H}_0 : R(\beta^o) = r,$$

where $R(\cdot)$ is a $J \times 1$ continuously differentiable vector-valued function, $J \leq K$, and the $J \times K$ matrix $\frac{dR(\beta^o)}{d\beta} = R'(\beta^o)$ is of full rank J. Note that $R(\beta^o) = r$ covers both linear and nonlinear restrictions on model parameters. An example of nonlinear restriction is $\beta_1^o\beta_2^o = 1$.

Question: Why do we need $J \leq K$, namely the number of restrictions is less than that of unknown parameters?

Question: How to construct a test statistic for $\mathbf{H}_0$?

The basic idea is to check whether $R(\hat{\beta}) - r$ is close to 0. How large the difference $R(\hat{\beta}) - r$ should be in order to be considered as significantly different from 0 will be determined by the sampling distribution of $\sqrt{n}[R(\hat{\beta}) - r]$.

By a Taylor series expansion and $R(\beta^o) = r$ under $\mathbf{H}_0$, we have

$$\begin{aligned}\sqrt{n}[R(\hat{\beta}) - r] &= \sqrt{n}[R(\beta^o) - r] + R'(\bar{\beta})\sqrt{n}(\hat{\beta} - \beta^o) \\ &= R'(\bar{\beta})\sqrt{n}(\hat{\beta} - \beta^o) \\ &\xrightarrow{d} R'(\beta^o) \cdot N(0, \Omega_o) \sim N[0, R'(\beta^o)\Omega_o R'(\beta^o)'],\end{aligned}$$

where $\bar{\beta}$ lies between $\hat{\beta}$ and β^o, i.e., $\bar{\beta} = \lambda\hat{\beta} + (1 - \lambda)\beta^o$ for some $\lambda \in [0, 1]$.

Because $R'(\bar{\beta}) \xrightarrow{p} R'(\beta^o)$ given continuity of $R'(\cdot)$ and $\bar{\beta} - \beta^o \xrightarrow{p} 0$, and

$$\sqrt{n}(\hat{\beta} - \beta^o) \xrightarrow{d} N(0, \Omega_o) \text{ as } n \to \infty,$$

we have

$$\sqrt{n}[R(\hat{\beta}) - r] \xrightarrow{d} N[0, R'(\beta^o)\Omega_o R'(\beta^o)'].$$

by Slutsky's theorem. It follows that for $J \geq 1$, the quadratic form

$$\sqrt{n}[R(\hat{\beta}) - r]'[R'(\beta^o)\Omega_o R'(\beta^o)']^{-1}\sqrt{n}[R(\hat{\beta}) - r] \xrightarrow{d} \chi^2_J.$$

The Wald test statistic is then

$$W = n[R(\hat{\beta}) - r]'[R'(\hat{\beta})\hat{\Omega}_o R'(\hat{\beta})']^{-1}[R(\hat{\beta}) - r] \xrightarrow{d} \chi^2_J$$

where the convergence in distribution to χ^2_J follows from Slutsky's theorem.

When $J = 1$, we can define a t-test statistic

$$T = \frac{\sqrt{n}[R(\hat{\beta}) - r]}{\sqrt{R'(\hat{\beta})\hat{\Omega}_o R'(\hat{\beta})'}} \xrightarrow{d} N(0, 1) \text{ as } n \to \infty.$$

Theorem 8.7. ***[t-Test and Wald Test]:*** *Suppose Assumptions 8.1 to 8.7 hold. Then under* $\mathbf{H}_0 : R(\beta^o) = r$ *and as* $n \to \infty$, *we have:*
(1) when $J = 1$,

$$T \equiv \frac{\sqrt{n}[R(\hat{\beta}) - r]}{\sqrt{R'(\hat{\beta})\hat{\Omega}_o R'(\hat{\beta})'}} \xrightarrow{d} N(0, 1) \ ;$$

(2) when $J \geq 1$,

$$W \equiv n[R(\hat{\beta}) - r]'[R'(\hat{\beta})\hat{\Omega}_o R'(\hat{\beta})']^{-1}[R(\hat{\beta}) - r] \xrightarrow{d} \chi^2_J.$$

Both the t-test and Wald test statistics in Theorem 8.7 are based on an asymptotically optimal GMM estimator. One could also construct t-test and Wald test statistics using a consistent but suboptimal GMM estimator. (How?) However, in finite samples, the test statistics based on an asymptotically suboptimal GMM estimator are expected to be less powerful against $\mathbf{H}_0$ (i.e., to have a larger Type II error). (Why?)

8.9 Model Specification Testing

As pointed out earlier, many dynamic economic theories can be formulated as a moment condition or a set of moment conditions. Thus, to test validity of an economic theory, one can check whether the related moment condition holds.

Question: How to test whether the econometric model or economic theory as characterized by

$$\mathbf{H}_0 : E\left[m_t(\beta^o)\right] = 0 \text{ for some unknown parameter value } \beta^o$$

is correctly specified?

We can test correct model specification by checking whether the above population moment condition holds. We can define the sample moment

$$\hat{m}(\hat{\beta}) = n^{-1} \sum_{t=1}^{n} m_t(\hat{\beta})$$

and see if it is significantly different from zero (the value of the population moment evaluated at the true parameter value β^o). For this purpose, we need to know the asymptotic distribution of $\sqrt{n}\hat{m}(\hat{\beta})$.

Consider the test statistic

$$\sqrt{n}\hat{m}(\hat{\beta}) = \sqrt{n}\hat{m}(\beta^o) + \frac{d\hat{m}(\bar{\beta})}{d\beta}\sqrt{n}(\hat{\beta} - \beta^o)$$

which follows from a first order Taylor series expansion, and $\bar{\beta}$ lies between $\hat{\beta}$ and β^o. The asymptotic distribution of $\sqrt{n}\hat{m}(\hat{\beta})$ is contributed from two sources.

Recall that the two-stage GMM estimator

$$\hat{\beta} = \arg\min_{\beta \in \Theta} \hat{m}(\beta)'\tilde{V}^{-1}\hat{m}(\beta),$$

where $\tilde{V}$ is a preliminary consistent estimator for V_o. The FOC of the two-stage GMM estimation is given by

$$0 = \frac{d}{d\beta}\left[\hat{m}(\hat{\beta})'\tilde{V}^{-1}\hat{m}(\hat{\beta})\right].$$

It is very important to note that $\tilde{V}$ is not a function of β, so it has nothing to do with the differentiation with respect to β. By a Taylor series expansion, we have

$$\begin{aligned} 0 = &\frac{d\hat{m}(\hat{\beta})}{d\beta'}\tilde{V}^{-1}\sqrt{n}\hat{m}(\beta^o) \\ &+ \frac{d\hat{m}(\hat{\beta})}{d\beta'}\tilde{V}^{-1}\frac{d\hat{m}(\bar{\beta})}{d\beta}\sqrt{n}(\hat{\beta}-\beta^o). \end{aligned}$$

It follows that for n sufficiently large, we have

$$\sqrt{n}(\hat{\beta}-\beta^o) = -\left[\frac{d\hat{m}(\hat{\beta})}{d\beta'}\tilde{V}^{-1}\frac{d\hat{m}(\bar{\beta})}{d\beta}\right]^{-1}\frac{d\hat{m}(\hat{\beta})}{d\beta'}\tilde{V}^{-1}\sqrt{n}\hat{m}(\beta^o).$$

Hence,

$$\begin{aligned} &\tilde{V}^{-1/2}\sqrt{n}\hat{m}(\hat{\beta}) \\ &= \tilde{V}^{-1/2}\sqrt{n}\hat{m}(\beta^o) + \tilde{V}^{-1/2}\frac{d\hat{m}(\bar{\beta})}{d\beta}\sqrt{n}(\hat{\beta}-\beta^o) \\ &= \left[I - \tilde{V}^{-1/2}\frac{d\hat{m}(\bar{\beta})}{d\beta}\left[\frac{d\hat{m}(\hat{\beta})}{d\beta'}\tilde{V}^{-1}\frac{d\hat{m}(\bar{\beta})}{d\beta}\right]^{-1}\frac{d\hat{m}(\hat{\beta})}{d\beta'}\tilde{V}^{-1/2}\right]\tilde{V}^{-1/2}\sqrt{n}\hat{m}(\beta^o) \\ &= \hat{\Pi}[\tilde{V}^{-1/2}\sqrt{n}\hat{m}(\beta^o)], \end{aligned}$$

where

$$\hat{\Pi} = I - \tilde{V}^{-1/2}\frac{d\hat{m}(\bar{\beta})}{d\beta}\left[\frac{d\hat{m}(\hat{\beta})}{d\beta'}\tilde{V}^{-1}\frac{d\hat{m}(\bar{\beta})}{d\beta}\right]^{-1}\frac{d\hat{m}(\hat{\beta})}{d\beta'}\tilde{V}^{-1/2}.$$

By CLT for $\{m_t(\beta^o)\}$ and Slutsky's theorem, we have

$$\tilde{V}^{-1/2}\sqrt{n}\hat{m}(\beta^o) \xrightarrow{d} N(0, I),$$

where I is an $l \times l$ identity matrix. Also, we have

$$\hat{\Pi} \xrightarrow{p} I - V_o^{-1/2}D_o(D_o'V_o^{-1}D_o)^{-1}D_o'V_o^{-1/2} \equiv \Pi,$$

where Π is an $l \times l$ symmetric matrix which is also idempotent (i.e., $\Pi^2 = \Pi$) with $\mathrm{tr}(\Pi) = l - K$. (How to show this?) We emphasize that the idempotent matrix Π arises due to the choice of the asymptotically optimal weighting matrix $\hat{W} = \tilde{V}$ in the second stage estimation. If the weighting matrix $\hat{W}$ in the second stage does not converge to the asymptotic variance $V_o = \text{avar}[\sqrt{n}\hat{m}(\beta^o)]$, we will not be able to obtain the idempotent matrix Π. Instead, we will obtain a nonsingular $l \times l$ matrix.

It follows that under correct model specification, we have the test statistic

$$\begin{aligned} n[\hat{m}(\hat{\beta})'\tilde{V}^{-1}\hat{m}(\hat{\beta})] &= [\tilde{V}^{-1/2}\sqrt{n}\hat{m}(\beta^o)]'\hat{\Pi}^2[\tilde{V}^{-1/2}\sqrt{n}\hat{m}(\beta^o)] + o_P(1) \\ &\xrightarrow{d} G'\Pi G \sim \chi^2_{l-K} \end{aligned}$$

by Lemma 3.2 for the quadratic forms of normal random variables, where $G \sim N(0, I)$.

We emphasize that the adjustment of degrees of freedom from l to $l-K$ for the asymptotic Chi-square distribution is due to the impact of the sampling variation of the two-stage asymptotically optimal GMM estimator $\hat{\beta}$. In other words, the use of the two-stage asymptotically optimal GMM estimator $\hat{\beta}$ (obtained from choosing $\hat{W} = \tilde{V}$) instead of any other asymptotically suboptimal GMM estimator renders the degrees of freedom to change from l to $l-K$. If an asymptotically suboptimal GMM estimator is used, the quadratic form $n[\hat{m}(\hat{\beta})'\tilde{V}^{-1}\hat{m}(\hat{\beta})]$ will not follow an asymptotic χ^2 distribution $\mathbf{H}_0$.

Theorem 8.8. *[**Overidentification Test**]: Suppose Assumptions 8.1 to 8.6 hold, and $\tilde{V} \xrightarrow{p} V_o \equiv avar[\sqrt{n}\hat{m}(\beta^o)]$ as $n \to \infty$. Then under the null hypothesis that $\mathbf{H}_0 : E[m_t(\beta^o)] = 0$ for some unknown β^o, the overidentification test statistic*

$$J \equiv n \cdot \hat{m}(\hat{\beta})'\tilde{V}^{-1}\hat{m}(\hat{\beta}) \xrightarrow{d} \chi^2_{l-K} \text{ as } n \to \infty.$$

This test is often called the J-test or the test for overidentification in the GMM literature (e.g., Hansen 1982), because it requires $l > K$. This test can be used to check if the model characterized as the moment condition $E[m_t(\beta^o)] = 0$ is correctly specified.

It is important to note that the fact that the GMM objective function

$$n\hat{m}(\hat{\beta})'\tilde{V}^{-1}\hat{m}(\hat{\beta}) \to G'\Pi G$$

where Π is an idempotent matrix is due to the fact that $\hat{\beta}$ is an asymptotically optimal GMM estimator that minimizes the objective function $n\hat{m}(\beta)'\tilde{V}^{-1}\hat{m}(\beta)$. If a suboptimal GMM estimator is used, we would not be able to obtain such a result. In other words, the GMM objective function is no longer asymptotically χ^2_{n-K} under correct model specification. Instead, we need to use a different asymptotic variance estimator to replace $\tilde{V}$ in order to obtain an asymptotically χ^2_l distribution under correct model specification. Because the critical value of χ^2_{l-K} is smaller than that of χ^2_l when $K > 0$, the use of an asymptotically optimal estimator $\hat{\beta}$ leads to an asymptotically more powerful test, i.e., it will have a higher probability to reject model misspecification.

We note that when $l = K$, the exact identification case, the moment conditions cannot be tested by the two-stage asymptotically optimal GMM estimator $\hat{\beta}$, because $\hat{m}(\hat{\beta})$ will be identically zero, no matter whether $E[m(\beta^o)] = 0$.

Question: In constructing the J test statistic, we have used the preliminary weighting matrix $\tilde{V}$, which is evaluated at the first-stage preliminary parameter estimator $\tilde{\beta}$. Can we use $\hat{V}$, a consistent estimator for V_o that is evaluated at the two-stage asymptotically optimal estimator $\hat{\beta}$ instead of the first stage preliminary estimator $\tilde{\beta}$?

With the preliminary matrix $\tilde{V}$, the J-test statistic can be conveniently defined as n times the minimum value of the objective function—the quadratic form in the second stage of GMM estimation. Thus, the value of the test statistic $n\hat{m}(\hat{\beta})'\tilde{V}^{-1}\hat{m}(\hat{\beta})$ is directly available as a by-product of the second stage GMM estimation. For this reason and for its asymptotic χ^2 distribution, the J-test is also called the minimum chi-square test.

We can use $\hat{V}$ to replace $\tilde{V}$ in constructing a test statistic, and the resulting test statistic $n\hat{m}(\hat{\beta})'\hat{V}^{-1}\hat{m}(\hat{\beta})$ is also asymptotically χ^2_{l-K} under correct model specification (please verify!). However, this statistic is less convenient to compute than the test statistic $n\hat{m}(\hat{\beta})'\tilde{V}^{-1}\hat{m}(\hat{\beta})$, because the latter is the objective function of the second stage GMM estimation. This is analogous to the F-test statistic, which is based on the SSR of linear regression models.

As an application of the overidentification test, we now consider how to test for validity of instruments in an endogenous linear regression model

$$Y_t = X_t'\beta^o + \varepsilon_t,$$

where $E(\varepsilon_t|X_t) \neq 0$. Suppose there exists a set of instrument candidates for Z_t. To estimate the true parameter value β^o, we use the moment function

$$m_t(\beta) = Z_t(Y_t - X_t'\beta).$$

Then the overidentification test can be used to check the validity of the moment condition

$$E[m_t(\beta^o)] = E[Z_t(Y_t - X_t'\beta^o)] = 0.$$

This essentially checks whether Z_t is a valid instrument vector, that is, whether the instrument vector Z_t is orthogonal to $\varepsilon_t = Y_t - X_t'\beta^o$ in the sense that

$$\mathbf{H}_0 : E(\varepsilon_t|Z_t) = 0.$$

Recall that when the weighting matrix $\hat{W} = \mathbf{Z}'\mathbf{Z}/n$, the GMM estimator $\hat{\beta}$ delivers the 2SLS estimator $\hat{\beta}_{2SLS}$, namely,

$$\hat{\beta} = \hat{\beta}_{2SLS} = \arg\min_{\beta}(Y - \mathbf{X}\beta)'\mathbf{Z}(\mathbf{Z}'\mathbf{Z})^{-1}\mathbf{Z}'(Y - \mathbf{X}\beta).$$

When $\{Z_t\varepsilon_t\}$ is an MDS with $E(\varepsilon_t^2|Z_t) = \sigma^2$, the weighting matrix $\hat{W} \to Q_{ZZ} \propto V_o = \sigma^2 Q_{ZZ}$ is an asymptotically optimal weighting matrix. It follows that $\hat{\beta}_{2SLS}$ is asymptotically optimal estimator of β^o.

Assuming that $\{Z_t\varepsilon_t\}$ is a stationary MDS and $E(\varepsilon_t^2|Z_t) = \sigma^2$, we now use $\hat{\beta}_{2SLS}$ to construct a test statistic for the null hypothesis $\mathbf{H}_0$: $E(\varepsilon_t|Z_t) = 0$. Put $\hat{e} = (\hat{e}_1, ..., \hat{e}_n)'$, where $\hat{e}_t = Y_t - X_t'\hat{\beta}_{2SLS}$. We define the following test statistic

$$S \equiv \frac{\hat{e}'Z(Z'Z)^{-1}Z'\hat{e}}{\hat{e}'\hat{e}/n},$$

where the numerator

$$\hat{e}'Z(Z'Z)^{-1}Z'\hat{e} = n \cdot \hat{m}(\hat{\beta}_{2SLS})'\hat{W}^{-1}\hat{m}(\hat{\beta}_{2SLS})$$

is n times the value of the objective function of the GMM minimization with the choice of $\hat{W} = (Z'Z/n)$, which is an optimal choice when $\{m_t(\beta^o)\}$ is a stationary MDS with conditional homoskedasticity (i.e., $E(\varepsilon_t^2|Z_t) = \sigma^2$). In this case,

$$\frac{\hat{e}'\hat{e}}{n}\frac{Z'Z}{n} \xrightarrow{p} \sigma^2 Q_{zz} = V_o.$$

It follows that the test statistic

$$\frac{\hat{e}'Z(Z'Z)^{-1}Z'\hat{e}}{\hat{e}'\hat{e}/n} \xrightarrow{d} \chi^2_{l-K}$$

under the null hypothesis $\mathbf{H}_0$: $E(\varepsilon_t|Z_t) = 0$. This test is proposed by Sargan (1958) and so is called Sargan's test.

Theorem 8.9. ***[Sargan's Test]:*** *Suppose Assumptions 7.1, 7.3, 7.4(c), 7.6 and 7.7 hold, and $l > K$. Then under the null hypothesis that $\mathbf{H}_0$: $E(\varepsilon_t|Z_t) = 0$, the Sargan test statistic*

$$S \xrightarrow{d} \chi^2_{l-K} \text{ as } \to \infty.$$

In fact, the overidentification test statistic in Theorem 8.9 is equal to nR^2_{uc}, where R^2_{uc} is the uncentered R^2 from the auxiliary regression

$$\hat{e}_t = \alpha' Z_t + w_t.$$

Thus, Sargan's test can be viewed as testing whether the $l \times 1$ parameter vector α is a zero vector under the conditions that $\{Z_t\varepsilon_t\}$ is an MDS with $E(\varepsilon_t^2|Z_t) = \sigma^2$. In fact, it can be shown that under the null hypothesis of $E(\varepsilon_t|Z_t) = 0$, nR^2_{uc} is asymptotically equivalent to nR^2 in the sense that

$$nR^2_{uc} = nR^2 + o_P(1),$$

where R^2 is the uncentered R^2 of the auxiliary regression of $\hat{e}_t$ on Z_t. This provides a more convenient way to calculate the test statistic. However, it is important to emphasize that this convenient procedure is asymptotically valid only when $\{Z_t\varepsilon_t\}$ is an MDS with conditional homoskedasticity (i.e., $E(\varepsilon_t^2|Z_t) = \sigma^2$). If there exists conditional heteroskedasticity (i.e., $E(\varepsilon_t^2|Z_t) \neq \sigma^2$) or $\{Z_t\varepsilon_t\}$ is not an MDS, then we need to robustify Sargan's test statistic.

It may be pointed out that Sargan's (1958) test will have no asymptotic unit power against all alternatives to the null hypothesis $\mathbf{H}_0 : E(\varepsilon_t|Z_t) = 0$. This happens when $E(\varepsilon_t|Z_t) \neq 0$ but $E(Z_t\varepsilon_t) = 0$. This undesired feature is similar to Hausman's (1978) test for model specification, which also has no asymptotic unit power when $E(\varepsilon_t|X_t) \neq 0$ but $E(X_t\varepsilon_t) = 0$.

8.10 Conclusion

Most economic theories have implications on and only on a moment restriction

$$E[m_t(\beta^o)] = 0,$$

where $m_t(\beta)$ is an $l \times 1$ moment function. This moment condition can be used to estimate the true model parameter value β^o via the GMM estimation method. The GMM estimator is defined as:

$$\hat{\beta} = \arg\min_{\beta \in \Theta} \hat{m}(\beta)' \hat{W}^{-1} \hat{m}(\beta),$$

where

$$\hat{m}(\beta) = n^{-1}\sum_{t=1}^{n} m_t(\beta).$$

Under a set of regularity conditions, it can be shown that

$$\hat{\beta} \xrightarrow{p} \beta^o$$

and

$$\sqrt{n}(\hat{\beta} - \beta^o) \xrightarrow{d} N(0, \Omega),$$

where

$$\Omega = (D_o' W^{-1} D_o)^{-1} D_o' W^{-1} V_o W^{-1} D_o (D_o' W^{-1} D_o)^{-1},$$

with $D_o = E[\frac{d}{d\beta} m_t(\beta^o)]$. The asymptotic variance Ω of the GMM estimator $\hat{\beta}$ depends on the choice of weighting matrix W. An asymptotically most efficient GMM estimator is to choose

$$W = V_o \equiv \text{avar}[\sqrt{n}\hat{m}(\beta^o)].$$

In this case, the asymptotic variance of the GMM estimator is given by

$$\Omega_o = (D_o' V_o^{-1} D_o)^{-1},$$

which is a minimum variance. This is similar in spirit to the GLS estimator in a linear regression model. This suggests a two-stage asymptotically optimal GMM estimator $\hat{\beta}$: (a) one can first obtain a consistent but possibly suboptimal GMM estimator $\tilde{\beta}$ by choosing some convenient weighting matrix $\tilde{W}$; (b) then one uses $\tilde{\beta}$ to construct a consistent estimator $\tilde{V}$ for V_o, and uses it as a weighting matrix to obtain the second stage GMM estimator $\hat{\beta}$.

To construct confidence interval estimators and hypothesis test statistics, one has to obtain a consistent asymptotic variance estimator for the GMM estimator. A consistent asymptotic variance estimator for an asymptotically optimal GMM estimator is

$$\hat{\Omega}_o = (\hat{D}' \hat{V}^{-1} \hat{D})^{-1},$$

where

$$\hat{D} = n^{-1}\sum_{t=1}^{n} \frac{dm_t(\hat{\beta})}{d\beta},$$

and the construction of $\hat{V}$ depends on the properties of $\{m_t(\beta^o)\}$, particularly on whether $\{m_t(\beta^o)\}$ is an ergodic stationary MDS process.

Suppose a two-stage asymptotically optimal GMM estimator is used. Then the associated Wald test statistic for the null hypothesis of interest

$$H_0 : R(\beta^o) = r,$$

is given by

$$\begin{aligned} W &= n[R(\hat{\beta}) - r]'[R'(\hat{\beta})(\hat{D}'\hat{V}^{-1}\hat{D})^{-1}R'(\hat{\beta})']^{-1}[R(\hat{\beta}) - r] \\ &\xrightarrow{d} \chi^2_J. \end{aligned}$$

Here, the asymptotic χ^2_J distribution holds under the null hypothesis $\mathbf{H}_0$: $R(\beta^o) = r$. Similarly, we can construct a t-test statistic when $J = 1$.

The moment condition $E[m_t(\beta^o)] = 0$ also provides a basis to check whether an economic theory or economic model is correctly specified. This can be done by checking whether the sample moment $\hat{m}(\hat{\beta})$ is close to zero. A popular model specification test in the GMM framework is the J-test statistic

$$J = n\hat{m}(\hat{\beta})'\tilde{V}^{-1}\hat{m}(\hat{\beta}) \xrightarrow{d} \chi^2_{l-K},$$

where convergence in distribution is obtained under correct model specification, where $\hat{\beta}$ is an asymptotically optimal GMM estimator. (What will happen if a consistent but suboptimal GMM estimator is used?) This is also called the overidentification test. The J-test statistic $n\hat{m}(\hat{\beta})\tilde{V}^{-1}\hat{m}(\hat{\beta})$ is rather convenient to compute, because it is the objective function of the two-stage GMM estimator. As a special case of the overidentification test, we also introduce Sargan's (1958) test for validity of IV under the MDS condition with conditional homoskedasticity in a linear regression model. If there exists conditional heteroskedasticity or $\{Z_t\varepsilon_t\}$ is not an MDS, Sargan's test statistic has to be robustified.

GMM provides a convenient unified framework to view most econometric estimators. In other words, most econometric estimators can be viewed as a special case of the GMM framework with suitable choices of moment function and weighting matrix. We have seen that the OLS and 2SLS estimators are special cases of the class of GMM estimators in a linear regression model, and in particular, the 2SLS estimator is asymptotically optimal when (and only when) $\{Z_t\varepsilon_t\}$ is an MDS with conditional homoskedasticity.

Exercise 8

8.1. A GMM estimator is defined as

$$\hat{\beta} = \arg\min_{\beta\in\Theta} \hat{m}(\beta)'\hat{W}^{-1}\hat{m}(\beta),$$

where β is a $K \times 1$ parameter vector, $\hat{W}$ is a possibly stochastic $l \times l$ symmetric and nonsingular matrix,

$$\hat{m}(\beta) = n^{-1}\sum_{t=1}^{n} m_t(\beta),$$

is an $l \times 1$ sample moment vector and $m_t(\beta)$ is an $l \times 1$ moment function of parameter β and random vector Z_t, and $l \geq K$. We make the following assumptions:

Assumption 1: β^o is the unique solution to $E[m(Z_t, \beta^o)] = 0$, and β^o is an interior point in Θ.

Assumption 2: $\{Z_t\}$ is an ergodic stationary process and $m(Z_t, \beta^o)$ is an MDS in the sense that

$$E\left[m(Z_t, \beta^o)|\, Z^{t-1}\right] = 0,$$

where $Z^{t-1} = \{Z_{t-1}, Z_{t-2}, ..., Z_1\}$ is the information available at time $t-1$.

Assumption 3: With probability one, $m(Z_t, \beta)$ is continuously differentiable with respect to $\beta \in \Theta$ such that

$$\sup_{\beta\in\Theta} \|\hat{m}'(\beta) - m'(\beta)\| \xrightarrow{p} 0,$$

where $\hat{m}'(\beta) = \frac{d}{d\beta}\hat{m}(\beta)$ and $m'(\beta) = \frac{d}{d\beta}E[m(Z_t, \beta)] = E[\frac{\partial}{\partial\beta}m(Z_t, \beta)]$.

Assumption 4: $\sqrt{n}\hat{m}(\beta^o) \xrightarrow{d} N(0, V_o)$ as $n \to \infty$ for some finite and positive definite matrix V_o.

Assumption 5: $\hat{W} \xrightarrow{p} W$ as $n \to \infty$, where W is a finite and positive definite matrix.

From these assumptions, one can show that $\hat{\beta} \xrightarrow{p} \beta^o$, and this result can be used in answering the questions in Parts (1) to (4). Moreover, you can make additional assumptions if you feel appropriate and necessary.

(1) Find the expression of the asymptotic variance-covariance matrix V_o in terms of $m(Z_t, \beta^o)$.

(2) Find the FOC of the above GMM minimization problem.

(3) Derive the asymptotic distribution of $\sqrt{n}(\hat{\beta} - \beta^o)$.

(4) Find the optimal choice of $\hat{W}$. Explain why your choice of $\hat{W}$ is optimal.

8.2. Suppose we use GMM to estimate an endogenous linear regression model $Y_t = X_t'\beta^o + \varepsilon_t$ by choosing a moment function $m_t(\beta) = Z_t(Y_t - X_t'\beta)$, where β is a $K \times 1$ parameter vector, X_t is a $K \times 1$ regressor vector, and Z_t is a $K \times 1$ instrument vector such that $Q_{ZX} = E(Z_t X_t)$ is a finite and nonsingular matrix. Assume that all necessary regularity conditions hold.

(1) Show that $\hat{\beta} = (Z'X)^{-1}Z'Y$ is a GMM estimator with a suitable choice of weighting matrix $\hat{W}$. Give your reasoning.

(2) Compare the relative efficiency between $\hat{\beta}$ from Part (1) and $\hat{\beta}_{2SLS}$ when $\{Z_t\varepsilon_t\}$ is an MDS and $E(\varepsilon_t^2|Z_t) = \sigma^2$. Give your reasoning.

(3) Does your conclusion in Part (2) hold when $\{Z_t\varepsilon_t\}$ is an MDS but $E(\varepsilon_t^2|Z_t) \neq \sigma^2$? Explain.

8.3. (1) Show that the 2SLS estimator $\hat{\beta}_{2SLS}$ for the parameter β^o in the regression model $Y_t = X_t'\beta^o + \varepsilon_t$ is a special case of the GMM estimator with suitable choices of moment function $m_t(\beta)$ and weighting matrix $\hat{W}$.

(2) Assume that $\{Z_t\varepsilon_t\}$ is an ergodic stationary MDS. Obtain the two-stage asymptotically optimal GMM estimators by choosing weighting matrix $\hat{W} = \tilde{V}$, under conditional homoskedasticity and conditional heteroskedasticity respectively. Give your reasoning.

(3) Compare the relative efficiencies of the asymptotically optimal GMM estimators obtained in Part (2) with $\hat{\beta}_{2SLS}$ under conditional homoskedasticity and conditional heteroskedasticity respectively. Give your reasoning.

8.4. Suppose $\{m_t(\beta)\}$ is an ergodic stationary MDS, where with probability one, $m_t(\cdot)$ is continuous on a compact parameter set Θ, and $\{m_t(\beta)m_t(\beta)'\}$ follows UWLLN, and $V_o = E[m_t(\beta^o)m_t(\beta^o)']$ is finite and nonsingular. Let $\hat{V} = n^{-1}\sum_{t=1}^{n} m_t(\hat{\beta})m_t(\hat{\beta})'$, where $\hat{\beta}$ is a consistent estimator of β^o. Show $\hat{V} \xrightarrow{p} V_o$ as $n \to \infty$.

8.5. Suppose $\tilde{\beta}$ is a preliminary GMM estimator with weighting function $\tilde{W} \xrightarrow{p} W$, where W is an $l \times l$ nonstochastic, symmetric, finite and nonsingular matrix, and $W \neq V_o = E[m_t(\beta^o)m_t(\beta^o)']$.

(1) Use $\tilde{\beta}$ to construct a Wald test statistic for the null hypothesis $\mathbf{H}_0 : R(\beta^o) = r$, and derive its asymptotic distribution under $\mathbf{H}_0$. Give your reasoning. Assume that all necessary regularity conditions hold.

(2) Compare the relative efficiency between the Wald test statistic in Part (1) and the Wald test statistic in Theorem 8.7 which employs the two-stage asymptotically optimal GMM estimator. Which test is expected to have better power in finite samples when $\mathbf{H}_0$ is false? Explain.

8.6. Consider testing the null hypothesis $\mathbf{H}_0 : R(\beta^o) = r$ under the GMM framework, where $R(\beta^o)$ is a $J \times K$ nonstochastic matrix, r is a $J \times 1$ nonstochastic vector, and $R'(\beta^o)$ is a $J \times K$ matrix with full rank J, with $J \leq K$. We can construct an LM test based on the Lagrange multiplier $\hat{\lambda}^*$, where $\hat{\lambda}^*$ is the optimal solution of the following constrained GMM minimization problem:

$$(\hat{\beta}^*, \hat{\lambda}^*) = \arg \min_{\beta \in \Theta, \lambda \in R} \left\{ \hat{m}(\beta)' \tilde{V}^{-1} \hat{m}(\beta) + \lambda' [r - R(\beta)] \right\},$$

where $\tilde{V}$ is a preliminary consistent estimator for $V_o = \text{avar}[\sqrt{n}\hat{m}(\beta^o)]$ that does not depend on β. Construct the LM test statistic and derive its asymptotic distribution in each of the following three cases:

(1) $\{m_t(\beta^o)\}$ is an ergodic stationary MDS. Give your reasoning.

(2) $\{m_t(\beta^o)\}$ is an ergodic stationary non-MDS. Give your reasoning. Assume that all regularity conditions hold.

8.7. *[Nonlinear IV Estimation]:* Consider a nonlinear regression model

$$Y_t = g(X_t, \beta^o) + \varepsilon_t,$$

where $g(X_t, \cdot)$ is twice continuously differentiable with respect to β, $E(\varepsilon_t|X_t) \neq 0$ but $E(\varepsilon_t|Z_t) = 0$, where Y_t is a scalar, X_t is a $K \times 1$ vector of explanatory variables and Z_t is an $l \times 1$ vector of IVs with $l \geq K$. Suppose $\{Y_t, X_t', Z_t'\}$ is an ergodic stationary process, and $\{Z_t \varepsilon_t\}$ is an MDS.

The unknown parameter value β^o can be consistently estimated based on the moment condition

$$E[m_t(\beta^o)] = 0,$$

where $m_t(\beta) = Z_t[Y_t - g(X_t, \beta^o)]$. Suppose a nonlinear IV estimator solves the minimization problem

$$\hat{\beta} = \arg \min_{\beta} \hat{m}(\beta)' \hat{W}^{-1} \hat{m}(\beta),$$

where $\hat{m}(\beta) = n^{-1}\sum_{t=1}^{n} Z_t[Y_t - g(X_t, \beta)]$, and $\hat{W} \to^p W$, a finite and positive definite matrix.

(1) Show $\hat{\beta} \xrightarrow{p} \beta^o$ as $n \to \infty$.

(2) Derive the FOC.

(3) Derive the asymptotic distribution of $\hat{\beta}$. Discuss the cases of conditional homoskedasticity and conditional heteroskedasticity respectively.

(4) What is the optimal choice of W so that $\hat{\beta}$ is asymptotically most efficient?

(5) Construct a test for the null hypothesis that $\mathbf{H}_0 : R(\beta^o) = r$, where $R(\beta)$ is a $J \times K$ nonstochastic matrix with $R'(\beta^o)$ of full rank, r is a $J \times 1$ nonstochastic vector, and $J \leq K$.

8.8. *[NLS Estimation]:* Consider a nonlinear regression model

$$Y_t = g(X_t, \beta^o) + \varepsilon_t,$$

where β^o is an unknown $K \times 1$ parameter vector and $E(\varepsilon_t|X_t) = 0$. Assume that $g(X_t, \cdot)$ is twice continuously differentiable with respect to β with the $K \times K$ matrices $E[\frac{\partial g(X_t,\beta)}{\partial \beta}\frac{\partial g(X_t,\beta)}{\partial \beta'}]$ and $E[\frac{\partial^2 g(X_t,\beta)}{\partial \beta \partial \beta'}]$ finite and nonsingular for all $\theta \in \Theta$.

The NLS estimator solves the minimization of the SSR problem

$$\hat{\beta} = \arg\min_{\beta} \sum_{t=1}^{n} [Y_t - g(X_t, \beta)]^2 .$$

The FOC is

$$D(\hat{\beta})'e = \sum_{t=1}^{n} \frac{\partial g(X_t, \hat{\beta})}{\partial \beta}[Y_t - g(X_t, \hat{\beta})] = 0,$$

where $D(\beta)$ is an $n \times K$ matrix, with the t-th row being $\frac{\partial}{\partial \beta} g(X_t, \beta)$. This FOC can be viewed as the FOC

$$\hat{m}(\hat{\beta}) = 0$$

for a GMM estimation with moment function

$$m_t(\beta) = \frac{\partial g(X_t, \beta)}{\partial \beta}[Y_t - g(X_t, \beta)]$$

in an exact identification case ($l = K$). In general, there exists no closed form expression for $\hat{\beta}$. Assume that all necessary regularities conditions hold.

(1) Show $\hat{\beta} \xrightarrow{p} \beta^o$ as $n \to \infty$.

(2) Derive the asymptotic distribution of $\sqrt{n}(\hat{\beta} - \beta^o)$.

(3) What is the asymptotic variance of $\sqrt{n}(\hat{\beta} - \beta^o)$ if $\{\frac{\partial g(X_t,\beta)}{\partial \beta}\varepsilon_t\}$ is an ergodic stationary MDS with conditional homoskedasticity (i.e., $E(\varepsilon_t^2|X_t) = \sigma^2$)? Give your reasoning.

(4) What is the asymptotic variance of $\sqrt{n}(\hat{\beta} - \beta^o)$ if $\{\frac{\partial g(X_t,\beta)}{\partial \beta}\varepsilon_t\}$ is an ergodic stationary MDS with conditional heteroskedasticity (i.e., $E(\varepsilon_t^2|X_t) \neq \sigma^2$)? Give your reasoning.

(5) Suppose $\{\frac{\partial g(X_t,\beta)}{\partial \beta}\varepsilon_t\}$ is an ergodic stationary MDS with conditional homoskedasticity (i.e., $E(\varepsilon_t^2|X_t) = \sigma^2$). Construct a test for the null hypothesis $\mathbf{H}_0 : R(\beta^o) = r$, where $R(\beta)$ is a $J \times K$ nonstochastic matrix such that $R'(\beta^o) = \frac{\partial}{\partial \beta}R(\beta^o)$ is a $J \times L$ matrix with full rank $J \leq L$, and r is a $J \times 1$ nonstochastic vector.

(6) Suppose $\{\frac{\partial g(X_t,\beta)}{\partial \beta}\varepsilon_t\}$ is an ergodic stationary MDS with conditional heteroskedasticity (i.e., $E(\varepsilon_t^2|X_t) \neq \sigma^2$). Construct a test for the null hypothesis $\mathbf{H}_0 : R(\beta^o) = r$, where $R(\beta)$ is a $J \times K$ nonstochastic matrix such that $R'(\beta^o) = \frac{\partial}{\partial \beta}R(\beta^o)$ is a $J \times L$ matrix with full rank $J \leq L$, and r is a $J \times 1$ nonstochastic vector.

8.9. Suppose $\hat{V}$ is a consistent estimator for $V_o = \text{avar}[\sqrt{n}\hat{m}(\beta^o)]$ using the second stage GMM estimator $\hat{\beta}$. Show that replacing the first stage preliminary variance estimator $\tilde{V}$ by $\hat{V}$ has no impact on the asymptotic distribution of the overidentification test statistic $n\hat{m}(\hat{\beta})'\tilde{V}^{-1}\hat{m}(\hat{\beta})$, namely, show

$$n\hat{m}(\hat{\beta})\tilde{V}^{-1}\hat{m}(\hat{\beta}) - n\hat{m}(\hat{\beta})\hat{V}^{-1}\hat{m}(\hat{\beta}) \xrightarrow{p} 0$$

as $n \to \infty$ under correct model specification. Assume all necessary regularity conditions in Theorem 8.8 hold.

8.10. Suppose $\tilde{\beta}$ is a suboptimal but consistent GMM estimator, say the first stage preliminary GMM estimator in a two-stage asymptotically optimal GMM procedure. Our interest is to test the null hypothesis that $\mathbf{H}_0 : E[m(X_t, \beta^o)] = 0$. Assume that all necessary regularity conditions hold. Could we simply replace the two-stage asymptotically optimal GMM estimator $\hat{\beta}$ by $\tilde{\beta}$ and still obtain the asymptotic χ^2_{l-K} distribution for the overidentification test statistic $J = n \cdot \hat{m}(\hat{\beta})'\tilde{V}^{-1}\hat{m}(\hat{\beta})$ under $\mathbf{H}_0$? That is, will the test statistic $n \cdot \hat{m}(\tilde{\beta})'\tilde{V}^{-1}\hat{m}(\tilde{\beta})$ follow the asymptotic χ^2_{l-K} distribution under $\mathbf{H}_0$? Give your reasoning.

8.11. Suppose $\tilde{\beta}$ is a consistent but asymptotically suboptimal GMM estimator of β^o which is based on the weighting matrix $\tilde{W}$, where $\tilde{W} \xrightarrow{p} W$, an $l \times l$ symmetric, finite and nonsingular matrix. We now use $\tilde{\beta}$ to construct a test statistic for the null hypothesis

$$\mathbf{H}_0 : E[m_t(\beta^o)] = 0.$$

The idea is to use the sample moment $\hat{m}(\tilde{\beta}) = n^{-1}\sum_{t=1}^{n} m_t(\tilde{\beta})$ and check whether it is significantly different from zero. Assume that all necessary regularity conditions hold.

(1) Derive the asymptotic distribution of $\sqrt{n}\hat{m}(\tilde{\beta})$ under $\mathbf{H}_0$.

(2) Construct a quadratic form test statistic $\tilde{J}$ of $\sqrt{n}\hat{m}(\tilde{\beta})$ so that it is asymptotically Chi-squared under $\mathbf{H}_0$. Give your reasoning.

(3) Compare the test statistic $\tilde{J}$ with the overidentification test J statistic proposed in Theorem 8.8. Which test is expected to be more powerful against model misspecification? *[Hint: Compare the degrees of freedom between the two test statistics under* $\mathbf{H}_0$*.]*

8.12. Suppose Assumptions 7.1 to 7.3, 7.4(c), 7.6 and 7.7 in Chapter 7 hold. To test the null hypothesis $\mathbf{H}_0 : E(\varepsilon_t|Z_t) = 0$, where Z_t is an $l \times 1$ instrument vector, one can consider the auxiliary regression

$$\hat{e}_t = \alpha' Z_t + w_t,$$

where $\hat{e}_t = Y_t - X_t'\hat{\beta}_{2SLS}$, and test whether all coefficients $\{\alpha_j\}$ are jointly zero.

(1) Show that Sargan's test statistic S in Theorem 8.9 is equal to nR_{uc}^2, where R_{uc}^2 is the uncentered R^2 in the above auxiliary regression of $\hat{e}_t$ on Z_t.

(2) Show $nR_{uc}^2 = nR^2 + o_P(1)$ as $n \to \infty$ under the null hypothesis $\mathbf{H}_0$, where R^2 is the centered R^2 in the auxiliary regression of $\hat{e}_t$ on Z_t.

(3) Explain why Sargan's test generally has asymptotic unit power when the null hypothesis $\mathbf{H}_0$ is false.

(4) Does Sargan's test have asymptotic unit power when $E(\varepsilon_t|Z_t) \neq 0$ but $E(Z_t\varepsilon_t) = 0$? Explain.

8.13. Given Assumptions 7.1, 7.2, 7.3, 7.4(c) and 7.6 in Chapter 7, $E(Z_{jt}^4) < \infty$ for $j \in \{1, ..., l\}$, $E(\varepsilon_t^4) < \infty$, and $l > K$. Construct a test statistic for the null hypothesis $\mathbf{H}_0 : E(\varepsilon_t|Z_t) = 0$, and derive its asymptotic distribution under $\mathbf{H}_0$. This is a robust Sargan's test which is valid under conditional heteroskedasticity.

Chapter 9

Maximum Likelihood Estimation and Quasi-Maximum Likelihood Estimation

Abstract: Conditional probability distribution models have been widely used in economics and finance. In this chapter, we introduce two closely related popular methods to estimate conditional distribution models—Maximum Likelihood Estimation (MLE) and Quasi-MLE (QMLE). MLE is a parameter estimator that maximizes the model likelihood function of the random sample when the conditional distribution model is correctly specified, and QMLE is a parameter estimator that maximizes the model likelihood function of the random sample when the conditional distribution model is misspecified. Because the score function is an MDS and the dynamic Information Matrix (IM) equality holds when a conditional distribution model is correctly specified, the asymptotic properties of MLE is analogous to those of the OLS estimator when the regression disturbance is an MDS with conditional homoskedasticity, and we can use the Wald test, LM test and Likelihood Ratio (LR) test for hypothesis testing, where the LR test is analogous to the $J \cdot F$ test statistic. On the other hand, when the conditional distribution model is misspecified, the score function has mean zero, but it may no longer be an MDS and the dynamic IM equality may fail. As a result, the asymptotic properties of QMLE are analogous to those of the OLS estimator when the regression disturbance displays serial correlation and/or conditional heteroskedasticity. Robust Wald tests and LM tests can be constructed for hypothesis testing, but the LR test can no longer be used, for a reason similar to the failure of the F-test statistic when the regression disturbance displays serial correlation and/or conditional heteroskedasticity. We discuss methods to test the MDS property of the score function, and the dynamic IM equality, and correct specification of a conditional distribution model.

Keywords: ARMA model, Censored data, Conditional probability distribution model, Discrete choice model, Duration model, Dynamic IM test, GARCH model, Hessian matrix, IM equality, IM test, Likelihood function, LM test, Log-likelihood function, LR test, Martingale, MDS, MLE, Probability Density Function (PDF), Probability Mass Function (PMF), Pseudo likelihood function, QMLE, Score function, Survival analysis, Truncated data, Value at Risk (VaR), Variation-free parameters, Vector AutoRegression (VAR), Wald test

9.1 Motivation

So far we have focused on econometric models for conditional mean or conditional expectation, either linear or nonlinear. When do we need to model the conditional probability distribution of Y_t given X_t?

We first provide a number of economic examples which call for the use of a conditional distribution model.

Example 9.1. [Value at Risk (VaR)]: In financial risk management, how to quantify extreme downside market risk has been an important issue. Let $I_{t-1} = (Y_{t-1}, Y_{t-2}, ..., Y_1)$ be the information set available at time $t-1$, where Y_t is the return on a portfolio in period t. Suppose

$$\begin{aligned} Y_t &= \mu_t(\beta^o) + \varepsilon_t \\ &= \mu_t(\beta^o) + \sigma_t(\beta^o)z_t, \end{aligned}$$

where $\mu_t(\beta^o) = E(Y_t|I_{t-1}), \sigma_t^2(\beta^o) = \text{var}(Y_t|I_{t-1})$, $\{z_t\}$ is an IID sequence with $E(z_t) = 0$, $\text{var}(z_t) = 1$, and PDF $f_z(\cdot|\beta^o)$. An example is that $\{z_t\} \sim$ IID $N(0, 1)$.

The Value at Risk (VaR), $V_t(\alpha) = V(I_{t-1}, \alpha)$, at the significance level $\alpha \in (0, 1)$, of the portfolio, is defined as

$$P\left[Y_t < -V_t(\alpha)|I_{t-1}\right] = \alpha.$$

Intuitively, VaR is the threshold that unexpected actual loss will exceed with probability α. Given $Y_t = \mu_t + \sigma_t z_t$, where for simplicity we have put $\mu_t = \mu_t(\beta^o)$ and $\sigma_t = \sigma_t(\beta^o)$, we obtain

$$\begin{aligned} \alpha &= P\left[\mu_t + \sigma_t z_t < -V_t(\alpha)|I_{t-1}\right] \\ &= P\left[z_t < \frac{-V_t(\alpha) - \mu_t}{\sigma_t}\right| I_{t-1}\Bigg] \\ &= F_z\left[\frac{-V_t(\alpha) - \mu_t}{\sigma_t}\right], \end{aligned}$$

where the last equality follows from the independence assumption of $\{z_t\}$. It follows that

$$\frac{-V_t(\alpha) - \mu_t}{\sigma_t} = -C_\alpha$$

or

$$V_t(\alpha) = -\mu_t + \sigma_t C_\alpha,$$

where C_α is the absolute value of the left-tailed critical value of the distribution $F_z(\cdot)$ at level α, namely

$$P\left[z_t < -C_\alpha\right] = \alpha$$

or

$$\int_{-\infty}^{-C_\alpha} f_z(z|\beta^o)dz = \alpha.$$

For example, $C_{0.05} = 1.65$ and $C_{0.01} = 2.33$.

Obviously, we need to model the conditional probability distribution of Y_t given I_{t-1} in order to calculate $V_t(\alpha)$, which is a popular quantitative measure for downside market risk.

For example, J. P. Morgan's RiskMetrics uses a simple conditional normal distribution model for asset returns:

$$\begin{aligned} Y_t &= \sigma_t z_t, \\ \sigma_t^2 &= (1-\lambda)\sum_{j=1}^{t-1} \lambda^j Y_{t-j}^2, \qquad 0 < \lambda < 1, \\ \{z_t\} &\sim IID\ N(0,1), \end{aligned}$$

where the conditional variance σ_t^2 is a weighted average of past volatilities. This is called an exponential smoothing volatility model, where parameter λ controls the degree of smoothing. Here, the conditional distribution of $Y_t|I_{t-1}$ is $N(0, \sigma_t^2)$, from which we can obtain

$$V_t(0.05) = 1.65\sigma_t.$$

Example 9.2. [Binary Probability Modeling]: Suppose Y_t is a binary variable taking values 1 and 0 respectively. For example, a business turning point or a currency crisis may occur under certain circumstance; households may buy a fancy new cell phone; and default risk may occur for some financial firms. In all these scenarios, the variables of interest can take only two possible values. Such variables are called binary.

We are interested in the probability that some economic event of interest occurs ($Y_t = 1$) and how it depends on some economic characteristics X_t. It may well be that the probability of $Y_t = 1$ differs among individuals or across different time periods. For example, the probability of students' success depends on their intelligence, motivation, effort, and the environment. The probability of buying a new product may depend on income, age, and preference.

To capture such individual effects (denoted as X_t), we consider a model

$$P(Y_t = 1|X_t) = F(X_t'\beta^o),$$

where $F(\cdot)$ is a prespecified CDF. An example of $F(\cdot)$ is the logistic function, namely,

$$F(u) = \frac{1}{1+\exp(-u)}, \qquad -\infty < u < \infty.$$

This is the so-called logistic regression model. This model is useful for modeling, e.g., credit default risk and currency crisis.

An economic interpretation for the binary outcome Y_t is a story of a latent variable process. Define

$$Y_t = \begin{cases} 1 & \text{if } Y_t^* \leq c, \\ 0 & \text{if } Y_t^* > c, \end{cases}$$

where c is a constant, the latent variable

$$Y_t^* = X_t'\beta^o + \varepsilon_t,$$

and $F(\cdot)$ is the CDF of the IID disturbance ε_t. If $\{\varepsilon_t\} \sim$ IID $N(0, \sigma^2)$ and $c = 0$, the resulting model is called a probit model. If $\{\varepsilon_t\} \sim$ IID Logistic$(0, \sigma^2)$ and $c = 0$, the resulting model is called a logit model. The latent variable could be the actual economic decision process. For example, Y_t^* can be the credit score and c is the threshold with which a lending institute makes its decision on loan approvals.

This model can be extended to the multinomial model, where Y_t takes discrete multiple integers instead of only two values.

Example 9.3. [Duration or Survival Models]: Suppose we are interested in the time length it takes for an unemployed person to find a job, the time length that elapses between two trades or two price changes, the time length of a strike, the time length before a cancer patient dies, the time length before a financial crisis (e.g., credit default risk) comes out, the time length before a startup technology firm goes bankrupt, and the time length before a family gets out of poverty. Such analysis is called duration analysis or survival analysis.

In practice, the main interest often lies in the question of how long the duration of an economic event will continue, given that it has not finished yet. An important concept called hazard rate or hazard function measures the probability that the duration will end now, given that it has not ended before. This hazard rate therefore can be interpreted as the chance to find a job, to trade, to end a strike, etc.

Suppose Y_t is the duration of some event (e.g., unemployment) from a population with PDF $f(y)$ and CDF $F(y)$. Then the survival function is defined as

$$S(y) = P(Y_t > y) = 1 - F(y),$$

and the hazard rate is defined as

$$\begin{aligned}\lambda(y) &= \lim_{\delta \to 0^+} \frac{P(y < Y_t \leq y + \delta | Y_t > y)}{\delta} \\ &= \lim_{\delta \to 0^+} \frac{P(y < Y_t \leq y + \delta)/P(Y_t > y)}{\delta} \\ &= \frac{f(y)}{S(y)} \\ &= -\frac{d}{dy} \ln S(y) \\ &= \frac{f(y)}{S(y)}.\end{aligned}$$

Hence, we have $f(y) = \lambda(y)S(y)$. The specification of $\lambda(y)$ is equivalent to a specification of $f(y)$. But $\lambda(y)$ is more interpretable from an economic perspective. For example, suppose we have $\lambda(y) = r$, a constant; that is, the hazard rate does not depend on the length of duration. Then

$$f(y) = r \exp(-ry)$$

follows an exponential distribution.

The hazard rate may not be the same for all individuals (i.e., it may depend on individual characteristics X_t). To control heterogeneity across individuals, we assume a conditional hazard function

$$\lambda_t(y) = \exp(X_t'\beta)\lambda_0(y),$$

where $\lambda_0(y)$ is called the baseline hazard rate or the baseline hazard function. This specification is called the proportional hazard model, proposed by Cox (1972). The parameter

$$\begin{aligned}\beta &= \frac{\partial}{\partial X_t}\ln \lambda_t(y) \\ &= \frac{1}{\lambda_t(y)}\frac{\partial}{\partial X_t}\lambda_t(y)\end{aligned}$$

is the marginal relative effect of X_t on the hazard rate of individual t. The survival function of the proportional hazard model is

$$S_t(y) = [S_0(y)]^{\exp(X_t'\beta)}$$

where $S_0(y)$ is the survival function of the baseline hazard rate $\lambda_0(y)$.

The conditional PDF of Y_t given X_t is

$$f(y|X_t) = \lambda_t(y)S_t(y).$$

To estimate parameter β, we need to use the Maximum Likelihood Estimation (MLE) method, which will be introduced below.

Example 9.4. [Ultra-High Frequency Financial Econometrics and Autoregressive Conditional Duration (ACD) Model]: Suppose we have a sequence of tick-by-tick financial data $\{P_i, t_i\}$, where P_i is the price traded at time t_i, where i is the index for the i-th price change. Define the time interval between price changes

$$Y_i = t_i - t_{i-1}, \qquad i = 1, ..., n.$$

Question: How to model serial dependence of the duration Y_i?

Engle and Russell (1998) propose a class of ACD model:

$$\begin{cases} Y_i = \mu_i(\beta^o)z_i, \\ \mu_i(\beta^o) = E(Y_i|I_{i-1}), \\ \{z_i\} \sim \text{IID}\,EXP(1), \end{cases}$$

where I_{i-1} is the information set available at time t_{i-1}. Here, $\mu_i = \mu_i(\beta^o)$ is called the conditional expected duration given I_{i-1}. A model for μ_i is

$$\mu_i = \omega + \alpha\mu_{i-1} + \gamma Y_{i-1},$$

where $\beta = (\omega, \alpha, \gamma)'$.

From this model, we can write down the model-implied conditional PDF of Y_i given I_{i-1} :

$$f(y|I_{i-1}) = \frac{1}{\mu_i}\exp\left(-\frac{y}{\mu_i}\right), \qquad y > 0.$$

From this conditional PDF, we can compute the conditional intensity of Y_i (i.e., the instantaneous probability that the next price change will occur at time t_i), which is important for, e.g., options pricing.

Example 9.5. [Continuous-Time Diffusion Models]: The dynamics of the spot interest rate Y_t is fundamental to pricing fixed income securities. Consider a diffusion model for the spot interest rate

$$dY_t = \mu(Y_t, \beta^o)dt + \sigma(Y_t, \beta^o)dW_t,$$

where $\mu(Y_t, \beta^o)$ is the drift model, and $\sigma(Y_t, \beta^o)$ is the diffusion model, β^o is an unknown $K \times 1$ parameter value, and W_t is the standard Brownian motion. Note that the time t is a continuous variable.

Question: What is the Brownian motion?

Continuous-Time models have been popular in mathematical finance and financial engineering. First, financial economists have the belief that informational flow into financial markets is continuous in time. Second, the mathematical treatment of derivatives pricing is elegant when a continuous-time model is used.

The following are three well-known examples of the diffusion model:

- The random walk model with drift,

$$dY_t = \mu dt + \sigma dW_t;$$

- Vasicek's (1977) model,

$$dY_t = (\alpha + \beta Y_t)dt + \sigma dW_t;$$

- Cox, Ingersoll, and Ross' (1985) model,

$$dY_t = (\alpha + \beta Y_t)dt + \sigma Y_t^{1/2} dW_t.$$

These diffusion models are important for hedging, derivatives pricing and financial risk management.

Question: How to estimate model parameters of a diffusion model using a discretely sampled data $\{Y_t\}_{t=1}^n$?

Given the drift function $\mu(Y_t, \beta)$ and the diffusion function $\sigma(Y_t, \beta)$, we can determine the conditional PDF $f_{Y_t|I_{t-1}}(y_t|I_{t-1}, \beta)$ of Y_t given I_{t-1}. Thus, we can estimate β^o by MLE or asymptotically equivalent methods using discretely observed data. For the random walk model, the conditional PDF of Y_t given I_{t-1} is

$$f(y|I_{t-1}, \beta) = \frac{1}{\sqrt{2\pi\sigma^2 t}} \exp\left[-\frac{(y - \mu t)^2}{2\sigma^2 t}\right].$$

For Vasicek's (1977) model, the conditional PDF of Y_t given I_{t-1} is

$$f(y|I_{t-1}, \beta) = \frac{1}{\sqrt{-\frac{\pi\sigma^2}{\gamma}(1 - e^{2\gamma t})}} \exp\left\{\frac{\left[y - y_0 e^{\gamma t} + \frac{\alpha}{\gamma}(1 - e^{\gamma t})\right]^2}{\frac{\sigma^2}{\gamma}(1 - 2e^{2\gamma t})}\right\}.$$

For Cox, Ingersoll and Ross' (1985) model, the conditional PDF of Y_t given I_{t-1} is

$$\begin{aligned} f(y|I_{t-1}, \beta) &= \frac{1}{\sqrt{2\pi\left[\frac{y_0\sigma^2}{-\gamma}(e^{\gamma t} - e^{2\gamma t}) + \frac{\sigma}{2\gamma^2}(1 - e^{\gamma t})^2\right]}} \\ &\quad \times \exp\left\{\frac{\left[y - y_0 e^{\gamma t} + \frac{\alpha}{2\gamma^2}(1 - e^{\gamma t})^2\right]}{2\left[-\frac{y_0\sigma^2}{\gamma}(e^{\gamma t} - e^{2\gamma t}) + \frac{\alpha}{2\gamma^2}(1 - e^{\gamma t})^2\right]}\right\}. \end{aligned}$$

It may be noted that many continuous-time diffusion models do not have a closed form expression for their conditional PDF, which makes the MLE estimation infeasible. Methods have been proposed in the literature (e.g., Ait-Sahalia 2002) to obtain some accurate approximations to the conditional PDF so that MLE becomes feasible.

9.2 Maximum Likelihood Estimation (MLE) and Quasi-MLE (QMLE)

Recall that a random sample of size n is a sequence of random vectors $\{Z_1, ..., Z_n\}$, where $Z_t = (Y_t, X_t')'$. We denote the random sample as follows:

$$\mathbf{Z}^n = (Z_1', ..., Z_n')'.$$

A realization of $\mathbf{Z}^n$ is a data set, denoted as $\mathbf{z}^n = (z_1', ..., z_n')'$. A random sample $\mathbf{Z}^n$ can generate many realizations (i.e., data sets).

Question: How to characterize the random sample $\mathbf{Z}^n$?

All information in $\mathbf{Z}^n$ is completely described by its joint PDF/PMF $f_{\mathbf{Z}^n}(\mathbf{z}^n)$. (For discrete random variables, we have $f_{\mathbf{Z}^n}(\mathbf{z}^n) = P(\mathbf{Z}^n = \mathbf{z}^n)$.) By sequential partitioning (repeatedly using the multiplication rule that $P(A \cap B) = P(A|B)P(B)$ for any two events A and B), we have

$$\begin{aligned} f_{\mathbf{Z}^n}(\mathbf{z}^n) &= f_{Z_n|\mathbf{Z}^{n-1}}(z_n|\mathbf{z}^{n-1}) f_{\mathbf{Z}^{n-1}}(\mathbf{z}^{n-1}) \\ &= \prod_{t=1}^{n} f_{Z_t|\mathbf{Z}^{t-1}}(z_t|\mathbf{z}^{t-1}), \end{aligned}$$

where $\mathbf{Z}^{t-1} = (Z_{t-1}', Z_{t-2}', ..., Z_1')'$, and $f_{Z_t|\mathbf{Z}^{t-1}}(z_t|\mathbf{z}^{t-1})$ is the conditional PDF/PMF of Z_t given $\mathbf{Z}^{t-1}$. As a convention, we set $f_{Z_1|\mathbf{Z}^0}(z_1|\mathbf{z}^0) = f_{Z_1}(z_1)$, the marginal PDF/PMF of Z_1. Also, given $Z_t = (Y_t, X_t')'$ and using the formula that $P(A \cap B|C) = P(A|B \cap C)P(B|C)$ for any events A, B and C, we have

$$\begin{aligned} f_{Z_t|\mathbf{Z}^{t-1}}(z_t|\mathbf{z}^{t-1}) &= f_{Y_t|(X_t,\mathbf{Z}^{t-1})}(y_t|x_t, \mathbf{z}^{t-1}) f_{X_t|\mathbf{Z}^{t-1}}(x_t|\mathbf{z}^{t-1}) \\ &= f_{Y_t|\Psi_t}(y_t|\Psi_t) f_{X_t|\mathbf{Z}^{t-1}}(x_t|\mathbf{z}^{t-1}), \end{aligned}$$

where

$$\Psi_t = (X_t', \mathbf{Z}^{t-1\prime})',$$

an extended information set which contains not only the past history $\mathbf{Z}^{t-1}$ but also the current X_t. It follows that

$$\begin{aligned} f_{\mathbf{Z}^n}(\mathbf{z}^n) &= \prod_{t=1}^{n} f_{Y_t|\Psi_t}(y_t|\Psi_t) f_{X_t|\mathbf{Z}^{t-1}}(x_t|\mathbf{z}^{t-1}) \\ &= \prod_{t=1}^{n} f_{Y_t|\Psi_t}(y_t|\Psi_t) \prod_{t=1}^{n} f_{X_t|\mathbf{Z}^{t-1}}(x_t|\mathbf{z}^{t-1}). \end{aligned}$$

Often, the interest is in modeling the conditional distribution of Y_t given $\Psi_t = (X_t', \mathbf{Z}^{t-1'})'$.

We now examine some important special cases.

- **Case I: Cross-Sectional Observations**
  Suppose $\{Z_t\}$ is IID. Then $f_{Y_t|\Psi_t}(y_t|x_t, \mathbf{z}^{t-1}) = f_{Y_t|X_t}(y_t|x_t)$ and $f_{X_t|\mathbf{Z}^{t-1}}(x_t|\mathbf{z}^{t-1}) = f_{X_t}(x_t)$. It follows that

$$f_{\mathbf{Z}^n}(\mathbf{z}^n) = \prod_{t=1}^{n} f_{Y_t|X_t}(y_t|x_t) \prod_{t=1}^{n} f_{X_t}(x_t),$$

  where $f_{X_t}(x_t)$ is the marginal PDF/PMF of X_t.

- **Case II: Univariate Time Series Analysis**
  Suppose X_t does not exist, namely $Z_t = Y_t$. Then $\Psi_t = (X_t', \mathbf{Z}^{t-1\prime})' = \mathbf{Z}^{t-1} = \mathbf{Y}^{t-1} = (Y_{t-1}, ..., Y_1)'$, and as a result,

$$f_{\mathbf{Z}^n}(\mathbf{z}^n) = \prod_{t=1}^{n} f_{Y_t|\mathbf{Y}^{t-1}}(y_t|\mathbf{y}^{t-1}).$$

In general, we assume a parametric conditional distribution model

$$f_{Z_t|\mathbf{Z}^{t-1}}(z_t|\mathbf{z}^{t-1}) = f_{Y_t|\Psi_t}(y_t|\Psi_t, \beta) f_{X_t|\mathbf{Z}^{t-1}}(x_t|\mathbf{z}^{t-1}, \gamma),$$

where $f_{Y_t|\Psi_t}(\cdot|\Psi_t, \beta)$ is a known functional form up to some unknown $K \times 1$ parameter vector β, and $f_{X_t|\mathbf{Z}^{t-1}}(\cdot|\mathbf{z}^{t-1}, \gamma)$ is a known or unknown parametric function with some unknown parameter γ. Note that $f_{Y_t|\Psi_t}(y_t|\Psi_t, \beta)$ is a function of β rather than γ while $f_{X_t|\mathbf{Z}^{t-1}}(x_t|\mathbf{z}^{t-1}, \gamma)$ is a function of γ rather than β. This is called a variation-free parameters assumption. It follows that the model log-likelihood function

$$\ln f_{\mathbf{Z}^n}(\mathbf{z}^n) = \sum_{t=1}^{n} \ln f_{Y_t|\Psi_t}(y_t|\Psi_t, \beta) + \sum_{t=1}^{n} \ln f_{X_t|\mathbf{Z}^{t-1}}(x_t|\mathbf{z}^{t-1}, \gamma),$$

where the first term contains sample information about parameter β, and the second term contains the sample information about parameter γ. If we are interested in using the extended information set $\Psi_t = (X_t', \mathbf{Z}^{t-1\prime})'$ to predict the probability distribution of Y_t, then β is called a *parameter of interest*, and γ is called a *nuisance parameter*. In this case, to estimate β, we only need to focus on modeling the conditional PDF/PMF $f_{Y_t|\Psi_t}(y|\Psi_t, \beta)$. This follows because the second part of the likelihood function does not depend on β so that the maximization of $\ln f_{\mathbf{Z}^n}(\mathbf{z}^n)$ with respect to β

is equivalent to the maximization of the first part of the likelihood with respect to β.

We now introduce various conditional distribution models. For simplicity, we only consider IID observations so that $f_{Y_t|\Psi_t}(y|\Psi_t,\beta) = f_{Y_t|X_t}(y|X_t,\beta)$.

Example 9.6. [Linear Regression Model with Normal Errors]: Suppose $Z_t = (Y_t, X_t')'$ is IID, $Y_t = X_t'\alpha^o + \varepsilon_t$, where $\varepsilon_t|X_t \sim N(0,\sigma_o^2)$. Then the conditional PDF of $Y_t|X_t$ is

$$f_{Y_t|X_t}(y|x,\beta) = \frac{1}{\sqrt{2\pi\sigma^2}} e^{-\frac{1}{2\sigma^2}(y-x'\alpha)^2},$$

where $\beta = (\alpha', \sigma^2)'$. This is a classical linear regression model discussed in Chapter 3. The unknown regression parameter value α^o can be estimated by the Quasi-MLE (QMLE) method to be proposed below, and it can be shown that QMLE is identical to the OLS estimator for α^o.

Example 9.7. [Logit Model]: Suppose $Z_t = (Y_t, X_t')'$ is IID, Y_t is a binary random variable taking either value 1 or value 0, and

$$P(Y_t = y|X_t) = \begin{cases} \psi(X_t'\beta^o) & \text{if } y = 1, \\ 1 - \psi(X_t'\beta^o) & \text{if } y = 0, \end{cases}$$

where

$$\psi(u) = \frac{1}{1+\exp(-u)}, \qquad -\infty < u < \infty,$$

is the CDF of the logistic distribution. We have

$$f_{Y_t|X_t}(y|X_t,\beta) = \psi(X_t'\beta)^y[1-\psi(X_t'\beta)]^{1-y}, \quad y = 0, 1.$$

Example 9.8. [Probit Model]: Suppose $Z_t = (Y_t, X_t')'$ is IID, and Y_t is a binary random variable such that

$$P(Y_t = y|X_t) = \begin{cases} \Phi(X_t'\beta^o) & \text{if } y = 1, \\ 1 - \Phi(X_t'\beta^o) & \text{if } y = 0, \end{cases}$$

where $\Phi(\cdot)$ is the N(0,1) CDF. We have

$$f_{Y_t|X_t}(y|X_t,\beta) = \Phi(X_t'\beta)^y[1-\Phi(X_t'\beta)]^{1-y}.$$

There are wide applications of the logit and probit models. For example, a consumer chooses a particular brand of car, or a student decides to go to PhD study.

Example 9.9. [Censored Regression (Tobit) Models]: A dependent variable Y_t is called censored when the response Y_t cannot take values below (left censored) or above (right censored) a certain threshold value. For example, the investment can only be zero or positive (when no borrowing is allowed). The censored data are generated from mixed continuous and discrete probability distributions. Suppose the DGP is

$$Y_t^* = X_t'\alpha^o + \varepsilon_t,$$

where $\{\varepsilon_t\} \sim \text{IID}N(0, \sigma_o^2)$. When $Y_t^* > c$, we observe $Y_t = Y_t^*$; when $Y_t^* \leq c$, we only have the record $Y_t = c$, where constant c is known. The parameter α^o should not be estimated by regressing Y_t on X_t based on the subsample with $Y_t > c$, because the data with $Y_t = c$ contain relevant information about α^o and σ_o^2. More importantly, in the subsample with $Y_t > c$, ε_t is a truncated distribution with nonzero mean (i.e., $E(\varepsilon_t|Y_t > c) \neq 0$ and $E(X_t\varepsilon_t|Y_t > c) \neq 0$) even if $E(\varepsilon_t|X_t) = 0$. Therefore, the OLS estimator is not consistent for α^o if one only uses the subsample consisting of observations of $Y_t > c$ and throws away observations with $Y_t = c$.

Question: How to estimate α^o using an observed sample $\{Y_t, X_t'\}_{t=1}^n$ where some observations of Y_t are censored?

Suppose $Z_t = (Y_t, X_t')'$ is IID, with the observed dependent variable

$$Y_t = \begin{cases} Y_t^* & \text{if } Y_t^* > c, \\ c & \text{if } Y_t^* \leq c, \end{cases}$$

where $Y_t^* = X_t'\alpha^o + \varepsilon_t$ and $\varepsilon_t|X_t \sim \text{IID}N(0, \sigma_o^2)$. We assume that the threshold c is known. Then we can write

$$\begin{aligned} Y_t &= \max(Y_t^*, c) \\ &= \max(X_t'\alpha^o + \varepsilon_t, c). \end{aligned}$$

Define a dummy variable indicating whether $Y_t^* > c$ or $Y_t^* \leq c$,

$$D_t = \begin{cases} 1 & \text{if } Y_t > c \text{ (i.e., if } Y_t^* > c), \\ 0 & \text{if } Y_t = c \text{ (i.e., if } Y_t^* \leq c). \end{cases}$$

Then the PDF of $Y_t|X_t$ is

$$f_{Y_t|X_t}(y|x,\beta) = \left[\frac{1}{\sqrt{2\pi\sigma^2}} e^{-\frac{1}{2\sigma^2}(y_t - x'\alpha)^2}\right]^{D_t} \left[\Phi\left(\frac{c - x'\alpha}{\sigma}\right)\right]^{1-D_t},$$

where $\Phi(\cdot)$ is the $N(0,1)$ CDF, and the second part is the conditional probability

$$\begin{aligned} P(Y_t = c|X_t = x) & \\ &= P(Y_t^* \leq c|X_t = x) \\ &= P(\varepsilon_t \leq c - X_t'\alpha|X_t = x) \\ &= P\left(\frac{\varepsilon_t}{\sigma} \leq \frac{c - X_t'\alpha}{\sigma}\middle| X_t = x\right) \\ &= \Phi\left(\frac{c - x'\alpha}{\sigma}\right), \end{aligned}$$

given the fact that $\frac{\varepsilon_t}{\sigma}$ follows an $N(0,1)$ distribution conditional on X_t.

Question: Can you give some examples where this model can be applied?

One example is a survey on unemployment spells. At the terminal date of the survey, the recorded time length of an unemployed worker is not the duration when his layoff will last. Another example is a survey on cancer patients. The life of those who have survived up to the ending date of the survey will usually be longer than the survival duration recorded.

Example 9.10. [Truncated Regression Models]: A random sample is called truncated if we know before hand that observations can come only from a restricted part of the underlying population distribution. The truncation can come from below, from above, or from both sides. We now consider an example where the truncation is from below with a known truncation point. More specifically, assume that the DGP is

$$Y_t^* = X_t'\alpha^o + \varepsilon_t,$$

where $\varepsilon_t|X_t \sim \text{IID}N(0,\sigma_o^2)$. Suppose only those of Y_t^* whose values are larger than or equal to constant c are observed, where c is known. That is, we observe $Y_t = Y_t^*$ if and only if $Y_t^* = X_t'\alpha^o + \varepsilon_t \geq c$. The observations with $Y_t^* < c$ are not recorded. Assume the resulting sample is $\{Y_t, X_t'\}_{t=1}^n$, where $\{Y_t, X_t'\}$ is IID. We now analyze the effect of truncation for this model. For the observed sample, $Y_t^* \geq c$ and so ε_t comes from the truncated version of the $N(0,\sigma_o^2)$ distribution with $\varepsilon_t \geq c - X_t'\alpha^o$. It follows that $E(X_t\varepsilon_t|Y_t^* \geq c) \neq 0$ and therefore the OLS estimator based on the observed sample $\{Y_t, X_t'\}$ is not consistent. One can use MLE to estimate the true parameter value α^o consistently, and for this purpose, one needs to know the conditional PDF of Y_t given X_t.

Because the observation Y_t is recorded if and only if $Y_t^* \geq c$, the conditional distribution of Y_t given X_t is the same as the conditional distribution of Y_t^* given X_t and $Y_t^* > c$. Moreover, for any events A, B and C, we have $P(A \cap B|C) = P(A|B \cap C)P(B|C)$ by the multiplication rule. Putting $A = \{Y_t^* \leq y\}, B = \{Y_t^* > c\}$ and $C = \{X_t = x\}$, we have

$$P\left(Y_t^* \leq y, Y_t^* > c|X_t = x\right) = P(Y_t^* \leq y|Y_t^* > c, X_t = x)P(Y_t^* > c|X_t = x).$$

It follows that

$$\begin{aligned} &F_{Y_t^*|X_t}(y|x) - F_{Y_t^*|X_t}(c|x) \\ &= F_{Y_t^*|(X_t=x,Y_t^*>c)}(y|X_t = x, Y_t^* > c)P(Y_t^* > c|X_t = x). \end{aligned}$$

Differentiating the equation with respect to y, we obtain that for any $y > c$,

$$\begin{aligned} f_{Y_t|X_t}(y|x,\beta) &= f_{Y_t^*|(X_t=x,Y_t^*>c)}(y|X_t = x, Y_t^* > c) \\ &= \frac{f_{Y_t^*|(X_t=x,Y_t^*>c)}(y|X_t = x, Y_t^* > c)P(Y_t^* > c|X_t = x)}{P(Y_t^* > c|X_t = x)} \\ &= \frac{f_{Y_t^*|X_t}(y|X_t = x)}{P(Y_t^* > c|X_t = x)} \\ &= \frac{1}{\sqrt{2\pi\sigma^2}} e^{-\frac{1}{2\sigma^2}(y_t - x_t'\alpha)^2} \frac{1}{1 - \Phi\left(\frac{c - x_t'\alpha}{\sigma}\right)}, \end{aligned}$$

where $\beta = (\alpha', \sigma^2)'$, and the conditional probability

$$\begin{aligned} P(Y_t^* > c|X_t = x) &= 1 - P(Y_t^* \leq c|X_t = x) \\ &= 1 - P\left(\frac{\varepsilon_t}{\sigma} \leq \frac{c - X_t'\alpha}{\sigma}\middle| X_t = x\right) \\ &= 1 - \Phi\left(\frac{c - x'\alpha}{\sigma}\right). \end{aligned}$$

Question: Can you give some examples where this model can be applied?

One example is loan applications in banks: only those successful loan applications will be recorded. Another example is students' application to colleges. Suppose we are interested in investigating how the entrance examination scores of students depend on their effort, family support, and high schools, and we have a sample from those who have been admitted to colleges. This sample is obviously a truncated sample because we do not observe those who are not admitted to colleges because their scores are below certain minimum requirements.

Question: How to estimate β in a conditional PDF/PMF model $f_{Y_t|\Psi_t}(y|\Psi_t, \beta)$?

We first introduce the likelihood function.

Definition 9.1. [Likelihood Function]: The joint PDF/PMF of the random sample $\mathbf{Z}^n = (Z_1, Z_2, ..., Z_n)$ as a function of (β, γ)

$$L_n(\beta, \gamma; \mathbf{z}^n) = f_{Z^n}(\mathbf{z}^n, \beta, \gamma)$$

is called the likelihood function of $\mathbf{Z}^n$ when $\mathbf{z}^n$ is observed. Moreover, $\ln L_n(\beta, \gamma, \mathbf{z}^n)$ is called the log-likelihood function of $\mathbf{Z}^n$ when $\mathbf{z}^n$ is observed.

The likelihood function $L_n(\beta, \gamma; \mathbf{z}^n)$ is algebraically identical to the joint PDF/PMF $f_{\mathbf{Z}^n}(\mathbf{z}^n, \beta, \gamma)$ of the random sample $\mathbf{Z}^n$ taking the value $\mathbf{z}^n$. Thus, given (β, γ), $L_n(\beta, \gamma; \mathbf{z}^n)$ can be viewed as a measure of the probability or likelihood with which the observed sample $\mathbf{z}^n$ will occur.

Lemma 9.1. ***[Variation-Free Parameter Spaces]:*** *Suppose β and γ are variation-free over parameter spaces $\Theta \times \Gamma$, in the sense that for all $(\beta, \gamma) \in \Theta \times \Gamma$, we have*

$$f_{Z_t|\mathbf{Z}^{t-1}}(z_t|\mathbf{Z}^{t-1}, \beta, \gamma) = f_{Y_t|\Psi_t}(y_t|\Psi_t, \beta) f_{X_t|\mathbf{Z}^{t-1}}(x_t|\mathbf{Z}^{t-1}, \gamma),$$

where $\Psi_t = (X_t', \mathbf{Z}^{t-1\prime})'$. Then the likelihood function of $\mathbf{Z}^n$ given $\mathbf{Z}^n = \mathbf{z}^n$ can be written as

$$L_n(\beta, \gamma; \mathbf{z}^n) = \prod_{t=1}^{n} f_{Y_t|\Psi_t}(y_t|\Psi_t, \beta) \prod_{t=1}^{n} f_{X_t|\mathbf{Z}^{t-1}}(x_t|\mathbf{Z}^{t-1}, \gamma),$$

and the log-likelihood function

$$\ln L_n(\beta, \gamma; \mathbf{z}^n) = \sum_{t=1}^{n} \ln f_{Y_t|\Psi_t}(y_t|\Psi_t, \beta) + \sum_{t=1}^{n} \ln f_{X_t|\mathbf{Z}^{t-1}}(x_t|\mathbf{Z}^{t-1}, \gamma).$$

Suppose we are interested in predicting Y_t using the extended information set $\Psi_t = (X_t', \mathbf{Z}^{t-1\prime})'$. Then only the first part of the log-likelihood is relevant, and β is called a parameter of interest. The other parameter γ, appearing in the second part of the log-likelihood function, is called a nuisance parameter.

We now define an estimation method based on maximizing the conditional log-likelihood function $\sum_{t=1}^{n} \ln f_{Y_t|\Psi_t}(y_t|\Psi_t, \beta)$.

Definition 9.2. [Maximum Likelihood Estimator (MLE) and Quasi-MLE (QMLE)]: Define the estimator $\hat{\beta}$ for $\beta \in \Theta$ as

$$\hat{\beta} = \arg\max_{\beta\in\Theta} \prod_{t=1}^{n} f_{Y_t|\Psi_t}(Y_t|\Psi_t, \beta) = \arg\max_{\beta\in\Theta} \sum_{t=1}^{n} \ln f_{Y_t|\Psi_t}(Y_t|\Psi_t, \beta),$$

where Θ is a parameter space.

(1) When the conditional PDF/PMF model $f_{Y_t|\Psi_t}(y|\Psi_t, \beta)$ is correctly specified in the sense that there exists some parameter value $\beta^o \in \Theta$ such that with probability one, $f_{Y_t|\Psi_t}(y|\Psi_t, \beta^o)$ coincides with the true conditional PDF/PMF of Y_t given Ψ_t, then $\hat{\beta}$ is called the Maximum Likelihood Estimator (MLE).

(2) When $f_{Y_t|\Psi_t}(y|\Psi_t, \beta)$ is misspecified in the sense that there exists no parameter value $\beta \in \Theta$ such that with probability one, $f_{Y_t|\Psi_t}(y|\Psi_t, \beta)$ coincides with the true conditional PDF/PMF of Y_t given Ψ_t, then $\hat{\beta}$ is called the Quasi-MLE (QMLE).

Under the variation-free parameters assumption, the second term of the log-likelihood function $\ln L_n(\beta, \gamma|\mathbf{Z}^n)$ does not depend on β (see Lemma 9.1). As a result, $\hat{\beta}$ in Definition 9.2 is also the solution to maximization of

$\ln L_n(\beta, \gamma|\mathbf{Z}^n)$, namely,

$$\begin{aligned}\hat{\beta} &= \arg\max_{\beta \in \Theta} \sum_{t=1}^{n} \ln f_{Y_t|\Psi_t}(Y_t|\Psi_t, \beta) \\ &= \arg\max_{\beta \in \Theta} \ln L_n(\beta, \gamma|\mathbf{Z}^n).\end{aligned}$$

Thus, by the nature of the objective function, MLE/QMLE gives a parameter estimate which makes the observed sample $\mathbf{z}^n$ most likely to occur. By choosing a suitable parameter value $\hat{\beta} \in \Theta$, MLE/QMLE maximizes the probability that $\mathbf{Z}^n = \mathbf{z}^n$, that is, the probability that the random sample $\mathbf{Z}^n$ takes the value of the observed data $\mathbf{z}^n$. Note that MLE and QMLE may not be unique.

MLE is obtained over Θ, where Θ may be subject to some restriction. An example is the GARCH model where some parameters have to be restricted in order to ensure that the estimated conditional variance is non-negative (e.g., Nelson and Cao 1992).

Question: When does MLE/QMLE exist?

Suppose the likelihood function is continuous in $\beta \in \Theta$ and parameter space Θ is compact. Then a global maximizer $\hat{\beta} \in \Theta$ exists.

Theorem 9.1. ***[Existence of MLE/QMLE]:*** *Suppose for each $\beta \in \Theta$, where Θ is a compact parameter space, $f_{Y_t|\Psi_t}(Y_t|\Psi_t, \beta)$ is a measurable function of (Y_t, Ψ_t), and for each t, $f_{Y_t|\Psi_t}(Y_t|\Psi_t, \cdot)$ is continuous in $\beta \in \Theta$ with probability one. Then MLE/QMLE $\hat{\beta}$ exists.*

This result is analogous to the Weierstrass Theorem in multivariate calculus that any continuous function over a compact support always has a global maximum and a global minimum.

Example 9.11. [MLE/QMLE for a Linear Regression Model with Normal Errors]: Suppose $Z_t = (Y_t, X_t')'$ is IID, $Y_t = X_t'\alpha^o + \varepsilon_t$, where $\varepsilon_t|X_t \sim N(0, \sigma_o^2)$. Then the conditional PDF of $Y_t|X_t$ is

$$f_{Y_t|X_t}(y|x, \beta) = \frac{1}{\sqrt{2\pi\sigma^2}} e^{-\frac{1}{2\sigma^2}(y - x'\alpha)^2},$$

where $\beta = (\alpha', \sigma^2)'$. It follows that

$$\sum_{t=1}^{n} \ln f_{Y_t|\Psi_t}(Y_t|\Psi_t, \beta) = -\frac{n}{2}\ln 2\pi - \frac{n}{2}\ln \sigma^2 - \frac{1}{2\sigma^2}\sum_{t=1}^{n}(Y_t - X_t'\alpha)^2.$$

Solving the FOCs:

$$\frac{\partial \sum_{t=1}^{n} \ln f_{Y_t|\Psi_t}(Y_t|\Psi_t, \hat{\beta})}{\partial \alpha} = \frac{1}{2\hat{\sigma}^2} \sum_{t=1}^{n} X_t(Y_t - X_t'\hat{\alpha}) = 0,$$

$$\frac{\partial \sum_{t=1}^{n} \ln f_{Y_t|\Psi_t}(Y_t|\Psi_t, \hat{\beta})}{\partial \sigma^2} = -\frac{n}{2\hat{\sigma}^2} + \frac{1}{2\hat{\sigma}^4} \sum_{t=1}^{n} (Y_t - X_t'\hat{\alpha})^2 = 0,$$

we obtain

$$\hat{\alpha} = (\mathbf{X}'\mathbf{X})^{-1}\mathbf{X}'Y,$$

$$\hat{\sigma}^2 = \frac{e'e}{n},$$

where $e = Y - X\hat{\alpha}$. Therefore, the MLE/QMLE $\hat{\alpha}$ for α is exactly the same as the OLS estimator in Chapter 3.

The MLE/QMLE $\hat{\beta} = (\hat{\alpha}', \hat{\sigma}^2)'$ in Example 9.11 has a closed form solution. Generally, we can only characterize MLE/QMLE by FOC, and like the GMM estimator, there is usually no closed form for the MLE/QMLE $\hat{\beta}$. The solution $\hat{\beta}$ has to be searched by computers. The most popular computing methods used in economics are the BHHH algorithm (Berndt *et al.* 1974) and the Gauss-Newton algorithm.

9.3 Statistical Properties of MLE/QMLE

For notational simplicity, from now on we will write the conditional PDF/PMF of Y_t given Ψ_t as

$$f_{Y_t|\Psi_t}(y|\Psi_t, \beta) = f(y|\Psi_t, \beta), \quad -\infty < y < \infty.$$

We first provide a set of regularity conditions.

Assumption 9.1. [Parametric Probability Distribution Model]: (a) $\{Z_t = (Y_t, X_t')'\}_{t=1}^n$ is an ergodic stationary process; (b) $f(y_t|\Psi_t, \beta)$ is a conditional PDF/PMF model of Y_t given $\Psi_t = (X_t', \mathbf{Z}^{t-1\prime})'$, where $\mathbf{Z}^{t-1} = (Z_{t-1}', Z_{t-2}', ..., Z_1')'$, and β is a $K \times 1$ parameter vector. For each β, $\ln f(Y_t|\Psi_t, \beta)$ is measurable with respect to (Y_t, Ψ_t), and for each t, $\ln f(Y_t|\Psi_t, \cdot)$ is continuous in $\beta \in \Theta$ with probability one, where Θ is a finite-dimensional parameter space.

Assumption 9.2. [Compactness]: Parameter space Θ is compact.

Assumption 9.3. [UWLLN]: $\{\ln f(Y_t|\Psi_t, \beta) - E\ln f(Y_t|\Psi_t, \beta)\}$ obeys UWLLN, i.e.,

$$\sup_{\beta\in\Theta}\left|n^{-1}\sum_{t=1}^{n}\ln f(Y_t|\Psi_t,\beta) - l(\beta)\right| \xrightarrow{p} 0,$$

where the population log-likelihood function

$$l(\beta) = E\left[\ln f(Y_t|\Psi_t,\beta)\right]$$

is continuous in $\beta \in \Theta$.

Assumption 9.4. [Identification]: The parameter value

$$\beta^* = \arg\max_{\beta\in\Theta} l(\beta)$$

is the unique maximizer of $l(\beta)$ over Θ.

Question: What is the interpretation of β^*?

Assumption 9.4 is an identification condition which states that β^* is a unique solution that maximizes $l(\beta)$, the expected value of the logarithmic conditional likelihood function $\ln f(Y_t|\Psi_t, \beta)$. So far, there is no economic interpretation for β^* since we do not know whether $f(y|\Psi_t, \beta)$ is correctly specified for the conditional distribution of Y_t given Ψ_t. This is analogous to the best linear least squares approximation coefficient $\beta^* = \arg\min_\beta E(Y - X'\beta)^2$ in Chapter 2, where it cannot be interpreted as the expected marginal effect of X on Y if one does not know whether the linear regression model is correctly specified for $E(Y_t|X_t)$.

We now consider the consistency property of $\hat{\beta}$ for β^*. Because we assume that Θ is compact, $\hat{\beta}$ and β^* may be corner solutions. Thus, we have to use the extremum estimator lemma to prove the consistency of MLE/QMLE $\hat{\beta}$.

Theorem 9.2. ***[Consistency of MLE/QMLE]:*** *Suppose Assumptions 9.1 to 9.4 hold. Then as $n \to \infty$,*

$$\hat{\beta} - \beta^* \xrightarrow{p} 0.$$

Proof: Applying the extremum estimator lemma in Chapter 8, with

$$\hat{Q}(\beta) = n^{-1}\sum_{t=1}^{n}\ln f(Y_t|\Psi_t,\beta)$$

and

$$Q(\beta) = l(\beta) \equiv E[\ln f(Y_t|\Psi_t, \beta)].$$

Assumptions 9.1 to 9.4 ensure that all conditions for $\hat{Q}(\beta)$ and $Q(\beta)$ in the extremum estimator lemma are satisfied. It follows that $\hat{\beta} \xrightarrow{p} \beta^*$ as $n \to \infty$. This completes the proof.

9.4 Correct Model Specification and Its Implications

To discuss similarities and differences between MLE and QMLE, we first define correct specification of a conditional probability distribution model and discuss its implications.

Definition 9.3. [Correct Model Specification for Conditional Probability Distribution]: The model $f(y_t|\Psi_t, \beta)$ is correctly specified for the conditional PDF/PMF of Y_t given Ψ_t if there exists some parameter value $\beta^o \in \Theta$ such that with probability one, $f(y_t|\Psi_t, \beta^o)$ coincides with the true conditional PDF/PMF of Y_t given Ψ_t.

A conditional distribution model characterizes a family (or class) of conditional distributions. Each parameter value β yields a conditional distribution of Y given Ψ, and different parameter values for β yield different conditional distributions. A correctly specified conditional distribution model means that the family of conditional distributions it characterizes contains the true conditional distribution of Y_t given Ψ_t. Under correct specification of $f(y|\Psi_t, \beta)$, the parameter value β^o is usually called the true model parameter value. It will have a valid economic interpretation.

Question: What are the implications of correct specification of a conditional distribution model $f(y|\Psi_t, \beta)$?

Theorem 9.3. *Suppose Assumption 9.4 holds, and the model $f(y_t|\Psi_t, \beta)$ is correctly specified for the conditional probability distribution of Y_t given Ψ_t. Then with probability one, $f(y_t|\Psi_t, \beta^*)$ coincides with the true conditional PDF/PMF $f(y_t|\Psi_t, \beta^o)$ of Y_t given Ψ_t, where β^* is as given in Assumption 9.4 and β^o is the true parameter value. In other words, when the model $f(y_t|\Psi_t, \beta)$ is correctly specified for the conditional probability distribution of Y_t given Ψ_t, the population log-likelihood maximizer β^* coincides with* *the true parameter value* β^o, *namely*

$$\beta^* = \beta^o.$$

Proof: Because $f(y|\Psi_t, \beta)$ is correctly specified for the conditional distribution of Y_t given Ψ_t, there exists some $\beta^o \in \Theta$ such that

$$\begin{aligned} l(\beta) &= E[\ln f(Y_t|\Psi_t, \beta)] \\ &= E\{E[\ln f(Y_t|\Psi_t, \beta)|\Psi_t]\} \\ &= E\int_{-\infty}^{\infty} ln[f(y|\Psi_t, \beta)] f(y|\Psi_t, \beta^o)dy, \end{aligned}$$

where the second equality follows from the law of iterated expectations and the expectation $E(\cdot)$ in the third equality is taken with respect to the true probability distribution of the random variables in Ψ_t.

By Assumption 9.4, we have $l(\beta) \leq l(\beta^*)$ for all $\beta \in \Theta$. By the law of iterated expectations, it follows that for all $\beta \in \Theta$,

$$E\int_{-\infty}^{\infty} \ln[f(y|\Psi_t, \beta)] f(y|\Psi_t, \beta^o)dy \leq E\int_{-\infty}^{\infty} \ln[f(y|\Psi_t, \beta^*)] f(y|\Psi_t, \beta^o)dy,$$

where $f(y_t|\Psi_t, \beta^o)$ is the true conditional PDF/PMF. Hence, by choosing $\beta = \beta^o$, we have

$$E\int_{-\infty}^{\infty} \ln[f(y|\Psi_t, \beta^o)] f(y|\Psi_t, \beta^o)dy \leq E\int_{-\infty}^{\infty} \ln[f(y|\Psi_t, \beta^*)] f(y|\Psi_t, \beta^o)dy. \tag{9.1}$$

On the other hand, by Jensen's inequality and the concavity of the logarithmic function, we have

$$\begin{aligned} &\int_{-\infty}^{\infty} \ln[f(y|\Psi_t, \beta^*)] f(y|\Psi_t, \beta^o)dy - \int_{-\infty}^{\infty} \ln[f(y|\Psi_t, \beta^o)] f(y|\Psi_t, \beta^o)dy \\ &= \int_{-\infty}^{\infty} \ln\left[\frac{f(y|\Psi_t, \beta^*)}{f(y|\Psi_t, \beta^o)}\right] f(y|\Psi_t, \beta^o)dy \\ &\leq \ln\left\{\int_{-\infty}^{\infty} \left[\frac{f(y|\Psi_t, \beta^*)}{f(y|\Psi_t, \beta^o)}\right] f(y|\Psi_t, \beta^o)dy\right\} \\ &= \ln\left\{\int_{-\infty}^{\infty} f(y|\Psi_t, \beta^*)dy\right\} \\ &= \ln(1) \\ &= 0, \end{aligned}$$

where we have made use of the fact that $\int_{-\infty}^{\infty} f(y|\Psi_t,\beta)dy = 1$ for all $\beta \in \Theta$. Therefore, we have

$$\int_{-\infty}^{\infty} \ln\left[f(y|\Psi_t,\beta^*)\right] f(y|\Psi_t,\beta^o)dy \le \int_{-\infty}^{\infty} \ln[f(y|\Psi_t,\beta^*)]f(y|\Psi_t,\beta^o)dy.$$

Therefore, by taking the expectation with respect to the probability distribution of Ψ_t, we obtain

$$E\int_{-\infty}^{\infty} \ln[f(y|\Psi_t,\beta^*)]f(y|\Psi_t,\beta^o)dy \le E\int_{-\infty}^{\infty} \ln[f(y|\Psi_t,\beta^o)]f(y|\Psi_t,\beta^o)dy. \tag{9.2}$$

Since the inequalities in (9.1) and (9.2) hold simultaneously, we must have $\beta^* = \beta^o$ given Assumption 9.4; otherwise β^* cannot be the the maximizer of $l(\beta)$ over Θ. This completes the proof.

Theorem 9.3 provides an interpretation of β^* in Assumption 9.4. That is, the population log-likelihood maximizer β^* coincides with the true model parameter value β^o when $f(y|\Psi_t,\beta)$ is correctly specified. Thus, by maximizing the population model log-likelihood function $l(\beta)$, we can obtain the true parameter value β^o.

Under Theorem 9.2, we have $\hat{\beta} \xrightarrow{p} \beta^*$ as $n \to \infty$. Furthermore, by correct specification for conditional distribution, we know $\beta^* = \beta^o$, where β^o is the true model parameter value. Therefore, we have $\hat{\beta} \xrightarrow{p} \beta^o$ as $n \to \infty$.

This is essentially equivalent to the consistency in the linear regression context, in which, the OLS estimator always converges to β^* no matter whether the linear regression model is correctly specified for conditional mean. And when the linear regression model coincides with the true conditional mean function, we have $\beta^* = \beta^o$ from Theorem 2.4 and then the OLS estimator will converge to the true model parameter β^o.

Below, we examine two additional important implications of correct model specification for conditional distribution. For this purpose, we assume that the true parameter value β^o is an interior point of the parameter space Θ, so that we can impose a differentiability condition on the log-likelihood function $\ln f(y|\Psi_t,\beta)$ at β^o:

Assumption 9.5. $\beta^o \in \text{int}(\Theta)$, where β^o is as in Definition 9.3.

Question: Why do we need this assumption?

This assumption is needed in order to take a Taylor series expansion for $f(y|\Psi_t, \beta)$.

We first state an important implication of a correctly specified conditional distribution model for Y_t given Ψ_t.

Theorem 9.4. *[MDS Property of Score Function]: Suppose that for each t, $\ln f(Y_t|\Psi_t, \cdot)$ is continuously differentiable with respect to $\beta \in \Theta$ with probability one. Define a $K \times 1$ score function*

$$S_t(\beta) = \frac{\partial}{\partial \beta} \ln f(y_t|\Psi_t, \beta).$$

If $f(y|\Psi_t, \beta)$ is correctly specified for the conditional probability distribution of Y_t given Ψ_t, then

$$E\left[S_t(\beta^o)|\Psi_t\right] = 0,$$

where β^o is as in Definition 9.3 and satisfies Assumption 9.5, and $E(\cdot|\Psi_t)$ is the expectation taken over the true conditional probability distribution of Y_t given Ψ_t.

Proof: We shall only consider the case of a conditional continuous distribution for Y_t. Note that for any given $\beta \in \Theta$, $f(y|\Psi_t, \beta)$ is a valid PDF. Thus we have

$$\int_{-\infty}^{\infty} f(y|\Psi_t, \beta)dy = 1.$$

When $\beta \in \text{int}(\Theta)$, by differentiation, we have

$$\frac{\partial}{\partial \beta} \int_{-\infty}^{\infty} f(y|\Psi_t, \beta)dy = 0.$$

By exchanging differentiation and integration, we have

$$\int_{-\infty}^{\infty} \frac{\partial}{\partial \beta} f(y|\Psi_t, \beta)dy = 0,$$

which can be further written as

$$\int_{-\infty}^{\infty} \frac{\partial \ln f(y|\Psi_t, \beta)}{\partial \beta} f(y|\Psi_t, \beta)dy = 0.$$

This relationship holds for all $\beta \in int(\Theta)$, including β^o. It follows that

$$\int_{-\infty}^{\infty} \frac{\partial \ln f(y|\Psi_t, \beta^o)}{\partial \beta} f(y|\Psi_t, \beta^o)dy = 0,$$

where

$$\frac{\partial \ln f(y|\Psi_t, \beta^o)}{\partial \beta} = \left. \frac{\partial \ln f(y|\Psi_t, \beta)}{\partial \beta} \right|_{\beta=\beta^o}.$$

Because $f(y|\Psi_t, \beta^o)$ is the true conditional PDF/PMF of Y_t given Ψ_t when $f(y|\Psi_t, \beta)$ is correctly specified for the conditional distribution of Y_t given Ψ_t, we have

$$E[S_t(\beta^o)|\Psi_t] = 0.$$

This completes the proof.

Note that $E[S_t(\beta^o)|\Psi_t] = 0$ implies that $E[S_t(\beta^o)|Z^{t-1}] = 0$, namely $\{S_t(\beta^o)\}$ is an MDS. As will be seen later, this MDS property is crucial to understand the asymptotic properties of the MLE $\hat{\beta}$.

Question: Suppose $E[S_t(\beta^o)|\Psi_t] = 0$ for some $\beta^o \in \Theta$. Can we claim that the conditional PDF/PMF model is correctly specified?

No. The MDS property is one of many implications of correct model specification for conditional probability distribution. In certain sense, the MDS property is equivalent to correct specification for conditional mean. Misspecification of $f(y|\Psi_t, \beta)$ may occur in higher order conditional moments of Y_t given Ψ_t. Below is an example in which $\{S_t(\beta^o)\}$ is an MDS but the model $f(y_t|\Psi_t, \beta)$ is misspecified.

Example 9.12. Suppose $\{Y_t\}$ is a univariate time series process that follows the DGP

$$Y_t = \mu_t(\beta^o) + \sigma_t(\beta^o)z_t,$$

where $\mu_t(\beta^o) = E(Y_t|\Psi_t)$ and $\sigma_t^2(\beta^o) = \text{var}(Y_t|\Psi_t)$ depend on $\Psi_t = \mathbf{Y}^{t-1} = (Y_{t-1}, Y_{t-2}, ..., Y_1)'$, and $\{z_t\} \sim$ IID $N(0,1)$. Suppose further $\{Y_t\}$ has a unit variance.

We now consider the following model

$$Y_t = \mu_t(\beta) + \varepsilon_t, \quad \{\varepsilon_t\} \sim \text{ IID } N(0,1).$$

This model is correctly specified for conditional mean $E(Y_t|\Psi_t)$, because there exists some $\beta^o \in \Theta$ such that $\mu_t(\beta^o) = E(Y_t|\Psi_t)$. However, it is misspecified for conditional variance $\text{var}(Y_t|\Psi_t)$, because $\text{var}(Y_t|\Psi_t) = \sigma_t^2(\beta^o) \neq 1$. Given the assumption that $\{\varepsilon_t\} \sim$ IID $N(0,1)$, we can write the conditional PDF of the model as follows:

$$f(y|\Psi_t, \beta) = \frac{1}{\sqrt{2\pi}} \exp\left\{-\frac{1}{2}\left[Y_t - \mu_t(\beta)\right]^2\right\}, \quad -\infty < y < \infty.$$

It is straightforward to verify that

$$E\left[S_t(\beta^o)|\Psi_t\right] = E[S_t(\beta^o)|I_{t-1}] = 0,$$

although there exists misspecification in volatility dynamics.

Next, we state another important implication of a correctly specified conditional distribution model for Y_t given Ψ_t.

Theorem 9.5. ***[Conditional Information Matrix (IM) Equality]:*** *Suppose Assumptions 9.1 to 9.5 hold, $f(y|\Psi_t, \beta)$ is twice continuously differentiable with respect to $\beta \in int(\Theta)$ with probability one, and $f(y_t|\Psi_t, \beta)$ is correctly specified for the conditional probability distribution of Y_t given Ψ_t. Then*

$$E\left[S_t(\beta^o)S_t(\beta^o)' + H_t(\beta^o)|\Psi_t\right] = 0,$$

where

$$\begin{aligned} H_t(\beta) &\equiv \frac{d}{d\beta} S_t(\beta) \\ &= \frac{\partial^2}{\partial\beta\partial\beta'} \ln f(Y_t|\Psi_t, \beta), \end{aligned}$$

or equivalently,

$$\begin{aligned} &E\left[\frac{\partial}{\partial\beta} \ln f(Y_t|\Psi_t, \beta^o) \frac{\partial}{\partial\beta'} \ln f(Y_t|\Psi_t, \beta^o)\right| \Psi_t\bigg] \\ &= -E\left[\frac{\partial^2}{\partial\beta\partial\beta'} \ln f(Y_t|\Psi_t, \beta^o)\right| \Psi_t\bigg]. \end{aligned}$$

Proof: For all $\beta \in \Theta$, we have

$$\int_{-\infty}^{\infty} f(y|\Psi_t, \beta)dy = 1.$$

By differentiation with respect to $\beta \in int(\Theta)$, we obtain

$$\frac{\partial}{\partial \beta} \int_{-\infty}^{\infty} f(y|\Psi_t, \beta) dy = 0.$$

Exchanging differentiation and integration, we have

$$\int_{-\infty}^{\infty} \frac{\partial f(y|\Psi_t, \beta)}{\partial \beta} dy = 0,$$

$$\int_{-\infty}^{\infty} \frac{\partial \ln f(y|\Psi_t, \beta)}{\partial \beta} f(y|\Psi_t, \beta) dy = 0.$$

With further differentiation of the above equation again, we have

$$\begin{aligned}
&\frac{\partial}{\partial \beta} \int_{-\infty}^{\infty} \frac{\partial \ln f(y|\Psi_t, \beta)}{\partial \beta} f(y|\Psi_t, \beta) dy \\
&= \int_{-\infty}^{\infty} \frac{\partial}{\partial \beta} \left[\frac{\partial \ln f(y|\Psi_t, \beta)}{\partial \beta} f(y|\Psi_t, \beta) \right] dy \\
&= \int_{-\infty}^{\infty} \frac{\partial^2 \ln f(y|\Psi_t, \beta)}{\partial \beta \partial \beta'} f(y|\Psi_t, \beta) dy \\
&\quad + \int_{-\infty}^{\infty} \frac{\partial \ln f(y|\Psi_t, \beta)}{\partial \beta} \frac{\partial f(y|\Psi_t, \beta)}{\partial \beta'} dy \\
&= \int_{-\infty}^{\infty} \frac{\partial^2 \ln f(y|\Psi_t, \beta)}{\partial \beta \partial \beta'} f(y|\Psi_t, \beta) dy \\
&\quad + \int_{-\infty}^{\infty} \frac{\partial \ln f(y|\Psi_t, \beta)}{\partial \beta} \frac{\partial \ln f(y|\Psi_t, \beta)}{\partial \beta'} f(y|\Psi_t, \beta) dy \\
&= 0.
\end{aligned}$$

The above relationship holds for all $\beta \in \Theta$, including β^o. This and the fact that $f(y|\Psi_t, \beta^o)$ is the true conditional PDF/PMF of Y_t given Ψ_t imply the desired conditional IM equality PDF/PMF. This completes the proof.

The $K \times K$ matrix

$$\begin{aligned}
&E[S_t(\beta^o) S_t(\beta^o)' | \Psi_t] \\
&= E\left[\frac{\partial \ln f(Y_t|\Psi_t, \beta^o)}{\partial \beta} \frac{\partial \ln f(Y_t|\Psi_t, \beta^o)}{\partial \beta'} \middle| \Psi_t \right]
\end{aligned}$$

is called Fisher's conditional IM of Y_t given Ψ_t. It measures the content of the information contained in the random variable Y_t conditional on the information set Ψ_t. The larger the conditional expectation is, the more information Y_t contains.

Question: What is the implication of the conditional IM equality?

In certain sense, the conditional IM equality could be viewed as equivalent to correct specification of conditional variance. It has important implications on the form of the asymptotic variance of MLE. More specifically, the conditional IM equality will simplify the asymptotic variance of MLE in the same way as conditional homoskedasticity simplifies the asymptotic variance of the OLS estimator.

9.5 Asymptotic Distribution of MLE

To investigate the asymptotic distribution of $\sqrt{n}(\hat{\beta} - \beta^o)$, we need the following conditions.

Assumption 9.6. (a) For each t, $\ln f(y_t|\Psi_t, \cdot)$ is continuously twice differentiable with respect to $\beta \in \Theta$ with probability one.

(b) Given β^* as in Assumption 9.4, $\{S_t(\beta^*)\}$ obeys CLT, i.e.,

$$\sqrt{n}\hat{S}(\beta^*) \equiv n^{-1/2} \sum_{t=1}^{n} S_t(\beta^*) \xrightarrow{d} N(0, V_*)$$

for some $K \times K$ matrix $V_* \equiv \text{avar}[n^{-1/2} \sum_{t=1}^{n} S_t(\beta^*)]$ which is symmetric, finite and positive definite.

(c) $\{H_t(\beta) \equiv \frac{\partial^2}{\partial\beta\partial\beta'} \ln f(y_t|\Psi_t, \beta)\}$ obeys UWLLN over Θ. That is, as $n \to \infty$,

$$\sup_{\beta\in\Theta} \left\| n^{-1} \sum_{t=1}^{n} H_t(\beta) - H(\beta) \right\| \xrightarrow{p} 0,$$

where the $K \times K$ Hessian matrix

$$\begin{aligned} H(\beta) &\equiv E\left[H_t(\beta)\right] \\ &= E\left[\frac{\partial^2 \ln f(Y_t|\Psi_t, \beta)}{\partial\beta\partial\beta'}\right] \end{aligned}$$

is symmetric, finite and nonsingular, and is continuous in $\beta \in \Theta$.

No matter whether the conditional distribution model $f(y|\Psi_t, \beta)$ is correctly specified, Assumption 9.6 will be used. When $f(y|\Psi_t, \beta)$ is correctly specified, we have $\beta^* = \beta^o$ by Theorem 9.3 and so $\sqrt{n}\hat{S}(\beta^*) = \sqrt{n}\hat{S}(\beta^o)$ and $V_* = V_o \equiv avar[\sqrt{n}\hat{S}(\beta^o)]$.

Question: What is the structure of the asymptotic variance V_o of $\sqrt{n}\hat{S}(\beta^o)$ when $f(y|\Psi_t, \beta)$ is correctly specified?

By the stationary MDS property of $S_t(\beta^o)$ with respect to Ψ_t, we have

$$\begin{aligned}
V_o &\equiv \text{avar}\left[n^{-1/2}\sum_{t=1}^{n} S_t(\beta^o)\right] \\
&= E\left\{\left[n^{-1/2}\sum_{t=1}^{n} S_t(\beta^o)\right]\left[n^{-1/2}\sum_{\tau=1}^{n} S_\tau(\beta^o)\right]'\right\} \\
&= n^{-1}\sum_{t=1}^{n}\sum_{\tau=1}^{n} E[S_t(\beta^o)S_\tau(\beta^o)'] \\
&= E[S_t(\beta^o)S_t(\beta^o)'],
\end{aligned}$$

where the expectations of cross-products, $E[S_t(\beta^o)S_\tau(\beta^o)']$, are identically zero for all $t \neq \tau$, as implied by the MDS property of $\{S_t(\beta^o)\}$ from Theorem 9.4.

Furthermore, from the conditional IM equality, we have

$$\begin{aligned}
V_o &= E[S_t(\beta^o)S_t(\beta^o)'] \\
&= -H_o
\end{aligned}$$

by the law of iterated expectations, where the population Hessian matrix $H_o = H(\beta^o)$ is a $K \times K$ symmetric negative definite matrix.

We now derive the asymptotic normality of MLE.

Theorem 9.6. ***[Asymptotic Normality of MLE]:*** *Suppose Assumptions 9.1 to 9.6 hold, and $f(y_t|\Psi_t, \beta)$ is correctly specified for the conditional distribution of Y_t given Ψ_t. Then as $n \to \infty$,*

$$\sqrt{n}(\hat{\beta} - \beta^o) \xrightarrow{d} N(0, -H_o^{-1}).$$

Proof: Because β^o is an interior point in Θ and $\hat{\beta} - \beta^o \xrightarrow{p} 0$ as $n \to \infty$, we have $\hat{\beta} \in int(\Theta)$ for n sufficiently large. It follows that the FOC of maximizing the log-likelihood holds when n is sufficiently large:

$$\begin{aligned}\hat{S}(\hat{\beta}) &\equiv n^{-1}\sum_{t=1}^{n}\frac{\partial \ln f(Y_t|\Psi_t,\hat{\beta})}{\partial\beta}\\ &= n^{-1}\sum_{t=1}^{n} S_t(\hat{\beta})\\ &= 0.\end{aligned}$$

The FOC provides a link between MLE and GMM: MLE can be viewed as a GMM estimation with the moment condition

$$E[m_t(\beta^o)] = E[S_t(\beta^o)] = 0 \text{ for some parameter value } \beta^o$$

in an exact identification case.

By a first order Taylor series expansion of $\hat{S}(\hat{\beta})$ around the true parameter value β^o, we have

$$\begin{aligned}0 &= \sqrt{n}\hat{S}(\hat{\beta})\\ &= \sqrt{n}\hat{S}(\beta^o) + \hat{H}(\bar{\beta})\sqrt{n}(\hat{\beta}-\beta^o),\end{aligned}$$

where $\bar{\beta}$ lies between $\hat{\beta}$ and β^o, namely, $\bar{\beta} = a\hat{\beta} + (1-a)\beta^o$ for some $a \in [0,1]$, and the sample Hessian matrix

$$\begin{aligned}\hat{H}(\beta) &= n^{-1}\sum_{t=1}^{n} H_t(\beta)\\ &= n^{-1}\sum_{t=1}^{n}\frac{\partial^2 \ln f(Y_t|\Psi_t,\beta)}{\partial\beta\partial\beta'}\end{aligned}$$

is the derivative of $\hat{S}(\beta)$. Given that $\hat{\beta}-\beta^o \xrightarrow{p} 0$, we have

$$\begin{aligned}||\bar{\beta}-\beta^o|| &= ||a(\hat{\beta}-\beta^o)|| \leq ||\hat{\beta}-\beta^o||\\ &\xrightarrow{p} 0.\end{aligned}$$

Also, by the triangle inequality, UWLLN for $\{H_t(\beta)\}$ over Θ, and continuity of the population Hessian matrix $H(\beta)$, we obtain

$$\begin{aligned}&\left\|\hat{H}(\bar{\beta}) - H_o\right\|\\ &= \left\|\hat{H}(\bar{\beta}) - H(\bar{\beta}) + H(\bar{\beta}) - H(\beta^o)\right\|\\ &\leq \sup_{\beta\in\Theta}\left\|\hat{H}(\bar{\beta}) - H(\bar{\beta})\right\| + ||H(\bar{\beta}) - H(\beta^o)||\\ &\xrightarrow{p} 0.\end{aligned}$$

Because H_o is nonsingular, so is $\hat{H}(\bar{\beta})$ for n sufficiently large. Therefore, from the FOC we have

$$\sqrt{n}(\hat{\beta} - \beta^o) = -\hat{H}^{-1}(\bar{\beta})\sqrt{n}\hat{S}(\beta^o)$$

for n sufficiently large. (Compare with the OLS estimator $\sqrt{n}(\hat{\beta} - \beta^o) = \hat{Q}^{-1}\sqrt{n}\frac{X'\varepsilon}{n}$!)

Next, we consider $\sqrt{n}\hat{S}(\beta^o)$. By CLT, we have

$$\sqrt{n}\hat{S}(\beta^o) \xrightarrow{d} N(0, V_o),$$

where, as we have shown above,

$$\begin{aligned} V_o &\equiv \text{avar}\left[\sqrt{n}\hat{S}(\beta^o)\right] \\ &= E[S_t(\beta^o)S_t(\beta^o)'] \end{aligned}$$

given that $\{S_t(\beta^o)\}$ is a stationary MDS with respect to Ψ_t.

It follows by Slutsky's theorem that

$$\begin{aligned} \sqrt{n}(\hat{\beta} - \beta^o) &= -\hat{H}^{-1}(\bar{\beta})\sqrt{n}\hat{S}(\beta^o) \\ &\xrightarrow{d} N(0, H_o^{-1}V_oH_o^{-1}) \sim N(0, -H_o^{-1}) \end{aligned}$$

or equivalently

$$\sqrt{n}(\hat{\beta} - \beta^o) \xrightarrow{d} N(0, H_o^{-1}V_oH_o^{-1}) \sim N(0, V_o^{-1})$$

using the IM equality that $V_o = E[S_t(\beta^o)S_t(\beta^o)'] = -H_o$, which is implied by the conditional IM equality. This completes the proof.

Now it is easy to understand why $V_o = E[S_t(\beta^o)S_t(\beta^o)'] = -H_o$ is called the IM of Y_t given Ψ_t. The larger $-H_o$ is, the smaller the variance of $\hat{\beta}$ is (i.e., the more precise the estimator $\hat{\beta}$ is). Intuitively, as a measure of the curvature of the population log-likelihood function, the absolute value of the magnitude of the Hessian matrix H_o characterizes the sharpness of the peak of the population log-likelihood function at β^o. Figure 9.1 illustrates the relationship between the efficiency of MLE and the curvature of the population likelihood function.

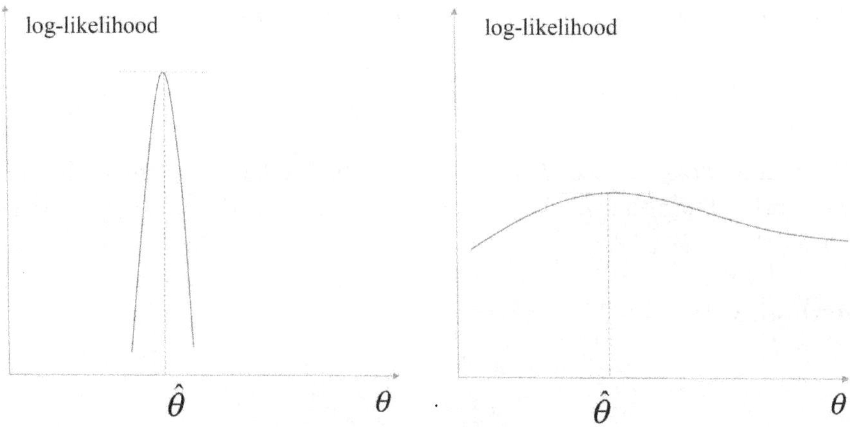

Figure 9.1 MLE efficiency and curvature of population log-likelihood function.

The asymptotic variance avar$(\sqrt{n}\hat{\beta}) = -H_o^{-1}$ is rather similar in structure to the asymptotic variance $\sigma^2 Q^{-1}$ of the $\sqrt{n}$-scaled OLS estimator, where $Q = E(X_t X_t')$, when there exists no autocorrelation nor conditional heteroskedasticity. In deriving the asymptotic variance avar$(\sqrt{n}\hat{\beta})$ for MLE, we have made use of the MDS property of the score function and conditional IM equality, which play a similar role to zero autocorrelation and conditional homoskedasticity in simplifying the asymptotic variance of the OLS estimator.

From statistical theory, it is well-known that the asymptotic variance of the MLE $\hat{\beta}$ achieves the Cramer-Rao lower bound. Therefore, the MLE $\hat{\beta}$ is asymptotically most efficient.

Question: What is the Cramer-Rao lower bound?

9.6 Consistent Estimation of Asymptotic Variance-Covariance Matrix of MLE

We now discuss consistent estimation of the asymptotic variance-covariance matrix of MLE.

When the model $f(y|\Psi_t, \beta)$ is correctly specified,

$$avar(\sqrt{n}\hat{\beta}) = V_o^{-1} = -H_o^{-1}.$$

Therefore, there are two methods to estimate avar$(\sqrt{n}\hat{\beta})$ of MLE.

Method 1: Use $\hat{\Omega} \equiv -\hat{H}^{-1}(\hat{\beta})$, where the sample Hessian matrix

$$\hat{H}(\beta) = \frac{1}{n}\sum_{t=1}^{n} \frac{\partial^2 \ln f(Y_t|\Psi_t, \beta)}{\partial\beta\partial\beta'}.$$

This requires taking second derivatives of the log-likelihood function. By Assumption 9.6(c) and $\hat{\beta} \xrightarrow{p} \beta^o$ as $n \to \infty$, we have $\hat{\Omega} \xrightarrow{p} -H_o^{-1}$. (Please verify it!)

Method 2: Use $\hat{\Omega} \equiv \hat{V}^{-1}$, where

$$\hat{V} \equiv \frac{1}{n}\sum_{t=1}^{n} S_t(\hat{\beta})S_t(\hat{\beta})'.$$

This requires the computation of the first derivatives (i.e., score functions) of the log-likelihood function.

Suppose the $K \times K$ process $\{S_t(\beta)S_t(\beta)'\}$ obeys UWLLN, namely,

$$\sup_{\beta \in \Theta} \left\| n^{-1}\sum_{t=1}^{n} S_t(\beta)S_t(\beta)' - V(\beta) \right\| \xrightarrow{p} 0,$$

where

$$V(\beta) = E[S_t(\beta)S_t(\beta)']$$

is continuous in β. Then if $\hat{\beta} \xrightarrow{p} \beta^o$, we can show that $\hat{V} \xrightarrow{p} V_o = V(\beta^o)$.

Question: Which asymptotic variance estimator, based on either Method 1 or Method 2, is better in finite samples?

9.7 Parameter Hypothesis Testing Under Correct Model Specification

Suppose $f(y|\Psi_t, \beta)$ is correctly specified for the conditional distribution of Y_t given Ψ_t. We are interested in testing the hypothesis of interest

$$\mathbf{H}_0 : R(\beta^o) = r,$$

where $R(\cdot)$ is a $J \times 1$ continuously differentiable vector function with the $J \times K$ matrix $R'(\beta^o)$ being of full rank. Like in Chapter 8, we allow both linear and nonlinear restrictions on parameters. Note that in order for $R'(\beta^o)$ to be of full rank, we need the condition that $J \leq K$, that is, the number of restrictions is smaller than or at most equal to the number of unknown parameters.

We will introduce three test procedures, namely the Wald test, LR test, and LM test. We now derive these tests respectively.

(1) Wald Test

By a Taylor series expansion, the null hypothesis $\mathbf{H}_0 : R(\beta^o) = r$, and the Slustky theorem, we have

$$\begin{aligned}\sqrt{n}[R(\hat{\beta}) - r] &= \sqrt{n}[R(\beta^o) - r] \\ &\quad + R'(\bar{\beta})\sqrt{n}(\hat{\beta} - \beta^o) \\ &= R'(\bar{\beta})\sqrt{n}(\hat{\beta} - \beta^o) \\ &\xrightarrow{d} N[0, -R'(\beta^o)H_0^{-1}R'(\beta^o)'],\end{aligned}$$

where $\bar{\beta} = a\hat{\beta} + (1-a)\beta^o$ for some $a \in [0, 1]$. It follows that the quadratic form

$$n[R(\hat{\beta}) - r]'[-R'(\beta^o)H_0^{-1}R'(\beta^o)']^{-1}[R(\hat{\beta}) - r] \xrightarrow{d} \chi^2_J.$$

By Slutsky's theorem, we have the Wald test statistic

$$W = n[R(\hat{\beta}) - r]'[-R'(\hat{\beta})\hat{H}^{-1}(\hat{\beta})R'(\hat{\beta})']^{-1}[R(\hat{\beta}) - r] \xrightarrow{d} \chi^2_J,$$

where again the sample Hessian matrix

$$\hat{H}(\beta) = n^{-1}\sum_{t=1}^{n} \frac{\partial^2}{\partial\beta\partial\beta'} \ln f(Y_t|\Psi_t, \beta).$$

Note that only the unconstrained MLE $\hat{\beta}$ is needed in constructing the Wald test statistic.

Theorem 9.7. ***[MLE-Based Wald Test]:*** *Suppose Assumptions 9.1 to 9.6 hold, and the model $f(y_t|\Psi_t, \beta)$ is correctly specified for the conditional probability distribution of Y_t given Ψ_t. Then under $\mathbf{H}_0 : R(\beta^o) = r$, we have as $n \to \infty$,*

$$\begin{aligned}W &\equiv n[R(\hat{\beta}) - r]'[-R'(\hat{\beta})\hat{H}^{-1}(\hat{\beta})R'(\hat{\beta})']^{-1}[R(\hat{\beta}) - r] \\ &\xrightarrow{d} \chi^2_J.\end{aligned}$$

Question: Do we have the following result: Under $\mathbf{H}_0$

$$\begin{aligned}\tilde{W} &= n[R(\hat{\beta}) - r]'[R'(\hat{\beta})\hat{V}^{-1}R'(\hat{\beta})']^{-1}[R(\hat{\beta}) - r] \\ &= [R(\hat{\beta}) - r]'[R'(\hat{\beta})[S(\hat{\beta})'S(\hat{\beta})]^{-1}R'(\hat{\beta})']^{-1}[R(\hat{\beta}) - r] \\ &\xrightarrow{d} \chi^2_J \, ?\end{aligned}$$

Here, unlike the Wald test statistic in Theorem 9.7, we use an alternative asymptotic variance estimator

$$\hat{V} = n^{-1}\sum_{t=1}^{n} S_t(\hat{\beta})S_t(\hat{\beta})' = \frac{S(\hat{\beta})'S(\hat{\beta})}{n},$$

where $S(\beta) = [S_1(\beta), S_2(\beta), ..., S_n(\beta)]'$ is an $n \times K$ matrix.

(2) Likelihood Ratio (LR) Test

Theorem 9.8. *[LR Test]: Suppose Assumptions 9.1 to 9.6 hold, and $f(y|\Psi_t, \beta)$ is correctly specified for the conditional probability distribution of Y_t given Ψ_t. Define the average log-likelihoods*

$$\hat{l}(\hat{\beta}) = n^{-1}\sum_{t=1}^{n} \ln f(Y_t|\Psi_t, \hat{\beta}),$$
$$\hat{l}(\tilde{\beta}) = n^{-1}\sum_{t=1}^{n} \ln f(Y_t|\Psi_t, \tilde{\beta}),$$

where $\hat{\beta}$ is the unconstrained MLE and $\tilde{\beta}$ is the constrained MLE subject to the constraint that $R(\tilde{\beta}) = r$. Then under $\mathbf{H}_0 : R(\beta^o) = r$, we have

$$LR = 2n[\hat{l}(\hat{\beta}) - \hat{l}(\tilde{\beta})] \xrightarrow{d} \chi^2_J \text{ as } n \to \infty.$$

Proof: We shall use the following strategy to prove $LR \xrightarrow{d} \chi^2_J$ as $n \to \infty$:

(1) Use a second order Taylor series expansion to approximate $2n[\hat{l}(\hat{\beta}) - \hat{l}(\tilde{\beta})]$ by a quadratic form in $\sqrt{n}(\tilde{\beta} - \hat{\beta})$.

(2) Link $\sqrt{n}(\tilde{\beta} - \hat{\beta})$ with $\sqrt{n}\tilde{\lambda}$, where $\tilde{\lambda}$ is the Lagrange multiplier of the constrained MLE.

(3) Derive the asymptotic distribution of $\sqrt{n}\tilde{\lambda}$.

Then combining (1) and (2) will yield an asymptotic χ^2_J distribution for the LR test statistic $LR = 2n[\hat{l}(\hat{\beta}) - \hat{l}(\tilde{\beta})]$.

We first consider (1). Note that the unconstrained MLE $\hat{\beta}$ solves for

$$\max_{\beta \in \Theta} \hat{l}(\beta).$$

The corresponding FOC is

$$\hat{S}(\hat{\beta}) = 0.$$

On the other hand, the constrained MLE $\tilde{\beta}$ solves the maximization problem

$$\max_{\beta \in \Theta} \left\{ \hat{l}(\beta) + \lambda'[r - R(\beta)] \right\},$$

where λ is a $J \times 1$ Lagrange multiplier vector. The corresponding FOCs are

$$\begin{aligned} \hat{S}(\tilde{\beta}) - R'(\tilde{\beta})'\tilde{\lambda} &= 0, \\ (K \times 1) - (K \times J) \times (J \times 1) &= K \times 1, \\ R(\tilde{\beta}) - r &= 0. \end{aligned}$$

(Recall $R'(\beta)$ is a $K \times J$ matrix.)

(2) We now take a second order Taylor series expansion of $\hat{l}(\tilde{\beta})$ around the unconstrained MLE $\hat{\beta}$:

$$\begin{aligned} -LR &= 2n[\hat{l}(\tilde{\beta}) - \hat{l}(\hat{\beta})] \\ &= 2n[\hat{l}(\hat{\beta}) - \hat{l}(\hat{\beta})] + 2n\hat{S}(\hat{\beta})'(\tilde{\beta} - \hat{\beta}) \\ &\quad + \sqrt{n}(\tilde{\beta} - \hat{\beta})'\hat{H}(\bar{\beta}_a)\sqrt{n}(\tilde{\beta} - \hat{\beta}) \\ &= \sqrt{n}(\tilde{\beta} - \hat{\beta})'\hat{H}(\bar{\beta}_a)\sqrt{n}(\tilde{\beta} - \hat{\beta}) \end{aligned}$$

where $\bar{\beta}_a$ lies between $\tilde{\beta}$ and $\hat{\beta}$, namely $\bar{\beta}_a = a\tilde{\beta} + (1-a)\hat{\beta}$ for some $a \in [0, 1]$. It follows that

$$LR \equiv 2n[\hat{l}(\hat{\beta}) - \hat{l}(\tilde{\beta})] = \sqrt{n}(\tilde{\beta} - \hat{\beta})'[-\hat{H}(\bar{\beta}_a)]\sqrt{n}(\tilde{\beta} - \hat{\beta}). \tag{9.3}$$

This establishes the link between the LR test statistic and $\sqrt{n}(\tilde{\beta} - \hat{\beta})$.

We now consider the relationship between $\sqrt{n}(\tilde{\beta} - \hat{\beta})$ and $\sqrt{n}\tilde{\lambda}$. By a Taylor expansion for $\hat{S}(\tilde{\beta})$ around the unconstrained MLE $\hat{\beta}$ in the FOC that $\hat{S}(\tilde{\beta}) - R'(\tilde{\beta})'\tilde{\lambda} = 0$, we have

$$\hat{S}(\hat{\beta}) + \hat{H}(\bar{\beta}_b)(\tilde{\beta} - \hat{\beta}) - R'(\tilde{\beta})'\tilde{\lambda} = 0,$$

where $\bar{\beta}_b = b\hat{\beta} + (1-b)\tilde{\beta}$ for some $b \in [0,1]$. Given $\hat{S}(\hat{\beta}) = 0$, we have

$$\hat{H}(\bar{\beta}_b)\sqrt{n}(\tilde{\beta} - \hat{\beta}) - R'(\tilde{\beta})'\sqrt{n}\tilde{\lambda} = 0$$

or

$$\sqrt{n}(\tilde{\beta} - \hat{\beta}) = \hat{H}^{-1}(\bar{\beta}_b)R'(\tilde{\beta})'\sqrt{n}\tilde{\lambda} \tag{9.4}$$

for n sufficiently large. This establishes the link between $\sqrt{n}\tilde{\lambda}$ and $\sqrt{n}(\tilde{\beta} - \hat{\beta})$. It implies that the Lagrange multiplier $\tilde{\lambda}$ is an indicator for the magnitude of the difference $\tilde{\beta} - \hat{\beta}$.

(3) We now derive the asymptotic distribution of $\sqrt{n}\tilde{\lambda}$. By a Taylor expansion of $\hat{S}(\tilde{\beta})$ around the true parameter value β^o in the FOC $\sqrt{n}\hat{S}(\tilde{\beta}) - R'(\tilde{\beta})'\sqrt{n}\tilde{\lambda} = 0$, we have

$$\begin{aligned} R'(\tilde{\beta})'\sqrt{n}\tilde{\lambda} &= \sqrt{n}\hat{S}(\tilde{\beta}) \\ &= \sqrt{n}\hat{S}(\beta^o) + \hat{H}(\bar{\beta}_c)\sqrt{n}(\tilde{\beta} - \beta^o), \end{aligned}$$

where $\bar{\beta}_c$ lies between $\tilde{\beta}$ and β^o, namely, $\bar{\beta}_c = c\tilde{\beta} + (1-c)\beta^o$ for some $c \in [0,1]$. It follows that

$$\hat{H}^{-1}(\bar{\beta}_c)R'(\tilde{\beta})'\sqrt{n}\tilde{\lambda} = \hat{H}^{-1}(\bar{\beta}_c)\sqrt{n}\hat{S}(\beta^o) + \sqrt{n}(\tilde{\beta} - \beta^o) \tag{9.5}$$

for n sufficiently large. Now, we consider a Taylor series expansion of $R(\tilde{\beta}) - r = 0$ around β^o :

$$\sqrt{n}[R(\beta^o) - r] + R'(\bar{\beta}_d)\sqrt{n}(\tilde{\beta} - \beta^o) = 0,$$

where $\bar{\beta}_d$ lies between $\tilde{\beta}$ and β^o. Given that $R(\beta^o) = r$ under $\mathbf{H}_0$, we have

$$R'(\bar{\beta}_d)\sqrt{n}(\tilde{\beta} - \beta^o) = 0. \tag{9.6}$$

It follows from Eqs. (9.5) and (9.6) that

$$\begin{aligned} R'(\bar{\beta}_d)\hat{H}^{-1}(\bar{\beta}_c)R'(\tilde{\beta})'\sqrt{n}\tilde{\lambda} &= R'(\bar{\beta}_d)\hat{H}^{-1}(\bar{\beta}_c)\sqrt{n}\hat{S}(\beta^o) + R'(\bar{\beta}_d)\sqrt{n}(\tilde{\beta} - \beta^o) \\ &= R'(\bar{\beta}_d)\hat{H}^{-1}(\bar{\beta}_c)\sqrt{n}\hat{S}(\beta^o). \end{aligned}$$

By CLT for $\sqrt{n}\hat{S}(\beta^o)$ given in Assumption 9.6(b) where $\beta^* = \beta^o$, the MDS property of $\{S_t(\beta^o)\}$ given in Theorem 9.4, the conditional IM equality given in Theorem 9.5, and Slutsky's theorem, we have as $n \to \infty$,

$$\sqrt{n}\tilde{\lambda} = \left[R'(\bar{\beta}_d)\hat{H}^{-1}(\bar{\beta}_c)R'(\tilde{\beta})'\right]^{-1} R'(\bar{\beta}_d)\hat{H}^{-1}(\bar{\beta}_c)\sqrt{n}\hat{S}(\beta^o)$$
$$\xrightarrow{d} N(0, [-R'(\beta^o)H_0^{-1}R'(\beta^o)']^{-1}). \quad (9.7)$$

We emphasize that the MDS property of $\{S_t(\beta^o)\}$ and the conditional IM equality play a crucial role in obtaining the asymptotic variance of $\sqrt{n}\hat{S}(\beta^o)$ and so $\sqrt{n}\tilde{\lambda}$.

Therefore, from Eqs. (9.4) and (9.7), we have

$$\hat{H}(\bar{\beta}_a)^{1/2}\sqrt{n}(\tilde{\beta} - \hat{\beta}) = \hat{H}(\bar{\beta}_a)^{1/2}\hat{H}^{-1}(\bar{\beta}_b)R'(\tilde{\beta})'\sqrt{n}\tilde{\lambda}$$
$$\xrightarrow{d} N(0, \Pi) \sim \Pi^{1/2} \cdot N(0, I), \quad (9.8)$$

where I is a $K \times K$ identity matrix,

$$\Pi = H_o^{-1/2}R'(\beta^o)'[-R'(\beta^o)H_o^{-1}R'(\beta^o)']^{-1}R'(\beta^o)H_o^{-1/2}$$

is a $K \times K$ symmetric and idempotent matrix ($\Pi^2 = \Pi$) with rank equal to J (this can be verified using the formula that $\text{tr}(ABC) = \text{tr}(BCA)$).

Recall from Lemma 3.2 that if a $K \times 1$ random vector $v \sim N(0, \Pi)$, where Π is a symmetric and idempotent matrix with rank $J \leq K$, then the quadratic form $v'\Pi v \sim \chi^2_J$. It follows from Eqs. (9.3) and (9.8) that

$$2n[\hat{l}(\tilde{\beta}) - \hat{l}(\hat{\beta})] = \sqrt{n}(\tilde{\beta} - \hat{\beta})'[-\hat{H}(\bar{\beta}_a)]^{1/2}[-\hat{H}(\bar{\beta}_a)]^{1/2}\sqrt{n}(\tilde{\beta} - \hat{\beta})$$
$$\xrightarrow{d} \chi^2_J.$$

This completes the proof.

The LR test is based on comparing the objective functions, the log-likelihood functions under the null hypothesis $\mathbf{H}_0$ and the alternative to $\mathbf{H}_0$. Intuitively, when $\mathbf{H}_0$ holds, the likelihood $\hat{l}(\hat{\beta})$ of the unrestricted model is similar to the likelihood $\hat{l}(\tilde{\beta})$ of the restricted model, with the little or small difference subject to sampling variations. When $\mathbf{H}_0$ is false, the likelihood $\hat{l}(\hat{\beta})$ of the unrestricted model will be sufficiently larger than the likelihood $\hat{l}(\tilde{\beta})$ of the restricted model at least for large samples. Therefore, we can test $\mathbf{H}_0$ by checking whether $\hat{l}(\hat{\beta}) - \hat{l}(\tilde{\beta})$ is significantly different from zero. How large a difference between $\hat{l}(\hat{\beta})$ and $\hat{l}(\tilde{\beta})$ is considered as sufficiently large to reject $\mathbf{H}_0$ is determined by the asymptotic χ^2_J distribution of the LR test.

The LR test statistic is similar in spirit to the F-test statistic in the classical linear regression model, which compares the objective functions—the SSRs under the null hypothesis $\mathbf{H}_0$ and the alternative to $\mathbf{H}_0$ respectively. In other words, the negative log-likelihood is analogous to the logarithm of SSR. In fact, the LR test statistic and the $J \cdot F$ statistic are asymptotically equivalent under $\mathbf{H}_0$ for a linear regression model

$$Y_t = X_t'\alpha^o + \varepsilon_t,$$

where $\varepsilon_t|\Psi_t \sim$ IID $N(0, \sigma_o^2)$. To see this, put $\beta = (\alpha', \sigma^2)'$ and note that

$$f(Y_t|\Psi_t, \beta) = \frac{1}{\sqrt{2\pi\sigma^2}} e^{-\frac{1}{2\sigma^2}(Y_t - X_t'\alpha)^2},$$

$$\begin{aligned}\hat{l}(\beta) &= n^{-1}\sum_{t=1}^{n} \ln f(Y_t|\Psi_t, \beta) \\ &= -\frac{1}{2}\ln(2\pi\sigma^2) - \frac{1}{2\sigma^2}n^{-1}\sum_{t=1}^{n}(Y_t - X_t'\beta)^2.\end{aligned}$$

It is straightforward to show (please verify it!) that

$$\hat{l}(\hat{\beta}) = -\frac{1}{2}\left[1 + \ln(2\pi) + \ln\left(\frac{e'e}{n}\right)\right],$$

$$\hat{l}(\tilde{\beta}) = -\frac{1}{2}\left[1 + \ln(2\pi) + \ln\left(\frac{\tilde{e}'\tilde{e}}{n}\right)\right],$$

where e and $\tilde{e}$ are the $n \times 1$ unconstrained and constrained estimated residual vectors respectively. Therefore, under $\mathbf{H}_0$, we have

$$\begin{aligned}2n[\hat{l}(\tilde{\beta}) - \hat{l}(\hat{\beta})] &= n\ln(\tilde{e}'\tilde{e}/e'e) \\ &= \frac{(\tilde{e}'\tilde{e} - e'e)}{e'e/n} + o_P(1) \\ &= J \cdot F + o_P(1),\end{aligned}$$

where we have used the inequality that $|\ln(1+z) - z| \le z^2$ for small z, and the asymptotically negligible ($o_P(1)$) reminder term is contributed by the quadratic term in the expansion. This implies that the LR test statistic is asymptotically equivalent to the F-test statistic under $\mathbf{H}_0$.

In the proof of Theorem 9.8, we see that the derivation of the asymptotic distribution of the LR test statistic depends on correct model specification of $f(y|\Psi_t, \beta)$, because it uses the MDS property of the score function and the conditional IM equality. In particular, these two important properties ensure that avar$[\sqrt{n}\hat{S}(\beta^o)] = V_o = -H_o$. If the conditional distribution model $f(y|\Psi_t, \beta)$ is misspecified such that the MDS property of the score function or the conditional IM equality does not hold, then the LR test statistic will not be asymptotically χ^2-distributed. This is similar to the fact that the test statistic $J \cdot F$ does not follow an asymptotic χ^2_J distribution when there exist(s) autocorrelation and/or conditional heteroskedasticity in the disturbance $\{\varepsilon_t\}$ of a linear regression model (see Chapter 4).

(3) LM or Efficient Score Test

We now use the Lagrange multiplier $\tilde{\lambda}$ to construct an LM test, which is also called Rao's (1948) efficient score test in statistics. Recall the Lagrange multiplier λ is introduced in the constrained MLE problem:

$$\max_{\beta \in \Theta} \hat{L}(\beta) + \lambda'[r - R(\beta)],$$

where the $J \times 1$ Lagrange multiplier $\tilde{\lambda}$ measures the effect of the restriction of $\mathbf{H}_0 : R(\beta^o) = r$ on the maximized value of the model likelihood. When $\mathbf{H}_0 : R(\beta^o) = r$ holds, the imposition of the restriction results in little change in the maximized likelihood. Thus the value of the Lagrange multiplier $\tilde{\lambda}$ for a correct restriction should be small. When $\mathbf{H}_0 : R(\beta^o) = r$ is false, we will obtain a sufficiently large Lagrange multiplier $\tilde{\lambda}$ at least for large samples. This indicates that the maximized likelihood value of the restricted model is sufficiently smaller than that of the unrestricted model, thus leading to the rejection of $\mathbf{H}_0 : R(\beta^o) = r$. Therefore, we can use $\ddot{\lambda}$ to construct a test for $\mathbf{H}_0 : R(\beta^o) = r$. How large the value of $\tilde{\lambda}$ should be in order to be considered as sufficiently different from zero will be determined by the sampling distribution of $\sqrt{n}\tilde{\lambda}$.

In deriving the asymptotic distribution of the LR test statistic, we have obtained

$$\begin{aligned}\sqrt{n}\tilde{\lambda} &= \left[R'(\bar{\beta}_d)\hat{H}^{-1}(\bar{\beta}_c)R'(\tilde{\beta})'\right]^{-1} R'(\bar{\beta}_d)\hat{H}^{-1}(\bar{\beta}_c)\sqrt{n}\hat{S}(\beta^o) \\ &\xrightarrow{d} N(0, [-R'(\beta^o)H_o^{-1}R'(\beta^o)']^{-1})\end{aligned}$$

as $n \to \infty$. It follows that the quadratic form

$$n\tilde{\lambda}'[-R'(\beta^o)H_o^{-1}R'(\beta^o)']\tilde{\lambda} \xrightarrow{d} \chi^2_J,$$

and so by Slutsky's theorem, we have

$$n\tilde{\lambda}'[-R'(\tilde{\beta})\hat{H}^{-1}(\tilde{\beta})R'(\tilde{\beta})']\tilde{\lambda} \xrightarrow{d} \chi^2_J$$

as $n \to \infty$. We have actually proven the following theorem.

Theorem 9.9. ***[LM/Efficient Score Test]:*** *Suppose Assumptions 9.1 to 9.6 hold, and the model $f(y|\Psi_t, \beta)$ is correctly specified for the conditional probability distribution of Y_t given Ψ_t. Then under $\mathbf{H}_0 : R(\beta^o) = r$, we have as $n \to \infty$,*

$$LM \equiv n\tilde{\lambda}'R'(\tilde{\beta})[-\hat{H}^{-1}(\tilde{\beta})]R'(\tilde{\beta})'\tilde{\lambda} \xrightarrow{d} \chi^2_J.$$

The LM test statistic only involves estimation of the model $f(y_t|\Psi_t, \beta)$ under $\mathbf{H}_0$, so its computation may be simpler than the computation of the Wald test statistic or the LR test statistic in most cases.

Question: Do we have the following result: under $\mathbf{H}_0$,

$$\begin{aligned}\tilde{LM} &= n\tilde{\lambda}'R'(\tilde{\beta})\tilde{V}^{-1}R'(\tilde{\beta})'\tilde{\lambda} \\ &= n^2\tilde{\lambda}'R'(\tilde{\beta})[S(\tilde{\beta})'S(\tilde{\beta})]^{-1}R'(\tilde{\beta})'\tilde{\lambda} \\ &\xrightarrow{d} \chi^2_J?\end{aligned}$$

Here, unlike the LM test statistic in Theorem 9.9, we use an alternative asymptotic variance estimator

$$\begin{aligned}\tilde{V} &= n^{-1}\sum_{t=1}^{n} S_t(\tilde{\beta})S_t(\tilde{\beta})' \\ &= \frac{S(\tilde{\beta})'S(\tilde{\beta})}{n},\end{aligned}$$

where $S(\beta) = [S_t(\beta), ..., S_t(\beta)]'$ is an $n \times K$ matrix.

Question: What is the relationship among the Wald, LR and LM test statistics?

It could be shown that the Wald test statistic W, the LR test statistic LR, and the LM test statistic LM are asymptotically equivalent to each other under the null hypothesis $\mathbf{H}_0$. Figure 9.2 provides a geometric interpretation of the relationships among the there test statistics.

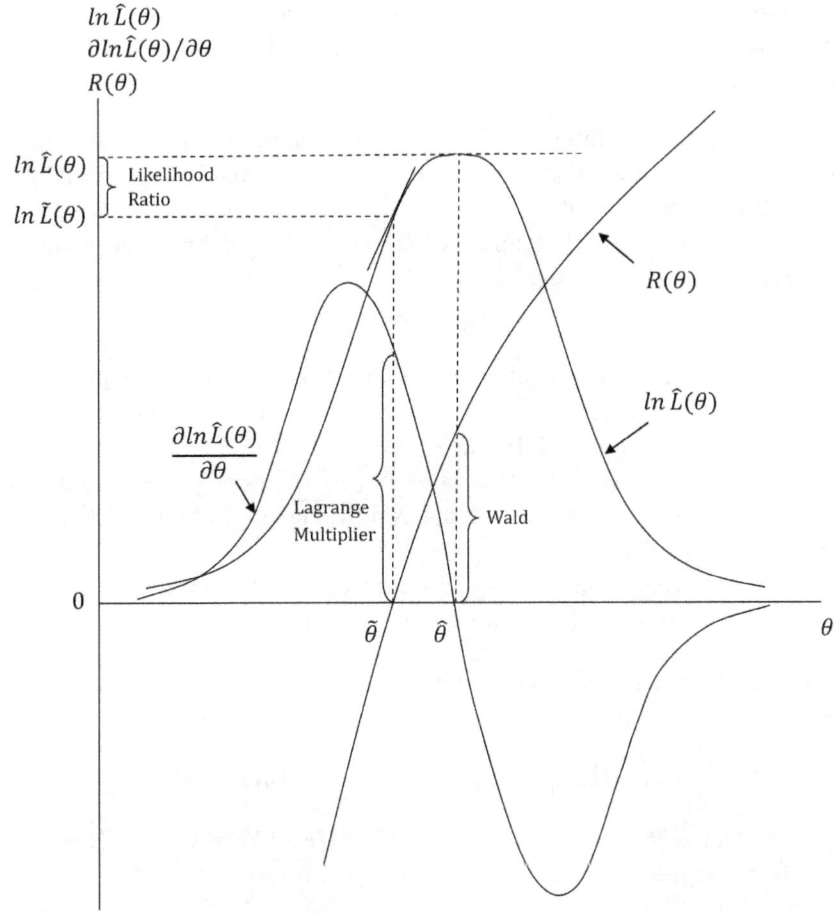

Figure 9.2 Geometric interpretation of the relationships among the Wald test, LR test and LM test.

9.8 Model Misspecification for Conditional Probability Distribution and Its Implications

When $f(y_t|\Psi_t, \beta)$ is misspecified for the conditional PDF/PMF of Y_t given Ψ_t, then for any parameter value $\beta \in \Theta$, $f(y|\Psi_t, \beta)$ is not equal to the true conditional PDF/PMF of Y_t given Ψ_t with probability one.

Question: What happens if $f(y_t|\Psi_t, \beta)$ is misspecified for the conditional PDF/PMF of Y_t given Ψ_t? In particular, what is the interpretation for parameter β^* when $f(y|\Psi_t, \beta)$ is misspecified, where $\beta^* = \arg\max_{\beta\in\Theta} l(\beta)$ is the maximizer of the population log-likelihood function as defined in Assumption 9.4?

We can no longer interpret β^* as the true model parameter value, because $f(y|\Psi_t, \beta^*)$ does not coincide with the true conditional probability distribution of Y_t given Ψ_t.

It should be noted that for QMLE, we no longer have the following equality:

$$\beta^* = \beta^o,$$

where β^* is as defined in Assumption 9.4 and β^o is the true model parameter value such that $f(y|\Psi_t, \beta^o)$ coincides with the true conditional distribution of Y_t given Ψ_t with probability one.

Although it always holds that $\hat{\beta} \xrightarrow{p} \beta^*$, as $n \to \infty$, we no longer have $\hat{\beta} \xrightarrow{p} \beta^o$, as $n \to \infty$, given that the conditional probability distribution model is misspecified.

Below, we provide an alternative interpretation for parameter β^* when $f(y|\Psi_t, \beta)$ is misspecified from an econometric perspective.

Theorem 9.10. *Suppose Assumptions 9.1 and 9.4 hold. Define the conditional relative entropy*

$$I(p : f|\Psi_t) = \int \ln\left[\frac{p(y|\Psi_t)}{f(y|\Psi_t, \beta)}\right] p(y|\Psi_t)dy,$$

where $p(y|\Psi_t)$ is the true conditional PDF/PMF of Y_t given Ψ_t. Then $I(f : p|\Psi_t)$ is nonnegative with probability one for all β, and

$$\beta^* = \arg\min_{\beta\in\Theta} E[I(p : f|\Psi_t)],$$

where $E(\cdot)$ is taken over the probability distribution of Ψ_t.

Proof: By the definition of relative entropy and the law of iterated expectations, we have

$$\begin{aligned}
E\left[I(p : f|\Psi_t)\right] &= E\left\{\int \ln\left[p(y|\Psi_t)\right] p(y|\Psi_t)dy\right\} \\
&\quad - E\left\{\int \ln\left[f(y|\Psi_t, \beta)\right] p(y|\Psi_t)dy\right\} \\
&= E\left\{E\left[\ln p(Y_t|\Psi_t)|\Psi_t\right]\right\} - E\left\{E\left[\ln f(Y_t|\Psi_t, \beta)|\Psi_t\right]\right\} \\
&= E\left[\ln p(Y_t|\Psi_t)\right] - E\left[\ln f(Y_t|\Psi_t, \beta)\right],
\end{aligned}$$

where the first term does not depend on β, and therefore, choosing β to minimize $E[I(p : f|\Psi_t)]$ is equivalent to choosing β to maximize the second term $E[\ln f(Y_t|\Psi_t, \beta)] = l(\beta)$. Given Assumption 9.4, the maximizer of $l(\beta)$ is β^*. On the other hand, the proof of $I(f_o : f|\Psi_t) \geq 0$ is analogous to the proof of Theorem 9.3, and so we will not repeat it. This completes the proof.

Theorem 9.10 suggests that the parameter value β^* that maximizes the population log-likelihood minimizes the "distance" of the model PDF/PMF $f(\cdot|\cdot, \beta^*)$ from the true conditional PDF/PMF $p(\cdot|\cdot)$ in terms of conditional relative entropy. Relative entropy is a divergence measure for two alternative distributions. It is not a distance measure but it has similar properties to a distance: it is always nonnegative and is zero if and only if two distributions coincide with each other. There are many distance/divergence measures for two distributions. Relative entropy has the appealing information-theoretic interpretation and the invariance property with respect to any one-to-one continuous transformation. It has been widely used in economics and econometrics. Figure 9.3 provides a geometric representation of correct model specification and model misspecification respectively.

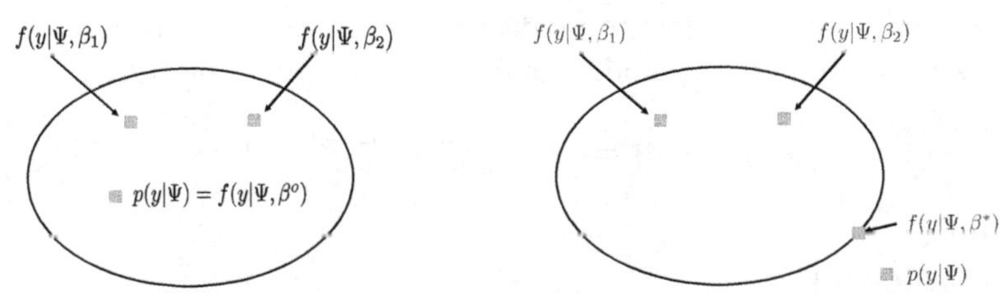

(a) Correct model specification for probability distribution

(b) Model misspectication for probability distribution

Figure 9.3 Illustration of correct model specification and model misspectication.

Question: Why is a misspecified PDF/PMF model $f(y_t|\Psi_t, \beta)$ still useful in economic applications?

In many applications, misspecification of higher order conditional moments does not render inconsistent the estimators for the parameters appearing in the lower order conditional moments. For example, suppose a conditional mean model is correctly specified but the conditional higher order moments are misspecified. We can still obtain consistent estimators for the parameters appearing in the conditional mean model. Of course, the parameters appearing in the higher order conditional moments cannot be consistently estimated.

We now consider a few illustrative examples.

Example 9.13. [Nonlinear Regression Model]: Suppose $\{(Y_t, X_t')'\}_{t-1}^n$ is an observable IID random sample, with

$$Y_t = g(X_t, \alpha^o) + \varepsilon_t,$$

where $E(\varepsilon_t|X_t) = 0$.

Here, the regression model $g(X_t, \alpha)$ is correctly specified for $E(Y_t|X_t)$ since $E(\varepsilon_t|X_t) = 0$, but we do not know the probability distribution of $\varepsilon_t|X_t$.

Question: How to estimate the true parameter value α^o when the conditional mean model $g(X_t, \alpha)$ is correctly specified for $E(Y_t|X_t)$?

In order to estimate the true parameter value α^o that appears in a correctly specified conditional mean model $g(X_t, \alpha^o)$, we assume that $\varepsilon_t|X_t \sim$ IID $N(0, \sigma^2)$, which is likely to be incorrect (and we know this possibility). Then we can obtain the pseudo conditional likelihood function

$$f(y_t|x_t, \beta) = \frac{1}{\sqrt{2\pi\sigma^2}} e^{-\frac{1}{2\sigma^2}[y_t - g(x_t, \alpha)]^2},$$

where $\beta = (\alpha', \sigma^2)'$.

Define QMLE

$$\hat{\beta} = (\hat{\alpha}', \hat{\sigma}^2)' = \arg\max_{\alpha, \sigma^2} \sum_{t=1}^{n} \ln f(Y_t|X_t, \beta).$$

Then $\hat{\alpha}$ is a consistent estimator for α^o. In this example, misspecification of IID $N(0, \sigma^2)$ for $\varepsilon_t|X_t$ does not render inconsistent the parameter estimator for α^o. The QMLE $\hat{\alpha}$ is consistent for α^o as long as the conditional mean model $g(X_t, \alpha)$ of Y_t is correctly specified in $f(y|X_t, \beta)$. Of course, the parameter estimator $\hat{\beta} = (\hat{\alpha}', \hat{\sigma}^2)'$ cannot consistently estimate the true conditional distribution of Y_t given Ψ_t if the conditional distribution of $\varepsilon_t|X_t$ is misspecified.

On the other hand, suppose the true conditional distribution $\varepsilon_t|X_t \sim$ IID $N(0, \sigma_t^2)$, where $\sigma_t^2 = \sigma^2(X_t)$ is a function of X_t, but we assume

$\varepsilon_t|X_t \sim$ IID $N(0,\sigma^2)$. Then we still have $E[\frac{\partial}{\partial\alpha}\ln f(Y_t|X_t,\beta^*)|X_t] = 0$ but the conditional IM equality does not hold.

Example 9.14. [CAPM]: Define Y_t as an $L \times 1$ vector of excess returns for L assets (or portfolios of assets). For these L assets, the excess returns can be explained using the standard CAPM:

$$\begin{aligned} Y_t &= \alpha_0^o + \alpha_1^o Z_{mt} + \varepsilon_t \\ &= \alpha^{o\prime} X_t + \varepsilon_t, \end{aligned}$$

where $X_t = (1, Z_{mt})'$ is a bivariate vector, Z_{mt} is the excess market portfolio return, α^o is a $2 \times L$ parameter matrix, and ε_t is an $L \times 1$ disturbance, with $E(\varepsilon_t|X_t) = 0$, which implies that there is no systematic pricing bias in any time period t. Under this condition, the standard CAPM is correctly specified for the expected excess return $E(Y_t|X_t)$.

To estimate the unknown parameter matrix α^o, one can assume

$$\varepsilon_t|\Psi_t \sim N(0,\Sigma),$$

where $\Psi_t = \{X_t, Y_{t-1}, X_{t-1}, Y_{t-2}, ...\}$ and Σ is an $L \times L$ symmetric and positive definite matrix. Then we can write the pseudo conditional PDF of Y_t given Ψ_t as follows:

$$\begin{aligned} f(Z_t|\Psi_t,\beta) &= (2\pi)^{-\frac{L}{2}}\,|\Sigma|^{-\frac{1}{2}} \\ &\quad \times \exp\left[-\frac{1}{2}(Y_t - \alpha' X_t)'\Sigma^{-1}(Y_t - \alpha' X_t)\right], \end{aligned}$$

where $\beta = (\alpha', \mathrm{vech}(\Sigma)')'$.

Although the IID normality assumption for $\{\varepsilon_t\}$ may not hold, the QMLE based on the pseudo Gaussian likelihood function will be consistent for parameter matrix α^o appearing in CAPM.

Example 9.15. [Univariate ARMA(p,q) Model]: In Section 5.1 of Chapter 5, we introduced a class of time series models called ARMA(p,q). Suppose

$$Y_t = \alpha_0^o + \sum_{j=1}^{p}\alpha_j^o Y_{t-j} + \sum_{j=1}^{q}\alpha_{p+j}^o\varepsilon_{t-j} + \varepsilon_t,$$

where ε_t is an MDS with mean 0 and variance σ^2. Then this ARMA(p,q) model is correctly specified for $E(Y_t|I_{t-1})$, where $I_{t-1} = \{Y_{t-1}, Y_{t-2}, ..., Y_1\}$ is the information set available at time $t-1$. Note that the probability distribution of ε_t is not specified.

Question: How can we estimate parameters $\alpha^o = (\alpha_0^o, \alpha_1^o, ..., \alpha_{p+q}^o)'$?

Assuming that $\{\varepsilon_t\} \sim$ IID $N(0, \sigma^2)$, then the pseudo conditional PDF of Y_t given Ψ_t is

$$f(y|\Psi_t, \beta) = \frac{1}{\sqrt{2\pi\sigma^2}} \exp\left[-\frac{(y - \mu_t \alpha)^2}{2\sigma^2}\right],$$

where $\Psi_t = \mathbf{Y}^{t-1}$, $\beta = (\alpha', \sigma^2)', \alpha = (\alpha_0, \alpha_1, ..., \alpha_{p+q})'$, and

$$\mu_t(\alpha) = \alpha_0 + \sum_{j=1}^{p} \alpha_j Y_{t-j} + \sum_{j=1}^{q} \alpha_{p+j}\varepsilon_{t-j}.$$

Although the IID normality assumption for $\{\varepsilon_t\}$ may be false, the QMLE that maximizes the above pseudo Gaussian likelihood function will be consistent for the true parameter value α^o appearing in the ARMA(p, q) model.

In practice, we have a random sample $\{Y_t\}_{t=1}^n$ of size n to estimate an ARMA(p, q) model and we need to assume some initial values for $\{Y_t\}_{t=-p}^0$ and $\{\varepsilon_t\}_{t=-q}^0$. For example, we can set $Y_t = \bar{Y}_n$ for $-p \leq t \leq 0$ and $\varepsilon_t = 0$ for $-q \leq t \leq 0$. The pseudo conditional PDF of Y_t given Ψ_t also depends on these assumed initial values. When an ARMA(p, q) is a stationary process, the choice of initial values does not affect the asymptotic properties of the QMLE $\hat{\beta}$ under regularity conditions.

Example 9.16. [Vector Autoregression (VAR) and Structural VAR Models]: Suppose $Y_t = (Y_{1t}, ..., Y_{Lt})'$ is an $L \times 1$ stationary autoregressive process of order p, denoted as VAR(p):

$$Y_t = \alpha_0^o + \sum_{j=1}^{p} \alpha_j^{o\prime} Y_{t-j} + \varepsilon_t, \qquad t = p+1, ..., n,$$

where α_0^o is an $L \times 1$ parameter vector, α_j^o is an $L \times L$ parameter matrix for $j = \{1, ..., p\}$, and $\{\varepsilon_t = (\varepsilon_{1t}, ..., \varepsilon_{Lt})'\}$ is an $L \times 1$ MDS with $E(\varepsilon_t) = 0$ and $E(\varepsilon_t \varepsilon_t') = \Sigma^o$, an $L \times L$ finite and positive definite matrix. When Σ^o is not a diagonal matrix, there exist contemporaneous correlations between different components of ε_t. This implies that a shock on ε_{1t} will be spilled over to other variables. With the MDS condition for $\{\varepsilon_t\}$, a VAR(p) model is correctly specified for $E(Y_t|I_{t-1})$, where $I_{t-1} = \{Y_{t-1}, Y_{t-2}, ..., Y_1\}$. Note that a VAR$(p)$ model can be equivalently represented as follows:

$$\begin{aligned}
Y_{1t} &= \alpha_{10} + \textstyle\sum_{j=1}^{p} \alpha_{11j} Y_{1t-j} + \cdots + \sum_{j=1}^{p} \alpha_{1Lj} Y_{Lt-j} + \varepsilon_{1t}, \\
Y_{2t} &= \alpha_{20} + \textstyle\sum_{j=1}^{p} \alpha_{21j} Y_{1t-j} + \cdots + \sum_{j=1}^{p} \alpha_{2Lj} Y_{Lt-j} + \varepsilon_{2t}, \\
\cdots & \cdots\cdots \\
Y_{Lt} &= \alpha_{L0} + \textstyle\sum_{j=1}^{p} \alpha_{L1j} Y_{1t-j} + \cdots + \sum_{j=1}^{p} \alpha_{LLj} Y_{Lt-j} + \varepsilon_{Lt}.
\end{aligned}$$

VAR, popularized by Sims (1980) in macroeconomics, is an autoregressive model used to capture linear interdependencies among multiple time series $\{Y_{it}\}_{i=1}^{L}$. VAR models generalize the univariate AR model by allowing for more than one evolving variable. All variables in a VAR model enter the model in the same way: each variable has an equation explaining its evolution based on its own lagged values, the lagged values of the other model variables, and an error term. VAR modeling does not require as much knowledge about the forces influencing a variable as economic structural models do with the system of simultaneous equations. The only prior knowledge required is a list of variables which can be hypothesized to affect each other intertemporally.

Let β^o denote a parameter vector containing all components of unknown parameters from $\alpha_0^o, \alpha_1^o, ..., \alpha_p^o$, and Σ^o. To estimate β^o, one can assume

$$\varepsilon_t | I_{t-1} \sim \text{IID } N(0, \Sigma).$$

Then $Y_t | I_{t-1} \sim N(\alpha_0 + \sum_{j=1}^{p} \alpha_j' Y_{t-j}, \Sigma)$, and the pseudo conditional PDF of Y_t given $\Psi_t = Y^{t-1}$ is

$$\begin{aligned}
f(Y_t | \Psi_t, \beta) = & \frac{1}{\sqrt{(2\pi)^L \det(\Sigma)}} \\
& \times \exp\left\{ -\frac{1}{2} [Y_t - \mu_t(\alpha)]' \Sigma^{-1} Y_t - \mu_t(\alpha) \right\},
\end{aligned}$$

where $\mu_t(\alpha) = \alpha_0 + \sum_{j=1}^{p} \alpha_j' Y_{t-j}$.

VAR(p) is not an economic structural model. In macroeconomics, the following Structural VAR (SVAR(p)) model is often considered:

$$A_0^o Y_t = c^o + \sum_{j=1}^{p} A_j^{o\prime} Y_{t-j} + u_t, \qquad t = p+1, ..., n,$$

where A_j^o is an $L \times L$ parameter matrix for $j = 0, 1, ..., p$, and c^o is an $L \times 1$ intercept vector. The diagonal elements of A_0^o are normalized to be unity, and the off-diagonal elements of A_0^o are generally nonzero, implying that the components in Y_t have contemporaneous impacts on each other. The $L \times 1$ innovation vector u_t represents economic structural shocks, and it is often assumed to be an MDS and the economic shocks contained in u_t are mutually independent or at least uncorrelated. For example, it is reasonable to assume that an oil price shock (a supply shock) and a consumer preference shift for cell phones (a demand shock) are mutually independent.

A SVAR(p) model can be transformed into a reduced form:

$$Y_t = A_0^{o-1}c^o + \sum_{j=1}^{p} A_0^{o-1}A_j^{o\prime}Y_{t-j} + A_0^{o-1}u_t, \qquad t = p+1, ..., n,$$

where the components of the new innovation vector $\varepsilon_t = A_0^{o-1}u_t$ are generally correlated with each other. Suitable conditions have to be imposed to ensure identifiability of the original parameters in the SVAR(p) model.

Example 9.17. [Volatility Model]: Time-Varying volatility is an important empirical stylized facts for many macroeconomic and financial time series. For example, it has been well-known that there exists volatility clustering in financial markets, that is, a large volatility today tends to be followed by another large volatility tomorrow; a small volatility today tends to be followed by another small volatility tomorrow, and the patterns alternate over time. In financial econometrics, the following volatility model has been used to capture volatility clustering or more general volatility dynamics. Suppose $(Y_t, X_t')'$ is a strictly stationary process with

$$Y_t = \mu(\Psi_t, \alpha^o) + \sigma(\Psi_t, \alpha^o)z_t,$$

$$E(z_t|\Psi_t) = 0,$$

$$E(z_t^2|\Psi_t) = 1.$$

The models $\mu(\Psi_t, \alpha)$ and $\sigma^2(\Psi_t, \alpha)$ are correctly specified for $E(Y_t|\Psi_t)$ and $\text{var}(Y_t|\Psi_t)$ if and only if $E(z_t|\Psi_t) = 0$ and $\text{var}(z_t|\Psi_t) = 1$. We need not know the conditional distribution of $z_t|\Psi_t$ (in particular, we need not know the higher order conditional moments of the standardized innovation z_t given Ψ_t).

An example for $\mu(\Psi_t, \beta)$ is the ARMA(p, q) in Example 9.15. We now provide some popular models for $\sigma^2(\Psi_t, \alpha)$. For notational simplicity, we put $\sigma_t^2 = \sigma^2(\Psi_t, \alpha)$.

- Engle's (1982) ARCH(q) model:

$$\sigma_t^2 = \alpha_0 + \sum_{j=1}^{q} \gamma_j \varepsilon_{t-j}^2.$$

- Bollerslev's (1986) GARCH(p, q) model:

$$\sigma_t^2 = \alpha_0 + \sum_{j=1}^{p} \alpha_j \sigma_{t-j}^2 + \sum_{j=1}^{q} \gamma_j \varepsilon_{t-j}^2.$$

- Nelson's (1990) Exponential GARCH(p, q) model:

$$\ln \sigma_t^2 = \alpha_0 + \sum_{j=1}^{p} \alpha_j \ln \sigma_{t-j}^2 + \sum_{j=0}^{q} \gamma_j g(z_{t-j}),$$

where $g(z_t)$ is a nonlinear function defined as

$$g(z_t) = \theta_1(|z_t| - E|z_t|) + \theta_2 z_t.$$

- Glosten *et al.*'s (1993) Threshold GARCH(p, q) model:

$$\sigma_t^2 = \alpha_0 + \sum_{j=1}^{p} \alpha_j \sigma_{t-j}^2 + \sum_{j=1}^{q} \gamma_j \varepsilon_{t-j}^2 \mathbf{1}(z_{t-j} > 0) + \sum_{j=1}^{q} \theta_j \varepsilon_{t-j}^2 \mathbf{1}(z_{t-j} \leq 0),$$

where $\mathbf{1}(\cdot)$ is the indicator function.

- Zakoian's (1994) Threshold ARCH(1) model:

$$\sigma_t = \alpha_0 + \alpha_1 \sigma_{t-1} + \gamma_1 |\varepsilon_{t-1}| \mathbf{1}(z_{t-1} > 0) + \gamma_2 |\varepsilon_{t-1}| \mathbf{1}(z_{t-1} \leq 0).$$

This is a specification for the conditional standard deviation $\sigma_t = \sigma(I_{t-1})$.

For ARCH(q) and GARCH(p, q) models, the shock ε_{t-j}, no matter positive or negative, has the same impact on the volatility σ_t^2. For Exponential GARCH(p, q), Threshold GARCH(p, q) and Threshold ARCH models, the impact of the shock ε_{t-j} on volatility σ_t^2 depends on whether the standardized innovation z_{t-j} is positive or negative. There exist asymmetric volatility dynamics in these three models.

Question: In a GARCH model, both conditional mean and variance models are assumed to be correctly specified for conditional mean and conditional variance respectively, but we do not know the conditional distribution of Y_t given Ψ_t (because we do not know the conditional distribution of z_t). In this case, how to estimate α^o, the true parameter value appearing in the first two conditional moments?

A most popular approach is to assume that $z_t|\Psi_t \sim$ IID $N(0, 1)$. Then $Y_t|\Psi_t \sim N(\mu_t(\Psi_t, \alpha), \sigma^2(\Psi_t, \alpha))$, and the pseudo conditional PDF of Y_t

given Ψ_t is

$$f(y|\Psi_t, \beta) = \frac{1}{\sqrt{2\pi}\sigma(\Psi_t, \alpha)} e^{-\frac{1}{2\sigma^2(\Psi_t,\alpha)}[y-\mu(\Psi_t,\alpha)]^2},$$

where $\beta = \alpha$. It follows that the log-likelihood function

$$\sum_{t=1}^n \ln f(Y_t|\Psi_t, \beta) = -\frac{n}{2}\ln 2\pi - \sum_{t=1}^n \ln \sigma_t(\Psi_t, \alpha) - \frac{1}{2}\sum_{t=1}^n \frac{[Y_t - \mu(\Psi_t, \alpha)]^2}{\sigma^2(\Psi_t, \alpha)}.$$

The IID $N(0, 1)$ innovation assumption does not affect correct specification of the conditional mean $\mu(\Psi_t, \alpha)$ and conditional variance $\sigma^2(\Psi_t, \alpha)$, so it does not affect the consistency of QMLE for the true parameter value α^o appearing in the conditional mean and conditional variance models. In other words, ε_t may not be IID $N(0, 1)$ but this does not affect the consistency of the Gaussian QMLE.

In addition to $N(0, 1)$, the following two error distributions have also been often used in practice:

- Standardized Student's$\sqrt{(\nu - 2)/\nu} \cdot t(\nu)$ Distribution.
  Here, ν is the number of degrees of freedom, and the scale factor $\sqrt{(\nu - 2)/\nu}$ ensures that z_t has unit variance. The PDF of z_t is

$$f(z) = \sqrt{\frac{\nu}{\nu - 2}} \frac{\Gamma\left(\frac{\nu+1}{2}\right)}{\sqrt{\pi\nu}\Gamma\left(\frac{\nu}{2}\right)} \left(1 + \frac{z^2}{\nu}\right)^{-\frac{\nu+1}{2}}, \quad -\infty < z < \infty,$$

  where $\Gamma(\cdot)$ is the Gamma function. In this example, $\beta = (\alpha', \nu)'$.
- Generalized Error Distribution.
  The PDF of z_t is given by

$$f(z_t) = \frac{c}{2b\Gamma\left(\frac{1}{c}\right)} \exp\left[-\left(\frac{|z - a|}{b}\right)^c\right], \quad -\infty < z < \infty,$$

  where a, b and c are the location, scale and shape parameters respectively. In this example, $\beta = (\alpha', a, b, c)'$. Note that both standardized t-distribution and generalized error distribution include $N(0, 1)$ as a special case. Figure 9.4 plots the PDF of N(0,1), standardized Student's t-distribution, and standardized generalized error distribution with $(a, b, c) - (0, 1, 2)$, respectively.

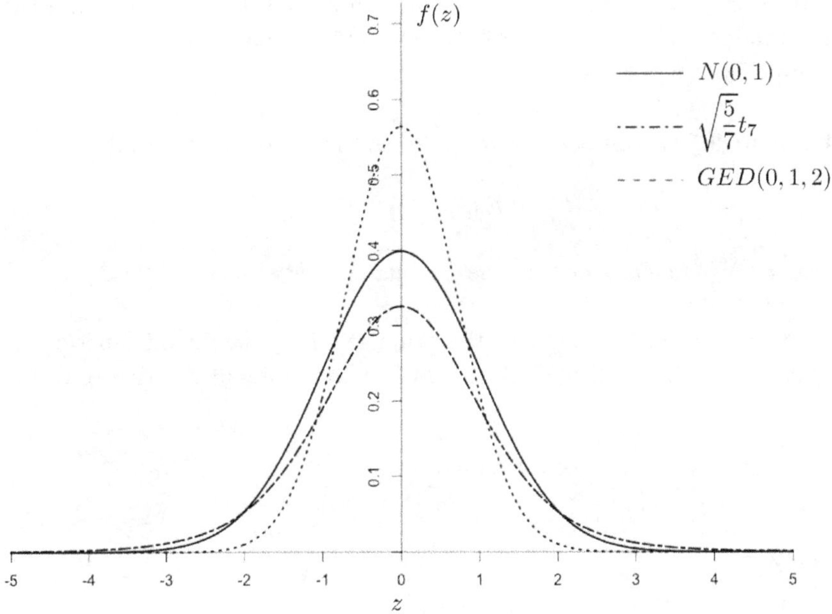

Figure 9.4 Probability density functions of standardized innovations.

Like in the estimation of ARMA(p, q) models, we may have to choose initial values for some variables in estimating GARCH models. For example, in estimating a GARCH(1,1) model, we will encounter the initial values problem for the conditional variance $\sigma_0^2 = \sigma^2(\Psi_0, \alpha)$ and ε_0 when time period $t = 0$. One can set σ_0^2 to be the unconditional variance $E(\sigma_t^2) = \omega/(1 - \alpha_1 - \gamma_1)$, and set $\varepsilon_0 = 0$.

We note that the ARMA model in Example 9.15 can be estimated via QMLE as a special case of the GARCH model by setting $\sigma^2(\Psi_t, \beta) = \sigma^2$.

Question: What is the implication of a misspecified conditional distribution model?

Although misspecification of $f(y_t|\Psi_t, \beta)$ may not affect the consistency of QMLE for some parameter value α^o (i.e., a subset of parameter vector β^*) under suitable regularity conditions, it does affect the asymptotic variance (and so the asymptotic efficiency) of the QMLE $\hat{\beta}$. This is a price which we have to pay for a misspecified conditional distribution model $f(y|\Psi_t, \beta)$.

We first investigate the implication of a misspecified conditional distribution model $f(y|\Psi_t, \beta)$ on the MDS property of the score function and the dynamic IM equality.

Theorem 9.11. *Suppose Assumptions 9.4 to 9.6(a) hold. Then*

$$E\left[S_t(\beta^*)\right] = 0,$$

where $E(\cdot)$ is taken over the true probability distribution of the DGP.

Proof: Because β^* maximizes the population log-likelihood function $l(\beta)$ and is an interior point in Θ given Assumptions 9.4 and 9.5, the FOC holds at $\beta = \beta^*$:

$$\frac{dl(\beta^*)}{d\beta} = 0,$$

namely,

$$\frac{dE[\ln f(Y_t|\Psi_t, \beta^*)]}{d\beta} = 0.$$

Exchanging differentiation and integration yields the desired result:

$$E\left[\frac{\partial \ln f(Y|\Psi_t, \beta^*)}{\partial \beta}\right] = 0.$$

This completes the proof.

No matter whether the conditional distribution model $f(y|\Psi_t, \beta)$ is correctly specified, the score function $S_t(\beta^*)$ evaluated at β^* always has mean zero. This is due to the consequence of the FOC of the maximization of $l(\beta)$. This is analogous to the FOC of the best linear least squares approximation where the FOC of minimizing MES$(\beta) = E(Y_t - X_t'\beta)^2$ is $E(X_t u_t) = 0$, with $u_t = Y_t - X_t'\beta^*$ and $\beta^* = [E(X_t X_t')]^{-1} E(X_t Y_t)$. However, different from Theorem 9.4, the score function $S_t(\beta^*)$ generally does not have the property of $E[S_t(\beta^*)|\Psi_t] = 0$; in particular, $\{S_t(\beta^*)\}$ is generally no longer an MDS.

When $\mathbf{Z}^n$ is an IID random sample, or $\mathbf{Z}^n$ is not independent but $\{S_t(\beta^*)\}$ is a stationary MDS (note that $\{S_t(\beta^*)\}$ could still be a stationary MDS when $f(Y_t|\Psi_t, \beta)$ is misspecified for the conditional distribution of Y_t

given Ψ_t; see Example 9.12), we have

$$\begin{aligned}
V_* &\equiv \text{avar}\left[n^{-1/2}\sum_{t=1}^{n} S_t(\beta^*)\right] \\
&= E\left\{\left[n^{-1/2}\sum_{t=1}^{n} S_t(\beta^*)\right]\left[n^{-1/2}\sum_{\tau=1}^{n} S_\tau(\beta^*)\right]'\right\} \\
&= n^{-1}\sum_{t=1}^{n}\sum_{\tau=1}^{n} E[S_t(\beta^*)S_\tau(\beta^*)]' \\
&= n^{-1}\sum_{t=1}^{n} E[S_t(\beta^*)S_t(\beta^*)]' \\
&= E[S_t(\beta^*)S_t(\beta^*)'] \equiv var[S_t(\beta^*)].
\end{aligned}$$

Thus, even when $f(y|\Psi_t, \beta)$ is a misspecified conditional distribution model, we do not have to estimate a long-run variance-covariance matrix for V_* as long as $\{S_t(\beta^*)\}$ is an MDS.

Question: Can you give a time series example in which $f(y|\Psi_t, \beta)$ is misspecified but $\{S_t(\beta^*)\}$ is an MDS?

Consider a conditional distribution model which correctly specifies the conditional mean of Y_t but misspecifies higher order conditional moments (e.g., conditional variance).

In the time series context, when the conditional PDF/PMF $f(y|\Psi_t, \beta)$ is misspecified, $\{S_t(\beta^*)\}$ may not be an MDS. In this case, we have

$$\begin{aligned}
V_* &\equiv \text{avar}\left[\sqrt{n}\hat{S}(\beta^*)\right] \\
&= n^{-1}\sum_{t=1}^{n}\sum_{\tau=1}^{n} E[S_t(\beta^*)S_\tau(\beta^*)'] \\
&= \sum_{j=-\infty}^{\infty} E[S_t(\beta^*)S_{t-j}(\beta^*)'] \\
&= \sum_{j=-\infty}^{\infty} \Gamma(j),
\end{aligned}$$

where

$$\Gamma(j) = E[S_t(\beta^*)S_{t-j}(\beta^*)'] \text{ for } j \geq 0,$$

and $\Gamma(j) = \Gamma(-j)'$ for $j < 0$. In other words, we have to estimate a long-run variance-covariance matrix for V_* when $\{S_t(\beta^*)\}$ is not an MDS.

Question: If the model $f(y|\Psi_t, \beta)$ is misspecified for the conditional distribution of Y_t given Ψ_t, do we have the conditional IM equality?

Generally, the answer is no. That is, we generally have neither $E\left[S_t\left(\beta^*\right)|I_{t-1}\right] = 0$ nor

$$E\left[S_t(\beta^*)S_t(\beta^*)'|\Psi_t\right] + E\left[\left.\frac{\partial^2 \ln f(Y_t|\Psi_t, \beta^*)}{\partial\beta\partial\beta'}\right|\Psi_t\right] = 0,$$

where $E(\cdot|\Psi_t)$ is taken under the true conditional distribution which differs from the model distribution $f(y_t|\Psi_t, \beta^*)$ when $f(y_t|\Psi_t, \beta)$ is misspecified. An important implication of the failure of the conditional IM equality is that $\text{var}[S_t(\beta^*)] \neq -H(\beta^*)$ even if $\{S_t(\beta^*)\}$ is an MDS.

Question: Can you provide an example for which the conditional IM equality does not hold when the model $f(y|\Psi_t, \beta)$ is misspecified for the conditional distribution of Y_t given Ψ_t?

9.9 Asymptotic Distribution of QMLE

When the conditional distribution model $f(y|\Psi_t, \beta)$ is misspecified, the MDS property for the score function and the conditional IM equality generally do not hold. This has impact on the structure of the asymptotic variance $\text{avar}(\sqrt{n}\hat{\beta})$ of the QMLE $\hat{\beta}$.

Theorem 9.12. ***[Asymptotic Normality of QMLE]:*** *Suppose Assumptions 9.1 to 9.6 hold. Then as $n \to \infty$,*

$$\sqrt{n}(\hat{\beta} - \beta^*) \xrightarrow{d} N(0, H_*^{-1}V_*H_*^{-1}),$$

where $V_* \equiv \text{avar}[\sqrt{n}\hat{S}(\beta^*)]$ *and* $H_* \equiv H(\beta^*) = E\left[\frac{\partial^2 \ln f(Y_t|\Psi_t, \beta^*)}{\partial\beta\partial\beta'}\right]$.

Proof: According to the proof of Theorem 9.6, when n is sufficiently large we have

$$\sqrt{n}(\hat{\beta} - \beta^*) = -\hat{H}^{-1}(\bar{\beta})\sqrt{n}\hat{S}(\beta^*),$$

where $\bar{\beta} = a\hat{\beta} + (1-a)\beta^*, a \in [0, 1]$. By the triangle inequality and Assumption 9.6, we have as $n \to \infty$,

$$\hat{H}(\hat{\beta}) \xrightarrow{p} H(\beta^*) = H_*.$$

On the other hand, by Assumption 9.6(b) we have as $n \to \infty$,

$$\sqrt{n}\hat{S}(\beta^*) \xrightarrow{d} N(0, V_*),$$

where $V_* = \text{avar}[\sqrt{n}\hat{S}(\beta^*)]$. It follows from Slutsky's theorem that

$$\sqrt{n}(\hat{\beta} - \beta^*) \xrightarrow{d} N(0, H_*^{-1}V_*H_*^{-1}).$$

This completes the proof.

Without the MDS property of the score function, we have to estimate $V_* \equiv \text{avar}[\sqrt{n}\hat{S}(\beta^*)]$ by, e.g., Newey and West's (1987, 1994) long-run variance estimator in the time series context. Without the conditional IM equality (even if the MDS holds), we cannot simplify the asymptotic variance of QMLE from $H_*^{-1}V_*H_*^{-1}$ to $-H_*^{-1}$ even if the score function is an IID sequence or an MDS. In certain sense, the MDS property of the score function is analogous to no autocorrelation in a regression disturbance, and the conditional IM equality is analogous to conditional homoskedasticity.

The asymptotic variance $H_*^{-1}V_*H_*^{-1}$ of QMLE is more complicated than the asymptotic variance $-H_*^{-1}$ of MLE, because we cannot use the conditional IM equality to simplify the asymptotic variance even when $\{S_t(\beta^*)\}$ is an IID sequence or an MDS sequence. Moreover, V_* has to be estimated using a long-run variance estimator when $\{S_t(\beta^*)\}$ is not an MDS.

In the literature, the variance $H_*^{-1}V_*H_*^{-1}$ is usually called the robust asymptotic variance-covariance matrix of QMLE. It is robust to misspecification of model $f(y_t|\Psi_t, \beta)$. That is, no matter whether $f(y_t|\Psi_t, \beta)$ is correctly specified, $H_*^{-1}V_*H_*^{-1}$ is always the correct asymptotic variance of MLE or QMLE.

Question: Is QMLE asymptotically less efficient than MLE?

Yes. The asymptotic variance of MLE, equal to $-H_o^{-1}$, the inverse of the negative Hessian matrix, achieves the Cramer-Rao lower bound, and therefore is asymptotically most efficient. On the other hand, the asymptotic variance $H_*^{-1}V_*H_*^{-1}$ of QMLE is not the same as the asymptotic variance $-H_o^{-1}$ of MLE and therefore does not achieve the Cramer-Rao lower bound. It is asymptotically less efficient than MLE. This is the price one has to pay with use of a misspecified PDF/PMF model, although some model parameter value α^o still can be consistently estimated and has a valid economic interpretation.

9.10 Asymptotic Variance Estimation of QMLE

Question: How to estimate the asymptotic variance $H_*^{-1}V_*H_*^{-1}$ of QMLE?

First, it is straightforward to estimate H_* by the sample Hessian matrix

$$\hat{H}(\hat{\beta}) = n^{-1}\sum_{t=1}^{n}\frac{\partial^2 \ln f(Y_t|\Psi_t,\hat{\beta})}{\partial\beta\partial\beta'}.$$

UWLLN for $\{H_t(\beta)\}$ and continuity of $H(\beta)$ ensure $\hat{H}(\hat{\beta}) \xrightarrow{p} H_*$ as $n \to \infty$.

Next, how to estimate $V_* = \text{avar}[n^{-1/2}\sum_{t=1}^{n} S_t(\beta^*)]$?

We consider two cases, depending on whether $\{S_t(\beta^*)\}$ is an MDS:

Case I: $\{Z_t = (Y_t, X_t')'\}$ Is IID or $\{Z_t\}$ Is Not Independent But $\{S_t(\beta^*)\}$ Is a Stationary MDS

In this case,

$$V_* = E[S_t(\beta^*)S_t(\beta^*)']$$

so we can use

$$\hat{V} = n^{-1}\sum_{t=1}^{n} S_t(\hat{\beta})S_t(\hat{\beta})'.$$

Under the regularity conditions given in this chapter, we can show that $\hat{V}$ is consistent for V_*.

Case II: When $\{Z_t\}$ Is Not IID and $\{S_t(\beta^*)\}$ Is a Stationary Non-MDS

In this case, we have

$$V_* = \sum_{j=-\infty}^{\infty}\Gamma(j),$$

where $\Gamma(j) = \text{cov}[S_t(\beta^*), S_{t-j}(\beta^*)]$ for $j \geq 0$, and $\Gamma(j) = \Gamma(-j)'$ for $j < 0$. We can use a kernel-based long-run variance-covariance matrix estimator

$$\hat{V} = \sum_{j=1-n}^{n-1} k(j/p)\hat{\Gamma}(j),$$

where

$$\hat{\Gamma}(j) = n^{-1} \sum_{t=j+1}^{n} S_t(\hat{\beta}) S_{t-j}(\hat{\beta})' \text{ for } j \geq 0,$$

and $\hat{\Gamma}(j) = \hat{\Gamma}(-j)'$ for $j < 0$.

Taking into account both cases, we directly assume that $\hat{V}$ is consistent for V_*.

Assumption 9.7. $\hat{V} \xrightarrow{p} V_*$ as $n \to \infty$, where $V_* = \text{avar}[\sqrt{n}\hat{S}(\beta^*)]$ is a $K \times K$ symmetric, finite and nonsingular matrix.

Lemma 9.2. ***[Asymptotic Variance Estimator for QMLE]:*** *Suppose Assumptions 9.1 to 9.7 hold. Then as $n \to \infty$,*

$$\hat{H}^{-1}(\hat{\beta})\hat{V}\hat{H}^{-1}(\hat{\beta}) \xrightarrow{p} H_*^{-1} V_* H_*^{-1}.$$

9.11 Hypothesis Testing Under Model Misspecification

With a consistent asymptotic variance estimator for QMLE, we can now construct suitable hypothesis test statistics under a misspecified conditional distribution model.

Again, we consider the null hypothesis

$$\mathbf{H}_0 : R(\beta^*) = r,$$

where $R(\beta)$ is a $J \times 1$ nonstochastic continuously differentiable vector function with the $J \times K$ matrix $R'(\beta^*)$ being of full rank, r is a $J \times 1$ nonstochastic vector, with $J \leq K$.

(1) Robust Wald Test Under Model Misspecification

We first consider a robust Wald test.

Theorem 9.13. ***[QMLE-Based Robust Wald Test]:*** *Suppose Assumptions 9.1 to 9.7 hold. Then under $\mathbf{H}_0 : R(\beta^*) = r$, we have as $n \to \infty$,*

$$\begin{aligned} W_r &\equiv n[R(\hat{\beta}) - r]'\{R'(\hat{\beta})[\hat{H}^{-1}(\hat{\beta})\hat{V}\hat{H}^{-1}(\hat{\beta})]^{-1}R'(\hat{\beta})'\}^{-1}[R(\hat{\beta}) - r] \\ &\xrightarrow{d} \chi^2_J. \end{aligned}$$

Proof: By a first order Taylor series expansion, we obtain

$$\begin{aligned}\sqrt{n}[R(\hat{\beta})-r] &= \sqrt{n}[R(\beta^*)-r]+R'(\bar{\beta})\sqrt{n}(\hat{\beta}-\beta^*)\\ &= R'(\bar{\beta})\sqrt{n}(\hat{\beta}-\beta^*)\\ &\xrightarrow{d} N(0, R'(\beta^*)H_*^{-1}V_*H_*^{-1}R'(\beta^*)'),\end{aligned}$$

where $\bar{\beta}=a\hat{\beta}+(1-a)\beta^*$, $a\in[0,1]$, so that $||\bar{\beta}-\beta^*||\le||\hat{\beta}-\beta^*||\to 0$ as $n\to\infty$, and we have made use of Theorem 9.12 ($\sqrt{n}(\hat{\beta}-\beta^*)\xrightarrow{d} N(0,H_*^{-1}V_*H_*^{-1})$ and Slutsky's theorem. Therefore, as $n\to\infty$, the quadratic form

$$\sqrt{n}[R(\hat{\beta})-r]'\left[R'(\beta^*)H_*^{-1}V_*H_*^{-1}R'(\beta^*)'\right]^{-1}\sqrt{n}[R(\hat{\beta})-r]\xrightarrow{d}\chi^2_J.$$

The desired result for the robust Wald test statistic W_r follow immediately from Lemma 9.2, $R'(\hat{\beta})\xrightarrow{p} R'(\beta^*)$ as $n\to\infty$, and Slutsky's theorem again. This completes the proof.

The robust Wald test statistic W_r is applicable when the conditional probability distribution model $f(y|\Psi_t,\beta)$ is misspecified. Only the unconstrained QMLE $\hat{\beta}$ is used in constructing the robust Wald test statistic W_r. We note that the robust Wald test statistic W_r under model misspecification differs from the Wald test statistic W under correct model specification. The robust Wald test statistic under model misspecification is similar in structure to the robust Wald test statistic W_r in linear regression modeling that is robust to conditional heteroskedasticity (under the IID or MDS assumption) or that is robust to conditional heteroskedasticity and autocorrelation (under the non-MDS assumption). Indeed, the robust Wald test statistic W_r in Theorem 9.13 can be viewed as a generalization of the robust Wald test statistic from a linear regression model to a nonlinear context. We note that the robust Wald test statistic W_r is different in structure from the MLE-based Wald test W in Theorem 9.7. The latter is not robust to model misspecification.

(2) Robust LM Test Under Model Misspecification

Question: Can we construct a robust LM test statistic for $\mathbf{H}_0: R(\beta^*)=r$ when $f(y|\Psi_t,\beta)$ is misspecified?

Yes, we can still derive the asymptotic distribution of $\sqrt{n}\tilde{\lambda}$, with a suitable asymptotic variance, which of course will be generally different from that under correct model specification. Then we can construct a quadratic form in $\sqrt{n}\tilde{\lambda}$ which follows an asymptotic Chi-square distribution under the null hypothesis $\mathbf{H}_0$. Therefore, we need to robustify the LM test statistic LM of Theorem 9.9 in Section 9.7.

Recall that from the FOCs of the constrained MLE $\tilde{\beta}$,

$$\hat{S}(\tilde{\beta}) - R'(\tilde{\beta})'\tilde{\lambda} = 0,$$
$$R(\tilde{\beta}) - r = 0.$$

In deriving the asymptotic distribution of the LR test statistic in Section 9.7, we have obtained

$$\sqrt{n}\tilde{\lambda} = \left[R'(\bar{\beta}_d)\hat{H}^{-1}(\bar{\beta}_c)R'(\tilde{\beta})'\right]^{-1} R'(\bar{\beta}_d)\hat{H}^{-1}(\bar{\beta}_c)\sqrt{n}\hat{S}(\beta^*)$$

for n sufficiently large, where $\bar{\beta}_c$ and $\bar{\beta}_d$ are linear combinations of $\tilde{\beta}$ and β^* respectively. This expression still holds when $f(y|\Psi_t, \beta)$ is misspecified.

By CLT (Assumption 9.6(b)), we have $\sqrt{n}\hat{S}(\beta^*) \xrightarrow{d} N(0, V_*)$ as $n \to \infty$, where $V_* = \text{avar}[\sqrt{n}\hat{S}(\beta^*)]$. Therefore, using Slutsky's theorem, we can obtain

$$\sqrt{n}\tilde{\lambda} \xrightarrow{d} N(0, \Omega) \text{ as } n \to \infty$$

under $\mathbf{H}_0$, where

$$\begin{aligned}\Omega &= [R'(\beta^*)H_*^{-1}R'(\beta^*)']^{-1} \\ &\times R'(\beta^*)H_*^{-1}V_*H_*^{-1}R'(\beta^*)' \\ &\times [R'(\beta^*)H_*^{-1}R'(\beta^*)']^{-1}.\end{aligned}$$

Then we can construct a robust LM test statistic

$$LM_r \equiv n\tilde{\lambda}'\tilde{\Omega}^{-1}\tilde{\lambda},$$

where the asymptotic variance estimator

$$\begin{aligned}\tilde{\Omega} &= [R'(\tilde{\beta})\hat{H}^{-1}(\tilde{\beta})R'(\tilde{\beta})']^{-1} \\ &\times [R'(\tilde{\beta})\hat{H}^{-1}(\tilde{\beta})\tilde{V}\hat{H}^{-1}(\tilde{\beta})R'(\tilde{\beta})'] \\ &\times [R'(\tilde{\beta})\hat{H}^{-1}(\tilde{\beta})R'(\tilde{\beta})']^{-1},\end{aligned}$$

and $\tilde{V}$ satisfies the following condition:

Assumption 9.8. $\tilde{V} \xrightarrow{p} V_*$ as $n \to \infty$, where $\tilde{V}$ is defined as $\hat{V}$ in Assumption 9.7 with $\hat{\beta}$ replaced with $\tilde{\beta}$.

Under Assumptions 9.1 to 9.6 and 9.8, we can show $\hat{\Omega} \xrightarrow{p} \Omega$. It follows from Slustky's theorem that under $\mathbf{H}_0$,

$$LM_r \xrightarrow{d} \chi^2_J \text{ as } n \to \infty.$$

The robust LM test statistic LM_r will only involve estimation of the conditional PDF/PMF model $f(y|\Psi_t, \beta)$ under the null hypothesis $\mathbf{H}_0$. Often it is relatively easy to estimate the model $f(y|\Psi_t, \beta)$ under $\mathbf{H}_0$.

Theorem 9.14. ***[QMLE-Based Robust LM Test]:*** *Suppose Assumptions 9.1 to 9.6 and 9.8 and $\mathbf{H}_0 : R(\beta^*) = r$ hold. Then as $n \to \infty$,*

$$LM_r \equiv n\tilde{\lambda}'\tilde{\Omega}^{-1}\tilde{\lambda} \xrightarrow{d} \chi^2_J.$$

The QMLE-based robust LM test statistic LM_r differs from the MLE-based LM test statistic LM in that they employ different asymptotic variance estimators. The QMLE-based LM test statistic LM_r is robust to misspecification of the conditional PDF/PMF model $f(y|\Psi_t, \beta)$. The structure of the robust LM test statistic LM_r is similar to the robust LM test statistic in a linear regression model with conditional heteroskedasticity and/or autocorrelation. Like the robust Wald test statistic W_r, the robust LM test statistic LM_r can be viewed as a generalization of the robust LM test statistic from a linear regression model to a nonlinear model.

Question: Are the robust Wald test W_r and LM test LM_r applicable when the model $f(y|\Psi_t, \beta)$ is correctly specified for the conditional distribution of Y_t given Ψ_t?

Question: When the model $f(y|\Psi_t, \beta)$ is misspecified, are the robust Wald test statistic W_r and robust LM test statistic LM_r asymptotically equivalent in the sense that $W_r - LM_r \xrightarrow{d} 0$ as $n \to \infty$ under the null hypothesis $\mathbf{H}_0 : R(\beta^*) = r$?

Question: Can we use the LR test statistic $LR = 2n[\hat{l}(\hat{\beta}) - \hat{l}(\tilde{\beta})]$ under model misspecification?

The answer is no. This is because in deriving the asymptotic distribution of the LR test statistic, we have used the MDS property of the score function $\{S_t(\beta^*)\}$ and the conditional IM equality (so $V_* = -H_*$), which may not hold when the conditional distribution model $f(y|\Psi_t, \beta)$ is misspecified. If the MDS property of the score function or the conditional IM equality fails, the LR statistic will not be asymptotically χ^2_J under $\mathbf{H}_0 : R(\beta^*) = r$. This is similar to the fact that J times the F-test statistic does not converge to χ^2_J when there exists serial correlation in $\{\varepsilon_t\}$ or when there exists conditional heteroskedasticity. Like the $J \cdot F$ test statistic, it is impossible to modify the LR statistic LR. This is different from the Wald test and LM test statistics. The latter can be modified to be robust to model misspecification.

In many applications (e.g., estimating CAPM models), both GMM and QMLE could be used to estimate the same parameter vector. In general, by making fewer assumptions on the DGP and making use of less sample information, GMM will be generally less efficient than QMLE if the pseudo-model likelihood function is close to the true conditional distribution of Y_t given Ψ_t.

9.12 Specification Testing for Conditional Probability Distribution Model

It is important to check whether a conditional probability distribution $f(y|\Psi_t, \beta)$ is correctly specified. There are several reasons for doing so:

- A misspecified PDF/PMF model $f(y|\Psi_t, \beta)$ implies suboptimal forecasts of the true probability distribution of the underlying DGP.
- The QMLE based on a misspecified PDF/PMF model $f(y|\Psi_t, \beta)$ is less efficient than the MLE which is based on a correctly specified PDF/PMF model.
- A misspecified PDF/PMF model $f(y|\Psi_t, \beta)$ implies that we have to use a robust version of the asymptotic variance of QMLE, because the conditional IM equality and even the MDS property for the score function generally no longer hold. As a result, the resulting statistical inference procedures are more tedious and perform less satisfactorily in small and finite samples.

Question: How to check whether a conditional probability distribution model $f(y|\Psi_t, \beta)$ is correctly specified?

Here, the null hypothesis of interest $\mathbf{H}_0$ is that there exists some unknown parameter value β^o such that with probability one, $f(y|\Psi_t, \beta^o)$ coincides with the true conditional distribution of Y_t given Ψ_t. We now introduce a number of specification tests for conditional distribution model $f(y|\Psi_t, \beta)$.

We consider two cases respectively.

Case I: $\{Z_t = (Y_t, X_t')'\}$ Is an IID Sequence

In this case, a popular test is White's (1982) IM test.

In the IID random sample context, White (1982) proposes a specification test for $f(y|\Psi_t, \beta) = f(y|X_t, \beta)$ by checking whether the IM equality holds:

$$E\left[S_t(\beta^o)S_t(\beta^o)'\right] + E[H_t(\beta^o)] = 0.$$

This is implied by correct model specification. If the IM equality does not hold, then there is evidence of model misspecification for the conditional distribution of Y_t given X_t.

Define the $\frac{K(K+1)}{2} \times 1$ sample average

$$\hat{m}(\beta) = \frac{1}{n}\sum_{t=1}^{n} m_t(\beta),$$

where

$$m_t(\beta) = \text{vech}\left[S_t(\beta)S_t(\beta)' + H_t(\beta)\right].$$

Let $\hat{\beta}$ be the MLE for β^o. Then as $n \to \infty$,

$$\hat{m}(\hat{\beta}) \xrightarrow{p} E\left[m_t(\beta^o)\right]$$

by UWLLN. Therefore, when the IM equality holds, we have $E\left[m_t(\beta^o)\right] = 0$ and so $\hat{m}(\hat{\beta})$ will be close to zero as $n \to \infty$. On the other hand, when the IM equality does not hold, $\hat{m}(\hat{\beta})$ will converge in probability to a nonzero moment as $n \to \infty$. Therefore, one can test model specification for $f(y|\Psi_t, \beta)$ by checking whether the sample average $\hat{m}(\hat{\beta})$ is close to zero. How large the magnitude of $\hat{m}(\hat{\beta})$ should be in order to be considered as significantly larger than zero can be determined by the asymptotic distribution of $\sqrt{n}\hat{m}(\hat{\beta})$.

Question: How to derive the asymptotic distribution of $\sqrt{n}\hat{m}(\hat{\beta})$?

White (1982) proposes an IM test using a suitable quadratic form of $\sqrt{n}\hat{m}(\hat{\beta})$ that is asymptotically $\chi^2_{K(K+1)/2}$ under correct model specification. Specifically, White (1982) shows that as $n \to \infty$,

$$n^{1/2}\hat{m}(\hat{\beta}) = n^{-1/2}\sum_{t=1}^{n}[m_t(\beta^o) - D_0 H_0^{-1} S_t(\beta^o)] + o_P(1)$$
$$\xrightarrow{d} N(0, \Sigma),$$

where $D_o \equiv D(\beta^o) = E\left[\frac{\partial m_t(\beta^o)}{\partial \beta}\right]$, and the asymptotic variance

$$\Sigma = \text{var}\left[m_t(\beta^o) - D_o H_o^{-1} S_t(\beta^o)\right].$$

It follows that a test statistic can be constructed by using the quadratic form

$$IM = n\hat{m}(\hat{\beta})'\hat{\Sigma}^{-1}\hat{m}(\hat{\beta})$$

for some consistent variance estimator $\hat{\Sigma}$ for Σ. Putting $\hat{W}_t = m_t(\hat{\beta}) - \hat{D}(\hat{\beta})\hat{H}^{-1}(\hat{\beta})S_t(\hat{\beta})$, we can construct a consistent variance estimator

$$\hat{\Sigma} = \frac{1}{n}\sum_{t=1}^{n}\hat{W}_t\hat{W}_t'.$$

It can be shown that under correct specification of $f(y|\Psi_t, \beta)$, and as $n \to \infty$,

$$IM \xrightarrow{d} \chi^2_{K(K+1)/2}.$$

Question: If the IM equality holds, is the model $f(y|X_t, \beta)$ correctly specified for the conditional distribution of Y_t given X_t?

Correct model specification implies the IM equality but the converse may not be true. The IM equality is only one of many (possibly infinite) implications from the correct specification of $f(y|\Psi_t, \beta)$. Therefore, when the IM test fails to reject the null hypothesis of correct model specification, one cannot claim that the model $f(y|\Psi_t, \beta)$ is correctly specified. Instead, one can only say that no evidence is found against correct model specification.

When White's (1982) IM test fails to reject the null hypothesis of correct specification of $f(y|\Psi_t, \beta)$ for a large sample size n, the IM equality still holds even if $f(y|\Psi_t, \beta)$ is misspecified. In this case, we can still use the simple asymptotic variance formula $\text{avar}(\sqrt{n}\hat{\beta}) = -H_*^{-1}$ or $\text{avar}(\sqrt{n}\hat{\beta}) = V_*^{-1}$, where $\hat{\beta}$ is actually the QMLE. In this sense, it is more appropriate to interpret White's (1982) IM test in the following way: it is a consistent test for the validity of the IM equality rather than a consistent test for model specification of $f(y|\Psi_t, \beta)$.

Although White (1982) considers IID random samples only, the IM test is applicable to test the hypothesis of IM equality for both cross-sectional and time series models as long as the score function $\{S_t(\beta^o)\}$ is an ergodic stationary MDS.

Case II: $\{Z_t = (Y_t, X_t')'\}$ Is an Ergodic Stationary Process

In a time series context, White (1994) proposes a dynamic IM test for correct model specification of $f(y|\Psi_t, \beta)$. This test essentially checks the MDS property of the score function $\{S_t(\beta^o)\}$:

$$H_0 : E[S_t(\beta^o)|\Psi_t] = 0,$$

which is implied by correct model specification of $f(y|\Psi_t, \beta)$. If evidence is found that $\{S_t(\beta^o)\}$ is not an MDS, then there exists model misspecification in $f(y|\Psi_t, \beta)$.

Define a $pK^2 \times 1$ moment function

$$m_t(\beta) = \text{vech}[S_t(\beta) \otimes S^{t-1}(\beta)],$$

where $S^{t-1}(\beta) = [S_{t-1}(\beta)', S_{t-2}(\beta)', ..., S_{t-p}(\beta)']'$ is a $pK \times 1$ weighting vector, and $\otimes$ is the Kronecker product. Then the MDS property of $\{S_t(\beta^o)\}$ implies

$$E[m_t(\beta^o)] = 0.$$

This moment condition essentially checks whether $\{S_t(\beta^o)\}$ is a WN up to lag order p. If $f(y|\Psi_t, \beta)$ is correctly specified, then $E[m_t(\beta^o)] = 0$. If $E[m_t(\beta^o)] \neq 0$, i.e., if there exists serial correlation in $\{S_t(\beta^o)\}$, then there is evidence of model misspecification.

White (1994) considers the sample average

$$\hat{m} = n^{-1} \sum_{t=1}^{n} m_t(\hat{\beta})$$

and checks if this is close to zero, where $\hat{\beta}$ is MLE. White (1994) develops a so-called dynamic IM test by using a suitable quadratic form of $\sqrt{n}\hat{m}$ that follows an asymptotic Chi-square distribution under correct dynamic model specification. The construction of such a quadratic form is similar to the IM test statistic IM, so we omit it here.

Question: If $\{S_t(\beta^o)\}$ is an MDS, can we conclude that $f(y|\Psi_t, \beta)$ is correctly specified for the conditional distribution of Y_t given Ψ_t?

No. Correct model specification implies that $\{S_t(\beta^o)\}$ is an MDS but the converse may not be true. It is possible that $S_t(\beta^o)$ is an MDS even when the model $f(y|\Psi_t, \beta)$ is misspecified for the conditional distribution of Y_t given Ψ_t; see Example 9.12 in Section 9.4. A better approach is to test the conditional PDF/PMF model itself, rather than only the properties of its derivatives (e.g., the MDS of the score function or the conditional IM equality).

Next, we consider a test that directly checks the conditional distribution of Y_t given Ψ_t.

Suppose Y_t is a continuous random variable, and $f(y|\Psi_t, \beta)$ is a conditional PDF model of Y_t given Ψ_t. We define the dynamic probability integral transform

$$U_t(\beta) = \int_{-\infty}^{Y_t} f(y|\Psi_t, \beta)dy.$$

Lemma 9.3. ***[Dynamic Probability Integral Transform]:*** *If, with probability one, $f(y|\Psi_t, \beta^o)$ coincides with the true conditional PDF of Y_t given Ψ_t, then*

$$\{U_t(\beta^o)\} \sim \text{ IID } U[0, 1].$$

Proof: Left as an exercise.

The dynamic probability integral transform $U_t(\beta)$ can be interpreted as a generalized residual of the conditional PDF model $f(y|\Psi_t, \beta)$. Intuitively, in a time series context, a conditional PDF model $f(y|\Psi_t, \beta)$, if correctly specified, will fully capture the dynamics of time series $\{Y_t\}$, so there will be no serial dependence left in the generalized residual series $\{U_t(\beta^o)\}$. Furthermore, the PDF model $f(y|\Psi_t, \beta)$ also correctly characterizes the probability distribution of Y_t over its entire domain in each time period, so the generalized residual $U_t(\beta^o)$ follows a uniform distribution. Therefore, one can test whether $\{U_t(\beta^o)\}$ is IID $U[0,1]$. If it is not, there exists evidence of model misspecification.

Hong and Li (2005) use a nonparametric kernel estimator for the joint PDF of $\{U_t(\beta^o), U_{t-j}(\beta^o)\}$ and compare the joint PDF estimator with $1 = 1 \cdot 1$, the product of the marginal standard uniform densities of $U_t(\beta^o)$ and

$U_{t-j}(\beta^o)$ under correct model specification. The proposed test statistic follows an asymptotic $N(0,1)$ distribution. See Hong and Li (2005) for more discussion.

Question: Suppose $\{U_t(\beta^o)\}$ is IID $U[0,1]$. Is the PDF model $f(y|\Psi_t, \beta)$ correctly specified for the conditional distribution of Y_t given Ψ_t?

For univariate time series (so $\Psi_t = \mathbf{Y}^t\{Y_{t-1}, Y_{t-2}, ...\}$), the IID $U[0,1]$ property holds if and only if the conditional PDF model $f(y_t|\Psi_t, \beta)$ is correctly specified.

9.13 Conclusion

Conditional probability distribution models have wide applications in economics and finance. For many applications, one is required to specify the entire probability distribution of the underlying DGP. If the probability distribution model is correctly specified, the resulting estimator $\hat{\beta}$ which maximizes the likelihood function is called the MLE.

For other applications, one may be only required to specify certain aspects (e.g., the conditional mean and conditional variance) of the probability distribution of the DGP. One important example is volatility modeling for financial time series. To estimate model parameters, one usually makes some auxiliary assumptions on the probability distribution of the DGP that may be false so that one can estimate β by maximizing the pseudo likelihood function. This is called the QMLE. MLE is asymptotically more efficient than QMLE, because the asymptotic variance of MLE attains the Cramer-Rao lower bound.

The likelihood function of a correctly specified conditional distribution model has different properties and implications from that of a misspecified conditional distribution model. In particular, for a correctly specified conditional distribution model, the score function is an MDS and the conditional IM equality holds. As a consequence, the asymptotic distributions of MLE and QMLE are different (more precisely, their asymptotic variances are different). In particular, the asymptotic variance of MLE is analogous to that of the OLS estimator under MDS regression disturbances with conditional homoskedasticity, whereas the asymptotic variance of QMLE is analogous to that of the OLS estimator under conditional heteroskedasticity and/or autocorrelation.

Hypothesis tests can be developed using MLE or QMLE. For hypothesis testing under a correct specified conditional distribution model, the Wald, LM, and LR tests can be used, and in fact they are asymptotically equivalent to each other under the null hypothesis. When a conditional distribution model is misspecified, the robust Wald and LM test statistics can be constructed. Like the F-test statistic in the regression context, the LR test statistic is valid only when the conditional distribution model is correctly specified. The reason is that the LR statistic test utilizes the MDS property of the score function and the conditional IM equality which may not hold under model misspecification.

It is important to test correct specification of a conditional distribution model. We introduce some specification tests for conditional distribution models under IID and time series observations respectively. In particular, White (1982) proposes an IM test for IID observations and White (1994) proposes a dynamic IM test that essentially checks the MDS property of the score function of a correctly specified conditional distribution model with time series observations. Hong and Li (2005) develop a nonparametric test for a dynamic conditional PDF model using probability integral transforms.

Exercise 9

9.1. For the probit model $P(Y_t = y|X_t) = \Phi(X_t'\beta^o)^y[1 - \Phi(X_t'\beta^o)]^{1-y}$, where $y = 0, 1$. Show that

(1) $E(Y_t|X_t) = \Phi(X_t'\beta^o)$.

(2) $\text{var}(Y_t|X_t) = \Phi(X_t'\beta^o)[1 - \Phi(X_t'\beta^o)]$.

9.2. Consider Example 9.3 in Section 9.2. Suppose the hazard rate $\lambda(y) = \alpha$, where $\alpha > 0$. Show that the PDF $f(y) = \alpha e^{-\alpha y}$ if $y \geq 0$, and $f(y) = 0$ if $y < 0$. That is, the underlying probability distribution is $\text{EXP}(\frac{1}{\alpha})$. Give your reasoning.

9.3. Consider a censored regression model as described in Example 9.9 of Section 9.2.

(1) Show that $E(X_t\varepsilon_t|Y_t > c) \neq 0$, where c is a constant. Thus, the OLS estimator based on a censored subsample that excludes the observations of $\{Y_t = c\}$ is not consistent for the true model parameter value β^o.

(2) Obtain the log-likelihood function of the conditional PDF of Y_t given X_t. Give your reasoning.

(3) Show that the MLE $\hat{\beta}$ is consistent for β^o. Give your reasoning.

9.4. A random sample is called truncated if the observations can come only from a restricted part of the underlying population distribution. We consider an example where the truncation is from below with a known truncation point c. Specifically, assume that the DGP is

$$Y_t^* = X_t'\alpha^o + \varepsilon_t,$$

where $\varepsilon_t|X_t \sim \text{IID}N(0, \sigma_o^2)$. Suppose only those of Y_t^* whose values are larger than or equal to constant c are observed. That is, we observe $Y_t = Y_t^*$ if and only if $Y_t^* = X_t'\alpha^o + \varepsilon_t \geq c$. The observations with $Y_t^* < c$ are not recorded. Assume the resulting sample is $\{Y_t, X_t'\}_{t=1}^n$, where $\{Y_t, X_t'\}$ is IID.

(1) Show $E(X_t\varepsilon_t|Y_t^* \geq c) \neq 0$. This implies that the OLS estimator $\hat{\beta}$ based on the observed sample $\{Y_t, X_t'\}_{t=1}^n$ is not consistent for β^o.

(2) Obtain the log-likelihood function for the conditional PDF of Y_t given X_t.

(3) Show that the MLE $\hat{\beta}$ is consistent for β^o. Give your reasoning.

9.5. Suppose $f(y|\Psi_t, \beta)$ is a conditional PDF model for Y_t given Ψ_t, where $\beta \in \Theta$, a parameter space. Show that for all β and $\tilde{\beta} \in \Theta$,

$$\int_{-\infty}^{\infty} \ln[f(y|\Psi_t, \beta)] f(y|\Psi_t, \tilde{\beta}) dy \leq \int_{-\infty}^{\infty} \ln[f(y|\Psi_t, \tilde{\beta})] f(y|\Psi_t, \tilde{\beta}) dy.$$

9.6. (1) Suppose $f(y|\Psi_t, \beta)$, $\beta \in \Theta$, is a correctly specified model for the conditional PDF of Y_t given Ψ_t, such that with probability one, $f(y|\Psi_t, \beta^o)$ coincides with the true conditional PDF of Y_t given Ψ_t. We assume that with probability one, $f(y|\Psi_t, \beta)$ is continuously differentiable with respect to β, and β^o is an interior point in Θ. Show that

$$E\left[\left.\frac{\partial \ln f(Y_t|\Psi_t, \beta^o)}{\partial \beta}\right| \Psi_t\right] = 0.$$

(2) When $f(y|\Psi_t, \beta)$ is a misspecified model for the conditional PDF of Y_t given Ψ_t, the result proven in Part (1) usually does not hold. Provide an example.

(3) Assume that Part (1) holds, i.e., the conditional expectation of the score function given the extended information set Ψ_t is zero at some parameter value. Can one conclude that $f(y|\Psi_t, \beta)$ is correctly specified for the conditional distribution of Y_t given Ψ_t? If yes, give your reasoning. If not, give a counter example.

9.7. Suppose $f(y|\Psi_t, \beta)$, $\beta \in \Theta \subset \mathbf{R}^K$, is a correctly specified PDF/PMF model for the conditional distribution of Y_t given Ψ_t, such that for some parameter value β^o, $f(y|\Psi_t, \beta^o)$ coincides with the true conditional PDF/PMF of Y given Ψ_t with probability one. We assume that with probability one, $f(y|\Psi_t, \beta)$ is continuously differentiable with respect to β and β^o is an interior point in Θ.

(1) Show that

$$E\left[\left.\frac{\partial \ln f(Y_t|\Psi_t, \beta^o)}{\partial \beta} \frac{\partial \ln f(Y_t|\Psi_t, \beta^o)}{\partial \beta'}\right| \Psi_t\right] + E\left[\left.\frac{\partial^2 \ln f(Y_t|\Psi_t, \beta^o)}{\partial \beta \partial \beta'}\right| \Psi_t\right] = 0,$$

where $\frac{\partial}{\partial \beta} \ln f(y|\Psi_t, \beta)$ is a $K \times 1$ vector, $\frac{\partial}{\partial \beta'} \ln f(y|\Psi_t, \beta)$ is the transpose of $\frac{\partial}{\partial \beta} \ln f(y|\Psi_t, \beta)$, $\frac{\partial^2}{\partial \beta \partial \beta'} \ln f(y|\Psi_t, \beta)$ is a $K \times K$ matrix, and the expectation $E(\cdot)$ is taken under the true conditional distribution of Y_t given Ψ_t.

(2) When $f(y|\Psi_t, \beta)$ is a misspecified model for the conditional distribution of Y_t given Ψ_t, the conditional IM equality proven in Part (1) usually does not hold. Provide an example.

(3) Assume that the conditional IM equality in Part (1) holds at some parameter value. Can one conclude that the model $f(y|\Psi_t, \beta)$ is correctly specified for the conditional distribution of Y_t given Ψ_t? If yes, provide your reasoning. If not, given a counter example.

9.8. Put $V_* = E[S_t(\beta^*)S_t(\beta^*)']$ and $H_* = E[\frac{\partial}{\partial\beta}S_t(\beta^*)]$, where $S_t(\beta) = \frac{\partial}{\partial\beta}\ln f(Y_t|\Psi_t, \beta)$, and $\beta^* = \arg\min_{\beta\in\Theta} l(\beta) = E[\ln f_{Y_t|\Psi_t}(Y_t|\Psi_t, \beta)]$. Under what circumstances will $H_*^{-1}V_*H_*^{-1} - (-H_*^{-1})$ be PSD? Give your reasoning and you can provide any necessary regularity conditions. Note that the formula $H_*^{-1}V_*H_*^{-1}$ is the asymptotic variance of QMLE and the formula $-H_*^{-1}$ is the asymptotic variance of MLE.

9.9. Suppose a conditional PDF/PMF model $f(y|\Psi_t, \beta)$ is misspecified for the conditional distribution of Y_t given Ψ_t, namely, there exists no $\beta \in \Theta$ such that with probability one, $f(y|\Psi_t, \beta)$ coincides with the true conditional distribution of Y_t given Ψ_t. Show that generally,

$$E\left[\frac{\partial \ln f(Y_t|\Psi_t, \beta^o)}{\partial\beta}\frac{\partial \ln f(Y_t|\Psi_t, \beta^o)}{\partial\beta'}\middle|\Psi_t\right] + E\left[\frac{\partial^2 \ln f(Y_t|\Psi_t, \beta^o)}{\partial\beta\partial\beta'}\middle|\Psi_t\right] = 0,$$

does not hold, where β^o satisfies Assumptions 9.4 and 9.5. In other words, the conditional IM equality generally does not hold when the conditional PDF/PMF model $f(y|\Psi_t, \beta)$ is misspecified for the conditional distribution of Y_t given Ψ_t. Use some example(s) to illustrate.

9.10. Consider a DGP

$$Y_t = \mu(\Psi_t, \alpha^o) + \sigma(\Psi_t, \alpha^o)z_t, \quad \{z_t\} \sim \text{IID}\sqrt{\frac{\nu-2}{\nu}} \cdot t_\nu.$$

Assume that we specify the following conditional PDF model for $Y_t|\Psi_t$:

$$f(y|\Psi_t, \beta) = \frac{1}{\sqrt{2\pi\sigma^2(\Psi_t, \alpha)}}\exp\left[-\frac{[y - \mu(\Psi_t, \alpha)]^2}{2\sigma^2(\Psi_t, \alpha)}\right],$$

where the conditional mean model $\mu(\Psi_t, \alpha)$ and conditional variance model $\sigma^2(\Psi_t, \alpha)$ are correctly specified for $E(Y_t|\Psi_t)$ and $\text{var}(Y_t|\Psi_t)$ respectively. However, the normalized Student's t_ν distribution of $\{z_t\}$ is misspecified as an $N(0, 1)$ distribution, and so the model $f(y|\Psi_t, \beta)$ is misspecified for the conditional distribution of Y_t given Ψ_t.

(1) Check if the score function $\{S_t(\beta)\}$ is an MDS. Give your reasoning.

(2) Check if the conditional IM equality holds. Give your reasoning.

9.11. Consider the following MLE problem:

Assumption 1: $\{Y_t, X_t'\}$ is an ergodic stationary process, and $f(y|\Psi_t, \beta)$ is a *correctly specified* conditional PDF/PMF model of Y_t given $\Psi_t = (X_t', \mathbf{Z}^{t-1\prime})'$, where $\mathbf{Z}^{t-1} = (Z_{t-1}', Z_{t-2}', ..., Z_1')'$ and $Z_t = (Y_t, X_t')'$. For each β, $\ln f(Y_t|\Psi_t, \beta)$ is measurable of (Y_t, Ψ_t), and for each t, $\ln f(Y_t|\Psi_t, \cdot)$ is twice continuously differentiable with respect to $\beta \in \Theta$ with probability one, where Θ is a compact set.

Assumption 2: $l(\beta) = E[\ln f(Y_t|\Psi_t, \beta)]$ is continuous in $\beta \in \Theta$.

Assumption 3: (a) $\beta^o = \arg\max_{\beta\in\Theta} l(\beta)$ is the unique maximizer of $l(\beta)$ over Θ, and (b) β^o is an interior point of Θ.

Assumption 4: (a) $\{S_t(\beta^o) \equiv \frac{\partial}{\partial\beta} \ln f(Y_t|\Psi_t, \beta)\}$ obeys CLT, i.e.,

$$\sqrt{n}\hat{S}(\beta^o) = n^{-1/2} \sum_{t=1}^{n} S_t(\beta^o)$$

converges to a multivariate normal distribution with some $K \times K$ variance-covariance matrix as $n \to \infty$; (b) $\{H_t(\beta) \equiv \frac{\partial^2}{\partial\beta\partial\beta'} \ln f(Y_t|\Psi_t, \beta)\}$ obeys UWLLN over Θ. That is,

$$\lim_{n\to\infty} \sup_{\beta\in\Theta} \left\| n^{-1} \sum_{t=1}^{n} H_t(\beta) - H(\beta) \right\| = 0,$$

where the $K \times K$ Hessian matrix $H(\beta) \equiv E[H_t(\beta)]$ is symmetric, finite and nonsingular, and is continuous in $\beta \in \Theta$.

The MLE is defined as $\hat{\beta} = \arg\max_{\beta\in\Theta} \hat{l}(\beta)$, where $\hat{l}(\beta) \equiv n^{-1}\sum_{t=1}^{n} \ln f(Y_t|\Psi_t, \beta)$. Suppose we have had $\hat{\beta} \to \beta^o$ almost surely, and this consistency result can be used in answering the following questions in Parts (1) to (4). Show your reasoning in *each* step.

(1) Find the FOC of MLE.

(2) Derive the asymptotic distribution of $\sqrt{n}(\hat{\beta} - \beta^o)$. Note that the asymptotic variance of $\sqrt{n}(\hat{\beta} - \beta^o)$ should be expressed as the Hessian matrix $H(\beta^o)$.

(3) Find a consistent estimator for the asymptotic variance of $\sqrt{n}(\hat{\beta}-\beta^o)$ and justify why it is consistent.

(4) Construct a Wald test statistic for the null hypothesis $\mathbf{H}_0 : R(\beta^o) = r$, where r is a $J \times 1$ constant vector, and $R(\cdot)$ is a $J \times 1$ vector with the

derivative $R'(\beta)$ is continuous in β and $R'(\beta^o)$ is of full rank. Derive the asymptotic distribution of the Wald test under $\mathbf{H}_0$.

9.12. Suppose Assumptions 9.1 to 9.5 hold, the model $f(y|\Psi_t, \beta)$ is correctly specified for the conditional distribution of Y_t given Ψ_t, and the $K \times K$ process $\{S_t(\beta)S_t(\beta)'\}$ follows UWLLN, i.e., $\sup_{\beta\in\Theta} \|n^{-1}\sum_{t=1}^n S_t(\beta)S_t(\beta)' - V(\beta)\| \xrightarrow{p} 0$, where $V(\beta) = E[S_t(\beta)S_t(\beta)']$ is continuous in β. Define $\hat{V} \equiv \frac{1}{n}\sum_{t=1}^n S_t(\hat{\beta})S_t(\hat{\beta})'$, where $\hat{\beta}$ is the MLE.

(1) Show $\hat{V} \xrightarrow{p} V_o = V(\beta^o)$ as $n \to \infty$.

(2) Define a Wald test statistic $\tilde{W} = n[R(\hat{\beta}) - r]'[R'(\hat{\beta})\hat{V}^{-1} R'(\hat{\beta})']^{-1}[R(\hat{\beta}) - r]$ for the null hypothesis $\mathbf{H}_0 : R(\beta^o) = r$, where $R(\cdot)$ is a $J \times K$ continuously differentiable nonstochastic matrix with $R'(\beta^o)$ being full rank, and r is a $J \times 1$ nonstochastic vector, and $J \leq K$. Derive the asymptotic distribution of $\tilde{W}$ under $\mathbf{H}_0$.

9.13. Suppose Assumptions 9.1 to 9.6 hold, and the conditional PDF/PMF model $f(y|\Psi_t, \beta)$ is correctly specified for the conditional distribution of Y_t given Ψ_t. Construct a t-type test statistic for the null hypothesis $\mathbf{H}_0 : R(\beta^o) = r$, where $R(\cdot)$ is a $1 \times K$ continuously differentiable nonstochastic matrix. Derive the asymptotic distribution of the proposed t-type test statistic under $\mathbf{H}_0$.

9.14. Suppose Assumptions 9.1 to 9.7 hold, and the conditional PDF/PMF model $f(y|\Psi_t, \beta)$ is misspecified for the conditional distribution of Y_t given Ψ_t. Construct a t-type test statistic for the null hypothesis $\mathbf{H}_0 : R(\beta^*) = r$, where $R(\cdot)$ is a $1 \times K$ continuously differentiable nonstochastic matrix. Derive the asymptotic distribution of the proposed t-type test statistic under $\mathbf{H}_0$.

9.15. Suppose $\{(Z_t = Y_t, X_t')'\}_{t=1}^n$ is an IID random sample. Consider a linear regression model $Y_t = X_t'\alpha^o + \varepsilon_t$, where $\varepsilon_t|X_t \sim N(0, \sigma_o^2)$. Put $\beta = (\alpha', \sigma^2)'$ and note that

$$
\begin{aligned}
f(Y_t|X_t, \beta) &= \frac{1}{\sqrt{2\pi\sigma^2}} e^{-\frac{1}{2\sigma^2}(Y_t - X_t'\alpha)^2}, \\
\hat{l}(\beta) &= n^{-1}\sum_{t=1}^n \ln f(Y_t|X_t, \beta) \\
&= -\frac{1}{2\sigma^2}\ln(2\pi) - \frac{1}{2\sigma^2} n^{-1}\sum_{t=1}^n (Y_t - X_t'\beta)^2.
\end{aligned}
$$

Suppose $\mathbf{H}_0 : R\beta^o = r$ is the hypothesis of interest, where R is a $J \times K$ nonstochastic matrix with full rank, r is a $J \times 1$ nonstochastic vector, and $J \leq K$.

(1) Show

$$\hat{l}(\hat{\beta}) = -\frac{1}{2}\left[1 + \ln(2\pi) + \ln\left(\frac{e'e}{n}\right)\right],$$

$$\hat{l}(\tilde{\beta}) = -\frac{1}{2}\left[1 + \ln(2\pi) + \ln\left(\frac{\tilde{e}'\tilde{e}}{n}\right)\right],$$

where $\hat{\beta}$ is the unconstrained MLE, $\tilde{\beta}$ is the constrained MLE under $\mathbf{H}_0$, and e and $\tilde{e}$ are $n \times 1$ unconstrained and constrained estimated residual vectors respectively.

(2) Show that under $\mathbf{H}_0 : R\beta^o = r$,

$$\begin{aligned} 2n[\hat{l}(\tilde{\beta}) - \hat{l}(\hat{\beta})] &= n\ln(\tilde{e}'\tilde{e}/e'e) \\ &= J \cdot \frac{(\tilde{e}\tilde{e} - e'e)/J}{e'e/n} + o_P(1) \\ &= J \cdot F + o_P(1), \end{aligned}$$

where $o_P(1)$ denotes the reminder term that vanishes to zero in probability as $n \to \infty$.

9.16. Suppose Assumptions 9.1 to 9.6 hold, and the conditional PDF/PMF model $f(y|\Psi_t, \beta)$ is correctly specified for conditional distribution of Y_t given Ψ_t. We are interested in testing the hypothesis of interest

$$\mathbf{H}_0 : R(\beta^o) = r,$$

where $R(\cdot)$ is a $J \times 1$ continuously differentiable vector function with the $J \times K$ matrix $R'(\beta^o)$ being of full rank. Show that the Wald test statistic W, the LM test statistic LM and the LR test statistic LR are asymptotically equivalent under $\mathbf{H}_0$ in the sense that as $n \to \infty$, $W - LM = o_P(1), W - LR = o_P(1)$, and $LM - LR = o_P(1)$.

9.17. Suppose Assumptions 9.1 to 9.8 hold, and $f(y|\Psi_t, \beta)$ is a misspecified model for the conditional distribution of Y_t given Ψ_t. We are interested in testing the hypothesis of interest

$$\mathbf{H}_0 : R(\beta^*) = r,$$

where $R(\cdot)$ is a $J \times 1$ continuously differentiable vector function with the $J \times K$ matrix $R'(\beta^*)$ being of full rank. Are the robust Wald test statistic

W_r and robust LM test statistic LM_r are asymptotically equivalent under $\mathbf{H}_0$ in the sense that $W_r - LM_r = o_P(1)$ as $n \to \infty$.

9.18. Suppose $\{Z_t = (Y_t, X_t')'\}$ is a stationary time series process. Show that the dynamic probability integral transform $\{U_t(\beta^o)\}$ is IID $U[0,1]$ if the conditional PDF model $f(y|\Psi_t, \beta)$ is correctly specified for the conditional PDF of Y_t given Ψ_t, where $\Psi_t = (X_t, \mathbf{Z}^{t-1})$, and $\mathbf{Z}^{t-1} = (Z_{t-1}, Z_{t-2}, ..., Z_1)$.

9.19. Suppose $\mathbf{Y}^n = (Y_1, Y_2, ..., Y_n)$ is an observed random sample of size n. Consider an AR(1) model

$$Y_t = \beta Y_{t-1} + \varepsilon_t, \quad t = 1, ..., n,$$

where $\{\varepsilon_t\}_{t=1}^n \sim$ IID $N(0, \sigma_\varepsilon^2)$, $Y_0 \sim f_0(y)$, and β is an unknown scalar parameter. The PDF $f_0(y)$ of Y_0 is known.

In statistics, the so-called Bayesian school of statistics develops an important method to estimate the unknown parameter β. The first step is to assume that parameter β is random and follows a prior distribution. Suppose the prior distribution of β is an $N(0, \sigma_\beta^2)$ distribution, and σ_ε^2 and σ_β^2 are known constants.

(1) Derive the joint PDF $f(\beta, \mathbf{y}^n)$ of random vector $(\beta, \mathbf{Y}^n)$, where $\mathbf{y}^n = (y_1, y_2, ..., y_n)$.

(2) Derive the conditional PDF $f(\beta|\mathbf{y}^n)$ of β given that the sample $\mathbf{Y}^n = \mathbf{y}^n$. This is called the posterior probability density.

(3) The Bayesian estimator $\hat{\beta} = \hat{\beta}_n(\mathbf{y}^n)$ minimizes the following average mean squared error

$$\hat{\beta} = \arg\min_a \int (a - \beta)^2 f(\beta, \mathbf{y}^n) d\beta.$$

Find the Bayesian estimator of β.

In each step, please state your reasoning clearly.

9.20. Suppose $\{Y_t, X_t'\}$ is a strictly ergodic stationary time series process, $Y_t = X_t'\beta^o + \varepsilon_t, \varepsilon_t = h_t^{1/2} z_t, h_t = \alpha_0 + \alpha_1 \varepsilon_{t-1}^2$, and the unobservable innovation sequence $\{z_t\} \sim$ IID $N(0,1)$. Moreover, $\{X_t\}$ and $\{z_t\}$ are mutually independent. A random sample $\{Y_t, X_t'\}_{t=1}^n$ of size n is observed. Assume that all regularity conditions are satisfied.

(1) Find the OLS estimator $\hat{\beta}$ for β.

(2) Show that the OLS estimator $\hat{\beta}$ is BLUE.

(3) Find the MLE $\tilde{\beta}$ for β.

(4) Discuss the relative efficiency between $\hat{\beta}$ and $\tilde{\beta}$. Give your reasoning.

Chapter 10

Modern Econometrics: Retrospect and Prospect

Abstract: This chapter aims to summarize the theories, models, methods and tools of modern econometrics which we have covered in the previous chapters. We first review the classical assumptions of the linear regression model and discuss the historical development of modern econometrics by various relaxations of the classical assumptions. We also discuss the challenges and opportunities for econometrics in the Big data era and point out some important directions for the future development of econometrics.

Keywords: Asymptotic analysis, Big data, Causal inference, Conditional heteroskedasticity, Endogeneity, Exogeneity, High-dimensional data, Instrumental Variable (IV), Linear regression model, Machine learning, Model ambiguity, Model misspecification, Model uncertainty, Nonexperimental design, Nonlinear model, Normal distribution, Panel data analysis, Policy evaluation, Program evaluation, Stationarity, Structural change

10.1 Summary of Book

The econometric theory developed in this book is built upon the following fundamental axioms:

- Any economy can be viewed as a stochastic DGP governed by some probability law.
- Any economic phenomenon, often in form of data, can be viewed as a realization of the stochastic economic process.

The probability law of the DGP can be called the *law of economic motions*. The objective of econometrics is to infer the probability law of economic motions using observed data and then use the obtained knowledge to explain what has happened, to predict what will happen, to test economic theories and hypotheses, to conduct policy evaluation and make policy recommendations, etc.

Suppose the conditional probability distribution of an economic variable of interest is available. Then one can obtain various attributes of the conditional distribution, such as its conditional mean, conditional variance, conditional skewness, conditional kurtosis, and conditional quantile. Here, an important question is: what aspect of the conditional distribution will be important in economics? Generally speaking, the answer is dictated by the nature of the economic problem one has at hand. For example, EMH states that the conditional expected asset return given the past information is equal to the long-run market average return; rational expectations theory suggests that conditional expectational errors given the past information should be zero. In unemployment duration analysis, one should model the entire conditional distribution of the unemployment duration given the economic characteristics of unemployed workers. For all of these, econometrics can provide an analytic framework, methods and tools when combined with observed data.

It should be emphasized that the conditional distribution or its various attributes indicate a predictive relationship between economic variables, that is, a statistical association under which one can use some explanatory variables to predict other variables. A predictive relationship may or may not be a causal relationship among economic variables, which is often of central interest to economists. Economic theory often hypothesizes a causal relationship and such economic theory can then be used to interpret the predictive relationship as a causal relationship. Moreover, economic theory can be formulated as an empirically testable restriction on the conditional distribution of the DGP. Such a restriction can be used to validate economic theory empirically, and to improve forecasts if the restriction is valid.

Motivated by the fact that most economic theories often have implications on and only on the conditional mean of economic variables, we have first provided a probabilistic theoretic foundation for linear regression modeling in Chapter 2. We then consider the classical linear regression model in Chapter 3, for which we develop a finite sample statistical theory when the regression disturbances are IID normally distributed and are independent of regressors. The normality assumption is crucial for the finite sample econometric theory. The essence of the classical theory for linear regression models is the IID assumption for disturbances, which implies conditional homoskedasticity and serial uncorrelatedness, and ensures the BLUE property of the OLS estimator. When conditional heteroskedasticity and/or autocorrelation exist(s), the GLS estimator illustrates how to restore the BLUE property by correcting conditional heteroskedasticity and/or differencing out serial correlation.

Using the classical linear regression model as a benchmark, we develop an econometric theory for linear regression models by relaxing the classical assumptions in subsequent chapters. First, we relax the normality assumption in Chapter 4. This calls for asymptotic (or large sample) analysis as the sample size $n \to \infty$ because the finite sample theory is no longer possible. It is shown that for a large sample size, the classical results in Chapter 3 are approximately applicable to linear regression models with independent observations under conditional homoskedasticity. Under conditional heteroskedasticity, however, the classical results, such as the popular t-test and F-test statistics, are no longer applicable, even if the sample size goes to infinity. This is due to the fact that the asymptotic variance of the OLS estimator has a different structure under conditional heteroskedasticity. One has to use White's (1980) heteroskedasticity-consistent variance-covariance matrix estimator and uses it to develop robust hypothesis tests. It is therefore important to test conditional homoskedasticity, and White (1980) proposes a regression-based test procedure among many others.

The asymptotic theory for linear regression models with independent observations in Chapter 4 is extended to linear regression models with time series observations in Chapter 5. This covers two types of linear regression models: one is a static regression model where regressors are exogenous variables, and the other is a dynamic regression model where regressors contain lagged dependent variables and exogenous variables. It is shown that the asymptotic theory of Chapter 4 is applicable to stationary time series regression models when the regression disturbance is an MDS. Because of its importance, we introduce tests for the MDS property of regression disturbances by checking serial correlation in the disturbances. These include the popular LM test for serial correlation. We have also considered an LM test for ARCH and discussed its implications on the inference of static and dynamic regression models respectively.

For many static regression models, it is evident that regression disturbances display serial correlation. This affects the asymptotic variance of the OLS estimator. When serial correlation is of a known structure up to a few unknown parameters, we can use the Ornut-Cochrance procedure to obtain a two-stage asymptotically efficient estimator for regression parameters. When serial correlation is of unknown form, we have to use a long-run variance-covariance matrix estimator to estimate the asymptotic variance of the OLS estimator. A leading example is the kernel-based estimator such as those of Newey and West (1987) and Andrews (1991). With such a long-run variance-covariance matrix estimator, robust test statistics for hypotheses of interest can be constructed. These are discussed in Chapter 6.

Estimation and inference of linear regression models become complicated when the orthogonality condition that $E(\varepsilon_t|X_t) = 0$ does not hold, which can arise due to measurement errors, simultaneous equations bias, omitted variables, and so on. In Chapter 7 we discuss a popular IV-based estimation method—a 2SLS procedure—to estimate model parameters in such scenarios. IV regression has been a main methodology to identify economic causal relationships using nonexperimental data.

Chapter 8 introduces GMM, which is particularly suitable for estimating linear and nonlinear econometric models that can be formulated as a set of moment conditions. A prime economic example is the rational expectations theory, which is often characterized by a set of Euler equations. In fact, GMM provides a convenient framework to view most econometric estimators, including the OLS and 2SLS estimators.

Chapter 9 considers conditional probability distribution models and other econometric models that can be estimated by using pseudo likelihood function methods. Conditional distribution models have found wide applications in economics, and MLE is the asymptotically most efficient method to estimate parameters for conditional distribution models. On the other hand, many econometric models can be conveniently estimated by using a pseudo likelihood function approach. These include nonlinear regression models, ARMA models, GARCH models, as well as models for limited dependent variables and discrete choices. Such an estimation method is called QMLE. There is an important difference between MLE and QMLE: the structures of their asymptotic variances are different. In certain sense, the asymptotic variance of MLE is similar in structure to the asymptotic variance of the OLS estimator under conditional homoskedasticity and serial uncorrelatedness, while the asymptotic variance of QMLE is similar in structure to the asymptotic variance of the OLS estimator under conditional heteroskedasticity and/or autocorrelation.

Chapters 2 to 9 are treated in a unified and coherent manner. The econometric theory is developed progressively from the classical linear regression models to nonlinear expectations models and conditional distributional models. The book has emphasized the important implications of conditional heteroskedasticity and autocorrelation as well as misspecification of conditional distributional models on the asymptotic variances of the related econometric estimators. With a good command of the econometric theory developed in Chapters 2 to 9, one can conduct a variety of empirical analysis in economics, including all motivating examples introduced in Chapter 1 and subsequent chapters. In addition to the econometric theory, we also train students how to do asymptotic analysis via the progressive development of the asymptotic theory in Chapters 2 to 9. We have introduced a variety of basic asymptotic analytic tools, including various convergence concepts, limit theorems, and basic time series concepts and models. We have seen that how modern econometrics emerges from the classical econometrics by relaxing classical assumptions for linear regression modeling to allow for conditional heteroskedasticity and autocorrelation, endogeneity, nonlinearity, model misspecification, as well as models of conditional higher order moments and conditional distribution.

To provide further insights into the logical links among Chapters 2 to 9 and present a relatively comprehensive but selective overview of the core theory and methods in modern econometrics, we will discuss the development of modern econometrics from a historical perspective in subsequent sections. We will also point out some important directions for future development of econometrics in the Big data era.

10.2 Assumptions of Classical Econometrics

While econometrics has a history of nearly one century, modern econometrics has not emerged from classical econometrics until four decades ago. Thus, classical econometrics could be used as a starting point to understand modern econometrics. One of the core ingredients of classical econometrics is the classical linear regression model, which is based on the following assumptions:

- *Linear Regression Model:* $Y_t = X_t'\beta^o + \varepsilon_t$, $t = 1, ..., n$, where Y_t is the dependent variable, X_t is a K-dimensional regressor vector, β^o is a K-dimensional vector of unknown parameters, ε_t is an unobservable disturbance representing the total impact of all other factors, aside from the regressor vector X_t, on Y_t, and n is the sample size.

- *Strict Exogeneity:* $E(\varepsilon_t|\mathbf{X}) = 0$, where $\mathbf{X} = (X_1, X_2, ..., X_n)'$ is an $n \times K$ matrix. This implies that the average impact of the disturbance ε_t on Y_t does not depend on $\mathbf{X}$. A sufficient condition is that the disturbance sequence $\{\varepsilon_t\}$ and $\mathbf{X}$ are mutually independent.
- *Homoskedasticity and Zero-Autocorrelation:* $E(\varepsilon\varepsilon'|\mathbf{X}) = \sigma^2\mathbf{I}$, where $\varepsilon = (\varepsilon_1, ..., \varepsilon_n)'$, $\mathbf{I}$ is an $n \times n$ identity matrix, and $\sigma^2 > 0$ is a constant. This condition implies that conditional variance of ε_t is independent of $\mathbf{X}$. In addition, no autocorrelation in $\{\varepsilon_t\}$ exists. Again, a sufficient condition is independence between $\{\varepsilon_t\}$ and $\mathbf{X}$.
- *Conditional IID Normality:* $\varepsilon|\mathbf{X} \sim N(0, \sigma^2\mathbf{I})$. This assumption implies that ε and $\mathbf{X}$ are mutually independent. It facilitates statistical inferences in finite samples (i.e., when the sample size n is finite). Since many important parameter estimators, such as the OLS and GLS estimators, are weighted averages of the disturbances $\{\varepsilon_t\}$, their sampling distributions are normal distributions. As a result, the classical finite sample statistical inference theory is available.
- *Nonsingularity of Sample Regressor Matrix* $\mathbf{X}'\mathbf{X}$. This condition is a restriction on the random sample, which implies that any regressor should not be a linear combination of others, excluding the possibility of multicollinearity.

Under the nonsingularity condition, the OLS estimator exists. Under strict exogeneity, the OLS estimator is unbiased for the unknown parameter vector β^o. Given conditional homoskedasticity and zero-autocorrelation, the OLS estimator is BLUE. When the disturbances $\{\varepsilon_t\}$ are an IID sequence with a conditional normal distribution, the OLS estimator has a normal distribution in finite samples, provided $n > K$. This finite sample distribution could be used to construct confidence interval estimators and hypothesis test statistics for the unknown parameter vector β^o, including the well-known Student's t-test and F-test statistics. See Chapter 3 for detailed discussion.

Modern econometrics emerges from relaxing the classical assumptions of the linear regression model. Its assumptions become more realistic and general, and it covers various econometric models. As a result, the scope of application has been extended greatly, and the econometric theory has become more rigorous. Below, we will describe the historical development and core contents of modern econometrics by relaxing each classical assumption of the linear regression model.

10.3 From Normality to Nonnormality

The assumption that the disturbance ε_t follows a conditional normal distribution is made in order to derive the finite sample distributions of the OLS estimator and related statistics, and to facilitate statistical inferences. In finite samples, the classical t-test and F-test statistics follow the Student's t-distribution and F-distribution respectively only when the conditional normality assumption holds.

However, an empirical stylized fact of most economic and financial data is that they do not follow the normal distribution and often have heavy tails, as indicated by the fact that the kurtosis is usually larger than 3. As a result, the finite sample distribution theory based on the normality assumption is no longer applicable. Various tests have been proposed to check whether the estimated residuals of a linear regression model follow the normal distribution. One well-known example is Jarque and Bera's (1980) test.

One major development of modern econometrics is to abandon the normality assumption for the disturbance term. Using asymptotic analysis, econometricians have shown that when the sample size $n \to \infty$, the OLS and other estimators are consistent for unknown parameters, and after suitable standardization, they have an asymptotic normal distribution. In fact, it can be shown that for a linear regression model with IID observations, if the disturbances are not conditionally normally distributed but display conditional homoskedasticity, the OLS estimator is asymptotically BLUE, and the classical t-test and F-test statistics remain applicable when the sample size is sufficiently large. In other words, the classical OLS theory is applicable to large samples when conditional homoskedasticity holds. This conclusion also holds for a stationary time series linear regression model when the disturbances are an MDS with conditional homoskedasticity. See Chapter 4 and Chapter 5 for more discussion. Together with many others, Halbert White played an important role for asymptotic analysis in econometrics. His book, *Asymptotic Theory for Econometricians*, published in 1984 and re-printed in 2001, has been a classic reference for asymptotic analysis in econometrics.

It is convenient to apply the asymptotic theory in empirical studies, but when the sample size is finite, the asymptotic distributions of parameter estimators and test statistics may be different from the unknown finite sample distributions, which may lead to large Type I and Type II errors in statistical inference and thus yield misleading conclusions. To improve the approximation to the finite sample distributions, econometricians (e.g., Klein and Spady 1993, Phillips 1977a, 1977b and 1977c, Ullah 1990) have devoted themselves to developing theories and methods for inferences in finite samples, using the Edgeworth expansion and saddle point approximation. However, these methods are rather tedious and have not been applied extensively. With the rapid development of computer technology, bootstrap methods instead have been proposed and used widely to approximate finite sample distributions. The basic idea of bootstrap methods is to use computers to repeatedly resample the observed data to generate a large number of so-called bootstrap random samples. These bootstrap samples are then used to approximate the finite sample distributions of parameter estimators and test statistics. A main theoretical foundation of bootstrap methods is the Edgeworth expansion. It has been shown that bootstrap methods can greatly improve the degree of approximation to the finite sample distributions so that they can provide more accurate and reliable statistical inferences in finite samples. More discussion on bootstrap methods could be found in Hall (1992) and Horowitz (2001).

10.4 From Independent and Identically Distributed Disturbances to Conditional Heteroskedasticity and Autocorrelation

Another important assumption in classical linear regression modeling is conditional homoskedasticity and zero-autocorrelation for disturbances. This assumption implies that the conditional variance of disturbance ε_t dose not change with the value of $\mathbf{X}$. Under this assumption, the OLS estimator is BLUE. When conditional homoskedasticity or zero-autocorrelation fails, the OLS estimator is no longer BLUE, and furthermore, the classical t-test and F-test statistics do not follow the well-known Student's t-distribution and F-distribution respectively. Therefore, the classical t-test and F-test are not applicable any more even if the sample size is large.

For a long time, econometricians have realized the limitation of the conditional homoskedasticity and zero-autocorrelation assumption, and so the

GLS estimator has been proposed. The GLS theory assumes that there exist(s) conditional heteroskedasticity and/or autocorrelation in disturbances and the form of the variance-covariance matrix for disturbances is known up to some constant. As a result, conditional heteroskedasticity and autocorrelation could be eliminated by correcting conditional heteroskedasticity and differencing out autocorrelation via suitable transformations. In this way, the original linear regression model can be transformed into a linear regression model with conditional homoskedasticity and zero-autocorrelation for new disturbances. Then, the classical linear regression theory is applicable to the transformed model. For instance, in a static time series linear regression model, if disturbances follow a stationary AR process of a fixed order, then autocorrelation in disturbances could be eliminated by the Cochrane-Orcutt method with estimated AR coefficients. The resulting adaptive feasible GLS estimator will become asymptotically BLUE when the sample size goes to infinity.

However, the assumption that the form of conditional heteroskedasticity and autocorrelation is known up to a constant is rather restrictive for most economic and financial data, because conditional heteroskedasticity and autocorrelation is usually of unknown form. Under the zero-autocorrelation assumption (which usually holds for cross-sectional data), an adaptive feasible GLS estimator could be obtained by plugging into the GLS estimator formula a conditional variance estimator of OLS residuals. The latter can be consistently estimated using smoothed nonparametric methods (see, e.g., Robinson 1988 and White and Stinchcombe 1991).

Nevertheless, the OLS estimator and its statistical inference procedures are often preferred in practice, due to its simplicity. White (1980) derives the asymptotic variance of the OLS estimator under conditional heteroskedasticity, and proposes a consistent variance estimator. This is called White's (1980) heteroskedasticity-consistent variance-covariance matrix estimator in the literature. With this variance estimator, the classical t-statistic can be modified to become applicable when the sample size is large, even if there exists conditional heteroskedasticity of unknown form. This modified t-test statistic is called a robust t-test statistic. Unfortunately, the classical F-test statistic could not be modified. Consequently, the classical F-test becomes not applicable any more under conditional heteroskedasticity, even if the sample size is large. However, a robust Wald test statistic and a robust LM test statistic can be constructed by using White's (1980) heteroskedasticity-consistent variance-covariance matrix estimator.

For stationary time series linear regression models, when conditional heteroskedasticity and autocorrelation of disturbances is of unknown form, the asymptotic variance of the OLS estimator becomes a long-run variance-covariance matrix. Newey and West (1987, 1994) and Andrews (1991) propose smoothed nonparametric kernel methods to estimate the long-term variance-covariance matrix. These methods have been extensively used in empirical studies. However, it has been documented, in both simulation and empirical studies, that when relatively persistent autocorrelation exists, kernel-based estimators for the long-run variance-covariance matrix often lead to strong overrejection for robust test statistics, even if the sample size is large. This issue has not been resolved satisfactorily yet, although many improvement and refinement methods have been proposed in the literature.

10.5 From Linear to Nonlinear Models

In econometrics, a linear regression model $Y_t = X_t'\beta^o + \varepsilon_t$ indicates a linear relationship between dependent variable Y_t, regressor vector X_t, and parameter vector β^o, where the regressor vector may consist of one or more explanatory variables and their nonlinear transformations. Therefore, it does not necessarily imply a linear relationship between Y_t and the original explanatory variables. For example, when the conditional mean of Y_t is a polynomial of some explanatory variable, it can be considered as a linear regression model. In this case, Y_t remains as a linear function of parameter vector β^o. However, when the conditional mean of Y_t is not a linear function of parameter vector β^o, the relationship between Y_t and regressor vector X_t is generally nonlinear. Moreover, if the model is not a specification for the conditional mean of Y_t, but one for the conditional variance, or the conditional quantile, or even the entire conditional distribution, then Y_t will be typically nonlinear in both parameters and explanatory variables.

In time series econometrics, linear time series models, such as ARMA models, usually indicate a linear relationship between dependent variable Y_t, lagged dependent variables, and lagged disturbances. So far, popular nonlinear time series models in the literature include Threshold AutoRegressive (TAR) models, Markov Chain Regime Switching (MCRS) models and Smooth Transition AutoRegressive (STAR) models. All of these models specify the conditional mean dynamics of a time series process in a nonlinear manner. They could be viewed as a combination of different linear models in different states, which implies that the dependent variable follows a linear process in one state but may change to another linear process in another state. These nonlinear features are determined by the assumptions of mechanisms under which different states switch to each other. Nonlinear conditional mean models can be widely used to characterize nonlinear features in economic time series, such as asymmetric business cycles and asymmetric spillover effects among different financial markets. Readers are referred to Hamilton (1994), Tong (1990) and Teräsvirta, Tjøtheim and Granger (2010) for introduction to nonlinear time series models.

In the 1970s, the oil crisis, the emerging floating foreign exchanges system, and the high-interest rate policy by the U.S. Federal Reserve Board have stimulated tremendous uncertainties into the world economy. How to measure these uncertainties and their impacts on economic agents' decision-makings becomes an important issue. As a key instrument to quantify uncertainty and risk, econometricians have proposed various models for conditional variance dynamics, including Engle's (1982) ARCH model, Bollerslev's (1986) GARCH model, Nelson's (1991) Exponential GARCH model, and Glosten *et al.*'s (1993) Threshold GARCH model. These volatility models do not specify the entire conditional distribution, but only model the first two conditional moments of a time series process. Therefore, MLE cannot be employed to estimate unknown parameters. In order to estimate unknown parameters in a volatility model, some auxiliary assumptions can be imposed to obtain the conditional distribution of the time series process, so that the MLE procedure can be implemented. Since the auxiliary assumptions might be false (and researchers are aware of this possibility), the likelihood function of a volatility model is likely to be misspecified. As a result, the estimation method is called a Quasi-MLE or QMLE. As long as the first two conditional moments are correctly specified, QMLE can consistently estimate the unknown parameters in a volatility model, even if the likelihood function is incorrectly specified (e.g., Bolleslev and Wooldridge 1992, Lee and Hansen 1994, Lumsdaine 1996). Of course, a price of QMLE is that its asymptotic variance is larger than that of MLE. The latter is based on the true conditional distribution and is asymptotically most efficient. Hence, QMLE is asymptotically less efficient than MLE. The structure of the asymptotic variance of QMLE is analogous to that of the asymptotic variance of the OLS estimator in a linear regression model with conditional heteroskedasticity and/or autocorrelation, while the structure of the asymptotic variance of MLE is analogous to that of the OLS estimator under conditional homoskedasticity and zero-autocorrelation. Therefore, it is necessary to employ a robust variance estimator for QMLE, which will be applicable even if the likelihood function is misspecified. Analogous to the F-test statistic for a linear regression model, the popular LR test can no longer be applicable when the likelihood function is misspecified, since it is equivalent to using an asymptotic variance estimator of MLE. Robust test statistics, such as a robust Wald test statistic and a robust LM test statistic, can be constructed using a consistent variance estimator for QMLE. See Chapter 9 for more discussion.

A large class of econometric models (including linear and nonlinear regression models) can be characterized by a set of population moment conditions. The population moment conditions often arise from economic theory. For example, the rational expectations theory in macroeconomics implies that the stochastic pricing error for assets follows an MDS process, namely that there exists no systematic pricing error in each time period. Based on this MDS property, researchers can choose proper IVs to generate a set of population moments whose values are zero when evaluated at the true parameter value. Since the conditional distribution of the DGP is unknown, MLE cannot be used. Hansen (1982) proposes GMM to estimate unknown parameters in a set of moment conditions. The basic idea of GMM is to define a set of sample moments, whose dimension is larger than or at least equal to that of unknown parameters, and then to select a suitable parameter value as its estimator to make the sample moments as close as possible to the zero population moments. In mathematics, the GMM estimator minimizes a weighted quadratic form of the sample moments, where the weighting matrix generally affects the asymptotic variance of the GMM estimator. An asymptotically most efficient weight matrix is the asymptotic variance-covariance matrix of the sample moments, which plays a similar role to the weighting matrix in GLS estimation, because it eliminates correlations between the sample moments and their heteroskedasticity. GMM could be viewed as a generalization of the classical MME in statistics, but it is motivated by estimating and testing economic models, such as the rational expectations models in macroeconomics. Most estimation methods in econometrics can be formulated as special cases in a GMM framework, including the OLS and 2SLS estimators. It may be noted that QMLE and GMM are the two most popular methods to estimate nonlinear econometric models.

10.6 From Exogeneity to Endogeneity

The classical linear regression model assumes that the conditional mean of the disturbance ε_t given any values of all regressors $\{X_t\}$ is zero, which implies that the current, past and future values of regressors $\{X_t\}$ do not affect the average value of ε_t, if t is an index for time. This condition is called strict exogeneity. There are various definitions of exogeneity in econometrics. If the stochastic disturbance sequence $\{\varepsilon_t\}$ and the regressor sequence $\{X_t\}$ are mutually independent, or if regressor vector X_t is nonstochastic, then one can say that there exists strong exogeneity. If the conditional mean of ε_t given the current value of regressor vector X_t is zero, it is called weak exogeneity. Weak exogeneity implies that the linear regression model is correctly specified for conditional mean $E(Y_t|X_t)$. In other words, the conditional mean $E(Y_t|X_t)$ is a linear function of regressor vector X_t.

The strict exogeneity assumption of the classical linear regression model lies between the strong exogeneity condition and the weak exogeneity condition. Strong exogeneity implies strict exogeneity, which in turn implies weak exogeneity, but the converse is not true. The primary aim of the strict exogeneity assumption for a linear regression model is to facilitate derivation of the sampling distributions of the OLS estimator and related test statistics in finite samples. For the asymptotic or large sample theory, the weak exogeneity condition suffices.

When weak exogeneity fails, the conditional mean of the stochastic disturbance ε_t given the current regressor vector X_t is not zero, which usually indicates that endogeneity exists. In this case, it is said that there exist endogenous variables in regressor vector X_t. Endogeneity may occur due to various reasons, including measurement errors of explanatory variables, the existence of omitted variables, and simultaneous equations bias. The so-called simultaneous equations bias means that besides the regression equation for the dependent variable that is being considered, there exist one or more omitted equations that characterize how the dependent variable and other variables determine explanatory variables. In this case, there usually exists a two-way causality between the dependent and explanatory variables, which implies that the dependent and explanatory variables affect each other simultaneously. When correlation between the regressor vector and the disturbance is caused by the existence of two-way causality, one says that there exists endogeneity, since it implies that regressor vector X_t contains one or more endogenous variables to be determined by simultaneous equations. Endogeneity leads to the failure of the orthogonality condition that $E(\varepsilon_t|X_t) = 0$, and so the OLS estimator is no longer consistent for the unknown parameter vector β^o. Other reasons may also cause $E(\varepsilon_t|X_t) = 0$ to fail, such as measurement errors of explanatory variables, omitted variables and function form misspecification. Strictly speaking, these reasons are irrelevant to endogeneity. Nevertheless, for simplicity, the assumption of $E(\varepsilon_t|X_t) = 0$ is loosely referred to as the exogeneity condition.

If researchers are only interested in estimating a linear regression model, which characterizes how explanatory variables in X_t determine dependent variable Y_t, the OLS estimator will not be consistent for the unknown parameter values when endogeneity exists. Instead, the 2SLS method can be employed. A consistent estimator for the parameters in the one-way causality from X_t to Y_t can be obtained by regressing the dependent variable on the projection variables which are obtained by projecting regressor vector X_t on Z_t, a set of IVs. These IVs must be uncorrelated with disturbance ε_t but closely correlated with regressor vector X_t. This is called the 2SLS method, which has been proposed for quite a long time ago. See, e.g., Stock and Trebbi (2003) for a historical review.

The key of 2SLS is how to find a set of effective IVs. In empirical studies in economics, it has been often documented that correlations between regressors and IVs are rather low, leading to unstable and even inconsistent estimation of unknown parameter values. This phenomenon is called "weak IVs" (see Staiger and Stock 1997). Studies of weak IVs have been an important direction of econometrics in the last two decades.

Endogeneity may exist not only in linear regression models, but also in models for conditional variance, conditional quantile, and conditional distribution. In addition, nonparametric and semiparametric regression models with endogeneity have been drawing attention in the literature. Endogeneity takes a central position in econometrics, since the main objective of economic analysis is to identify and quantify the causal relationships between economic variables. It has been sometimes claimed that, in the Big data era, only correlation is needed, and causality is not important. Obviously, this is not the case in economics.

Because of the nonexperimental nature of economic phenomena and observed economic data, one cannot simply adapt controlled experiment methods to study a casual relationship under the *ceteris paribus* condition. In other words, one cannot investigate whether a change in the dependent variable is caused by changes in some explanatory variables, while holding fixed the values of other explanatory variables by controlled experiments. How to identify a causal relationship is a challenge in empirical studies in economics. In the past two decades, the so-called "treatment effect" analysis has been a popular focus in microeconometrics. Studies in this field have borrowed the ideas and methods of randomized experiments from statistics, especially from biostatistics and medical statistics, and have developed a class of econometric theories and methods to identify and estimate economic causal effects. A new discipline, econometrics of program evaluation, has emerged, which can evaluate various economic policies and programs by conducting counterfactual analysis under the nonexperimental conditions. The basic idea to evaluate the effect of an economic policy is to, *ceteris paribus*, compare the outcome of policy implementation with the counterfactual outcome under the assumption that the policy had not been implemented, and the difference between the actual and counterfactual outcomes is the estimated effect of the policy. The key challenge here is how to estimate the counterfactual outcome under the assumption that the policy had not been implemented, given the fact that it has actually been implemented. Many methods, such as Difference-In-Difference (DID), Regression Discontinuity Design (RDD), Propensity Score Matching (PSM) and panel data approach to program evaluation, have been developed to evaluate various policies and programs (see Imbens and Wooldridge 2009 for a review). For example, Hsiao *et al.* (2011) propose a panel data approach to policy evaluation and apply it to evaluate the effects of the Hong Kong turnover to China and the signing of Closer Economic Partnership Arrangement (CEPA) between Hong Kong and Mainland China in 2003 on Hong Kong's economy. On the other hand, in the past three decades or so, the emerging experimental economics has developed a new approach to exploring economic causalities by controlled experiments. A closely related approach is the field study, which is a quasi-experimental method, imposing some experimental interventions under real social-economic environments to track and study causal effects in economics.

10.7 From Correct Model Specification to Model Misspecification

If there exists an unknown parameter value β^o such that $E(Y_t|X_t) = X_t'\beta^o$, a linear regression model is correctly specified for conditional mean and the unknown parameter value β^o is called the true model parameter. On the other hand, if there exists no parameter value β such that $E(Y_t|X_t) = X_t'\beta$, then a linear regression model is misspecified for conditional mean. Model misspecification can occur for various reasons, such as omitted variables and function form misspecification.

When a linear regression model is misspecified for conditional mean, the parameter β can neither be called the true model parameter, nor be given any economic interpretation. For example, if a linear consumption function is misspecified, then the parameter cannot be interpreted as the MPC, since the latter is the expected partial derivative of consumption with respect to income. When the true consumption function is not linear, the MPC is not a constant. In general, if a model is misspecified for conditional mean or other attributes of conditional distribution (e.g., conditional variance, conditional quantile, and even conditional distribution itself), parameters cannot be called the true model parameters or be given any economic interpretation. The validity of economic interpretation for model parameters depends on whether a model is correctly specified. In addition to the validity of economic interpretation, model misspecification may also cause serious consequences in applications. In finance, for example, the use of a misspecified model may lead to the so-called "model risk". A main cause for the 2008 subprime mortgage crisis has been attributed to the use of a Gaussian copula model, which was widely used in the Wall Street to price financial derivatives but could not correctly characterize the asymmetric linkages among financial markets in volatile periods.

However, model misspecification does not imply that any misspecified model cannot be used. For example, suppose the dynamic evolution of an economic time series consists of about 80% of linear components and about 20% of nonlinear components. Obviously, a linear regression model neglects the nonlinear components and therefore is misspecified, but it still has rather good predictive ability, although its parameters cannot be interpreted as the expected marginal effect of regressors. On the other hand, some parameters of a misspecified model may still be given economic interpretation. For example, in a linear regression model for the rate of return to education, where the dependent variable is income and explanatory variables include education and work experience only, there may exist such omitted variables as personal ability, which is unobservable but correlated with education and work experience. This is a misspecified linear regression model. However, if one is mainly interested in the rate of return to education, the 2SLS method can be used to estimate the parameter value for education consistently.

Model misspecification can also occur in other scenarios. In a correctly specified linear regression model, if observed data is defective, for example, some observations are censored or truncated, then the OLS estimator will not be consistent for the true model parameter. In this case, auxiliary assumptions, such as the regression disturbance following a normal distribution, can be made so that MLE can be used to estimate unknown parameters. Since the data is defective, the relationship between the dependent variable and regressors becomes highly nonlinear. However, MLE delivers consistent estimation for the unknown parameters in the original linear regression model, provided the auxiliary assumptions hold. On the other hand, a volatility model specifies the first two conditional moments of a time series process. Even if a volatility model is correctly specified, the conditional distribution of the time series process is still unknown. Here, one can make some auxiliary assumptions (such as the standardized innovation following the standard normal distribution), so that the likelihood function can be obtained and QMLE can be adopted to estimate unknown parameters. Although the auxiliary assumptions might be false and so the likelihood function could be misspecified, QMLE still delivers consistent estimation for unknown parameters in a volatility model, provided that the conditional mean and variance models are correctly specified. This is different from the case that correct auxiliary assumptions are needed to obtain consistent estimation for parameters in a linear regression model with censored or truncated data. However, misspecification for the likelihood function affects the asymptotic efficiency of QMLE, and a consistent robust variance-covariance matrix estimator for QMLE is needed for valid statistical inference. See Bollerslev and Wooldridge (1992), Lee and Hansen (1994) and Lumsdaine (1996).

Since model misspecification (i.e. $E(\varepsilon_t|X_t) = 0$ fails) affects the validity of economic interpretations as well as the efficiency and even the consistency of model parameters, Hausman (1978) proposes a test to check whether a linear regression model is misspecified. This is called Hausman's test in the literature. White (1981), Newey (1985), Tauchen (1985) and White (1990) generalize this method to develop more general model specification tests based on moment conditions, which are called moment specification tests or m-tests. These tests are not consistent tests, in the sense that they may miss some misspecified models even for large samples. Bierens (1982,

1990), Hong and White (1995), Fan and Li (1996) and Hong and Lee (2013) propose various consistent model specification tests using nonparametric methods. These tests can detect any model misspecification if the sample size is large enough.

In statistics and econometrics, there is another form of model checking called "model validation", where a data set is split into a training data set and a test data set. The training data set is used to estimate model parameters and the test data set is used to evaluate the predictive ability of the estimated model. This model validation method is mainly used to evaluate the out-of-sample predictive ability of a model and is widely used in time series forecasting and machine learning. Out-of-sample evaluation can avoid in-sample overfitting. Furthermore, if the DGP of a training data set is substantially different from that of a test data set, a model may not predict the test data set well even if it is correctly specified for the DGP of the training data set.

10.8 From Stationarity to Nonstationarity

For a stationary time series linear regression model with conditionally homoskedastic MDS disturbances, the OLS theory of a classical linear regression is applicable for large samples. When heteroskedasticity and/or autocorrelation exist(s), the OLS estimator is no longer BLUE and the classical t-test and F-test statistics are no longer applicable either, even if the sample size is large. Nevertheless, the classical test statistics, especially the t-test and F-test statistics, can be modified, and the resulting robust test statistics become valid in large samples.

However, the OLS theory is generally not applicable when the dependent and explanatory variables are nonstationary time series processes. Granger and Newbold (1974) document the so-called spurious regression phenomenon via simulation studies, where for any two mutually independent nonstationary unit root time series, if one regresses one series to the other, the t-test statistic of the OLS estimator will be statistically significant based on the conventional distribution theory. Phillips (1986) offers a rigorous explanation from a theoretical perspective. Nelson and Plosser (1982), by applying the Dickey and Fuller (1979) test, document that most macroeconomic and financial time series are nonstationary unit root processes. Thus, econometricians have been devoting themselves to developing nonstationary time series econometric theories and methods, including the cointegration theory by Engle and Granger (1987) and the unit root theory by Phillips (1987a, 1987b). For linear regression models, the asymptotic theory for nonstationary unit root time series is totally different from that for a stationary time series which we establish in the present book. See Hamilton (1994) for detailed discussion.

Apart from nonstationary unit root processes, nonstationary time series can also take the form of a trend-stationary process. The mean of a so-called trend-stationary time series is changing over time, so it is not stationary. When the mean is a linear function of time, this time series will show a long-run linear trend. If the time trend is eliminated, the demeaned time series will become stationary. If the sample size is not large, the data generated from a trend-stationary process and those from a unit root process may look similar and therefore are difficult to distinguish from each other. In empirical studies of macroeconomics, it is important to check whether macroeconomic time series are unit root or trend-stationary processes, because they have different policy implications. For examples, it is related to whether macroeconomic fiscal and monetary policies have long-term effects (for unit root processes) or short-term effects (for trend-stationary processes).

Nonstationary time series can also arise due to structure changes. There are mainly two forms of structural changes, namely abrupt structural breaks and smooth or evolutionary structural changes. Observations generated from a time series process with structural breaks may resemble those generated from a unit root process. Since Chow (1960) proposes an F-test for a single structure break with known break point, econometricians have devoted great effort to testing various structural breaks over the past several decades. In particular, they have developed tests for whether there exist structural breaks with multiple unknown break points, and established a relatively satisfactory asymptotic distribution theory. See, e.g., Andrew and Ploberger (1994, 1995) and Bai and Perron (1998).

Besides abrupt structural breaks, structure changes can also arise in form of smooth changes, which implies that model parameters change continuously over time. An example is the so-called time-varying STAR model in time series econometrics. A trend-stationary process is another example, if its unconditional mean is a smooth function of time. Changes of economic agents' preferences, technology innovations, institutional reforms and policy shifts often lead to changes of economic agents' behaviors and economic structures. In particular, economic agents can rationally predict or perceive policy changes, and then adjust their behaviors accordingly, leading to economic structural changes. This is exactly the well-known Lucas (1976) critique. Moreover, while some external shocks may occur suddenly, due to habit formations, adjustment costs and other reasons, the behaviors of economic agents and economic structures may change slowly. Even if the behaviors of economic agents change abruptly, if each individual behavior changes at a different time point, then the aggregated macroeconomic time series may display a slowly changing structure. As a result, smooth structure changes may appear to be a better approximation to economic reality in many scenarios.

A typical example of smooth structural changes in economics is the "Great Moderation" phenomenon in the U.S. macroeconomic volatility dynamics. Since the mid-1980s, the U.S. GDP growth rate and inflation rate have displayed a trend of diminishing volatilities in a continuous manner. This is called the "Great Moderation" phenomenon (e.g., Bernanke 2004). In fact, there exists a similar "Great Moderation" phenomenon in the Chinese economy: the GDP growth rate and inflation rate in China have also displayed a trend of slowly diminishing volatilities since 1992 and 1999 respectively (Sun, Hong and Wang 2018).

Chen and Hong (2012, 2016) propose tests to check whether there exist smooth structural changes in a time series linear regression model and a GARCH model respectively. Their empirical studies suggest that structural changes could be an important source for the poor predictive power of a linear regression model for asset returns. Smooth structural changes may cause a spurious long memory phenomenon as well, in the sense that a long memory phenomenon of economic time series may appear due to smooth structural changes in mean. Hong, Wang and Wang (2017) propose a class of tests for strict stationarity and weak stationarity, and apply these tests to check stationarity of most macroeconomic and financial time series. They document that the first differenced macroeconomic and financial time series do not satisfy the stationarity condition, which has been a standard assumption in nonstationary time series econometrics. In particular, the mean and variance of the first differenced economic time series change over time.

In the past two decades, a new discipline in time series analysis, namely locally stationary time series analysis (e.g., Dahlhaus 1996), has emerged. It is another kind of nonstationary processes, where its structures or parameters change slowly over time. Thus, in a short period, it could be approximated reasonably well by a stationary time series model, but segments in different time periods have to be approximated by different stationary time series models. The availability of high-frequency time series data is expected to contribute to the literature of smooth structural changes and locally stationary time series modeling.

10.9 From Econometric Models to Economic Theories

The roles that economic theory plays in econometric modeling seem absent in the discussion so far. We have seen that there are various econometric models, including conditional mean models, conditional variance models, conditional quantile models, conditional moment models, conditional distribution models, and generalized linear regression models, such as Probit models, Logit models, Cox's (1972) proportional hazard models, and Poisson regression models. In empirical studies in economics, the choice of a model depends on the nature of the economic problem under study. It is impossible that a single econometric model or method be universally applied to study all economic problems. For example, to study financial market efficiency or predictability, one needs to model the conditional mean dynamics of asset returns; to study volatility spillover between financial markets, one needs to model the conditional variance dynamics of multiple markets; and to study Value at Risk (VaR) or extreme downside risk in financial markets, one needs to model the conditional quantile or even the conditional distribution of asset returns.

Economic theory plays a crucial role in selecting explanatory variables in econometric modeling. The choice of explanatory variables in an econometric model should rely on economic theory, apart from empirical experience and data-driven statistical analysis. To identify causality between economic variables, econometric tools alone are inadequate; economic theory has to be relied upon. Moreover, when an econometric model is correctly specified, economic theory can provide valid economic interpretations for model parameters. It is crucial to interpret econometric models and empirical findings of statistical analysis from an economic perspective.

On the other hand, how can one test whether economic theory can explain observed economic phenomena? In other words, how can one test the validity of economic theory? A basic idea is to transform economic theory into a set of empirically testable restrictions on an econometric model, and then test whether these restrictions are consistent with observed data. We emphasize that certain auxiliary assumptions, such as functional form specification of an econometric model, are needed in testing economic theory. Therefore, when a statistical hypothesis is rejected, one needs to distinguish whether it is due to the failure of economic theory or the failure of the auxiliary assumptions. Generally speaking, economic theory or hypothesis is model-free. Therefore, when one transforms economic theory into statistical restrictions of an econometric model, there usually exists a gap between the original economic theory or hypothesis and the resulting statistical hypothesis. In other words, the economic hypothesis and the statistical hypothesis are not equivalent. As a result, caution is needed in interpreting the empirical results of statistical hypothesis testing. Consider EMH as an example: if the historical information of an asset return has no predictive power for the expected future asset return, one says that the weak form of EMH holds (Malkiel and Fama 1970). This economic hypothesis is model-free. Now, suppose one uses an AR model of a finite order to test this hypothesis. If EMH holds, the AR model will have no predictive power and so all autoregressive coefficients are jointly zero. As long as at least one autoregressive coefficient is not zero, the weak form of EMH will be rejected. However, if the statistical hypothesis that all autoregressive coefficients are zero is not rejected, can one accept the weak form of EMH? No, because the AR model is only one of possibly infinitely many ways to predict asset returns. When the statistical hypothesis that all autoregressive coefficients are zero is not rejected, it only indicates that the AR model has no predictive ability and does not imply that the historical data of asset returns has no predictive ability for future asset returns. Therefore, when all autoregressive coefficients are zero, one can only conclude that no evidence has been found against the weak form of EMH. In general, one has to pay attention to the gap between economic and statistical hypotheses and the difference between the evidence from data and the evidence from a model.

Econometrics plays a key role in advancing the development of economic theories. With data being accumulated and new econometric methods invented, the chance will be higher to find evidence against existing economic theories. In other words, the existing economic theory may not be able to explain the newly available observed data, and therefore it will eventually be rejected by accumulating data evidence and new economic theory will be called for.

Due to various reasons, such as small sample sizes of observed data and limited powers of econometric tests, two or more economic theories may coexist in the sense that they all pass statistical tests simultaneously. In other words, it is possible that several economic theories or models coexist and all of them can explain the same economic phenomenon to certain extent. But then, which economic theory or model truly captures or characterizes the DGP? This is called model uncertainty or model ambiguity in economics. In the Big data era, there usually exist a large number of potential explanatory variables, so multicollinearity is likely to occur in practice. As a result, multiple econometric models (e.g., models with different sets of explanatory variables, or models with different functional forms) may have the same or very similar performance according to some statistical criterion. On the other hand, for some data set, an econometric model may perform best, but if the data is perturbed, such as by adding or deleting a few observations, then the best-performing model may change. This phenomenon is a form of model uncertainty, and may be called model instability in a time series context. It is an important but challenging task to interpret model uncertainty and model instability, and to examine their implications on econometric inference.

10.10 From Traditional Data to Big Data

With nowadays information technologies, such as the internet and mobile internet, being developed rapidly and applied extensively, the amount of observed data has been increasing exponentially, which is called Big data. Besides traditional numerical structured data, Big data also includes multitudinous unstructured data and semi-structured data, such as text, graph, audio and video data. Even for the numerical structured data, there include data of new forms, such as functional data, interval data and symbolic data. The sources of Big data include transaction records from e-commerce companies, websites of enterprises and governments, and various social platforms, sensors and satellite images. Most of these Big data are recorded in real-time or near real-time, so their volume is massive, whereas the information density may be usually low.

Big data provides much information that traditional data does not have, and such information can be used to construct important variables which could not be measured accurately before. For example, investor sentiment index (Baker and Wurgler 2006, 2007), economic policy uncertainty index

(Baker *et al.* 2016) and economic policy change index (Chan and Zhong 2018) could be constructed, based on text data from social platforms and news media. Then the impact of these variables on real economy and financial markets can be investigated.

Big data also makes it possible to construct important high-frequency economic indices or variables. For example, so far the highest sampling frequency of macroeconomic price indices, such as Consumer Price Index (CPI) and Producer Price Index (PPI), is monthly. Based on the internet-based price information of consumer goods and producer goods, it is possible to construct weekly or daily CPI and PPI by using Artificial Intelligence (AI) methods. These high-frequency macroeconomic variables can play an important role in studying short-run macroeconomic dynamics. It is conceivable that high-frequency macroeconomics is likely to emerge. In this new discipline, high-frequency interactions between macroeconomy and financial markets could be explored. In fact, Big data has help bring nowcasting into time series econometrics. The term "nowcasting" is originated from meteorology and it means weather forecasting in a very short time period, usually up to 2 hours. "Nowcasting" in econometrics usually means predicting the current quarterly GDP and other macroeconomic indices. Since the release date of quarterly GDP is lagged behind in practice, nowcasting the current quarterly GDP and other macroeconomic indices is of great importance for monitoring macroeconomic trends and changes in a timely manner. Many central banks in the world have started nowcasting their own countries' GDPs. For more discussion on nowcasting, see Giannone *et al.* (2008).

Big data include numerous new forms of data which are different from the traditional data, such as tick-by-tick transaction data, functional data and interval data. These data of new forms call for the development of new econometric models and methods. In the past two decades, high frequency and ultra-high frequency data have promoted the rapid development of high-frequency financial econometrics. For example, based on ultra-high frequency transaction data, Engle and Russell (1998) proposed a new model called ACD, to capture the time duration dynamics between consecutive price changes or transactions. This model can predict the timing of, e.g., the next price change and the instantaneous probability of a price change at each future time point. These predictions could be used to design algorithm-based trading strategies and to price financial derivatives. Furthermore, by using intraday data of asset returns, financial econometricians have proposed new methods to estimate daily volatilities and covariances of asset returns. These high-frequency volatilities and covariances could be used to improve portfolio management and financial risk management. See Ait-Sahalia *et al.* (2010), Andersen *et al.* (2001, 2003, 2004), Barndorff-Nielsen and Shephard (2002, 2004), Noureldin, Shephard and Sheppard (2011) and Shephard and Sheppard (2010) for detailed discussion.

Big data also includes the so-called functional data, such as the temperature as a function of time in a day and a stock price as a function of time from the opening hour to the closing hour in a trading day. Panel data is a special case of functional data. Functional data has spawned a family of functional data models (see Muller 2005, Muller and Stadtmuller 2005 and Ramsay and Silverman 2002, 2005). Another new form of data is the interval data, which is a set of numbers ranging from the maximum to minimum values of a variable. Almost all data used in econometric modeling are point-valued data. Compared with a point-valued data, an interval-valued data contains more information but it has not been used effectively. Interval-valued data are not uncommon; examples include daily observations on the highest and lowest temperatures, systolic and diastolic blood pressures, high and low stock price indices and bid-ask asset price spreads. Interval-valued data is a special case of the so-called symbolic data. Han, Hong and Wang (2017) propose an AutoRegressive Conditional Interval (ACI) model for an interval-valued time series process. This can be viewed as the interval version of an ARMA model in time series analysis. See Han *et al.* (2016) and Sun *et al.* (2018) for more discussion on interval data modeling.

In most cases, the volume of a Big data is huge, especially a high-frequency Big data. If the sample size is much larger than the number of potential explanatory or predictive variables in a Big data, then the Big data is called a "Tall Big data". Compared with traditional data, a Tall Big data offers more potential to explore subtle relationships, especially nonlinear relationships, among variables in the Big data. Many machine learning methods for Big data analysis, such as decision trees, support vector machines, random forests and artificial neural networks, are all nonlinear algorithms. To a great extent, these algorithms are analogous in spirit to nonparametric analysis in econometrics and statistics. Halbert White together with many others, has established the econometric theory of nonparametric artificial neural network modeling (see, e.g., White 1992). Artificial neural networks have been widely used in empirical studies in economics and finance. In fact, the most important feature of Big data is not its large sample size but its large number of potential explanatory or predictive variables. It is possible that the number of potential explanatory or predictive variables in a Big data surpasses the sample size. Such a Big data is called a "Fat Big data". A high-dimensional set of explanatory variables provides various possibilities for variable or model selection. In a Fat Big data, it is possible that only a few explanatory variables have significant predictive power for the dependent variable. Many algorithms (such as decision trees and random forests) have been invented in machine learning to select important predictive variables (see, e.g., Varian 2014). One important method is the so-called LASSO method, which can select important predictive variables from a high-dimensional set of potential variables, most of which are assumed to have zero coefficients. This is a "statistical learning" method combined with machine learning. Based on a high-dimensional set of explanatory variables, one can investigate many important topics in econometrics by machine learning methods. Examples include: how to select the most important IVs from a high-dimensional set of potential instruments, so as to enhance efficient IV estimation and avoid the weak IV problem? How to select important leading indicators that have the best predictive power from a high-dimensional set of leading indicators whose number may exceed the sample size, so as to achieve best out-of-sample forecasts? For CAPM, how to select important risk factors of each asset from a high-dimensional set of potential risk factors, where each asset has only a few risk factors but different assets have different risk factors? Finally, in nonparametric estimation with a relatively large number of explanatory variables, how to employ machine learning methods to reduce the dimension of the nonparametric estimator so as to obtain an optimal estimation?

Big data and machine learning are also expected to be of great help in estimating causal effects in economics. As introduced earlier, the basic idea of policy evaluation, based on observed nonexperimental data in economics, is to compare the observed outcome when a policy has been implemented with the counterfactual outcome under the assumption that the policy had not been implemented, *ceteris paribus*. Since the policy has been implemented, the counterfactual outcome cannot be observed and so has to be estimated. Obviously, the quality of policy evaluation depends on the efficiency of estimation of the counterfactual outcome. Counterfactual estimation is essentially an out-of-sample prediction. Since a main advantage of machine learning is its ability to provide excellent out-of-sample predictions based on the massive information contained in a Big data, machine learning can therefore offer new approaches to efficient policy evaluation. As is well known, machine learning algorithms are not necessarily based on causal relationships. They often look like a "black box". Nevertheless, as Varian (2014) points out, machine learning combined with Big data could accurately and precisely predict counterfactual outcomes, so it can make significant improvement on causal analysis and policy evaluation.

It may be emphasized that Big data does not imply that it contains a full information about a population distribution of the DGP. For example, because of heterogeneity, insatiability and uncertainty of an economy, out-of-sample forecasts for the trend of the economy may not be accurate and precise, even if all existing data have been fully utilized. In fact, if a Big data is a Fat Big data, then this high-dimensional data is actually a "small sample" from the perspective of econometric modeling and inference.

When modeling a Tall Big data, one perhaps does not have to focus on parameter estimation uncertainty caused by random sampling, unlike the case in traditional data analysis. For example, suppose the sample size is as large as millions in a Tall Big data but t-test statistics of some parameter estimator are just marginally significant at the 5% significance level. Then how much of variations in the dependent variable can be explained by this explanatory variable? In fact, with such a large sample size, a statistically significant explanatory variable does not necessarily mean that it is economically significant as well. It is most likely that model uncertainty is more important than parameter uncertainty when the sample size is extraordinarily large. Thus, more attention may be paid to model selection and model uncertainty when modeling a Big data.

10.11 Conclusion

Starting from the classical linear regression model, this chapter has outlined the development of core theory and methods of modern econometrics in the past four decades, by sequentially relaxing the classical assumptions of linear regression models, especially those of normal distribution, homogeneity and zero-autocorrelation, strict exogeneity, correct model specification, linearity, and stationarity. It has also discussed some important directions for the future development of econometrics in the Big data era. As one can see, modern econometrics has greatly expanded the scope of application of econometrics by developing more econometric models, methods and tools, and by rigorously establishing more general econometric theory. Over the past four decades or so, economics has witnessed the so-called "empirical revolution" in its research peridium, which advocates to look for truths in economic causal relationships via rigorous analysis of observed data. Developed in the same period, modern econometrics has become the most important scientific methodology of empirical studies in economics.

The econometric theory presented in this book has laid a relatively solid foundation in econometrics. However, it is impossible to cover all important econometric models, methods and tools. For example, we only cover stationary time series models, but nonstationary time series models, such as unit root models and cointegrated models, have not been covered, which call for a different asymptotic theory (see, e.g., Hamilton 1994). Panel data models also require a separate and independent treatment (see, e.g., Hsiao 2003). Due to the unique features of financial time series, particularly high-frequency financial time series, financial econometrics has emerged as a new field in econometrics most of which is not covered by standard time series econometrics. On the other hand, although our theory can be applied to models for limited dependent variables and discrete choice variables, more detailed treatment and comprehensive coverage on microeconometrics are needed (e.g., Cameron and Trivedi 2005). Moreover, topics on asymptotic analytic tools may be covered to train students' asymptotic analytic skills in a more comprehensive manner. For more discussion on asymptotic theory, see White (1984, 2001) and Davidson (1994). Therefore, this book has better to be considered as an introduction to modern econometrics.

Finally, it may be noted that most materials of this chapter are based on Hong (2020).

Exercise 10

10.1. Summarize the main results of this book in a unified manner.

10.2. One of the most important objectives of economic analysis is to identify causal relationships among economic variables. Discuss the relationship between a statistical (e.g., predictive) relationship and an economic causal relationship.

10.3. What are the roles of economic theory in econometric modeling?

10.4. Discuss the importance of correct model specification on economic interpretation of empirical results. Can a misspecified econometric model be useful in empirical studies in economics?

10.5. Econometric modeling involves modeling various aspects of the conditional distribution of economic variables, such as conditional mean, conditional variance, conditional quantile, and conditional distribution. In a specific empirical study in economics, which moment(s) should be used in econometric modeling?

10.6. Conditional heteroskedasticity and autocorrelation in regression disturbances are a key to understanding the regression theory in econometrics. Discuss the implications of relaxing conditional homoskedasticity and no autocorrelation to conditional heteroskedasticity and/or autocorrelation.

10.7. Model misspecification is a key to understanding econometric theory of conditional probability distribution modeling. Discuss the implications of relaxing correct model specification to model misspecification for conditional distribution modeling.

10.8. Most nonlinear econometric models can be estimated by GMM and QMLE methods. Discuss the motivations, natures, advantages and disadvantages of these two important econometric methods.

10.9. Discuss the impacts, in terms of both opportunities and challenges, Big data and machine learning may bring to the development of econometric theory, methods and tools.

10.10. What are the advantages and limitations of econometric analysis in the empirical studies of economics?

10.11. Discuss the scientific foundation of econometrics as a main methodology in empirical studies in economics.

Bibliography

Akaike, H., (1973). Information Theory and an Extension of the Maximum Likelihood Principle, *Selected Papers of Hirotugu Akaike*, 199-213.

Ait-Sahalia, Y., (2002). Maximum-Likelihood Estimation of Discretely-Sampled Diffusions: A Closed-Form Approximation Approach, *Econometrica*, 70, 223-262.

Ait-Sahalia, Y., J. Fan and D. Xiu, (2010). High-Frequency Covariance Estimates with Noisy and Asynchronous Financial Data, *Journal of American Statistical Association*, 105, 1504-1517.

Andersen, T. G., T. Bollerslev, F. X. Diebold and H. Ebens, (2001). The Distribution of Realized Stock Return Volatility, *Journal of Financial Economics*, 61, 43-76.

Andersen, T. G., T. Bollerslev, F. X. Diebold and P. Labys, (2001). The Distribution of Realized Exchange Rate Volatility, *Journal of American Statistical Association*, 96, 42-55.

Andersen, T. G., T. Bollerslev, F. X. Diebold and P. Labys, (2003). Modeling and Forecasting Realized Volatility, *Econometrica*, 71, 579-625.

Andersen, T. G., T. Bollerslev and N. Meddahi, (2004). Correcting the Errors: Volatility Forecast Evaluation Using High-Frequency Data and Realized Volatilities, *Econometrica*, 73, 279-296.

Andrews, D., (1991). Heteroskedasticity and Autocorrelation Consistent Covariance Matrix Estimation, *Econometrica*, 59, 817-858.

Andrews, D. W. K. and W. Ploberger, (1994). Optimal Tests When a Nuisance Parameter Is Present Only Under the Alternative, *Econometrica*, 62, 1383-1414.

Andrews, D. W. K. and W. Ploberger, (1995). Admissibility of the Likelihood Ratio Test When a Nuisance Parameter Is Present Only Under the Alternative, *Annals of Statistics*, 23, 1609-1629.

Bai, J. and P. Perron, (1998). Estimating and Testing Linear Models with Multiple Structural Changes, *Econometrica*, 66, 47-78.

Baker, M. and J. Wurgler, (2006). Investor Sentiment and the Cross-Section of Stock Returns, *Journal of Finance*, 61, 1645-1680.

Baker, M. and J. Wurgler, (2007). Investor Sentiment in the Stock Market, *Journal of Economic Perspectives*, 21, 129-152.

Baker, S. R., N. Bloom and S. J. Davis, (2016). Measuring Economic Policy Uncertaintyt, *Quarterly Journal of Economics*, 131, 1593-1636.

Barndorff-Nielsen, O. E. and N. Shephard, (2002). Estimating Quadratic Variation Using Realized Variance, *Journal of Applied Econometrics*, 17, 457-477.

Barndorff-Nielsen, O. E. and N. Shephard, (2004). Econometric Analysis of Realized Covariation: High Frequency Based Covariance, Regression, and Correlation in Financial Economics, *Econometrica*, 72, 885-925.

Bernanke, B., (2004). The Great Moderation, in *The Taylor Rule and the Transformation of Monetary Policy*, E. F. Koenig (Ed.), Chapter Five, Hoover: Hoover Press.

Berndt, E., B. Hall, R. Hall and J. Hausman, (1974). Estimation and Inference in Nonlinear Structural Models, *Annals of Economic and Social Measurement*, 3, 653-665.

Bierens, H. J., (1982). Consistent Model Specification Tests, *Journal of Econometrics*, 20, 105-134.

Bizer, D. and S. N. Durlauf, (1990). Testing the Positive Theory of Government Finance, *Journal of Monetary Economics*, 26, 123-141.

Blundell, R. W. and J. L. Powell, (2004). Endogeneity in Semiparametric Binary Response Models, *Review of Economic Studies*, 71, 655-679.

Bollerslev, T., (1986). Generalized Autoregressive Conditional Heteroskedastcity, *Journal of Econometrics*, 31, 307-327.

Bollerslev, T. and J. M. Wooldridge, (1992). Quasi-Maximum Likelihood Estimation and Inference in Dynamic Models with Time-Varying Covariances, *Econometric Reviews*, 11, 143-172.

Box, G.E.P. and D.A. Pierce, (1970). Distribution of Residual Autorrelations in Autoregressive Moving Average Time Series Models, *Journal of American Statistical Association*, 65, 1509-1526.

Breiman, L., (2001). Statistical Modeling: The Two Cultures (with Comments and a Rejoinder by the Author), *Statistical Science*, 16, 199-231.

Breusch, T. S., (1978). Testing for Autocorrelation in Dynamic Linear Models, *Australian Economic Papers*, 17(31), 334-355.

Breusch, T. S. and A. Pagan, (1980). The Lagrange Multiplier Test and Its Applications to Model Specification in Econometrics, *Review of Economic Studies*, 47, 239-253.

Brockwell P. J. and R. A. Davis., (1991). *Time Series: Theory and Methods, 2nd Edition*, New York: Springer.

Campbell, J. Y., A. W. Lo and A. C. MacKinlay, (1997). *The Econometrics of Financial Markets*, Princeton: Princeton University Press.

Campbell, J.Y. and J. Cochrance, (1999). By Force of Habit: A Consumption-Based Explanation of Aggregate Stock Market Behavior, *Journal of Political Economy*, 107, 205-251.

Cameron, A. C. and T. Pravin, (2005). *Microeconometrics: Methods and Applications*, Cambridge: Cambridge University Press.

Chan, J. T. and Zhong, W., (2018). Reading China: Predicting Policy Change with Machine Learning, *Working Paper*, Bates-White Economic Consulting.

Chen, B. and Y. Hong, (2012). Testing for Smooth Structural Changes in Time Series Models via Nonparametric Regression, *Econometrica*, 80, 1157-1183.

Chen, B. and Y. Hong, (2016). Detecting for Smooth Structural Changes in GARCH Models, *Econometric Theory*, 32, 740-791.

Chen, D. and Y. Hong, (2003). Has Chinese Stock Market Become Efficient? Evidence from a New Approach, *China Economic Quarterly (in Chinese)*, 1, 249-268.

Chow, G. C., (1960). Tests of Equality Between Sets of Coefficients in Two Linear Regressions, *Econometrica*, 28, 591-605.

Christensen, L. R., Jorgenson, D. W. and Lau, L. J. (1971). Conjugate Duality and the Transcendental Logarithmic Production Function, *Econometrica*, 39, 255-256.

Christensen, L. R., Jorgenson, D. W. and Lau, L. J. (1973). Transcendental Logarithmic Production Frontiers, *Review of Economics and Statistics*, 55, 28-45.

Cochrane, J. H., (1988). How Big is the Random Walk in GNP?, *Journal of Political Economy*, 96, 893-920.

Cochrane, J. H., (2001). *Asset Pricing*, Princeton: Princeton University Press.

Cournot, A., (1838). *Researches into the Mathematical Properties of the Theory of Wealth*, New York: McMillan.

Cox, D. R., (1962). *Renewal Theory*, New York: John Wiley.

Cox, D. R., (1972). Regression Models and Life Tables (with Discussion), *Journal of Royal Statistical Society, Series B*, 34, 187-220.

Cox, J. C., J. E. Ingersoll and S. A. Ross, (1985). A New Theory of the Term Structure of Interest Rates, *Econometrica*, 53, 385-407.

Dahlhaus, R., (1996). Maximum Likelihood Estimation and Model Selection for Locally Stationary Processes, *Journal of Nonparametric Statistics*, 6, 171-191.

Davidson J., (1994). *Stochastic Limit Theory: An Introduction for Econometricians*, Oxford: OUP Oxford.

Dickey, D.A., and W.A. Fuller, (1979). Distribution of the Estimators for Autoregressive Time Series with A Unit Root, *Journal of American Statistical Association*, 74, 427-31.

Durbin, J., (1970). Testing for Serial Correlation in Least Squares Regression When Some of the Regressors are Lagged Dependent Variables, *Econometrica*, 38, 422-421.

Durbin, J. and G. S. Watson, (1950). Testing for Serial Correlation in Least Squares Regression: I, *Biometrika*, 37, 409-428.

Durbin, J. and G. S. Watson, (1951). Testing for Serial Correlation in Least Squares Regression: II, *Biometrika*, 38, 159-178.

Durlauf, S. N., (1991). Spectral Based Testing of the Martingale Hypothesis, *Journal of Econometrics*, 50, 355-376.

Engle, R., (1982). Autoregressive Conditional Hetersokedasticity with Estimates of the Variance of United Kingdom Inflation, *Econometrica*, 50, 987-2008.

Engle, R. F., Granger, C. W. J., Rice, J. and Weiss, A., (1986). Semiparametric Estimation of the Relation Between Weather and Electricity Sales, *Journal of American Statistical Association*, 81, 310-320.

Engle, R., and C.W.J. Granger, (1987). Cointegration and Error-Corretion Representation, Estimation and Testing, *Econometrica*, 55, 251-276.

Engle, R. F., and J. R. Russell, (1998). Autoregressive Conditional Duration: A New Model for Irregularly Spaced Transaction Data, *Econometrica*, 66, 1127-1162.

Fama, E. F., (1965). The Behavior of Stock-Market Prices, *Journal of Business*, 38(1), 34-105.

Fan, J., and Li, R., (2006). Statistical Challenges with High Dimensionality: Feature Selection in Knowledge Discovery, *arXiv preprint math/0602133.*

Fan, J. and I. Gijbels, (1996). Local Polynomial Modelling and Its Applications, in *Monographs on Statistics and Applied Probability 66*, New York: Chapman and Hall.

Fan, Y. and Q. Li, (1996). Consistent Model Specification Tests: Omitted Variables and Semiparametric Functional Forms, *Econometrica*, 64, 865-890.

Ferson, W. E., and S. R. Foerster, (1994). Finite Sample Properties of the Generalized Methods of Moments in Tests of Conditional Assets Pricing Models, *Journal of Financial Economics*, 36, 29-55.

Fisher, R. A., (1922). The Goodness of Fit of Regression Formulae, and the Distribution of Regression Coefficients, *Journal of Royal Statistical Society*, 85, 597-612.

Fisher, R. A., (1925). *Statistical Methods for Research Workers, 1st Edition*, Edinburgh: Oliver and Boyd.

Fisher, I., (1933). Editor's Note, *Econometrica*, 1, 1-4.

Frisch, R., (1933). Propagation Problems and Impulse Problems in Dynamic Economics, in *Economic Essays in Honour of Gustav Cassel*, London: Allen and Unwin.

Friedman, M., (1957). The Permanent Income Hypothesis, in *A Theory of the Consumption Function*, Princeton: Princeton University Press.

Gauss, C. F., (1809). *Theoria Motus Corporum Coelestum*, Hamburg: Perthes und Besser.

Gauss, C. F., (1821). Theoria Combinationis Observationum Erroribus Minimis Obnoxiae, Parts 1, 2 and Supplement, *Werke*, 4, 1-108.

Galton, F., (1877). Typical Laws of Heredity, *Nature*, 15, 492-495, 512-514 and 532-533.

Galton, F., (1885). Types and Their Inheritance (Presidential Address, Section H, Anthropology), *Nature*, 32, 506-510.

Giannone, D., L. Reichlin and D. Small, (2008). Nowcasting: The Real-Time Informational Content of Macroeconomic Data, *Journal of Monetary Economics*, 55, 665-676.

Glosten, L. R., R. Jagannathan and D. E. Runkle, (1993). On the Relation Between the Expected Value and the Volatility of the Nominal Excess Return on Stocks, *Journal of Finance*, 48, 1779-1801.

Godfrey, L. G., (1978). Testing Against General Autoregressive and Moving Average Error Models When the Regressors Include Lagged Dependent Variables, *Econometrica*, 46, 1293-1302.

Granger, C. W. J., (1969). Investigating Causal Relations by Econometric Models and Cross-Spectral Methods, *Econometrica*, 37, 424-438.

Granger, C. W. J., (1980). Testing for Causality: A Personal Viewpoint, *Journal of Economic Dynamics and Control*, 2, 329-352.

Granger, C. W. J., (2001). Overview of Nonlinear Macroeconometric Empirical Models, *Journal of Macroeconomic Dynamics*, 5, 466-481.

Granger, C. W. J. and M. Machina, (2006). Structural Attribution of Observed Volatility Clusterin, *Journal of Econometrics*, 135:15-29.

Granger, C. J. W. and P. Newbold, (1974). Spurious Regressions in Econometrics, *Journal of Econometrics*, 2, 111-120.

Granger, C. J. W. and T. Teräsvirta, (1993). *Modelling Nonlinear Economic Relationships*, Oxford: Oxford University Press.

Groves, T., Y. Hong, J. McMillan and B. Naughton, (1994). Incentives in Chinese State-Owned Enterprises, *Quarterly Journal of Economics*, CIX, 183-209.

Gujarati, D. N., (2006). *Essentials of Econometrics, 3rd Edition*, Boston: McGraw-Hill.

Hall, P., (1992). *The Bootstrap and Edgeworth Expansion*, Berlin: Springer Science and Business Media.

Hamilton, J. D., (1994). *Time Series Analysis*, Princeton: Princeton University Press.

Han, A., Y. Hong and S. Wang, (2017). Autoregressive Conditional Models for Interval-Valued Time Series Data, *Working Paper*, Department of Economics, Cornell University.

Han, A., Y. Hong, S. Wang and X. Yun, (2016). A Vector Autoregressive Moving Average Model for Interval-Valued Time Series Data, in Essays in Honor of Aman Ullah, *Advances in Econometrics*, 36, 417-460.

Hansen, L. P., (1982). Large Sample Properties of Generalized Method of Moments Estimators, *Econometrica*, 50, 1029-1054.

Hansen, L. P. and K. Singleton, (1982). Generalized Instrumental Variables Estimation of Nonlinear Rational Expectations Models, *Econometrica*, 50, 1269-1286.

Härdle, W., (1990). *Applied Nonparametric Regression*, Cambridge: Cambridge University Press.

Hastie, T., R. Tibshirani and M. Wainwright, (2015). *Statistical Learning with Sparsity: The Lasso and Generalizations*, London: Taylor & Francis Group.

Hausman, J. A., (1978). Specification Tests in Econometrics, *Econometrica*, 46, 1251-1271.

Hayashi, F., (2000). *Econometrics*, Princeton: Princeton University Press.

Hong, Y., (1996). Consistent Testing for Serial Correlation of Unknown Form, *Econometrica*, 64, 837-864.

Hong, Y., (1997). One-Sided Testing for Autoregressive Conditional Heteroskedasticity in Time Series Models, *Journal of Time Series Analysis*, 18, 253-277.

Hong, Y., (2001). A Test for Volatility Spillover with Application to Exchange Rates, *Journal of Econometrics*, 103, 183-224.

Hong, Y., (2017). *Probability and Statistics for Economists*, Singapore: World Scientific Company.

Hong, Y., (2020). Understanding Modern Econometrics, Forthcoming in *Journal of Econometrics and Finance* [in Chinese].

Hong, Y., Y. Liu and S. Wang, (2009). Granger Causality in Risk and Detection of Extreme Risk Spillover Between Financial Markets, *Journal of Econometrcss*, 150, 271-287.

Hong, Y. and T. H. Lee, (2003). Diagnostic Checking for the Adequacy of Nonlinear Time Series Models, *Econometric Theory*, 19, 1065-1121.

Hong, Y. and Y. J. Lee, (2005). Generalized Spectral Testing for Conditional Mean Models in Time Series with Conditional Heteroskedasticity of Unknown Form, *Review of Economic Studies*, 72, 499-451.

Hong, Y. and Y. J. Lee, (2013). A Loss Function Approach to Model Specification Testing and Its Relative Efficiency, *Annals of Statistics*, 41, 1166-1203.

Hong, Y. and H. Li, (2005). Nonparametric Specification Testing for Continuous-Time Models with Applications to Spot Interest Rates, *Review of Financial Studies*, 18, 37-84.

Hong, Y., X. Wang and S. Wang, (2017). Testing Strict Stationarity with Applications to Macroeconomic Time Series, *International Economic Review*, 58, 1227-1277.

Hong, Y. and H. White, (1995). Consistent Specification Testing via Nonparametric Series Regression, *Econometrica*, 63, 1133-1160.

Horowitz, J. L., (2001). The Bootstrap, In J. J. Heckman and E. Leamer (Eds.), Chapter 52, *Handbook of Econometrics*, 5, 3159-3228.

Hsiao, C., (2002). *Analysis of Panel Data*, Cambridge: Cambridge University Press.

Hsiao, C., (2003). *Panel Data Analysis, 2nd Edition*, Cambridge: Cambridge University Press.

Hsiao, C., S. H. Ching and S. K. Wan, (2011). A Panel Data Approach for Program Evaluation: Measuring the Benefits of Political and Economic Integration of Hong Kong with Mainland China, *Journal of Applied Econometrics*, 27, 705-740.

Imbens, G. W. and J. M. Wooldridge, (2009). Recent Developments in the Econometrics of Program Evaluation, *Journal of Economic Literature*, 47, 5-86.

Jarque, C. M. and A. K. Bera, (1980). Efficient Tests for Normality, Homoscedasticity and Serial Independence of Regression Residuals, *Economics Letters*, 6, 255-259.

Jennrich, R. I., (1969). Asymptotic Properties of Non-Linear Least Squares Estimators, *Annals of Mathematical Statistics*, 40, 633-643.

Judge, G. G., Griffiths, W. E., Hill, R. C., Lutkepohl, H.and T. C. Lee, (1985).

The Theory and Practice of Econometrics, New York: John Wiley and Sons.

Kendall, M. G. and A. Stuart, (1961). *The Advanced Theory of Statistics*, Frome: Butler & Tanner.

Keynes, J. M., (1936). *The General Theory of Employment, Interest and Money*, Cambridge: McMillan Cambridge University Press.

Kiefer, N., (1988). Economic Duration Data and Hazard Functions; *Journal of Economic Literature*, 26, 646-679.

Klein, R. W. and R. H. Spady, (1993). An Efficient Semiparametric Estimator for Binary Response Models, *Econometrica*, 61, 387-421.

Lancaster, T., (1990). *The Econometric Analysis of Transition Data*, Cambridge: Cambridge University Press.

Lee, S. W. and B. E. Hansen, (1994). Asymptotic Theory for the GARCH (1, 1) Quasi-Maximum Likelihood Estimator, *Econometric Theory*, 10, 29-52.

Legendre, A. M., (1805). *Nouvelles Méthodes Pour la Détermination des Orbites des Comètes*, Paris: Courcier.

Ljungqvist, L. and Sargent, T. J., (2002). *Recursive Macroeconomic Theory*, Cambridge: MIT Press.

Ljung, G. M. and Box, G. E. P., (1978). On a Measure of a Lack of Fit in Time Series Models, *Biometrika*, 65, 297-303.

Lo, A. W. and A. C. MacKinlay, (1988). Stock Market Prices Do Not Follow Random Walks: Evidence from a Simple Specification Test, *Review of Financial Studies*, 1, 41-66.

Lucas, R. E., (1976). Econometric Policy Evaluation: A Critique, *Carnegie-Rochester Conference Series on Public Policy*, 1, 19-46.

Lucas, R., (1977). Understanding Business Cycles, in *Stabilization of the Domestic and International Economy*, Karl Brunner and Allan Meltzer (eds.), *Carnegie-Rochester Conference Series on Public Policy*, 5, Amsterdam: North-Holland.

Lumsdaine, R. L., (1996). Consistency and Asymptotic Normality of the Quasi-Maximum Likelihood Estimator in IGARCH (1, 1) and Covariance Stationary GARCH (1, 1) Models, *Econometrica*, 64, 575-596.

Malkiel, B. G. and E. F. Fama, (1970). Efficient Capital Markets: A Review of Theory and Empirical Work, *Journal of Finance*, 25, 383-417.

Mandelbrot, B., (1963). The Variation of Certain Speculative Prices, *Journal of Business*, 36(4), 394-419.

Mehra, R. and E. Prescott, (1985). The Equity Premium: A Puzzle, *Journal of Monetary Economics*, 15, 145-161.

Muller, H. G., (2005). Functional Modelling and Classification of Longitudinal Data, *Scandinavian Journal of Statistics*, 32, 223-240.

Muller, H. G. and U. Stadtmuller, (2005). Generalized Functional Linear Models, *Annals of Statistics*, 33, 774-805.

Nelson, C. R. and C. R. Plosser, (1982). Trends and Random Walks in Macroeconmic Time Series: Some Evidence and Implications, *Journal of Monetary Economics*, 10, 139-162.

Nelson, D. B., (1990). Stationarity and Persistence in the GARCH(1,1) Model, *Econometric Theory*, 6.

Nelson, D. B., (1991). Conditional Heteroskedasticity in Asset Returns: A New Approach, *Econometrica*, 59, 347-370.

Nelson, D. B. and Cao, C. Q., (1992). Inequality Constraints in the Univariate GARCH Model, *Econometrica*, 10, 229-235.

Newey, W. K., (1985). Generalized Method of Moments Specification Testing, *Journal of Econometrics*, 29, 229-256.

Newey, W. and K. West, (1987). A Simple, Positive Semi-definite, Heteroskedasticity and Autocorrelation Consistent Covariance Matrix, *Econometrica*, 55, 703-08.

Newey, W. and K. West, (1994). Automatic Lag Selection in Covariance Matrix Estimation, *Review of Economic Studies*, 61, 631-653.

Noureldin, D., N. Shephard and K. Sheppard, (2011). Multivariate High-Frequency-Based Volatility (HEAVY) Models, *Journal of Applied Econometrics*, 27, 907-933.

O'hara, M., (1995). *Market Microstructure Theory*, New Jersey: Wiley.

Pagan, A. and A. Ullah, (1999). *Nonparametric Econometrics*, Cambridge: Cambridge University Press.

Pearson, K., (1903). The Law of Ancestral Heredity, *Biometrika*, 2, 211–236.

Phillips, A. W., (1958). The Relation Between Unemployment and the Rate of Change of Money Wage Rates in the United Kingdom, *Economica*, 25, 283-299.

Phillips, P. C. B., (1977a). An Approximation to the Finite Sample Distribution of Zellner's Seemingly Unrelated Regression Estimator, *Journal of Econometrics*, 6, 147-164.

Phillips, P. C. B., (1977b). Approximations to Some Finite Sample Distributions Associated with a First-Order Stochastic Difference Equation, *Econometrica*, 45, 463-485.

Phillips, P. C. B., (1977c). A General Theorem in the Theory of Asymptotic Expansions as Approximations to the Finite Sample Distributions of Econometric Estimators, *Econometrica*, 45, 1517-1534.

Phillips, P. C. B., (1986). Understanding Spurious Regressions in Econometrics, *Journal of Econometrics*, 33, 311-340.

Phillips, P. C. B., (1987a). Time Series Regression with a Unit Root, *Econometrica*, 55, 277-301.

Phillips, P. C. B., (1987b). Towards a Unified Asymptotic Theory for Autoregressiot, *Biometrika*, 74, 535-547.

Phillips, P.C. and Perron, P., (1988). Testing for a Unit Root in Time Series Regression, *Biometrika*, 75, 335-346.

Pons, O. M.T., (2019). *Orthonormal Series Estimators*, Singapore: World Scientific.

Poterba, J. M. and Summers, L. H., (1988). Mean Reversion in Stock Prices: Evidence and Implications, *Journal of Financial Economics*, 22(1), 27-59.

Priestley, M. B., (1981). *Spectral Analysis and Time Series*, London: Academic Press.

Ramsay, J. and B. W. Silverman, (2002). *Applied Functional Data Analysis: Methods and Case Studies*, Berlin: Springer.

Ramsay, J. and B. W. Silverman, (2005). *Functional Data Analysis, 2nd Edition*, Berlin: Springer.

Ranga Rao, R., (1962). Relations Between Weak and Uniform Convergence of Measures with Applications, *Annals of Mathematical Statistics*, 33, 659-680.

Rao, C. R., (1948). Large Sample Tests of Statistical Hypotheses Concerning Several Parameters with Applications to Problems of Estimation, *Proc. Cambridge Philos. Soc*, 44, 50-57.

Reiersøl, O., (1945). Confluence Analysis by Means of Instrumental Sets of Variables, *Akiv för Matematik Astronomi och Fysik*, 32a: 1-119

Robinson, P. M., (1988). Root-N-Consistent Semiparametric Regression, *Econometrica*, 56, 931-954.

Robinson, P. M., (1994). Efficient Tests of Nonstationary Hypotheses, *Journal of the American Statistical Association*, 89, 1420-1437.

Samuelson, L., (2005). Economic Theory and Experimental Economics, *Journal of Economic Literature*, XLIII, 65-107.

Samuelson, P., (1939). Interactions Between the Multiplier Analysis and the Principle of Acceleration, *Review of Economic Studies*, 21, 75-78.

Sargan, J. D., (1958). The Estimation of Economic Relationships Using Instrumental Variables, *Econometrica*, 26, 393-415.

Sargent, T. J., (1987). *Dynamic Macroeconomic Theory*, Cambridge: Harward University Press.

Schwarz, G., (1978). Estimating the Dimension of a Model, *The Annals of Statistics*, 6, 461-464.

Shao, X., (2010). The Dependent Wild Bootstrap, *Journal of the American Statistical Association*, 105, 218-235.

Shephard, N. and K. Sheppard (2010). Realising the Future: Forecasting with High-Frequency-Based Volatility(HEAVY) Models, *Journal of Applied Econometrics*, 25, 197-231.

Sims, C. A., (1980). Macroeconomics and Reality, *Econometrica*, 48, 1-48.

Smith, A., (1776). *An Inquiry into the Nature and Causes of the Wealth of Nations*, New York: The Modern library.

Staiger, D. and J. H. Stock, (1997). Instrumental Variables Regression with Weak Instruments, *Econometrica*, 65, 557-586.

Stock, J. and F. Trebbi, (2003). Retrospectives: Who Invented Instrumental Variable Regression?, *Journal of Economic Perspectives*, 17, 177-194.

Sun, Y., A. Han, Y. Hong and S. Wang, (2018). Threshold Autoregressive Models for Interval-Valued Time Series Data, *Journal of Econometrics*, 206, 414-446.

Sun, Y., Y. Hong and S. Wang, (2019). Out-of-Sample Forecasts for China's Economic Growth and Inflation Using Rolling Weighted Least Squares, *Journal of Management Science and Engineering*, 4, 1-11.

Tauchen, G., (1985). Diagnostic Testing and Evaluation of Maximum Likelihood Models, *Journal of Econometrics*, 30, 415-443.

Teräsvirta, T., Tjøtheim, D. and Granger, C. W. J., (2010). *Modelling Nonlinear Economic Time Series.*, Oxford: Oxford University Press.

Tong, H., (1990). *Non-Linear Time Series: A Dynamical System Approach.*, Oxford: Oxford University Press.

Tibshirani, R., (1996). Regression Shrinkage and Selection via the Lasso, *Journal of Royal Statistical Society Series B*, 58, 267-88.

Ullah, A., (1990). *Finite Sample Econometrics: A Unified Approach*, Berlin: Springer.

Varian, H. R., (2014). Big Data: New Tricks for Econometrics, *Journal of Economic Perspectives*, 28, 3-28.

Vasicek, O. A., (1977). An Equilibrium Characterisation of the Term Structure, *Journal of Financial Economics*, 5, 177-188.

Vinod, H. D., (1973). Generalization of the Durbin-Watson Statistic for Higher Order Autore- gressive Processes, *Communications in Statistics*, 2, 115-144.

Von Neumann, J. and O. Morgenstern, (1944). *Theory of Games and Economic Behavior*, Princeton: Princeton University Press.

Wallis, K. F. (1972). Testing for Fourth Order Autocorrelation in Quarterly Regression Equations, *Econometrica*, 40, 617-636.

Walras, L., (1874). *Elements of Pure Economics, or, The Theory of Social Wealth*, Cambridge: Cambridge University Press.

Wang, S., L. Yu and K. K. Lai, (2005). Crude Oil Price Forecasting with TEI@I Methodology, *Journal of Systems Science and Complexity*, 18, 145-166.

Wang, X. and Y. Hong, (2018). Characteristic Function Based Testing for Conditional Independence: A Nonparametric Regression Approach, *Econometric Theory*, 34, 815-849.

White, H., (1980). A Heteroskedasticity-Consistent Covariance Matrix Estimator and a Direct Test for Heterokedasticity, *Econometrica*, 48, 817-838.

White, H., (1981). Consequences and Detection of Misspecified Nonlinear Regression Models, *Journal of American Statistical Association*, 76, 419-433.

White, H., (1982). Maximum Likelihood Estimation of Misspecified Models, *Econometrica*, 50, 1-26.

White, H., (1984). *Asymptotic Theory for Econometricians*, Pittsburgh: Academic Press.

White, H., (1990). A Consistent Model Selection Procedure Based on M-Testing, in *Modelling Economic Series: Readings in Econometric Methodology*, 369-383, Oxford: Oxford University Press.

White, H., (1992). *Artificial Neural Networks: Approximation and Learning Theory*, London: Blackwell Publisher.

White, H., (1994). *Estimation, Inference and Specification Analysis*, Cambridge: Cambridge University.

White, H. and M. Stinchcombe, (1991). *Adaptive Efficient Weighted Least Squares with Dependent Observations*, Berlin: Springer.

White, H., (2001). *Asymptotic Theory for Econometricians (Revised Edition)*, Pittsburgh: Academic Press.

Wright, P. G., (1928). *Tariff on Animal and Vegetable Oils*, New York: Macmillan Company.

Yule, G. U., (1897). On the Theory of Correlation, *Journal of Royal Statistical Society Series B*, 60, 812-54.

Zakoian, J. M., (1994). Threshold Heteroskedastic Models, *Journal of Economic Dynamics and Control*, 18, 931-955.

Index

χ^2 distribution, 98, 111
2SLS, *see* Two-stage least squares

ACD, *see* Autoregressive conditional duration
ACD model, 388
Adaptive feasible GLS, 132
Adjusted R^2, 84, 138
Affine function, 43, 44, 58
AI, *see* Artificial intelligence
AIC, *see* Akaike information criterion
Akaike information criterion, 83, 84, 135
Almost sure convergence, 158–161
AR model, *see* Autoregressive model
AR(p), 286–288, 292
ARCH, *see* Autoregressive conditional heteroskedasticity
ARCH model, 16, 17
ARMA model, *see* Autoregressive-moving average model, 433
ARMA(p, q) model, 427, 428, 433
Artificial intelligence, 480
Artificial neural network, 481
Asymptotic analysis, 151, 161, 165, 188
Asymptotic distribution, 409, 416, 418, 420, 421, 436, 440–442, 444, 448, 453, 454
Asymptotic efficiency, 168, 361
Asymptotic independence, 220, 221
Asymptotic normality, 168, 170, 171, 227, 228, 278, 279, 311–313, 315, 323, 356, 357, 410, 436
Asymptotic theory, 149, 151, 166, 189
Asymptotic variance, 170, 172, 173, 175, 191, 296, 306, 312, 316, 317, 322, 323, 326, 329
Asymptotic variance estimation, 173, 229, 438
Asymptotic variance estimator, 175, 177, 178, 192, 230, 232, 364, 365, 367, 372, 375, 414, 416, 422, 439, 441, 442
Asymptotic variance-covariance matrix estimation, 413
Autocorrelation, 74, 125, 126, 134–136
Autocorrelation function, 207, 256
Autocorrelogram, 207
Autocovariance function, 207, 257, 269, 270, 272, 274, 285, 290, 291
Autoregressive conditional duration model, 388
Autoregressive conditional heteroskedasticity, 210–212, 214, 218, 219, 239, 241–244, 248, 255, 258, 261–263
Autoregressive model, 70, 118, 197, 205–207, 211, 212, 218, 219, 224, 246

Autoregressive process, 205, 206
Autoregressive-moving average, 207
Autoregressive-moving average model, 206
Autoregressive-moving average process, 206
Auxiliary regression, 185, 186, 194, 195
Auxiliary regression model, 195

Balanced panel data, 330
Bartlett kernel, 275–277, 285
Bayesian information criterion, 84, 135
Best linear least squares approximation coefficient, 46, 47, 52, 58, 59, 61, 62
Best linear least squares prediction, 45, 47
Best linear least squares predictor, 45, 47, 52, 53, 58, 61, 62
BIC, *see* Bayesian information criterion
Big data, 461, 470, 479–483, 485
Binary probability modeling, 385
Bivariate linear regression model, 46, 47
Bivariate normal distribution, 38, 60, 61
Boundedness in probability, 155
Box-Pierce portmanteau test, 254
Box-Pierce test, 253
Breusch-Godfrey test, 247
Brownian motion, 389
Business cycles, 208, 209
Buy-and-hold trading strategy, 154

Capital asset pricing model, 51, 80, 347, 427, 443
CAPM, *see* Capital asset pricing model
Cauchy-Schwarz inequality, 168, 169
Causal relationship, 29, 30, 38
Causality, 469, 470, 477
Censored data, 394
Censored regression models, 450
Centered R^2, 80, 83, 146
Central limit theorem, 94, 161, 163, 165, 172, 304, 311, 326
Ceteris paribus, 68, 93
Characteristic function, 162, 163
Chebyshev's inequality, 154, 157
Cholesky's decomposition, 127
Cholesky's factorization, 127
Classical linear regression, 72, 141, 459, 461, 464, 469, 483
Classical linear regression model, 68, 134, 135, 458, 459, 461, 464, 469, 483
CLT, *see* Central limit theorem
Cobb-Douglas function, 13, 14
Cochrane-Orcutt procedure, 292
Coefficient of determination, 78, 139, 143, 145
Compactness, 353, 400
Complete stationarity, 202
Conditional distribution, 29, 31, 384, 385, 392, 393, 396, 401–407, 410, 414, 421, 424, 426, 430, 431, 433–436, 439, 442–445, 447–449, 451, 452, 454, 455
Conditional distribution model, 384, 392, 393, 402, 405, 407, 410, 421, 433–436, 439, 442, 443, 448, 449
Conditional expectation, 31
Conditional heteroskedasticity, 14, 16, 18, 40–42, 71, 116, 125, 126, 128, 131, 134, 135, 141, 144, 167, 168, 173, 175, 177–179, 182–185, 187, 188, 192, 193, 195, 229, 231, 232, 240–242, 244, 248, 255, 459–461, 464–467, 485
Conditional heteroskedasticity and autocorrelation, 464
Conditional homoskedasticity, 14, 16, 18, 39–41, 73, 116, 119, 122, 151, 168, 172, 173, 175, 177–180, 184, 187, 188, 193–196, 225, 228–230, 233, 234, 236, 239, 241–243, 248, 254, 258, 259, 312, 313, 316–318, 320, 322–325, 329, 331, 459, 460,

462–465, 467, 485
Conditional IM equality, 408–410, 412, 413, 418, 419, 427, 436, 437, 442, 443, 447–449, 451, 452
Conditional kurtosis, 28
Conditional mean, 27–31, 34, 36, 37, 40, 42, 43, 52, 57, 58, 60–62
Conditional median, 29, 36, 61
Conditional moment, 29, 30, 42
Conditional non-autocorrelation, 74
Conditional normality, 94, 135
Conditional probability distribution, 27, 29
Conditional probability distribution model, 332, 402, 424, 440, 443, 448
Conditional quantile, 31
Conditional skewness, 28
Conditional variance, 28, 29, 37, 39, 40, 42, 61
Consistency, 86, 168–170, 176, 226, 231, 246, 251, 275, 277, 293, 295, 306, 309–311, 318, 320–322, 336, 353, 355, 356
Consistent estimation, 229, 230
Consistent estimator, 229, 262
Constant return to scale, 1, 13, 14
Consumption function, 1, 5, 11, 31, 50, 62, 119
Continuity, 160, 170, 359, 368
Continuous time diffusion model, 389, 390
Control variable, 120
Convergence in distribution, 105, 160, 161
Convergence in mean squares, 152, 157, 160, 161, 190
Convergence in probability, 153, 155–157, 160, 161, 190
Convergence in probability one, 158
Convergence in quadratic mean, 152, 157, 190
Convergence with probability approaching one, 153
Correct model specification, 14, 52, 58, 59, 65, 166, 170, 223, 224, 245–247, 255, 269, 402, 471, 483, 485
Correct model specification for conditional distribution, 404
Correct model specification for conditional mean, 49
Correlation analysis, 46, 61
Cost function, 32
Counterfactual analysis, 471
Counterfactual estimation, 482
Counterfactual outcome, 471, 482, 483
Covariance stationarity, 204
Cox's proportional hazard model, 388
Cox, Ingersoll and Ross' model, 390
Cramer's representation, 208
Cramer-Wold device, 163
Critical value, 102, 103, 105, 107, 108, 115, 120, 146
Cross-sectional observations, 392
Cross-spectral density, 273
Cross-spectral density function, 273
Cross-spectrum, 273
Cumulative distribution function, 156, 160, 161

Daniell kernel, 276, 277
Data Generating Process, 7, 12, 20, 21
Decision rule, 102, 105, 107, 108
Delta method, 164, 165
Dependent variable, 31, 38, 44
DGP, *see* Data Generating Process
DID, *see* Difference-in-difference
Difference-in-difference, 471
Difference-stationary process, 213, 217, 218
Diffusion model, 389, 390
Distributional lag model, 223
Disturbance, 39, 48, 51, 63, 65, 68–70, 74, 77, 93, 94, 137
Dummy variable, 33
Duration analysis, 2, 18, 19
Durbin's h-test, 252, 253
Durbin-Watson test, 252
Dynamic asset pricing, 1
Dynamic asset pricing model, 11

Dynamic capital asset pricing model, 347, 348
Dynamic CAPM, *see* Dynamic capital asset pricing model
Dynamic information matrix equality, 434
Dynamic probability integral transform, 447, 456
Dynamic regression model, 223, 236, 246, 247, 249, 251, 254, 255, 259–262

Econometrics, 1–4, 6–11, 17, 20, 24–26
Economic duration, 18
Economic reform, 1, 14, 15, 20
Economic relationship, 3, 8, 21
Efficiency, 86, 93, 119, 145
Efficient market hypothesis, 2, 15, 16
Efficient score test, 421, 422
Eigenvalue, 72, 73, 144
EMH, *see* Efficient market hypothesis
Empirical stylized fact, 2, 3, 8, 16
Empirical validation, 6
Endogeneity, 300, 307, 324, 328, 331, 461, 469, 470
Engel curve, 2
Equity premium puzzle, 13
Ergodic stationarity, 222, 268, 303
Ergodic stationary MDS, 312, 323, 326, 336
Ergodic stationary MDS process, 228
Ergodic stationary non-MDS, 313, 321, 324
Ergodic stationary process, 221, 223, 227, 230, 232, 400, 446, 453
Ergodic stationary random sample, 221
Ergodicity, 220, 221, 223, 256
Errors in expectations, 296
Errors in variables, 294
Estimated residual, 77, 81, 85, 99, 137
Euler equation, 9, 12, 348, 349
Exact identification, 352, 372, 380
Exclusion restriction, 305
Exogeneity, 462, 469, 470
Expected marginal effect, 50, 59
Experimental economics, 471
Explanatory variable, 30, 31, 38, 44, 50, 51, 59
Exponential GARCH model, 431
Exponential smoothing, 385
Extremum estimator, 355, 356

F-distribution, 99, 111, 115, 134
F-test, 112, 113, 117, 122, 140, 142, 151, 175, 178, 180, 188, 192
F-test statistic, 99, 112, 116, 119, 121–124, 127, 131, 133, 135, 139, 142, 143, 146, 175, 180, 188, 192
Fat Big data, 482, 483
Field study, 471
First order condition, 12, 45, 48, 58, 64
Fitted value, 77, 81
FOC, *see* First order condition
Forward exchange rates, 266, 267
Fourier coefficient, 54, 55, 64
Fourier transform, 207, 209, 257, 258, 272
Frequency domain analysis, 209
Functional data, 479–481

GARCH model, 399, 431, 433
Gauss-Markov theorem, 89, 93, 131
Gaussian distribution, 94
Gaussian process, 205, 217, 257
GDP, *see* Gross domestic product
general equilibrium, 5
general equilibrium theory, 4–6
Generalized error distribution, 432
Generalized least squares estimation, 124, 127, 130, 131, 146
Generalized least squares estimator, 128, 131, 132, 135, 144, 145
Generalized method of moments, 355, 357, 361, 365, 371–373, 376, 378, 379, 381, 460, 468, 485
Generalized method of moments estimation, 343, 346, 350, 363, 365, 370, 372, 374, 380
Generalized method of moments

estimator, 349–353, 355–357, 360–363, 365–367, 369, 371–379, 381, 382
GLS, *see* Generalized Least Squares
GMM, *see* Generalized method of moments
Goodness of fit, 78, 82–84
Granger causality, 122, 235–237
Great moderation, 21, 476
Gross domestic product, 5, 20–24, 200, 235, 268, 272

Hausman's test, 324, 325, 327, 328, 340, 341
Hausman's test for endogeneity, 327
Hazard function, 18, 387, 388
Hazard rate, 18, 19, 387, 388, 450
Hessian matrix, 46, 409–412, 437, 453
Heteroskedasticity, 129, 133, 135, 136
Heteroskedasticity and autocorrelation consistent variance-covariance matrix estimation, 133, 134
Heteroskedasticity-consistent variance-covariance matrix estimator, 459, 465
High-dimensional data, 483
High-dimensional linear regression, 86
Hypothesis testing, 87, 96, 99–101, 168, 178, 233, 279, 322, 331, 337

$I(1)$, 218
Idempotent, 87, 88, 96, 97, 137, 419
Idempotent matrix, 419
Identification, 353, 401, 411
IID Cauchy sequence, 203
IID observations, 166, 188
IID random sample, 71, 77, 154, 155, 159, 161, 166, 167, 169, 170, 191, 192, 195, 197
IM, *see* Information Matrix
Impulse response function, 207, 213
Independence and identical distribution, 71, 72, 98, 129
Information matrix equality, 434
Innovation, 206, 207, 211, 212, 214, 218, 219
Instrumental variables, 15, 304–306, 329, 334–336, 338, 349, 376, 379, 460, 468, 470, 482
Instrumental variables regression, 293, 305, 306
Instruments, 304–306, 324, 328, 336
Integrated process of order 1, 218
Interiorness, 356
Interval-valued data, 481
invertibility, 207
IV, *see* Instrumental variables
IV conditions, 304
IV estimation, 346
IV estimator, 352, 379

J. P. Morgan's RiskMetrics, 385
Joint significance, 117

Kernel, 276, 283, 285, 288, 289, 291
Kernel estimator, 132
Kernel function, 275–277, 285
Kernel smoothing, 56, 57
Keynesian model, 10
Keynesian theory, 5
Kronecker delta, 54, 74

Lag order, 204, 207, 249
Lagged dependent variable, 223 225, 244, 246, 247, 249, 250, 254
Lagrange multiplier, 113–115, 142, 416–418, 421
Lagrange multiplier test, 242, 248, 253, 415, 421–423, 440–443, 449, 455, 456
Lagrangian function, 113
LASSO, *see* Least absolute shrinkage and selection operator, 482
Law of iterated expectations, 32–35, 169, 173, 178
Law of large numbers, 165
Least absolute shrinkage and selection operator estimator, 86
Likelihood function, 392, 397, 399, 401, 412, 426, 448

Likelihood ratio test, 415, 416, 420–423, 442, 449, 455
Linear IV estimation, 351
Linear IV estimator, 351–353
Linear regression model, 37, 44, 47–53, 58, 59, 62, 63, 65, 458–477, 483
Linear regression model with normal errors, 393, 399
Linear regression modeling, 43, 61
Linear restriction, 123, 135
Linearity, 68, 166, 191, 223, 268, 304, 337
Ljung-Box test, 254
LLN, *see* Law of large numbers
LM test, *see* Lagrange multiplier test
LM test statistic, 422, 441–443, 455, 456
Locally stationary time series, 476, 477
Log-likelihood, 392, 397, 398, 401, 404, 412–414, 419, 424, 432, 434, 450
Log-likelihood function, 392, 397, 398, 401, 404, 412–414, 419, 424, 432, 434, 450
Logistic function, 386
Logistic map, 198
Logit model, 386, 393, 394
Long horizon return, 267, 268
Long horizon return predictability, 267
Long memory, 285
Long-run variance estimator, 274, 276, 277, 281–283, 286, 289, 291
Long-run variance-covariance matrix estimation, 270, 282
Long-run variance-covariance matrix estimator, 282, 288
LR test statistic, 416, 420–422, 442, 449, 455
Lucas' critique, 476

MA, *see* Moving-average
MA model, 206, 207
MA process, 239, 246, 256, 259
Machine learning, 474, 481–483, 485
MAE, *see* Mean Absolute Error
Marginal effect, 52–54
marginal effect, 19
Marginal propensity to consume, 1, 5, 11, 31, 50, 62
Market microstructure noises, 297, 298
Martingale, 213, 214
Martingale difference sequence, 213–217, 221–224, 226, 228, 232, 239, 241, 245–248, 254, 255, 257, 259–261
Martingale process, 213, 214, 217, 218
Mathematical model, 3, 4, 6
Mathematical modeling, 2–4, 6, 24
Maximum likelihood estimation, 9, 12, 17–19, 388, 391
Maximum likelihood estimator, 390, 396, 398–402, 406, 409–413, 415–417, 421, 437, 441–444, 446, 448–450, 452–456
MDS, *see* Martingale difference sequence
Mean Absolute Error, 35, 36, 61
Mean square error, 34, 35, 43, 48, 52, 58, 60, 61
Measurement errors, 294–296, 305, 306
Method of moments estimation, 343–346, 468
MLE, *see* Maximum likelihood estimation
MLE-based Wald test, 415, 440
MME, *see* Method of moments estimation
Model misspecification, 54, 425, 439, 440, 442–444, 446, 447, 449, 461, 471–474, 485
Model misspecification for conditional distribution, 423
Model selection criterion, 135
Model specification, 51, 473, 474
Model specification test, 369, 376
Model uncertainty, 479, 483

moment conditions, 346, 347, 349, 353, 369, 371–374, 376, 379
Moment matching, 345, 346
Money supply, 268
Moving-average process, 206
MPC, *see* Marginal propensity to consume
MSE, *see* Mean square error
Multicollinearity, 72, 138, 139, 462, 479
Multiplier, 1, 10, 11
Multiplier effect, 5
Multivariate central limit theorem, 170
Multivariate CLT, *see* Multivariate central limit theorem

N-th order stationarity, 204
Near-multicollinearity, 73, 85, 94, 95, 108, 139
Nonexperimental nature, 2
Nonexperimental observations, 15, 30
Nonlinear IV estimation, 379
Nonlinear MA process, 215, 257
Nonlinear model, 466
Nonlinear regression model, 331, 332, 426, 460, 468
Nonlinear regression model with endogeneity, 332
Nonnormality, 463
Nonparametric analysis, 57
Nonparametric artificial neutral net model, 481
Nonparametric estimation, 273
Nonparametric modeling, 54, 57
Nonparametric series regression, 56, 57
Nonsingularity, 72, 166, 223, 269, 304, 337
Nonstationarity, 474
Nonstationary process, 210, 213
Nonstationary time series, 210, 223, 224, 474–476, 484
Normal distribution, 94, 95, 97, 125, 126, 135, 462, 463, 473, 483
Normality, 86, 94, 95, 128, 458, 459, 462, 463
Nowcasting, 480

OLS, *see* Ordinary least squares
Omitted variables, 120–122, 145, 294, 298, 305, 307, 329, 330
Optimal GMM estimator, 365–367, 369, 371, 372, 375, 376, 378, 379, 381
Optimal prediction, 101
Optimal weighting matrix, 350, 362, 371, 373
Optimality, 34
Ordinary least squares, 73–79, 81, 82, 85–87, 93–96, 99, 108, 113, 114, 117, 125, 127, 131–133, 135, 137–145, 147
Ordinary least squares estimation, 74, 78, 79, 86, 93, 99, 138, 142, 144
Ornut-Cochrane procedure, 286
Orthogonality, 89, 131
Orthogonality condition, 39, 48, 52, 58, 59
Overidentification, 371–374, 376, 381, 382
Overidentification test, 371–374, 376, 381, 382

P-value, 107, 108, 144
Panel data, 328, 330, 331
Partially linear regression model, 329
PDF, *see* Probability Density Function
Phillips curve, 2
Policy evaluation, 458, 471, 482, 483
Population moments, 344, 345, 369
Positive definite, 76, 110, 125, 127, 145
Positive semi-definite, 89, 91, 93, 141, 144
Power, 285, 289
Power function, 107
Power spectral density function, 208
Prais-Winsten transformation, 130
Predictive relationship, 28–30

Probability Density Function, 27
Probability distribution, 27, 29
Probability law, 7, 8, 19
Probability limit, 153
Probit model, 386, 393, 394, 450
Production function, 13–15, 31, 32
Production-bonus causality, 299
Program evaluation, 471
Projection matrix, 87, 137
Propensity score matching, 471
PSD, *see* Positive semi-definite
pseudo likelihood function, 448
PSM, *see* Propensity score matching

Quadratic form, 96, 97, 111, 112, 115, 116, 142
Quadratic form of normal random variables, 96, 110
Quadratic-Spectral kernel, 276, 277
Quantitative analysis, 2
Quasi-maximum likelihood estimation, 18
Quasi-MLE, 391, 393, 398

R^2, 78–83, 85, 135, 137, 138, 143, 145
Random coefficient process, 42
Random walk, 213, 214, 217, 218, 389, 390
Random walk model with drift, 389
Rational expectations, 1, 9, 11, 12, 222, 224, 247, 296, 306, 332, 347
Rational expectations model, 332
RDD, *see* Regression discontinuity design
Realized volatility, 298
Regressand, 30
Regression analysis, 30, 31, 38, 40, 46, 59
Regression discontinuity design, 471
Regression function, 30–32, 34–39, 43, 47, 52, 58
Regression identity, 38, 51
Regressor vector, 30, 44, 58, 59
Regressors, 50, 54, 57
Relative entropy, 424, 425
Reserved causality, 300
Response variable, 31
Restricted model, 113, 115, 117, 123, 143
Return on portfolio, 80
Ridge regression, 86
Ridge regression estimator, 86
RiskMetrics, 385
Robust t-test, 134, 183, 240, 266, 280–282, 289
Robust t-test statistic, 182, 183, 266, 280–282, 289
Robust Wald test, 116, 134, 183, 240, 241, 281, 282, 289, 323, 324, 439, 440, 442, 455
Robust Wald test statistic, 116, 134, 183, 281, 282, 289, 323, 324, 440, 442, 455

Sample autocorrelation function, 253
Sample autocovariance, 253
Sample autocovariance function, 253, 274, 290, 291
Sample Hessian matrix, 411, 414, 415, 438
Sample path, 198, 210
Sample residual variance estimator, 89, 92, 96
Sample variance, 80, 92, 99, 137
Sampling distribution, 86, 87, 94, 96, 99, 102, 103, 105, 146, 148
Score function, 405, 413, 414, 420, 421, 434, 436, 437, 442, 443, 446–449, 451, 452
Second order condition, 46
Self-normalization, 289
Serial correlation, 74, 125, 128, 129, 131–134, 245, 247–255, 257, 259, 260
Serial dependence, 207, 209, 246, 247
Significance level, 102, 105–108, 120, 140, 146
Simultaneous equations bias, 300, 303
Size, 67, 68, 72, 73, 77, 84, 86, 94, 95, 102, 105, 107, 108, 132, 133, 274, 275, 288–291
SLLN, *see* Strong Law of Large

Numbers
Slutsky's theorem, 163, 165, 172, 179, 180, 182, 183
Smooth change, 475
Smooth structural change, 476, 477
Smooth Transition AutoRegressive, 466, 475
SOC, *see* Second order condition
Spectral density function, 207–210, 257, 258
Spectral density matrix, 272, 273
Spherical error variance, 73
Spot exchange rates, 101, 267
Spurious regression, 82, 223, 224
Spurious regression model, 224
Spurious relationship, 30
SSR, *see* Sum of squared residuals
Standardized spectral density, 208, 258
Standardized spectral density function, 208, 258
Standardized Student's t-distribution, 432
STAR, *see* Smooth Transition AutoRegressive
Static regression model, 223, 246, 250–255, 259
Stationarity, 202, 474, 476, 483
Stationary time series, 459, 463, 466, 474–477, 484
Statistical learning, 482
Statistics, 10, 14, 24
Stochastic process, 208, 222, 223, 257
Stochastic time series process, 198, 202, 204
Strict exogeneity, 69, 70, 92
Strict stationarity, 202–205, 219
Strictly exogenous variable, 71
Strong convergence, 159
Strong exogeneity, 71
Strong Law of Large Numbers, 159, 167
Structural break, 475
Structural change, 123, 143, 475, 476
Structural VAR model, 428, 429
Student's t-distribution, 99, 104, 127, 146
Sum of squared residuals, 75, 77, 113, 115, 142–144
Survival analysis, 18, 387
Survival function, 387, 388
Symmetric and idempotent matrix, 419
Symmetric matrix, 419, 427, 439

t-test, 106, 108, 112
t-test statistic, 99, 104, 107, 109, 111, 131, 135, 139, 140, 146, 179
Tall Big data, 481, 483
Taylor series approximation, 165
Taylor series expansion, 162, 165, 405, 411, 415–418, 440
Threshold ARCH model, 431
Threshold GARCH model, 431
Time domain analysis, 209
Time series, 197, 208, 209, 222, 255
Time series analysis, 197, 208, 209, 222, 255
Time series data, 199–202, 207
Time series data set, 199–202, 207
Time series random sample, 199
Time-varying STAR, 475
Tobit model, 394
Trace operator, 92
Traditional data, 479–481, 483
Translog function, 31
Treatment effect, 471
Trend-stationary process, 210–212, 218, 220
True model parameter, 50, 59, 61, 64
True parameter value, 49, 52, 396, 402–404, 411, 418, 426, 428, 431, 432
Truncated kernel, 276, 277
Truncated regression model, 395
Two-stage least squares, 302, 303, 306–314, 324, 325, 329, 331, 334–336, 338, 341
Type I error, 106, 107
Type II error, 107

Ultra-high frequency financial econometrics, 388
Unbalanced panel data, 330
Unbiasedness, 88
Unbiasedness hypothesis, 266, 267
Unbiasedness property, 92
Uncentered R^2, 78
Uniform convergence, 353–355, 364
Uniform strong law of large numbers, 354
Uniform WLLN, 401, 409, 411, 414, 438, 444, 453, 454
Unit root, 217–220
Unit root process, 217–220
Univariate ARMA model, 427
Univariate time series analysis, 392
Unrestricted model, 113, 115, 118, 142, 143
Uptailed critical value, 106
USLLN, *see* Uniform strong law of large numbers
UWLLN, *see* Uniform WLLN

Value at risk, 384
Vanishing variance, 88, 135
VaR, *see* Value at risk
VAR model, 429
Variance estimation, 96
Variance ratio, 284–286, 290, 291
Variance ratio test, 284–286, 290, 291
Variation-free parameter, 392, 398
Variation-free parameter space, 397
Vasicek's model, 389, 390
vech, 185, 186, 194, 195
vech operator, 185
Volatility, 2, 17, 24
Volatility clustering, 2, 9, 16, 17

Wage determination, 124, 237
Wage-Price spiral model, 301
Wald test, 116, 234, 240, 241, 323, 324, 368, 369, 376, 379
Wald test statistic, 116, 184, 323, 324, 368, 369, 376, 379, 415, 416, 422, 440, 442, 453–455
Weak convergence, 153
Weak exogeneity, 469
Weak instrumental variables, 470, 482
Weak law of large numbers, 154, 155, 169, 174, 176, 177
Weak stationarity, 204, 205
Wealth effect, 119
Weighting matrix, 350, 352, 353, 361–363, 365, 371–373, 375, 376, 378, 382
White noise, 205, 209, 210, 215–217, 239, 257, 259
White's heteroskedasticity-consistent variance-covariance matrix estimator, 177, 188, 192
White's test for conditional heteroskedasticity, 187, 188
Within estimator, 331
WLLN, *see* Weak law of large numbers
WN, *see* White noise
Wold's decomposition, 205, 207

Zero mean ergodic stationary process, 278

CPSIA information can be obtained
at www.ICGtesting.com
Printed in the USA
BVHW062320220720
584324BV00005B/14

9 789811 220180